Table of Contents

3   Color by the Numbers

Convincing color correction isn't out of the reach of the color-blind. The rest of us can do better, but not without abiding by certain rules

4   Color, Contrast, Canyons, and LAB

A channel structure that separates color from contrast offers decisive advantages for certain images.

5   The Key Is the K

The black channel is the most potent weapon in the CMYK arsenal. Those who understand GCR have a powerful RGB tool as well.

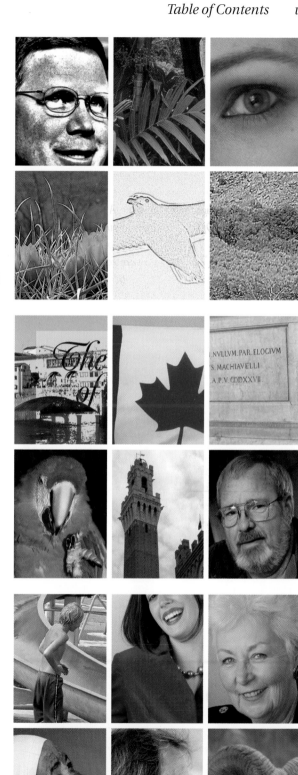

6 Sharpening with a Stiletto

Whether in conventional or high Radius, low Amount form, the Unsharp Mask filter appears to add focus—but it's based on a blur.

use Bl's White method - in CS3

7 Keeping the Color In Black and White

Any contrast in hue or saturation won't survive the transition. We have to convert it to luminosity contrast.

8 Keeping the Black and White in Color

The same techniques that enable better luminosity in a B/W conversion work well in color, too.

9

Inferences, Illusions, and When to Bet the Image

When the target numbers aren't obvious, do some detective work. Every image has its own clues.

10

Every File Has Ten Channels

CMYK, LAB, and RGB each have strengths and weaknesses. We need to learn not just to work in all three—but to think in them.

11

Making Things Look Alike

The second half of the book commences by exploring how to make the monitor match the print and concluding: open your eyes.

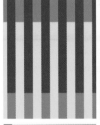

12 Managing Color Settings

Choosing wisely depends on understanding not only the theory, but also the choices that others make, and where the process can break down.

13 Politics, Printing, and the Science of the Skosh

The key to success in preparing files for offset printing is to hope for the best and prepare for the worst.

14 Resolution for the Multimegapixel Era

We don't need as much data today as in the age of film—but sometimes we don't have enough.

15

The Art of the False Profile

If an image appears too dark, it could be because your expectations are too light. Change the definition of RGB, and a Wonderland opens up.

16

What Comes Around, Goes Around

Camera Raw and similar acquisition modules permit us to bypass some dubious camera logic.

17

Blurs, Masks, and Safety in Sharpening

Channel structure can be exploited to mix conventional and hiraloam USM into one harmonious whole.

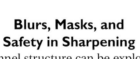

18 — Overlays, Hiraloam, and Shadow/Highlight

The image's endpoints need resuscitation today much more frequently than they did in the age of film.

19 — Color, Contrast, and Safety in Masking

The best masks are based on existing channels—and maybe not in the colorspace you're currently using.

20 — There Are No Bad Originals

The thought process for approaching images summarized, one new and one old correction, and speculation about the future of our field.

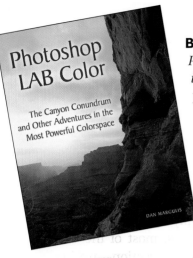

By the Same Author:

Photoshop LAB Color: The Canyon Conundrum and Other Adventures in the Most Powerful Colorspace (2006) unleashed the considerable potential of LAB, revolutionized workflows, and became an immediate best seller. It is neither a companion to nor a substitute for the present volume. *Photoshop LAB Color* treats LAB-related issues in more depth than *Professional Photoshop* does. It also discusses areas that are beyond the scope of this book, such as overlay blends using the A and B channels, and advanced retouching and selection techniques. It does not cover the CMYK and RGB fundamentals that are the foundation of *Professional Photoshop.* The Table of Contents is as follows:

Introduction

"Here is a meta thought," wrote one of the beta readers—the volunteers who read this book on your behalf before it was published. "People who are reading your books for the first time may take a while to understand what you are about. I have to explain all the time that you are not offering recipes the way other Photoshop authors do, but rather teaching people how to think about color correction. In the process, you consider case studies and offer techniques. But the successful reader will come away with much more than just a catalog of techniques. I'd like to see a statement like this near the beginning of the book."

*   *   *

Now that we've made *him* happy, let's talk about you. You may be a professional retoucher. You may be a professional photographer. You may be a professional something else, who has to create good digital images as part of your job. Or you may be ignoring the daunting first word of the title, because you aren't a professional at all, but you wish to create work that *looks* professional.

In late 2005, Microsoft, which ought to know, stated flatly: "Digital cameras are the fastest-growing consumer device category in history." A marketing research firm estimated that in that year, in North America alone, 26 million digicams would be sold.

Some of these 26 million digicam owners are potential readers of this book. Far more are not, which has far-reaching consequences for digicam marketing that we will be discussing throughout, particularly in the second half.

No matter which category of reader you fall into, you have purchased this book because you want to make your images look better, just as I do with my own. Crude ways of doing this are known: Adobe Photoshop's Image: Adjustments>Auto Contrast usually works, but we would never use it, because we want something better than it can deliver. And, even though applying it would apparently improve the image, most of the time it would *hamper* a later correction—we'd be better off starting from scratch than picking up from where it left off.

Similarly, the automated adjustments that digicams use—which we are often unaware of—are successful at making most images look better out of the box. Sometimes they are to our benefit; at others we have to take steps to reverse them.

This book is the fifth and final edition of a series that began in 1994. It teaches how to make pictures look very much better than any automated method can, and always has. But it can't stop there, and never has, hence the reader's warning.

Many are not satisfied with merely making obvious improvements. They would like to know that their images don't look pitiful in comparison to what I, or someone with similar skills, might produce. Unfortunately, that target is moving. Every year, better techniques are uncovered, and we gain a deeper understanding of what we are trying to accomplish in the first place.

The technical challenges change, too. The files that professionals face today, for example, almost always arrive in RGB. They can be of any level of quality and, in many cases, are shot by amateurs. In 1994, they arrived in CMYK, usually had been professionally shot, and often had been improved during the process of drum scanning, which was standard practice at the time.

What we do today in Photoshop derives directly from what painters have been doing for nearly a millennium. They have been learning more about their art throughout that time. We have more tools than they ever dreamed of. Anyone who supposes that we will ever run out of new ways to make pictures look better is only fooling himself.

In sum, I write the way I do because I think you should aspire to be able to handle imaging problems that don't exist today, and to be better at color correction in the future than I currently am.

The Changes in This Edition

It is therefore the tradition of this series that each new title is drastically expanded and rewritten. The second (1998) edition was around 80 percent new; the third (2000) and fourth (2002) were each more than half new. This one takes the prize: it's around 90 percent new content compared to *Professional Photoshop Fourth Edition.*

The page size has been enlarged to permit larger comparison images. The text is half again as long as in the previous edition. While many chapters correspond, and even open with the same jokes, almost all the interior content has changed.

The most potent weapons in the color-correction war are curves, channel blending, and sharpening. These are covered comprehensively in the first 10 chapters in a way that I hope will be accessible to most readers. The second half of the book is much harder. Chapters 11–14 have to do with color settings, resolution, and calibration issues, and the war between photographers and printers. Chapter 16 is about Camera Raw, and Chapters 15 and 17–20 cover advanced topics, mostly sharpening. The beta readers say they are both hard and the most rewarding chapters in the book.

The curves section has been overhauled, but the basic techniques haven't changed.

The channel blending and sharpening sections are rebuilt from the ground up and feature many previously unpublished strategies.

Channel blending as an adjunct to curves is a concept originated in this series, as indeed LAB color correction itself is. Time has shown that both concepts are more powerful than I originally thought. I now feel that channel blending is right up there with curves in terms of overall importance.

I'm not the only one who thinks that. By far the most common request for this edition was increased coverage of channel moves. In fact, many suggested that it be a book *entirely* about channel blending.

These changes happened because of extensive online commentary about the series. I run the large Applied Color Theory discussion group, details of which are in the Notes & Credits section. There I asked for and got a lot of opinions about what to do with this edition. Furthermore, the unexpectedly great commercial success of my book *Photoshop LAB Color* (2006) indicated some errors in the way I had been approaching things.

The second most common request was for more than the single chapter I had previously devoted to unsharp masking. This was convenient, because a significant, closely related command, Shadow/Highlight, was introduced in Photoshop CS in 2003 and so was not covered last time. Four chapters now examine the sharpening issue closely.

The third request, a plaintive call for help, was to discuss why commercial printing is such a minefield for photographers and others whose background is RGB only. This implies not just summarizing the sad realities of printing, such as its inherent variability, and not just providing strategies to avoid losing color during the conversion to CMYK, but also engaging in some frank commentary on the politics of the situation.

Fourth, we needed a discussion of how to handle files that are in a raw format, a problem that didn't exist at the time of the last edition. This involved probably the most work of the entire book, because I needed to carefully examine many different varieties of raw images from many different models of cameras, and to compare methods of correcting them both with and without the use of Camera Raw or some other module.

Fifth, there was a request for more explanation of my own thought process in choosing certain techniques for specific images. I've tried to do that, and also have added a series of quizzes to try to keep you honest as you plow through the text.

In addition to these reader requests, it must be acknowledged that camera technology has changed so much in the last five years that most of the images discussed in the last edition are less instructive today. That was still the age of film in the professional world; now we are almost entirely digital. The two classes of images are similar, but certain problems are now far more common than they used to be. Plus, any file produced by scanning film has had some human correction. Files from digital cameras haven't.

A bit over a dozen of the film-based images in the last edition were so useful that I couldn't bear to part with them. The others have been replaced with ones that are more typical of modern practice. And here is where having such a devoted readership is helpful. I already had a truckload of useful images from photographers who had volunteered to help with *Photoshop LAB Color,* but I was greedy for more.

I said as much on my list, and asked those interested in participating to make themselves known, and to describe what equipment they were using and what sort of image they specialized in. The response was very great. I asked several people, most of them strangers to me, to send me libraries of uncorrected images that they would be willing to let me examine and use—and, especially

to place on the attached CD, so that you could follow along with the exercises. That's another big change—every image for which a correction is illustrated (with one ancient exception) is now available to you.

You and I owe thanks to Darren Bernaerdt, Stuart Block, David Cardinal, Ric Cohn, David Moore, Kim Müller, John Ruttenberg, Gerry Shamray, Marty Stock, and David Xenakis, who each submitted DVDs of material, and to several other photographers who offered individual images. The library of images from which I chose the ones for this book occupies nearly 100 gigabytes.

Above all, we must recognize the contribution of the *Knoxville News Sentinel,* which offered me use of an archive of thousands of files that its imaging director, Clarence Maslowski, had chosen as being especially problematic. No photographer is exempt from having to work with images that are less than optimal for one reason or another. But a newspaper on deadline shoots under every known disastrous condition—and often has to use the results in print, no matter how bad the exposure. I could easily have written an entire second book using nothing but other pictures from this archive.

*   *   *

Google this or my other titles, or search the photography discussion boards, and you'll get more information than can conveniently be read. Most like what I say, a few don't, but there's unanimity on the basics.

Everybody agrees that these writings form the assumed foundation for today's professional practice. Further, that I make a highly technical subject sound irritatingly easy by the cheap trick of using simple English to describe it, rather than the polysyllabic gobbledygook that others seem to feel makes lame ideas sound more impressive. However, I am not noted for hand-holding.

To assist in making the text less opaque, I again solicited help from the list. As with both the last edition and *Photoshop LAB Color,* a very dedicated group of beta readers scrutinized and criticized the manuscript. We had ten people this time, some of whom had beta-read one or more of the other titles. I selected this group from more than 30 volunteers, trying to make it represent *your* interests as much as possible. Here's how it broke out—notice how many of these people fall into more than one category.

Three current or former professional photographers, and three serious amateurs. Two people who work for service providers that accept jobs from the public, one of which outputs in RGB and the other CMYK. Five people who have been professional retouchers, four who say they currently work four hours or more a day in Photoshop, three who say they have to be at least as skilled in another application as they are in Photoshop, and three who identify themselves as being beginning or intermediate Photoshoppers. Three have taught Photoshop professionally; three have taught other subjects professionally, and five are or have been professional writers or editors. Three have taken courses with me and seven have not. I have socialized with three people; have never met three others but feel that I know them well through correspondence; and have only a vague acquaintance with four. Four have a background in the hard sciences and five in fine art. Three almost always have to produce CMYK files, two almost always RGB, and five could be asked for either one. Six hail from the United States, two from Canada, and one each from Brazil and New Zealand. One person is color-blind.

This group's members proved as aggressive as they are diverse. They generally saw things the same way. On the first draft, they were most impressed by Chapters 7, 8, 15, 16, 18, and 19. They were extremely unimpressed by certain other parts, which, upon rereading, didn't impress me very much, either. Those parts didn't make it into the final book, needless to say.

The amount of effort these people went through was no joke—I got seriously marked-up versions of every chapter from each one of them. You will be getting to meet most of them, because when they've said something provocative that offers a different perspective from mine, I quote them by name, although the three whose words appear in this introduction will remain anonymous.

For the record, we should all thank Les De Moss, Fred Drury, André Dumas, Bruce Fellman, George Harding, André Borges Lopes, Clarence Maslowski, Clyde McConnell, John Ruttenberg, and Nick Tressider. They, along with my wife, Cathy Panagoulias, who saw the chapters before the editing team did, and Elissa Rabellino, who picked up the ball on Peachpit's behalf after the team had torn the drafts to shreds, have made the book much easier to read, and prevented many errors. Most authors would say at this point that any remaining flaws are theirs alone. I, in accord with the longstanding tradition of the prepress industry in which I grew up, state that any surviving errors in this text are the fault of the photographer.

On Mutual Expectations

Many poor ways of handling images are publicly advocated, often passionately. This is not because anybody deliberately wishes to peddle inferior methodology. Quite the contrary: the people who advance these methods have convinced themselves that they work, which is understandable. If some sequence of commands produces an obviously better image, it's easy to conclude that it was the right thing to do, and to recommend it to others.

Deciding that a picture has been made better is easy. The hard part is to imagine how much better it might be. In this respect, I have an enormous advantage, thanks to the contributions of another group.

I teach master classes in color correction, including some that are for experts only, by invitation only. Regardless of level, I've found that the best approach is to have everyone work on the same images using techniques of their own choosing, and then compare results side by side. That way, deficiencies in technique are immediately apparent. The objective is not to win so much as it is to avoid being disgraced by producing an image that is blatantly worse than somebody else's.

I get to play, too, if I like, and I almost always *do* play when the opponents are experts. I rehearse a lot of the content of this book that way. The edge I have over other authors is that, before I say that the following method is the best one and that you won't be able to come close any other way, I may have actually seen 50 people try that other way and fail.

Likewise, you don't get to see the techniques that I thought were really, really good right up until the day they put my image in fifth place. When I recommend a technique, generally I *know* that it works because I have access to the efforts of people who are approximately as skilled as I am and can't do better some other way.

The other huge advantage these classes provide is that I've participated in around 5,000 small-group discussions and votes on which image looks best. As a result, I have rather a good sense of when one image is going to be a near-unanimous choice, and when there may be a difference of opinion.

Early in my magazine writing career, I presented two different results and recommended the method that had produced the first, since, I said, it was obvious that nobody could possibly be so stupid as to prefer the second. It took around 500 angry responses for me to understand that some people are so anxious that the color be right that they are willing to forgive poor contrast, whereas others take the opposite view.

Today, I would never make such a mistake, and in any event I now have a better handle on how to package good color *and* good contrast in one happy container. With every edition, I discard certain techniques in favor of better ones. On page 486, if you get that far, is a box summarizing how my approach has changed since last time.

* * *

Now that you know what can be expected of me, more or less, what about *you?*

First, you have to want good images enough to get involved in a wrestling match. If not, you should buy one of those step-by-step recipe books.

If you really want to make your images look better, it is not necessary that you know exactly what you want in advance of doing it, but it *is* necessary that you be willing and able to state what you like when you see it.

[Another beta reader: "I disagree. If you don't know what you want to achieve, you won't know if you have achieved it. When do you stop correcting an image? When it looks 'good enough' or when it cannot be better? It is necessary that you be able to know what you *don't like* about the image and make corrections until you are willing and able to state that you like what you see."]

At one extreme, I assert that if you don't do things in the by-the-numbers method shown in Chapters 2–4 or something reasonably close thereto, you will not get competitive results. At the other are the sharpening chapters, where the only test is what looks good to you, which may not agree with what looks good to me. In this edition you will likely get tired of reading that my opacity settings or whatever are only my own personal preference and not a firm recommendation. Such disclaimers are necessary because of past experience that some readers are baffled by why I am using 53% layer opacity and not the 57% that looks better to them.

Also, when the word *Professional* appears

in the title, you have little choice but to cut the author a little slack with respect to explaining how Photoshop works. Yes, there are adequate explanations of the commands that we use over and over, but I often refer to certain command structure or retouching techniques as if everybody is supposed to know them, when in fact I am perfectly aware that even some experts don't and am merely trying to avoid wasting three pages on a tangential topic by explaining in depth.

If you find yourself lost at any point, then you'll be in good company. The ability to deal with frustration is a prerequisite to using this book, and it's not just when I omit explaining something. As you can see from the Stumbling Blocks boxes in most chapters, even sophisticated readers have blind spots. Don't worry. You'll get back on track.

Again, Google my titles and you'll find one telling phrase that is repeated by reader after reader—one that you won't find about any other Photoshop books, and precious few in any technical field.

Here it is: you get more out of these books on the second and third reading. And sometimes more. [A third beta reader: "And how. I'd put that in ital or maybe even bold. And you can quote me: like good Italian food, it gets better the second or third time around."] So, relax. If you're serious about image enhancement, you're in it for the long haul.

The Lifelong Learning Curve

As those who have suffered through past titles will attest, my own reading interests are diverse. This allows me to savor the preceding paragraph, because I am in a position to know in what company these books are being placed. And that answers at least one of the questions that the beta reader posed in the opening lines of this introduction.

Most correction techniques don't date. The fanciest new stuff in this book is there because I didn't know how to do it before, not because it couldn't have been done in Photoshop 3. This is why, unlike in other series, there is no Photoshop version number in the title. Nor do I indulge in planned obsolescence by discussing specific makes of cameras, printers, or third-party software. The section on Camera Raw will age rapidly as the young module improves, but other than that, these techniques should last for a while.

Note that Photoshop itself, which is a mature program, continues to improve at a time when it might be expected to stand pat. The last edition featured zero in the way of new Photoshop capabilities, because there were none important enough to include. Not this time—Shadow/Highlight, Surface Blur, Camera Raw: these are significant improvements. They are food for thought for the rest of us.

But what you'll find in the next 500 pages is not version-specific. When I wrote the introduction to the last edition, I said, "The next revision will come not when there's new software, but when there are new or better tricks to present."

That time is now. I hope you find the tricks useful and the presentation comprehensible. To close, let's repeat the last three paragraphs of the aforementioned 2002 introduction.

* * *

If you decide to go farther, good luck, because it is a treacherous, if rewarding, passage you're heading for.

If it ever gets too difficult, too discouraging, remember that what we are after is surpassingly simple. After we're done with the correction, we want to ask ourselves, *does this picture look better now?*

I hope your answer will be the same as mine: not only does it look better, it looks better than if I had done this same picture two years ago.

Professional Photoshop

FIFTH EDITION

Color, Contrast, And Channels

Before tackling color correction, a fundamental question must be answered: is the idea to reproduce a photograph as accurately as possible, or to reproduce what a viewer who was in the position of the camera would have seen?

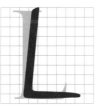et there be light, the Lord said, and since then there's been nothing but trouble for graphic artists.

The dome of St. Peter's Cathedral is the brilliant concept and execution of His servant Michelangelo Buonarroti, sculptor, poet, painter, architect, and the greatest graphic artist of the millennium. My wife and I, checking into our Rome hotel, discovered that the balcony overlooked it. Naturally, like any other tourist, I whipped out my digicam and shot Figure 1.1A.

The reasons for wanting to improve this picture were sentimental, not professional. My wife and I wanted to make a decent print of the scene, plus we wanted to give away some copies to friends. So I had at it for a few minutes in Adobe Photoshop, and produced Figure 1.1B.

The picture looks better now. Let's pause and agree on this point. If you're thinking that you could make an even better version yourself, that's certainly possible. It's only to be expected that you think so. After all, the title of this book contains the word *professional*. Graphic arts professionals are notorious for overrating their own work.

Set that aside. For present purposes, there is no third alternative. You have to vote for one of these two.

How people react to different versions of the same image is a topic that I've been interested in for a while. I've done a lot of testing with juries and with classes, so I know how people tend to vote, and I know what kinds of images win overwhelmingly and what kinds lead to split verdicts. This pair hasn't gone to any jury, but it doesn't need to—I'm quite confident that, given only these two choices, almost everyone would prefer Figure 1.1B.

Figure 1.1 Which version of this scene looks better? What are the criteria for deciding?

This book's topic is color correction. The word *correction* means roughly to make better. The word *better* is problematic. No rulebook, no computer program, can ever decide which of two versions of a photograph is the better one. People often reach different conclusions, which is awkward.

In such cases, the rule is a simple one for the professional users at whom this book is aimed. The better of the two images is the one that your client says is better.

Unfortunately, your client isn't looking over my shoulder as I type this, so I can't ask him. But we can ask a lot of other people, and if there's an overwhelming consensus—as I believe there would be with this image—then it's an excellent prediction of how the client would feel.

Figure 1.1B, therefore, is better—not the best conceivable, but better. It's better because I used certain techniques that are known to make images look better, and because Figure 1.1A has certain defects that I did not permit to survive. The next five hundred pages will try to help you do the same: to detect problems that need to be fixed, and to identify the appropriate techniques to get rid of them.

Pearls Before Swine

You are undertaking a notoriously difficult subject by reading a notoriously expensive, opinionated, unforgiving, and technical book. This identifies you as someone who is serious, not to say obsessive, about image quality. Yet your goal is the same as that of any amateur, any advertiser, any proud parent with a picture of a child, anyone with a product to advertise or a scene to remember. Whether a scintillating work of art, the most stiflingly mundane commercial photo, or a second-rate photograph with first-rate sentimental value, we always want to enhance quality.

Sometimes the decision about which version is better is not as easy as in our first example. Figure 1.2 offers three contenders, not just two. The question this time is not just which is the best, but also which is the worst. I've asked around 500 people who were involved in the graphics industry. How do you think the vote went?

Some of these people were experts and others were beginners. Some judged the pictures outdoors, others in graphic arts lighting booths, others under incandescent lighting, and still others under fluorescent. None of these factors had any bearing on the results.

The people came from all over North America, and occasionally from other parts of the world. Surprisingly, this mattered. Those hailing from the southeastern part of the United States were more or less evenly divided between Figures 1.2B and 1.2C as best. Those from other regions preferred Figure 1.2C by a ratio of nearly 3 to 1.

All 500 people who looked at this image declared that Figure 1.2A is the worst of the three. And so, of course, it is. But as to which of the other two is better, your vote is as good as mine, and your client's vote counts more than either one.

This is the first salvo of the never-ending battle between color and contrast. Those preferring Figure 1.2B almost always conceded that the detailing in the hog's coat is better in Figure 1.2C. However, they thought the animal is too orange overall in that image. Southerners are probably more aware of the proper color of hogs than others are, hence the different vote by geographic origin.

Similarly, many of those who liked Figure 1.2C admitted that hogs aren't really that color but said that Figure 1.2B, let alone Figure 1.2A, was too flat.

In sum, we may not have a consensus on which is the best version, but the basics aren't in dispute. Figure 1.2B is better for color but Figure 1.2C is better for contrast. Some people favor one factor more than the other, up to a point. After all, Figure 1.2A is

approximately the same color as Figure 1.2B, but nobody in the world prefers it to the much livelier Figure 1.2C.

So, which flawed version is better? It depends on how your client juggles the relative importances of color and contrast. But one thing is for sure. If a fourth version combined the color of Figure 1.2B with the detailing of Figure 1.2C, it would get all the votes. Part of the mission of this book is to explain how to create just such a version.

The Natural Look

The key to having viewers like our images is to understand how cameras and human eyes differ.

Returning to Michelangelo's dome, Figure 1.1B has better color *and* better contrast. Without getting into the specifics of how it was done, let's talk about other areas that might cause disagreement.

Certain technical defects in Figure 1.1A have been corrected, yielding better detail in Figure 1.1B. Everybody likes detail: after all, when was the last time you heard somebody say that a picture would have looked better if you had run the Gaussian Blur filter before you printed it?

Color, on the other hand, is sometimes subjective, sometimes not. The sky in Figure 1.1B is markedly bluer than in Figure 1.1A. Whether it has gotten *too* blue is subjective. Whether it should actually be a little more

Figure 1.2 *Hundreds of people were asked which of these versions was the best and which the worst. How do you think they voted?*

A

Figure 1.3 *The woman's chin is purplish because the camera sees a reflection from her turtleneck. The Venetian canal has a similar reflection of the buildings. A human observer would not see either of these colors. Yet a warm reflection in water seems romantic and a purple chin does not.*

purple is subjective; whether it should be green is not. If I provided alternatives to Figure 1.1B where the major difference was a purpler or a grayer sky, some would favor them and others would not. Nobody would vote for a green sky.

If asked to describe why Figure 1.1B is better than Figure 1.1A, a layperson would probably use imprecise terms like *crisper* or *cleaner*. This is as opposed to a professional, who would use more technically correct words, such as *more bite* or *snappier*.

Either group, if pressed, might use the phrase *more natural*. In other words, more like what we would have seen, had we been in the position of the camera.

Figure 1.1A is hazy. The human visual system cuts right through haze. Furthermore,

when we humans concentrate on a certain object, we lose perception in other areas as we force our vision to become more sensitive to the things that interest us. Notice that the foreground of Figure 1.1B seems sharply focused in comparison to the background. In Figure 1.1A the two areas are more alike. If we were there looking at the scene, we'd be concentrating more on the foreground, too, and less on the background.

Also, the human visual system is self-calibrating. We always perceive the ambient lighting as being neutral, not colored. Pictures taken under fluorescent lighting usually have an undesirable green-yellow tinge that professionals describe as a *cast*. The question of whether the cast is actually present is academic; the camera sees it, we don't.

Green color casts, as a rule, look stupid. One of the main goals of color correction is to take them out. In every language on earth, as far as I am able to determine (and I've checked around 20), greens and blues are known as *cool colors* and reds, oranges, and sometimes yellows as *warm colors.* Warm casts are sometimes tolerable or even preferable. Cool casts are rarely acceptable.

This cast-reduction procedure is so universally accepted today that it's hard to believe that less than 15 years ago, a significant minority believed it to be wrong. Their misguided mantra was "match the art"—that the original photograph had some mystic power that made it the desired target for the final output.

Most art directors who parroted this line relied on, shall we say, an imaginative view of what the original art represented. As one who worked in prepress houses during the period, I can report that when clients complained we were not "matching the art," it was usually because we had already moved away from a literal match, but not far enough to suit them. In effect, they were asking that we move even further away from it.

Times have changed. Nowadays everyone understands that an image printed in a newspaper or on a large-format printer or posted on the Web is not going to match the original photograph exactly and that there is no reason to want it to. As more photographers have taken over the preparation of their own work for print, they've come to realize that it's another bite at the apple. What the photograph used to be is history; it's now in a new form into which many things don't translate properly and in which there are occasionally opportunities to do things that weren't possible in the original film, such as killing color casts when we feel like it.

Measurements of areas where the desired colors are known reveal that, strictly speaking, Figure 1.1A has a mild yellowish cast. I

could have neutralized it, and in principle I should have, but I replaced it with a slight warm (reddish) cast anyway, because I thought it would look better that way.

Certain rules are absolute. I absolutely wouldn't allow the image to have a green cast. But others are relative. Sometimes we deliberately leave things in that people wouldn't actually see, not because it makes the picture more believable but because it sets a mood.

The woman's chin in Figure 1.3A shows a reflection of the purple of her blouse. Such is the camera's opinion, at any rate. Mine is that purple reflections off chins look ridiculous because human observers don't see any such thing. So I would take it out.

Something similar happens in the Venetian scene of Figure 1.3B. A pink building is casting a reflection in the canal. A human observer wouldn't see nearly so pronounced a color. I think it looks romantic as shot, and would leave the reflection alone.

Sliding Down a Slippery Slope

Most serious users now accept the philosophy of trying to match what a human observer would see, but many haven't yet come to grips with all its logical ramifications. In 500 years, people will laugh at how little we knew about the astonishingly complex human visual system. But even today, we know about many more peculiarities than *chromatic adaptation,* its obsession with neutralizing ambient lighting.

We evaluate colors in context, not absolutely. The presence of a background color provokes the effect known as *simultaneous contrast.* We force the foreground color into a different direction to exaggerate its distinction from the background. As cameras don't play by these rules, any photograph taken of something full of similar colors has to be corrected if it is to look natural. For example, if we find ourselves in a forest, we cheerfully and unconsciously visualize all kinds of

Figure 1.4 Our visual system dislikes harsh reflections. Cameras do not. They frequently see catchlights that a human observer would not perceive. Should they be retouched out?

variations in its greens and browns, much to the frustration of photographers whose best forest shots lack that reality.

We also adjust to different lighting intensities more rapidly and accurately than any artificial instrument. Shots taken indoors often look too dark, because if we had been there, we would have seen the room as lighter than the camera did.

And we have a sophisticated filtering mechanism, lacking in cameras, that reduces the intensity of reflections and flashes of light. We have all seen photos like Figure 1.4, full of hot spots in the face. As we wouldn't see such catchlights ourselves if we were there, they look unnatural. This is one of the reasons why makeup is used so heavily during studio portrait shoots.

Furthermore,

• When humans concentrate on one object, that object gains contrast and everything else loses it, but the camera is egalitarian.

• The human observer loses color perception in uninteresting background areas. The camera doesn't.

• When an image reaches print, the less colorful an object is, the more it seems to recede into the background.

• The darkest parts of a scene are usually seen as colorless by humans, even when those areas are part of something with a pronounced color, such as the darkest folds of a green garment. A camera sees such folds as a very dark green.

Catering to these whims of human visualization is tough. Yet anyone who believes in reducing casts really has to believe in retouching out the catchlights and introducing more color variation in the forest and neutralizing unimportant background objects.

If we alter the photograph to make it look like what we would have seen had we been in the position of the camera, it will look better. That's the whole case for aggressive color correction in a nutshell.

The Weapons in the Arsenal

As Photoshop has matured, the number of tools has proliferated. Even though this is an advanced textbook, we're going to be concentrating on just a few of them—the ones that really make the difference.

• *Curves* are the principal and indispensable tool in establishing what is often called *color by the numbers.* We use them to be sure that we have a full range of tonality in every image, to assign added detail to the most important parts of the image, and to avoid colors that can't possibly be right. We will define how curves work in Chapter 2 and then spend two more chapters refining the approach. Curves permeate the rest of the book, even when they are not the main topic.

• *Channel blending* attacks certain problems that curves cannot solve. The typical use is in fixing up channels that are weak in contrast. We will introduce that application in Chapter 7, which discusses a seemingly irrelevant topic, creation of good black and whites. Then we will extend the technique into color images in Chapter 8. More esoteric channel blends are also valuable, but they can safely be put off until our final chapters.

● Most images require *sharpening,* because limitations in the capture process usually produce a slight impression of blurriness, no matter how well focused the camera may be. The traditional kind of sharpening is discussed in Chapter 6. But there are alternate types of sharpening—and many possible combinations of the different types. We'll touch on these alternate methods then, and expand on them in Chapters 17, 18, and 19.

● The advent of digital cameras has been a mixed blessing. One of the biggest issues, one that we didn't face to nearly so great an extent in the age of film, is that extreme *highlights and shadows* tend to get blown out as the camera software looks to maximize midtone contrast. All three methods listed above can be used as effective counters. However, the Shadow/Highlight command, which is closely related to sharpening, saves a lot of time. Without a good grasp of how the basic sharpening filter works, though, it's difficult to get the best results with S/H. Consequently we will be deferring discussion of it until Chapter 18.

Now that we've looked at the commands that the book focuses on, a few words about the ones it doesn't. Some methods, like Image: Adjustments>Brightness/Contrast, should be avoided because they are inferior. Others are tempting but overused. Chief among these is the ability to "select" areas of an image to be worked on in isolation, so that any changes will affect only the selected region and not the rest of the image.

Experienced people examine images for clues that there's something wrong with an image. A green cow, for example, might be such a clue. Less experienced folk are also capable of detecting and disliking green cows but often fall into the selection snare in trying to fix them.

If the cow is green, other things are greener than they should be as well. The grass the cow is standing on will be too green, but there's no way of knowing that in isolation: there are lots of kinds of grass and lots of degrees of greenness. Somewhere in the world, grass is probably found that's as green as what's underneath the cow. But in the context of this hypothetical picture, it wouldn't look right.

It's a mistake, therefore, to wheel out selection tools and isolate the cow.

When Do the Eyes Adjust?

If somebody turns on the lights without a warning while you're sitting in a dark room, you'll rub your eyes. That's the nutshell answer to why photos that you expect to look good as shot, and which do look good on a computer screen, often seem the wrong color when printed.

Look at the same room from outside, and it will seem darker than when you're inside it. The environment provokes the adjustment, but you have to be immersed in it. Humans evolved to adjust to new lighting conditions quickly and seamlessly. Once inside the room, we adapt unconsciously and automatically, sensitizing ourselves to dark areas so that we can perceive detail, and desensitizing ourselves to the brightness that is not present. No camera would see the room as being as light as we do.

Adjusting—or, better said, calibrating—to aberrant lighting conditions works similarly. If the ambient light is green, we desensitize ourselves to it and become acutely sensitive to magenta, its opponent. This balancing act lets us perceive neutrality where the camera sees green.

When we stare into a monitor, we are so isolated from other light sources that the same effect can take place. If the image being displayed is too green, the more we stare at it the less green it looks. If we were to take ten paces backward, it would be green again.

On a printed page, though, we can't be fooled by green casts. The offending image is surrounded by white—not green—paper. Nothing causes us to adjust to a single photograph instead of the surroundings as a whole. We see the greenness, the imbalance, and we don't like it.

Not that selections and masks are useless. If we are silhouetting part of an image or extending a background, ordinarily a selection is in order. When a shot has two conflicting light sources, a selection is usually the only way of reconciling the color throughout the image. If the model is wearing a blue shirt and the client says to make it red, a selection will often be needed.

Selections are, however, somewhat more necessary today than they were when the last edition of this book appeared, due to the supremacy of digital photography. Film simply records incoming light, for better or worse. Digital cameras incorporate various tricks to massage their data into something that the manufacturer hopes will be more attractive. Most of the time this works fairly well, but often a counter-correction is needed to reverse what the camera's logic did. Some of these counter-corrections require selections, masks, or the use of Photoshop's Blend If options for layers. Examples of each appear throughout the book, and Chapter 19 summarizes the reasons and best techniques for making such selections.

Similarly, the Hue/Saturation and Selective Color commands are important, but overused. Our premise is that global curves will correct whatever ails the image. In practice, they don't always do so. In those cases, a supplementary hit of the other commands is indicated, but not before curves have been given a chance to fall short.

Three junior versions of curves, Photoshop's Brightness/Contrast, Color Balance, and Levels commands, will not be discussed. Color correction is a competitive sport. Those wishing to swim with the sharks must paddle along with real curves, which alone can keep images afloat when the water gets deep and threatening.

Finally, we have to consider two areas that can't be described as "commands" and can't really be compared to any of the items discussed above. First is the question of how to make things look alike: how do we know that the printed result will be what we were expecting? This topic takes up Chapters 11–13, and related materials appear in several subsequent chapters.

Second is the possibility of manipulating the image before opening it in Photoshop proper, using an acquisition module such as Photoshop's Camera Raw, Apple's Aperture, Adobe's Lightroom, or similar software offered by camera vendors. Some of us don't have the option because our files are already in some other format, usually JPEG, when we get them; others have only the raw file, and still others have the choice of either.

This area of software is rapidly evolving. At present, its main disadvantages are that it's slow and its subcommands are clunky in comparison to Photoshop proper. The advantage is that we can quickly bring images closer to where we want them before starting work in earnest elsewhere. In Chapter 16, we'll discuss, using Camera Raw as a model, where such software is and isn't helpful.

But Who Is the Reader?

This book is the fifth and installment in a series of books entitled *Professional Photoshop*. Most such series offer revisions with every release of Photoshop. This one, which began in 1994, updates when there are significant new techniques to discuss, or when recommended workflows change. While other series are often little changed between editions, this one always has at least 50 percent new content. This time sets the record—it's around 90 percent.

It isn't that the basics of color correction have changed much. They haven't, although Shadow/Highlight, Camera Raw, and the Surface Blur filter didn't exist when the last edition appeared.

The changes are needed because I've learned more about the topic, meaning that certain recommendations have to be discarded. Also, because this book is so prominent in its field, it gets a lot of online commentary, plus I have my own discussion group with around 3,000 members. That feedback indicates which sections are making their points well and which need improvement. Because of it, there is a "Stumbling Blocks" section in most chapters—a box that reemphasizes points that have a history of confusing certain readers.

Even before publication, this edition has already undergone major changes, thanks to the efforts of a staff of ten readers with diverse backgrounds, who, I believe, fairly represent the reading audience. Much of the time, their effort is invisible. You don't get to see a lot of the stuff they objected to, because I agreed with them and axed it. You will, however, meet these beta readers from time to time, because sometimes their comments add a useful counterpoint to my own.

The broader audience that these beta readers represent has also changed. "Professional" never has actually meant someone who makes a living by using Photoshop. Rather, it means someone sufficiently interested in image quality to aspire to create images that are competitive with those that professionals might prepare.

So, the reader might be the typical one of 1994—a full-time retoucher, working with high-quality originals, probably for the preparation of print advertising. Or he could be a designer, or some other graphic arts generalist who wears the retouching hat along with several others. Such a person was rare in 1994, but common today.

Or the reader might be a professional photographer. Unlike 1994, today any photographer who can't manipulate images in Photoshop won't remain a professional for very much longer.

Professional photographers work almost exclusively with fairly good originals. That can be a bad thing, for a couple of reasons. First, the same techniques that make poor pictures into good ones make good originals into excellent ones. Second, if you work only with images that look pretty good to start with, it's easy to become passive and never discover how much better they can be. If forced to start with garbage that obviously can't sail without correction, one develops the proper buccaneering attitude.

Those who have to deal with poor originals are a rapidly growing group, and no less professional than the people we just spoke of. Most companies today create publications or Web pages featuring images shot by their own employees, who are usually not very good photographers. Images like the man in Figure 1.4 are the stock in trade of such work. Yet the demand for quality there is just as real as it is for the highest-end retouching and photography. Or, here's a sampling of some of the more unusual types who have taken my three-day intensive color-correction course:

- Newspaper production people, who must work with news events shot under horrible lighting conditions, often by reporters, not photographers
- A scientist who wishes to enhance images produced by electron microscopy
- A professor of architecture who wants to help his students produce dynamite-looking portfolios to show prospective employers
- Police forensic scientists, who must try to make the best of crime scene images shot by police officers, often in the very dark settings that criminals seem to prefer
- Employees of a large funeral home, who nowadays are often asked to produce posters or other memorabilia based on 50-year-old images of the deceased

Each of these applications is not only arguably more difficult than those of the first two groups, but more important socially as well. Not to mention, speaking as somebody who has had to deal with some very difficult

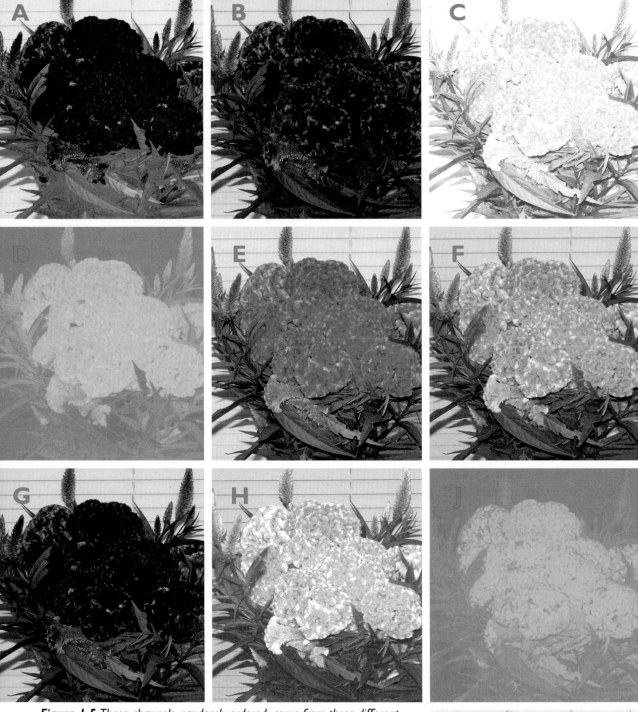

Figure 1.5 *These channels, randomly ordered, come from three different files, one each in CMYK, LAB, and RGB. The color images aren't shown, but they look alike. Can you identify each of the ten channels?*

clients, how would you like to disappoint somebody who's just lost a loved one?

As the readership has changed, however, there's always been one constant in the first chapter—and in this edition, it's more important than it ever has been before.

As mentioned earlier, I run a large online discussion group. When it was time to start thinking about how to

change this edition, I solicited commentary, and got a ton. Two items were mentioned more than any others, and they are the ones that receive the most additional attention in this book.

The second of these is more information on how to coax the best results out of commercial printers, particularly with respect to brilliant colors that are often out of the CMYK gamut. The request was to aim this information not at experienced prepress types but at photographers and others who have little experience in this minefield, and to emphasize the practical as opposed to the theoretical.

We will get to that in the second half of the book, starting in Chapter 11. Meanwhile, the most requested improvement by far, coming from every segment of the readership, was extra coverage of channel structure and channel blending. We'll spend much of the rest of the chapter laying a foundation for it. Let's start off with a quiz.

The Guide Goes Out the Window

It says in the how-to-be-a-technical-author guide that we should be kind and gentle at first. We are supposed to make sure that the opening exercise is not too difficult, so that the unfortunate reader will not be discouraged and put the book down.

Forget about it. The meek inherit the earth in other disciplines. Graphics professionals have to be tough. You want to work in this field, you may as well get used to being sandbagged once in a while.

CMYK files have four channels; LAB and RGB have three apiece. That's a total of ten channels that may confront us as we correct. I have extracted these ten channels from three identical-looking copies of a picture of a bouquet and jumbled them into a random order for Figure 1.5. It's your job to unscramble them. You don't get to see the composite, but if you did, there would be no surprises, no trickery, no crazy-looking colors.

If you're feeling bold, stop now and fill out the worksheet. If you'd like a hint, I will shortly describe what color the flowers are, and you can take it from there. But if you master the techniques of this book, you won't need that information—the color of the flowers can be deduced from these ten channels, without any composite image.

If you don't think you can be positive which channel is which even after getting the hint, this quiz can give you the irritating feeling that the author is getting onto a holier-than-thou tangent of no particular value.

Not so. If you can't solve a problem like this, your image quality will suffer. As you slog through the rest of the book, you'll see why.

Usually the problem is presented in

Figure 1.5 Worksheet

Each contestant on the facing page is a single channel taken from one of three files—CMYK, LAB, and RGB. The three original color images look identical. Identify the ten channels. (Answers on page 19.)

Channel	Version
A (LAB)	
B (LAB)	
Black	
Blue	
Cyan	
Green	
Lightness	
Magenta	
Red	
Yellow	

Figure 1.6
A hint for solving the previous puzzle. The flowers in Figure 1.5 are approximately the same color as this one.

reverse. That is, you look at a color picture, and you visualize what the channels look like. You may object that it isn't necessary. You can look at them whenever you like by displaying the Channels palette and clicking the channel you want to see. There's even a keyboard shortcut: Command–1 displays the first channel (red in RGB, cyan in CMYK, L in LAB) and so on; Command–~ (tilde character, U.S. English keyboards only) returns you to the composite color display.

But if you have an RGB file, how do visualize what the black channel of CMYK would look like? What about the L of LAB? You may need to know these things to squeeze the most out of the image.

Successful color correction relies heavily on three Photoshop maneuvers: curves, channel blending, and sharpening. All depend on knowing what the channels look like—not just because it helps us visualize the forthcoming steps, but because it may make us realize that we're currently in the wrong colorspace.

Why the Quiz Matters

Professionals of 1994 worked in a CMYK world. The Web technically existed but it was a nonfactor. The big money was in images that were commercially printed. The only serious RGB output was that of film recorders, but it was a tiny fraction of the overall CMYK market.

Input, also, was generally CMYK, in the form of drum scans. Digital cameras were in their infancy, as were desktop scanners. Photographers seldom used Photoshop at all. They supplied film; the film got scanned, a prepress house color-corrected it, and a printer printed it.

CMYK output was still the rule by the time of the second edition in 1998. The rumblings of change, which some took as ominous and others welcome, were coming from the input side. The prepress industry was floundering, and methods of capturing in RGB were becoming more reliable.

Developments surrounding the third (2000), fourth (2002), and fifth (2006) editions of *Professional Photoshop* can be compressed into a few sentences. The prepress industry vanished. Film did not vanish altogether, but it became an endangered species. Drum scanning almost disappeared. With the advent of really excellent digital cameras at prices that are absurdly low by 1994 standards, almost all input today is RGB. The Web requires RGB output, and so do most desktop color printers. Commercial printing in CMYK is still a very big deal. High-end non-impact printers sometimes want CMYK files and sometimes RGB.

Until recently, most of the professional world worked in *either* RGB or CMYK, not both. The fear factor was in play, resulting in a lot of insults being hurled. Many professional photographers describe CMYK editing as a counterintuitive abomination. CMYK aficionados commonly retort that working in RGB is like attempting to do brain surgery while wearing boxing gloves.

Regardless of the truth of these jibes, the trend is for professionals to need to know both spaces. A person working for a firm whose only output is commercial printing may think he needs to know only CMYK, yet the files still arrive in RGB. A desktop color printer may require that the incoming file be RGB, but it prints in CMYK just like a press does, and any photographer who doesn't understand basic CMYK principles will not have as good luck with it as one who does.

And, probably the biggest factor: the cameras being sold to amateurs today are impressive instruments, capable of work to the highest professional level—in the right hands, which an amateur's are not. These images get passed on to professionals like us, who have to do the best they can with them.

One of the main purposes of this chapter, and indeed of this book, is to convince you that if you know either RGB or CMYK, you already know how to work in the other.

With that, the hint for the quiz is: the flowers in Figure 1.5 are roughly the same red as the rose in Figure 1.6. We'll show the composite image and return to the quiz later, but now it's time to discuss why RGB and CMYK are the same.

I'm Beginning to See the Light

Our sensation of color does not depend on ink hitting paper. Instead, it has to do with how light hits our eye. The light may originate from the sun, or from a light fixture, or from something else that generates its own light, such as a monitor. More commonly, the light comes from somewhere else and bounces off things we're looking at.

The colors of light to which we are sensitive are, approximately, red, green, and blue. When all these colors hit our eyes in equal quantities, we perceive neutrality, or an absence of color: whites, blacks, grays. When they don't, we see a color. To portray the intense red of Figure 1.6, we have to arrange for a lot more red light to hit the viewer's eye than any other flavor.

Doing that on a screen is straightforward. CRT monitors have red, green, and blue phosphors; LCD monitors achieve the same result by using filters that modify emitted white light. Whatever the technology, we turn the red light source on almost full blast and leave the other two almost completely off.

On the printed page, a more guileful approach is needed.

Blank paper reflects almost all light that hits it. That ambient light, in our minds although not in that of the camera, is equally balanced between red, green, and blue. Therefore, the paper seems neutral—to us.

To reproduce red flowers, we must block the reflection of almost all of the green and the blue light, while allowing almost as much red light to reflect as if the paper were blank. We could accomplish that by mixing up a red ink, but that would create some problems that only become obvious when we discuss

Figure 1.7 *The relationships of colors.*

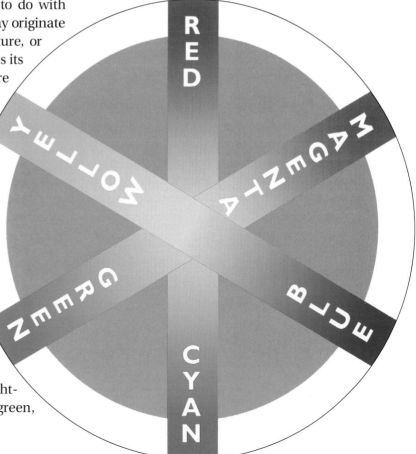

some of the other colors that we might wish to print.

Vivid reds, greens, and blues appear when one type of light reflects almost completely and the other two scarcely do at all. More subtle colors occur when the imbalance isn't quite so stark. Navy blue, for example, is close to black. Little light hits our eye, and what does is only slightly more blue than green and red. Brick red is close to the color of these flowers, but is composed of less red light and more green and blue, which contaminate the red and make it less intense.

Substitute a can of your favorite soft drink and analyze it in the same way. While you're at it, list the colors found in your nation's flag, and perhaps those of a few other countries.

The purpose of this request is to point out how common the colors red, green, and blue are in comparison to the colors known roughly as purple, aqua, and yellow, which fall between them. No doubt flags are a special case, but I actually did some research on the point. I own a stock-photo CD called *Flags of the World,* which contains images from the hundred most populous nations. I opened them all and set up a spreadsheet.

I classified each design element as one of the six major colors shown in Figure 1.7. By my count, 77 nations out of 100 make some major use of red in their flag. Blue appears in 44 flags, and green in 26.

The secondary colors really were secondary. Yellow put in the only respectable showing, being found in 22 flags. Fiji, Ukraine, and the United Nations use aqua. Sri Lanka is apparently the only country in the world making extensive use of a purple in its flag. Thus, there were 147 uses of primary colors, but only 27 of intermediates. Does this make any statistical sense?

If pixels were produced by random-number generator, an intermediate color would be just as likely as a primary one. Yet red, green, and blue objects are much more common than yellow, aqua, and purple ones. If you don't believe it, walk down the street and make note of what color shirts people are wearing.

Why, then, don't printers use red, green, and blue ink on their presses? They could certainly produce our flowers and the flags of most nations, without any help from CMY.

In most texts, this is an occasion for a jargonfest concerning additive and subtractive colors, and an entirely false implication that red, green, and blue ink would be useless. The actual reason we don't use this combination is that there would be no way to create bright intermediate colors like yellow.

In a perfect world, a red ink would reflect all the red light and absorb all the green and blue. A blue ink would reflect blue and absorb green and red. These are useful attributes indeed when reproducing the flags of France, the United Kingdom, and the United States, among others. A dark purple would also be practical with, say, 70 percent coverage of blue and red inks. But what of a lighter, richer purple? To produce that color, we have to reflect all the red, all the blue, and none of the green light from the page. Starting out with our hypothetical red ink would immediately eliminate some of the necessary blue light. Starting with blue would kill some of the red light, which is also essential. Hence, we have a problem without a solution.

Red, green, and blue inks each reflect one variety of light and absorb two. Our mission, which is to be able to control each type of light individually, requires the opposite: inks that absorb only one of the three primary kinds of light and reflect two. Instead of an ink that reflects green only, we need one that *absorbs* green only, reflecting red and blue simultaneously—to wit, magenta. We need one that absorbs only blue light—yellow— and we need one that theoretically absorbs all the red light but in real life leaves a lot to be desired, namely cyan.

Whether photographic, inkjet, toner, offset, or some more eccentric printing model, any process that deposits a reliable image on any substrate has to use, at least, these three colorants. There may be others, too—normally, though not necessarily, black, plus whatever other colors there may be room for and a desire to experiment with. But the first three colors are always cyan, magenta, and yellow.

Several cheaper desktop printers (and some that are not so cheap) appear to the casual observer to be RGB devices. They aren't. They may require that incoming files be RGB, but they print with cyan, magenta, and yellow colorants just like everyone else.

As Figure 1.7 shows, cyan is the opposite of red, green the opposite of magenta, and yellow the opposite of blue. The whole discussion almost becomes one of semantics. In a perfect world, red *is* cyan, and RGB *is* CMY.

In our vale of mortal sorrows, the two are slightly different. The most notable example is discussed in Chapter 3: we can't make a very good blue in CMYK. Also, it doesn't have nearly the range of pastel colors that RGB does. Inks aren't pure, printing has dot gain, and the presence of a black channel plays a role, but still each RGB channel has a first cousin in CMYK.

Telling the Channels Apart

Time for the answers to the quiz of Figure 1.5. There are ten channels, and we are given as a hint that the flowers are a deep red.

For those unfamiliar with LAB, the L channel is roughly equivalent to a black and white rendition of the color file, and the A and B are weird-looking blurry gray messes. That description permits us to set aside Figures 1.5D and 1.5J, which are so unlike the others that they have to be the A and B, although we don't yet know which is which.

The black channel of CMYK, at least in the style that this book recommends and which is the traditional practice of color separators, is

called a *skeleton black,* meaning that it shows only the outlines of lighter areas of the image. In a test like this, the black would always be the lightest of any of the ten channels. It's mildly difficult to evaluate this from the flowers only, but since Figure 1.5C is blank where the background falls, it's certainly the black.

To construct a deep red in RGB, the red channel must be quite light. As we do not want to contaminate the color with green and/or blue light, those two channels must be nearly solid. In CMYK, the magenta and yellow channels would also be nearly solid, because these inks prevent green and blue light from reflecting from the page. The cyan would have to be very light, as cyan kills the desired red. Figures 1.5F and 1.5H are the only ones with light flowers, so one must be the red and the other the cyan, which is which to be determined later.

Four of the remaining channels have dark flowers. Figure 1.5E is the loner, a mugwump. It straddles the fence, with its mug on the dark side and its wump on the light one. It's an average of the other channels, and therefore is the L channel of LAB.

To tell the surviving four channels apart, we resort to the other known color in the image—the one you got no hint about.

No hint is required, though, to understand that leaves like the ones underneath the flowers must be some species of green. These leaves aren't a brilliant green. If they were, the green channel would be almost blank where the leaves are, and the red and blue would be almost solid. Blanks and solids make for brilliant colors. Six channels have blanks or solids for their flowers, but none where the leaves are.

So, the leaves are a dull green, but the green channel in RGB and the magenta of CMYK still have to be lighter than their two partners. Of the four versions with dark flowers, Figures 1.5A and 1.5G have relatively light leaves. They must be the magenta and the

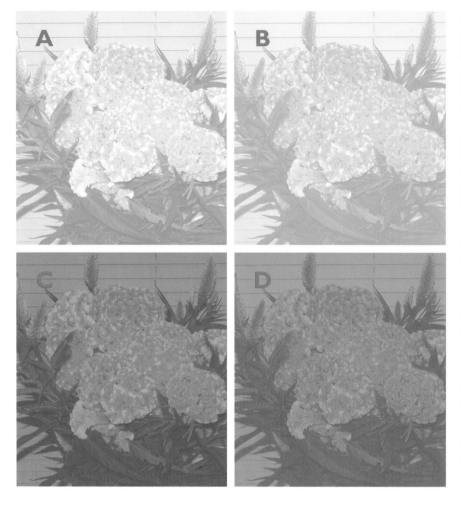

Figure 1.8 Top left, in a blank CMYK document, Figure 1.5H is pasted as the cyan channel. Top right, an RGB document using Figure 1.5F as the red and blank channels in the green and blue. Bottom left, Figure 1.5H as the cyan channel and flat 50% gray inserted in the magenta and yellow. Bottom right, Figure 1.5F as the red channel and flat 50% gray inserted in the green and blue.

contrast migrates to the black. Nothing of the kind occurs in RGB.

To tell an RGB channel from its CMYK cousin, therefore, look for the extra detail in the shadows. Since the leaves seem to have gotten flattened somewhat in Figure 1.5H, that one is the cyan, and Figure 1.5F is the red. And we can easily see the similar effects that differentiate the green from the magenta and the blue from the yellow.

green. Figures 1.5B and 1.5K, with much darker leaves, are the blue and the yellow.

We thus have three pairs of cousins. The differentiation between those cousins is an important one to appreciate, because it leads later to many decisions on whether to work in RGB or CMYK. In CMYK, much of the weight of the darker parts of the image is carried in the black. Also, in CMYK there is an ink limit, expressed as the sum of the coverage percentages in all four inks in the darkest area. The highest conceivable value is 400%—each of the four inks at 100%—but no offset printer will accept anything like that value; 300% is the most common maximum. To meet that limit, the cyan, magenta, and yellow channels have to be suppressed somewhat in dark neutral areas. When that happens, all

Now, let's start combining these channels, so that we can see how they interact to create color. Figure 1.8A puts the cyan channel into an otherwise blank CMYK document; Figure 1.8B puts the red into an otherwise blank RGB file, which is then, for purposes of this book, converted into CMYK for printing.

That the red and cyan channels are cousins is now even more apparent—but considering that the only thing we've put into Figure 1.8B is detail in the *red* channel, how come the only color we see is green-blue?

When Two Are Maxed Out

When the green and blue channels are blank, as they are in the RGB file that's the ancestor of Figure 1.8B, it means that as much green

Figure 1.9 *Top left: Figure 1.5F as the red channel, green channel blank, and Figure 1.5B as the blue. Top right, Figure 1.5F as the red, blue channel blank, and Figure 1.5B "accidentally" used as the green. Bottom left, the composite color image. Bottom right, the composite color image with the black channel deleted.*

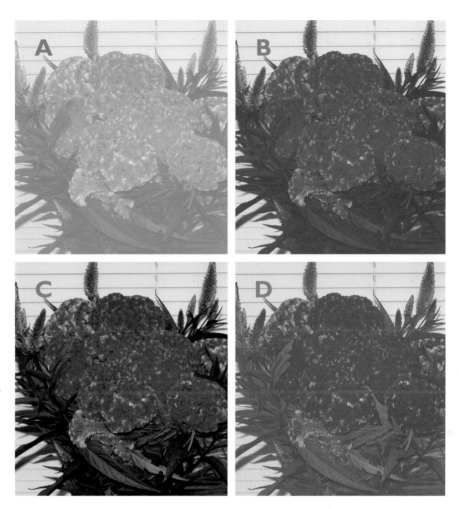

and blue light as possible is hitting our eyes. What we call the *red* channel in RGB is more like the *anti-red* channel, in that it's only as red as possible where it's blank. Everywhere else, it *reduces* the amount of red that we see. So, since we are seeing maximum amounts of green and blue light, but something less than the maximum red, the result is green-blue—until we start filling in the other channels.

In Figures 1.8C and 1.8D, the blank channels of these two images, except the black of CMYK, are filled with 50% gray. Now, the backgrounds are red in CMYK, because the magenta and yellow are darker than the cyan, and in RGB because the green and the blue are darker than the red. The flowers are even redder. But the leaves are not red at all, because the two red-killing channels (red and cyan) are darker than the four red-favoring ones (green, magenta, blue, and yellow).

Notice also that the two colorspaces, although they have a pronounced similarity, aren't identical. The CMYK "red" background in Figure 1.8C is more orange than the corresponding parts of the RGB file in Figure 1.8D. As we'll see in Chapter 3, CMYK is generally a warmer colorspace than RGB, something that we need to take account of when defining things that are neutral or near-neutral.

As we add the last channel (blue in RGB, its cousin yellow in CMYK), further secrets reveal themselves. These two are the channels with dark flowers and dark leaves. To tell

Quiz Answers

The text discusses how to identify which channel is which in Figure 1.5, but to summarize, the correct answers are as follows:

A–Magenta	C–Black	F–Red	J–B (LAB)
B–Blue	D–A (LAB)	G–Green	K–Yellow
	E–Lightness	H–Cyan	

least that they seem to be. Yet logically, they *can't* be red. In Figure 1.9A they can only be yellow-green, or cyan, because the magenta component that a green channel would provide is absent. In Figure 1.9B they can only be magenta, blue, or cyan, because there is none of the yellow that the absent blue channel would add.

The effect of redness in the flowers is even stronger if you cover one of the images and look only at the other. That's simultaneous contrast at work, as our visual systems force us to imagine a bigger distinction between the flowers and the background. A camera, a spectrophotometer, or any other artificial color-measuring device would not see this redness. Unless your audience is one of machines and not people, you have to bear in mind that what such instruments perceive is often not what we do.

Strange Channels, Strange Lighting

We mop up by naming the correct green and magenta, Figures 1.5G and 1.5A respectively. Figure 1.9C shows the composite image; Figure 1.9D is the same except that the black channel has been deleted, so that you can see how critical it is to shadow detail.

As a housekeeping matter, we complete the quiz by announcing that Figure 1.5D is the A of LAB and Figure 1.5J is the B. 50% gray is a neutral in the A and B channels; anything lighter is warmer and anything darker is cooler. That's the clue we need to tell which is which in this image.

The A is a magenta-green channel, so its

them apart, we look for the characteristic loss of shadow detail in CMYK. We find it in Figure 1.5K, which is therefore the yellow, and not in Figure 1.5B, which is the blue.

The Importance of the Green Channel

To save space, the next pair of example images is derived from RGB channels only; a CMYK exercise would yield similar results. I start with a real red and blank blue and green, as in Figure 1.8B. Now, in Figure 1.9A, I put Figure 1.5B into the blue channel, which is where it belongs. In Figure 1.9B, it goes into the green channel instead.

The error is apparent because the leaves are purple instead of green, but there are two other points to consider. First, in the overall scheme of things, the green channel is a great deal more important than the blue, and somewhat more important than the red. Look at how much fuller Figure 1.9B is than 1.9A. It's the same two channels, but the green is given much more weight than the blue. This is a critical thing to bear in mind when color-correcting. Added contrast in the blue is likely to be almost unnoticeable. Detailing in the green is a big deal.

Second, observe how the flowers are starting to get red in both versions—or, at green leaves are much darker than the heavily magenta flowers. The B is yellow-blue. Both the flowers and the leaves are more yellow than they are blue. Therefore the distinction between the flowers and leaves must be less than that seen in the A.

It is not important, at least not yet, to have a full grasp of what the A and B channels do. To show why understanding the others *is* important, let's move to our first color correction, which features the same quiz, except in reverse.

Like almost all of the exercises we'll be facing in coming chapters, this one is real-world, an unsabotaged image that has to be improved for a professional context. When such an image is introduced, I'll tell you what I know about it, which is often not much.

Figure 1.10 is shot in a nightspot where the lighting is strange enough to turn the man's skin distinctly green—quite appropriate for a Martian, not nearly as desirable for a human being. It arrives in RGB, but the image is to be prepared for publication, so we need a CMYK file sooner or later.

We don't have to make the thing look like it was taken in broad daylight,

but we have to do something, because thanks to the phenomenon of chromatic adaptation that we've previously discussed, a human being in attendance at this performance wouldn't see anything like this green fleshtone.

With the flower quiz, we saw the individual channels and had to imagine what the

Figure 1.11 *Top, the cast is sharply reduced by blending the blue channel into the green. As this darkens the image overall, a further correction with curves is needed (bottom).*

composite color image looked like. Here, it's the reverse. You see the color—now tell me what the channels look like currently, and what they *should* look like, how we might get them to that happy point, and what the likely obstacles are to our attempts. So, let's ask ourselves these questions about channel structure in the RGB file:

- *Why is the skintone (and the watch, and the guitar strap) green?* Because the green channel is lighter than the other two.

- *Which channel should be the lightest, if the green should not?* Human skin is red. The red channel should be the lightest.

- *How do we make that happen?* By blending the blue channel into the green, making it

darker than the red. We know that the blue is currently darker than the red because Figure 1.10 is more easily described as yellow than as blue-green.

- *What problem will show up when we blend the blue into the green?* As we just saw in Figure 1.10, the green channel has an inordinate role in the weight of the image. If we make the green as dark as the blue, the image will become too dark, and will have to be adjusted further.

The commands that I'm about to gloss over are fully fleshed out in the next few chapters, so please forgive the lack of step-by-step instructions in favor of an explanation of concept.

Over the rest of the book, we'll be trying to develop a generalized method of improving images. For everyday images, this may consist of nothing more than curves. Unusual images, of which this is surely one, often need unusual treatments.

Here, as is frequently true when images have serious casts, the best approach is to cut the cast with a preliminary RGB channel blend. In Figure 1.11A, the green channel has been replaced by a hybrid: one-third of the old green, and two-thirds of the blue. The blue and red channels are unchanged.

The greenness has been muted, but the image is still too dark. But going from Figure 1.11A to 1.11B is easy and routine, although we haven't introduced the exact steps yet. There are many ways to do it in Photoshop. There are also at least three ways to go from Figure 1.10 to Figure 1.11A, but each requires imagination—and a knowledge of what the channels must look like—to realize that each step is needed.

Consequently, although most experienced retouchers could get to something like Figure 1.11B if they were starting with 1.11A, I believe that most professionals would not be able to get there starting with the actual original, Figure 1.10.

The Bottom Line

The purpose of color correction is to make images look better. Unfortunately there is no definition of *better.* An image is better if a strong majority of people who look at it say that it's better. This creates a problem when a panel of viewers is unavailable to evaluate our "correction."

All viewers tend to prefer images that have a full range of detail in their most important areas. Also, where the technologies of a camera and of the human visual system result in a scene being evaluated differently, viewers prefer the version that portrays what a human would have seen had he been in the position of the camera. For example, human vision is self-calibrating to the color of the ambient light. Cameras often pick up color casts that humans are unaware of. Almost all viewers prefer that these casts be reduced or eliminated.

Viewers often disagree as to which version is better when there is a choice of colors that might be correct. Skies, for example, have many possible colors. Nobody would accept a green sky, but some people prefer darker or bluer or purpler skies than others do.

Many subsequent corrections are made easier by a knowledge of how channels interact to produce color. The close relation between the RGB and CMY channel structure can often be exploited.

You Be the Judge

A book about color manipulation is not like other instructional books. There is much more room for the reader's opinion. The basic question, after any color move, must be, *does the picture look better now?* You do not need fifty years of experience and twelve advanced degrees to answer this.

The powerful channel-blending approach to color will play an important part in our corrections. For the next three chapters, however, we will study how to correct the traditional way: by the numbers, with curves.

It's the traditional way because it gives dramatic quality gains and, if not a walk in the park, is accessible to an ambitious amateur. It is how the best color has been produced since the advent of scanning, and no workflow that ignores it will produce first-rate results.

Some of us, annoyingly, are not satisfied with duplicating the best quality available ten years ago. Furthermore, some of us now have to work with appalling garbage that would never have even been considered for professional reproduction back then.

If you find yourself in one of these prideful but unenviable categories, the chapters mentioned above won't quite be enough for you. And as you progress into bizarre techniques that are usually senseless but occasionally salvage otherwise unmanageable images, you will be surprised at how often you will recollect Figure 1.5, and marvel at how the results are so much better when all files have ten channels.

Review and Exercises

Boxes like this appear at the end of most chapters. You're on your own for the suggested exercises, but the factual questions are answered in the Notes & Credits section, which begins on page 493.

✓ What is simultaneous contrast?

✓ What is chromatic adaptation?

✓ Which RGB channel contains the most powerful contrast information?

✓ Pair each RGB channel with its closest CMY counterpart.

✓ Figures 1.8A and 1.8B show images that are based on only one channel, with the other two blank. Why is Figure 1.8B, based only on the red channel, not red? Why is it darker than Figure 1.8A?

✓ What do you think the ramifications of chromatic adaptation are in terms of your ability to evaluate colors on your own monitor?

✓ You have an RGB file containing an object that you know should be neutral (white, gray, or black). If you measure its RGB values in the Info palette, how will you know that the file doesn't contain an undesired bias toward color?

The Steeper the Curve, The More the Contrast

Writing curves is a form of horsetrading. Most improvements in the image come at a price. Fortunately, the price is sometimes quite reasonable. Look for the areas you wish to emphasize, and then figure out how you will pay for the improvement.

olor on automatic pilot is an attractive concept. Shoot the picture, pop it into the computer, and presto! perfection every time.

But we can't do that, right? Getting a believable color image is an art form, isn't it? How could a computer do a better job than an artistically motivated human?

Figure 2.1A isn't exactly a real-world kind of problem, but it is an actual, unretouched original, representing what you get when you point and shoot a high-quality digicam into an extremely hazy area of Sequoia National Park. Figure 2.1B is Photoshop's take at fixing it automatically, with the simplest correction of all, Image: Adjustments>Auto Levels.

By the standards of the human interventions we saw in the last chapter, this is an impressive fix. The algorithm has found plenty of detail in the middle of a blur. It has found believably green leaves where there appears to be no color at all.

The next two chapters will discuss why this simple move works so well, what the cases are where it would work badly, and how we can modify it when the task isn't quite as easy as this one was. This chapter concentrates on contrast issues; Chapters 3 and 9 will tackle color fidelity.

The most important command in Photoshop is the curve, of which Figure 2.2A is one. Call it up with Image: Adjustments>Curves or with the keyboard shortcut Command–M. The horizontal axis represents the values as they currently are. The vertical axis indicates the new values that will replace them should we click OK.

Figure 2.1 *(opposite) The original, top, is so flat and colorless that it's difficult to believe that the bottom version can be created by computer, rather than human, intervention.*

This figure happens to show the Lightness channel of a hypothetical file in LAB, one of the four color models that Photoshop supports, along with RGB, CMYK, and grayscale (black and white). We should go through some options at this point, so that your curves will match those in the remainder of the book.

Figure 2.2A is the default setting. Its grid is divided by lines at increments of 25 percent. Some people like it that way. Other people, like me, prefer a finer grid with lines at 10 percent increments, as seen in Figure 2.2B. That's the style we'll show henceforth. To toggle back and forth, Option–click anywhere inside the grid.

At bottom right is a clickable icon that toggles between a relatively large Curves dialog and a smaller one. Personally, I use the larger one when working in LAB, where some curves require a delicate touch, and the smaller one in the other three colorspaces. This book shows the smaller dialog throughout.

Left, Right, Up, and Down

The setting that throws a lot of people is the curve orientation, which is defined by the gradient bar below the grid. In Figure 2.2A, darkness is to the left. The lower left corner of the grid represents black. The upper right represents white. If we click a point into the center of the curve and raise it, we move toward white, so the picture gets lighter.

To reverse this, click the gradient, changing darkness to the right, as shown in Figure 2.2B. And why do so? Because it's the Photoshop equivalent of Valium: it saves considerable stress later.

For reasons of tradition, the default in LAB and RGB is that darkness is to the left. The default in CMYK and in grayscale is that darkness is to the right. For anyone who has to work in more than one colorspace (and you qualify for that, as a reader of this book), this

is a recipe for early dementia praecox. The L channel and a grayscale version of the image are quite similar, yet applying the same curve to each one lightens one and darkens the other. Ditto for RGB and CMYK. As we saw in Chapter 1, they are kissing cousins. The same curve shapes ought to get something like the same results, but they won't, unless you reverse the orientation of one of them.

Therefore, I strongly recommend that you choose one orientation and stick with it in all four colorspaces. Darkness to the right is what we'll use throughout the book. If you grew up with RGB and are uncomfortable doing it that way, there's no technical problem with keeping darkness to the left—provided you realize that the curves shown here are going to seem inverted.

This brings up three topics of political correctness. First, it has been seriously suggested in previous editions that there should be a second printing of the book with the curves inverted for the benefit of those who can't stand looking at darkness to the right.

Second, Figure 2.2, along with every other screen grab in this book, comes from a Macintosh. This practice was thought to be so offensive that the publisher of the Spanish translation of a previous edition published two versions, one labeled for PC users and one for Macheads. The only difference was the screen grabs.

Third, when keyboard shortcuts are mentioned, I use the Mac, not the PC, terminology. To prove that people have violent opinions about this topic, on the enclosed CD there is a lengthy thread from my color-theory list where I asked for suggestions on how to refer to such shortcuts in print.

Despite the Photoshop default of random-generator orientations for its curves, I believe that having all the curves treat darkness in the same way is the only sane approach. Darkness to the right is more traditional in professional color correction, a relic of the

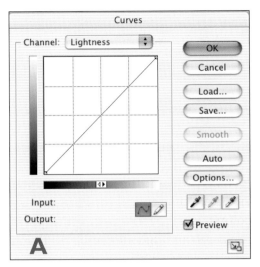

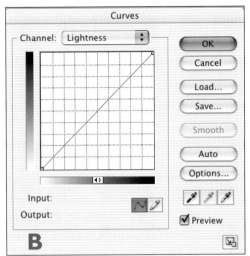

Figure 2.2
*Left, Photoshop
defaults for the
Curves dialog.
Right, the
settings suggested
in this book.*

days when CMYK and grayscale reigned jointly. That's the only reason it's chosen.

Similarly, it is typographically and editorially extremely annoying to repeatedly indicate how to duplicate one platform's commands on another. The Mac's Command key is equal to the PC's Ctrl, and the PC's Alt is the Mac's Option. The Mac also has a key called Control (Ctrl on some keyboards), which has nothing to do with the Ctrl key on a PC. This would be a source of ambiguity if we used the PC commands as the standard, so we go the Mac route.

As noted by several participants in the thread that's on the CD, anyone who finds it unduly difficult to adjust to a different set of keyboard shortcuts (or, by implication, to adjust to a different curve orientation) is likely to be reading the wrong book.

When There's a Choice of Shape

Before finalizing a curve, we analyze the numbers that currently exist in the file, and force them to become more acceptable. That topic is addressed more in the next chapter than in this one, which discusses shape.

Now, a hypothetical assignment. Imagine that you have a CMYK file. I inform you that values that are currently 70 percent of the maximum value of cyan ink—we will use the shorthand 70^C in the future—need to be

increased, darkened, to 80^C. The exercise being hypothetical, you don't need to ask why, but rather how.

First, call up the Curves dialog and switch over to the cyan curve. The most straightforward approach is to count seven gridlines up, and seven gridlines over, to find the point that is currently 70^C. Click a point there, and drag it directly upward, due north, until it reaches the eighth line. That produces the curve shown in Figure 2.3A. I've put a yellow square at the critical point.

However, you could do it a different way. You could forget about clicking a point into the curve. Instead, click and drag the top right endpoint to the left, as in Figure 2.3B, until the curve (or, better stated, straight line, since it has no middle point that would make it a curve) crosses the same 70=80 point that we saw in the first curve.

A third option: click a point at a location that's much lower than the one chosen in Figure 2.3A. Raise it until 70^C becomes 80^C. That's Figure 2.3C.

A final alternative: rather than raising that point, lower it. Then sweep the upper right endpoint to the left. Figure 2.3D completes the quartet. The curves are superimposed on one another in Figure 2.4. Each one causes the requisite change from 70^C to 80^C. So, which is best?

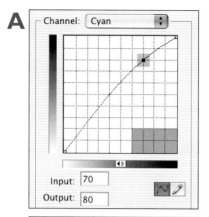

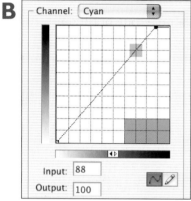

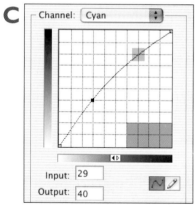

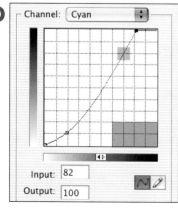

To that question, there is an answer that is as accurate as it is clear and concise.

It depends.

A New Angle on Contrast

These curves illustrate the principal concept in professional color reproduction: *the steeper the curve, the more the contrast.*

The default curve is a straight line at an angle of 45 degrees, because every value will remain unchanged if we click OK. 10^C will become 10^C, 20^C will become 20^C, and so forth.

When we start sticking points in, the shape changes. All of the four curves we've just discussed, and every other curve you or I will ever write, have certain areas that are steeper than 45 degrees, and certain other areas that are flatter.

Any objects that fall into the steeper areas gain contrast, and look better than they did in the original image. Any objects that fall into the flatter areas lose contrast, and look worse. That's the whole concept in a nutshell.

Color correction therefore is a form of horsetrading. We decide what parts of the image are important enough that we'd like them to gain contrast—but then we have to figure out a way to finance it, by finding other areas that we are willing to sacrifice.

The machine correction of Figure 2.1 was so effective because it didn't sacrifice anything. The original was extremely flat because it occupied only the middle third of the curve in all three RGB channels. When we move the lower left and upper right points inward—which is all that the Auto Levels command does—every part of the curve that affects the original becomes much steeper than 45 degrees. Every point is now farther away from its neighbors, and the leaves and the trees pop away from the background.

Adding contrast is one thing, and getting appropriate color another. Just as an auto mechanic occasionally solves a difficult problem by accidentally hitting something with his elbow, the Auto Levels command inadvertently wrought reasonable color out of the appallingly flat Figure 2.1. It isn't always that easy.

In fact, the color issue would probably disqualify one or more of the curves we've just been discussing. Figures 2.3A and 2.3C would add more cyan to the picture than the other two curves would. That may be acceptable, or it may introduce a disagreeable cast. But we still could have two or three curve shapes to choose from, so we choose the one that will assign the most contrast to the interest object. If this were a picture of a polar bear in a snowstorm, we would prefer the

Figure 2.3 *Four different ways to approach the assignment of making a value of 70^C become 80^C.*

curve shown in Figure 2.3C. It's steepest in the lightest part of the curve, where the bear and the snow live.

As Long As It Catches Mice

In Spanish, there is a saying that goes, in the nighttime every cat is a gray one. Entirely too many computer artists amend this to say that all cats are gray as long as the highlight and shadow are correct.

Consider Figure 2.5. The top row is the original version of each of three felines. I have preadjusted each to have a good highlight and shadow, a topic that will be discussed in Chapter 3. Each of the other three rows shows what happens when a certain curve is applied to each of the three images. As you can see, the original was not the best possible reproduction of any of the three cats, because in each of the lower three rows, there is one cat that's better—and two that are worse. You'll see the three curves that made these rows in a minute. Meanwhile, can you figure out what they must look like?

These images are easy to handle because they have a single object of interest. Certain images are more *busy,* a term that means they contain several important objects or colors. Some images are busy, but many more are not. Product shots, fashion shots, images of animals, food shots—all generally have only one or two color ranges that are important. The rest is just background.

So it is with Figure 2.5. Each image is about a *cat,* not a background. If the price for improving the cat is losing some detail in the background, so be it. Just as I have only a certain amount of money to spend on computer hardware, I have only a certain amount of contrast to spend on this image. And, in these pictures, I propose to spend it on cats, not backgrounds.

A white cat lives in the light end of a curve; a black cat, in the dark end; a gray cat, somewhere in the middle. That's enough

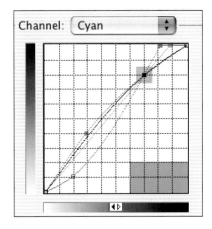

Figure 2.4 Over-printing all four curves of Figure 2.3 demonstrates that all pass through the same point in the yellow square, meaning that all make the desired change in shadow value.

information for this example, but normally one would like to narrow it down a little and find the exact range. This can be done by running the cursor over the lightest and darkest areas of each cat and recording the resulting Info palette numbers. Alternatively, with a curve open, we can move across the image while holding down the mouse button. This generates a movable circle on the curve, a technique that we will discuss shortly.

Granted that the highlight and shadow start out correct, it still is possible to write curves, as Figure 2.6 shows, that are steep where a specific cat is found. Provided, that is, that we agree with what any of these cats would say, which is, anyplace a cat is not is a place unworthy of our attention.

Now, one last question before we look at the curves. Each of these three curves is intended to make a single cat purr, at the expense of the other two. The first part of the question is, which row hosts the two *worst* cats? I assume you agree that it's the second row from the bottom. The gray cat is great, but the other two felines are much the worse for wear.

Why are the black and the white cats so poor in the row that favors the gray one, even compared to what happened to the white and the gray cat in the row that favored the black one?

There is a big difference between a single image of three cats, and three separate

images of one cat each. If all three cats some-how managed to pose for a single picture without clawing each other to death, we could do little more than make sure the high-light and shadow values were correct.

But if even one cat is missing, it opens up space to maneuver. Retouching is much like shopping: it's one thing to know what you'd like to buy, and another to find the money to pay for it. To get what you want, you need to find something you're willing to part with.

Figure 2.6's curves each get steeper in the region occupied by one cat. To pay for it, they get flatter in the tonal ranges of the other two, squashing contrast. It would also be possible to write a curve that helped *two* cats at once, paying for it by damaging the third.

And why are the black and the white cats hurt so disproportionately by the curve that is aimed at improving the gray cat? It's all a matter of range. The gray cat originally had the most variation in its color of any of the three. The area it occupies on the curve is longer, more expensive to correct, requiring more of a sacrifice elsewhere.

Maximizing Detail Is No Accident

This adventure in cat herding evades one of the biggest problems in curvewriting. This chapter is about adding contrast. Since curves can't affect color when there's no color to affect, it's most convenient that these are grayscale images. In grayscale, we can steepen away to our hearts' content. If the image has color, however, we have to be more careful—some of the time. Yet in some im-ages the color makes no difference at all.

The car of Figure 2.7 has just been involved in an accident. While parked, it was hit by another vehicle. An insurance adjuster must now decide whether this was a mere love tap

or something that requires authorizing thou-sands of dollars for a new fender.

Dispatching an adjuster to the scene is a very 1990s thing to do. Far better, in today's world, to whip out a digital camera, take a picture, and e-mail it for a quick decision.

In the original, however, one practically has to be told that there's a dent to be able to find it. Surely, if the adjuster is to make an intelligent call, we need to find a way to enhance the detail.

In doing so, we concern ourselves not a bean for what it does to the color. The ad-juster doesn't care whether this car is bur-gundy or green, or whether the tire is black or orange. He only wants to see detail, and as much of it as possible.

Therefore, we focus on the damaged area, ignoring such normally vital questions as highlight, shadow, and neutrality.

In an ordinary product shot, our usual ap-proach is to trade in some of the detail in the background for extra pop in the foreground. There are normally limits to our enthusiasm, however; we don't want to blow the back-ground away completely, or to radically change its color.

This image is the exception: everything but the dent is utterly irrelevant. If anything else turns a weird hue or even vanishes altogether, that's just fine.

The file arrives in an unknown RGB. An RGB file is what the adjuster, who probably doesn't even know how to spell CMYK, wants.

The objective—in this picture, the *only* objective—is to get the curves as steep as possible where the car falls. If you followed the quiz concerning Figure 1.5, you know where that is: as the car is purple, the blue and especially the red channels must be light; since it is not green at all, the green channel must be relatively dark. But there's an easy way to find out if you're in any doubt.

Open the Curves dialog. Ignore the master curve—we'll discuss why later—and switch

Figure 2.5 *The top row contains the three original images. In each row beneath, one curve was applied to each of the three. Can you guess the shape of the curves that produced each of the bottom three rows?*

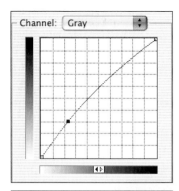

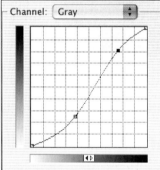

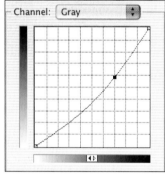

Figure 2.6 *The three curves that created the rows of Figure 2.5. Left, steepening the highlight produces a better white cat in the second row. Bottom left, the curve is steepest in the midtone, favoring the gray cat in the third row. Bottom right, the curve is steepest in the shadows, creating a snappier black cat in the bottom row.*

What's Important and What's Not

Shooting for advertising is merely a more complicated version of Figure 2.7. The interest object in Figure 2.8 is not a dent but two bottles. However, if the advertisement is to be successful, we need to focus the viewers' eyes on the products, just as we needed to focus on the dent. The method is the same: we extend their range with curves. Irritatingly, we have to be more careful: we can't have gross color changes this time. We also need to be aware of where the collateral damage will fall. In Figure 2.7B, the tire, molding, and underbody all took a hit in detail that dwarfs the one the fender took from the other car. In the context of that image, we didn't care. In advertising work, we can accept some losses in non-interest areas, but not that much.

As always in this book, the image arrives uncorrected. It is tagged ColorMatch RGB, which, again as always, is not an endorsement of that particular RGB, but merely reports how I received the file.

You can find the existing range by opening each curve and mousing over the bottles. Again, though, if you got the channel-identifying exercise of Figure 1.5 right, you already know what the moving circles will show. The towel and both caps are neutral. They will therefore look the same in all three channels. The products are both green. They must be significantly lighter in the green channel than in the red and blue.

If you prefer to think in CMYK, the magenta will be the light channel, and the cyan and yellow darker. The choice of colorspace doesn't affect the concept that a steeper curve gives a more detailed object. We will be staying in RGB for most of the rest of the chapter.

CMYK, LAB, RGB, or grayscale, success in curve-based correction is not possible without good endpoints. That's why the automatic correction in Figure 2.1B worked so well.

to the red. Click, hold, and mouse over the entire dent. As long as the mouse button is depressed, a circle appears on the curve, indicating where the point underneath the mouse falls. As the mouse moves, so will the circle. By watching how high and low the circle reaches as we mouse over the area, we get a good idea of the range. So we establish points that create as much steepness as possible there. Then we repeat the process in the green and blue channels.

I've put red lines in each of the curves to indicate what I found to be the range of the damaged area. These slapdash curves are nearly vertical there, opening the door to a finding that the door can't open, and that the whole fender needs to be replaced.

The average picture doesn't give us quite as much flexibility, but we still shoot for curves that are as steep in the interest areas as they can be, consistent with our other responsibilities. The rule applies not just to snapshot-type images like the one of the damaged vehicle, but also to high-quality professional photography.

We'll be falling all over this topic in the next chapter, so to save time I'll ask you to just take my word for it that the endpoints in Figure 2.8—the whitest area of the towel and the blackest area of the cap—are fine as is.

That means two things. First, Auto Levels wouldn't work on this original, as if our pride would permit us to even consider such an atrocity. Second, we can't increase range in the bottles by making their light areas lighter. They're already as light as the top of the towel is, and we can't make that any lighter without blowing out the texture. Instead, we have to make the relatively dark areas darker. That's what the curves above Figure 2.9 do. They're all at slightly different angles, because the affected area varies in each channel, being shortest in the green and longest in the blue. But the entirety of the bottles (and, coincidentally, the towel) are found in the steepest parts of these curves.

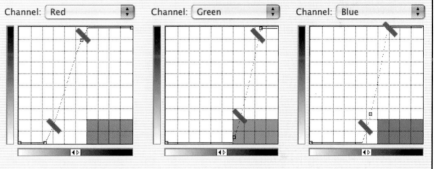

Presumably, the advertiser will be happier with the more assertive Figure 2.9 than with 2.8, even though there's a slight loss of detail in the black cap, which falls into the inevitable areas of the curves that are flatter than 45 degrees.

How to Correct, Sight Unseen

The digital revolution has given us many opportunities for better image quality. Occasionally, it gives us opportunities to work in the opposite direction.

The subject of this chapter is *contrast*. The desire for more of it is not limited to Photoshop experts, or even to Photoshop users.

Figure 2.7 *The car in the original, above, has been involved in an accident. If color fidelity is no object, detail in the damaged area can be brought out by extremely steep curves in all three channels.*

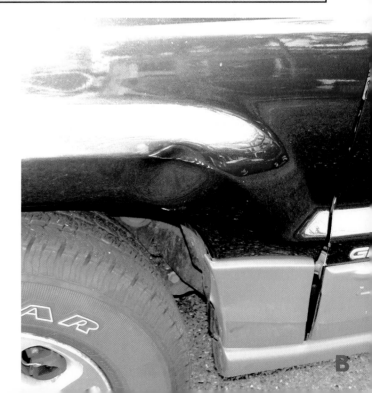

Almost every computer user owns a monitor that somewhere contains a knob or a controllable setting that allows us to increase contrast, or such is the claim. If you don't own a computer, your television probably has such a control, and if you don't own a television you presumably have much more entertaining books to read than this one.

You can't literally increase a monitor's contrast, unless you can make it create something either brighter than its own full intensity, or darker than when it's turned off. The only thing that can be done—and these controls do it—is to *reallocate* the contrast. The logical way to do so is to transfer it away from the lightest and darkest tones and into the midrange, which is much more likely to contain the subject of the image.

The usual way is as in the curve shown as Figure 2.3B: move the top right and/or bottom left endpoints inward, leaving not a curve but a straight line. That's the approach, for example, of Photoshop's Image: Adjustments>Brightness/Contrast command, which was developed during the administration of Rutherford B. Hayes, and is justifiably shunned by all right-thinking persons.

Add "contrast" with that command or by some similar control on a monitor or television, and you may make the majority of images look somewhat better. Those that don't will look worse, often a lot worse.

To illustrate, we mow down the flowers we first saw in Figure 1.5, by applying Brightness/Contrast to them at settings of +50 in both fields of the dialog. Figures 2.10A and 2.10B show the impact on a file that has first been converted to grayscale. The command blows

Figure 2.8 *An original studio capture for advertising work.*

Figure 2.9 *These curves emphasize contrast in the light half of the image, where all the important detail lies.*

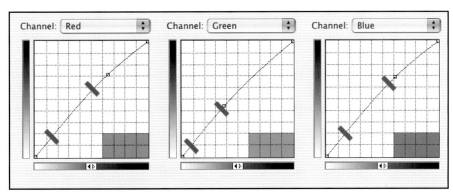

out a great deal of Figure 2.10B, but there's still enough detail to make out what the background must be. The leaves surrounding the flowers are plugged completely, but the flowers themselves are arguably better.

Returning to the world of color imaging, it's much harder to try to make a case for Figure 2.10D as opposed to 2.10C. All semblance of shape in the flowers has been blasted. The red channel is now blank, and the green and blue are almost solid.

This is what might be called the steamroller method of color correction. Any fragile detail that stands in the way of the needed lightening and darkening gets flattened. There are two ways to avoid this.

First, we could use some artificial intelligence. The Brightness/Contrast command has no clue whether +50 is too much. The Auto Levels command does. It measures the darkest and lightest parts of each channel, and moves the endpoints out only far enough for them to hit the limit, avoiding the nightmare of Figures 2.10B and 2.10D.

Second, even if we were to go farther than these prudent points, the damage could be ameliorated somewhat by a curve resembling the letter *S,* like the gray cat one of Figure 2.6. Such an S curve would cost detail in the lightest and darkest areas rather than blowing them out completely.

This observation leads us to a question that sounds ridiculous but whose ramifications affect every professional.

Ask a Silly Question, Get a Silly Answer

Suppose you had to color-correct a bunch of images sight unseen? What method would you use to squeeze the best quality out of them most of the time?

The answer is: Auto Levels, followed by a mild S curve to all three channels, possibly followed by some mild sharpening.

I am sure that, as a reader of this book, you would sooner give up digital photographs in favor of daguerreotypes than correct images without looking at them. And yet, thanks to the politics that pervades our profession, the topic is of extreme interest to manufacturers of digicams, who do not care particularly about readers of such books as this.

Yes, manufacturers do care about professional photographers. Their top-of-the-line models have all the manual controls that a dedicated shooter needs. But for each professional or serious amateur who buys a digital camera, there are at least a score of folk who don't intend to do anything more than point and shoot.

The graphic arts profession is noted for how well it plays the blame game, a fact that has been a driving force behind the financial success of my color-correction classes.

● If you are a photographer who has to deal with commercial printing firms, you are aware that all bad printing is actually the fault of the photographer. If you don't believe this, ask the printer.

● If you manufacture desktop printers, you are aware that all terrible input that reproduces terribly is the fault of your printer. If you doubt this, ask the client.

● And if you are a digicam manufacturer, you are aware that all incompetently shot images that look as if they were incompetently shot are actually the fault of your camera. The photographer will inform you of this, if you ask him.

These sad realities provoke predictable responses. Photographers—see Chapter 13—learn about CMYK so that they can argue intelligently when a printer tries to blame them for inadequate printing. Printer manufacturers send their technicians to color-correction classes because it's cheaper to do that than accept a lot of returned machines from users who don't know how to send them good color. And digicam manufacturers build capture algorithms that they think will make bad shots look as good as possible.

So, if you just point and shoot a modern digicam, you're going to get some "help": a blunderbuss expansion of range that usually is a good thing but gets ugly when it isn't, and an added S curve that could be a good thing if your image features relatively dull colors but certainly won't be otherwise.

The same goes if you allow an acquisition module to make aesthetic decisions for you. Mini-applications like Photoshop's Camera Raw, Apple's Aperture, Adobe's Lightroom, or the proprietary methods of camera manufacturers usually have their own automated methods of correction, which we often are best advised to turn off. (See Chapter 16 for more information on this topic.)

If you're more accustomed to correcting files that originate with scanned film, you can expect the digital changeover to offer the following surprises:

● Files that have seemingly correct lights and darks, but a color cast everywhere else. In the days of film, casts tended to be uniform throughout the range. We'll discuss this

effect in later chapters, along with its counterpart: files in which the light and dark areas *should* have a color but have been neutralized by the digicam and/or the acquisition software.

● Certain types of unsharp masking that would work if the original had been shot in film will instead turn slight imperfections into ugly artifacts. We'll be covering this in Chapter 5.

● And, most pertinent to the present discussion, you're likely to be handed a file in which detail in highlights and shadows has been artificially suppressed. If you happen to have control of the acquisition process, you can sometimes turn this helpful feature off. If you're handed a fait accompli, then there's nothing to do but learn techniques to enhance detail in highlight and shadow areas. That's why this edition of *Professional Photoshop* has three extra chapters on this topic—it is much more important now than in the age of film. Also, knowing about this effect is important if you happen to be using Camera Raw, which we'll be discussing in Chapter 16, or some other acquisition module.

Turning a Blind Eye to the Catchlight

Our next example shows why machines, even those with the kindest of intentions, need human guidance.

Figure 2.11A, in an unspecified RGB, is the work of a professional whose idea of a honeymoon is to get soaked. The camera's logic has done its thing, forcing a nearly white and a nearly black point into the image, just as Photoshop itself did back in Figure 2.1. In the mind of the machine, contrast has been maximized.

The major difference between a teenager and an algorithm is that the teenager lacks judgment only most of the time. The literal-minded camera went looking for the lightest point in the image and found the reflections in the blue slickers.

This is an idiotic choice. An experienced retoucher would have pretended not to notice those reflections (retouchers call them *specular highlights,* or *catchlights)* and instead chosen the lightest part of the falls as the highlight point.

Choosing something other than the lightest portion of an image as the highlight is frequently a good way to ruin images. Imagine what would have happened in Figure 2.8, for example, if we had chosen a relatively dark part of the towel. Every lighter part of the towel would be gone—all you would see is blank paper. And Figures 2.10B and 2.10D show the danger of randomly blowing out light areas of channels.

Figure 2.10 *Top, an original grayscale image. Second from top, after the Brightness/Contrast command is applied at settings of +50, +50. Bottom two images: the same exercise is repeated with an RGB version of the image.*

But if the reflections in Figure 2.11A blow out, who cares? The highlight is defined as the lightest *significant* area of the image. If you agree that it's not necessary to hold detail in these reflections, then they aren't significant. We look elsewhere.

The curve that produced Figure 2.11B uses the simple approach of Auto Levels, except

Levels and the S Curve

Being a mature program that has developed in a complex fashion, Photoshop often gives us several ways to accomplish the same thing. The most blatant example in this book is Chapter 7, where many of the moves could be made just as effectively in half a dozen ways beyond the ones being illustrated. There are many variations, similarly, in applying curves.

Two prominent and powerful commands, however, should be avoided. One is discussed on the facing page—using the master curve rather than separate curves for each channel. This other, the Image: Adjustments>Levels (not Auto Levels) command, hasn't yet been mentioned in this text. These two methods are undesirable for opposite sides of the same reason.

Levels is nothing more than a curve with only three points: the two endpoints and a point in the exact center. Like curves, it can be applied to each channel individually. Effective moves are possible with it. High key and low key images can be handled with Levels by moving the midpoint up or down. This adjustment isn't quite as accurate as raising or lowering the exact point at which the main object of interest ends, but this is a technical argument.

When the interest object happens to fall in the center of the tonal range, rather than at the ends, we need an S curve, but an S curve needs four points, which Levels can't provide.

An S curve suppresses detail in highlights and shadows in the interest of developing it in the midtones. That's usually OK, but blowing the highlights and shadows out altogether, as Levels would do, is not.

Almost invariably, at least one channel of a color image needs an S curve, and at least one needs a different shape. Levels can't produce an S curve, and to all intents and purposes the master curve can't produce anything but. So, stick to channel-by-channel curving.

that it ignores the catchlights in favor of the top right of the falls. The curves are straight lines; all I did was move the lower left points to the right.

Personally, I don't think that's enough. I perceive this picture as being about Niagara Falls, not the spectators, not the sky. I would rather allocate more contrast to the water. So instead of the simple straight lines, I propose using the curves of Figure 2.12. They all bulge in the center, making the lighter halves of the curves steeper and the darker halves flatter. The points above the ones that set the steepness head north in an effort to prevent the picture from getting too dark overall.

The falls, being light, reside in the lower halves of all three channels, so these curves emphasize them more than the ones in Figure 2.11 do. The gain is evident in the falls, but the price being paid is apparent, also. I financed the better water by allocating less contrast to the people, who are therefore snappier in Figure 2.11B.

In Chapter 1, I pointed out that certain moves are matters of taste but certain others are absolutely the right thing to do. These two corrected images illustrate one of each kind. Whether Figure 2.12 looks better than Figure 2.11B is a point on which reasonable people may differ. Whether Figure 2.11B looks better than 2.11A is not. You like it better and so do I.

Also, you may feel that I didn't go far enough in Figure 2.12, or perhaps that I went too far. You may think that the best way to handle this picture is to make something halfway between the two. Something halfway (or three-quarters, or nine-tenths of the way) between Figures 2.11A and 2.11B, however, will be universally rejected. Figure 2.11B is unconditionally better, and unless you lighten the waterfall, your version of the image just won't be competitive with that of someone who has.

Now that we've found a way of treating

this image that is clearly right, let's move on to other images to discuss methods that are clearly wrong.

√ High and Low Key Images

In describing the character of an image, professionals often use the word *keyness*. A picture of a white cat is *high key*. The term means not that the image is too light, but rather that it is a picture of something that by its nature *is* light. A black cat, similarly, is *low key*.

We use these terms to differentiate them from the average image, which has most of its detail in the midrange. These average images often are helped by S curves. High key and low key images are hurt by them.

Figure 2.13 is a rare specimen, an image that's simultaneously high key and low key. The areas of importance are either light or dark—nothing is in the middle. Consequently, the S curve that the camera secretly applies damages everything we're interested in: white and black areas both fall in flat areas of the unseen curve.

It's tempting to compensate as I did in Figure 2.13, by making an inverted S out of the master curve: flat in the center, steep on the ends. No question that it brings out more detail in the white and black feathers, but it's a misuse of curves, for two reasons.

First, all the curves we've done so far have emulated

Stumbling Blocks: The Shape of the Curve

In learning color correction, everybody has certain personal blind spots: the inability to grasp certain concepts that other people find clear. That isn't surprising. The subject is complicated, and there are lots of little rules whose importance is not immediately evident. Plus, when we concentrate on a difficult concept, it's easy to overlook one or two key phrases. We've already alluded to a huge one: people try to force things that should be approximately neutral to be absolutely neutral.

You yourself undoubtedly suffer from one of the blind spots, where you understand the difficult parts and somehow miss a simple concept. Because this book has already gone through four iterations, each of which has gotten a lot of feedback, it's become clear what some of these stumbling blocks are. So, most chapters have a box like this one, where we reemphasize specific points that have a history of tripping up at least a few readers. The first two of the four items below can turn curvewriting into a minefield if you don't get them.

If a *lot* of readers are having problems with one topic, that's the author's fault, of course. The bottom two items bewildered a lot more readers than I would have liked in the last edition, so the text explanations have been fleshed out considerably. But I'm leaving the points here, too, just to be on the safe side.

•**East-west and north-south.** To add contrast to an object, click points that approximate its range into the curve. Lower the lower point and raise the upper one to create a steeper angle where the object lives. But lower and raise them straight up and down, north and south. Moving the points diagonally changes the range that's being affected.

•**When to move the endpoints.** When a highlight is too dark, sometimes we move the white endpoint to the right. At other times we leave it alone and instead lower a point placed about a quarter of the way up the curve. This isn't a random process. Move the endpoint to emphasize detail in the highlights; use the quartertone drop when you're more interested in the midtones. Moving the lower endpoint to the right obliterates anything found to the left of it. Moving the quartertone point down (but not all the way to the baseline of the grid) damages detail in the lightest areas of the image without blowing it out completely.

•**The omnipotent S curve.** There is a misconception that an S-shaped curve is always the way to add contrast. Of course, it is the way to add contrast *in the midtones.* Since that's where contrast is needed in the typical image, one can see how the error developed. Different shapes are needed whenever highlight and/or shadow detail is important.

•**Why avoid the master curve?** In CMYK, using the master curve is catastrophic, because the black channel can't possibly behave as the CMY do. In RGB, it's not a guaranteed disaster, but it's an inferior way to work, because we can't maximize contrast as well as with channel-by-channel curves. Also, anything other than a neutral color will change. Some will get more and others less saturated. Hue will shift as well. Random changes in color are a bad idea.

A

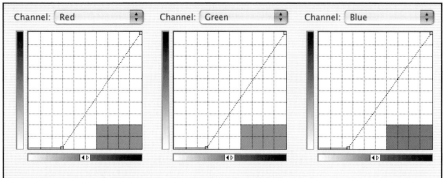

Channel:	Red	▲▼
Channel:	Green	▲▼
Channel:	Blue	▲▼

Figure 2.11 In the original digital capture, above, the camera has already set a white point in the reflections on the slickers. The curves that created the bottom version ignore these areas and set the white point in the falls.

B

human vision. If we're looking at light-colored products on a background of a white towel, or the Niagara River cascading over the grandest waterfall in the world, we sensitize ourselves to lightness. We assign more contrast to it in our minds, and less to anything darker, approximately as the curves of Figures 2.9 and 2.12 do.

We can't make ourselves sensitive to light and dark simultaneously, however. When evaluating the pelican of Figure 2.13A, we concentrate either on his white half or his black half, and the other half suffers.

If we were to try to emulate that in print, we'd get either a pelican with great black feathers and blown-out white ones, or vice versa, and nobody would be happy. Instead, we are forced to choose some sort of unhappy compromise.

The problem with the

Figure 2.12 An alternate version adds contrast to the lightest areas of the picture, while retaining the lightening effect of Figure 2.11B.

curve shown is not in the pelican but in the background. The rocks fall in the center of the curve, which happens to be the flat part of the inverted S, so they lose a lot of detail in comparison to the original. That's not the way we'd see it if we were there, so the printed image looks unnatural. There are better ways to handle these shadow/highlight issues, as we'll be seeing throughout the book, particularly in Chapters 17–19.

Avoiding the Master Curve

The second dubious practice of Figure 2.13 is the use of the master curve, which applies identical corrections to all three channels (note the RGB selected in the pop-up menu

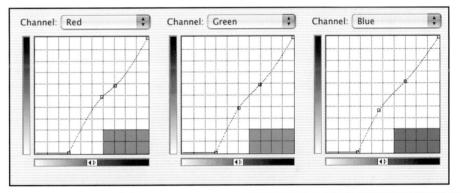

above the curve). In this particular image, there's no harm in using it. The important parts are neutrals—whites, blacks, and grays—and in neutral areas all three channels are alike, so the same curve works for all. In the other 99.99 percent of images, using the master curve results in second-rate quality. It does as well as that only in RGB, where channels are often similar to one another. In CMYK, the critical black channel always behaves differently from the other three, so applying a master curve is disastrous.

Let's show a modest gain for channel-by-channel curves first, before getting into the types of images where it's essential. Figure 2.14, which arrives in an unknown RGB, presents important yellows and

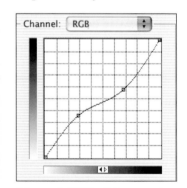

Figure 2.13 *The lightest and darkest areas of the original, top, are more important than its midrange. This suggests the type of inverted S curve shown above—but it kills detail in the background (bottom).*

greens. However, the background is significant enough that we can't afford to blow it out, nor are we inclined to accept plugging of the shadows.

Unlike those of the pelican of Figure 2.13, the channels aren't particularly alike. The yellow areas are dark in the blue channel but light in the other two. The greenery is light in the green channel but dark in the other two, particularly the blue. The background is generally light, but it is slightly darker in the red than in the other two channels.

I've ticked off the areas of importance in each curve of Figure 2.15, and I can also tell you that the original highlight and shadow values were within reason. So it just becomes a matter of steepening the appropriate areas.

We can start by observing that the red has the longest range and the green the shortest. As everything important shows up in its midrange, the green channel takes an S curve. But that won't work in either of the other two channels. In the blue, both areas of interest fall in the dark half of the curve. And in the red, the background is dark enough that the lower left point of the curve can be moved over, adding steepness to the lightest areas that actually exist.

Now, consider how this would be done if we decided to use the RGB master curve. We couldn't use the shape of the red curve because it would obliterate the background. We couldn't use the blue curve because it would kill the greenness of the leaves by darkening the green channel excessively.

The only possibility remaining is our good friend the S curve, as shown in Figure 2.16. It can't be as tight as the S curve in the green channel of Figure 2.15, because that would put the yellow areas into a flat part of the red channel, hurting detail.

Figure 2.16, no doubt, looks a lot better

than Figure 2.14. That's why so many people are seduced by the master curve, which, unfortunately, gives results that are as lacking in depth as many seducers are—check out the differences in the greenery of the enlarged portions of Figures 2.15 and 2.16.

Before leaving, here are three tips that aren't important yet, but will demonstrate their merit in chapters to come.

Figure 2.14 *This original has important detail in its green and yellow areas, but the background should not vanish, either.*

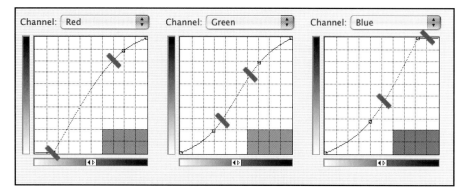

First, the blue channel of RGB and its CMYK cousin, the yellow, add very little contrast. There's a technical defect in the blue curve of Figure 2.15, in that the darkest part of the interest area falls to the right of the darkest point of the curve. Anything lying between the two loses all detail. We could never get away with that in either of the other channels, but it's unnoticeable in the blue. Or at least, I can't see it. If it's there, it would be in the yellowest areas of the field, where you'd see more contrast in Figure 2.16.

Second, in any green object, the two darkest channels are the red and blue of RGB or the cyan and yellow of CMYK. Note that the range is higher (darker) in the blue than in the red. This is normal. Natural greens are always biased toward yellow. So, from darkest to lightest, the order in RGB is blue, red, green; in CMYK it's yellow, cyan, magenta.

In constructing curves, we have to be careful that we don't force the red to be as dark as the blue, as otherwise the trees will turn bluish green rather than the green the viewer expects.

Figure 2.15 *Left, an image corrected by the RGB curves shown above. Below, an enlarged segment.*

Third, the master curve that I've been trashing may work deceptively well in largely neutral areas like Figure 2.13's pelican. It starts to lose its appeal in images with subdued colors, or with more than one important color, like Figure 2.14. It really does badly where there's only one important color, as in the damaged car of Figure 2.7. Refer back to those curves, and note how different the ranges of the three channels are. If you were crazy enough to try to use the master curve, you couldn't bring the bottom left point any farther to the right than the red curve is, or the top right point any farther to the left than in the green curve. So, you could gain only a fraction as much contrast as the set of three curves did.

Admittedly, that was a poor image to begin with, and we didn't much care about quality. But now let's examine the workflow when we face the same color in a setting where quality *is* desired.

How Far to Go?

Figure 2.17A is headed for a clothing catalog. Like most such images, this one was shot by a professional in a studio. If he didn't like his result, he could have shot it again. And yet it requires correction, as all similar shots do.

It's not a question of the blouse being the wrong color. The controlled lighting of the studio should eliminate that possibility. In

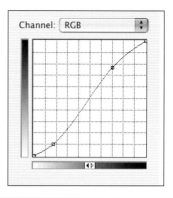

Figure 2.16 *The master curve is an inferior way to correct. Because the individual channels occupy different ranges, only an S curve is possible. The results are not as snappy as in Figure 2.15.*

any case, the photographer has also captured some color-control swatches, a prudent measure that sometimes helps and never hurts unless it's taken too seriously.

There is, however, a simultaneous contrast issue. When confronted by a large area of similar color, human beings sensitize themselves to it and see more variety than the camera does. And so the camera's version always looks flat.

As in the damaged car image of Figure 2.7, there's only one interest object. That car and the blouse happen to be about the same color, the background is irrelevant in both, the objective of increasing contrast is the same in both, and the obvious method of doing it is to find the object's range in every channel and make the curves steep there.

The question is, how steep? In the car image, the answer was, absolutely as steep as possible, no matter what happens to the color or to detail elsewhere in the image. That to-the-max approach won't work in a clothing catalog. We can't have parts of this blouse going white or blue, as the car did. So again: how far do we go?

I don't know. Neither do you. Furthermore, we probably wouldn't agree with each other even if we thought we did know.

This is therefore a very different exercise from the car photograph, and it's different, too, from the Auto Levels exercise that started the chapter. There, we (or, rather, Photoshop's

presets) had specific target values in mind for the lightest and darkest areas of the image. Here, we haven't got much of a clue.

In such circumstances, indulge in overkill. That is, I'd suggest treating this blouse almost exactly as we did the car, bringing out as much detail as possible, and then deciding how to split the difference between the original and the ultra-high-contrast version.

As with most things in Photoshop, there are several ways to accomplish this, but a curves adjustment layer screams out as being the best. To review: standard layers have all the attributes that an unlayered image would have. Adjustment layers contain commands only, which affect the layers beneath. Both types of layer can employ opacities less than 100%, allowing some of the underlying image to show through; both can be restricted to certain areas of the image by means of layer masks and/or layer Blending Options; and both can access many different blending modes. The disadvantages of adjustment layers are that they usually don't survive changes in colorspace and that painting and other retouching tools don't work; the disadvantage of conventional layers is that we can't edit our curves (or other commands) once we apply them.

Therefore, we establish a curves adjustment layer, either by clicking the handy icon at the bottom of the Layers palette and choosing Curves or with Layer: New Adjustment

Review and Exercises

✓ In the red-channel curve that produced the punchier Niagara Falls image of Figure 2.12, there's a funky twist in the top quarter. What is the purpose of the point that creates that twist? (Hint: what objects would fall in the area that this point artificially makes steeper?)

✓ What is the difference between a standard layer and an adjustment layer?

✓ Why do we usually not want to set the endpoints of an image to their extremes—that is, to $255^R255^G255^B$ and $0^R0^G0^B$ in RGB?

Layer>Curves. The Curves dialog opens automatically, and we apply drastic curves to
each channel, like the ones used for Figure
2.7's car.

Figure 2.18 is excessive, but it's all
part of the plan. If it has too much
contrast, we can easily dial it back. If
it has too little, we have a problem.
But before doing so, we should
consider a different approach.

The CMYK Alternative

To keep this chapter simple, so
far we've stuck with RGB. If this
file were headed for a photo lab
or a desktop printer, that's where we'd stay.
But it isn't. In real life, the image's destination
is a catalog. For that, a CMYK file is required,
just as I have to prepare CMYK files for the
printer of this book.

Becoming reasonably good at color
correction is mostly a matter of avoiding
mistakes, like forgetting to set highlights or leaving impossible
colors in the image. Becoming very good is more about
making the best choice when several good methods
are available.

This image is a foretaste of chapters to
come. We start with RGB, we must end
with CMYK, and in the middle we have to
improve the picture. But when, where,
and how?

Rather than go through a disserta-
tion on which colorspaces do what
better and when, or bring in other
options like doing the work in LAB,

Figure 2.17 *When trying to bring out
detail, it often helps to engineer in more
than is
needed
on an
adjustment
layer. The opacity can
then be lowered to taste.
Above, the original.
Below, a corrected
version.*

partially in RGB and partially in CMYK, or with channel blending, let's pretend that there are only two possibilities: correct in RGB and then convert to CMYK, or convert to CMYK first and then correct. As we have already had a look at the first possibility, let's start over and try the second.

The approach is the same. After Mode: CMYK, we establish a curves adjustment layer, locate the blouse in all channels, of

which we have four now, not three, and steepen away.

We already know about the similarity between the RGB channels and their CMY counterparts, but comparing the curves of Figure 2.18 to those of Figure 2.19 makes the relationship even more obvious. The shapes of the red and cyan curves are almost identical, as are those of the green and magenta.

The big difference, of course, is the presence of a black curve. In an object like this, its original range is short, easy pickings for a curve. And one of the many advantages of the black channel (which we will be discussing at length in Chapter 5) is that it can't change color. The blouse is not going to turn green or yellow no matter how hard we hit the black.

Remembering that both are intended to be overkill, Figure 2.19 seems better detailed and more believable than Figure 2.18. So, I would now throw Figure 2.18 away, and reduce the opacity of the adjustment layer in Figure 2.19 to taste. I used 70% to produce Figure 2.17B.

CMYK Before RGB

The concept is simple: steepen the curve, get better contrast. As we get deeper into color correction, the choices become more complex. Choosing which colorspace to work in has so many gotchas and exceptions that we won't actually summarize what we know about it until the final pages of the book. But making the right

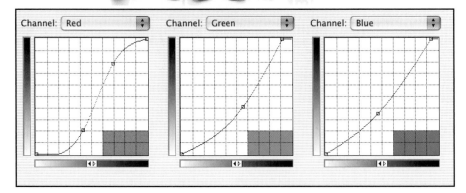

Figure 2.18 These RGB curves aim at increasing contrast throughout the range of the blouse.

choice can pay off, as it did here. RGB does well with this image, but CMYK does better.

In fact, we can make one of our first generalizations here. If you're trying to bring out critical detail with curves, CMYK works best. The quick technical explanation is that the ranges are shorter in the CMY channels because a lot of detail migrates into the black. So, not only do we have the opportunity to work the black channel, but in the CMY channels the interest objects fall in smaller ranges on the curve, which can then be steepened more than the RGB counterpart could.

Now, let's turn the example on its head. Suppose that we don't need a CMYK file at all, but that we require an RGB file at the end of the process. Is there a case to be made for converting the file to CMYK, correcting it there, and reconverting it back to RGB?

First, you'd need to ask yourself whether the improvement in Figure 2.19 is big enough, and the picture important enough, to warrant these extra steps, considering that Figure 2.18 is not bad. Second, unless you're quite experienced in this area, you should be really cautious about converting from RGB to CMYK and back again, because there's usually nothing to gain and there are some hidden traps.

The main problem is that many colors exist in RGB that don't exist in CMYK, or, to use the technical term, are *out of CMYK gamut*. When the RGB file goes into CMYK, those colors have to change to something else. If, having wiped out these illegal colors during the conversion to CMYK, we now bring the file back to RGB, they won't be there anymore, and we'll have to figure out a way to restore them.

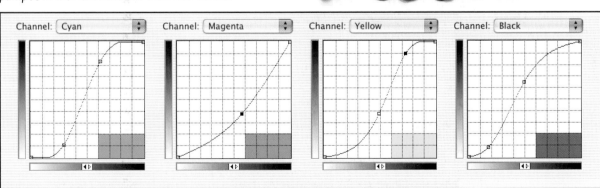

Figure 2.19 *Somewhat more detail can be pumped in with CMYK rather than RGB curves.*

| Channel: Cyan | Channel: Magenta | Channel: Yellow | Channel: Black |

These out-of-gamut colors tend to be blues, brilliant colors, and pastels. None of those exist in the original we've just been working on; the blouse is a rather dull, dark color. So, converting into CMYK isn't going to lose anything. It would be safe to return to RGB afterward, and if I were doing the job and needed an RGB file in the end, that's exactly what I'd do.

A Vote for Auto Levels

In color correction, certain fundamentals always work. We always try to get interest objects into steep parts of the curve, for example, which implies that we always are going to set light and dark points. That's why Auto Levels works: we usually can do better ourselves, but setting light and dark points is always right. In the next chapter, we'll look at how to avoid impossible colors, which is also always the right thing to do but is beyond the ken of an automated correction.

Unfortunately, many of our best weapons are effective only some of the time. Working in CMYK when the goal is an RGB file certainly qualifies.

For example, suppose we were dealing not with the purple blouse but rather with the green products of Figure 2.8. The objective is the same: more detail in the product. But this time there would be no advantage in working in CMYK. The black channel would be blank where these products appear, so it would be useless to apply a curve. If the goal is a CMYK file, it wouldn't matter whether this correction took place in RGB or CMYK. And the RGB original contains pastel colors that are unprintable and would get lost during the conversion to CMYK. So, if an RGB file is the goal, converting to CMYK to correct and then back again is quite mad—in this particular image.

Figuring out what strategy to use (and when) is frustrating, particularly when we discover after the picture has been printed that there would have been a better way. I'll be trying to give some hints as to the better ways in forthcoming chapters. Meanwhile, just sticking to the proper curve shape should pay big dividends. All you have to do is remember why Auto Levels works so well.

The Bottom Line

Curves can correct problems both with color and with detail; this chapter considers detail only.

The default curve is a straight line at an angle of 45 degrees. Any change we make results in some areas that are steeper than, and others that are flatter than, 45 degrees. The steep areas gain contrast; the flat ones lose it. Proper curving is therefore a form of horsetrading, where we try to gain contrast in significant areas at the expense of ones we don't care about.

The exception is if an image's highlight and/or shadow aren't set properly. Bringing them to their appropriate values steepens the interior of the curve and flattens only areas that don't exist in the image. This is why the Image: Adjustments>Auto Levels command is often so effective—although a human being can do much better.

Color by the Numbers

Artistic judgment or monkey work? Convincing color correction isn't out of the reach of the color-blind, provided they follow certain numerical rules. The rest of us can do better, but those who don't base their technique on meeting the numbers will not even compete.

Monkeying around with the color balance of photographic images is not a sport for the timid, or so goes the conventional wisdom. Believing this, people go through the most simian sorts of shenanigans trying to make their color look believable. They select this area, sharpen that one, call up histograms, apply strange filters, and generally try to demonstrate that if an infinite number of art directors employ an infinite number of digital tweaks somebody somewhere may throw them a banana.

And yet, most color correction could be handled by monkeys. This chapter introduces a numerical, curve-based approach calling for little artistic judgment. To be sure, one can go much farther, but all the advanced techniques are inevitably based on these surpassingly simple ones.

The by-the-numbers rules can be stated in a single sentence.

Use the full range of available tones every time, and don't give viewers any colors that they will know better than to believe.

*   *   *

The itinerant color scientist Dr. Lemuel Gulliver once remarked, "Undoubtedly Philosophers are in the right when they tell us, that nothing is great or little otherwise than by Comparison." That's a good thing to keep in mind when we compare corrected versions to the original—not just with photographs, but with text.

The call to arms that starts this chapter exploded onto the graphic arts scene in 1994, in the first edition of *Professional Photoshop*. Not content with suggesting that a monkey could do this kind of work, I taught a

Figure 3.1 In the original, left, the macaque is greenish yellow. The curves shown create a neutral animal, but do nothing to add contrast.

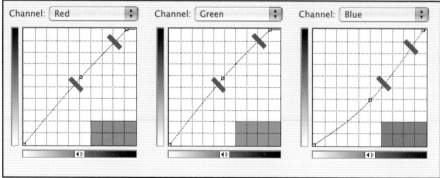

#1 R:	132/ 115	#2 R:	88/ 68
G:	138/ 115	G:	94/ 68
B:	92/ 115	B:	60/ 74

#3 R:	60/ 40	#4 R:	34/ 15
G:	63/ 38	G:	39/ 15
B:	30/ 34	B:	17/ 15

color-blind man to do it, and published some of his results, which were a good deal better than many professionals could produce at that benighted point in history.

Today, every professional accepts the need to set light and dark points, to maintain control of neutrals, and to use curves as the principal color-correction tool. In 1994, these concepts were unknown to desktop publishers, although drum scanner operators were aware of them. It was an age of primitive desktop scanners, almost no digital cameras, a Photoshop with no layers, and very expensive preparation for print.

It was, in short, a Lilliputian world by today's standards, and by the numbers was as revolutionary as a visiting giant. Those who adopted it made monkeys out of their competitors who didn't.

Since then, natural selection has done what it does best, and our Missing Link ancestors are extinct, helped along by cameras that set their own light and dark points and to some extent balance colors. In this more sophisticated world, saying that professional-level color correction can be done by apes is substantially less accurate than it was in the Photoshop Stone Age.

Nevertheless, by-the-numbers color correction remains the indispensable starting point. To see how it works in its simplest form, we'll travel farther than Gulliver ever did, into the forests of Indonesia.

Figure 3.1A is a portrait not of one of those vendors who says that all you need to get good color is a calibrated monitor, but rather of a primate known as a black macaque. I will indulge in the wild speculation that there may be a reason why he is not called a yellow-green macaque.

The camera faithfully recorded what it saw, but cameras don't have the sense of chromatic adaptation that we discussed in Chapter 1. This is a jungle scene, with lots of green light reflecting first off the leaves and then off the animal's face. If we were there ourselves, our self-calibrating vision would adjust to the lighting, and we'd see him as black.

Figure 3.2 *Substituting these curves for those of Figure 3.1 puts the macaque in steeper areas and results in better detail.*

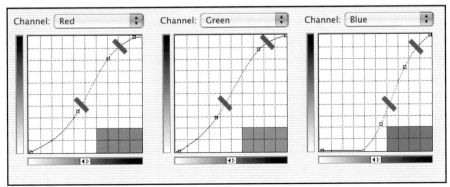

Black, white, and gray are described not as colors but as *neutrals.* In RGB, but not in CMYK, the rule is easy to remember: where all three channels are equal, the result is neutral. If all three channels are identical everywhere, the image is grayscale.

In a few pages, we'll go over how to measure values, but for this exercise I'll just tell you what they are. We never measure just a single point, which can be deceptive. I've measured four points in the animal's face in this file, which arrives in an unspecified

A Plan for Using This Book and Its CD

This book is divided into two halves. Chapters 1–10 stand independently of the rest of the book, giving the basics of global color correction. Chapter 1 is an introduction, and Chapters 9 and 10 suggest a workflow and how to analyze images before correcting them. Chapters 2–8 discuss the actual tools, which are almost entirely curves, channel blending, sharpening, and layer Blend If options. There are no selections or masks in use in the first half, nor is there anything from the toolbox except the color sampler tool. Nor do we discuss any calibration or resolution issues, or the possibility of using Camera Raw. We give only cursory attention to Color Settings. These things get covered in Chapters 11–15 because I believe it is helpful to understand the basics of image manipulation before attacking them. Chapters 16–20 are not particularly reader-friendly; enter at your own risk.

In contrast to previous editions, all but one of the images that are corrected on these pages are on the CD. They are, however, at lower resolutions, so the numbers you measure will not necessarily correspond exactly to those in the text. I recommend that you *not* use the CD for Chapters 2–6 and use your own images instead. The techniques in these chapters apply to almost all images. I think you'll be more impressed if you apply them to ones you're more familiar with. In later chapters, which show techniques that are right for certain images and not for others, you may wish to use the ones on the CD.

This book has a long history of being found both rewarding and frustrating. In order to help you avoid the second category, the following is advice that, after four editions, I can give with considerable confidence.

•Be sure you understand the terminology and the way numbers are used. From lightest to darkest, we say *highlight, quartertone, midtone, three-quartertone, shadow.* These are loose terms corresponding to regions on the curve: there is no firm line where the quartertone ends and the midtone begins. RGB and CMYK numbers are always positive, but LAB has negatives as well; numbers in parentheses, like $50^L(10)^A10^B$, denote this. In CMYK, we don't bother to attach values of 0^K to the end of the CMY numbers.

•By the end of Chapter 4, which discusses LAB, you will need to be able to identify colors by their numbers in any of the three colorspaces. I am not talking about subtle distinctions between, say, greens. But you need to be able to distinguish a green from a cyan or a yellow. Without this ability, color correction will take much longer. If you need it, there's a cheat sheet on page 98.

•Few people are equally proficient in RGB and CMYK. Make it a point of trying to work in the one in which you consider yourself weaker. I recommend that you choose one lightness/darkness orientation for curves that you use in every colorspace.

•Most chapters have Stumbling Blocks boxes highlighting areas that have confused previous readers.

•Don't be afraid to disagree with me on aesthetic points. When I am stating a rule that I regard as absolute— for example, that you can't get competitive work without using a full range every time—I am not shy about saying so. Choices of color or blending percentages are a different story, and your mileage may vary.

•If you get completely stuck, just skip the section and move on, and if you find that suggestion to be intensely frustrating, Google any one of my previous books and check out how many readers were in your shoes and claim that it all became clear on a second reading.

RGB. Going from lightest to darkest, they read $132^R138^G92^B$, $88^R94^G60^B$, $60^R63^G30^B$, and $34^R39^G17^B$. That last value, found near the ear, is also the darkest significant point of the image. The lightest significant point is a large yellow area in a leaf under the chin, at $245^R252^G173^B$, remembering that pure white is $255^R255^G255^B$ and pure black $0^R0^G0^B$.

We'd like to see three approximately equal numbers throughout the animal. Instead, the green is always highest, meaning that we see more green light. The blue is always lowest, meaning that we see less blue light, meaning more yellow. The darkest part of the face is also currently too light. We'd prefer $15^R15^G15^B$, for reasons to be discussed later.

The top half of each curve contains values from 128 to 0, the top quarter from 64 to 0. According to our numbers, the macaque lives mostly in the third quarter in the red and green, and in the top quarter in the blue. Recall that all curves in this book show darkness to the right, which is not the Photoshop default for RGB.

By the Numbers vs. By the Numbers

The words *by the numbers* suggest a child's coloring book, a wooden, invariable approach. In reality, there are many types of by-the-numbers corrections, some of which are better than others.

Since the blue values are always darker than the other two, the logical approach would seem to be to bring them together by lightening the blue and darkening the red and green. That's what I did to make Figure 3.1B, moving the center points up or down, watching the Info palette change until I saw a properly neutral $115^R115^G115^B$ where $132^R138^G92^B$ had been. Then, I moved the top right point of each curve to the left, darkening what had been $34^R39^G17^B$ into $15^R15^G15^B$. After verifying that the two other points I had looked at were also close to equal in all three channels, I called it quits.

By the numbers, Figure 3.1B is correct. There's nothing obviously wrong with it, which is more than can be said for Figure 3.1A. Yet there's something missing—more detail in the macaque.

Chapter 2 does not appear in this book because the publisher wanted me to inflate the page count so that the book would seem heftier. It's there because using curves to get better contrast is at least as important as using them to get better color.

When suddenly confronted by a wild animal that looks like it might be able to inflict bodily harm on us if so inclined, we don't stop to admire the background greenery. All our concentration is devoted to the creature. Our eyes open wider so that we can learn more about this dark potential threat, and we lose perception of anything that doesn't happen to be its color.

The pitiable camera, perhaps reasoning that even a monkey is not going to try to bite into a lens, has no such reaction. It sees only what's in front of it, with no special emphasis on nasty-looking foul-smelling bipeds with a sharp set of teeth. So there is a fundamental disconnect between what the camera saw and what *we* would have.

The response has to be a combination of the methods of this chapter and the last: the curves must be steepest where the macaque is, but the relation between the curves must result in a neutral animal. Hence, the subtler curves, and the better result, of Figure 3.2. Each curve establishes and lowers a point near the bottom of the macaque's range, forcing the entire top half of the curve to take on a steeper angle.

The tickmarks on the curves are in the same horizontal locations in Figures 3.1 and 3.2. Clearly, there's more distance between them vertically in Figure 3.2, and that's making all the difference. A color-blind person would have no difficulty achieving this result, as it's all numbers and logic.

Not that I'm saying this is the perfect correction. The points on these curves could be placed in different areas or pulled up and down by different amounts. And in that case, you might get something you like better than Figure 3.2. That's the creative part of by the numbers. But you can't get by without the basics. Figure 3.1A violates both of the basic rules stated at the beginning of the chapter: it doesn't use full range, and it gives the viewers a color that they know better than to believe.

Setting Up the System

By-the-numbers rules, as you might expect, encompass a lot more than neutral colors. But before we get into further specifics, we need to take care of some system housekeeping and to clarify why certain techniques are favored over others.

• The Info palette is our guide as we meander down the curving path. To make sure that it doesn't send you down a blind alley, click the eyedropper tool, and change the setting in the options bar (Figure 3.3) to something other than the default Point Sample. I use 3 by 3 myself, but the other option, 5 by 5, is workable.

This change is needed because we want the Info palette to report average values in an area. Point Sample makes it report a single pixel, which for all we know can be a speck of dust on the camera lens. 3 by 3 reports an average of nine pixels; 5 by 5 averages 25.

• Now, we configure the Info palette itself. Its top half is divided into two sides, each of which can be defined with its own eyedropper.

Figure 3.3 *Photoshop's default for Info palette readings is Point Sample, which reports the value of the single pixel that's beneath the cursor. It's better to alter this setting to get a more accurate idea of the sampled area's characteristics.*

One side should be set to Actual Color, so that the numbers being reported are those of the file's own colorspace. The other, in my opinion, should be set to whatever colorspace you are personally most comfortable in. We're going to be working in this chapter in both RGB and CMYK, and in the next chapter we'll be adding LAB. Few people can instantaneously assign a meaning to numbers in all three. Set the second side of the Info palette to give you equivalents in something you're certain of, as shown in Figure 3.4. Notice that, for ease in evaluating whether objects are really neutral, I've set the four fixed points to read in LAB. We'll talk about why in the next chapter.

Photoshop is a rich and often redundant program. There may be several ways of accomplishing the same thing. Sometimes they're equivalent and sometimes not. If I suggest doing things a certain way and you prefer something different, there are three possible outcomes, in my opinion.

• Your way is as good as mine. (Pride does not permit me to say it might be better.)

• Your way may work but it's a kludge.

• Your way is a bad one.

       *   *   *

The following practices are all acceptable and give substantially the same results as what I recommend.

• **Curves and adjustment layers**. People who need the flexibility to edit curves quickly put them on adjustment layers. Those who don't think they need to edit the curves but want to leave themselves an out save copies of the curves separately from the file. And those who are certain that their curves are final just apply the curves and move on. Your workflow may dictate one method or another.

• **Typing in the numbers**. To add a point to a curve, click where it's supposed to go and drag up or down. Or, Command–click inside the image, and the curve point will be placed automatically at the point in the

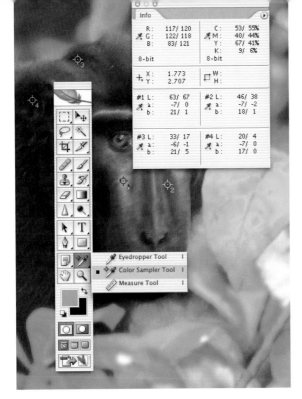

Figure 3.4 *Left, the color sampler tool places up to four fixed points (shown in the macaque). These points expand the Info palette and change as corrections are applied. Right, any section of the palette can be configured to display equivalents in other colorspaces.*

channel corresponding to what's underneath the cursor. If instead we Shift-Command–click, the point goes into the curves in all channels. It's also possible to click a random point and then key in input and output numbers in the bottom left corner of the Curves dialog. I don't like doing this because I hate when my hand leaves the mouse. If you are more coordinated, typing the numbers in works fine.

- **Fixed density points in the Info palette.** In the macaque image, I activated the color sampler tool (it lives in the same box as the eyedropper tool) and clicked four areas of different darkness in the animal's face. Those four were added to the Info palette, more than doubling its size, but enabling me to see what was happening to all four simultaneously as I adjusted curves. It was a useful move here so that you could see what was happening, but in real life I rarely use this feature, preferring to mouse over the affected area, looking at a lot more than four points.
- **Two sets of curves.** For efficiency's sake we try to get everything done with one set of curves. If the result isn't quite what you want, the world doesn't come to an end if you apply

a second set or even a third set. If the second and/or subsequent sets are drastic corrections, however, it probably means that the first set stunk more than a macaque does.

- **RGB and CMYK.** If you have an RGB file that is destined to remain in RGB, you should rarely go into CMYK with it—LAB, which we'll discuss in Chapter 4, is much more likely. But if the RGB file is eventually headed for CMYK, you could conceivably do most of the correcting in either space, or even in LAB. All these colorspaces have strengths and weaknesses, but speaking generally, CMYK is the best curving space and RGB the worst. No matter how good the RGB or LAB original is, quality output almost invariably requires minor tweaks to the file after it enters CMYK. If you accept the necessity for minor tweaking afterward, there's no reason to avoid doing the tough part in RGB.

*   *   *

The following practices are sometimes effective, but I turn my nose up at them.

- **The Levels crutch.** Levels is a weaker version of curves. It can be as effective in some cases, but it can't make an S curve, which is critical (see box, page 38). The sooner you jump into the deep water, the quicker you'll learn to swim. So I recommend using curves exclusively, particularly if you are currently not as agile at curvewriting as you'd like to be. Practice makes perfect.
- **Setting highlights and shadows with the eyedropper.** An eyedropper tool within the Curves dialog allows you to click the image area where you want to set an endpoint, and you can finish the curve from

there. It works fine, provided you in fact want the curve to start at that point—which you usually won't, because most of the time you'll want an S curve, not something that starts steep from the outset.

*   *   *

The following practices identify you as a yahoo and should be avoided.

● **Using the master curve.** In CMYK, doing so always costs contrast because the black channel never resembles the other three. In RGB, at best it doesn't add detail as well as channel-by-channel curves; at worst it changes color and harms detail in highlights and shadows.

● **Using other commands too soon.** Getting all the numbers right always creates a perfect image—so goes the theory. You should give the theory a chance to prove itself before indulging in any monkeyshines that would derail subsequent by-the-numbers correction, particularly Image: Adjustments> Hue/Saturation or Selective Color. If your curves have produced correct numbers and you're still dissatisfied, then, and only then, should you use them.

Similarly, it's dangerous to sharpen or to use Image: Adjustments>Shadow/Highlight while there's still major curving to be done. These commands increase apparent focus by creating artifacts that are, we hope, too subtle to detect. Minor curve adjustments probably won't hurt, but big curves may emphasize these artifacts in a disagreeable way.

*   *   *

If you're going to be doing your own separations into CMYK, for purposes of this book you'll need to check some of your choices under color settings. This topic is explored in Chapter 12; the complex CMYK choices are fleshed out in Chapter 13 and you should defer any final choice until you read it. However, if you are now using the Photoshop default CMYK definition, U.S. Web Coated (SWOP) v2, you need to make a change.

Otherwise, your separations will have too much black in them and will not be compatible with many of the methods in this book. As a quick fix, jump ahead to Figure 5.2 and copy it into your own settings.

The RGB setting is another controversial topic, but we don't have to address it yet. Many of the RGB originals in this book contain an embedded profile identifying the type of RGB that the photographer was using. Provided you have your RGB color management policy set to Preserve Embedded Profiles, you'll be working in that space too if you decide to open the file from the CD. If there isn't a profile, your guess is as good as mine; I have no more information about the file than you do. For what it's worth, I open such files in Apple RGB, for reasons explained in Chapter 12.

So much for theory. Let's roll up our sleeves and correct some color. Please remember that a lot of the high-octane stuff that you'll encounter in other chapters isn't in use yet. We will not consider sharpening, channel blending, false profiles, selections, masks, or layering shenanigans, or the use of LAB. Could some of those things make the corrected versions here even better? Undoubtedly. But this chapter is the foundation. Ignore it, and all those tools, powerful as they are, won't give you competitive results.

The Magic Numbers

As most professionals today occasionally have to work in both CMYK and RGB, we'll do the same, with three examples coming up of each variety. RGB users who venture into CMYK often have difficulty with a particular concept, which should be clarified before giving suggested numbers.

The cyan ink throws a monkey wrench into the CMYK works. It reflects considerable red light, which it wouldn't do in a perfect world. Because of this, CMYK printing can't make good blues, a deficiency that is hard to adjust to, and the neutrality definition is different, which is easy to manage with practice.

RGB users know that to create a neutral color—gray, white, black—the values of all three channels need to be the same. One would think that (ignoring black, which is neutral already) the same rule would apply in CMY. It doesn't. To make a neutral, magenta and yellow should be equal, but cyan higher. This explains the suggested shadow and highlight values below.

Make your images meet the following four guidelines, and be prepared for startling improvements.

● The **shadow** is the darkest significant neutral area of an image. Almost all images have *something* we can use for a shadow.

In principle, the shadow should be the heaviest value we believe can be held with detail. If your final file is RGB, use $15^R15^G15^B$ unless you've seen that your output device retains detail well at a darker value. For CMYK, the value gets darker as printing conditions get better. For jobs printed on a web press, as this book is, I recommend $80^C70^M70^Y70^K$. Sheetfed presses could accept a higher shadow, but newspapers would need a lower one, at least in the CMY.

Most commercial printers impose a limit on the sum of all four inks, to avoid drying problems on press. The better the printing conditions, the higher the number they'll accept. SWOP, the industry-standard Specifications for Web Offset Publications, mandates a 300 maximum, which most magazines tweak down to 280. My $80^C70^M70^Y70^K$ suggestion sums to 290, close enough.

However, 290 is not close enough when preparing images for a newspaper, which is apt to ask for 240, or even for some inkjet printers. If a lower number is necessary, we reduce the CMY colors and increase black in roughly equal amounts.

People don't have good color perception in areas this dark, so, if need be, we can take liberties with one or two of the ink values. Don't do this without a good reason, though. An unbalanced shadow often is a symptom of a color cast that may be subtly hurting other parts of the image.

Also, your CMY values can be as high as you like in areas outside of shadows. Navy blue, for instance, might be $95^C65^M15^Y30^K$. The only reason cyan is limited to 80^C in the shadows is that otherwise the ink limit might be exceeded because all four inks are heavy. The navy blue above sums to only 205, way below any possible ink limit.

● The **highlight** is the lightest significant part of the image, with two qualifications. First, it cannot be a reflection or a light source. These things are called *speculars, specular highlights,* or *catchlights,* and we ignore them. Second, it must be something that we are willing to represent to the viewer as being *white.* Assuming such an area can be found (and it isn't always there to be found) use $245^R245^G245^B$ or $5^C2^M2^Y$.

Other experts suggest different CMY values. They may say $4^C2^M2^Y$, $3^C1^M1^Y$, $5^C3^M3^Y$, or $6^C3^M3^Y$. But everyone agrees that magenta and yellow should be equal, and cyan a couple of points higher, to maintain neutrality. Such universal agreement exists because this highlight value is critical. We humans are quite sensitive to light colors. A variation of three or four points in any ink could result in an unacceptable cast.

Guessing is what we do when we aren't sure. And because we hate being tossed about in a sea of guesses, we always have to be on the lookout for anchors, sure things. The most common such anchor is a color that logic tells us must be neutral.

Looking for the Sure Thing

● Areas that are supposed to appear **neutral,** that is, white, black, or any shade of gray, need to have equal values in all three channels in RGB. In CMYK, they need equal magenta and yellow, higher cyan. Black ink, being neutral itself, is irrelevant.

In teaching classes, I've observed that around half the students think that locating neutrals is the easiest part of color correction. The other half drive themselves berserk. They force neutrals to happen where no neutral should be; they find one neutral and ignore another; and they often would be better off if they handed the file off to a gibbon who knew how to launch Auto Levels.

To try to prevent such monkey business, I offer Figure 3.5. The cat is in RGB, the statue in CMYK. Can you guess which has been sabotaged, intentionally given an incorrect color?

I trust that you have no difficulty with the question, no matter how little confidence you have in your ability to identify neutral colors—but you may be surprised at why.

We force neutrality when we are sure, by logic and experience, that we are looking for neutrality. We just had that experience with the macaque. If that animal isn't neutral, a very dark gray or black, he must be very close. And the same is true of Figure 3.5's cat. You may never have met him, but if you've ever seen a cat before, you know that the light fur on his face, paws, and belly has to be white. White—not lavender, not turquoise, not tangerine—and we force a

white if the original capture features one of these or any other impossible color.

In deciding that the cat picture was the sabotaged one, however, you weren't relying on the light fur, which is in fact white in this image. You were clued in by the *dark* fur, not because you know that it's neutral, but because you know that cats are never purple.

A cat with these tiger markings might indeed be gray, but we aren't sure of it in the sense that we're sure his lighter fur is white and the macaque is black. This is a standard quandary when dealing with near-neutrals. We don't know what color it is—but we know what it's not.

Russian Blue is the name of a breed of cat that is a lot more expensive than this one. The present cat could be a rich brown, or a mousy-looking brown, but he can't possibly be any other color than brown or gray. This gives us enough information to start looking at numbers.

If the cat is gray, then the RGB values are all equal. Brown is a species of red. If the cat is brown, then the red channel must be lighter than the other two. If either the green or blue shows a higher number than the red, it's an impossible color. Cats don't have even slightly green or blue fur.

We can go further. If the red is lighter and

Figure 3.5 Even someone who's never seen these objects in real life can decide that certain colors are impossible—a purple cat, for example. But for these two cases, what color should we assume?

the other two are equal, the cat's a pure brown. If the other two aren't equal but the green is lighter than the blue, then the cat is a yellowish brown. I'll buy that as a possibility. But if the blue is lighter than the green, then it's a purplish brown. No sale, not to me.

To summarize: if you're going by the numbers, the white fur should have nearly equal RGB values. The dark fur may have equal values, too, but if it doesn't, then the red has to be the highest number of the three; the green value may be equal to the blue but it can't be lower. Anything else, you have to correct—but to what?

Like Gulliver, we are sometimes adrift in a sea without appropriate navigational tools and in doubt as to our destination. It's frustrating, perhaps, to learn that sometimes by-the-numbers means we have to wing it. I see no other internal indication of what color the cat is, so I would have to resort to the time-tested prepress technique of taking a guess. You might make a better one—but not if your numbers don't comply with those in the paragraph above.

Now, let's turn to the statue. It's currently gray. I've measured a point in the neck as $20^C15^M15^Y$; other points are comparable.

But is this the only possibility? Could this not be yellowed with age as well, or perhaps brownish? Here's a quiz. Let's reduce each ink, in turn, by 5 percent. There are a total of six possibilities, counting combinations of two inks. For example, $20^C10^M10^Y$ would imply a slight cyan cast. $15^C15^M15^Y$ doesn't have the extra cyan that's needed for neutrality. It is therefore a reddish, or warm, or brownish feel, because it's unbalanced in favor of magenta and yellow, which combine to make red. I might accept one but not the other. Even slight cyan casts are disagreeable. Slight casts in the direction of a warm color are often pleasing.

The other four possibilities are $20^C15^M10^Y$, $20^C10^M15^Y$, $15^C15^M10^Y$, and $15^C10^M15^Y$. They yield (but not in this order; you have to figure it out) yellow, green, magenta, and blue.

That part is so easy that I won't waste space on the answers. The harder question is, which, if any, of these six possibilities do you think is a reasonable alternative to pure gray? Come up with a response before you turn to Figure 3.6.

● **Fleshtones** should, in CMYK, have at least as much yellow as magenta, and up to a third again as much in extreme cases. Where the yellow is equal to or only slightly higher than the magenta, this implies a very light-skinned person, such as a small child or a blond. For Caucasians, the cyan value should be a fifth to a third as heavy as the magenta, depending upon how bronzed a person is. For someone dark-skinned, $15^C50^M65^Y$ will do; lighter-skinned Caucasians can go $6^C30^M35^Y$ or even lower.

Persons of Hispanic or Asian parentage share a skintone range that's smaller than Caucasians as a whole. Yellow is always significantly higher than magenta, commonly 10 to 15 points in those of Asian descent. Cyan begins at one-quarter the magenta value and can be greater even than one-third.

Beta reader André Lopes, who hails from São Paulo, offers this warning: "'Hispanic or Asian parentage' is a dangerous expression. There are many 'mongolian Asians,' such as Chinese, Vietnamese, and Japanese. But there are also at least a billion Indians and Pakistanis who have 'brownish gray' skins, very different from northern Asians. And Latin American Hispanics who have some native blood (particularly in Central America and the Andes region) have skintones very similar to those of bronzed mongolians. But the inhabitants of Buenos Aires, if I may use some Brazilian humor, are a bunch of Italians who speak Spanish and believe they are British."

The race commonly (and inaccurately) referred to as *black* exhibits more diversity than any other group. Lighter-skinned

individuals compare to Hispanics, with yellow distinctly higher than magenta. However, as the skintone gets darker, the difference compresses. The darkest-skinned persons often have equal magenta and yellow. As for cyan and black, there is no limit.

References to the original human inhabitants of the North American continent brings up issues of political correctness. *Redskin* is considered pejorative by almost everyone except football fans. To me, that word is less offensive than people asking what the "typical" Native American fleshtone should be. Presumably for evolutionary reasons, large variations are seen depending upon the strength of the sun in the area. The Seminoles of Florida, and my own Chickasaw ancestors in Oklahoma, are accurately described as redskins—they have distinctly more of a magenta component than other ethnic groups. The Makah people of western Washington state have a lighter complexion than most Asians. Between a Seminole and a Makah the typical difference is greater than between a Swede and an Italian.

Locating and measuring suitable fleshtones is easy with experience,

Figure 3.6 *Even when the precise color of a near-neutral object is unknown, logic and experience can exclude certain possibilities. This garden statue could be gray, but it might have a slight color. Here are six possibilities, all generated by five-point increments in the CMY values at a certain point in the neck. Top row, red and magenta casts. Middle row, blue and cyan. Bottom row, green and yellow casts. Which ones do you think are plausible? And what is the impact of each on the sky?*

but if you haven't tried it before, some snares must be avoided. Choose only normally lit skin, not a shadow or a semireflection. Also, avoid areas where makeup may have been applied, such as a woman's cheeks.

Except in persons of African descent, it is not customary to have black ink in a fleshtone, but it sometimes happens, particularly when using nonstandard GCR settings (see Chapter 5 for more on this). If black is present, count it as additional cyan, because it does the same thing: it pushes the color away from red and toward gray.

You may notice that there are no RGB numbers given. They depend on your choice of working space. A spreadsheet on the CD will let you find equivalences. In the interim, you can always refer to the CMYK numbers even if working in RGB, by setting up one side of the Info palette to read CMYK values.

Picking Significant Target Points

To start, we open the image and check the values in all of the key areas we've just been discussing. In simple pictures, we can keep these numbers straight in our heads, but as they get more complex, writing down the density values and what we propose to do with them can be helpful. To the extent the image does not meet our target numbers, we force it closer by applying curves.

To locate highlight

and shadow, I prefer to watch the Info palette as I run the cursor over several likely areas. This lets me choose the second-lightest area as a highlight, if I decide that the real lightest area is unimportant.

If you're uncomfortable with this, you can open Image: Adjustments>Threshold and move the slider until it becomes obvious where the light and dark points are. Remember, though, to look for the lightest and darkest *significant* areas, which are often a far cry from the areas that are *literally* lightest and darkest.

We'll now put that philosophy into action with four real-world images, two of which are reasonably good to start with and two of which aren't. We'll end with two CMYK images, and start with a pair of fleshtone exercises in RGB.

For an outdoor shot taken in a New England winter, Figure 3.7, which arrives in sRGB, isn't that bad. The camera has balanced the

Figure 3.7 *A cold-weather original can produce flesh-tones that are pinker than normal rules suggest.*

highlights and shadows nicely. They comply with our rules, but other parts of the image don't. Let's take stock.

The window frame is clearly the lightest significant point in the image, and also apparently is white. The camera agreed. It's hard to know exactly which point is the most representative, but the one I chose measures $244^R246^G247^B$, right in step with my $245^R245^G245^B$ recommendation.

The shadow is darker than we would like. The lining of her jacket and the area below her ear, below the hairline and just above the collar, are both in the neighborhood of $2^R2^G5^B$.

When measuring fleshtones, I usually around half a dozen readings just to make sure. Others make a rectangular selection of part of the forehead, run a huge blur filter, measure the result, and then cancel the blur. Definitely we don't want to measure this woman's cheeks because she might be wearing makeup. Also, we have to be careful because she has freckles. Anyway, the typical number I get is $173^R132^G130^B$. Since our rules require us to evaluate a CMYK number, the Info palette tells me that the equivalent is $32^C50^M39^Y1^K$—too cyan, too magenta.

There's one last known color to measure. It's not her shirt, which looks like it's blue but could be green or purple as far as we know. It's her hair. Certain colors are as impossible for this woman as they would be for the fur of the cat in Figure 3.5.

Undyed human hair ranges from yellow to black. It can never be on the green or blue side of gray. Granted, this is an uncorrected original. But no matter how bad the colors are, we can still see that the woman's hair is much too dark for her to be a blond. She can't have black hair, either, because lighter streaks, which people with very dark hair don't have, are found throughout.

We have a suggestion of a cool cast from the fleshtone reading. Possibly that cast is bad enough that this woman is actually a redhead. If not, her hair is brown. Either way, the red value has to be distinctly higher than either of the other two channels.

My reading, however, is $63^R62^G63^B$, equal values and therefore a pure gray. In the context of this image, that's an impossible color, a color that the viewer knows better than to believe.

The four by-the-numbers rules concern shadow, highlight, neutrals, and fleshtones. We ignore the third because there is nothing known to be neutral except for the window frame, which counts as a highlight. In the other three, we can use the rules as a starting point, but in each we should be careful not to take them too literally.

Neither the whites nor the blacks are an important part of this image, which distinguishes it from any of the three others we've seen in this chapter. I don't particularly care if the shadows plug around her collar area (you wouldn't say that about the macaque of Figure 3.1), and I don't particularly care if some of the whites blow out (you wouldn't say that about either the cat or the statue in Figure 3.5).

The skintone is too magenta for normal conditions, but these conditions may not be normal. If she were an athlete who'd just been exerting herself, we'd understand why—her skin would be redder than that of a fashion model shot in a studio. The same may apply here. This is a cold-weather shot; the color of her cheeks looks like a natural reaction to the temperature and not makeup. So while I would like to reduce the magenta component of the face, I'm not going to be doctrinaire about insisting that the yellow must be higher than the magenta, as it would in a normal photograph.

But I forgot—I'm using CMYK language, and this one will be corrected in RGB. If that's unfamiliar territory, just consider that the red is the cyan, the green the magenta, and the

Figure 3.8 *These curves increase contrast in the face and eliminate a bluish cast.*

blue the yellow. Here are the curving objectives as I see them.

• Leave the shadows alone but be more aggressive in the highlights, remembering that they have to be kept neutral because the window frame is white.

• Put the woman's face into the steepest part of each curve, recognizing that it is the most important area of the picture.

• Adjust the color balance of the face and the hair.

The green and blue curves are alike in that the face falls roughly in their middle. I started by mousing over the face to locate the exact range, and then placed points to surround that range, roughly a quarter and three-quarters of the

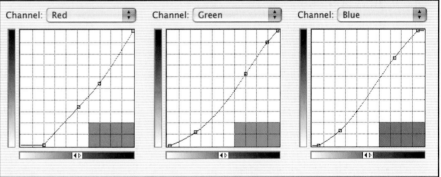

way up the green and blue grids. I lowered the lower point, which increased steepness in the facial range.

I would have liked to raise the upper point in both, too, but had to be content with doing it to the blue only, because the objective was to increase the yellow component to defeat the magenta cast measured earlier. At this stage, I was not trying for great precision, so I wasn't checking the Info palette.

The highlight in the green and blue had now been lightened. Also, because it fell in a flat part of the curves, it was losing contrast.

That's fine in the green and blue, but the face falls in a much lighter range in the red, and this curve shape would hurt it. So, in the red channel, rather than making an S, I moved the lower left point to the right, maintaining steepness in the lightest areas.

With the basic shapes of the curves established, it was time to fine-tune the color of the frame, the face, and the hair. My initial curve had wiped out the window frame in the red channel. As a result, the entire frame had a reddish cast. I countered this by raising the bottom point slightly from the bottom line of the grid. Now the lightest value anywhere in the image was 253ᴿ, not 255ᴿ.

Finally, I monkeyed around with the middle points in all three curves, trying to get acceptable values in both hair and face. Unlike the frame, where nearly equal values are definitely needed, here there's room for differences of opinion. I wound up inserting another point near the top of the green curve to darken the hair, which I thought was getting too yellow and not brown enough.

Figure 3.8 is the final result. My key areas measure as follows: highlight 253ᴿ253ᴳ254ᴮ; face 220ᴿ171ᴳ148ᴮ, which equates on my system to 9ᶜ38ᴹ39ʸ; and hair 97ᴿ75ᴳ55ᴮ.

The Lightest Significant Part

These by-the-numbers techniques work not just with originals of reasonable quality. When something is seriously wrong with the image, the results can be impressive.

Figure 3.7 wasn't intended for publication. Figure 3.9, a much worse original, is. This is a newspaper photograph from a small town in Tennessee. The town's Methodist church had been founded long ago by the father of the older man, who himself had served as pastor for a quarter of a century before his retirement. The church has just been burned down by an arsonist; a local firefighter has been arrested and charged with the crime.

Figure 3.9 *In principle, overly dark images can be corrected without human intervention, by adjusting the range automatically. Here, Photoshop's Auto Color command (inset) actually makes the image worse, because it identifies an insignificant part of the image (the light area at upper right) as being a highlight.*

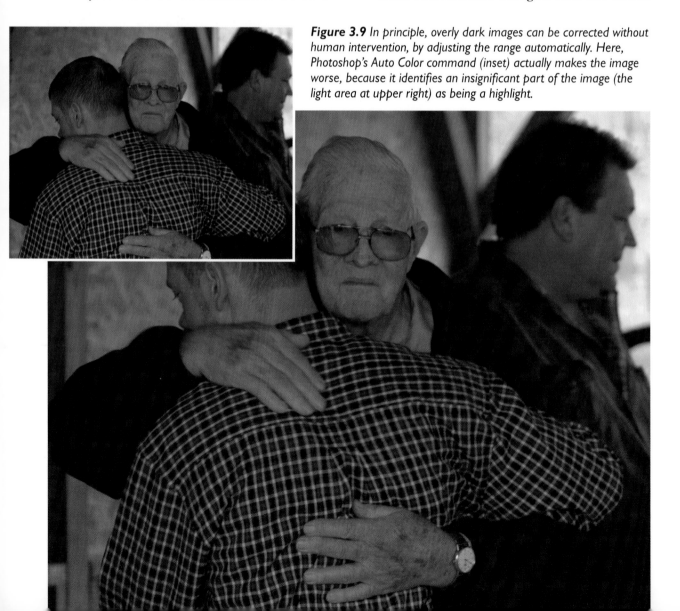

Figure 3.10 *An aggressive correction of Figure 3.9, choosing the man's white hair as the highlight and allowing anything lighter to vanish, while balancing the skintone.*

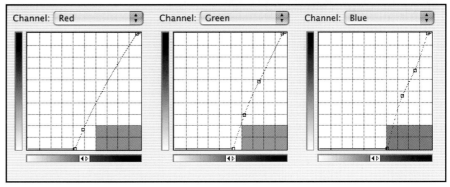

Naturally the photographer does not want to make himself obtrusive at this gut-wrenching moment; hence no flash. But the photo captures the emotion, and the newspaper wants to use it in print.

In this day and age, how can a professional camera deliver such a thing? The camera replies, "What makes you think it's bad?" And when we answer that it's way too dark, the camera says we're mistaken. And in its small mind, we are.

Image: Adjustments>Auto Color is a souped-up version of Auto Levels. Like Auto Levels, it sets proper endpoints, but it also tries to analyze and correct color casts. Yet as the inset shows, the Auto Color version is just as dark as the original and sports even worse color.

Such images make monkeys out of machines. The basis of Auto Color is a redacted version of by the numbers. To quote the definition given a few pages ago, "The

Stumbling Blocks: Tricks Numbers Play

•**Overreliance on a single sampling point**. If the highlight, or whatever it is you're sampling, is so small that only one point can be measured, then you shouldn't be worrying about it at all. It's better to run the cursor over several adjacent values, or similar areas elsewhere in the image, before deciding that the one you've chosen is correct.

•**Highlights/shadows that aren't significant**. If you don't care whether a certain light point is blown out or a certain dark point is totally plugged, choose different endpoints. Maximize detail by choosing as highlight and shadow the lightest/darkest points in which you desire to hold detail, rather than the literally lightest and darkest points of the image.

•**The curve that can only be made one way**. If a point must be changed from, say, 70% to 80%, this does not require that one choose specifically the 70% point on the curve and raise it. Other shapes are often necessary.

•**The 70%–80% CMY "limit."** Recommended shadow values of 80^{C}70^{M}70^Y don't mean that CMY inks can't be higher elsewhere. They're artificially low in shadows to stay within a total ink limit, usually 300% or so. A fire engine might be 0^{C}100^{M}100^Y, only 200% total ink as opposed to the 290% in the shadows.

•**"The" neutral point**. Not every image has one, and some have more than one. If you can't find one, don't force one to occur. And if you do find one, look for another.

•**Originals with high black values in the shadows**. These often indicate files that were separated using too high a black ink limit. Forcing the CMY values to 80^{C}70^{M}70^Y in the shadows in such cases may cause problems. Either correct to a lighter CMY shadow or reseparate the image using a proper setting.

•**My curves are not the gospel**. Quality results are impossible if the numbers are seriously off. But there are many ways to achieve the same or similar numbers. The way shown here is not guaranteed to be the best. Your curves don't have to be identical to mine. Chances are, though, that their shapes will be similar.

•**The magic fleshtone values**. The typical fleshtone values cited in this chapter are not target numbers for you to force all skin to match. Across all ethnicities, flesh can be light or dark. The relationship between the inks is what counts, not their exact values.

•**The power of positive guesswork**. The by-the-numbers philosophy looks for areas of known color, or where certain colors are inconceivable. Sometimes neither one is available. At such times, there is nothing to do but guess, based on feedback from the monitor.

highlight is the lightest significant part of the image…"

The word *significant* is not there to make the sentence sound more impressive. It is in fact the most consequential, the most far-reaching word in the entire definition. That's too bad for the machine, in whose dictionary no entry for *significant* appears.

An algorithm, whether the camera's or the computer's, looks for the lightest point of the image—not the lightest *significant* point—and sets it to a predetermined value. Here, it moors itself to the lightest spots in the upper right corner, and wakes up to find itself bound head and hair to the ground, because it doesn't realize that you and I have no interest in said area.

Dark as it is, the gray hair above the man's left ear is the lightest significant point of the image. Once we determine to set it to 245^{R}245^{G}245^B (it starts at 143^{R}123^{G}95^B in the sRGB original), the rest is easy. The curves in Figure 3.10 are similar to those of Figure 3.8, but simpler and more drastic. The bottom point in each curve sets the highlight, the next point ensures that the face falls in as steep an area as possible while maintaining a good color balance, and the upper point keeps the young man's hair brown.

A Modest Proposal or Two

Curves, as we learned in Chapter 2, come with a price. They improve certain areas at the expense of others. My curves blew out the upper right background altogether. I don't care, any more than I care about the light spot by the older

Figure 3.11 *By changing the bottom of each curve to the beginning of an S shape, some highlight detail is preserved, creating a less stark look than in Figure 3.10.*

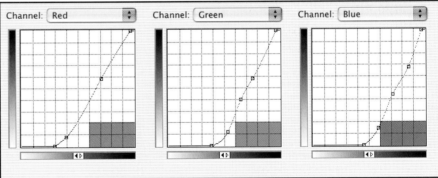

man's ear or the large reflections off his fingernails. I think the focus should be the man's emotions.

If any or all of these things bother you, there are two remedies. First, if you applied these curves on an adjustment layer, you already have a layer mask. By default, it's white, which means that it does nothing. If you activate a painting tool and paint a very light gray into the affected areas of the mask, it will bring back enough of the underlying original to fool the viewer into thinking that there's still detail there.

Rather than lessen the adjustment layer's opacity, another way to soften the blow is to modify the curves as in Figure 3.11, making their bottoms into the start of an S. This hurts detail in the lightest parts of the image but doesn't eliminate it altogether. Of course, it doesn't get the man's hair as white as in Figure 3.10, because nominally the highlight is now something else.

Figure 3.12 *The 1994 original at left features many colors that are known to be neutral, and one that some people mistakenly take to be so. The curves below produce the corrected version, right.*

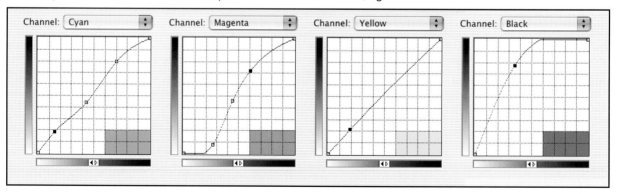

Of Free Speech and Figures of Speech

Gulliver was no great admirer of freedom of expression. He quoted "a Philosopher" as saying that "He knew no Reason, why those who entertain Opinions prejudicial to the Publick should be obliged to change, or should not be obliged to conceal them. And as it was Tyranny in any Government to require the first, so it was Weakness not to enforce the second: For, a Man may be allowed to keep Poisons in his Closet, but not to vend them about as Cordials."

If Gulliver had been in charge in 1994, not only would he have approved of my monkey comments, but he probably would have pushed for government scrutiny of stock photo agencies, because some of the things that were being vended around as cordials were poisonous indeed, as we will step back in time to discover.

Figure 3.12A, believe it or not, came from the biggest and theoretically most quality-oriented vendor in the then-novel field of royalty-free stock. It was delivered in CMYK, as most files were in those days, so that's where we'll work on it.

Before giving the measurements, the literally lightest area of Figure 3.12A is the near horse's forehead. The darkest area is a tie between the black stripe of the flag at top left and the harness at extreme lower left. Are these the areas we really want to use for highlight and shadow?

I say yes to the horse's forehead, but no to the flag and the harness. That horse is the whole focus of attention in the image. We want to retain detail throughout, and furthermore we know that he's white. If the stripe in the flag plugs, though, who cares? It's not a significant part of the image. The shadow should be the near blinder. It's dark, it's neutral, and it's significant.

There's no shortage of things that seem like they should be neutral in this image. Going from darkest to lightest, the original readings are: highlight in forehead, $2^C6^M2^Y$; closest horse's neck, beneath the mane, $7^C28^M6^Y$; background wall, $35^C40^M40^Y1^K$; and near blinder, $72^C58^M68^Y30^K$.

This is the easiest correction of the chapter, provided we work by the numbers. People who don't do so often try to select the horses. Such an action is to remove the horses from the context of the image and effectively paste them into a background to which they have no relation. The horses may be the most blatant things that are too pink in the original, but they aren't the only things.

Or, people might conclude that the whole image is too pink and drastically reduce magenta. That wouldn't work, because, presumably owing to the efforts of the baboon who "corrected" the image originally, the magenta cast affects only the light half. The dark half is actually too green. If you don't

believe it, check the blinder numbers again. Magenta and yellow are supposed to be equal in a neutral area, but here the magenta is 10 points too low. And if you still don't believe it, look at the Canadian flag in the background. If there were really a magenta cast, the flag would be too purple, instead of too orange.

There are two key curves here, one for color, one for contrast. The S curve in the magenta corrects the color, eliminating the pinkness in the horses while establishing 70^M in the blinder. And the ultra-steep curve that adds 40^K to the shadow provides punch.

The yellow curve needs nothing more than a slight increase in the light area where the horses are found, because the shadow value is near the desired 70^Y already. And the cyan needs slight increases both in the highlight and the shadow, nothing nearly as radical as what happened to the magenta. There's just one final trap to avoid.

Betting the Image

Our language is replete with misleading phrases involving color. The *whites of our eyes* are in reality pink. *Red wine* is purple, and *white wine* greenish yellow. *White people* and *black people* are both red.

Sometimes, however, the adjective needs to be taken seriously. That *black macaque* was, in fact, black. And Figure 3.12A was shot in New York City. The architectural material is typical of the area. It is known as *brownstone*. New Yorkers don't call it that because it's gray. Yet lots of professionals would take it for granted that it is, and would wreck the image by omitting the points in the center of the magenta and cyan curves that keep it brown.

If we've never heard of brownstone, we should ask ourselves whether this building is really gray. The answer to that is yes—probably. Most such walls would be close to gray. But the next question is the big one: are we really ready to bet the image that we're right?

I'm not willing to bet that the building is neutral, but I am willing to risk the image that the horses are. I'll also gladly bet that the light parts of the flags are neutral and that the horses' blinders are, too.

This image is the only one in this book that also appeared in the 1994 first edition of *Professional Photoshop,* the others having gone the way of Blefuscu's navy. In addition to being a good illustration of how to handle casts that change color as the image gets darker, it reminds us how far we've come as a field in a dozen years—and perhaps how far

we haven't gone. We'd never get such an image from a professional source today.

Every professional now knows to set a dark point somewhere in the image, so we have gotten the monkey of wildly flat images like Figure 3.12A off our backs. Color, I regret to say, remains a problem.

Some 21st-century people still open the image, discover that the horses are pink, and immediately wheel out the selection tools. The normal result is white horses that look like they've been cut out and pasted into a pink background.

Avoiding the Impossible: How the Pros Know the Numbers

There's a popular misconception that the best retouchers know exactly what numbers to shoot for no matter how esoteric the subject matter. In real life, the key is more to avoid numbers that can't possibly be right. If we find any such in the image, we have to twist curves or whatever to avoid them. Here's a brief guide to familiar colors, starting with the easiest.

GREENS almost always favor their yellow neighbor. Cyanish greens are rare. Often yellow is as much as half again higher than cyan. In the natural "green" of a plant, equal cyan and yellow would be impossible in CMYK, equal red and blue impossible in RGB. On the other hand, if the cyan/red is so light that it's closer to the magenta/green value than it is to the yellow/blue, then the resulting color is a greenish yellow rather than a yellowish green. That's impossible, too. If we discover either situation in our picture, we have to correct.

REDS are, in principle, equal combinations of magenta and yellow, with much less cyan. If the magenta is slightly higher than yellow, it's a rosier red. If yellow is higher, it's an angrier, more orange color. Faces are close to equal, but when they aren't, it's always a yellowish red. Reddish yellows, and magentaish reds, are impossible in faces. In other things that are red, anything goes.

BLUES would, in a perfect world, have equal amounts of cyan and magenta. Photoshop commands like Hue/Saturation and Selective Color that are capable of targeting "blues" in fact make this assumption. The sad fact is that equal cyan and magenta makes purple, so any real blue will have decidedly more cyan. The color of most skies is even more heavily skewed; many skies are better described as bluish cyan than cyanish blue.

Note that I am using CMYK numbers, because, at least for greens and reds, simple rules are available that don't work in RGB—namely, faces are never more magenta than yellow, growing things are never as cyan as yellow. These rules don't apply to the RGB cognates, because the blue channel is lighter than a CMYK user familiar with yellow channels would expect. Therefore, when working with fleshtones or natural greens, I recommend setting the right half of the Info palette to read CMYK, even when working in RGB.

Intelligent retouchers look at suspect areas of an image and ask, are these color values even *possible?* If they are, we don't try to mastermind the operation by guessing at how they might be better. But if the colors are impossible, we have to change them, even if we aren't positive of what to change them to.

For example, if you were asked to define the hair color known as *blond,* you would probably say it was yellow. Pure CMYK yellow, in the sense of equal cyan and magenta, is in fact possible if the hair is very light. More commonly, though, the hair is a *reddish* yellow, meaning yellow first, magenta second, cyan third. A greenish yellow, with cyan higher than magenta, is impossible. If the image features greenish yellow hair, this has to be changed. I can't tell you to what, but you can't let it stay where it is.

Others still recite the tired old mantra, "But it didn't look that pink on my calibrated monitor!" Of course it didn't—the viewer's villainous visual system calibrated itself to the picture on the screen. Chromatic adaptation, our subconscious determination to neutralize all incoming light, is why we have to correct casts in images where the camera failed to adjust as a human would have. It's also why a lot of pictures have to be recorrected due to objectionable casts that somebody who trusted the screen overlooked. The question is not whether the monitor is "calibrated" but whether the Info palette is.

And certainly, people still try too hard to find neutrals. I give this image as a class exercise, and way too many people force the brown walls to be gray, and then wonder why the whole image looks too cold. If you don't know for a fact that the object is neutral (and we *do* know this about the horses, the white part of the Canadian flag, the black stripe, and the leather blinder), leave it alone.

The bottom line about this image is the same as about the others in this chapter, and the same as it was in 1994. To be successful, we need a full range of tone, and Figure 3.12A doesn't give it to us. We can't give viewers colors that they know better than to believe. Pink horses qualify. So does gray brownstone—at least to New Yorkers.

Before going even further back in time for a different type of brownstone, a final example of by-the-numbers correction, we'll conclude discussion of these horses with a few words about them from the 1994 edition of *Professional Photoshop.*

In short, once he got the hang of curves, there is absolutely no reason that an orangutan could not get these results. Years of retouching experience, artistic talent, and mathematical aptitude wouldn't hurt him, but they are not really needed.

Notice how these numerical adjustments have the habit of helping areas of the image that we never even thought about. Things like the flags behind the horses…

Artists who worry their images to death tend to see such shortcomings immediately and plunge happily and vigorously into a morass of individual moves. They isolate the horses and work on them; they fix up the flags one by one; they tediously darken the harnesses, and after eight hours they have something nearly as good as what the orangutan would have gotten in 35 seconds. That may be the most persuasive kind of number there is.

When an Emerald Isle Turns Yellow

Gulliver was English, but his creator was Irish. Hundreds of years before Jonathan Swift was born, Dunluce Castle commanded the cliffs of the Antrim coast. The picture of it

Review and Exercises

✓ If you discover that a highlight area is too dark, what's the difference between lightening it by moving the lower left point of the curve to the right, and lowering a different, higher point?

✓ Why are there 256 steps in RGB (0–255) but only 101 in CMYK (0%–100%)? Does this make RGB correction more accurate?

✓ Why do we not set the shadow to the darkest possible value, $0^R0^G0^B$? Are there any circumstances under which we might do it, and if so, what are they?

in Figure 3.13, however, is as modern as it gets: a professional-quality digicam with a professional standing behind it, aided by good lighting conditions.

This image arrives in CMYK. Nothing large enough to be measured (and therefore nothing large enough to be significant) is white. The lightest measurable area is in the sky, $16^C7^M2^Y$. The shadow is in the large opening at the lower right of the near tower, at $80^C64^M71^Y75^K$. The grass near the rear fence measures $37^C21^M86^Y1^K$. A brown area in the castle is $39^C48^M70^Y$. The sea is $52^C28^M13^Y1^K$ about halfway up the picture.

The shadow value is slightly off. The yellow and magenta should be equal, but the magenta is seven points lower. Doesn't sound like a big deal, and certainly no sweat to correct, but it suggests that the dark parts of the image, at least, may be getting too green-yellow. And the suspicion is confirmed

elsewhere—in the trickiest part of the by-the-numbers technique.

Back in Figure 3.6, we looked at six different casts: cyan, magenta, yellow, red, green, blue. How did I identify which of the six was which before placing them in the page?

Here's a quick formula. Look at the CMY values, even if you're in some other color-space. The highest of the three is the dominating ink; the lowest, in combination with the black, is a contaminant and is sometimes known as the *unwanted color*.

The ink in the middle is the key. If it's closer to the contaminating ink, we're looking at a yellow, magenta, or cyan object. If closer to the dominating ink, the object is red, green, or blue. Therefore, $30^C80^M90^Y$ is a red—a yellowish, desaturated red. But $30^C50^M90^Y$ is a reddish yellow.

Do you see the problems in the readings for this image? I don't know specific numbers

Figure 3.13 *Dunluce Castle, County Antrim, Ireland.*

Figure 3.14 A corrected version of Figure 3.13, produced by the curves below.

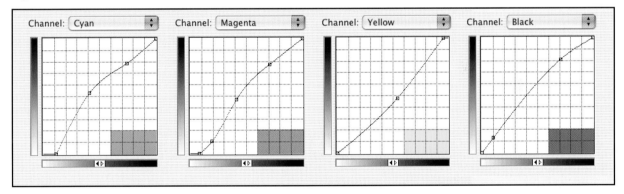

for Irish grass. However, one need not be a leprechaun to speculate that it's probably green. The measured values are not. As the middle ink, the cyan is 15 points away from the sum of the contaminating inks (magenta and black) but 49 points away from the dominant; the grass in the original is yellow, a greenish yellow admittedly, but still yellow and not green.

In the same way, the castle should be brown, which is a very desaturated red. Cyan must be the lowest CMY ink, as it is. The further the magenta and yellow are away from it, the more saturated the red is.

Like most browns, including all those we've seen in this chapter, if it isn't pure red (magenta and yellow equal), then we'd expect a yellowish brown rather than a purplish one. That is the case here, almost. The yellow is higher than the magenta—so much so that the color is no longer a red. Nine points separate cyan and magenta, but 22 are between magenta and yellow. It's a reddish yellow castle, not a yellowish red, not a brown one.

Otherwise Than by Comparison

We're about ready for the curves, but there's one last item, this time affecting contrast. As noted earlier, the sky is the lightest significant part of the image. If it were white, we'd know what to do, but you don't have to be Joyce or Shaw to realize that it isn't. It's currently cyan tending toward blue, which sounds right.

Nevertheless, we should change it, not to a different color, but to a different lightness. If we can't hit $5^C2^M2^Y$ because that would be white, fine, but we should try for something just as light. $6^C2^M0^Y$ or $7^C3^M0^Y$ ought to do it.

The final curves that produce Figure 3.14, then, are:
- Cyan: highlight gets lighter; midtone bulges upward to put more cyan in the grass, but also to get the castle in a steep area of the curve.
- Magenta: Lighter in the highlight, then reduced in the quartertone to take magenta out of the grass, and increased in the three-quartertone to put it into the castle.
- Yellow: reduced everywhere to lessen the imbalance in the castle and the grass.
- Black: bulges up, creating a steeper half

The Bottom Line

Much of color correction can be reduced to simple numerical rules. Images must have full range, which is accomplished by setting proper highlights and shadows coupled with the steepening techniques of Chapter 2. And they must avoid impossible colors. Sometimes we specifically know the desired color, as in a person whose hair clearly should be gray. At other times we don't know what the color is, but we know what it is not. A person's dark hair may be black or it may be brown, but it can't be dark green. A forest must always be green, even if we don't know the specific green.

By the numbers is not a wooden philosophy, but a means of avoiding obvious errors. Many different-looking versions of the same image can comply with the numerical requirements.

---

where the grass and castle are found. With so little shadow detail, there's no problem with going over the nominal 70^K limit.

*   *   *

Working by the numbers does not replace artistic judgment. It does replace a lot of bad color. The basic concepts are readily absorbed by the color-blind, if not by monkeys. In fact, around a dozen color-blind people have taken my three-day hands-on course, which is aimed at people who are very serious about color correction indeed. One of the beta readers of this book is color-blind, yet corrects color, by the numbers perforce.

It's understandable, I think. I certainly get a rush when I make something like Figure 3.9 look better than a nonexpert thinks is possible, and I suspect that most readers feel similar elation when they get praised for their work. Imagine how much more adrenaline flows when the viewer's jaw drops at learning that a color-blind person did the work!

Gulliver traveled for a little over 16 years. The journey of those doing professional color correction in Photoshop has a few years to go yet to meet that number. We have, however, met many strange life forms and learned a great deal, so much so that the practices of 1994 now seem to us to be Lilliputian.

If you find the challenges and intricacies of color correction to be Brobdingnagian, let me complete a quotation begun earlier. Here are Gulliver's thoughts upon encountering that gigantic species.

"Undoubtedly Philosophers are in the right when they tell us, that nothing is great or little otherwise than by Comparison. It might have pleased Fortune to let the *Lilliputians* find some Nation, where the People were as diminutive with respect to them, as they were to me. And who knows but that even this prodigious Race of Mortals might be equally over-matched in some distant Part of the World, whereof we have yet no Discovery?"

4

Color, Contrast, Canyons, and LAB

In RGB and CMYK, every channel affects both color and contrast. In LAB, they don't. Working in channels with no detail information at all gives a decisive advantage in certain types of images—like canyons.

he catchy title phrases of the last two chapters could reasonably have been compressed into one word apiece. Chapter 2, all about steepening curves, might have been called *Contrast*. Chapter 3, the by-the-numbers strategy aimed at avoiding things that the viewer would know better than to believe, could have been called *Color*. If the concepts could be blended into one unified whole, the two chapters together might be termed *Success*.

As we saw in the second half of Chapter 3, it isn't always easy to write the curves that will solve both problems at once. We were, however, working in RGB and CMYK, as most people do. In those two colorspaces, every channel affects both color and contrast.

We will now turn to LAB, which treats color and contrast as separate entities. In doing so, it may make our life very much easier, or very much harder. I have had mixed success in teaching how to use it. My current view calls for throwing the reader right into the deep end.

For the following exercise, select from one of your own images an uncorrected landscape or other subdued subject. Do not choose a picture that contains brilliant colors, or one with an obvious color cast.

Open the image and Image: Mode>Lab Color. You don't need the Info palette. Bring up the Curves dialog, on an adjustment layer if you wish. The first channel is Lightness, or L. This is where all the contrast, and none of the color, resides. You can consider it as a grayscale version of the file.

Do just what we did in Chapter 2. Mouse over the most important area of the picture to determine its range, and create a curve that's steepest there. I have done this in Figure 4.1; do yours to suit your image.

For the A and B curves, however, please just copy what you see in the curves below. No need to ask why, just do it. You can ask what the letters A and B stand for, which will yield the useful answer that they don't stand for anything. It's critical that their curves still cross the original center point. You must therefore be careful to bring the top and bottom endpoints inward by equal amounts. If you must experiment, the idea is that the AB curves are emphasizing color variation. The steeper the curves, the greater the effect.

Now try the technique again, with a different image, and with a third. By the third time you try it, you should have it down to less than a minute, which is what it took me to generate Figure 4.1B from 4.1A.

For one minute, that's a big difference. Try doing this in RGB or CMYK, and no matter how much time you allocate, you're unlikely to match this result. Figure 4.1B emulates what the human visual system does when confronted by a vista of similar colors: it breaks them apart, making some colors brighter and others duller, all in accord with the law of simultaneous contrast and in disaccord with the way that a camera works.

The Eyes-Glazed-Over Syndrome

This chapter is necessarily an abridged version of what LAB can do. If you'd like to read a little more about it—384 pages this size, to be exact—I happen to have written a book about it. When it came out in 2005,

both I and a lot of other people, notably the publisher of Peachpit Press, were in for a big surprise.

The virtues of LAB have been bruited about for a little over a decade. However, it developed such a fearsome reputation for complexity that its use was limited to the most serious professionals. That was the target audience for my book, which I anticipated would be significantly more difficult than previous versions of *Professional Photoshop*. As a sop to the less experienced, however, about a quarter of the text was deliberately gentle, featuring simple recipes like the one I just gave, and de-emphasizing explanations of why in favor of what works.

Photoshop is the hottest area in technical publishing, thanks to, among other things, the explosive growth of digital cameras. We were sure that there were enough advanced users who would be interested in LAB that the book wouldn't lose money, but in fact it did far better than anyone had expected, being for a time the top-selling title in the entire computer and Internet field.

Experts alone can't buy that many books. Most of them, one must surmise, were purchased by people whose eyes glaze over at technical descriptions like the one we will be getting to in a few pages. What amounted to an underground network of LAB aficionados manifested itself in online groups, sharing information about how the best techniques work and warning about the dangers.

Figure 4.1 *(opposite) The basic LAB move calls for steepening the A and B curves by rotating them counterclockwise around the center point, coupled with locating and steepening the most important range in the L curve.*

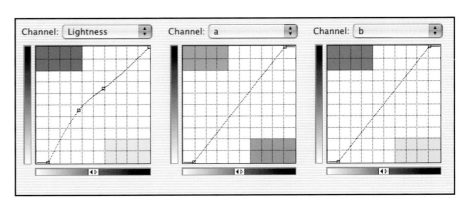

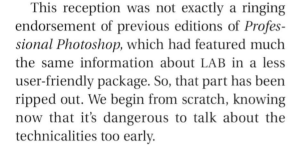

Figure 4.2 *Images with colors that are already very distinguishable from one another are poor candidates for LAB.*

LAB is often likened to a sledge-hammer. In working with it, we need to recognize that if you happen to be a hammer, everything else looks a lot like a nail. My title is *Photoshop LAB Color: The Canyon Conundrum and Other Adventures in the Most Powerful Colorspace.* The subtitle alludes both to LAB's strengths and its shortcomings.

This reception was not exactly a ringing endorsement of previous editions of *Professional Photoshop,* which had featured much the same information about LAB in a less user-friendly package. So, that part has been ripped out. We begin from scratch, knowing now that it's dangerous to talk about the technicalities too early.

The whole first chapter of that book features canyons like the one just shown as Figure 4.1A. Canyons are usually very monochromatic, and LAB's specialty is driving colors apart.

It follows that in images like Figure 4.2, LAB is a bad idea. Apply it to bright colors like those of these antique autos, and they may

Figure 4.3 *When an image has large areas of similar color, like the grassy foreground below, LAB can be helpful.*

be driven out of gamut, because LAB can specify not just colors that are beyond the capability of any conceivable output device to reproduce, but colors that don't exist at all.

The point is so important that it bears repeating. The value of LAB is usually to accentuate differences between colors, as it did in Figure 4.1 B. But there's plenty of differentiation of colors in Figure 4.2 already.

The Colorspace Confrontation

LAB has extensive retouching capabilities, too, but this book will concentrate on its curving advantages, starting with a faceoff to show what LAB brings to the table that other colorspaces do not.

Figure 4.3 is similar to, although not as dark as, the sad picture we saw earlier as Figure 3.9. The camera has hung its hat on an irrelevant highlight—in this case, clouds that are so far to the right of the barn that they are cropped out here. What's left is too dark and therefore too flat.

The flavor of RGB is not specified. The lightest significant point of the image is the tail of the windmill, which starts at an unconscionable $187^R187^G176^B$. The shadow is in the near door, $3^R4^G4^B$. The barn is the dull red that one might expect, $87^R54^G37^B$. The grass is a grayish yellow $103^R106^G49^B$.

With so little shadow detail, the overly dark reading is no problem. A true highlight needs to be set; we would like to have the grass and the barn fall in

steep parts of the curves; and we have to create a legal value for the greenery, much as we did in the Irish scene of Figure 3.13. To do this, the red curve needs to be raised more than the other two at around the midtone, forcing more of a cyan component into the green.

Otherwise, the curves are unremarkable. As the barn and grass seem more important than the light detail in the windmill, a slight flattening of the lightest parts of the curves is unobjectionable.

At this point, we set the RGB version aside, go back to the original, convert it to LAB, and start again. Before doing so, Figure 4.4 may help you visualize the mysterious goings-on in the A and B.

Both are *opponent-color* channels. Light areas in the A are more magenta than they are green, in the

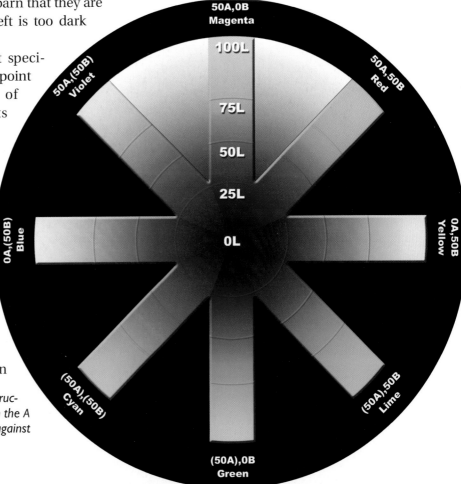

Figure 4.4 *The opponent-color structure pits magenta against green in the A channel (vertical bar) and yellow against blue in the B (horizontal bar).*

B more yellow as opposed to blue. These colors are positive in the weird LAB designation system; the more positive, the more colorful. The maximum is +127, but in practice we rarely get even half that high.

Darkness denotes green in the A, blue in the B. These get negative numbers, –128 being the most colorful, but again we never see so extreme a number in real life. For purposes of typographic sanity, negative numbers take parentheses rather than a minus sign, as in the legends of Figure 4.4.

There's one extra negative number because every Photoshop channel, LAB or otherwise, has exactly 256 levels. Zero is a legal value, leaving an odd number, 255, to be divided in half. That zero is a critical point, because it represents neutrality. That's why it's so important that the AB curves of Figure 4.1 pass through the original center point, which is the zero. Otherwise, things that were originally neutral would take on a cast.

We'll now use slightly more complex curves to correct this prairie image. The

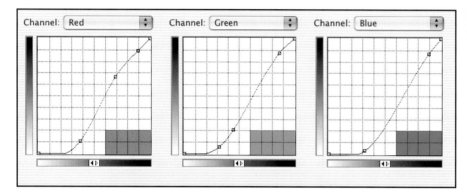

Figure 4.5 *An RGB correction of Figure 4.3.*

L curve is a simple straight line to establish the highlight. As the sky is quite light in the L, it isn't advisable to flatten the lightest parts of the curve as much as we did when the file was in RGB.

I've placed points at the center of both the AB curves, because I think that certain colors need to be emphasized more than others. Note that, like all other curves in this book, darkness is set to the right. The LAB default is the other way around. With this book's orientation, the cool colors (green and blue) are to the top and the warm ones (magenta and yellow) to the bottom.

I'd like to have more variation in the prairie, which is green in the A and yellow in the B. But I'm not particularly anxious to augment the magenta component of the barn, or to make the sky extremely vivid. So my angles are different in the two halves of each curve. We'll go over how this is done in a subsequent example, but for now, compare Figures 4.5 and 4.6. I have a decided preference for Figure 4.6, which, in addition to

Figure 4.6 *An LAB correction of Figure 4.3.*

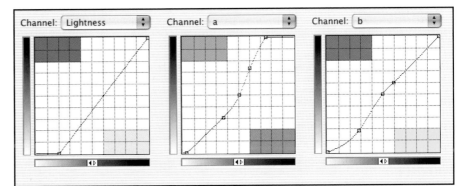

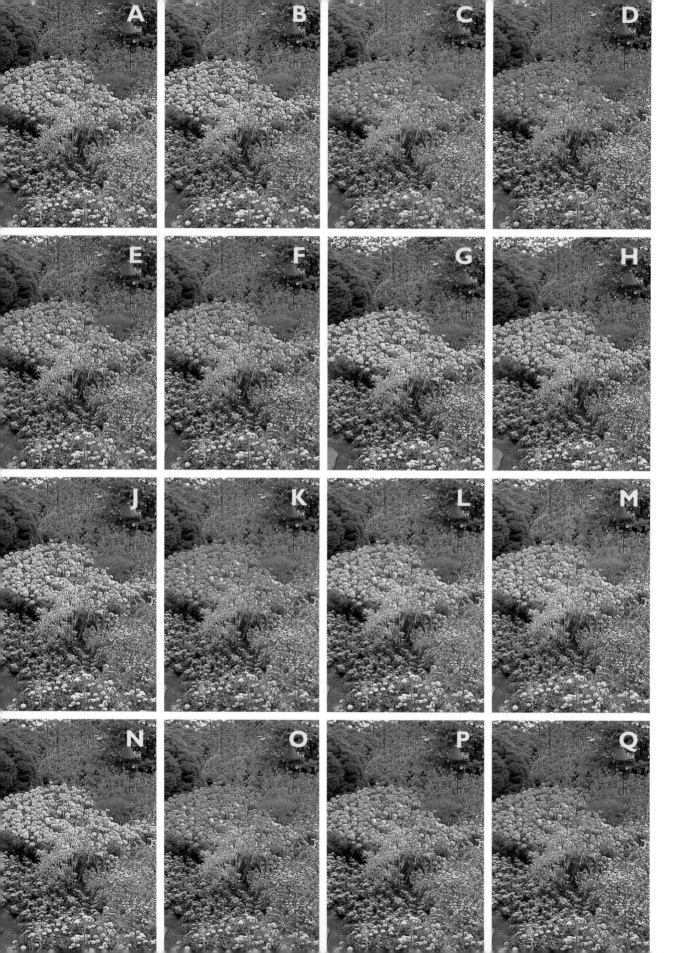

being more lively, has a better break between the green fields in the foreground and the yellow ones in the background. That's the sort of variation that LAB gives and CMYK and RGB do not.

The Relationship of the A and B

Channels that have no contrast information can be a daunting concept to master, let alone when the "white" point is actually a medium gray. If you can get the following challenge right, dealing with LAB will be much easier.

Figure 4.7 consists of variants of the same flowery image. The L channel is constant throughout. The A and B have been shuffled. Each one in each version can be

- its original self,
- the other original AB channel,
- an inverted (negative) copy of itself,
- the other original channel inverted.

Therefore, there are four possibilities for each channel, 16 possibilities in all, including cases where the two channels are identical. Figure 4.7A is the base—uninverted copies of the A and B right where they should be. The other 15 versions are in a random order. Your job is to sort them out. If you consider yourself an LAB master, stop right now, do the exercise, and check your answers on page 89. If you'd like some help getting started, read on.

* * *

If we were to invert one of the channels in an RGB file, the result would look odder than a flying submarine. Yet when we invert the A or B, the result is believable, if you don't mind a gross color change. It's not strikingly obvious here which of these 16 versions contain one or more inverted channels.

The inversions are credible because neutral colors don't change. They fall right in the

middle of each channel, at a value that matches the Photoshop setting of 50% gray. Inverting that doesn't change its value. If we invert the A, anything that was magenta

Figure 4.7 *Version A is the original image. The others, in a random order, are modified by replacing the original A and B channels each with one of four possibilities: the original A, the original B, or either one inverted. Can you pick out the right A and B for each version?*

Worksheet for Figure 4.7

For each version on the facing page, identify the source of the A and the B channel, which can be

1. a copy of the original A,
2. an inverted copy of the original A,
3. a copy of the original B,
4. an inverted copy of the original B.

Version A is known to be the original, so it's 1,3. (Answers, page 89.)

Version	A	B
A	1	3
B		
C		
D		
E		
F		
G		
H		
J		
K		
L		
M		
N		
O		
P		
Q		

(light, or positive) will become green (dark, or negative). The more colorful it used to be, the more colorful it will be after the inversion. But 0ᴬ remains 0ᴬ.

This information helps solve the puzzle. The yellow flowers are a good place to start. We know exactly what's going on there. The yellow-versus-blue B must be strongly

positive. The magenta-versus-green A must be nearly 0ᴬ.

We know that three other versions share this same B with Figure 4.7A. Two of them also use copies, one inverted, of the B where the A used to be. Those two can't possibly have yellow flowers, even though the original B is contributing a lot of yellow. Using either a standard or inverted copy of the B where the A used to be would drive the flowers strongly toward magenta or green, respectively.

Since 0ᴬ doesn't change by being inverted, it follows that the only other yellow flowers on the page come where the A is an inverted copy of itself and the B is the original. If you aren't yet convinced that Figure 4.7H is that one, check out the flowers in the bottom right corner, the ones that were magenta in Figure 4.7A. Now they're green.

Once we recognize that the original A does not contribute color to yellow areas, we can go further. In four of these images, both the A and B are copies or inverted copies of the original A. In those, the overall color must be nearly 0ᴬ0ᴮ—neutral. Do you see the four *least* colorful versions of these yellow flowers? Those are the ones where both channels are based on the A.

Apparently the yellow flowers were very slightly magenta in Figure 4.7A. We know this by observing a slight greenness in the yellow flowers in Figure 4.7H. You can use this information to further break down the versions, but there's an easier way. The flowers that were originally magenta can be treated just as the yellow ones were. Originally, they are strongly A–positive but near 0ᴮ. So, look for the

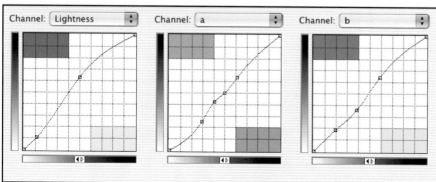

Figure 4.8 *LAB is at its best when the objects of interest have short ranges in the L curve and can easily be isolated in the A and B.*

Figure 4.9 Top, only the L curve is applied to Figure 4.8. Bottom, all three curves are applied.

four versions in which these flowers are nearly colorless. Those are the ones where both channels are based on the original B.

If you're still having trouble, you're not alone. The beta readers, who had no difficulty with the channel-identification quiz of Figure 1.5, thought this one extremely nasty, and told me so in no uncertain terms, including some that I cannot print. This was a surprise, because the group contains several LAB experts.

Due to this unexpected response, I've included a fuller explanation of how to finish this quiz in the Notes & Credits section at the back of the book.

Controlling the Blunt Instrument

Understanding how the AB channels combine to make color permits precise control. In the advertising photo of Figure 4.8, we don't have to look at the channels to be able to describe them. The duck is very light in the B channel, and neutral—about a 50% gray, or 0^A in the A, probably slightly positive, giving the yellow a slight reddish tinge. Its beak is positive in both AB channels. The seal is strongly negative in the B, somewhat positive in the A. The frog is strongly negative in the A and positive in the B. And the soap is close to $0^A 0^B$.

A specialty of LAB is that objects can often be isolated in certain ranges of the AB curves, allowing us to alter them almost as if they had been selected, with limited changes to anything else. (LAB also has great advantages in making formal selections, or in restricting changes with the Blend If sliders.)

Look at the A curve. From left to right, or bottom to top if you prefer, there are four internal points. The bottom one targets the duck's bill, making it more magenta and thus redder. The next one moves in the opposite

Figure 4.10 *Comparing the original RGB channels to the L shows why it is so effective to correct the contrast of this image through an L curve. In all three RGB channels, at least one of the floating toys is relatively dark. In the L channel, all three, plus the soap, occupy the same range, which can easily be isolated in the curve.*

Tip: A Bigger Curves Grid

As noted back in Figure 2.2, we have two choices for the size of the curves grid. To toggle between them, click the size icon at the lower right of the dialog.

Unless you have a two-monitor setup, it's a nuisance to use the larger size, because it takes up too much room on the screen, blocking a good view of the image. I always use the smaller size when working in CMYK or RGB.

In LAB, however, small moves have drastic consequences. We need greater precision than in the other colorspaces, particularly around the center point. So consider toggling to the larger grid when in LAB.

direction, moving the seal away from magenta and toward green. I did this because I felt the seal should be more blue and that it was verging on purple in Figure 4.8.

The third point locks 0^A. If it weren't there, the impact of the second point would push the curve upward, and the soap would become green. The fourth drives the frog away from magenta and toward a more vivid green.

Targeting specific colors in this manner is difficult in other colorspaces. In this particular image, it would also be hard to duplicate what's happening in the L. The curve is successful because it happens that all three of the floating toys fall in the area between the two internal points of the curve. As that area gets steeper, the most important part of the picture picks up contrast. You can see the impact of the L move alone in Figure 4.9A, and of the curves applied to all three channels in Figure 4.9B.

The reason behind the L's success is revealed in Figure 4.10, which compares it to the three original RGB channels. Objects that are strongly colored must be dark in at least one RGB channel and light in at least one other. In the blue, for example, the toys range from nearly white (the seal) to nearly black (the duck). No curve can steepen all these areas.

Because the L ignores color altogether, it doesn't have the problem. All three toys are rather light. They all land in the same narrow range, easy pickings for the curve shown in Figure 4.8.

When the focus of attention is a relatively dull color, avoiding the L makes more sense, as the range is probably longer there than in one or more RGB channels. Brighter colors—while they often deter use of the A and B—suggest that steepening the L may work better than increasing contrast in RGB.

The L is such a blunt instrument that we need to resist the temptation to overuse it. That's why I haven't given suggested highlight and shadow numbers yet. Most output devices won't accept an LAB file, so sooner or later you'll have to convert out, either to the RGB that most photo-processing devices want, or to the CMYK needed for commercial printing.

Unless you're in a big hurry, I'd suggest being conservative about setting highlight and shadow in the L, because it's easy to fix those things in other colorspaces, especially CMYK. The L can be clunky beyond all names of clunkiness. It blows out highlights and plugs shadows at the least provocation.

Use LAB primarily for the things it's good at, and leave the fine-tuning for later. The exception is when time is too short for a second round of curves. In that case, I'd set the highlights and shadows to an aggressive 98^L and 3^L. (In the LAB world, 100^L is absolutely white and 0^L absolutely black, the reverse of what's found in grayscale and in CMYK.) If you're going to have the opportunity to work on the file elsewhere, I wouldn't go beyond 94^L and 10^L, although if they were more extreme than that to begin with, I wouldn't change them.

You may be noticing by now a distinct difference of correction style between this chapter and the last. Correction in RGB and CMYK is usually by the numbers. LAB correction is more intuitive. As we slogged through Chapter 3, we checked reading after reading. Here, it's largely eyeballing. In Chapter 3, you didn't have to duplicate my work exactly, but you had to somehow come close to getting the same numbers that I did or the correction would fail. Here, the only reason that the frog is the particular green it is in Figure 4.9B is that's how green I decided to make it. You're entitled to your own opinion and to choose a different color.

Zero Plus Zero Makes Plenty

You do need to consult the Info palette, though, for one critical LAB value. Neutral colors should be at or near 0^A0^B. I passed over that point in describing the last curves. This soap, you probably agree, should be white. In the original, Figure 4.8, the typical measurement was 0^A4^B—slightly yellow. Do you detect that yellowness in Figure 4.9A?

The A curve, as noted previously, has a locking point right on the center, preserving any values of 0^A. If the B channel had been correct to begin with, I would have placed a similar point on its curve. Without it, notice that the curve passes slightly high of the center point, forcing more blueness, less yellowness, and achieving 0^B in Figure 4.9B.

Quiz Answers

In Figure 4.7, each version had A and B channels that were based on one of the following four possibilities:
1. a copy of the original A,
2. an inverted copy of the original A,
3. a copy of the original B,
4. an inverted copy of the original B.

Here is the answer key. (For an in-depth explanation of why, consult the Notes & Credits section.)

A	1,3	E	3,3	J	2,2	N	1,2
B	2,1	F	4,1	K	1,4	O	2,4
C	3,4	G	1,1	L	3,2	P	4,2
D	4,4	H	2,3	M	3,1	Q	4,3

The cast in this image was minor, but moving the center point kills big casts, too. It can also be used for artistic purposes.

Sunset in Yellowstone National Park is an awe-inspiring experience. Figure 4.11A doesn't really do it justice. It is exactly the sort of canyon-like image that LAB excels at. To produce Figure 4.11B, I used a stronger version of the simple curves of the canyon of Figure 4.1. However, in spite of finding that the original highlights and shadows were the appropriate 0^A0^B, I decided to warm the image up. The A curve runs slightly to the right of the center point, pushing things slightly away from green and toward magenta. The B curve is even farther to the right, emphasizing yellow at the expense of blue.

These moves transform values of 0^A0^B into 4^A10^B. The only difference between Figures 4.11B and 4.11C is that the latter version's AB curves were pushed back to the left and crossed the center point exactly.

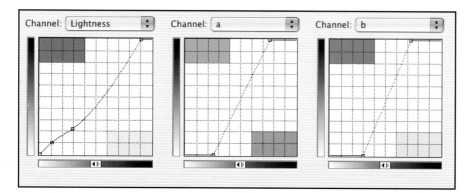

Figure 4.11 *The placement of the center point makes quite a difference in the result. Below, the original. Opposite top, the curves at left, where both AB curves pass slightly to the right of the center point, are applied. Opposite bottom, the curves are adjusted to pass exactly through the center.*

I prefer Figure 4.11B, but am sure that some readers will think Figure 4.11C is better. Or, you could second-guess my curves decision in any of the following ways.

● Redoing the curves at steeper angles, to make a more colorful version.

● Making them flatter, so that the image is more steel-gray.

● Increasing the angle of the A curve only, which would make the sunset more orange.

● Locking the center and lower half of the B curve, and increasing the steepness of its top half. This would create something of a hybrid of Figures 4.11B and 4.11C, with a bluer sky but widespread yellow reflections.

Plus, you could look for some combination. It's also often possible to target certain areas so precisely in LAB that to get an equivalent effect in RGB or CMYK (if one is even possible) would require making a selection. We'll close with two such examples.

A Jewel of a Shortcut

Figure 4.12A is another advertising shot. What it advertises is that when dealing with brilliant colors like those in jewelry, we need to get them as far away from their surroundings as possible. That suggests LAB.

In this image, maintaining neutrality isn't all that important. Several objects compete for our attention. First, when the scene is as fanciful as this one, there can be a terminology problem. These green stands for the jewelry look to me like mushrooms. The background blue-green stalks remind me of asparagus. So, those vegetable terms will be in use, which is fair enough since one would have to part with a lot of lettuce to purchase what's sitting on top of the mushrooms.

Command–clicking within the image with the Curves dialog open creates a point at whatever value is beneath the cursor. In LAB, where objects are more easily separated than in other colorspaces, it can be quite useful. Here, I went one step further, using Shift-Command–click, which puts the appropriate point not just in one channel, but in all three.

Stumbling Blocks: The Most Powerful Colorspace

•**Forget darkness: a neutral is a neutral**. In the A and B channels, white, black, and gray are all the same "color"—0ᴬ0ᴮ.

•**Overdoing it in the L**. The L channel is powerful but clumsy. Fine-tuning shadows and highlights is not its strong suit. Assuming that you're going to have a chance to make final corrections in RGB or CMYK, don't force extreme endpoints with the L curve—too much chance of loss of detail.

•**Colors that are out of two gamuts**. It's fairly easy to define colors that are unprintably vivid, but LAB is so huge that it can also call for colors that the monitor can't display. In either case, there will probably be detail loss the next time you convert, as Photoshop tries to match the unmatchable.

I count five objects of interest in this image, all yellows, greens, blues, and purples. No reds, inasmuch as I am disinterested in what happens to the background. The five are:

- the gold,
- the green mushrooms,
- the deep blue areas of the asparagus,
- the blue stones set into the jewelry (yes, there are several shades, but in the overall context of this image we can consider the duller ones as a single color, and the more vivid ones as similar to the asparagus),
- those stones that are clearly purple.

If we Command–click five times into each AB curve, or Shift-Command–click to put the point in all three channels, certain duplications are apparent, especially in the A. The mushrooms are certainly more green than magenta, but the blue stones have nearly the same A value. The purple stones and the

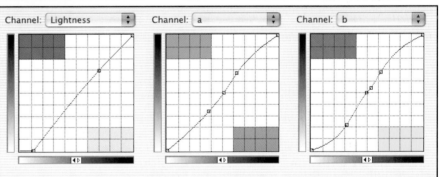

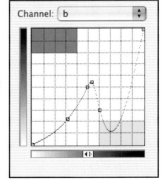

Figure 4.12 Opposite, the original image. Top left, a version prepared with the standard LAB curves shown above. Top right, the same LA curves are applied, but the B curve at right is added, illustrating LAB's ability to make enormous color changes believably.

blues of the asparagus are slightly positive, and the gold is almost 0^A.

The B hosts much more variation. The gold, of course, is all by itself at the bottom of the curve, far more yellow than it is blue.

The mushrooms, which are slightly more yellow than blue, are considerably higher up the curve. The purple and most of the blue stones share the same slightly negative B values. And the blue asparagus and the large blue stones are strongly negative, high up on the curve.

A lot of what follows has to do with where this file is going—in this case, to a book titled *Professional Photoshop Fifth Edition,* printed in the United States by a company specializing in book printing, nominally comporting with SWOP standards, on reasonably good but not outstanding paper.

As discussed in Chapter 1, such printing conditions don't handle blues well. This poses two problems: there may not be enough variation between the dull and vivid blues; and the asparagus may turn purple on us if we aren't careful.

I was worried enough about the purple possibility to keep the two halves of the A curve at different angles, emphasizing the greens more than the magentas. In the yellow half of the B, I liked the idea of adding yellowness to the gold, but not to the mushrooms, which are held by a locking point. In the blue half, the brighter and duller blues are forced apart by a move for which there is no counterpart in RGB or CMYK. The duller blues are moved down, toward neutrality; the more vivid ones are moved up, becoming more blue. The result is Figure 4.12B.

The Selection Without a Selection

Granted how far away the brightest blues are from anything else in the B channel, it's easy to adjust the curve to make them more blue. Give the matter a little thought and you'll realize that it's also easy to do whatever else we like with them.

Figure 4.12C, for example, depends on a psychotic curve in the shape of an inverted V, unthinkable in any other colorspace. It creates a sort of illegitimate progeny of the inverted A and B channels of the sadistic exercise of Figure 4.7.

Put yourself in the position of the eventual viewer of this advertisement. You have never seen Figure 4.12A, so you don't know that you're seeing yellow where the camera saw blue. Is there anything about Figure 4.12C that gives the show away?

We'll end the chapter with an exercise that amplifies two of the techniques of this last image: making certain colors more lively while closely similar ones get duller, plus taking advantage of the channel structure to isolate the correction to a single area.

The example image is, what else, a canyon. If you have never been to this particular one, let me explain that there are canyons and then there are canyons. There's nothing inherently unbelievable about the Grand Canyon except its scale. You can stand there looking at it and refuse to accept that it is as colossal as your eyes tell you it is.

Bryce Canyon, the subject of the next image, is much more compact. You can hike it in a day. At the end of the day, you won't believe that what you just hiked through exists at all. Orange and pink structures, molded by erosion into shapes from a fantasy world, range from tiny spires called *hoodoos* to massive cliffs like the one we're about to work on. It is truly like nothing else on earth.

Thanks to simultaneous contrast, chromatic adaptation, and various other phenomena, we know that human observers evaluate canyons far differently than cameras do. Most of our corrections in every chapter have been aimed at producing what a human would have seen as opposed to what the camera did see.

In a situation like Bryce, however, there's a third possibility: the scene that the human

Figure 4.13 (opposite) Bryce Canyon National Park is noted for its fantastically sculpted orange-and-pink structures. The original, top, doesn't evoke the same feeling as the corrected version at bottom.

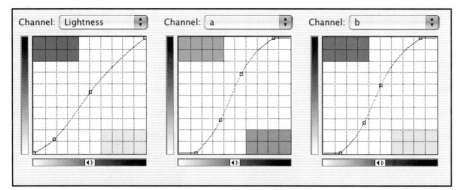

Figure 4.14 *These curves create greener trees and more variation in the hoodoos, but they also make the sky too cyan.*

did not actually see, but remembers having seen some weeks later when processing the image in Photoshop. Given enough time, human emotion trumps memory.

Figure 4.13A is what the camera saw. I certainly remember having seen more color variation. At the time, though, the camera and I probably perceived approximately the same *overall* color in the rocks and trees.

Now that it's been a while, though, I remember hiking this trail (it's called Fairyland) and being shocked at how vivid these orange formations were. I also remember green trees. In fact, I think I remember Figure 4.13B, which is probably not what I actually saw at the time.

Getting to that point requires a technique that we haven't addressed before, because the LAB curve we'd like to use massacres

the background. We need more variation between the relatively neutral and more orange areas of the rocks. It won't do to just make the whole area more colorful. Instead, we need something like the curves of Figure 4.14, which drive both AB channels into negative territory where they used to be neutral. That's great for the trees, which become greener, and for the lighter parts of the rock, which become more neutral, but it's very bad for the clouds, and not so hot for the background sky either. Both are driven toward green in the A and toward blue in the B, which combination produces cyan.

Fortunately, there's an easy way to restore the original background. It requires that the curve be applied on a standard or adjustment layer, because it makes use of the Blend If sliders that are located within layer Blending Options.

A quick preview for those unfamiliar with this powerful command. Before invoking it, we have a two-layered document. Figure 4.13A is on the bottom; Figure 4.14 (or curves that would create it) is on top. Layer mode is set to Normal. If we would like to blend the two layers, we can reduce opacity from its default 100%. Here, however, we don't want to blend, but rather exclude. We don't want to use the top layer at all in the sky. The only problem is how to explain this concept to Photoshop, which does not understand words like *clouds* and *sky*.

Consider the channel structure, and the formula that Photoshop wants may become

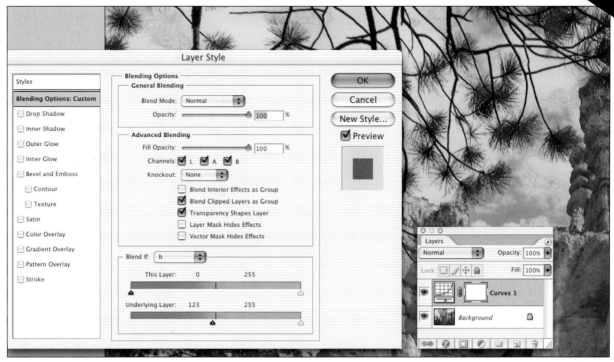

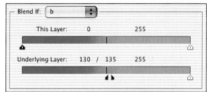

Figure 4.15 *Using the Blend If sliders to restore the original sky of Figure 4.13A. As the bottom slider moves to the right, things that were formerly negative in the B channel are excluded. Above, sharp breaks appear where the cyan sky of Figure 4.14 still shows through. As the slider moves farther to the right (final settings are at right), the breaks are eliminated, resulting in the smoother sky of Figure 4.13B.*

clear. In the L, the clouds are light. So are parts of the rock. The background sky is definitely at least as dark as other parts of the rocks. No luck in differentiating the two there.

In the A, the rock formation is clearly positive, being more magenta than green. Unfortunately, that makes the trees negative. Both clouds and sky fall somewhere in the middle, so again we're out of luck.

In the B, the rocks are entirely positive because they are more yellow than blue. So are the trees. The clouds are near 0^B and the sky itself is negative. That's the clear break we've been looking for. We can explain to Photoshop that we don't want to use the top layer anyplace that formerly was neutral or negative in the B channel.

To get that message across, we choose Layer: Layer Style>Blending Options, or choose Blending Options from the menu

accessed at the right of the Layers palette, or, simplest of all, double-click to the right of the top layer's icon. Any of the three brings up the same dialog used for special effects such as drop shadows and glows. We, however, only need the Blend If sliders at the bottom. We choose the B, Underlying Layer, and the left-hand slider.

As we move the slider to the right, things that were previously more blue than yellow are excluded. Figure 4.15 shows harsh breaks between sky areas that used to be blue and the clouds that used to be neutral. Because the slider setting has excluded the sky but has not reached the clouds yet, the clouds are now more cyan than the sky is. Life in LAB carries its share of surprises.

We continue moving the slider to the right until it makes a believable break, or close to one, between foreground and background.

Color Recipe Book

	CMYK	RGB	LAB
R...	Magenta and yellow about equal, cyan much lower.	Green and blue about equal, red much higher.	A and B both strongly positive and about equal.
Yellowish Red	Yellow highest, cyan lowest, magenta closer to yellow.	Blue lowest, red highest, green closer to blue.	A and B positive, B highest, A more than half as high.
Reddish Yellow	Yellow highest, cyan lowest, magenta closer to cyan.	Blue lowest, red highest, green closer to red.	A and B positive, B highest, A less than half as high.
Yellow	Yellow high, cyan and magenta about equal and much lower.	Blue low, red and green about equal and much higher.	A near zero, B strongly positive.
Greenish Yellow	Yellow high, magenta lowest, cyan closest to magenta.	Blue lowest, green highest, red closest to green.	A slightly negative, B strongly positive.
Yellowish Green	Yellow high, magenta lowest, cyan closest to yellow.	Blue lowest, green highest, red closest to blue.	A strongly negative, B slightly positive.
Green	Cyan and yellow about equal, magenta much lower.	Red and blue about equal, green much higher.	A strongly negative, B near zero.
Cyanish Green	Cyan highest, magenta lowest, yellow closest to cyan.	Red lowest, green highest, blue closest to green.	A strongly negative, B slightly negative.
Greenish Cyan	Cyan highest, magenta lowest, yellow closer to magenta.	Red lowest, green highest, blue closest to red.	A strongly negative, B not quite as negative.
Cyan	Cyan high, magenta and yellow about equal and much lower.	Red lowest, green and blue about equal and much higher.	A and B both strongly negative and about equal.
Bluish Cyan	Cyan highest, yellow lowest, magenta roughly in the middle.	Red lowest, blue highest, green closer to blue.	A not quite as negative as B.
Cyanish Blue	Due to the small CMYK gamut, about the same as bluish cyan.	Red lowest, blue highest, green closer to red.	A much less negative than B.
Blue	Cyan highest, magenta almost as high, yellow lowest.	Blue highest, red and green about equal and much lower.	A near zero, B strongly negative.
Magentaish Blue	Yellow lowest, magenta equal to or slightly more than cyan.	Blue highest, green lowest, red closer to green.	A slightly positive, B strongly negative.
Bluish Magenta	Magenta high, yellow lowest, cyan somewhere between.	Green lowest, blue highest, red closer to blue.	A strongly positive, B slightly negative.
Magenta	Magenta high, yellow and cyan about equal and much lower.	Green lowest, red and blue about equal and much higher.	A strongly positive, B near zero.
Reddish Magenta	Magenta high, cyan low, yellow closer to cyan.	Green lowest, red highest, blue closer to red.	A strongly positive, B slightly positive.
Magentaish Red	Magenta high, cyan low, yellow closer to magenta.	Green lowest, red highest, blue closer to green.	A slightly more positive than B.

We always then split the slider by Option–clicking it, and move the two halves slightly apart. Doing so creates a transition zone where the two layers are blended, eliminating hard edges.

Two final points about this image. First, working on an adjustment layer like this leaves open the possibility of reducing opacity after seeing how the Blend If exclusion works. Here, I dropped it to 70%, something that didn't seem like an obvious move when the sky was a brilliant cyan in Figure 4.14.

Second, this last Blend If move wouldn't be all that much more difficult in RGB. We would use the blue channel rather than the B. Both the clouds and the sky would be light enough in the blue to separate them from the rocks. Some of the lighter areas of the rocks would, however, be excluded. We would then have to enter the adjustment layer's layer mask, lasso them, and delete them to black. This would not take very long.

On the other hand, with this type of image you should be in LAB anyway, because as far as I know there isn't any way of duplicating the color variation without it. So you might as well use the quick way of selecting.

If you'd like to see a more striking illustration of LAB superiority, go back to the jewelry of Figure 4.12B and imagine you had to use Blend If to restrict a correction to the bluest stones. In other colorspaces it would be quite a chore, inasmuch as these blues range from quite light to quite dark. In LAB, there's no problem—no matter how light or dark they are, they're always more B–negative than any other part of the picture.

LAB and the Workflow

LAB is now well established among serious Photoshop users. People are still finding their own level of comfort with it. Then again, some RGB users are uncomfortable with CMYK, and vice versa.

Review and Exercises

✓ Open the original of Figure 4.1. Experiment with using the same straight-line AB curves, but use different angles for each one, making sure they still cross the center point. When the A is steeper, the redness of the canyon will be accentuated; the B emphasizes the yellowest areas.

✓ When the objective is to increase contrast, when is the L channel a better choice than trying to steepen the curves in RGB or CMYK?

✓ Find some images of flowers, or use the original of Figure 4.7 on the CD. Construct curves in the A and/or B by locking the center point and Command–clicking the flower. Then adjust the new point up or down to see how radically the colors can change.

✓ Match each of the following items in the printed files of this chapter to its typical LAB value. Numbers in parentheses are negative.

1. The tan foreground at the lower right of Figure 4.1B	A. $40^L 3^A (15)^B$
2. The foreground grass of Figure 4.5	B. $80^L 5^A 65^B$
3. The yellow duck of Figure 4.8	C. $75^L 15^A 25^B$
4. The deep sky at the top left of Figure 4.11B	D. $65^L (15)^A 30^B$
5. The gold surrounding the purple stone in Figure 4.12B	E. $35^L 25^A 25^B$
6. The orange rock in the upper right of Figure 4.13B	F. $75^L 12^A 60^B$

Today's professional world increasingly requires both RGB and CMYK, and quality considerations often require LAB as well. On page 98 is a recipe list: the definition of all the colors in all three colorspaces. In principle, you shouldn't need it. Your speed in correcting in each space will depend largely on how quickly you can identify what colors are impossible and need correction. So you may wish to cover up the answers and treat the page as a quiz—one that should be retaken from time to time.

Some have adopted a workflow that's LAB most of the time, and advocate LAB as a teaching tool for less experienced users. A more conservative approach concentrates on the following, which can be recommended to all users.

• When images are somewhat monochromatic, LAB brings out subtle distinctions in

color in a way that's difficult to match in other colorspaces. This advantage shows up particularly in landscape shots, like Figures 4.1A, 4.11A, and 4.13A.

• The basic LAB move—boosting contrast in the L, steepening the AB, and sharpening the L—is simple and fast. Certain images are important enough to demand that we spend as much time as we need to get them right. Others aren't. Realtors preparing catalogs containing hundreds of property images, newspaper photographers on deadline, and tourists getting ready to print a mountain of shots of their last trip are all examples of people who are in too big a hurry to devote more than a minute or two to each file. For such folks, an LAB workflow is quite attractive.

• Even if you don't work with LAB as such, you should learn its numbering system. Color by the numbers, the topic of Chapter 3, isn't notably easy, particularly for those who have to work both in CMYK and RGB. The LAB numbering system is simpler than either. Just knowing that anything 0^A0^B is white, gray, or black is a time-saver. Set up the right side of the Info palette to read LAB equivalents of whatever the colorspace you're working in, and you can save time in evaluating originals.

The fancy stuff with selections, gross color changes like those shown in the jewelry of Figure 4.12C, and advanced curving is optional. If you are inclined to study these things, you'll find them rewarding.

LAB separates color from contrast. Knowing the contexts in which to use it is a big step on the way to reuniting the two into one harmonious whole.

The Bottom Line

RGB and CMYK have many similarities, but LAB is a radical alternative. It completely separates color from contrast, enabling several specialized treatments that are not available in other colorspaces.

The most important use of LAB is in driving similar colors apart by steepening the A and B channels. It can also often avoid the need for selections when it is necessary to alter the color of a specific object. In principle, the L channel's functionality can be matched in RGB or CMYK, but some images correct better in the L, and others should avoid it.

For an in-depth treatment of LAB, consult my book *Photoshop LAB Color: The Canyon Conundrum and Other Adventures in the Most Powerful Colorspace.*

5

The Key Is the K

Manipulating the black channel is the most potent weapon in the CMYK arsenal. With it, we can control neutrality, add definition in shadows, and strengthen shape. Success requires a knowledge of gray component replacement, and of what colorspaces with four letters offer that those with three letters can't.

 six-year-old, a scientist, and a retoucher were each given the same test in logic. They were asked, what do the following have in common: RGB, xyY, LUV, LAB, LCH, XYZ, and HSB?

The six-year-old said, they all have three letters. The scientist said, each is a paradigmatic construct enabling expression of empirical visual data in the form of unique normative values of probative color equivalence. The retoucher said, each is a colorspace, but not CMYK, so to hell with 'em all.

That the six-year-old gave the most coherent and technically useful response is the theme of this chapter, in which we will discover how to make a weapon of the anomaly that sets CMYK apart from and above other color models: the presence of black ink.

Many techniques discussed in this chapter are not possible in colorspaces that have only three variables. Taking full advantage of a four-letter colorspace avoids a lot of four-letter words.

Black is not itself a color, but rather the total absence of color. That need not deter us from using it in color correction. In fact, it should encourage us. Since black ink blots out everything, small changes in the black content have a huge effect.

Those who have to prepare files for commercial printing, or for any other output condition that requires a CMYK file, plainly need to understand this chapter. Even if you never have to supply a CMYK file to anybody, however, it's a topic that can't safely be ignored, any more than you can ignore LAB.

The cyan, magenta, and yellow channels are close relatives of the red, green, and blue. From that, you might suppose that CMYK is just a form of

Figure 5.1 *This image uses cyan, magenta, and yellow inks only. It is not a conventional separation with the black channel deleted, but an image prepared on the assumption that black ink is unavailable.*

Instead, I prepared it specially for this unhappy circumstance. For example, the darkest areas are around $98^C 92^M 92^Y$, as opposed to the $80^C 70^M 70^Y$ that they would be if the black weren't AWOL.

Granted, those shadows are a little cheesy-looking. We could definitely improve them with the aid of black ink. On the other hand, we've all seen worse-looking stuff than this. Figure 5.1 is not all that horrible.

In short, CMY is a method that already works reasonably well. How much of an impact can a fourth ink have?

This question merits extended discussion not just because black is such a powerhouse, but because the same considerations apply if a fifth and/or sixth color is added to CMYK. Such added colors are now appearing in all kinds of printing devices.

Note how CMY, like the other colorspaces referred to earlier, has only three letters. As the six-year-old noted, there's something special about that: uniqueness.

Take RGB. We can define any color in terms of its red, green, and blue components, but only in one way. Every color is unique, and no other combination of red, green, and blue light can produce it.

LAB is very different, but it shares the same property. It assigns a darkness value (L), modified with values along two different opponent-color axes. Again, every color can be described this way, and again, each LAB color is unique.

And so on with the other color models,

RGB with a black channel tacked on for luck. The reality is considerably more complex. Even before we consider what the output will be, there are two glaring differences between CMYK and RGB files. They are:

• In RGB, objects can be as dark as we like. $0^R 0^G 0^B$ is legal. CMYK has an arbitrary limit on the amount of ink that can be used, one that has many ramifications.

• In RGB, all colors are unique; they can be created in only one way. CMYK usually offers many different possible formulations.

This chapter will show how to exploit these factors in two ways:

• As a defensive measure, to guard against an undesired result on press

• As an offensive measure, to make color correction simpler and more effective

A Hypothetical Colorspace

It would be a sad world if we had to print without black ink. We could, however, get by. Figure 5.1 is printed without any black ink at all. It is not a conventional separation from which the black channel has been deleted. We'll see examples of that in a little while.

including CMY, and so it will be with any other three-letter system that may be developed in the future. Each color in the system has a unique value.

Adding a fourth variable to any of these will create alternate ways to make colors that were already possible. It also will expand the gamut of colors that can be produced. That the fourth variable happens to be black has nothing to do with it. If the fourth color were (to suggest something off the wall) tangerine, the considerations would be the same.

Let's talk about, then, an imaginary world of CMTY. This would be very useful if we happened to represent citrus growers. Imagine the bangup oranges, grapefruits, and lemons we could produce if we could back up the basic yellow and magenta inks with a hit of tangerine. We might even be able to make brighter limes, because of the strong yellow component of tangerine ink.

$10^C50^M100^T100^Y$ is a brilliant orange, impossible to reproduce with CMY, or with CMYK for that matter. Similarly, we expand the gamut in the shadows. Tangerine is a light ink, but adding it to CMY shadows would help a little, creating a color darker than previously possible.

Brilliant oranges and marginally deeper shadows aren't all that tangerine has going for it. It also offers *options*—options to create colors that were already possible, but to create them with different mixes of ink.

Since tangerine could be described as a mixture of lots of yellow and a bit of magenta, in principle we could put it into any color that normally contains significant amounts of yellow and even a little magenta, provided we were willing to take some yellow and magenta out to make up for it.

For example, a fleshtone might fall in the neighborhood of $10^C40^M50^Y$, but $10^C39^M5^T47^Y$ should be practically the same thing. So should $10^C35^M25^T30^Y$. And so should many other possibilities. Don't hold me to these numbers; I'm guessing about dot gain and other variables, but you get the idea. If we had this problem in real life, we could certainly figure out the proper numbers.

Since there is no *theoretical* difference, we have to ask, is there a *practical* one? Would we put tangerine ink in fleshtones?

I will answer this quickly. Yes, we would. There would be less variation on press and a less pronounced screening pattern. Most important, it would reduce the range of the

A Message to the RGB-centric

When drafts of this book were circulating, the reaction was pretty uniform. Readers thought each chapter was either good or bad, either hard or easy. This chapter was the exception. Those with a CMYK background breezed through it; everyone else found it a nightmare.

Beta reader John Ruttenberg spoke up for this group, saying, "There really are two halves to Chapter 5: press independent and press specific. Everyone should be interested in the cowgirl correction [Figure 5.4]. This shows how to use CMYK to get better shadow detail, even for images destined for RGB. The last half is really aimed at prepress pros only. Consider making this clear, with some phrase like, 'We are about to swim in the deep end.'"

I would rephrase that. The first half of this chapter discusses CMYK concepts as they apply in a perfect world. Sometimes, as when an image has absolutely critical shadow detail, even files that are destined for RGB should spend a little time in CMYK—having a black channel in such cases is a lifesaver.

The second half is not about a perfect world, but rather about the world in which we currently live, where output on press is not particularly reliable. Those preparing files for press often need to adopt a defensive posture, using black ink as a shield against undesired color changes. If you never have to prepare files for press, then technically you don't have to read it. On the other hand, sometime in your professional career you are likely to be confronted with unusual output circumstances. In your case, it may be a press, or it may be something else. Either way, debating how to cope with conditions as unreasonable as what today's printing firms stick us with can be a valuable exercise.

magenta and yellow inks, making it easier to target them with curves like those shown in Chapter 2.

Sorry for such a brusque answer, but we don't print with tangerine, we print with black, and it's time to confront it.

Black as Tangerine

Like tangerine, black expands our gamut. It doesn't help at all with citrus fruit, but it does enable a far deeper shadow than was possible before. And like tangerine, it gives us options. Instead of substituting for lots of yellow and a little magenta, black substitutes for all three CMY inks simultaneously.

This discussion will be a lot easier if, for the moment, we forget about such tiresome practicalities as dot gain, different printing conditions, the anemic nature of cyan ink, and other obstacles to perfection.

In this best of all possible CMY worlds, equal parts of the three, say $25^C25^M25^Y$, would make a neutral gray—the same, in fact, as using 25^K alone. We can also split the difference: $20^C20^M20^Y5^K$ or $15^C15^M15^Y10^K$ ought to work just as well.

This principle applies not just to grays, but to anything with more than trace amounts of C, M, and Y. $75^C25^M85^Y$, a forest green, would thus be eligible.

$50^C0^M60^Y$ of this would be untouchable, since we couldn't put in more black than there was magenta originally. This is what makes the color green as opposed to lavender or whatever. It can therefore be described as the *color component*.

The remaining $25^C25^M25^Y$ is what pushes the color away from a brilliant green and more toward gray. People call it the *gray component*, and it is up for grabs. We can replace it with black ink totally, partially, or not at all. Hence, another three-letter acronym: *gray component replacement*, or GCR, usually coupled with another poorly understood concept, UCR.

Historically, artists looking for quality separations did not need to concern themselves with this topic. Drum scanners owned by somebody else produced a CMYK file, exactly what we needed to print with, and all this GCR/UCR stuff was taken care of by the time we got the files.

The age of digital photography ended what was left of that workflow. Cameras now always give us RGB files as a starting point. But we still often have to prepare them for commercial printing, or for some other application where a CMYK file is required. That means that GCR is no longer the scanner operator or the printer's problem, but ours.

Where GCR Is Mandatory

Most North American magazines claim to adhere to the Specifications for Web Offset Publications, or SWOP. Among other things, SWOP dictates that total ink values in any area cannot exceed 300%, which most publications adjust downward to 280%. The rule exists because, at the high speeds of a web press, greater volumes of ink can create drying problems. Also, inks may contaminate one another, resulting in, say, a yellow ink that is too orange.

The more absorbent (which in practice means the cheaper) the paper is, the worse the problem. Some titles, typically trade publications that print on uncoated paper, ask for an even lower maximum, like 260%. Newspapers commonly ask for 240%, because newsprint is second cousin to toilet paper.

By the same token, better printing conditions imply a higher maximum. For sheetfed printing on coated paper at reputable shops, 320% is certainly acceptable, if not 340%.

Many printers employ an ink police to enforce these rules. They behave a lot like their highway counterparts. For example, in my home state of New Jersey, there are interesting signs by the side of certain major highways reading *Speed Limit 65*.

State troopers do not enforce any such limit, because they can imagine what New Jersey drivers would say if they got stopped for doing 66 in a 65. Nevertheless, there actually is a speed limit, merely not the posted one. I won't tell you what it is, because some things are better learned by experience, as I did on a recent trip to Montana, where I underestimated the real speed limit.

Printers are more liberal than state troopers. The people that their ink police ticket are valued clients. The printer does not want an argument about whether 281% is over the limit. If some dark area of respectable size is found to be "in the neighborhood" of 280%, you are as likely to get stopped as if you go two miles an hour faster than the speed limit, but if the ink police find 300% or higher, your job will bounce. That may be more serious than a speeding ticket, especially if it happens late in the production cycle.

The problem gets really bad under poor printing conditions. This book's suggested shadow of $80^C70^M70^Y70^K$ is technically illegal for magazine work inasmuch as it sums to 290%. Again, though, no magazine printer would dare to cast the first citation at such a venial sin. A newspaper advertising department that is asking for a limit of 240% is a different story. They'll bounce that shadow for sure. Yet we don't wish to lighten it; the whole point of Chapter 2 was how important overall range is, and it's even more critical in poor printing conditions, where the paper isn't very white.

So much for the question of whether to use GCR. We *have* to use it in the dark areas of newspaper printing, because for every point of black we put in, we can (in a perfect world) kill three points of CMY. In theory, $75^C65^M65^Y75^K$ is the same darkness

as $80^C70^M70^Y70^K$, but it uses 10 points less total ink. In practice, 1^K is worth *more* than $1^C1^M1^Y$, so $60^C50^M50^Y80^K$, which sums to 240% and is therefore legal for newspapers, is as dark as we need.

Beta reader Clarence Maslowski, who supervises a newsprint operation, comments, "Adding more ink at this point does not make a darker shadow, visual or measured. It only [irritates] the pressman. You don't need a spectrophotometer to find it, either. A little setoff onto a paid ad and it becomes a problem that everyone knows about."

This mandatory GCR in shadows plus a tiny amount in slightly lighter areas to avoid an abrupt transition is the lightest black that Photoshop's standard settings will generate.

CMYKs Fixed and Editable

We choose Mode: CMYK, and Photoshop provides what is called a *color separation,* a term that made sense when scanner operators were breaking a transparency into four separate channels. Today, the file already consists of separate channels when we convert to CMYK, but the term *separation* persists.

The characteristics of the separation are governed by the CMYK working space settings in Color Settings unless we override them on a given image by using Convert to Profile. Many of the black maneuvers in this chapter require use of Custom CMYK, which is an option in either command.

If you have settings prepared in Custom CMYK loaded as your working space, you can edit them, either in Color Settings or in Convert to Profile. That is, if your workspace calls for Light GCR, but you wish to use Heavy GCR on a certain image, you can run it through Convert to Profile and change the setting. At first glance the result will look very close to what it would be with the normal setting, but it would have the stronger black that you decided you needed.

If you have loaded a named preset CMYK, such as the default, U.S. Web Coated (SWOP) v2, you can't edit it inside Photoshop. It may *appear* that you can, because if you switch to Custom CMYK, the familiar dialog will appear. If you switch it to, say, Heavy GCR, it looks like you're editing your working space's settings. In fact, you are editing the default setting of Photoshop 5. So, although you will be able to generate something with Heavy GCR, the color and darkness will not match what you are accustomed to.

It is for those who believe that black ink is toxic and want as little of it as is reasonable. To differentiate this species of shadow-only GCR from the picture-wide varieties, there is another term for it, a confusing one: *UCR*, for *undercolor removal.*

The above definition is generally but not universally accepted. Some people use UCR and GCR to mean the same thing. In Europe, and occasionally in the United States, another term, *achromatic reproduction*, is used to signify the use of heavy GCR.

Photoshop uses the traditional UCR definition, which is the lightest black that a reasonable person would ever use, consistent with the exigencies of the ink police and the necessity for a dark shadow. More black than that is called Light GCR, a term that has no precise meaning, except that it's lighter than the equally ill-defined Medium GCR, which is in turn less than Heavy GCR. There are also options for None, meaning printing without a black at all, and for Maximum, meaning what it says. Neither of these has a use in most photographs, although I used None to produce Figure 5.1. Maximum, as we will see later, is needed to avoid registration problems in artwork containing fine black lines.

To give an idea of how this works in practice, I created a color that was a bit less saturated than the forest green discussed earlier and separated it all four ways. While your values might vary slightly depending on various other settings, my results were UCR: $60^C27^M68^Y$; Light GCR: $58^C24^M66^Y4^K$; Medium GCR: $55^C19^M64^Y10^K$; Heavy GCR: $52^C15^M62^Y14^K$.

Notice that as GCR goes up, total ink usage goes down. In the above color, UCR produces 155 points total ink, Heavy GCR only 143.

The options are governed by Edit: Color Settings (in some versions, Photoshop: Color Settings)>Working Space>Custom CMYK. For now, I recommend you insert the values shown in Figure 5.2. This is a temporary fix; we will discuss fine-tuning the settings in Chapters 12 and 13. But you need to move away from Photoshop's default, U.S. Web Coated (SWOP) v2, which is unsuitable for professional work because we can't change its GCR settings.

The Need for a Lower Black Limit

If you have several different printing conditions, you may need several different Color Settings files. If not, you should be able to stick with one setting and never visit the dialog again. For GCR changes that are unique to one image, use Edit: Convert to Profile (CS2 and later; Image: Mode>Convert to Profile in previous versions). The Custom CMYK option shown in Figure 5.3 brings up the Figure 5.2 dialog, but it's strictly a one-shot deal that doesn't change our base settings. It can also be used to change the GCR of a file that's already in CMYK. That's what we'd have had to do in any of the images we've discussed in previous chapters if we had decided that their black generation was wrong. Merely changing the CMYK definition in Color Settings doesn't change the channels of existing CMYK files.

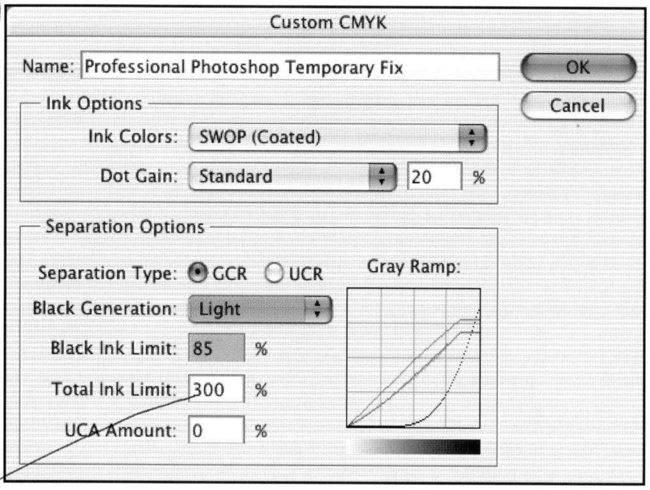

Figure 5.2 *Use these Custom CMYK settings as a starting point for working with the techniques of this chapter. The highlighted areas differ from Photoshop's defaults.*

Before going any further, we need to stress again that *in theory* it doesn't matter what kind of black generation we choose—Photoshop always will generate the same colors, although with different combinations of inks. Therefore, this is a *practical* chapter. It discusses things that wouldn't make any difference in a perfect world but nevertheless have have an impact when ink actually hits paper. We'll start by considering an original destined for a clothing catalog.

The Pure Play on Black

Back when we first examined channel structure in the flowers of Figure 1.5, we noted that the CMY shadows looked ghosted out. That's a CMYK peculiarity, the influence of the total ink limit. It makes almost no difference in curving—unless the color black happens to be critical to the image, as it is in Figure 5.4.

This original capture arrives in Adobe RGB. It is to print at about the size you see here in the catalog of a company that specializes in the fanciful (and expensive) attire that women employ to snare the attention of judges at horse shows. Consequently, while the woman should look attractive, too, the clothing is the focus.

As you can see, all the CMY detail in the clothing rode off into the sunset. Compare, for example, the cyan to its RGB cousin, the red, and the magenta against its cousin the green. The faces are similar—but what a difference in the garments. It's even hard to distinguish the gloves.

The culprit is the 300% total ink limit imposed by the settings of Figure 5.2. We can only get that much ink if the original is as black as it can possibly be, which these garments clearly aren't.

Figure 5.3 *The Convert to Profile command permits overriding the Custom CMYK settings for a single image.*

In Figure 5.1, which had no black ink at all, my shadow still summed up to 282%. Now that a fourth ink exists, I'd like to add around 70^K of it. That's a bronco we can't ride. Something has to give. Photoshop (or any other separation method, for that matter) can't stay within the limit without peeling back the CMY. In doing so, it wipes out all detail. And we can't unilaterally declare a higher limit, because the catalog printer, not to mention the printer of this book, won't accept it.

If the model were wearing navy blue rather than black, this effect would not occur. Yellow ink, which kills blue, would presumably drop down to about 30^Y. That would give us the wiggle room to increase cyan to as much as 100^C while still honoring the limit. All three CMY channels would have detail. But when the underlying color is black, they can't.

Believe it or not, this is good news. Consider how we would try to add detail to such blacks in RGB. There are opportunities to do so in the red and green channels, at a considerable price. The darkest parts of the clothing can't get much darker. To add more range, we'd have to lighten the lighter parts. When we did that, the face and the hair would go along for the ride.

CMYK comes galloping to the rescue of black objects. All shadow detail, and little else, migrates into the black. It's a lot easier to adjust that than three RGB channels that

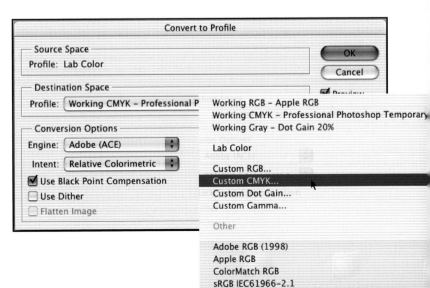

each have considerable detail in other areas, which would get in the way.

This black has room to make parts of the garments both lighter and darker, which is not the case in RGB. Not only can we add more shape, but doing so is almost cost-free. In RGB, we had to confront possible damage to the skin. Not so in the black, which has almost no skin to damage.

These factors explain the two high-lighted choices in Figure 5.2. Custom CMYK defaults to Medium GCR. The tradition in printing is for a lighter black than that, with good reason—it's easier to deal with images like Figure 5.4. In a heavier black channel, the face might carry important shape that would be easy to damage with a correction whose main target was the clothing.

The Custom CMYK default is for 100^K maximum, a poor choice that would produce a shadow of around $70^C 60^M 60^Y 90^K$. The CMY channels would look even worse than they do in Figure 5.4, and it would detract from our ability to apply a steepening curve to the black. The black ink limit belongs somewhere between 75^K and 90^K. Anything higher has nothing to gain and quite a bit to lose. The only exception is in cases that warrant Maximum GCR, which we'll get to in a few pages. First, though, this image is important because it serves as a stalking horse for any other that involves critical blacks. Let's put it through its paces.

Evaluating Neutrality

Getting more detail in the fabric is such a pressing priority that it can hide other problems. To me, the original is rather bland. Because so much of it is supposed to be neutral, LAB looks like the clear choice for at

Figure 5.4 *Above, an original digital capture for a catalog. Opposite: the CMYK channels, plus the RGB red and green.*

least part of the correction. We can hold the center point of the AB curves while making them steeper. That will retain the neutrality of the clothing no matter how dark it is or isn't. If we tried RGB or CMYK curves, we'd have to watch out that the light half of the clothing didn't take on a different color from the dark half.

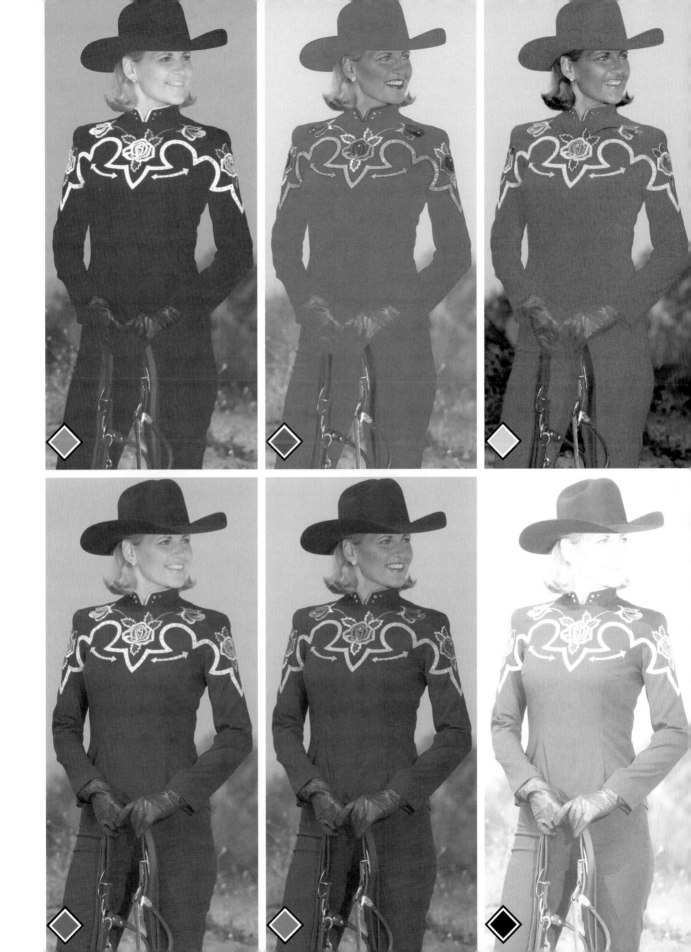

Also, working in LAB, or at least looking at LAB numbers in the Info palette, makes the initial evaluation of this image easier. The clothing doesn't fall in a short range. We need to look at lots of different points and would prefer not to take all day doing it. In addition to finding out whether the blacks are currently 0^A0^B—neutral—we should examine the possibility that some of them aren't supposed to be black in the first place. (To see an example of why LAB values are easier to read in the Info palette, turn back two chapters and check out the screen grab of Figure 3.4).

Yes, the riding outfit *looks* black. But it might, for example, have a dark purple sheen. Fortunately, we can figure out by context whether it does. The shirt and pants clearly are manufactured to match one another, but I doubt that the hat is. And we can

hang that hat on the fact that the gloves don't match any of the other three.

To uncover the truth, with the Info palette set to LAB, we run the cursor up and down, around and through the black areas. If we consistently find 0^A0^B or thereabouts, all is well. If the outfit measures something significantly other than what the gloves do, we know that it's not truly black. If outfit, hat, and gloves all measure the same AB, but it isn't black, then we've identified a cast. If all these objects are the same color, I refuse to believe it can be anything other than black.

The actual readings show that all three *are* the same color. They are always within two points of 0^A, in either direction. The B also has a five-point range, but it isn't similarly neutral—it runs from $(5)^B$ to 0^B, the parentheses denoting a negative (blue) value.

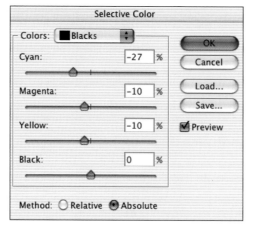

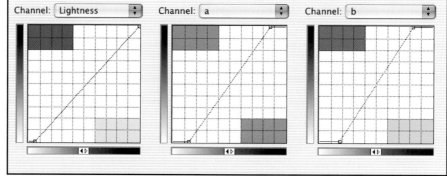

Figure 5.5 *The progression of correcting Figure 5.4. Clockwise from top: LAB curves enhance colors without changing neutral balance; after conversion to CMYK, a sharp curve to the black adds snap to the garments; a Selective Color move reduces all under-colors, particularly cyan; the final black channel.*

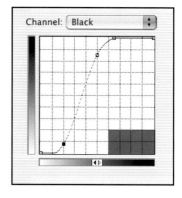

Figure 5.6 *Left, after the application of the LAB curves shown opposite. Right, the final correction.*

Chapter 9 is about drawing inferences about colors, things that aren't apparent at first glance but show up when we start comparing. We just saw one. Here's another: I infer that the photographer wasn't favored with good shooting weather. I know this because the sky measures the same single-digit negative B that the outfit does. If it had been a sunny day, the sky would be bluer.

I doubt that the company wants a gray sky. We could try to make it bluer with various forms of chicanery, but this picture allows an easier method. We just ignore the issue, pretending that the garments are properly neutral even though we know that the file has them slightly blue. Working in LAB, we apply the curves of Figure 5.5 and arrive at Figure 5.6A.

Now, Mode: CMYK. The LAB curves didn't do anything to alter the shape of the black channel, which looks about like it did in Figure 5.4. Observing that the maximum in the garments is around 62^K, we make a very steep curve to bring it to 95^K while lightening the lighter parts.

I'd show the state of the image now, but can't. The printer won't let me use it, because it's well over the ink limit. The 300% imposed by Figure 5.2 only holds for the moment of separation. The black curve of Figure 5.5 leaves it in the dust.

That's all right, though, because it suits us to reduce total ink anyway. Look again at the cyan, magenta, and yellow channels of Figure 5.4. What useful purpose do they serve?

We are better off removing some of these undercolors. The Selective Color dialog of Figure 5.5 does so. It instructs Photoshop to add or subtract specific inks wherever it encounters specific colors—in this case, anything that Photoshop considers to be black. Under normal circumstances, we'd reduce all CMY channels equally. Here, the clothing had a cool cast, so extra cyan comes out. Recall that we left that cast in while in LAB, to avoid neutralizing the sky. In the final image, Figure 5.6B, do you notice that the blacks are less cool than in Figure 5.6A?

Many corrections work equally well in different colorspaces. Large dark neutral areas belong in CMYK. Moves that are designed to keep them neutral while enhancing other colors are best accomplished in LAB. Certain types of channel blending, which we haven't

Figure 5.7 *GCR removes CMY and substitutes black. The higher the GCR setting, the more pronounced the effect. Below, two original images. Unlike other colorspaces, CMYK can construct the same color in several ways. Opposite, each row shows the CMY composite without the black channel, and next to it, the black alone. From top to bottom (lightest black to darkest, darkest CMY to lightest), the rows were prepared with UCR, Light GCR, Medium GCR, and Heavy GCR.*

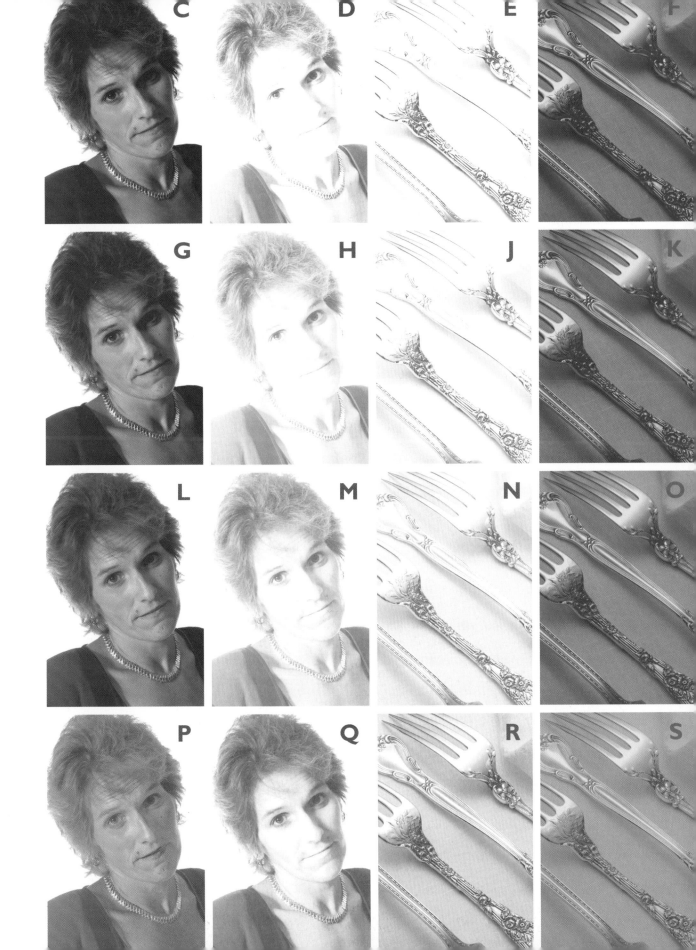

covered yet but which would be used in this picture if we had, work better in RGB.

Given that this image needs to be printed, the RGB to LAB to CMYK workflow just described is a painless one. But what if we needed an RGB file as a final product?

In that case, we'd do things in a different order. I'd still want to use both LAB and CMYK, because they offer things for this image that RGB doesn't. I'd go RGB to CMYK to LAB to RGB, though. Recall that the big danger of going in and out of CMYK is that certain vivid colors may get lost. Figure 5.4 is too dull for this to be a factor, but Figure 5.6A might not be. CMYK has trouble with light, bright colors like the pinks in the shirt. It's better to bring these out in LAB after the blacks have been enhanced.

Is this a complicated procedure? Certainly. I'd do it all in RGB, but I don't know how. Is going to CMYK politically correct? I don't care. The question is only relevant if somebody can come up with a better-looking final result in a different way.

When in Doubt, Do Without

The tradition in fine printing is a relatively light black plate, which people variously describe as *no GCR, minimum GCR,* or a *skeleton black.* Such terms have no exact meaning. However, in this general style, black ink starts to appear when each of the three process colors is printing more than 25% and the sum of all three values is 100 or more. If the three colors get heavier, the black gets heavy faster, so that the darkest area of the picture will have black values at least as high as those of the magenta and yellow, and perhaps even of the cyan. Photoshop's UCR and Light GCR settings make this traditional kind of separation.

Black ink is roughly as powerful as the other three put together. Any mistake or misunderstanding in its application will therefore be very bad—unless we use a skeleton black.

We have to be particularly cautious of a heavier black if the job is going to an offset press rather than some kind of digital printer, as black ink densities are notoriously unreliable in the pressroom. Similarly, black dot gain, which we'll discuss in Chapter 13, is underestimated in Photoshop's Custom CMYK default.

If black ink runs unexpectedly heavily, the problems are the same as if we had darkened the channel with a curve. If this happens and we're using a stronger black, colored areas become muddy. With a skeleton black, they're unaffected because they are at or around 0^K. Heavier ink coverage may actually make the skeleton-black image look better. It will show more contrast, although shadow detail will go down the tubes.

As a general rule, Photoshop's Light GCR has slight technical advantages over its UCR. Either, however, is a skeleton black, a satisfactory choice for nine out of ten images you'll face henceforth.

Naturally, we now need to deal with the one out of ten in which skeleton blacks *aren't* satisfactory. Let's study how the options might play out in the two images of Figure 5.7, and then formulate some general rules about when to use a heavier GCR.

The smaller versions show a progression in order of increasing black and, thus, of decreasing CMY. They are the four Custom CMYK settings (UCR, Light GCR, Medium GCR, and Heavy GCR), all with a maximum of 85^K. In principle, all four pairs of images look alike when you combine them.

The Politics of Presswork

This is not a book about printing, but printers are even less inclined to take credit for their own screwups than prepress people are, if possible. Instead, if the job looks lousy, they will blame the photographer, the art director, global warming, and, most especially, us. Worse, the client sometimes falls for this

Figure 5.8 *These images simulate what can happen when a heavier GCR combines with unexpectedly heavy ink density. Both were constructed by marrying the black channel from the bottom row of Figure 5.7 to the CMY of the second row. Which of these incorrect results looks worse, in comparison to the originals of Figures 5.7A and 5.7B?*

pap, or even comes to the same erroneous conclusion without anybody's help. Preventing pressroom problems is very much in our interest.

The presence of extra black has several pluses and several minuses. If the pluses seem to correspond to what we want to accomplish with our picture, it will pay to use GCR.

The most obvious way GCR can help is as a defensive measure against some of the chaos caused by ink-density variation. Presses and pressmen are not precision instruments, so this happens all the time. If you are working not with a press but with some kind of digital printer, some of these comments about black may not apply.

The nice thing about black ink is that it is almost perfectly neutral. The more of it, the

less likelihood that overinking of cyan, magenta, or yellow can affect the basic hue. The bad thing is that if black itself is overinked, it is much more noticeable than any of the other three.

Figure 5.8 emulates just such a tiresome occurrence. The two versions are created by joining the Heavy GCR blacks of Figure 5.7 with the CMY that was intended for Light GCR. That is, Figure 5.8A is a wedding of Figures 5.7G and 5.7Q.

That the fleshtones are now muddier isn't the biggest issue. Much detail is lost in the hair, which has also changed color, and the blouse. Plus, judging by the shiner she's sporting, it looks like somebody punched this woman in the eye.

You may say, suppose we don't use much black—wouldn't it be just as likely that the

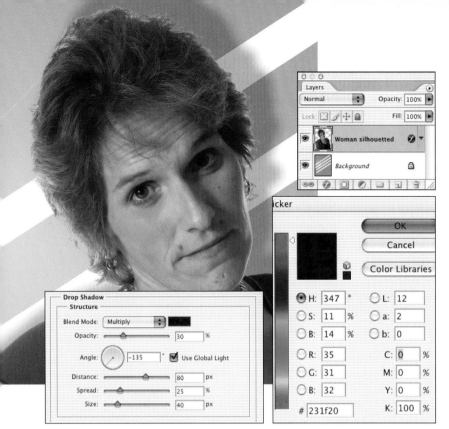

Figure 5.9 *Creating an artificial drop shadow in Photoshop requires that the shadow object be silhouetted on its own layer. If the shadow is created in RGB and then brought into CMYK, it will separate according to Color Settings, which will yield an overly light black. But if, as it should be, the shadow is invoked in CMYK, the default results in black only, which is undesirable.*

Such variation, as we will discuss in Chapter 13, is unfortunately par for the course in real-world printing. Oftentimes, though, it is inconvenient or impossible to redo the job.

The whole point of Figures 3.5 and 3.6 was to demonstrate what combination of CMY inks produces a neutral. In that unusual context, it was critically important that gray balance on press be correct, and editorially impossible to include black ink in the image.

In any circumstances in which that image appeared other than a technical treatise on color correction, this should not have been permitted to occur. A knowledgeable person would have separated the file with heavier GCR. It doesn't take much black ink to prevent grays from wandering.

cyan or some other color would print too heavily, achieving the same muddy mess? Yes, surely there could be too much cyan, but it wouldn't be nearly as bad. Each CMY ink darkens much less than the equivalent amount of black. And as for a cyan cast, in areas this dark our eyes are not particularly sensitive to colors. We would perceive added darkness, not blue hair.

From which, we derive:

- **Rule One**: When the image has an overall dark appearance or contains critical dark areas, avoid GCR.

* * *

In the second printing of *Professional Photoshop 6*, the publisher rejected an entire 16-page signature because an image of a statue (Figure 3.5 in today's edition) that was supposed to be gray, and had been in the first printing, became green.

Bridal gowns, gray animals, the forks of Figure 5.7B: if the image depends on holding light neutrals, use extra black.

- **Rule Two**: When the most important area is a neutral color lighter than the equivalent of 50^K, GCR guards against disaster.

* * *

GCR is also helpful when producing a duotone effect with process inks. A green duotone, for example, requires all four CMYK inks, but not much magenta or black. If cyan and/or yellow ink comes down too heavily on press, parts of the image may not have the uniform green tint we want. But the more black in the file, the less CMY, and the less pronounced the error will be.

This goes double for the most common kind of duotone there is: a grayscale image that we wish to print in all four process inks. The usual reason we would want to do this is

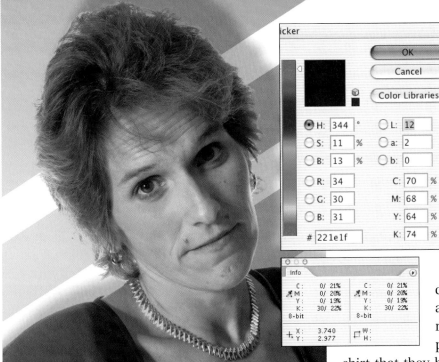

if it's mixed with color images on the same page. If the grayscale prints in black only, the screen pattern may seem coarse in comparison to the softer-looking CMYK files. But if you separate it with the customary skeleton black, and the ink balance on press turns out to be something other than what it should be, the file won't look like a grayscale any more.

In earlier editions of this book, we had a separate chapter on such multitones. In my opinion, not enough readers need this information to justify continuing to print it. However, the old chapter is still valid. It's included in PDF on the book's CD, in this chapter's folder.

● **Rule Three**: When creating a process duotone, tritone, quadtone, or 4/c black and white, use Heavy GCR.

*   *   *

Sometimes color fidelity is so critical that it justifies resorting to all kinds of horsing around on press. The best-known examples are mail-order clothing catalogs. If a shirt prints in slightly the wrong shade, tens of thousands of dollars' worth of merchandise will be returned by angry customers who believed the book.

In such stressful cases, pressmen and art directors do not rely on contract proofs, but on a real shirt that they hold in their hands as they try all kinds of inking shenanigans to match it.

This is not the time to use GCR, because black neutralizes everything. The more black ink, the less leeway there will be to make artistic changes on press.

● **Rule Four**: When you are expecting careful help for a critical color match during the pressrun, GCR is usually a hindrance.

*   *   *

But if you'd prefer added darkness to a color shift, the shoe is on the other foot. That foot may swell up painfully if you use Photoshop's defaults to create a drop shadow. We will demonstrate with a new version of an image we've just worked with.

This time, the assignment is to silhouette the woman and place her on a background gradient that contains some white lines, on which she throws a shadow.

In principle, we do this by making the gradient on the bottom layer, placing the woman on the top layer, and double-clicking the top layer's row in the Layers palette to bring up the same Layer Style menu that we use for Blend If options. The Drop Shadow dialog is shown in Figure 5.9. Settings govern the width, blurriness, and angle of the shadow.

The defaults call for the shadow to be a shade of black, and for it to blend with what's underneath in Multiply mode. These two settings are correct for most shadows.

Conversions between colorspaces are harmless enough if there's no gamut issue—provided that we're working with a natural photograph. Computer-generated graphics have quite different characteristics. The woman can be corrected in whatever colorspace you like. The background should be constructed in the final output space. If you're preparing for a device that expects, say, sRGB, you should convert your file to that before making the graphics. And, in the case of this book, the background should be constructed in CMYK, for two important reasons.

First, CMYK's gamut is very limited in pastel colors like the ones shown. It's difficult to stay within those limits in RGB. If the RGB file calls for any colors that CMYK can't handle, they'll get clipped and the gradient effect will vanish, or possibly band. If it's too conservative, the CMYK file will be too dull. These problems disappear if the gradient is made in CMYK, where it is impossible to call for out-of-gamut colors.

Also, because we can specify the colors directly, we can make them as pure as possible, meaning no contaminating inks. The entire background should be 0^Y, but if the graphic is constructed elsewhere, traces of yellow are sure to creep in. That's important. Under the best of circumstances, these CMYK pastels are pretty lame. We can't afford to lose any of the available color.

Second, I've specified the shadow's weight to be 30%. Since the default color is black, the shadow will be gray. Do this in RGB, and that gray will be treated like any other gray when the time comes to enter CMYK. Here, depending on your choices in Color Settings, you'd get $25^C20^M20^Y$ or thereabouts.

If this shadow is printed incorrectly, it's much better that it be too dark or too light rather than the wrong color. Black ink in this gray can prevent that.

Making the shadow in CMYK is therefore definitely correct, but there's a trap. Double-click the color icon to the right of the Blending Mode setting in the Drop Shadow dialog, and, as Figure 5.9 indicates, you'll learn that the default is $0^C0^M0^Y100^K$. My choice of 30% produces $0^C0^M0^Y30^K$.

Making the shadow entirely black is at least as bad as not having any black at all. It's inviting an offensive line of demarcation where the shadow fades into the background. If black ink prints too heavily, it's asking for a disastrously dark shadow rather than an acceptably dark one. Also, for reasons I'll discuss at the end of the chapter, such a shadow would have to be trapped to the gradient.

A little black goes a long way. I know some very good pressmen, but none who can make black ink print as other than a shade of gray.

To split the difference, double-click the shadow color as described above. In the Color Picker shown in Figure 5.9, $0^C0^M0^Y100^K$ is equivalent to $12^L2^A0^B$. Note that black ink, being manufactured by mortals, is not necessarily absolutely neutral.

If we type over any of those values (I typed over the 12^L, but any number in any of the other colorspaces will do), Photoshop thinks we're asking for a new color, and recomputes the CMYK equivalent. As shown in Figure 5.10, that's $70^C68^M64^Y74^K$ or something similar, depending upon your CMYK definition. Click OK and *that* becomes the base color of the shadow. And, as the Info palette shows, what used to be $0^C0^M0^Y30^K$ changes magically into $21^C20^M19^Y22^K$.

- **Rule Five**: When creating a drop shadow, specify almost as much black as CMY inks.

*   *   *

Project design can also affect GCR desirability if there are areas near the image that require heavy coverage. Ink gets hard to control when a lot of it hits the paper at once.

So, if our image is going to be placed on a solid black background, bet on the black coming down too heavily in the picture itself. Naturally, if one is fortunate enough to know about this before converting to CMYK, one uses less GCR.

Other hints that the black may be hard to handle are very bold headline type or text type that contains fine lines (see box, this page). Any of these factors may motivate the pressman to hike the flow of black ink.

* **Rule Six**: If there is reason to fear heavy black inking on press, avoid GCR.

*   *   *

Since black ink minimizes hue variation, if the same image appears more than once, there is a case for using GCR.

This principle seems so obvious that we may forget that an image doesn't have to be a photograph. Flat colors behave the same way. And many designs call for repetitions of the same color, usually a pastel, in large background areas.

Light colors scarcely seem like the place one would want to introduce black ink. But if we are trying to ensure color fidelity from one page to the next—as, for example, in a company logo—it can be an excellent idea.

* **Rule Seven**: When repeatability from page to page is an issue, don't forget GCR principles, even when specifying colors in linework and flat tints.

*   *   *

Many people wonder why K stands for black. Mainly, it's to avoid confusion: in the pressroom, cyan is referred to as *blue,* so B is ambiguous. But K is more elegant, anyway. It stands for *key,* and indeed it is the key to the final major uses of GCR.

Black is the key for registration, meaning that the other three colors are supposed to be adjusted to agree with it and not vice versa. When a job is printed out of register, then, the culprit is almost invariably one of the other colors.

This suggests an application for GCR in the growing volume of work for lower-print-quality applications, especially newspapers. Because of the speed of newspaper presses, misregistration is common. A beefy black will minimize it. Warning: before trying this, you must understand newspaper dot gain, which is greater than in other forms of printing. If the black is too heavy, the outcome will not be attractive.

* **Rule Eight**: Where misregistration is likely, use a heavier black to control it.

*   *   *

As the most powerful ink, black can add detail and contrast, muddy or clean up colors, and bulk up shadows very quickly. No matter how one corrects them, images with more black tend to remain more neutral. So,

Of Layouts and Densities

The different typeface of this box shows how design considerations sometimes influence print results. It is based on fonts cut by Giambattista Bodoni (1740–1813). This face is the variant known as Bauer Bodoni, which is the house type for, among others, IBM.

In the early 19th century, when Bodoni did his most notable work, it had just become technically possible to cut metal lines, such as those used in type, thinner than ever before. Bodoni was determined to show how far the envelope could be pushed. In the headline, note how thin the tops and bottoms of the letters are in comparison to their sides. Because of the thinness of these strokes, pressmen have been cursing Bodoni's name for 200 years. It's difficult to print his types without the letters breaking apart.

The pressmen printing this book won't dare increase black ink because it would make the rest of the text too dark in comparison to other pages. As a result, I predict this box will be hard to read. But under different circumstances, they would have a heavy hand on the black inking controls— and woe betide the person who has separated using anything other than a skeleton black.

Stumbling Blocks: Whom to Ask?

•**"Ask the printer."** Separating into CMYK is such an, er, black art, that those who don't understand it wimp out and suggest that we ask the printer what Photoshop settings to use. Personally, I would prefer to ask an electrician or a plumber, or possibly even a lawyer, because while these worthies probably know as little as the typical printer about the subject, they would be less inclined to bluster their way through an answer. Every modern printer deals successfully with many variants of GCR. The number of commercial printers who know their own dot gain is small, and the number who have any clue what GCR does is less.

•**When does black generation change?** Altering Color Settings does nothing to files that are already in CMYK. Only a conversion—from RGB or LAB to CMYK, or from one CMYK to another with Convert to Profile—will change the type of black in an existing file.

•**Black type and black shadow.** Where type or fine lines appear in an image, they should be, if possible, printed in black ink only. Some confuse this situation with drop shadows and assume that shadows should be made up only of black as well. While having large amounts of black in a shadow is a good idea because it prevents a color cast, constructing it of black ink only asks for a trapping problem or for a hard edge where the shadow ends. Type needs to be all black to avoid registration problems. If a shadow is slightly out of register, on the other hand, nobody will notice.

•**Specifying CMYK equivalents while still in RGB.** Trying to create an area in RGB that will have heavy GCR once it gets to CMYK doesn't work. Specifying CMYK values in the Color Picker or adding black in Selective Color won't help. As far as Photoshop is concerned, every RGB color is an RGB color even if you have defined it in terms of CMYK. It is reseparated according to whatever your Color Settings provide for GCR.

•**Attempting to edit an uneditable profile.** The GCR maneuvering in this chapter presupposes use of Custom CMYK, in which black generation, dot gain, and total ink limit are editable, theoretically producing the same color with different formulations of ink. Photoshop's preset profiles, such as the default U.S. Web Coated (SWOP) v2, can't be edited. You may get the impression by entering Custom CMYK that you're editing the profile, but you're starting anew with defaults from Photoshop 5. The color results won't match what you were expecting.

• **Rule Nine**: Before going into CMYK, ask yourself: do I want bright, happy colors in this picture? If not, choose a heavier black.

The archetype of such a picture is Figure 5.7B, the forks. It's clearly supposed to be neutral, but you can see in some of the CMY-only versions, notably Figure 5.7S, that colors are threatening to rear their hueful heads.

Everything suggests using a heavy black channel. If it prints too heavily, as it does in Figure 5.8B, it's not nearly the catastrophe that Figure 5.8A is. Too dark, yes, but I'd rather have that than too green.

Accordingly, if this job is going to press, any setting short of Heavy GCR is as goofy as it is cowardly. And the same goes in reverse for the woman of Figure 5.7A. Some people are stronger believers in GCR than others, but this isn't the time to use it. Remember, you will likely be blamed if the job blows up on press. Why hand the pressman the dynamite? Choose the GCR setting that makes the explosion less likely.

Notice that the above speaks only of GCR as a defensive measure. It happens that both of these images would correct better with the proper GCR. The cutlery would have lots of detail in the black channel, which is incapable of imparting any cast but whose contrast can easily be augmented. And the woman's eyes and hair would be prominent in a skeleton black, but there would be almost no detailing in her skin. This will be seen as a big advantage in our next chapter, which covers sharpening.

Mud and Custom CMYK

Beginners often go into attack mode the first time their color files hit press or printer. They are always disappointed by the lack of contrast in comparison to what they thought they saw on the monitor.

That lack of contrast is a fact of life. We compensate by using targeted curves that discard contrast where it isn't needed and augment it where it is. But the problem can't be eliminated totally.

It's easy to confuse this effect with something more insidious—a result that's darker and muddier than what was expected.

If this is happening to you consistently, the fault is almost certainly in your Custom CMYK. The principal suspect is the dot gain setting. We'll defer discussion of this until Chapters 12 and 13, except for two points:

• If your images consistently print too dark, you need a higher dot gain setting.

• Dot gain in black is ordinarily higher than in any of the CMY inks.

There are no right answers for the overall dot gain number. Everything depends on local conditions. But for the other Custom CMYK settings, there are definitely *wrong* answers. To recap the recommendations of Figure 5.2, here are Photoshop's defaults— and how to do better.

• **Ink Colors**. The default is SWOP Coated. That describes most of my work, but possibly not yours. If your seps are going to a newspaper, you can still use SWOP Coated, although you'll have to raise dot gain to 30% or so. However, it's probably better to switch to SWOP Newsprint. Photoshop bases its separation on its ideas of what colors result when inks overlap. The newsprint setting correctly assumes muddier colors. This yields a slightly better newspaper sep in my tests.

As to the other Ink Colors defaults, I will not pretend that I have carefully examined every one; it's unlikely that anybody ever has. But, if printing to uncoated paper or doing work in Europe, I'd use the appropriate ink settings as a start.

• **GCR Method**. Photoshop's default, "Medium" black, is heavier than the traditional standard, and should be avoided in most images for reasons stated earlier.

• **Black Ink Limit**. Whether they use inks, toners, waxes, or dyes, all output devices fail to hold detail when the aforementioned colorants reach a certain heaviness. The worse the output condition, the lighter the point at which the failure will occur. For a number of reasons, the failure point for black can be quite low. Under many conditions, even 80^K is likely to print as solid; even the finest presses occasionally fail at 90^K. I recommend an 85^K maximum for virtually all print conditions. Anything between 75^K and 90^K makes sense. Custom CMYK's default black ink limit, 100^K, is a recipe for mud.

• **Total Ink Limit**. The default is the SWOP standard, 300%. If your conditions are of better quality, the number can go up. For sheetfed printing, it can be 320% or even 340%. If worse, it'll have to go down. Most newspapers request 240%. Some go even lower.

Do remember, though, that this limit doesn't protect you once the file is in CMYK. If you correct aggressively after the conversions, your relations with the ink police are in your own hands. If you show up with a 330% shadow where the limit is 300%, good luck explaining that it *used* to be 300% before you fixed it up.

• **UCA** (for *undercolor addition)* artificially adds cyan, magenta, and yellow to the shadow. This would only make sense where the normal shadow value is much less than the total ink limit. If you need detail in the shadows, however, it makes much more sense to set a *low* black limit—70^K or so— and, after separation, apply a curve that brings 70^K into the 90s, as we did with the riding outfit of Figure 5.4.

The one exception to the above is in preparing files for gravure printing, something that need not concern you if you customarily print less than 100,000 copies. As the name suggests, this process uses engraved cylinders, rather than rubber blankets, to apply ink to paper. Because the ink lives in, rather than on, the cylinder, and because of the extreme pressure such a heavy cylinder applies, drying is a nonissue; use 400% ink coverage if you like. In fact, gravure printers want a *minimum,* not a maximum, ink coverage in shadows, as otherwise they look rather cheesy. Use UCA to make sure that even dark three-quartertones hit 300%.

Fine Lines and Maximum GCR

We have so far avoided Maximum GCR as we would the Image: Adjustments>Brightness/Contrast command or the smudge tool. Yet there's a category of images appearing throughout the book that always uses it. Can you name it?

Yes, indeed. I am referring to screen grabs such as Figures 5.2 and 5.3. Note the fine lines around the dialogs. With cartoons, which often have such fine black lines, we run into the same problem.

The quaint notion that four printing plates can always be kept in perfect register has derailed many a design. Natural photographs aren't usually sharp enough that a slight registration failure will be noticeable. Black type and fine lines are.

Photoshop doesn't care whether black areas are clothing, cutlery, or characters. They all get separated to the same value, $80^C70^M70^Y70^K$ or thereabouts.

Those values are inadequate for something as sharp as type or a fine line. Ideally, these should be $0^C0^M0^Y100^K$. If not, something like Figure 5.11 can emerge from beneath a rock.

This magazine page contains an article written by a "renowned Photoshop expert." His failure to separate the graphic with Maximum GCR was severely punished when the black plate printed a quarter of a mile too low.

The type above the graphic is a quarter of a mile too low as well, but nobody notices because there's nothing to compare it to. It's constructed of black ink only, just as most of the graphic should have been.

It's unusual to see registration quite this bad in the real world, but, as you can see, it does happen. Personally, I think it demonstrates that anyone who advocates correcting files by means of Levels in the RGB master setting runs a high risk of offending God, who has a great sense of humor.

Not wishing to add whatever this book's registration problems may be to the existing disaster, after scanning the magazine page I converted it using Maximum GCR. That one

Review and Exercises

✓Explain why the cyan, magenta, and yellow channels usually have no detail in shadow areas.

✓When a CMYK file is required, it usually doesn't matter whether the correction is done elsewhere. Why should CMYK drop shadows be specified in CMYK when possible?

✓What factors indicate that an image should be separated using a heavier GCR than normal?

✓What is the difference between a CMYK setting supplied as a Photoshop default, like U.S. Web Coated (SWOP) v2, and one that is generated by the Custom CMYK setting?

✓Under what circumstances would you separate using Maximum GCR?

✓A beta reader with little background in CMYK asks why I do not mention separating the Bodoni type in the box on page 118 using Maximum GCR. Can you help him out with the answer?

where the histogram begins. As you move these sliders, al
check the image on screen to ensure the color changes yo

where the histogram begins. As you move these sliders, always
check the image on screen to ensure the color changes you do

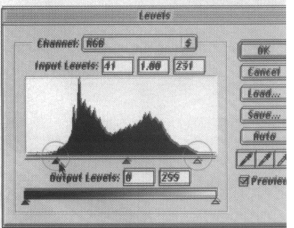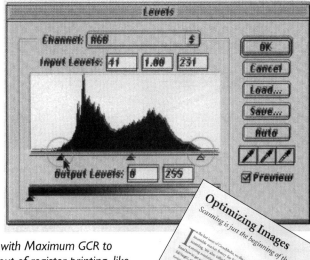

Figure 5.11 *Art with fine lines should usually be separated with Maximum GCR to ensure that the lines will print in black ink only. Otherwise, out-of-register printing, like that afflicting this magazine page, can make the lines illegible. The section shown above the full page appears at actual size and was reseparated for this book using Maximum GCR. Is this book's printer any better? The section at left above was reseparated in CMY only. Is the type as distinct as in the section at right?*

is the version on the right. But for sport, I also converted a second copy of the RGB file using the None setting in black generation. The left version has no black ink at all. It's CMY-only, just as Figure 5.1 was.

We live in an age of direct-to-plate printing, which ordinarily yields quite good registration. This graphic also appeared in the last edition, which went to press twice. One time, you'd have to look closely to see a difference in the type between the CMY and black versions. The other, the CMY looked bolder because the inks did not register properly. This book is being printed by a different company. How well did they do? Do you think it makes sense to take a chance that they'll have good registration, when a foolproof countermeasure is available?

Actions and Consequences

Screen grabs come up so often for me that I have an Action that automates their production. First, it changes Image: Image Size to 140 pixels per inch without resampling. This is the size I typically use in books. Then, it runs Convert to Profile, using Maximum GCR and assuming a special set of CMYK

"inks" that are defined as being considerably less pure than the SWOP recommendations. This is to provoke Photoshop into believing that more saturated values are needed to match the RGB colors.

No measurements or great expertise were needed to define these ink values—I made them up as I went along. This, of course, means that the colored areas of the screen grab won't be accurate. Little sleep need be lost over this. In a screen grab, one doesn't care whether the colors are dead on as long as they are bright. Maximum GCR makes muddiness likely. These bogus inks are a good countermeasure.

Finally, the Action runs Image: Trap on the CMYK file. Trapping is desirable when two totally different colors butt one another. Without trapping, a disagreeable white line can occur if the job should happen to be printed out of register.

To avoid the catastrophe of Figure 5.11, as we saw, the author needed to use Maximum GCR. This, however, would have introduced a trapping problem involving the red circles.

Assume for the sake of argument that those circles are $0^C100^M100^Y$. They butt three different neutral colors: a near-white within the histogram box, a gray outside it, and black in the histogram itself.

As executed by the author, that black area separated to a normal shadow and thus probably contained at least 60^M60^Y. It butts the circle, which has even more of both inks. Therefore, no matter how bad the registration, no white line could possibly appear between them. Theoretically, a small area of $0^C60^M60^Y$ might occur, but the chances are that no one would notice.

Doing the job correctly, though, requires that these neutral areas be handled differently. It is a Jack Sprat and his wife situation. The circles contain no black, and the background has nothing but. If the two misregister, the result will be blank paper where they miss one another.

To guard against such an ugly occurrence, the cognoscenti build in intentional overlaps.

The Bottom Line

Superficially, CMYK and RGB are similar. The CMYK structure is advantageous when working with blacks and dark grays, because all detail migrates into the black channel, where it can be handled aggressively without much harm to the rest of the image.

Unlike RGB and LAB, where all color values are unique, CMYK can usually express the same color in many different ways by substituting a certain amount of black for CMY, or vice versa. The idea of using more black and less CMY is loosely known as GCR. Traditionally, printers prefer a relatively light or "skeleton" black. There are some cases, both as an aid to color correction and as an insurance policy against color shifting on press, where a higher GCR setting is appropriate.

Where the circle butts the black, we'd thicken it without thinning the background, because nobody would likely see the extra red on top of the black. Where the background is lighter, we'd do the reverse: adding a little bit of black to the edge of the circle, making it impossible for a white line to show up.

Trapping is not one of the four or five easiest concepts in the graphic arts. Fortunately, most of the work discussed in this book doesn't require it.

Trap is unnecessary unless there is a knifelike edge between two colors that have almost nothing in common, such as pure magenta and pure cyan. In a photograph, that situation never happens. Edges are indistinct, and colors somewhat subtle. Neighboring colors always share certain common values.

While you'll probably never have to trap a photograph, most of us occasionally have other kinds of trapping problems. So I'm reluctant to let the subject drop, because Photoshop can be a big help in solving them.

Being lazy, I think that the best way to avoid trapping problems is to avoid situations that require a trap. Figure 5.12 is an enlarged version of the drop cap that appears on the first page of this chapter. It was constructed in Adobe Illustrator, not Photoshop. In this design, no possible turn of events can result in a white line. The background grid is cyan, but both letters have a significant cyan component. No trap is needed.

Suppose, though, that the background letter were not a bluish gray, but a gray, period. Now, it's a trap situation, if you happen to be an idiot. An idiot says that gray is a shade of black and constructs it entirely out of said ink. And, as there is no black ink in the grid, trapping becomes necessary.

You would not, of course, do this, because you are not an idiot, and you know the theory of GCR. You realize that you can make a gray just as well with the CMY inks as with black, and a CMY gray will have enough cyan in common with the grid that trapping will no longer be an issue.

It All Fits Together

For the first half of the 1990s, the conventional color wisdom was that correction in CMYK would become obsolete, a viewpoint much ridiculed in previous editions of *Professional Photoshop*.

The idea was that all conversion to CMYK would take place at the RIP, eliminating many of the tricks we've just seen.

It is now a dead idea. The market has rejected RGB chauvinism because it can't deliver quality.

At this point, however, we can go further. *Any* type of colorspace chauvinism is unduly limiting. These last two chapters have highlighted capabilities that are found only in CMYK and LAB.

The next one will, too: RGB is the worst of the three when it comes to sharpening. But RGB has strengths that the other colorspaces don't as well. We simply haven't gotten to them yet.

Every edition of this book has been at least half new content. Only one photograph (Figure 3.12) remains from the first, 1994 edition, along with two blocks of text. One consists of

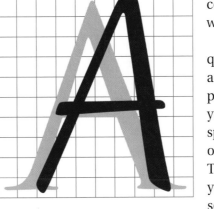

Figure 5.12 *When all graphic elements share large amounts of color (here, cyan), trapping is unnecessary.*

the first five paragraphs of this chapter. We'll end with the other, because today it's truer than ever.

*   *   *

If you are dead set and determined never to work in CMYK no matter what, you will be able to produce pretty good color if you are proficient at writing curves.

But if pretty good is not quite good enough for you, accept that your perpetual punishment for confining yourself to a single colorspace will be color that can only be pretty good, forever. Through eternity, a voice in your mind, whispering ever so softly, will torment you. As you wail and gnash your teeth over your lack of a good image backbone, your inability to hold neutral colors, the missing definition, the highlights that cannot be highlighted, and the shadows that can never be defined, the voice will continue to haunt you; and whatever your color correction talents, however close you get to the sacred territory that is better than pretty good, you will continue to hear it. And you will know and understand, even without the voice, that if you wish to unlock the cell of your pretty good prison, that if you wish to be set free into a better-looking world, the lifeless, gray door *can* be opened—and the key is the K.

Figure 6.1 *Unsharp masking seeks to improve the apparent focus of the image, as at top right. Its trick is introducing artifacts that intensify transition areas but are too small to call attention to themselves. Below, enlarged versions of the original and the sharpened version show how the characteristic halos work their magic.*

6
Sharpening
With a Stiletto

Unsharp masking, an artificial means of improving focus, is a powerful tool, especially for larger images. How much of it should you use? As much as you can get away with, of course. By choosing which channels to sharpen, you'll be able to get away with a lot more of it.

ou enter the boss's office under that most tense of circumstances: you are about to ask for a raise. It is possible that negotiations will ensue, so you have to be prepared with a number. How much more money should you ask for?

The stakes are all too clear. Ask for too little, and you may just get it; ask for too much, and you may get booted out of the office with nothing.

It's also clear that the amount you can get away with asking for is not fixed, but varies sharply depending on your technique. People who, during the meeting, tell the boss what a kind, sweet individual he is and what a joy to work with can, as a rule, ask for more than those who imply that, were it not for their own contribution, the boss's boss would realize what an incompetent dolt he is.

And it is also clear that it depends on the character of the boss. Should you mention that another company may make you an offer at a higher salary? Some bosses respond well to this type of thing. Others, like myself, are of the crabby variety, and are apt to suggest that, should you decide to leave, you not allow the door to hit you in the backside on the way out.

The fact is, you should ask for as much as you think you can get away with under the circumstances, but the circumstances are very much under your control. This is exactly analogous to unsharp masking.

There are at least as many strategies in the sharpening game as there are in playing office politics. Both games are rapidly evolving, as players think up new and better techniques. The options have become so bewildering that one chapter is no longer sufficient—after we go through the basics here, we will return to the topic in Chapters 17 and 18. Before

Figure 6.2 *Fleshtone images are dangerous because of the possibility of accentuating unwanted detail. Top, the original. Bottom left, when sharpened in RGB. Bottom right, sharpened only in the black of CMYK.*

we even start to discuss the options in the principal dialog, we'll try to set the agenda by answering the traditional journalistic questions: who, what, when, where, why, and how?

Who, What, and When?

The who involved is you. This chapter is important to you because its techniques make a decisive difference in believability, particularly of images output at a relatively large size.

The what is *unsharp masking,* henceforward known as USM, an artificial method of making images seem more in focus, as Figure 6.1B is in comparison to Figure 6.1A. Generally speaking, there's no such thing as an image that's too in focus, but there is such a thing as one that looks artificial. The function of this chapter is to show how to get focus without the artificial appearance.

The when is suggested by Figures 6.1C and 6.1D, which put the process under a microscope. USM does its thing by inserting attention-getting artifacts in areas of transition. Those artifacts, which are normally called *halos,* are painfully visible in Figure 6.1D, but of course we don't intend for viewers ever to see the image at that size. They will be looking at

Figure 6.1B, and our hope is that they'll fall for our scam because the halos are too small to perceive clearly.

When looking for a raise, as a matter of honor we try to squeeze the last tenth of a percent out of the company. With USM, it's the same thing. Brinksmanship is fun. We want to go as far as possible without triggering the telltale "Aha!" from the viewer who sees the obnoxious halos and knows when he's being taken.

It follows that sharpening needs to be done late in the correction process. The curving of Chapters 2–4 is highly effective at bringing out contrast—including in the artifacts of USM. It must therefore be done before we throw USM out onto the bargaining table.

There's no call to be doctrinaire and insist that USM be the very last step before we click OK in the print dialog. Mild correction after USM is acceptable. Gross changes ask for gross consequences.

Where?

USM is like color correction in LAB. There's a lot of room for differences in taste. I apply fairly drastic sharpening here to make sure that the effect is visible. You may think that I've gone too far, or not far enough, but you should be able to visualize how you could get the result you want.

That is, if there's no horrendous defect as the result of a stupid decision about where to sharpen. Figure 6.2B exemplifies just such a decision.

The skin of humans, even relatively young ones, is made not of alabaster, but rather of a flexible epidermoid integument, highly useful for insulation and in resisting injury, but somewhat unforgiving of acne scars, and entirely too prone to wrinkling.

Careless USM can age the skin more than 25 years of sunbathing. Figure 6.2B brings out impressive detail. This woman, not being a crocodile, would not want us to see it.

And yet, the original of Figure 6.2A seems too soft, especially in the hair. Note that even in the version with the reptilian skintone, the hair is not overfocused. The question is how to get such hair and at the same time a natural-looking, yet not overdetailed, skin.

If you're trying to get a raise, go to the person who can give it to you, not to some office politician who's liable to spread ugly rumors about you. It's the same way with USM. Half the battle has nothing to do with the settings, but with choosing where to apply them.

Here's the question you should always ask yourself: are all colors in this picture equally important for sharpening purposes, or is one more critical than others?

If there *is* a critical color, it's practically sure to be red or green. When blues are important, they're almost always skies or water, which are soft-looking by nature, not receptive to sharpening. Ditto purples, which are likely to be grapes, eggplants, or flowers. All of these objects should be smooth.

We occasionally find important yellow objects in an image, and every now and then one that's cyan. But these colors never dominate an image the way that green dominates Figures 6.1 and 6.3 and red dominates Figure 6.2. And once in a cyan moon we encounter clothing in one of these oddball colors, like the purple blouse of Figure 2.17.

Despite seeing three such images in a row, the fact is that most pictures aren't dominated by one color. The previous two chapters are a reasonable sample. They contain a dozen photos. The woman in Figure 5.7A and the image of Bryce Canyon in Figure 4.13 are both dominated by red. The shot of Yellowstone National Park in Figure 4.11 is dominated by blue but is the sort of moody image that doesn't require conventional sharpening. The other nine images are more typical, having no clear boss color.

Because these nine are typical, we would sharpen them in the typical way, using the entire image as the target if we are in RGB or CMYK. If we're in LAB, we always sharpen the L channel only, because the A and B just contain color information, no detail.

Unless you're never planning to leave RGB at all, it's best to avoid sharpening there. Both other alternatives have slight technical advantages in certain cases. Not enough, in my view, to warrant moving out of RGB if you have no other reason to do so. In around half of the images I've tested, I see no difference at all, and in the others the differences are small enough that if you can make use of them, you probably don't need me to tell you what sorts of images they will show up in.

But it would be fair to say that the best technical overall sharpen is in the L, and CMYK is not far behind. So, if the ultimate destination of the file is CMYK, you shouldn't be considering RGB sharpening, not that the world will end if you do.

Disasters like Figure 6.2B occur not because people sharpen in RGB but because they don't realize they shouldn't be sharpening certain channels at all.

If we are headed for CMYK anyway, and if the image has only one important color, we should forget about RGB and LAB altogether.

A face is red. The two channels that create red are magenta and yellow. Those channels are much darker than the other two, so they are rich in detail—detail like wrinkles, pores, scars, blemishes, and hairs.

In addition to accentuating these features, sharpening overall also caused the illusion that the woman's face was sprayed with fine droplets of white paint. The pinkness of the skin is actually breaking up, because without magenta and yellow, there is no red. The artifacts of sharpening have created areas where the two channels are too light for the color to be believable.

The solution may have suggested itself in the last chapter. Refer back to Figure 5.7H. That's what a person's face looks like in the black channel. And that's why Figure 6.2C, which sharpens only the black and not the CMY, doesn't damage the skin. There isn't any skin in that channel that *could* be damaged.

This philosophy doesn't stop with the black. The key color in Figure 6.3A is green, which is constructed of yellow and cyan. But the green areas are separated into tiny leaves, not an unbroken stretch of color like a face. So we don't get a snowy appearance by sharpening overall, but I still don't recommend it. Figure 6.3B is sharpened in the L of LAB, while Figure 6.3C hits not just the black but the magenta. The dominating yellow and cyan are never touched, so the leaves cannot get much lighter than they were originally.

In spite of these more realistic, less obviously sharpened leaves, Figure 6.3C seems to show more detail than Figure 6.3B does, because I was able to use heavier sharpening settings, a major advantage of using weak channels. Sharpen the cyan and yellow, and color and/or darkness can change. Sharpen the magenta and black as hard as you like, and the leaves can never become any color other than green.

The analogous move with red objects is to sharpen both the black and the cyan. That's what I would recommend with the Bryce Canyon shot of Figure 4.13. Faces, however, are a category unlike any other in imaging, in that we actually would like to suppress detail in favor of a smoother appearance, particularly if the subject is a young person or an adult female. Cyan carries some facial detail and is therefore dangerous. Black does not. It does contain hair, eyes, eyelids, and eyelashes, all things that we are very interested in sharpening.

In fact, sharpening the black only is an effective conservative approach with almost any image. You can use big settings with little risk of disaster.

Before moving on, some reminders and other housekeeping matters.

When I said that red is constructed of magenta and yellow, and green of yellow and cyan, did you agree instantaneously? If not, now might be a good time to go back and review Chapter 1. Visualizing how the channels look and interact is going to be more and more critical in subsequent chapters.

That we have gotten a quarter of the way through a sharpening chapter without seeing *how* to sharpen an image is an extension of the philosophy of discussing channel structure in Chapter 1 before putting it to use in blending. Sharpening is a topic that could easily fill an entire book. If you want to get good at it, you need the where and why stuff before getting into the how.

Because there are so many sharpening options, some rather esoteric, our study of it is split in two sections. This chapter gets us started with the basic command. In Chapters 17 and 18, we'll look at fancier options and discuss USM in conjunction with its close relative, the Image: Adjustments> Shadow/Highlight command. This is why I did not discuss how to sharpen Figures 6.2A and 6.3A if you do not wish to enter CMYK. It's doable, but would involve introduction of some topics that are best put off.

Figure 6.3 *Images dominated by a single color should be sharpened in the weak CMYK channels. Top, the original. Bottom left, sharpened in the L of LAB. Bottom right, sharpened in the magenta and black of CMYK.*

- Remember that sharpening is subjective, and I'm doing a lot of it to make sure you can see the impact. If you think that Figures 6.2C and 6.3C are oversharpened, then you can always lower the setting, or put them on a layer and lower the opacity. By contrast, Figures 6.2B and 6.3B have inherent defects that lowering opacity will help but not cure.

It would be reasonable to inquire at this point why photographers can't just get images in focus in the first place, so that we wouldn't have to unsharp mask them.

The brief answer is that they can't. The long answer involves throwing so many sharpening rocks at the gull of Figure 6.4 that you may accuse me of being the kind of guy who leaves no tern unstoned.

Why?

We have to sharpen for much the same reason that we have to color-correct: humans and cameras don't see things the same way. A flying bird does not blur into the sky, at least not for us. They are completely distinct entities: the bird ends and the sky begins with inconceivable suddenness.

The camera can't record this, for three

Tip: Blurring the Black

Sharpening the black can be quite effective. So can the reverse process. One of the most common give-aways of poor technique comes when a retoucher, in an attempt to accentuate the foreground object, selects and blurs the background.

This usually results in the appearance that the foreground object has been cut out of the picture and pasted back in, yet the desire to occasionally defocus the background is so strong that Photoshop now includes a Lens Blur filter to assist in doing it.

If you've ever tried and been dissatisfied with that or another technique, try this one: take the file into CMYK and blur the black only. That's a pure play on focus without smooshing all the colors together the way that other options do.

reasons. First, we see in three dimensions. We perceive the sky as being several miles above the gull, but the camera captures a flat image in which both are on the same plane.

Second, a digital file consists of pixels, which are not infinitely small. In the enlarged half of Figure 6.4 we can already see them. They are too clunky to make a believable edge. And even if they were infinitely small, we'd still be stuck, because whatever our output method is, it probably can't address a space nearly as small as the pixels we currently use. For example, a rectangular space of around .0003 square centimeters is reserved for each halftone dot printed in this book. That sounds very small, and indeed it is small enough that we can't see the dots easily without magnification, but it's three or four times larger than a pixel.

And third, we see whatever we feel like seeing. If the bird doesn't have sharp edges, our imagination provides them. Cameras do not take quite such a creative view of reality.

So, something needs to be done to emphasize edges, transitions. The solution is to put halos around the edges. Painters have been doing it for centuries. And it's quite standard in the photographic studio. The model in Figure 6.2 wears eyeliner, a clear use of edge enhancement before we ever get into Photoshop, forgetting about the unsharp maskara that we add afterward. Lip pencils and eyeshadow serve the same purpose. The fact that women wear these cosmetics even when not posing for glamour shots is a strong indication that even if our capture and printing process were absolutely perfect, we'd probably need USM anyway.

How?

Finally, it's time to get down to specifics. To sharpen an image, we first, if we're not planning to do it overall, select our target channels. Then, Filter: Sharpen>Unsharp Mask. Up pops the dialog of Figure 6.5. We throw

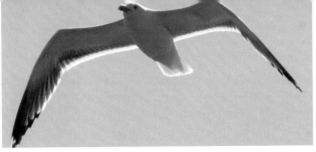

Figure 6.4 *Sharpening is needed because photographs do not portray edges with as much definition as the viewer expects to see. The original, left, is not obviously out of focus, but in the enlarged version at right, the edges seem soft.*

in some random numbers because we don't know what they mean yet, and click OK.

Photoshop now, without telling us anything about it, produces for its own nefarious purposes a blurred version of the image. It compares it to the original, exaggerates any differences it may find between the two, trashes the blurred version, and there you have it.

After explanations like that, my wife is fond of saying that if you ask a silly question, you get a silly answer. I don't dare argue with *her*, but a student once made the same remark, which led to a bet that I could sharpen an image to publication quality using no filter other than Gaussian Blur.

The student lost. The image I did it with is Figure 6.1B. It took only 23 steps (which are listed in the folder for this chapter on the CD, if you care), and around five times as long as it would with the USM filter; and I could have gotten a better result by sharpening the magenta and black only, as in Figure 6.3B, and with all that it can't be denied that the image got sharper in a believable way.

With a new image and a couple of steps omitted, we can get an idea of how this seemingly ridiculous concept gets the job done. Figure 6.4 arrives in sRGB. To it, I applied Filter: Blur>Gaussian Blur, Radius 1.0 pixels. That produced Figure 6.6B.

Figures 6.6A and 6.6C, after some fancy blending and contrast-boosting commands, show the result of comparing Figures 6.4 and 6.6B. Figure 6.6A shows the area in which the original image is darker than the blurred version. Figure 6.6C shows the lighter areas—and the bird seems to have changed shape.

Work out for yourself why this is happening. The bird's top half is darker than the sky, but most of the bottom, especially the tail feathers, is lighter. The blurred version wipes out some of these distinctions in favor of areas that are neither particularly light nor dark.

Therefore, the tops of the wings are darker in the original than in the blurred version, but lighter in the area just above. So, there is a sharp line in Figure 6.6A just inside the tops of the wings, and one in Figure 6.6C just outside. In the white tail feathers, the opposite occurs. The original is *lighter* than the blurred version there, but darker in the surrounding sky. The blur, after all, darkened the sky above the bird but lightened it below. So this time, the line is on the inside edge in Figure 6.6C and on the outside in Figure 6.6A.

Now that we've found the differences between the original and the blurred version, we proceed to exaggerate them. The lines in Figure 6.6A show where the original already is darker, and since this difference must be exaggerated, the original must be darkened more. The lines in Figure 6.6C show lighter areas. In these areas the original must get lighter still.

In short, we will in effect be stamping Figure 6.6A into the original, creating dark halos inside the top of the wings and outside the white tail feathers. Then, we'll use the lines in Figure 6.6C to create the lighter halos. This procedure certainly will emphasize the transition areas.

In many areas of the world, copies of Photoshop are unavailable in the local language, so users have to cope with English.

They often can't figure out why the term *unsharp* is used to describe how to sharpen. If you've ever wondered about it yourself, Figure 6.6B is an unsharp version of the original. The unsharp version generates the masks that create the sharpening effect.

USM by the Numbers

Figure 6.7A shows what happens when we forget about this cockamamie blurred version and apply the settings of Figure 6.5 directly to the original. You should be able to see how the lines of Figures 6.6A and 6.6C have translated into light and dark halos.

The Amount setting is the maximum 500%. If we wish to use the same haloing in a more subdued manner, we reduce it. Figure 6.7B has an Amount of 200% but otherwise the same two settings as Figure 6.7A.

The enlarged version of Figure 6.7A shows much more blue noise in the bird's belly than was in the original image. This noise developed, or rather was aggravated, when it was eliminated.

Read that last sentence again. It appears to make the same quantity of sense as the value found in Figure 6.5 next to the setting we're about to discuss. It is nevertheless true. The original, Figure 6.4, had modest noise. Blurring it in Figure 6.6B wiped that noise out. The comparison between original and blurred version therefore found, and enhanced, differences—small ones, in comparison to the ones at the edges. But fine noise is visible in Figures 6.6A and 6.6C, and that noise was emphasized in the sharpened version of Figure 6.7A.

If the USM filter didn't

exist and we had to try to establish our halos by blending Figures 6.6A and/or 6.6C into the original, we wouldn't have to worry. With each of the two, we'd open the Curves dialog and slide the lower left (highlight) point over to the right. That would be the end of the noise, which is light, but it would preserve the much darker halos that outline bird, eyes, and beak.

The Threshold setting of the USM filter does the same thing. A Threshold of 0 means the difference masks are used as is, noise and all. Higher numbers gradually exclude small differences, which often are noise. Figure 6.7C returns to 500% Amount, but with a 10 Threshold. It's approximately as sharp as Figure 6.7A, without the noisome noise.

The other question in the USM dialog is, how blurry is the blurred version used for comparison? The answer affects the width, but not the intensity, of the sharpening halos.

I created Figure 6.6B with a Gaussian Blur of Radius 1.0 pixels. This blur created areas where bird and sky met and became one. Those areas, neither bird nor sky, were very different than they were in the original, resulting in the clearly defined edges of Figures 6.6A and 6.6C.

Suppose that I had used a higher Radius, say 3.0, for the blur. The area that is neither bird nor sky would extend farther into both. The line of difference between original and blurred version would become wider.

The USM filter is based on a Gaussian Blur. The Radii of the two commands operate identically. Figures 6.7D, 6.7E, and 6.7F use the same Amount and Threshold settings as Figures 6.7A, 6.7B, and

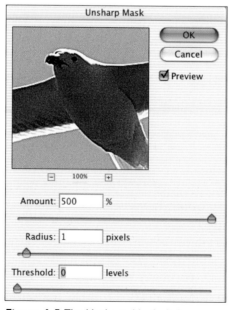

Figure 6.5 *The Unsharp Mask dialog.*

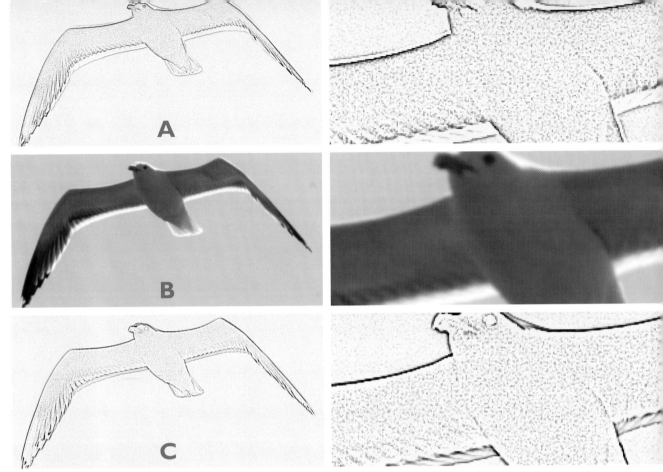

Figure 6.6 *The middle version, based on Figure 6.4, has been Gaussian Blurred at a Radius of 1.0 pixel. The top and bottom versions compare the before and after images. At top, with contrast greatly enhanced, are the areas in which Figure 6.4 is darker than the blurred version here. Bottom, the areas in which it is lighter.*

6.7C, but Radius has been increased to 3.0. The halos have widened to such an extent that we probably wouldn't accept these images. Sharpening should be hard to detect; we don't want the viewer to be conscious of the halos. The dark lines at the top and bottom of the gull in Figure 6.7F, which is the best of the three, are still too prominent in my view.

In Which Haloing Is Taken to the Max

Having discovered that a 3.0 Radius is too much, it would seem like the last thing we need is an even higher setting. Going *much* higher, however, opens new opportunities.

This image clearly needs a Threshold of around 10, so we'll use that from now on. Figure 6.7G is at 500% Amount and the wildly extravagant 15.0 Radius, resulting in half a mile of white space between gull and sky.

The key to sharpening is to hide the halo. In Figure 6.7C we hid very light and dark halos by making them narrow. When halos are extremely wide, we can do the opposite: they can be hidden by drastically lessening their intensity.

In Figure 6.7H, Amount has been reduced to 50% from 500%. The horrific 15-Radius haloing of Figure 6.7G is now invisible to all but the most suspicious viewer.

You should compare this version to the original, Figure 6.4. The impact of these wide, subdued halos is subtle, but it's there. I prefer this unusually sharpened version. I don't prefer it to Figure 6.7C, however. The effects are so different that what's happening in Figure 6.7H almost can't be called sharpening at all. It's not quite as effective as the normal low-Radius sharpening in this particular image, but it might be in other contexts.

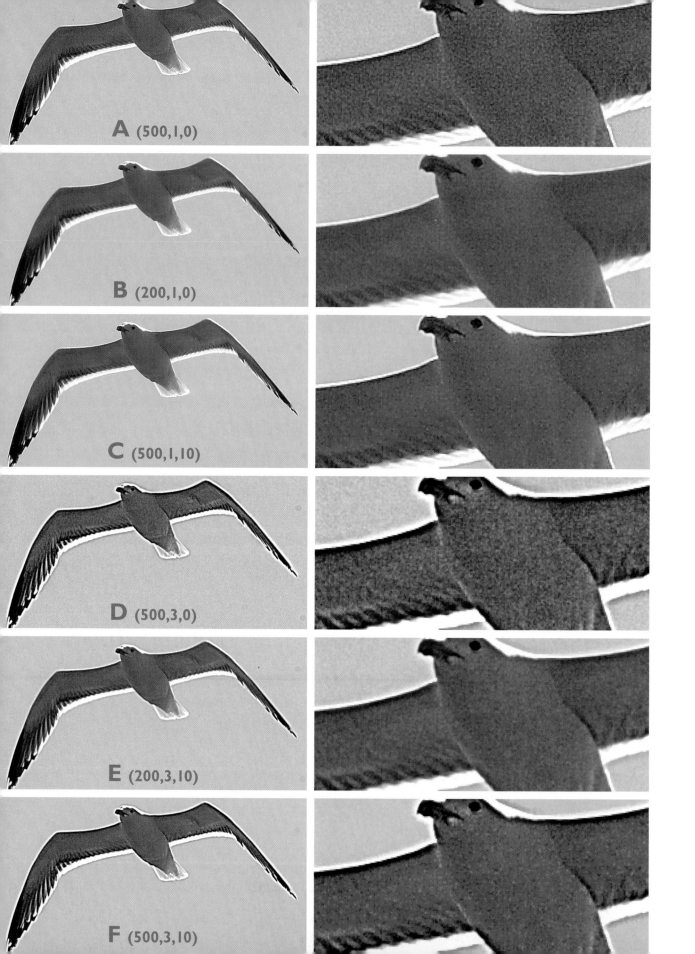

A (500,1,0)

B (200,1,0)

C (500,1,10)

D (500,3,0)

E (200,3,10)

F (500,3,10)

Before going there, though, let's look at the impact of an ultra-high Radius of 100.0 in Figure 6.7J. In a version that took a Gaussian Blur of 100.0 pixels on the chin, we wouldn't be able to see a bird at all. Hence, there's no haloing, but rather a general darkening of the bird and a wipeout of the surrounding sky. The result looks totally useless to the casual student and totally tempting to the Photoshop expert, who visualizes collages, selections, and layer masks where others see whites and blacks. But that can wait until Chapter 19.

Finalizing the Numbers

Now that we know how the numbers interrelate, we can start talking about right and wrong. Some of this is highly personal. I'm strongly of the view that most people don't sharpen their images enough (see box, page 139). There are, however, certain ideas that everyone would accept.

First, let's agree that the six versions from Figures 6.7A to 6.7F constitute a single group, and that Figures 6.7G, 6.7H, and 6.7J represent a radical alternative. The first group is traditional, similar but not identical to the sharpening that might have been gotten off drum scanners 15 years ago, or from process separation cameras 15 years before that. I call this *conventional* sharpening; the second group is *hiraloam,* for High Radius, Low Amount. Most images sharpen better conventionally; a smaller percentage takes to hiraloam the way seagulls take to fish. So the first decision is which general method to use.

Figure 6.7 *The impact of the changes in the USM settings. Opposite: version A is sharpened at 500% Amount, 1.0 Radius, 0 Threshold. B reduces Amount to 200%. C returns to 500% with a Threshold of 10. D, E, and F repeat A, B, and C except that Radius is set to 3.0. This page: high Radius sharpening. G uses values of 500%, 15.0, 10. H reduces Amount to 50%, and J uses values of 500%, 100.0, 10.*

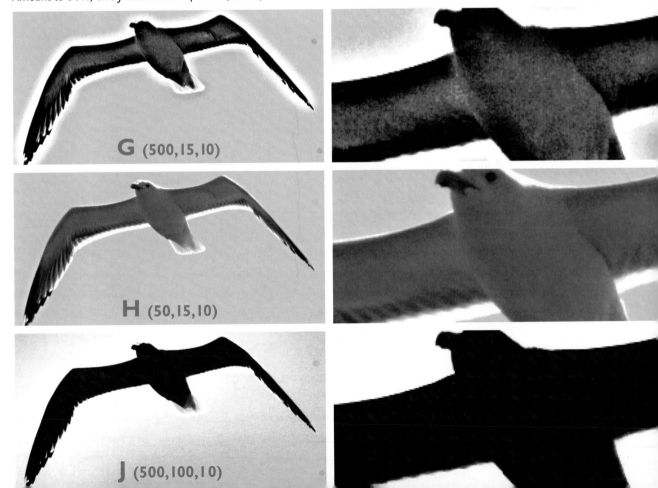

G (500,15,10)

H (50,15,10)

J (500,100,10)

We'll get back to that question later. Conventional appears to work better on this image, so let's stick with that for the moment.

It would be hard to construct a case for Figure 6.7A over 6.7C. Nobody likes random noise. This image requires a Threshold. Similarly, you could argue that the halos should be thicker than they are in Figure 6.7C, but it's tough to imagine that you would want to go as far as the 3.0 Radius of Figure 6.7F. As for Amount, that's up to you.

Different people are most likely to see eye to eye about Threshold, then about Radius, and are least likely to agree about Amount. That's the order I would suggest choosing the settings in.

Start the search by opening the image and View: Actual Pixels (also known as 100% magnification) so that your impression will not be warped by a Photoshop calculation that forces the picture to fit a strange monitor resolution. Don't go larger except for diagnostic purposes, because at a higher magnification, defects will show that are too small to appear on output. If you must go smaller, go to 50% magnification, which is more reliable than either 66.7% or 33.3%.

Beta reader André Lopes has a different perspective. He writes, "Most modern monitors have a resolution about 100 pixels per inch, more than the traditional 72 ppi but lower than the usual printing resolutions (normally 200 to 300 ppi in books and magazines). So, when we use 100% magnification in Photoshop, we see an image at least twice as big as the final printed version—and the halos become much more visible than they will really be.

"Instead of using a lower magnification, I usually recommend evaluating USM looking to the monitor from a greater distance. For example: we normally read a magazine or a book holding it about 16 inches away from our eyes. If the image on the monitor is three times larger, we look at it from a distance three times farther—about 50 inches in this case."

Whichever way you choose, commence hostilities by putting in values that are overkill for almost any image: 500% Amount, 5.0 Radius, 0 Threshold. Before reducing them, remind yourself that you are a tainted observer. Every year my doctor diagnoses herself with at least eight fatal diseases, because whenever a symptom shows up that might conceivably be associated with any of them, she imagines she has contracted it. Me, since I don't realize that a headache after obliterating most of a bottle of rum may indicate a brain tumor, I live a peaceful and worry-free life.

The same effect occurs here. You and I know what sharpening halos look like. Our clients generally don't. Pictures that look obviously sharpened to us don't to them.

Also, images look softer on output than they do on screen. Look again at Figure 6.6A. I don't defend its noisiness, but the correctly sized version is not all that terrible. Would you have predicted such a result from seeing all the noise in the enlarged version, or on a monitor?

If you are in a properly aggressive state of mind, you may now proceed to find the correct Threshold. At these extreme settings, it should be clear where you're sharpening noise and other detritus, if at all. The grainier the image, the higher the Threshold has to be. Sports photography probably needs at least a 15. Studio photography of something that doesn't move usually can get by with 0 or 1.

In their eternal search for mathematical verities, calibrationists have been known to suggest that the Radius should depend on the resolution of the scan. This is like saying that the larger a suitcase is, the heavier it will be. There is a kernel of truth there, but the fact is that the contents of the suitcase have a considerable impact, and that a small suitcase filled with lead weighs more than a

How Much Is Too Much? Readers, Author Duke It Out

Certain people appear to consider oversharpening an image as falling somewhere between arson and criminally negligent homicide on the scale of felonies. The phobia is particularly prevalent among professional photographers.

In deciding whether you've gone too far, trusting your instincts can be dangerous. You're a biased observer, because you know how sharpening works and have sensitized yourself to its artifacts. But you have to put yourself in the position of someone who doesn't realize that it's all a digital fraud. You detect the halos in Figure 6.7H because you've seen them in more obvious form right above. Would a casual observer know that Figure 6.7C has sharpening artifacts without having seen the difference masks of Figure 6.6?

Taste in sharpening is quite personal, but there is one reliable test. Whenever a photographer accuses me of oversharpening, I always ask whether any clients have ever rejected any of his images for being too sharp. The response is always an indignant "Certainly not"—almost as decisive as the "Yes" when asked whether they ever reject images as too soft.

Clients complain, sometimes because of an authentic difference of opinion and sometimes because we did poor work, but even if these were nonfactors, they would complain from time to time anyway, because they want to be a part of the creative process. Occasional complaints are inevitable, but if a professional finds that they follow a pattern, corrective action is needed. In 2005, I saw the following interesting online quote from the proprietor of a lab that serves photographers.

"Sharpening is actually a factor in returned prints, the current topic that consumes me. I know photographers live in fear of oversharpening and halos, but I must say that in nearly a million prints shipped, I don't have a record of any being returned for oversharpening (although I've been expecting them in the case of people with shiny skin and on-board flash). In critical portraits, my experience is you can go soft on the sharpening of the skin but the customer expects the eyes and lips to be sharp…We've received roughly 1,000 returned prints for too little sharpening and the customer always concludes our printers aren't good. That means another 9,000

prints were disappointing in terms of sharpness, but the customer didn't complain."

Worrying about oversharpening in a world that doesn't like soft images is like worrying about using LAB to boost colors in a world that hates drabness. If nobody ever complains that your colors are too loud and garish, they aren't loud and garish enough. If nobody ever says that your images are oversharpened, you need bigger numbers in the USM dialog.

The above remarks were unpopular with some of the beta readers. André Dumas, who is a photographer, termed it "a gross simplification of the subject."

He said, "If we are in fact talking about oversharpening, the question should be: has any client ever rejected an image because he didn't like the way it looked? The answer is Yes! And could it be that the image has been sharpened too much and what the client saw was something that he could not quite define but his reaction was: 'I don't know why…but I just don't like it'? Again the answer is Yes!

"Fear of oversharpening is not a phobia; it is a valid concern that good photographers have for very good reasons. My motto, when in doubt undersharpen, you will never kick yourself for it, but oversharpening is gross and will put you to shame."

Beta reader André Lopes, who is a production consultant, not a photographer, adds, "Another point to consider here, especially for retouchers with little experience in using USM: undersharpened images look slightly out of focus, and clients normally blame it on the photographer. Oversharpened images are an undoubted error in retouching and clients will blame it on you."

To the foregoing sentiments, I say fiddle-dee-dee. We are, of course, infinitely tasteful ourselves, but few professionals have gotten rich by assuming that unknown clients are similarly sophisticated. If the clients are consistently dissatisfied, I say move in a different direction.

The point about beginning retouchers is well taken. Experienced retouchers, like me, have had so much practice blaming photographers for our own foulups that we have little doubt we can fob it off again.

larger one filled with clothes. And so it is with images, even if we set aside the obvious point that certain photographs have more grain than others of the same size, and thus cannot be sharpened as much.

Imagine that Figure 6.2 was a woman shown from the waist up, rather than in a tight closeup of the face. One need not be Einstein to realize that this would present an entirely different sharpening problem, because the size of the detailing would not match, even if the two images themselves were of identical resolution.

Before wheeling out a big Radius, we have to be sure that there is nothing in what we are sharpening that has subtle detail, of which big Radii are the enemy.

Small and subtle are not the same thing. An eyelash is small, but not subtle. The variations in the leaves of Figure 6.3 are subtle, but they are not small.

The character of the image, therefore, plays a much bigger role in determining the best Radius than resolution does. Ask yourself, is there fine detail or not?

A person's hair or eyelashes, a wine bottle, the bubbles in a glass of soda: these things want a wide Radius. The bark of a tree, the skin of a fruit, a field of grass, fabric, the grain in wooden objects, all have subtle detail that a large Radius would kill.

Where both kinds of detail appear, we are forced to go with the least common denominator and choose a narrow Radius. Or we need to find a channel that does not have subtle detail. In a face, that's the black.

So, with the woman of Figure 6.2, I was able to use a Radius of 4.0 in the black channel, because as a practical matter, the black contains only the eye area and the hair. And the Amount? 500%, what else. In spite of the horrific oversharpening of Figure 6.2B, Figure 6.2C has more dramatic eyes. If you hit the ball accurately enough, it doesn't matter how hard you hit it.

And as for Amount, as the ancient Romans remarked, *de gustibus non est disputandum*, which means, if you think 500% was too much, just put in whatever number you like, click OK, and get on with your life.

Shapen, Not Blurred

Back to the question of when to use hiraloam in preference to—or as an adjunct to—conventional. The answer is straightforward: if you see a lot of clearly defined edges, think conventional. If not, think hiraloam.

Two sea pictures illustrate. In each, the original is at left, a conventional sharpen at center, and a hiraloam version at right.

To recapitulate: conventional USM typically employs Radii of .8 to 2.5. Amount settings vary, but values as high as the maximum, 500%, are by no means unheard of.

The hiraloam alternative is a much higher Radius—say 10 to 25. Such an enormous blur will cause devastation unless accompanied by a drastic reduction in Amount—say, to 50% or, rarely, 100%. The result is almost a shaping, not a sharpening. The effect can be pleasing—sometimes. It isn't in Figure 6.8C. All detail in the light areas of the boats has been sunk by a tsunami of lightening. The masts have been improved somewhat, but still, one could easily argue that Figure 6.8A, the original, is better.

The conventional sharpening, Figure 6.8B, has no such problem. It has merrily found, and emphasized, the 25 billion or so edges that litter this image, causing the desired appearance of better focus.

Figure 6.8D is a different story. There's no highlight to blow out, no shadow to plug, and nothing that looks like it needs to have a crisp edge. So, none of the factors that caused hiraloam to make a hash of Figure 6.8C are present. Figure 6.8E, the conventional sharpen, makes the water look grainier, but I like Figure 6.8F better, because it has added shape: the rolling shadows in the waves are darker, the reflections in the water lighter, all without loss of detail.

If we tried this shaping method on the palm leaf picture of Figure 6.1, it would lose to conventional again, but not as badly as in Figure 6.8C: the leaves would get lighter and there would be a pleasing darkening of the background surrounding them, but there wouldn't be any of the gain in snap in the leaves themselves.

That's usually how it is. Images where shape-sharpening is unequivocally better are rare, but they happen. Going back to the dozen images used in the last two chapters, only one is a clear case where hiraloam would be better—the Yellowstone sunset of Figure 4.11A.

Sharpening fanatics, however, look for the best of both worlds. Which method is better for the flags of Figure 6.9A?

To answer, we look for hard edges, which are good for conventional, and large areas of similar color, which are good for hiraloam. This image has a little of both. Where clouds meet sky, the edge is indistinct, and conventional sharpening has nothing to offer. Hiraloam is apt to make the

Figure 6.8 *Above center, conventional sharpening works well in emphasizing well-defined edges. But below center, with no real edges apparent, it simply makes the water look grainy. The right-hand versions use hiraloam sharpening; the originals are at left.*

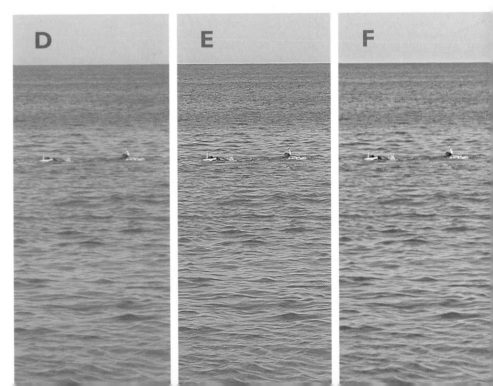

sky darker overall, which is good. But where whites meet reds in the Canadian flag (and similarly in all other flags), the transition is a crisp and immediate one. That calls for conventional USM. Yet the three nearest flags have relatively large blocks of similar color. To get a believable ripple, hiraloam would be better.

Figure 6.9B is conventional USM, done in RGB at settings of 450%, 1.0, 12. The hiraloam competition is in Figure 6.9C, at 50%, 20.0, 12. Both add considerable pop to the original, but in very different ways. Choosing between the two is like choosing between good color and good contrast, or between the spaghetti and the sauce. Successful sharpeners are swinish. We want both.

If you want to combine the two methods, the conventional USM has to come first, as hiraloam may bring out noise just enough for low-radius sharpening to notice it. Also, we need slightly lower settings for each than if they were applied by themselves, as to some extent the two reinforce one another. The result should be something like Figure 6.9D, which combines the crisper flags of Figure 6.9B with the better sky of Figure 6.9C.

Sharpening can be carried to extremes. With an infinite amount of time, you can test a cascade. You might try an *ultra*-high Radius sharpen, say a 100.0 Radius coupled with a

Beware of Presharpening

Applying USM to an image that somebody else has already tried to sharpen can be a frustrating experience. Artifacts of the first sharpening may be pronounced enough that they can't be excluded even with a high Threshold.

The somebody else who does this is nowadays quite likely to be a machine. If you are acquiring images through a camera manufacturer's module or through Camera Raw, light sharpening may be being applied by default. Check for it, and turn it off!

20% Amount, and then do hiraloam and then do conventional. It works sometimes. However, being aware of blending possibilities provides a bigger bang for the buck.

So Much for Newton's Third Law

The introduction of blending modes comes at a fortuitous time. The end of our discussion of the seagull of Figure 6.7 was really the end of the first part of this book. Further adventures lie ahead. They're important, but what got us up to this point is indispensable.

Let's jump ahead, and talk about how we will correct the original shown in Figure 21.1A. Inasmuch as the book has but 20 chapters, it is problematic to steal a glance at something in the 21st, but discuss it we must. How do we propose to correct an image we've never seen of an unknown subject that was shot when we were not present?

I can answer this.

We will try to make it look more like what a human would have seen if the human was in the position the camera was. We will seek out the lightest and darkest significant points and set them to the most extreme values that our process can hold. We will place the most important parts of the image in steep parts of the curve; we will consider whether RGB, CMYK, or LAB is the place to do the work; and we will make an intelligent decision about sharpening.

These rules will be as true for Figure 21.1A as for any other image we have worked on or ever will. If we don't follow them, we can't possibly produce professional work. People who do follow them will beat us every time.

From now on, we'll be looking at methods that work some of the time, but not always. Many of them involve blending, a topic that

Figure 6.9 (opposite) Different styles of sharpening the original, top. Second from top, a conventional sharpen with a 1.0 Radius. Third from top, an alternate version with a Radius of 20.0 and a low Amount of 50%. Bottom, a version combining the middle two.

will take us through the next several chapters. Here's a first foray into it.

For every action, said Newton, there is an equal and opposite reaction. While this is good physics, it's bad unsharp masking.

USM compares the original to a blurred copy of itself. Those parts where the original is darker (see Figure 6.6A) are made darker still. Areas where the original is lighter (Figure 6.6C) are lightened more. That equal and opposite reaction needs to be squashed.

In Figure 6.9B, conventional sharpening placed a dark halo in the red areas of the Canadian flag and a light one in the adjoining sky. The two are equally evil. Black lines in a red flag look bad, and so do white ones in a blue sky.

To its left, though, the flag of the province of Ontario sings a different song. Its dark blue can swallow a black line a lot easier than the sky can quaff a white one.

It turns out that there are many such cases, probably even the majority of images, where dark halos are more palatable than light ones. It happens practically any time that a

relatively dark object butts a medium-dark one. The concept is so vital to image quality that by 1986, every commercial drum scanner was able to use its massive (for those days) 16K of RAM to control the two kinds of halos on the fly, without going through the shenanigans that Photoshop requires of us two decades later.

The barrel cactus of Figure 6.10A is an example. We can forget about hiraloam; this image is full of well-defined edges, particularly at the business end of those spines, you may take it from someone who once fell into such a cactus in an effort to evade a conversation with a rattlesnake.

Dark halos around these spines are a good thing—they make them stand out. Light halos on the inside are bad, as they wipe out the characteristic dark red.

I offer Figure 6.10B, which required several steps, as a reasonable response. Figures 6.10C, 6.10D, and 6.10E are examples of things to avoid.

Disk space and RAM permitting, it's a good idea to make subjective edits like USM on a separate layer. You can always decide later that you've gone too far, and reduce the layer's opacity. I, in fact, generally go too far *deliberately*, reasoning that I can always reduce the opacity but I can't increase it beyond 100% if I decide that it isn't sharpened enough. We don't ever want to be in the position of having to sharpen conventionally twice, because sharpening an artifact can be deadly.

For the following procedure, the extra layer is not a recommendation but a requirement.

● Layer: Duplicate Layer.
● Give the new layer a stiff jolt of conventional USM. Hiraloam is irrelevant because light hiraloam halos are not usually objectionable, but light conventional ones often are.

Stumbling Blocks: Too Much, Too Soon

•When to sharpen. Generally, one saves sharpening for last, but this rule isn't firm. The reason to avoid sharpening early is that a later curve may exaggerate the halos too much. However, if you think the image needs just minor tweaks, it won't hurt to sharpen beforehand.

•Doesn't sharpening change the highlight/shadow values? Halos can indeed be lighter than normal highlights and/or darker than normal shadows. This means nothing. We choose highlights and shadows not because they are literally the lightest and darkest points of the image but because they are the lightest and darkest *significant* points. A sharpening halo can't be considered significant detail.

•Luminosity blues. Running a couple of chapters ahead, several readers have tried to sharpen a single channel and then use Edit: Fade>Luminosity to avoid color shifts. This is a sensible idea that doesn't happen to work. Instead, sharpen the channel(s) on a new layer set to Luminosity.

For this image I chose robust values of 450%, 1.2, 2. This produced Figure 6.10C, with the predicted dark halos around the spines and deterioration of the color and detail inside them.

The Layers palette has a mode indication to the left of the opacity setting. The default setting is Normal, which means that we see the top layer, not the bottom. The bad news is that there are 22 other possible settings as of Photoshop CS2; the good news is that a dozen of them will be referred to in this book as frequently as *Principia Mathematica,* which is to say, not at all.

Two of the useful ones are Darken and its sister Lighten. They are misnamed; Darken should really be called Don't Lighten. It works exactly as Normal does, except that no pixel is allowed to get lighter. So,

- Set the mode of the top layer to Darken. The only difference between the two layers is the sharpening halos. The dark halos, being darker than the bottom layer, are preserved, but you may kiss the light halos good-bye, inasmuch as the bottom layer cannot be made lighter anywhere.

We are now at Figure 6.10E. The light halos are completely gone, so the image looks unnaturally dark.

- With the top (Darken mode) layer still active, make another duplicate layer. The top two layers are now identical sharpened versions, both set to Darken mode. The overall appearance of the image is unchanged.

- Change mode of the top layer from Darken to Lighten (in this instance, changing to Normal would produce an identical result). Doing so doesn't lighten the dark halos, which are the same on the top two layers. It does restore the light halos that were disallowed in the middle layer by Darken mode. Overall appearance has now reverted to that of Figure 6.10C.

- Change opacity of the top (Lighten mode) layer to 50%.

Lightening and darkening have now been separated onto two independently controllable layers. I left Figure 6.10B as is, but could have tweaked the opacity of both sharpening layers further. Another possibility is to use not just different opacities but different sharpenings on the lightening and darkening layers. If the lightening half of the sharpening needs (in effect) a lower Amount, it probably could use a lower Radius as well.

Figure 6.10D is another advertisement for keeping channel structure in mind. It was prepared exactly as above, except all work was done in RGB, whereas Figure 6.10B was converted to CMYK before sharpening. The RGB version isn't bad, but the CMYK seems deeper. Without all this layering, RGB and CMYK sharpening would give almost identical results.

Inkjet and Other Printers

All but the noisiest images improve with judicious sharpening. The form of output, though, determines how much to use. This chapter has assumed offset printing. Here are three common variants, in order of poorest to best print quality.

- **Newspaper printing** is so inherently low-contrast that it calls for a heavier hand with USM, especially in the Amount field. Newsprint doesn't facilitate bright whites or rich blacks, so halos are less visible.

- Treatment of **large-format printers** depends on the use of the product. If it will be viewed at a distance, sharpening can be quite heavy. But if it also may be viewed closely (for example, if it is posted at a bus stop), you may wish to reduce the Radius.

- Inkjet and other **photo-quality printers** produce a softer look than offset, so in principle they can be sharpened more. However, they also support whiter whites and darker blacks. This combination suggests a slightly higher Radius, and lower Amount, than you would use for offset printing.

And, of course, if somebody else will correct the file after you're done with it, you shouldn't sharpen at all.

A Few New Wrinkles

USM offers extraordinary opportunities both to improve believability and to mess up the image beyond recognition. Its dangers can be finessed, provided we are willing to treat unsharp masking as a stiletto, not a shotgun. Photoshop can do everything we need, but sometimes requires kludgy two- or three-step operations that would not be necessary with a better implementation.

To put everything in, as it were, better focus, let's return to the cause of the worst catastrophe of the chapter. As noted back then, facial images, particularly those of women, are a real minefield, because any detail we bring

out in the skin is likely to be something that the model wants us to see about as much as love handles or varicose veins. Figure 6.2B proved the point.

And yet a certain amount of USM is clearly wanted. Check out Figure 6.11 for an illustration of how makeup artists and drum scanner operators think alike.

There are two distinct faces and two distinct styles of sharpening going on in both, the two kinds discussed in this chapter. The whites of the eyes are of course lighter than skin, so they need a dark halo. It would also be nice to get a light halo inside the eye, but the cosmetics industry hasn't yet figured out how to accomplish that; give them time and they'll probably do it with Botox.

Figure 6.10 Opposite top, the original. Opposite bottom, a version sharpened by emphasizing darkening more than lightening halos. Below, C uses the same sharpening settings as version B, but with no reduction of light halos. E is the same image with the light halos removed completely. D is an RGB repetition of the steps done in CMYK to produce version B.

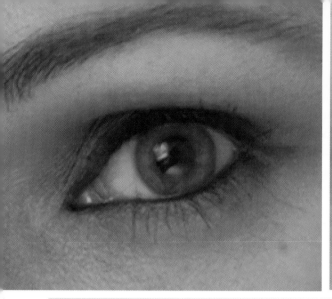

Figure 6.11 *Makeup applied to studio models parallels the use of USM. As the eyes are lighter than their surroundings, dark halos are desirable at their outside edges. The strong, relatively narrow application of eyeliner and mascara emulates conventional sharpening. The subtler, much wider haloing of the eye shadow has the same goals as hiraloam sharpening.*

Other Sharpening Filters

Photoshop features half a dozen sharpening filters other than the workhorse USM. The most interesting by far is Image: Adjustments>Shadow/Highlight, which was introduced in Photoshop CS. Most see this command as a method of opening shadow and/or highlight detail, but, as we will see when we give it serious study in Chapter 18, it has much in common with USM.

The filters Sharpen, Sharpen More, and Sharpen Edges, found along with USM under Filter: Sharpen, are greasy kid stuff. Non-beginners should stay away.

In the same subcategory is Smart Sharpen, introduced in Photoshop CS2. It grafts pieces of the Shadow/Highlight command onto the existing USM filter. The Amount and Radius are there, but the critical Threshold field is inexplicably missing, leaving a filter of limited utility. The real need is for independent control of light and dark halos throughout the range. USM is arguably Photoshop's most important filter, so it's hard to accept that it lacks a major capability that has been standard in the printing industry for 20 years.

Some people also sharpen by creating a new layer, applying Filter: Other>High Pass, and setting the layer to Overlay mode. At typical Radius settings for this filter, the result is substantially the same as with hiraloam USM. In addition to requiring extra steps, High Pass sharpening lacks a Threshold. Also, it's hard to pick the correct Radius because we can't exaggerate the Amount setting as in Figure 6.7G. Therefore, if you use this particular kludge, you should switch to straight hiraloam.

Eyeliner and mascara correspond to conventional sharpening. They accentuate the edge with a pronounced, nearly black, narrow line. Halos created by eye shadow, however, are much subtler and much wider. They accomplish exactly what hiraloam sharpening is supposed to.

In spite of the presharpening makeup, we still use USM on the black to try to accentuate the eyes even further. When working with a man's face, and we'll end this chapter with one, we sharpen even more. A certain amount of roughness is acceptable in a man's face. Also, men do not give us a head start by wearing eyeliner, mascara, and eyeshadow, at least not right now, but again, just give the cosmetics industry time.

This color-corrected image arrives in CMYK. The procedure with faces should be hiraloam first, conventional to the black channel next; discussion of what to do if you can't use CMYK to be deferred.

I reiterate an earlier suggestion that the easiest way to find the proper Threshold and Radius is to work on a wildly exaggerated version. For hiraloam purposes, the final

Amount is likely to be between 25% and 75%, but if we set it to the obscene 500% we'll be able to see a lot more of what's happening. To that, I add a 5.0 Radius. Figures 6.12A–C now test the impacts of Thresholds of 0, 10, and 20.

This man's skin has several natural red spots. It also features whiskers. No Threshold is going to be high enough to exclude them. However, we don't want to accentuate wrinkles and pores, as Figure 6.12A does. Figure 6.12B is a lot more like it. Figure 6.12C makes the whole face look unnaturally soft in comparison to the rest of the overly sharpened image. I judge that the truth should lie somewhere in the middle. Aggressive sharpeners tend to be lucky in print, so I tempted fate with my final choice.

With the Threshold thus locked into 13, Figures 6.12D–F present Radii of 25.0, 50.0, and 75.0. Figure 6.12D gives the man bags under his eyes and not much else. The huge Radius of Figure 6.12F lightens almost the entire face. We're trying to add shape. Figure 6.12E seems just about right. Two settings down, only the easy one to go.

Figure 6.12 *Before sharpening a face, use 500% Amount to evaluate how high to set Threshold (three trial settings at right) and, after finalizing it, Radius (below).*

In finalizing a hiraloam Amount, we key on the areas that may be lightened excessively. Here, we pay special attention to the teeth, the whites of the eyes, the end of the nose, and the top of the forehead. These are all understandably blown out in Figure 6.12E; our job is to make sure the final setting undoes that peccadillo. I chose an Amount of 45% to go with the 50.0 Radius and 13 Threshold. We have reached Figure 6.13B. Note that there appears to be no damage to the skin.

On the other hand, while it's shadowed the eyes attractively, it doesn't add the digital eyeliner and mascara we want. For that, the black is needed, but before getting to it we need a duplicate layer—that is, two copies of this hiraloam version on top of one another.

Ordinarily one works on the top layer; this time, although Photoshop offers other ways to do the same thing, the easiest way is to work on the bottom. So, in the Layers palette, click the bottom layer to activate it, and also click off the eye icon on the top layer so that what you're doing on the bottom won't be hidden by the top layer.

On this bottom layer, activate only the black, with the keyboard shortcut Command–4 or by clicking black in the Channels palette. You may also wish to click the CMYK eye icon to be able to watch the composite picture change during the time that you are only permitted to work on the black.

For this conventional sharpen, I found that a Threshold of 5 was needed to avoid giving the man a serious five-o'clock shadow. I used a 3.0 Radius, which is thick for conventional USM, and 500% Amount. That puts us at Figure 6.13C.

Darkening halos are preferable to lightening ones not just in overall sharpens of cacti, but in maneuvers with the black. You have to like what's happening to the eyes in Figure 6.13C, but the hair is problematic. If you agree with me that the black sharpen has made certain areas weirdly light, then it's time to activate the top layer, on which is a copy of Figure 6.13B. We set it to Darken mode, meaning that all the darkening being done below is retained, while all lightening is disallowed. Then we cut the opacity to 50%, bringing back half of the lightening. That's Figure 6.13D. We might have tried the same maneuver, or some equivalent, back in the last sharpening of hair, Figure 6.2C.

Location, Location, Location

In large images, judicious USM is every bit as potent as the other big weapons in the retoucher's arsenal: appropriate highlights and shadows, good allocation of contrast, and careful use of the black plate.

In smaller images, the various USM options aren't as important. Small images do need sharpening, don't get me wrong, but the exact setting won't make or break quality the

Review and Exercises

✓In Figure 6.3B, the version sharpened in the L of LAB, the leaves did not change color. Can you explain, though, why they are so much *lighter* than the leaves of either of the other versions?

✓What is the normal reason for deciding to sharpen only one or two channels in CMYK, rather than doing an overall sharpen in any convenient colorspace?

✓What is the difference between conventional sharpening with a high Radius setting, and hiraloam sharpening? What are the principal dangers of each?

✓Open a dozen or so random images from your own collection. Make a chart, and for each one say whether you would sharpen conventionally, hiraloam, both, or not at all. For those you would sharpen conventionally, state whether you would do so overall, in single channels, and/or with darkening halos emphasized more than lightening ones. Add up the results and see which method seems most common. Is there anything unusual about the types of images you work with that would suggest that other people might use other methods more frequently?

Figure 6.13 *Above left, the original. Above right, with hiraloam sharpening applied based on the results of Figure 6.12. Below left, after duplicating the hiraloam version to a new layer, heavy conventional USM is added to the black channel only. Below right, the original hiraloam version is applied to the hiraloam/black version at 50% opacity, Darken mode.*

way it will in large ones. Yet, almost all existing documentation illustrates the USM options with images the size of postage stamps.

The thumbnail approach is common because it's expensive to print large color pictures in books and magazines. I have that limitation here, too—note the excruciatingly tight crops to make everything fit—but it's just too hard to see the detail otherwise. Remember, if these images were printing larger, the sharpening defects would be even more evident than what you see here.

Also, unlike most other areas of color correction, here we really have to rely on the monitor to figure out whether our sharpening settings are sufficient or whether we have

gone overboard. That's a tall order, since the phosphors of a monitor don't correspond to the realities of either desktop printers or presses. We have to make the best of it, though, by being resolution-savvy. First of all, we should view the image in Photoshop at 100%. Lower magnifications are unreliable on most monitors; higher ones cause needless ulcers by seeming to display defects that will not be visible in print.

More important, though, if our file departs from the normal rules of resolution, we need to make an adjustment for it in our minds. Normal resolution, experts agree, is between 1.5 and 2 times the screen ruling, times the magnification percentage. This book, for example, uses a 150-line screen, so normal resolution for my digital file is between 200 and 266 pixels per inch. The images here are all around 240, and I am printing them all at 100% magnification. If I were printing one at 75% magnification, that would result in a higher effective resolution ($240/.75 = 320$).

When resolution is higher than normal, or if output is to an inkjet printer, the printed image will appear markedly softer than it will on the monitor. When resolution is lower than normal, the printed image will appear harsher. Be warned! If, as so many people do, you scan at 300 pixels per inch regardless of the screen ruling, your monitor will be lying to you about how effective your USM is.

Above all, in USM, be greedy at all times. Remember the strategy of asking for a raise. There's no fixed limit. The best amount of sharpening is the largest one you can get away with.

The Bottom Line

The Unsharp Mask filter adds apparent focus by introducing artifacts that the viewer interprets as crisper transitions. Careful control of the filter's settings is essential to avoid making the artificiality of the procedure obvious.

The sharpening approach is determined not by size or resolution but by the character of the image. Images dominated by a single color should be sharpened in their light channels rather than overall. Objects that don't have strong edges should be sharpened with a high Radius, low Amount (hiraloam) setting.

Images in this chapter are sharpened aggressively so that you can see what the technique does. In all likelihood you would want to reduce these settings somewhat in real work. When disk space and RAM permit, it's advisable to do the sharpening on a layer so that its intensity can be adjusted after the fact.

Keeping the Color In Black and White

In colored objects, we see variations in hue, saturation, and darkness. When they must be reproduced in black and white, two of these types of contrast are taken away. The key to an effective conversion is to translate them into the third kind before it happens.

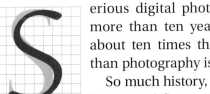

erious digital photography has been around for slightly more than ten years. Serious film-based photography is about ten times that old. Serious artwork in forms other than photography is about ten times older than that.

So much history, so little time to learn from it. We have to fit the workflow to the available time, a concept that was as true for Michelangelo as it is for us today. So, a certain selectivity about when to talk about past practices is necessary.

Nevertheless, permit me to state that the quality of graphic art in modern times is savagely underrated. If you want to rate centuries during the aforementioned millennium of the graphic arts, the 20th, in my estimation, ranks second in terms of creative quality. It is, however, not close at all to being the winner. That honor clearly goes to the 15th, particularly to the Florentine region of Italy. We have some very fine photographers, architects, and other artists today, but they had Michelangelo and Leonardo and Botticelli and Donatello and Ghiberti and Brunelleschi all in the same little town at practically the same time.

Careful examination of what these luminaries were trying to achieve with their images is a good use of your time. Learning how to paint a fresco yourself is not. We can admire what Ansel Adams tried to do with his images, but because we have Photoshop, we don't need to know the gory details of his darkroom practices.

I make this introduction because this is arguably the most important chapter in the book. Don't skip it even if you think it's irrelevant to the sort of work you do. It may seem that way on its face, but, as with the bells in Florence's campanile, there are reverberations everywhere.

Where Is the Life That Late I Led?

Here's the assignment: given a color original, produce the best possible black and white. As color printing has become cheaper and cheaper, fewer and fewer people need to have to do this—at least in theory.

The skill used to be a very big deal. My very first commissioned article about imaging, in 1992, was about conversion to black and white. It basically made my writing career. At that time, Photoshop had made color accessible, but even a skilled operator could not get better color than an equally skilled person running 1980s equipment. Black and white was, as the Florentines say, another pair of sleeves. With channel operations in Photoshop, we could suddenly produce B/Ws that were orders of magnitude better than anybody could get off a drum scanner or a Scitex system.

Admittedly, professionals don't need to produce nearly as many B/Ws today as they did in 1992. Unless they work for newspapers or other extremely cost-conscious organizations, they may never have to make a B/W at all. Nevertheless, the skill is more important than ever today. Before discussing why, let's have a quiz.

Given the parrot of Figure 7.1E, do you think that Figure 7.1A or 7.1B is the better conversion to B/W? In the accompanying image of the flag of Canada, do you prefer Figure 7.1C or 7.1D?

While you decide, here are the reasons why you really need to know what's in this chapter, other than the obvious one that you may need to create a B/W picture because you're working on a one-color job. These are listed from least to most important.

• Quality **duotones** depend on having a quality B/W to work with. (See the duotone chapter in PDF on the enclosed CD in the Chapter 5 folder.)

• The basic concepts and tradeoffs involved in **calibration** issues, which are often referred to as **color management**, show up in intensified and more understandable form in the conversion to grayscale. The only difference between converting an RGB image to CMYK and to grayscale is one of degree. In CMYK, we don't have a very good blue. In grayscale, we don't have a very good red or green either. The problems, and the solutions, are absolutely analogous, except that in grayscale the shortcuts and sacrifices are more evident.

• The techniques for making good B/Ws are the basis for the ridiculously powerful methods of **Chapters 8** and **10**.

• Today as in 1992, successful conversions to grayscale depend on **channel blending**. In 1992, nobody had even heard of this concept. Today, it is widely recognized as one of the most powerful forms of image correction, as well as the most difficult. Increased coverage of channel blending was the top reader request for this edition. Explaining how to put the principles into practice will take several chapters, but it all starts here, with black and whites.

But I'm Always True to You, Darling...

I've been lecturing using the images of Figure 7.1 for years. I've asked thousands of people their opinion. The vote is not unanimous, but it's lopsided. Around 95 percent of those asked prefer Figures 7.1B and 7.1C.

Figures 7.1A and 7.1D are default versions. They were produced by opening the original color image and Image: Mode>Grayscale. To understand why so many people think they are unsatisfactory, we have to ask ourselves what we're trying to accomplish.

The entire process of image capture and manipulation is like Medici politics: compromise after compromise, vain attempt after vain attempt to match what can't be matched.

A photograph is an attempt to match real life. Unfortunately, real life has three dimensions, and photographs only two.

Figure 7.1 *Is version A or B a better rendition of the color original at bottom right? Is a Canadian flag better portrayed in grayscale by version C or D?*

That may not be such a disadvantage in this parrot image, but in the last chapter (Figure 6.4) another bird was flying low against a strong sky. The difference between the enormously deep actual scene and the flat photographic result is at least as big, in my opinion, as between Figures 7.1B and 7.1E. The photographer has no more chance of literally matching a miles-deep scene than we have of literally matching the red of the parrot using black ink only.

For that matter, Figure 7.1E itself is a compromise. When the original file was in RGB, the blues were far more intense than can possibly be reproduced with the ratty cyan and magenta inks that commercial printers use. Yet once again, we are supposed to do our best to remind the viewer of what the RGB file looked like, just as the RGB file was intended to remind us of a real-world parrot, and the grayscale parrot is intended to remind us of the CMYK version.

When we choose Image: Mode>Grayscale, Photoshop, because it has no brain, no creativity, needs a formula. It's one you should memorize. No matter what colorspace the file is currently in, Photoshop creates an idealized RGB version of it, and from that a weighted average to make a single channel. The formula is 3–6–1: three parts red, six parts green, one part blue.

As we have just seen, this formula doesn't work. But what would be a better one? I chose these two images because they share a common color: the parrot's red chest is approximately the same red as that found in the flag of Canada. The formula converted to the same gray in Figures 7.1A and 7.1D. But human observers reject those two versions as inaccurate. Humans demand that identical reds convert into drastically different grays—as they do in Figures 7.1B and 7.1C—depending on the context of the image. As the word *context* is incomprehensible to a formula, the formula fails.

...in My Fashion

In a proper conversion, the B/W image should be crisp and legible. The viewer should be able to form a mental picture of what the color image looks like. If these are our objectives in the next example, another default conversion in Photoshop, we have obviously failed miserably. How could the formula go so far astray?

Figure 7.2A is basically an illustration of the colorspace known as HSB—hue, saturation, brightness. In the left third of the image, there is a big contrast in hue between the red and blue squares. Unfortunately, hue contrast is worth deedledy-bop in B/W, so the conversion doesn't work too well.

In the center third, there is a big contrast in saturation between the two greens. As saturation is also a meaningless concept in B/W, this conversion is lamentable as well.

In the right-hand third, the contrast is neither hue nor saturation, but lightness, or luminosity. Bingo! Not only does luminosity count in B/W, it's the *only* thing that counts. So this conversion is quite acceptable.

Here, then, is the principal secret to getting good grayscales: if the color image is full of luminosity contrast, we're in good shape. If not, we have to take action. We have to find the contrast that will vanish, and convert it into the kind of contrast that won't.

It's useful to think of B/W in terms of HSB. We just have to remember that H and S are now worthless.

If we convert Figure 7.2A and correct Figure 7.2B, we'll be in Selectionsville. The distinction between the top and bottom halves will be gone. Whatever we want to do has to be done *before* the fatal switchover—even if it makes the color look terrible. This is a most important concept. A good RGB file can produce an unacceptable B/W. Sometimes it takes an unacceptable RGB to produce a good one. We return to the two originals of Figure 7.1 to illustrate.

Success in the conversion depends on three things: identifying what will be lost when hue and saturation vanish; deciding approximately what the final result *should* look like; and figuring out how to get there.

Both originals feature the same problem shown in the left third of Figure 7.2A: much of what we perceive as contrast is the difference between red and blue, which will disappear when we enter B/W. That hue contrast needs to be converted into luminosity contrast.

We can see in the default conversions that the red flag is originally darker than the blue sky in Figure 7.1D, but the parrot's blue wings are darker than the red chest in Figure 7.1A. The task now is very reminiscent of the unsharp masking of Chapter 6: exaggerate the differences. In the flag image, the reds have to get even darker or the blues lighter, or both. In the parrot, it's just the opposite. The blues must get darker and/or the reds lighter.

Figure 7.2 *Certain types of contrast convert well to black and white, but other varieties completely dry up.*

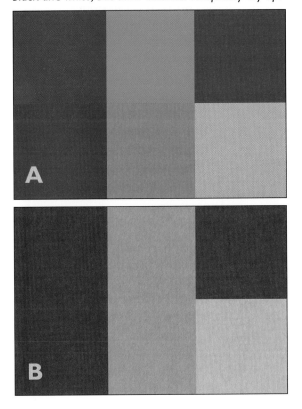

Curves and sharpening can help accomplish this, but the big gun is the blend. When there's this much color variation, it has to show up as colossal contrast in at least one of the RGB channels shown in Figure 7.3. The problem is that it's likely to be wiped out by Photoshop's 3–6–1 blend. If we use, in effect, some different formula, we may be able to retain the distinctions.

Who's Not with the Program?

While Florence was noted for its artists, it also had its practical politicians, who may be of more help with our grayscales.

Machiavelli wrote, "A prince ought either to be a true friend or a true enemy. He should stand wholeheartedly behind his friends, and just as wholeheartedly against his enemies. This is always smarter than staying neutral."

Although he was not a Photoshop user, Machiavelli would have done just fine with his B/W conversions. Success often depends on finding out who your enemies are, and arranging to have them liquidated, or at least eviscerated.

In short, we need to ask: friend or foe?

In the flag image, we've concluded that we need to darken the flag and lighten the sky. Unfortunately, the red channel has a different agenda. It is the foe. The green is somewhat lacking in detail, but it's our friend. The blue is our *good* friend.

In the parrot, the wings must be darker than the chest. The green and blue channels are on a different wavelength. They are the foe. They need to find out who's boss. Our only friend, the red, will teach them.

In Photoshop, like any mature application, different commands can often be used to get the same result. In the case of channel blending, a *lot* of different commands work. We could create a layered document and use blending modes there. We could use Image: Apply Image, or Image: Calculations, or Image: Adjustments>Channel Mixer.

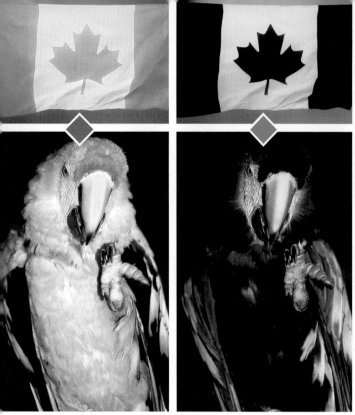

Figure 7.3 The red, green, and blue channels of the two original color images of Figure 7.1.

with alpha channels, channels on different layers, or ones from a different document. Apply Image and Calculations can; the only limitation is that the channels have to come from documents of the same size.

Considering that each of these commands has many suboptions, there are more ways of creating an effective grayscale than there are churches in Florence. Go Web surfing, and you'll see lots of recipes that have very different facades. But they all worship the same deity: luminosity contrast to make up for the lost souls of hue and saturation.

This chapter will take the sort of ecumenical approach that was not popular with Machiavelli's contemporaries. I'll show at least one example of each command, after the following quick summary.

Apply Image and Calculations are very similar. They both blend channels from any layer of any open document, offer most modes that layering does, allow the use of a mask, and have variable opacity. The only difference is that Calculations deposits its output in a separate channel, whereas Apply Image blends into one that already exists. You can always use either to replace the other if you don't mind an extra step or two.

Channel Mixer has a couple of esoteric uses that the others don't duplicate, but otherwise is not as effective. It can't blend

We don't need any new documents or new layers to do the Canadian flag image, though. We just have to remember that the formula is 3–6–1, and that the red is our enemy.

Machiavelli would know exactly what to do in a situation like this. He would have the enemy named to be Duke of Hackensack or to some other position where he would never be heard from again.

We can do the same with Channel Mixer, which can be set up to spit out a grayscale image with a 1–6–3 ratio if we like. I believe it is more instructive, however, to just swap the red and blue channels, attaining 1–6–3 in a more elegant fashion.

The Channel Mixer settings of Figure 7.4 do that. The old red channel—our foe—is now in the weaker position of being the blue. Our friend, the former blue, is now the red. So we have temporarily given Canada a blue flag. One of the attractions of grayscale, however, is that nobody cares what color the image used to be. Convert the blue flag to grayscale and you get Figure 7.1C; the red flag produces Figure 7.1D.

The Lion and the Fox

The parrot could be treated in the same way. This time, the green is the foe, but it is twice as important as our friend the red. We could swap the two with Channel Mixer, but this time we'll weaken the foe rather than transferring him to a new jurisdiction. Lucrezia Borgia's preferred method of weakening foes allegedly was to prick them with an arsenic-soaked ring. Today, we can administer the poison through Apply Image.

Throughout this chapter, we'll be cruising that amusing Ponte Vecchio, pictured in Figure 7.5. The photograph is on the bottom layer; the green rectangle and all the type on the top, which is otherwise transparent.

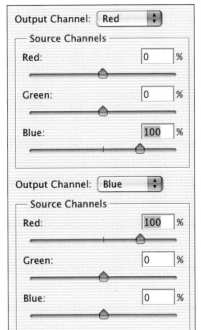

Figure 7.4 *These Channel Mixer moves exchange the red and blue channels, turning the original red flag into a blue one. The blue flag is better for a B/W conversion because it is darker than the red.*

The first two variants are the simplest. Figure 7.5A is the way layers behave by default: Normal mode, 100% opacity. Where the top layer exists, we see only it. The bottom layer is completely superseded.

Opacity can be jiggered however we like. Figure 7.5B is at 60%. This does not merely ghost out the top layer—it blends it with what's underneath. Every pixel in that area is a 60–40 average of the two layers. Everyplace else is unchanged because the top layer is transparent there.

This same blending technique can be used to prepare the parrot for a better grayscale conversion. Apply Image automatically blends into the open channel(s). If no particular channel is selected, it blends into the entire image.

Here, we want the blend to affect only the green, so we expose it with Command–2 or by clicking the green channel in the Channels palette. That makes the green the target, which can't be changed in the Apply Image

dialog of Figure 7.6. The source, however, can be any channel on any layer of any currently open image that's the same size as this one. No need for any such options here: we want

The Temptation of the L

Make two copies of a color file. Convert one to grayscale, the other to LAB. Compare the grayscale to the L channel. Most of the time, you'll like the L better. This is not, however, an effective way to create a B/W.

The L uses the same averaging formula that a direct move to grayscale does, so it shares the same strengths and weaknesses. The two are not identical, because the mathematical structure of LAB requires a relatively light L. Additionally, less contrast is assigned to highlights and shadows, and more to midtones.

A lighter, snappier version of a direct grayscale conversion is tempting, but if that's what you want, you can always convert to grayscale and apply a curve. It won't match the quality of a B/W version created by careful blending of channels.

to use the red channel of this same image. The mode and opacity are the same as in Figure 7.5B: Normal, 60%. If I had chosen 100%, the green channel would have been replaced by, rather than blended with, a copy of the red.

The result of this 60–40 blend is Figure 7.6A. We could have created a wildly different color version that would have produced substantially the same B/W by interchanging the red and green channels. That would have produced Figure 7.6B. Note that the differentiation between red and blue in both versions is much stronger than it was in the original, Figure 7.1E.

A Prince Must Keep an Open Mind

It goes without saying that both example images could have been made a whole lot better by the use of the techniques of earlier chapters. We haven't even set highlight and shadow, which for most B/W conditions should be 3^K and 90^K.

Targeted curves and creative sharpening are concepts that work as well in black and white as in color. Without the preliminary blends, though, satisfactory results are unlikely. The problem can be identifying friend and foe. Before turning the page, what would your strategy be for preparing to convert the playground scene of Figure 7.7 to B/W?

This image is our third consecutive conversion involving contrast between red (the boys' bodies and faces) and blue (the slide). As that contrast gets lost during the conversion, the default grayscale of Figure 7.8 is as tired-looking as a fresco that hasn't been cleaned in 500 years.

I gave this as one of a set of images testing grayscale conversions in an advanced color-correction class. Everybody recognized that something had to be done to increase the luminosity difference between the reds and the blues, but there are two ways to go. If you think the blues should be made darker and/or the reds lighter, then the original red channel is your friend and the blue your foe. If, like me, you'd rather do it the other way, you may wish to strike an alliance with the forces of cool colors.

Figure 7.9A is my take on it. Figure 7.9B is by Mark Bunger, one of the students who took the opposite view, going for a contrasty look with the boys distinctly lighter than the slide.

There was more politicking in Florence than in a convention of color consultants, so it would not be out of place for me to explain why you should be burned at the stake if you prefer Mark's version. Instead, I will make the innocuous but obvious statement that either of these decidedly different approaches is far superior to sticking with Figure 7.8.

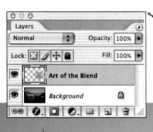

Figure 7.5 *This graphic will be repeated throughout the chapter to illustrate different methods of blending. The photo is on the bottom layer; the rectangle and the type are on an otherwise transparent top layer. Left, the default, Normal mode at 100% opacity. Right, opacity is reduced to 60%.*

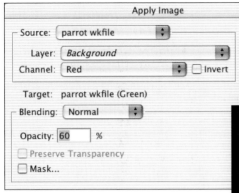

Figure 7.6 *The Apply Image command, left, blends the red channel into the green, producing the left-hand bird. At right, the red and green channels are swapped with the Channel Mixer, as they were in Figure 7.4.*

Two Confusing Mode Names

This image, being more complex than either of our first two, requires more complex blending modes.

Darken mode, illustrated in Figure 7.10A, should be called Don't Lighten. It operates just like Normal mode, except that it doesn't allow anything to get lighter. In those areas, we still see the bottom layer, or at least part of it. The mode operates channel by channel, so it often darkens one channel while leaving another alone, causing unexpected color changes, like the sky turning green where it intersects the box.

The black type is definitely darker than anything underneath it, so Darken mode preserves it. The waters of the Arno are darker than the light green box, which therefore vanishes. In the lightest structures on the

bridge, the box is slightly darker than the red, but lighter than the other two. So the red darkens, imparting a cyan flavor to the area.

In the sky, the box is darker than the blue channel only. Darkening the blue channel, as we know, adds a yellow component, so the sky has turned green. And if you would like to know why the word *blend* has turned purple, it hasn't. It's the same color it was in Figure 7.5A. Thanks to simultaneous contrast, things look bluer against a yellowish background and purpler against cyanish water.

Darken mode's sibling, Lighten, operates in reverse. In Figure 7.10B, the original background shows through where the black letters were, because all three channels were originally lighter than pure black. Parts of the bridge are now reddish, where the box lightened the green and blue channels but

Figure 7.7 *Another image involving contrast between reds and blues. They need to be differentiated, but which should be made darker?*

was not permitted to darken the red to match them. And the sky lost its blueness where the box blew out the dominating darkness in the red channel.

For Fortune Is a Woman

These two blending modes are needed when, as here, some of your friends are not quite as savory as you would like.

If you agree with my decision to darken the boys and lighten the slide, then the original red is the foe. The green appears to be a neutral party, and the blue to be our friend—as trustworthy a friend as Cesare Borgia. The trees in the background are plugged, almost unrecognizable.

We could try blending the green into the red, but the left-hand boy's bathing trunks are as bad in the green as the trees are in the blue. Plus, despite being the worst for our darkness plans, the red is the only one with good detailing in the slide, so we'd hate to eliminate it entirely.

In such cases, we look to blending modes to help us construct the perfect ally. My first step was to open the green channel and apply the blue to it, Lighten mode, 100% opacity. The point was to lighten the slide and the bathing trunks, while leaving the background alone. This created Figure 7.11A, which in itself is a big deal. Remember, the green counts for 60 percent of the eventual conversion, so lightening the slide is a major step in the right direction.

Figure 7.8 *Left, a default conversion of Figure 7.7. Below, the red, green, and blue channels.*

When sharpening, we discovered in the last chapter, it often pays to emphasize darkening while not eliminating lightening altogether. The same is true of blends. I now switched over to the red. Using Normal mode this time, I blended the new green channel in at 35% opacity, producing Figure 7.11 B. I felt I could not afford to make the slide any lighter than that without losing detail. But I had no objection to the boys becoming as dark in the red as they are in the green. So I repeated the green-into-red blend, Figure 7.11 A into 7.11 B, this time at 100% opacity, but Darken mode. That blend can't affect the slide or the background, both of which are already darker in Figure 7.11 B.

The result is Figure 7.11 C. With that for a red channel, Figure 7.11 A for a green, and the original, Figure 7.8 C, as the blue, we're booked for a pretty good result in grayscale—although the composite color image, Figure 7.12, looks rather strange. (Afterward, I applied some minor contrast-enhancing curves, and also USM, but the blends take both the lion's and the fox's share of the credit for Figure 7.9 A.)

If this example frustrated you, the following may be of interest.

This book has been heavily revised during the editing process, so nobody knows which chapters are currently good or bad. However, in first draft, the team thought overwhelmingly that this was the best of the first ten chapters, with the exception of one person who thought it was the worst.

Speaking for the majority, and defending his own failure to offer any constructive remarks about this chapter, Nick Tressider wrote, "It's rather perverse that I find myself unable (unwilling perhaps) to comment on a chapter containing subject matter that is pretty new to me. I understood this chapter

Figure 7.9 *Two different ideas on how to create more variation between objects that were formerly red and those that were blue.*

Figure 7.10 *The misleadingly named Darken and Lighten modes compare darknesses of the two layers.*

well, I believe, and was very impressed with the results where I worked through the exercises. I'd be interested to hear if other beta readers experience the same."

They didn't. Fred Drury was steaming right about here. He wrote, "It's one hell of a leap from the relatively simple, single step, Channel Mixer and Apply Image examples to a three step Apply Image in three different modes with varying opacity. I think you need another example in between."

My response is that I would agree, except that the insidious purpose of this chapter is not to teach black and white at all. It is, rather, a tease, an advance look at colorful things that come later. I am well aware that this last was a complicated example, but I don't care because it is more important that

you know such things are possible than exactly how to do them.

Another fellow named Nick commented in a different context, "I am certainly convinced of this: it is better to be bold than cautious, because fortune is a woman…and she gives herself more freely to impetuous men than to those who make cold advances, and then, being a woman, she is always the young man's friend, because they are less reticent, more rambunctious, and more reckless in their affections."

Niccolò the Magnificent

Having dealt with the mode called Darken that doesn't always darken, we turn to the one that always does. Multiply mode, shown in Figure 7.13, uses each layer to darken the

Figure 7.11 *Blending steps along the road to Figure 7.9A. Left, the blue channel is blended into the green, Lighten mode. Center, the result is blended into the red, Normal mode, 35% opacity. Right, the blend repeated in Darken mode at 100%.*

Figure 7.12 After the steps described in Figure 7.11, the composite color image is unattractive. Fortunately, as it will be converted into B/W, nobody will know that the RGB original looked like this.

other. The result is always darker than either layer, unless one of the layers is blank.

Multiply mode is useful in creation of drop shadows and other special effects. In color correction, it's a clumsy tool, much overused. It plugs shadows with the least provocation, it's not as flexible as curves, and a major use in restoring highlight detail was preempted by the introduction of the Shadow/Highlight command in Photoshop CS. There is, however, one trick left for it to perform.

Machiavelli stressed not just knowing who your enemies are, but choosing friends carefully. He wrote, "Any ally who is the prime force behind another's rise to power will himself be ruined. This is because the ally managed to effect the other's rise to power either by ingenuity or else by force, and the person so empowered distrusts both."

While past chapters have fluttered back and forth between colorspaces, this one has been exclusively RGB. That's as it should be. In

what we've covered so far—curves and sharpening—RGB correction is weaker than either CMYK or LAB.

Not so with this channel blending. LAB's separation of color and contrast rules it out in blending for all but the most experienced practitioners. And CMYK has the terrible issue of loss of detail in shadow areas. (If you need a reminder of how this effect works, review the discussions of Figures 1.5 and 5.4.) If you want to create quality B/Ws or do any other kind of contrast-enhancing blending, do it in RGB.

There is, however, one way in which CMYK can be a decisive ally, one that can bring us to power with ingenuity and force.

It is unclear whether Machiavelli would turn over in his grave at having his philosophy being used in a guide to color correction, but we'll shortly find out.

Florence's cathedral of Santa Croce is a treasure for the living, among other things, because of the honor it pays to the dead. No cemetery in the world houses such illustrious remains; indeed, only one, the Novodevichy Necropolis in Moscow, can be considered even remotely in the same league. Machiavelli, eminent as he was, is small potatoes next to some of the other luminaries entombed there: Galileo, Michelangelo, Ghiberti, and Rossini, among others. There's even an empty memorial for Dante. The lighting is not great, and flash photography is not permitted, so we get to work with Figure 7.14, from which a B/W is needed.

The original is simultaneously too soft and too noisy, a rarity that usually requires nasty lighting conditions like these. The inscriptions and the detailing in the marble are critical elements (after all, we want to know whose tomb

Figure 7.13 Multiply mode always produces a result darker than either layer.

it is). If we try to bring them out by curves, the whole image will get too dark, and if we try USM, it will be hard to avoid exacerbating the noise.

The easiest solution is to make a copy of the image and convert it to CMYK. The black channel should be approximately what we're looking for: nearly blank in the light areas, but plenty in the darker details. We can

Figure 7.14 *The tomb of Niccolò Machiavelli, along with the three RGB channels and an interloper.*

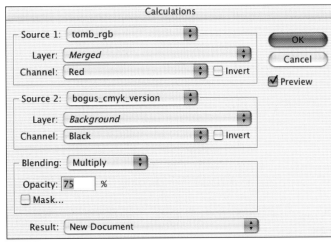

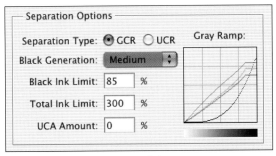

Figure 7.15 *Above, a copy of the RGB image goes into CMYK. Right, the resulting black channel is sharpened and then multiplied into the existing red. Below, enlarged, are the red, sharpened black, and combined versions.*

stamp those details into the RGB original just as the box and type are being stamped into the image in Figure 7.13. The Apply Image command does not care that one version is in RGB and the other in CMYK. A channel is a channel.

The skeleton black that we customarily use is not quite heavy enough for this type of blending. So, to the copy, Edit: Convert to Profile (CS2 and later; Image: Mode>Convert to Profile earlier versions)>Custom CMYK, where we enter the values shown in Figure 7.15 and click OK.

In the last chapter, we saw how sharpening faces is best in the black, which has almost no skin detail but a lot of the things we need to have sharper. The same applies to this black. We can apply a lot of USM (in this case, 500% Amount, 2.0 Radius, 5 Threshold).

In examining the RGB channels of Figure 7.14, the red seems to have the best definition in the background painting. To give that red even more snap, I propose to multiply it by the sharpened version of the black from the CMYK copy of the image.

With a reminder that there are at least a dozen other valid ways to sneak the detail from this sharpened black into either the red or the RGB as a whole, I used the Calculations command to create yet a third document, this one grayscale. Figure 7.15 shows the

steps, and the red, sharpened black, and resulting channel.

Note that the original image looks flat, because, as stupid machines are wont to do, the camera has found an inconsequential object, viz., the candlestick in the background, to be the lightest part of the picture, and has decided to make a highlight of it.

As discussed in Chapters 2 and 3, the highlight needs to be the lightest *significant* area of the image. I measured that to be in the wall above the tomb at about head level of the statue. So, I moved the lower left endpoint of the grayscale curve inward until that area was lightened to 3^K. As the focus of attention in this image is the relatively light marble, I also placed and raised a point in the center of the curve grid, making the light half of the curve steeper to gain contrast there at the expense of the shadow areas.

The new grayscale, together with a default conversion of the original, is in Figure 7.16. Now that the separate CMYK file has served its purpose as a faithful ally, it is only right to honor Machiavelli by dragging it to the Trash in the slowest and most painful manner possible, and to expect to meet it, at least in my case, on the second level of Inferno.

Figure 7.16 *Above, a default conversion to B/W. Below, the version produced by blending.*

The World's Fastest B/W Conversion

It took generations for the pious inhabitants of Florence to complete Santa Croce and even longer for the Duomo, the city's main cathedral. After looking at the last two examples, you may be wondering if B/W conversions take that long, too. Not usually, fortunately.

The image of Figure 7.17 does not show much of the color or saturation contrast that will be lost during the conversion to B/W. Examination of the channels shows that the green is better than the red or blue in every possible respect. So, why bother to average the poor channels in at all? Instead of a 3–6–1 blend, do a 0–10–0. Expose the green channel, then Mode: Grayscale, and in response to Photoshop's "Discard other channels?" query, click OK.

Figure 7.17 Most images don't need a procedure as complex as the last two. Here, the green channel is so much better than the other two that there's no point in looking for blends. The other two channels should be discarded.

If someone ordered me to pick the best channel in each of the five original images so far in this chapter, I would say that the red was best in two, the blue in two, and now the green is best in this one, and it's the only one of the five that I'd say could be used immediately as the B/W.

Nevertheless, the best channel is not determined randomly. If you know the subject, you may know the best channel before you even open the file, particularly if it falls into one of the following two common categories.

Normally lit human faces are usually best in the green, just as in Figure 7.17. A flat red and an overly dark blue are to be expected.

Skies are always best in the red. We sometimes underrate how important skies are in outdoor shots. They are often too weak in the original capture. The picture becomes more dramatic when they are emphasized, and exploiting the red channel is how to do it.

Figure 7.18 *Blend If options exclude portions of the top layer and expose the bottom.*

Stumbling Blocks: The Blend

•**Many ways to play the game.** There's no point in trying to scope out why the blends in this chapter are done the specific way they are. In each case, there are several different methods, and several different commands, that would get similar results. The important thing is to understand that all successful methods are based on finding detail in some channels and forcing it into the composite by hook or by crook.

•**Choosing the "best" channel too quickly.** If your plan calls for the whole image to depend on a single channel, throw more than a cursory glance at it before starting blending. A quick look usually tells us whether something is wrong with a *color* image. But a channel may have small defects that shouldn't be magnified. Look carefully for noise, and for loss of detail in strongly colored areas.

•**Forgetting the final steps.** Channel blending is an adjunct to, not a replacement for, curves and sharpening. Sometimes the gain from blending is so impressive that people forget to check highlight and shadow in the B/W, or that it has been sharpened properly.

Before attacking just such a sky, we need to study one more blending mode, or, better said, blending method.

Good Laws and Good Arms

In the beginning, there was the magic wand tool. It led our Photoshop progenitors into the lair of a snake called overselection, who talked them into trying to correct images as if they were several unrelated pieces.

Since then, their descendants have been paying for that original sin, in the form of images with objects that look as if they've been cut out of the picture and pasted back in. Be that as it may, occasions arise calling for us to treat one part of the picture differently than another. The crudest way to do this is with a selection. More believable results often come from use of a mask based on an existing channel. Sometimes that mask needs to be saved as a separate channel and edited, but that topic is ten chapters away. Sometimes such edited masks are crucial, but frequently they can be bypassed with Blend If sliders. We showed their function back in Figure 4.15, but in view of their importance, let's do it again with Figure 7.18.

These sliders allow exclusions from whatever blending the layer would ordinarily call for. Figure 7.18's top layer is set for convenience at Normal mode, 100%

opacity, but any mode and opacity can be used in combination with these sliders.

The sliders are usually accessed by double-clicking the icon of the target layer. If the sliders were left alone, Figure 7.18 would be identical to Figure 7.5A: the top layer would completely replace the bottom. Any one of eight sliders, however, can instruct Photoshop to ignore the top layer in certain ranges and use the bottom instead.

Here, the instruction is to exclude areas that are dark in the blue channel on the underlying layer. As we know, blue channels are dark in shadows, as well as in deep yellows, reds, and greens. Certainly they are not dark in skies, which is why the top layer is permitted to go about its business there. The top layer is excluded from the undersides of the arches, which are quite dark in every channel, including the blue.

Everywhere else, the top layer starts to dissolve. Parts of the bridge itself are tawny enough, or dark enough, to fall on the slider's left side, but other parts don't qualify.

Consequently, the image breaks apart sharply in several places; in real life, such breaks would be avoided by splitting the slider by Option–clicking it, creating a transition zone.

Today one can drive from the Ponte Vecchio to Siena in an hour, but in the 15th century it was a big enough distance by horseback for the two cities to become military and cultural rivals.

Were it not for being overshadowed by Florence, Siena would be appreciated as one of the great cultural cities. Its city hall, pictured in Figure 7.19, is likely the finest civic building in the world, eclipsing even the ducal palace of Venice shown in Figure 15.1. Its famed trilogy of wall paintings on the consequences of good and bad government should be required viewing for politicians today.

It's a pity we have to make a B/W conversion out of such a lousy original. It does give us a chance, however, to build a sky, because we certainly have to lighten the building if we are to add contrast to it, and when we do so, the sky will vanish.

It won't be difficult to put it back with the Blend If sliders, provided we have a good sky waiting in the wings. So we set aside one copy before the first blend. It seems that the green has the best contrast for the building,

Figure 7.19 *The building in this original is too dark, but any effort to add contrast to it prior to converting to B/W will wipe out what little there is of a sky.*

A **B** **C**

Figure 7.20 Three intermediate channels. Left, the original red applied to the green, 50% Lighten. Middle, a curve is applied to the new channel to enhance the building, but wipes out the sky. Right, the original red channel is applied to itself at 100% Multiply, creating a channel that will be used to restore the sky.

but it could stand to be lighter. Therefore, on a new layer, I applied the green to the entire document and then applied the red from the underlying layer to it at 50% opacity, Lighten mode (Figure 7.20A). This was followed by a curve to increase building detail at the expense of the sky. Figure 7.20B, the result, will be used for half of the final conversion.

To get the other half, I switched over to the reserved copy of the original. Figure 7.20C is the red channel applied to itself in Multiply mode, 100% opacity. The sky is great, the building horrible.

Now, the merge. It seems to me that the sky in Figure 7.20C is too strong, so, on a new layer, I applied it at 65% opacity to Figure 7.20B. It was then simple to create a Blend If to unify the two half-images. The final version is shown next to a default grayscale conversion in Figure 7.21.

To Those Who Understand

The screen grabs show that the image was in RGB while I was doing all this grayscale blending. It could have been done entirely with the Calculations command, without layers or a second RGB document.

However, as Machiavelli was fond of pointing out, prudence is everything. If you're

---

Review and Exercises

✓Why are all the blending exercises in this chapter done in RGB and not CMYK?

✓When we choose Mode: Grayscale, what formula does Photoshop use to generate the result?

✓In Figure 7.10B, explain, in terms of what's going on in each channel, why a background texture of sorts is visible behind the word *BLEND*.

✓Suggest a procedure for converting a color image of a United States flag into grayscale. Would the procedure change depending on the darkness of the sky behind it?

✓Assemble half a dozen pictures of people's faces, avoiding ones with obvious defects such as bad color or being taken in shadow. How many of them would you convert to grayscale by simply discarding the red and blue channels? If you find one or two that should use a different procedure, explain why.

positive that you won't need the flexibility that layers offer to change course later on, by all means use Calculations. Similarly, there was no need to use Lighten mode to make Figure 7.20A or Darken mode on the top layer of the document that made Figure 7.21B. In both cases, Normal mode would have done the same thing, I'm fairly sure. But why take a risk of overlooking some small area that might push the image in the opposite direction?

Managing the conversion to black and white is the same as converting a natural scene into a photograph, or an RGB file into

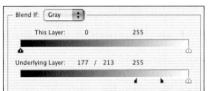

Figure 7.21 This structure produces a final version, below right, merging Figures 7.20B and 7.20C. Below left, a default grayscale conversion.

CMYK and its much smaller gamut. We're trying to stay as faithful as possible to the original, given the limitations of the process. The greater the difference between the original and the colorspace we have to convert it to, the more intervention will be necessary—but the point is the same. The 3–6–1 formula is probably the best for a generalized RGB-to-B/W conversion. But if you rely on it exclusively, you'll get fifth-rate results. If that isn't in your travel plans, you need to keep a few things in mind:

- Know what you're losing in the conver-

The Bottom Line

Images that move from color into grayscale appear to lose contrast because we no longer see variation between certain colors. If those color-related contrasts are important, they need to be translated into darkness-related contrasts before the file enters grayscale. This chapter advocates doing so by channel blending with the Apply Image command, although there are other methods available. Best blending results come in RGB rather than CMYK. However, sometimes a supplementary copy in CMYK is helpful because the black channel can often be used as a blending aid.

Those who never need to make black and whites still need this chapter, for two reasons. First, it's the foundation for Chapter 8, which extends the technique to color images. Second, the difficulties we face when entering grayscale—and the solutions—are analogous, although more extreme, than those we face when converting RGB to CMYK. Learning why we do what we do in one case makes it much easier to apply it to the other.

sion. Examine the original for places where the contrast you perceive is one of color and not of brightness.

- Get away from thinking that this is some kind of literal, formulaic conversion. It's perfectly all right for the same red to be of different darknesses in different grayscale images. It's perfectly all right for your idea of how dark each red should be to vary from mine.

"But my intention being to provide something of use to those of understanding," Machiavelli wrote, "it appears to me better to head for the truth of the matter than to something intangible. Many have imagined republics and principalities the like of which have never been seen or known to exist in reality; for how we live is so far removed from how we ought to live, that he who abandons what has to be done for what ought to be done, will rather learn to bring about his own ruin than his preservation. One who wishes to make a profession of goodness in everything must surely come to grief among so many who are not good. Therefore a prince must, in self-defense, learn how not to be good. Circumstances will dictate when he should use this knowledge, and when he should refrain from doing so."

As in the management of graphic arts firms, you sometimes need to be ruthless. When you encounter an individual—or a channel—with an attitude problem, if persuasion doesn't work, elimination is the next step. Your employees, and your B/Ws, will thank you for it.

Keeping the Black and White in Color

The battle is always to achieve both good color and good contrast. Black and whites don't have color, so we use channel blends to maximize their contrast. Those same blends can be the best way to add snap to an image that isn't a black and white.

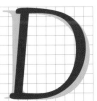

D eaf, despondent, dissolute, and disconsolate, Beethoven (the composer) produced, between 1823 and 1826, five string quartets that, as a group, were musically speaking at least a century ahead of their time. No other field of artistic endeavor has seen such a time-warping explosion.

Some of the dissonances were so shocking that the publisher would have none of them. The last movement of Opus 130, a massive, perverted fugue, was just over the top. Beethoven was forced to offer a much simpler alternate ending.

Charming, capricious, calculating, and canine, Beethoven (the dog) played, in 1992, the title role in a movie of somewhat less artistic merit than his namesake's late quartets. The original was so saccharine that the producers provided an alternate ending, too, and both are on the DVD, if you are sufficiently hard up to acquire it.

Alternate endings don't have an especially distinguished history in literary or musical works. Ibsen's *A Doll's House* has one, and John Fowles's *The French Lieutenant's Woman* a better one. The real hot field, however, has been in the movies: many new releases have them, so that the audience can be either cheered up or depressed as the mood may strike them.

In this book, we've had our own Great Fugue. The recurring themes are color and contrast, sung by different voices, in different keys, at different times. Contrast is the rhythm, color the melody. Together, they can make a harmonious whole, but if they don't meld together properly, the result will be out of tune.

Chapter 1, the prelude, talked about how they interrelate. Chapter 2, the introduction to curves, was about contrast. Chapter 3's curves were color with a contrasty accompaniment, and Chapter 4 was about LAB, which emphasizes the two themes by separating them completely. Chapter 5, the role of the black channel, was mostly contrast, and Chapter 6, sharpening, was entirely contrast, while color fiddled a counterpoint in the background.

Chapter 7, being about black and white, was also contrast only. We need only conclude the series of blending options shown in that chapter to bring the other theme back into the score.

The Alternate Ending

To understand Figure 8.1, think in LAB. Luminosity and Color modes split color and contrast. Luminosity mode directs Photoshop to combine the detail (or, if you prefer, the L channel) of the top layer with the color of the bottom. Color mode does the reverse.

The black type remains black in Figure 8.1A. The blueness of the blue type is gone, replaced by the color of the Arno. The light rectangle takes on the color of its background: blue-green in the river, blue in the sky. The bridge is represented by yellow, but a perfectly flat yellow, because the top layer is a flat tint, free of any detail.

The same black type has nearly vanished in Figure 8.1B. It's there if you look hard enough. It's neutral, whereas the rectangle is slightly green. If we see those script letters at all, they'll seem purplish rather than gray, the result of simultaneous contrast at work.

These two blending modes make it evident why Chapter 7, which is about converting color images into good black and whites, is so critical, even for people who never need black and whites. Do you see why?

Return for a moment to Figure 7.7. We were presented with a picture of boys on a slide. After a series of maneuvers, we produced Figure 7.12, a very detailed, but very green, version of the original.

The end of that story in Chapter 7 was simple. Figure 7.12 was transformed Cinderella-like into Figure 7.9A, a grayscale image so far superior to a default conversion that it is difficult to resist the temptation to say that everyone lived happily ever after.

Permit me to offer an alternate ending.

Instead of converting Figure 7.12 to grayscale, I propose pasting it on top of the original RGB file, which is reproduced here as Figure 8.2A. Changing the layer mode of the resulting file from Normal to Luminosity produces Figure 8.2B.

Transplanting a new ending onto a story can sometimes change the entire meaning of what came earlier. Indeed, it can lead the reader to suspect that the author had a different agenda than the one originally stated.

The Alternate Beginning

Figures 8.2A and 8.2B are two very different pictures, almost as if they had been shot under different lighting conditions. There's a question about how far to take this blend;

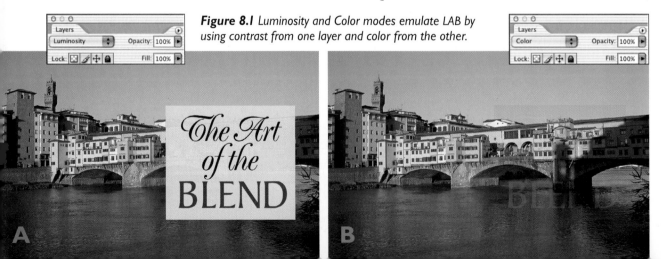

Figure 8.1 *Luminosity and Color modes emulate LAB by using contrast from one layer and color from the other.*

I used 90% opacity on the luminosity layer. But there's no question that the boys are the subject of the picture, or that they are more prominent in Figure 8.2B.

This effect could not have been achieved with curves or sharpening. These bright blues and reds must not blind us to seeing that the same changes in contrast that make for a good B/W also make for a good color image.

If you can separate color and contrast in the mind, then the horrible green color on the top layer won't intimidate you. If you've decided to use Luminosity mode, then it doesn't matter how bad the color is on the top layer—*it can even be a black and white.*

This image was the most difficult image in Chapter 7, but some B/W conversions are easy, such as the man with a canoe in Figure 7.17. I pointed out then that there are two common classes of image with one channel that is predictably better than the other two in every way. These are skies, in which the red channel is always best, and normally lit faces, in which the green almost always is. So, in Figure 7.17, the best B/W conversion was simply to throw the red and blue away.

If we also throw away the pretense that the objective of the exercise was a black and white and not a color image, a strategy similar to that of Figure 8.2 suggests itself. Not an alternate ending, but an alternate beginning. The principle that the green channel is the best of the three in faces crosses all lines of age, gender, and ethnicity. This chapter is full of flashbacks to earlier images, but rather than bringing back the medium-complexioned man of Figure 7.17, we'll move

Figure 8.2 *Top, the original shown in Figure 7.7. Bottom, Figure 7.12, which had been used to make a B/W conversion, is placed on a Luminosity layer above the original.*

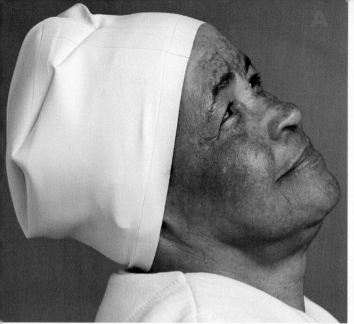

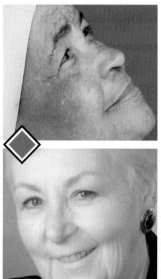
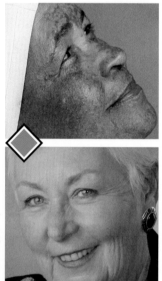

Figure 8.3 *In normally shot flesh-tones, the green channel is almost always the best. The originals, top, are improved by applying the green channel to a duplicate layer that is set to Luminosity mode. The results are at bottom.*

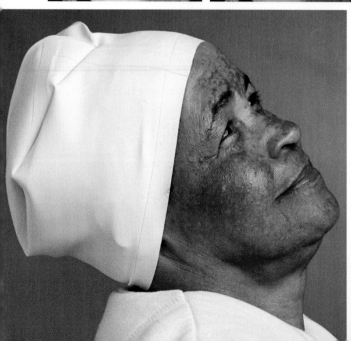

to two older women, one African-American, the other a Caucasian of light complexion.

We know by her blue eyes that the woman in Figure 8.3B has skin that is not only lighter than that of her counterpart in Figure 8.3A, but considerably pinker as well. In spite of these differences, the same characteristics show up when we examine the channels. The red is flat. The blue is dark.

Granted that the green shows the best contrast, we should open our attack on these images, and all those like them, by doing exactly what was done with Figure 7.17: trash the other two channels. Oh, we can't literally delete them, since we must retain credible colors. But we can do the equivalent, in three easy steps:

- Create a duplicate layer.
- To it, Apply Image, source Green, layer irrelevant, mode Normal, opacity 100%.
- Change layer mode to Luminosity.

The second move creates a grayscale image on the top layer. Remember, Apply Image writes to whatever channel is open. Since we didn't specify any particular channel, the entire RGB document is open. All three channels are replaced by a copy of the original green. Since all three channels are now identical, all three values are always identical, and equal values in all three channels make a gray.

The color is therefore not only worse than that of the bottom layer, but absent altogether. But who cares? The top layer has better contrast, and that's all that counts in Luminosity mode.

This blend is not the end of the story, but the beginning: a first step on the road to a final correction. But it seems obvious that whatever the next step is will be more effective if it starts with Figures 8.3C or 8.3D in preference to 8.3A or 8.3B.

The reproduction of skintone is critical to most professionals. These three simple steps at the start of processing the image have an impact that ranges from slight to awesome, always for the better. Yet people say that channel blending is rocket science. Not so. If you return here after finishing the entire book, you will have to agree that this chapter is the easiest of the 20. You open the image, look for a channel that has better contrast than the other two, and plug it into a luminosity layer. Game over.

Harmonious with the Background

Most wild animals, particularly those whose flesh is good to eat, have evolved to blend into their backgrounds to make life tougher on predators. It also makes life tough on wildlife photographers. The people who judge the photograph are the beneficiaries of another evolutionary gift: simultaneous contrast, which is a means of defeating the animal's deceptive-coloring defense.

I would advise giving the bighorns of Figure 8.4 a wide berth, particularly in mating season. Butting heads with the digital photograph, however, will be much easier if we first ask what we would do if the assignment were to convert to B/W.

Being roughly neutral, the rams' faces, horns, and bodies are almost the same in all three channels. The background is not. It's lighter in the red, darker in the blue. It's about the same darkness as the rams in the green, which means we should forget that flat-looking channel. If we were converting to B/W, either of the others is a better start, because the objects of interest stand out.

But which one? That's a matter of opinion, just as there was a matter of opinion back in Figure 7.9 as to whether the slide that we just looked at in Figure 8.2 should be made lighter or darker than the boys' bodies.

To help decide, I made a duplicate layer and applied the red channel to it to produce a grayscale layer, just as I did with the green in Figure 8.3. I changed the layer mode to Luminosity and produced Figure 8.5A. Then

I repeated the procedure with a new copy of the image, using the blue rather than the red, winding up with Figure 8.5B.

Remember, this is only the first page of the story. The question is not whether you like either of these pictures better than Figure 8.4, but whether you will like them better after applying curves. Figure 8.5A starts out lacking weight, so I'd place and raise a point around three-quarters of the way up the curve, darkening the image while adding steepness to the area the rams occupy.

I'd do the opposite with Figure 8.5B, dropping the quartertone to make a slightly lighter image overall. But I believe I could do more with either one of these images than with an unblended Figure 8.4, because they have the good break between rams and background that the original lacks. Personally, I would start with Figure 8.5B, which I find the most dramatic of the three.

The Sky's Not the Limit

Accentuating the foreground by playing tricks with the background is boilerplate material for the professional. The extra drama that darkening the background gives to the rams picture is a good example, but a more common one is to strengthen a tired-looking sky. We'll use another flashback image to illustrate, and also to start our discussion of how to incorporate some of the additional blending modes we saw in Chapter 7.

Figure 8.6A originally

Figure 8.4 In the composite color image, the rams blend into the background. In the red channel, though, the background is lighter than the animals. In the blue, it's darker. These differences can be exploited by luminosity blends.

appeared in our sharpening chapter as Figure 6.9D. For this exercise, assume that we need more punch in the sky.

The image remains in RGB, but there is little further point in showing the individual channels—by now you should be able to visualize them pretty well. As always, the sky is most pronounced in the red.

If we add a duplicate layer and then apply the red to it, however, after changing to Luminosity mode we wind up with Figure 8.6B. The red flags are red because they are so light in the channel of the same name. Applying that channel to the entire image makes them light in every channel, wrecking the image.

Since we don't want the red flags, or anything else for that matter, to get lighter, the mistake was blending the red into the RGB in Normal mode. We should have used Darken. That would have produced Figure 8.6C, half grayscale and half color. The effect occurs because in all blue areas, the red channel is darker than either of the others, which it replaces. That causes all three channels to have identical values throughout the sky, which is therefore a neutral gray.

The red flags, on the other hand, are darker in both other channels than in the red. As Darken mode doesn't permit any lightening, those two are left alone. And in the greenery, the green channel is replaced by the red, but the blue, being dark, is ignored. Changing the layer on which this mugwump image resides to Luminosity mode produces Figure 8.6D.

Figure 8.5 *Top, a version produced by applying the red channel to a luminosity layer on top of Figure 8.3. Bottom, a copy of the original blue channel is substituted on the luminosity layer.*

The Second Line of Defense

Darken and Lighten modes prevent undesired areas from being affected by the blend. They don't always work.

Whenever we see a face, we should consider using the green channel on a luminosity layer. Doing so in our next example creates the disastrous Figure 8.7B, owing to the subject's lamentable decision to wear a red jacket.

Figure 8.7 *Left, the original. Center, applying the green channel to a luminosity layer improves the face but drastically darkens the jacket. Right, the jacket is excluded from the blend with Blend If sliders.*

Stopping this by using Lighten mode would be useless, since that would prevent not just the jacket but the face from getting darker. Instead, we use layer Blending Options, specifically the Blend If sliders, to exclude use of the jacket from the top layer.

To explain this concept to Photoshop, we need to know our channels, and I reiterate that it should no longer be necessary to show them, as it should be obvious what they look like. The face and the jacket are both distinctly red, so they are both light in the red channel. However, because the jacket is much darker than the face, it follows that the two objects must be very different in both the green and blue channels. We'll use one of those for the sliders.

Figure 8.6 *(opposite) A, the original image. B, the red channel is blended into the RGB composite, Normal mode, on a layer with Luminosity mode selected. C, starting over, the red channel is blended into the RGB in Darken mode. D, version C's layer is changed from Normal to Luminosity mode.*

Here, the difference is so gross that it's a snap to distinguish them in either channel. As not every image is so obliging, we should discuss how to know which slider to use.

We are looking for the cleanest break between the darkest thing that we want to include in the blend and the lightest thing we wish to exclude. These are the darkest parts of the lips and the lightest parts of the jacket. We can choose one of eight different sets of sliders: red, green, blue, and a composite "gray," each on either This Layer or Underlying Layer. In this image, we in effect have four, not eight, choices. As the top layer is a copy of the green channel, all four of the This Layer sliders do the same thing as the green Underlying Layer ones.

Often the choice is clear. It's obvious here that there's little distinction in the red. Therefore it's also obvious that the gray is useless because it averages the red in with the others.

If this jacket were rosier, less of a fire engine red, then it would be obvious that the green is best. Faces are almost always darker in the blue than the green. The blue and green of this red jacket are about equal. So my guess is that the green is probably the best channel for this blend because there is more space between the face and the jacket, but let's make sure.

The file arrives in sRGB. According to my measurements, the darkest point of the lips is $186^R114^G99^B$. The lightest point of the jacket is $175^R38^G25^B$. The difference between the two is $11^R76^G74^B$. For the greatest chance of success in placing a point that will totally separate the two objects, the green is technically the best choice here, but in reality you could flip a coin to choose it or the blue.

Double-clicking to the right of the top layer's icon in the Layers palette brings up the Layer Style dialog with its Blend If sliders. I'd recommend resetting the top layer to Normal

mode if it isn't there already. Doing so displays a grayscale image. As you move the slider to the right, the red will start to show through. Against a gray background, it will be obvious if you are missing a piece of it or if you have gone too far. Against the background of Figure 8.7B it may not be so simple.

Finally, after finalizing the slider's placement, we should always split it by Option–clicking it and moving the halves apart. This avoids a harsh break where the layers meet. In this image, it isn't necessary, but usually it is, so it's good to get in the habit.

Once the position is finalized, change the top layer's mode back to Luminosity. The final result is Figure 8.7C.

Time for a Quiz

Trying to get blending into perspective as one of many tools in a workflow, we'll go to another flashback. Figure 8.8A is a copy of Figure 3.14, which was corrected only with CMYK curves. Figure 8.8B uses the same curves, but the story begins differently.

In Chapter 3, I stated that this image arrived in CMYK. In fact, it was a Camera Raw image that I had opened and converted immediately to CMYK. This time, I opened the file into sRGB and did some blending. If you are not familiar with how Camera Raw works, we'll be discussing it in Chapter 16. For now, you can ignore it and just assume we started with an sRGB file.

Reminder: unlike curves and sharpening, which generally can be done in any space but in which there are occasions where RGB is inferior, this type of blending should be done in RGB, period. As we know, ink limits kill shadow detail in the CMY channels, especially the magenta and yellow. This is not an advantage in

---

Stumbling Blocks: Alternate Beginnings

•**Looking for Luminosity.** The Apply Image and Calculations commands do not have Luminosity or Color as mode options, If you wish to use them for a luminosity blend and are very confident, you can apply them directly to the image and then Edit: Fade>Luminosity. The approach of applying them to a duplicate layer set to Luminosity mode is much more flexible.

•**Two blending modes, one image.** Figure 8.6B uses the red channel in both Darken and Luminosity modes. No command can apply both modes simultaneously. There are two steps: the Apply Image command to a duplicate layer in Darken mode, and then changing the layer mode to Luminosity. Thus, the Darken mode is contributed by Apply Image, the Luminosity mode by the layer itself.

•**The wrong colorspace.** These moves should not be attempted in CMYK because of the weird behavior in shadows caused by ink limit and described in Chapter 5. There are some occasions for blending in alternate types of RGB, though. These will be discussed in the second half of Chapter 15.

•**The wrong layer.** The Apply Image and Calculations commands think by default that you want to blend channels from a *merged* version of a layered document. That's wrong for most luminosity blending, where you need to specify that the channel must be picked up from the bottom layer instead.

Figure 8.8 *Above, a repeat of Figure 3.14, which was corrected from Figure 3.13 by curves only. Below, a version produced with the same curves but with a luminosity blend before they were applied.*

blending. Furthermore, in RGB neutral colors imply channels of equal strength, but in CMY they imply a heavier cyan. In a roughly gray object, the red matches the green and blue, but the cyan is higher than the magenta and yellow. This imbalance can cause problems with blends.

Also, remember that this type of blending is all a matter of taste. You can see in Figure 8.8B that I feel that the water needs to be made darker. You may think I went too far, or not far enough, or even that Figure 8.8A is better. There are so many options that, before discussing my own blends, we'll have a quiz.

Figure 8.9A is the original image. The other seven versions, which are in a random order, were produced by blending. In each case, I made a duplicate layer, applied a certain channel to it in a certain mode, 100% opacity, and then changed the layer mode to Luminosity, 100% opacity. In one case, I made a separate copy of the image, converted it to a Medium GCR Custom CMYK as described back in Figure 5.3, and used the resulting black channel to blend into the RGB original. The worksheet on this page shows the seven blends that were used; it's your job to figure out which version corresponds to each. If you want a challenge, stop now and fill out the worksheet; if you need a hint, read on. The answer key is on page 189.

This exercise shows how much control blending can give. Any of these could be combined with others, or used at a lower opacity. So there are infinite possibilities depending on your agenda for the image.

A Theme and Variations

This is an easy quiz, because it features large areas that are decidedly red, green, and blue, brown being a species of red. The channel of the same name as the color being portrayed

Figure 8.9 Luminosity blending offers many creative options. The original image is at top left. The others were each created with a single luminosity blend.

is always the lightest of the three. Therefore, the version with the lightest sea must have been made with the blue channel. And so on with the grass and the green channel, and the castle and the red.

For my own blend, I used the red channel, Normal mode, 60% opacity, but I felt that this lightened the castle too much. I could have used Darken mode instead. However, I got a more satisfactory result with a second blend into the same layer, the black channel from my CMYK copy in Multiply mode at 60% opacity.

Since most images in the last two chapters have featured either faces or skies, it's fitting that we should end with one that has both. And inasmuch as this chapter introduces the last basic correction concept, it's fitting we should have one that reviews ground we have covered in the preceding chapters.

Worksheet for Figure 8.9

Each version on the facing page was produced by creating a duplicate layer, blending a single channel into it, and changing mode to Luminosity. All blending is at 100% opacity. Version A is the original. Match each of the others to the following list of blend sources and modes. (Answers, page 189.)

Blend/Mode	Version
Black/Multiply	
Blue/Darken	
Blue/Normal	
Green/Lighten	
Green/Normal	
Original (No Blend)	A
Red/Darken	
Red/Normal	

Of Artifacts and Skies

Files from digital cameras generally are smoother than those produced by scanning film—with one important exception. Digicams produce a noisy red channel in clear sky images like the two shown here. The effect isn't noticeable if the file is handled normally, but luminosity blends of the sort discussed in this chapter can bring it out.

The problem exists in all cameras I've tested, including the dozen used by the photographers who contributed the images for this book, like these two. I therefore will not name the cameras, except to say that both are recent models from two prominent manufacturers. The left-hand image is from a camera popular among professional photographers. It was opened in Camera Raw. The right-hand file arrived as a JPEG. It is produced by a sub-$1,000 camera aimed at the high end of the consumer market.

All these versions show areas at normal size (300 pixels per inch resolution) and at 250% magnification. The top set is the originals, the middle the red channels only, and the bottom a new image produced by blending the red channel into the RGB on a luminosity layer. To my way of thinking, the defects are hidden well enough in a normal reproduction, but the blend brings them out objectionably.

Before hanging your hat on a luminosity blend, check the blending file for this kind of problem, particularly if you are thinking of blending with the blue channel, which is often quite noisy, or the red channel of a sky image.

If you need to correct a sky problem before blending, a nearly foolproof way is to create a duplicate layer and run Filter: Blur>Surface Blur (Photoshop CS2 and later) on the red channel. Then, move the document into LAB without flattening, and use the Blend If sliders to exclude anything that is not significantly negative in the B channel. Few things other than skies are, and if any occur in the image, they can be eliminated with a layer mask. The file can then be returned to RGB for the luminosity blend.

You have almost all the tools now. The book doesn't end here, because the hard part is figuring out how and when to use them— how to discipline the mind, how to visualize the likely course of the correction.

We've developed that kind of thought pattern in this chapter. If the picture features a face, we should be thinking about a luminosity blend from the green. If there's a sky, we should consider a darkening blend from the red. It's just a matter of extending the approach to other areas.

In addition to face and sky, Figure 8.10A contains a reminder of the lessons of every past chapter.

- In Chapter 1, we talked about how humans and cameras see things differently. We would focus on this man's face more, and would see it as considerably lighter than the camera did.
- Chapter 2 said to identify the interest object and stick it in a steep part of the curve. That's where the face has to go.
- Chapter 3 gave us target values for flesh-tones, which Figure 8.10A does not meet. Also, we have an area known to be neutral, namely the gray hair.
- When confronted by a lot of dull, similar colors as we are here, Chapter 4 suggests using LAB to break them apart.
- Chapter 5 points out that manipulations of the black channel are particularly valuable in faces because they avoid adding unwanted detail.
- Chapter 6 suggests using hiraloam rather than conventional USM on faces.

The image arrives in Adobe RGB. Before blending commences, we should check for color defects. I am suspicious of the gray hair, but especially of the light part of the sky.

In investigating large neutral areas like these, it makes life easier to set the right half of the Info palette to read LAB. As we mouse around the areas, the RGB numbers will be all over the map, because there is a lot of darkness variation. But the AB values, which aren't affected by darkness, will be fairly constant. 0^A0^B is neutral; single-digit positive values might be acceptable, but negative values, at least in the hair, are out, because hair is never blue or green.

The results show that the gray hair is only slightly off neutral, but parts of the light sky are around 10^A6^B. That's quite purple. And the face measures as too blue.

A cast that changes as the image gets darker can't be fixed in LAB without a mask or some other form of selection. So, my first step was to get rid of it in RGB. But, as seen in Figure 8.10B, I did it on an adjustment layer set to Color mode, the opposite of Luminosity. I was already committed to a luminosity blend later, so I did not want to worry about the shape of these curves altering contrast. Note, also, the extra copy of the base layer. That's because after applying the color curves, I need to merge the top two layers to create the luminosity layer. I need to retain a copy of the original image, so that I can use its channels for blending.

The LAB Denouement

Figure 8.11A, then, is the first blend. After Figure 8.10B's adjustment layer was flattened, the original green (taken from the bottom layer) went into a luminosity layer to produce Figure 8.11A. The result is too dark, but rich in facial detail. The curve of Figure 8.11B

Quiz Answers

Each version of Figure 8.9 was produced by blending a channel in a certain mode into a luminosity layer. Here is the answer key showing source and mode.

A	Original Image	E	Blue, Darken
B	Green, Normal	F	Red, Darken
C	Black, Multiply	G	Blue, Normal
D	Red, Normal	H	Green, Lighten

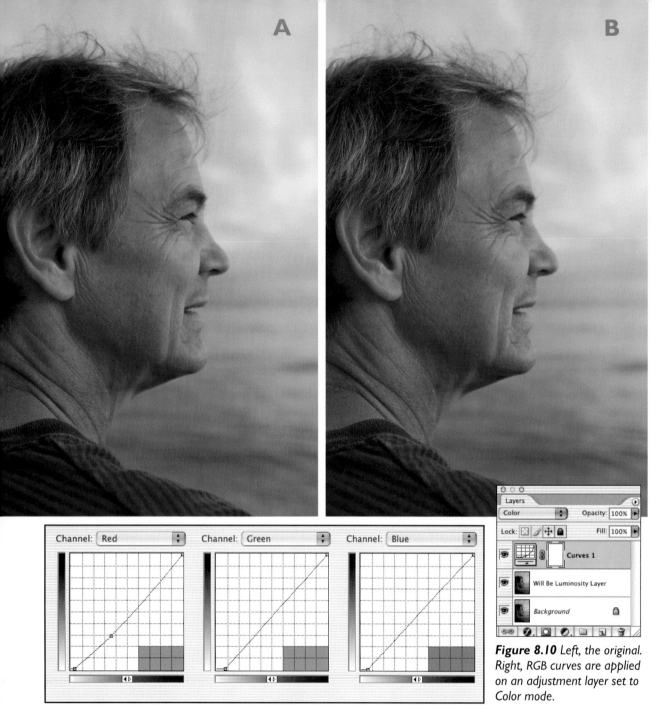

Figure 8.10 Left, the original. Right, RGB curves are applied on an adjustment layer set to Color mode.

kills two birds with one stone. It lightens the face while placing it into a steep part of the curve. It doesn't matter that it's the master RGB curve, as all three channels on the luminosity layer are identical, all copies of the green.

It also doesn't matter that the curve has almost wiped out the sky. That's why I saved a copy of the original. The next step is to duplicate the luminosity layer. I blended

the original red (being careful to specify the bottom layer as the source in the Apply Image dialog; the default is the merged image, which won't work) into this new top layer, choosing Darken mode so that the face would not lighten. This restores, yea rather enhances, the original sky.

In Figure 8.12A, though, check out what happened to the shirt. That's why I used a second luminosity layer instead of darkening the first one. With Blend If sliders, I excluded anything that was very dark in the red channel, Underlying Layer. That restored the shirt and softened the ocean under the chin.

The next stop is LAB. The L curve in Figure 8.12B adds even more range to the face; the A and B curves drive colors apart, especially in the blue range of the B. I moved the center points of both toward warmer colors, particularly toward yellow in the B, trying to get a sunnier effect in the background. It must be confessed that this reversed the effect of the color curve of Figure 8.10. That happens sometimes. It's harder to make color decisions on flat pictures than when they are getting close to the desired result.

The final move is the hiraloam sharpen, to the L channel. For Figure 8.13A, I used 40% Amount, 50.0 Radius, 8 Threshold.

The CMYK Coda

As Beethoven remarked, never deny the truth, even at the foot of the throne. Each colorspace has its strengths. RGB blends well, LAB drives colors apart, and CMYK is good for fine-tuning. That's why we haven't worried about exact numbers yet.

All we ask of Figure 8.13A is that it be closer to the desired color than the original, Figure 8.10A, was. Everything else can be accomplished in CMYK.

Figure 8.11 After the adjustment layer is flattened, a luminosity blend with the original green creates an overly dark face, left. Right, a steepening curve applied to the luminosity layer corrects the face but wipes out most of the background sky.

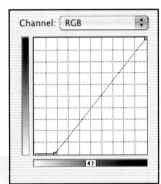

A

B

In Chapter 3, we talked about the impact of complexion on CMYK color balance, saying that the lightest-skinned Caucasians, and small children, have nearly equal magenta and yellow values. Everybody else has more yellow. The woman of Figure 8.3B has a light complexion, the woman of Figure 8.7 is slightly darker, and this man is darker still.

So we expect a pronounced imbalance in favor of yellow.

I was prepared to do some CMYK curving, but it turns out that almost all the numbers are already close enough, including the extra yellow in the skintone. The one exception: the typical value in the forehead is around $5^C45^M50^Y$. This violates the rule that the cyan

Figure 8.12 *Left, the red channel is blended into the luminosity layer in Darken mode. Right, after the shirt is excluded with Blend If sliders, the image is converted to LAB and the curves at right are applied.*

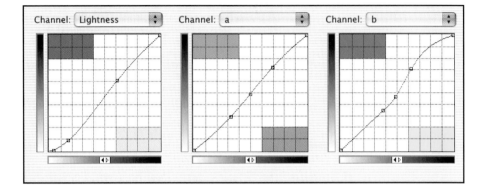

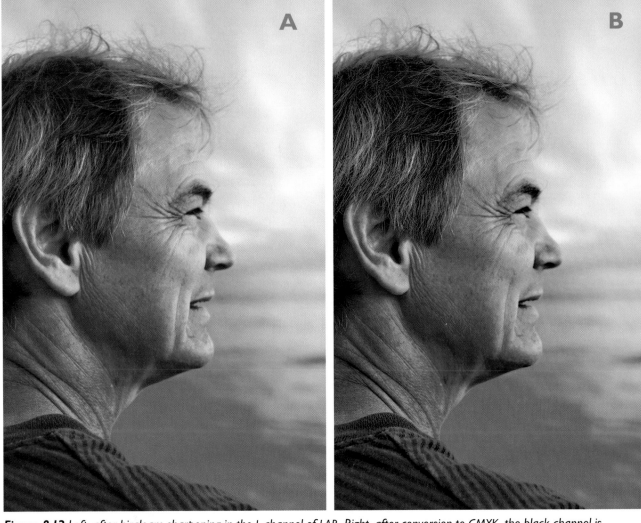

Figure 8.13 *Left, after hiraloam sharpening in the L channel of LAB. Right, after conversion to CMYK, the black channel is sharpened and the magenta channel blended in Darken mode at low opacity into the cyan to cut the redness of the face.*

should be at least a fifth of the magenta, and suggests that the face is too red. You can see this redness in the darkest areas of the neck, which are excessively hot in my view.

If you feel that the face is also too dark, a solution would be Image: Adjustments> Selective Color, choosing Reds and subtracting magenta. I don't; a relatively dark face is

Review and Exercises

✓ In Figure 8.6C, the idea was to strengthen the sky by blending the red channel in Darken mode onto a luminosity layer. This also darkened the blue flags and the greenery. If a client objected to these things, how would you eliminate them while retaining the darkening of the sky?

✓ In Chapter 2, we were warned against using the RGB master curve. Why is it used in Figure 8.11?

✓ Luminosity blends work better in RGB than in CMYK. The final blend of Figure 8.13B was not a luminosity blend, but one aimed at correcting color. In this specific case—blending into the lightest channel of a face in Darken mode—why might it be technically better to blend the magenta into the cyan, as shown here, than to make the cognate move in RGB (green into red)?

OK with me. The easiest and most accurate way of toning down the red is not just an alternate but a surprise ending: another blend, this time not on a luminosity layer.

We know that faces look best in the green channel, which corresponds to the magenta in CMYK. The magenta is also far darker than the cyan in a face. Blending it lightly into the cyan—at, say, 10% opacity, adds weight, kills red, and adds detail in one happy package. Of course, we use Darken mode, to avoid lightening the water, sky, and shirt.

To reach the final version, Figure 8.13B, I also applied conventional USM (settings: 300% Amount, 1.0 Radius, 8 Threshold) to the black channel only.

Before I wrap up, take two pieces of advice from the beta readers. André Dumas has an important warning about the foregoing image: "We know that nobody else would correct this image the same way you described here. Beginners and intermediates will be absolutely overwhelmed by this exercise *if* they think that what you are demonstrating is *the* only right way to correct this image. Of course it is not."

The other comment pertains to a sophisticated workflow that has been adopted by many users, including several beta readers, in recent years. I think it was too difficult to propose in Chapters 2 and 3, but we can extend the principles of *this* chapter to our curving. That is, once for color, once for contrast. Two sets of curves, two different layers.

In criticizing the earlier two chapters, Clarence Maslowski wrote, "For the last five years or more I usually perform my curving with two adjustment layers. The lower one is in Normal mode for the grunt work and the upper layer in Luminosity mode. Lately I find myself using Color mode in the lower layer rather than Normal. Reading these chapters and following along with your work reminds me how challenging and at some points awkward using one set of Normal curves can be. Certainly, it can be overwhelming for the beginner. You divided these chapters into contrast and color. I find the extension of this concept to be far and away more logical than a single round of curves. I hope you revisit this later."

If you think back to Figure 1.5, you might have wondered at the time what the point was of that ten-channel guessing game. Why should we have to be able to guess what the individual channels look like, when our business is to produce a good *composite* image?

These two last chapters should have given the answer. With a quick view of the color image, we can visualize the channels. If we instinctively know what they look like, we know what blends (let alone masks, which we'll discuss later on) are possible. And then we can think of some alternate beginnings, and decide which will produce the happiest ending.

The Bottom Line

The principles of color to black and white conversion of Chapter 7 have a powerful extension. Even if a color original has a good tonal range, it may make sense to alter the darkness relation between certain objects. To do so, on a duplicate layer create an image that would convert well to black and white. Then change the layer mode to Luminosity.

This blending is done in RGB, prior to other corrections unless there is a color imbalance that the blend may exacerbate.

In effect, the method requires us to think in LAB, separating color from contrast in our mind. Difficult images may become easier if we do two sets of corrections, once for color, once for shape.

Inferences, Illusions, and When to Bet the Image

This chapter is about detective work—looking for internal clues that tell us what the proper colors should be. It starts with known neutrals, but it doesn't end there. Draw the proper inferences, and the image yields up its mysteries.

Great bridge players seem to be able to see through the backs of the cards. The odds appear to call for one line of play, the expert chooses another, and presto! an opponent's king magically falls under the expert's ace.

This seemingly telepathic ability is so incredible to lesser players that allegations of cheating in top-level bridge are common. Since *we* couldn't deduce that the king would fall, the expert couldn't possibly have deduced it either. He must have peeked into the enemy hand!

We see the same thing in color correction. One of my lectures in 2001 created just such a sensation. I was accused of disguising deviltry as common sense, in that I had opened up an image in which there was a tree, taken one look at it, and decided that its value was $62^C 21^M 83^Y 3^K$.

Obviously (so it was said), such precision was far beyond the ability of mortal men. It was only, so it was said, that I had so many years of experience doing this, which nobody else could ever duplicate, etc., and what users really needed was to calibrate their monitors, to which end, as it happened, the speaker was prepared to sell them a profile.

Never mind that the number of years of experience I supposedly had would have placed a couple of past employers in violation of child labor laws. The point is, we experienced folk definitely are able to delude the rubes into thinking we've got hundreds of color formulas memorized.

In fact, now that we've gone through all the basics of curves, colorspaces, and blending, we need to review something even more fundamental: how do we decide what colors we're trying to achieve? This chapter discusses how to be a color detective.

The Red and the Black

Some inferences seem so preposterously easy that it never occurs to us that they are too sophisticated for a machine to make. We'll start with one of these no-brainers, a live restoration job showing a wedding in the heartland of Texas in the early 1960s. The original print has suffered serious damage. I wasn't there, yet I can divine what certain of the colors must have been. So, of course, can you.

In bridge textbooks, the custom is to ask the reader to cover up the opposing hands and figure out the answers to certain questions. Often, the question is of the food for thought variety and doesn't get answered right away.

So, please cover the two bottom versions before responding. Here goes:

♠ *What color do you think the bride's gown is supposed to be? How about the bow ties and pants the men are wearing?*

Before you throw the book against the wall in disgust, this is a legitimate question, sophisticated enough to presage much more challenging ones later on. You weren't at this wedding. How can you be so sure about these colors?

Vendors of automated color-correction systems often use this kind of image to illustrate how potent their products are. Indeed, Figure 9.1B, done with the simplest of all such methods, the Auto Levels command, is a stunning improvement. That command effectively forces a white and a black point to occur somewhere in the image. Disasters ensue when these endpoints aren't naturally

Figure 9.1 *Opposite: the 40-year-old original print, top left, hasn't been treated kindly by age. Bottom left, a version corrected in RGB with the Auto Levels command. This page, a curve correction that makes certain inferences about not just the bride and groom's clothing, but also the color of the wood.*

See what's NEW in LOCAL NEWS
BRETT HABER
ANGELA RAE
ERNIE ANASTOS
DAVID ROGERS
CBS 2
INFORMATION NETWORK
ANGELA RAE

Figure 9.2 *African-American hair is known to be black, and skin of any ethnic group is rarely green. The inset image is a curve correction of the large one—but there's one rather large catch.*

white or black. But you can't ask for much more emphatically white than a bridal gown or more decisively black than the bow tie of a man in semiformal attire.

Good as the Auto Levels move is, it falls short of what a human could do. Humans can find other colors of which they're just as certain. Even better, they can find colors that can be excluded—and they can use findings about one color to draw inferences about another. Watch.

♥ *What color gown is the second woman from the left wearing?*

We don't know, but we do know that it can't possibly be green or blue no matter how much fading has taken place over time. It has to be some kind of warm color: red, possibly orange, maybe purple.

While we can be as sure of this deduction as we are that the bride wears white, the information is useless. Nothing we are likely to do to the picture could create a green or blue dress. But what about the hair color? As bad as the original is, we can still tell that everyone's hair is much too dark for anyone pictured to be a blond. Therefore, according to the rules of Chapter 3, they would all have to have more yellow than magenta in their skintone. That's useful information. In the original image, none of them do. Furthermore, once we engineer more yellow into the skin, we can check that the hair has not gotten yellow, too.

♦ *There's one more known color in this image. Can you name it?*

By *color,* I don't mean burnt sienna as opposed to walnut brown. I mean white, black, red, green, blue, magenta, cyan, or yellow. I state positively that the desired color of the faces, whatever they may be now, is red. This is more than can be said, for example, about the gown we just spoke of, for which red is merely one of the possibilities.

True, *red* is not as specific a word as *white,* which requires a strict relationship between cyan, magenta, and yellow. *Red* merely means that magenta and yellow have to be significantly darker than cyan in CMYK, or that green and blue have to be significantly darker than red in RGB.

One can narrow it down further, though, by thinking in terms of its neighbors, yellow and magenta in the case of red. It's true that a face can be perfectly red, which is equal magenta and yellow and much less cyan. If it varies from that, however, it's always on the yellow side, at least in people with hair as dark as what you see here. Magenta can never be higher than yellow; otherwise the hair would be purple.

The other known color also falls somewhere between red and yellow. I refer to the pews. Certain kinds of wood are brown, which is a red. Others are more yellow. But purple wood is about as common as a green ace of hearts. And purple wood is what we get in Figure 9.1B.

The human correction, Figure 9.1C, is better because it takes the position that the wood has to be either yellowish red or reddish yellow. Not greenish, not purplish, but yellow highest, magenta second, and cyan way down.

Is this the best one can do with curves? Maybe not. I don't know if I've hit the wood color exactly. I do know that it's conceivably correct. Figure 9.1B is not. Notice the extra "detail" Figure 9.1C exposes: a yellow stain across the couple's chests.

♣ *How do you know it isn't all a setup? Perhaps some calibrationist paid all the men to wear brown ties and brown pants, the better to baffle by-the-numbers correction.*

Bridge experts sometimes pull off brilliant deceptions. Say that you, a defender, hold the ace and queen of a certain suit, and the opponent, whom you know also has the king, plays the jack ahead of you. If you win the trick with the ace, the opponent will never in a million years believe that you also hold the queen, and may be in for a most unpleasant experience later in the play.

Speaking as one who's been hornswoggled in this way many times, there's nothing for it but to take off one's hat to the person who pulled off the amazing falsecard.

People do crazy things at weddings and afterward. Who knows, this could be the first bride in the history of western culture to wear a cyan gown. Maybe somebody painted the pews green. Or perhaps all the attendees slathered their faces with blusher, in which case they're purple.

But what are the odds? In other words, exactly how confident are you that the gown is white, the ties black, the faces red?

Presumably the answer is somewhat less than 100 percent, but somewhat more than the point at which one would say, I may be wrong about this, but I'm so confident of

being right that I'm willing to risk a hideous result if I'm not.

It becomes, therefore, a matter of betting the image. If we're very certain that we know what an area should be—or very certain that it can't be what it currently is—then we place the bet. Otherwise, we pass and wait for the next deal. See if you can avoid being taken in by the following falsecard.

The Media Can't Be Trusted

Skintone, as we have just seen, can be an important marker of color accuracy. Also, we're always on the lookout for things that aren't just light or dark, but that are reliably *white* or *black* and not some off-color.

The poster in Figure 9.2 has some of these. The headlines and logo are certain to be blank paper. We can bet that they should not just be a kind of white but that they should specifically be $255^R255^G255^B$ or $0^C0^M0^Y$. Plus, not only are there skintones, but two people are African-American, which is an advantage for us. Leaving aside Dennis Rodman, African-American hair is reliably black.

One can therefore easily produce something like the inset, but unfortunately the

The Lesson of the Stain

Correcting by the numbers implies a serious effort to make sure that the numbers in fact mean something. Relying on a couple of slapdash samples doesn't always work, particularly if there is reason to suspect the quality of the original image.

Figure 9.1C offers a pointed example. Now that the image has been corrected, physical damage, in the form of a yellow stain across the upper bodies of bride and groom, is evident. That stain would have to be retouched out of the file.

The damage is hard to detect in the original, Figure 9.1A, which is why we should take measurements in several of the areas that we consider should be white. Measuring only inside the damaged area and neutralizing it would create a blue cast.

Figure 9.3 *When the poster is placed in context, it's easy to see why its colors can't be relied on: they've been bleached out by the sun.*

themselves, become purplish red. Furthermore, while we can't bet the image that the concrete is absolutely neutral, it certainly is fairly close. Yet the faces in the poster seem to be more green than the concrete. What gives?

The sun in the corrected version looks strong, and the advertiser placed its poster where it would get a lot of it, day after day.

poster doesn't exist in isolation. Try to treat Figure 9.3 this way, and you'll be in for a nasty surprise. Set these people's hair to be black, and the window frames, telephone, and station sign, which look like they might be black

If whoever printed this poster made some guarantee of color-fastness, he's sorry for it now. What happened here is exactly what happened to the old wedding print we just worked on. Expose the thing to an adverse environment, and one of the colorants is likely to bail. There, it was the cyan and to a lesser extent the yellow; here, the magenta. The faces measure blue-green in the original because they *are* blue-green.

LAB and the Info Palette

The Info palette's two halves can display color equivalencies. The left half is usually set to Actual Color, meaning the values in the file's current colorspace. When working in an unfamiliar environment, like LAB, people use the right half as a crutch by setting it to read CMYK or RGB. And CMYK users often set the right half to Total Ink, to be sure that they don't inadvertently go over the printer's limit.

Info			
R:	255	L:	98
G:	250	a:	-4
B:	201	b:	24
8-bit		8-bit	

Actual Color
Proof Color

Grayscale
RGB Color
Web Color
HSB Color
CMYK Color
Lab Color

Total Ink
Opacity

Regardless of what colorspace you work in, when investigating neutrality, set the right half to read LAB, because the AB values aren't affected either by darkness or by each other. You can sweep over the area quickly and see whether anything is far removed from 0^A0^B. In RGB, this procedure would be much slower because you'd have to compare three rapidly changing numbers.

Guessing the Distribution

At bridge, the expert delays decisions on where cards lie as long as possible. The more irrelevant cards are played, the more clues emerge to the location of the critical ones. If an opponent unexpectedly turns up very short in hearts, she becomes much more likely than her partner to have missing cards in the other suits.

The biggest problem for those who want to become color magicians is to determine when something is supposed to be neutral. Whether it *looks* neutral in the original is usually irrelevant.

♠ *In Figure 9.4A, what color do you predict for the light-colored trim around the windows? How about the dark car to the left in Figure 9.4B?*

Based on experience with people's taste in house colors, it's nearly certain that the trim is white. By the looks of it, the left-hand car is black, flanked by a dark green and two dark blue vehicles.

These are right-out-of-the-camera RGB files from which CMYK files are eventually needed. So we have our choice of colorspace to work them in. However, to help out the investigation, I'd set up the Info palette to read LAB (see box, facing page)—it's much easier to judge neutrality, because we're just looking for 0^A0^B, regardless of darkness.

Running the cursor over many areas of the trim shows current values of between 2^A and 5^A—slightly more magenta than green—and between $(6)^B$ and $(2)^B$, more blue than yellow. Thus, the trim starts as a bluish purple, somewhat less intense than the house itself, which is typically around $10^A(5)^B$.

As for the car, in its lighter areas at rear, it's typically $0^A(20)^B$. In the darker areas at center it's more like $0^A(15)^B$. Both are distinctly blue.

Now that we know that the measured values don't correspond with what we were expecting in either picture, we are ready to correct, which means that it's time for the critical question.

Figure 9.4 *Should the light trim in the top image be white, or light purple? How about the left-hand car in the bottom image? Is it as black as it looks?*

♥ *Are you sure enough of your previous answer to bet the image on it, by forcing either or both of these areas to become neutral?*

At first, the house seems like the better bet. A car could certainly be navy blue, no matter how black it looks, but light purple is an extremely unusual choice for house trim.

So what are the odds against? 10 to 1? At least. As great as the odds against the wedding celebrants wearing something other than whites and blacks in the wedding image of Figure 9.1A? Definitely not.

In life as at cards, bad breaks happen. Trumps split 6–0; the tasteless paint their houses light purple. The trim, as we are about to prove, is not white. At bridge or at color

Figure 9.5 *Above, the addition of a known color, the snow, demonstrates that Figure 9.4A's colors were correct. Below, the presence of known colors, the tires, can be used to verify that the shadows in Figure 9.4B had a cast.*

correction, percentage plays don't always work. At such times, virtue has to be its own reward.

As with the wedding image, we often overlook the thought process that renders the correct color obvious. In Figure 9.5A, we make the following analysis, probably without ever realizing we're making it: the snow is definitely white; we can bet the image on that. Certain parts of the snow are just as dark as the trim, yet the trim is distinctly purpler; wherefore the trim is known to be purple.

The presence of the snow, an object of whose color there can be no doubt, is what makes this deduction possible. That known color was what was missing in Figure 9.4A.

Figure 9.4B is another story. In isolation, we can't bet on any car being any particular color. But I am just as convinced that the tires are 0^A0^B as snow is. If those tires are the same color as any car, then that car is known to be black.

These tires typically measure $0^A(18)^B$, very like the left-hand car. Therefore, I am prepared to bet the image that the car is black and blow the current blueness away.

◆   *Even if the tires were absent, there are two other clues that demonstrate the car is neutral. Can you name them?*

To show that the car is currently wrong, we need to find something else of approximately the same darkness that we're more sure about. We're certain that tires should be black, and they're just about as dark as the car is. We know that the pedestrian markings on the pavement should be white, but whether they start out correct proves nothing about the car, which is much darker.

The background of the one-way sign, however, is as dark as the tires, and just as certainly black.

Figure 9.6 *The architecture of this region is known for its use of soft pastel tones. Under such circumstances, it's dangerous to assume that anything is neutral—or is it?*

And, while I have recommended keeping the right half of the Info palette reading LAB, shifting it temporarily to CMYK reveals the other impossibility. We don't know much about the specific green of these trees, but we know from Chapter 3 that all natural greens feature more yellow than cyan. Measuring the green area nearest to the car, right in the region of the wires above its roof, finds $85^C50^M60^Y15^K$. The cyan and magenta are both higher than they ought to be; cyan plus magenta make blue, therefore the trees are too blue; the trees are as dark as the car, therefore the car must be too blue as well.

And so, we are justified in transforming Figure 9.4B into 9.5B; note the more believable tree color and the elimination of the blue cast. We would normally pause to discuss how it was done, but before doing so, we have to take the neutrality hunt even further.

♣ *The Art Deco architecture of South Beach is noted for its flamboyant use of pastel tones, such as the one in the building at right in Figure 9.6. The hotel at center measures $(3)^A(5)^B$,* *a soft blue-green. Can this be correct, or should it be white?*

The best inference is often a negative one. The great bridge player thinks, "If my right-hand opponent had the queen of hearts, he would never have played the card he did six tricks ago, so the queen of hearts must be in his partner's hand."

First of all, if you need to know the name of this hotel, you can't afford to stay there. And if you do know it, you may know its color. But let's assume that you don't, and you don't.

In any other resort location, it would be almost a certainty that this hotel would be white. But we are in South Beach. As matters stand, however, we can only say that the greenish blue we've measured seems unlikely to be right. We have, however, seen many stranger things.

Unfortunately, there is no snow in South Beach, at least not of the precipitative variety, so we are unable to make the comparison that we did in Figure 9.5A. There are also no tires, or anything else of a known color, that we can rely on. The sunbather is of undetermined ethnicity, and in any event she may be so sunburned that normal fleshtone values may not apply. Yet inferences are available.

We do not know the color of the umbrellas, although we surmise they might be neutral. Ditto for the lounges near the sunbather, which are probably white, for the ones to her right, which are likely gray, and for the large background dome, which is, chances are, neutral as well.

That's a total of five independent items that we consider are probably neutral, counting the hotel. Consider the umbrellas alone, and the best we can say is that the odds are they're white. When we learn that they are in fact $(2)^A(4)^B$, we can't deny the possibility that this is their correct color. But when we measure the other four objects, and they all come out the same greenish blue, then we *can* deny it. That's the negative inference. We can't prove directly that any of these objects are neutral. We do it indirectly, by assuming that they aren't, and discovering that the assumption leads to a ridiculous result.

The odds against five unrelated objects truly being the same unusual color are greater than the odds against a bride wearing a white gown. We *can* bet the image that all five are neutral.

Counting Up the Points

Our last two images are representative of the correction challenges we face in today's digital world, types of problems that didn't exist with scanned film. We were able to identify casts in both, but only at one end of the tonal range. The dark cars were too blue, but the light pavement was correctly neutral. The light hotel was found to have a cool cast, but the dark windbreaks on the beach, which should probably be gray, measure as correct, and so do the presumed shadow points.

Our first eight chapters introduced many different approaches, many different tools, many different options. The purpose of this and the following chapter is to clarify when things are optional and when they are mandatory or nearly so.

An example of *optional* would be the sky in Figure 9.6. Personally, I think it's too dark, but opinions will vary, as they would with color: some might want it more purple, others more cyan. Whatever your choice, Photoshop offers at least a dozen different routes to get there.

Also, I really glossed over the corrections used to create the wedding picture of Figure 9.1C and the cars of Figure 9.5B. In past chapters, you'd have seen the curves. Here, it wasn't necessary, because my approach was optional. I corrected the wedding in RGB but would have gotten similar results in CMYK, in LAB, or even by channel blending to kill the cast. With the cars, I used the green channel for an early luminosity blend, and I steepened the AB curves of LAB to bring out more color in the trees.

Again, though, there are other ways to do it. I was afraid to show the exact steps, for fear you might think I was advocating them as the only way to play the hand. However, the inferences about what colors to use were indispensable. If you don't detect the magenta cast across the midrange of the wedding shot or the blue shadows of the cars image, you cannot, in my experience, produce a competitive image, any more than Figure 9.1B is competitive with 9.1C.

Unlike these two, however, certain images clearly suggest specific approaches—even after we've decided on the correct colors.

The play of a bridge hand starts with an opening lead by the declarer's left-hand opponent. Declarer's partner then puts his cards face up on the table for his partner to play. Experienced declarers now pause for thought for a minute or two, even if there is only one card that can legally be played at the moment. This pause for reflection to organize an overall strategy makes the rest of the play faster and more accurate. I recommend the same type of pause before beginning work on a difficult image, for much the same reasons.

Let's plan the play of this hotel image. The RGB file comes from an early-model digicam, with no profile embedded. We'll assume that a CMYK file is eventually required.

Knowing How the Cards Lie

We've already discovered a cool cast in the light areas of Figure 9.6. Everybody would agree that such a cast is undesirable for a beach image. In fact, some people might want to go further than just making it neutral, and deliberately incorporate a slight warm cast. On the other hand, as noted earlier, we might disagree on the proper color and darkness of the sky. But there are several additional points that we *should* agree on.

● The overall range is bad, because the camera has woodenly chosen the frames of the beach chairs as the white point. Nobody else cares whether these tiny areas blow out. The highlight should be set in the lightest *significant* object, probably the nearest umbrella. That easy step can be taken whenever we like, in any colorspace.

● Unlike the other images in this chapter, this one has a serious issue with separation of colors. South Beach pastels are vivid in real life, but dull in this image. The need to increase color variation suggests that we should use LAB.

● The image features a lot of distinct edges, such as the windows and the beach chairs. This suggests strong conventional sharpening as described in Chapter 6. There is no dominating color, so the sharpening should be applied overall. We know that RGB is a relatively poor sharpening space. As we already have decided to enter LAB, that's where we should sharpen.

● Unfortunately, this cast appears only in the light areas; the dark parts appear correct. That's an argument against LAB, which

can only change casts overall, unless we go to the trouble of using a selection or using the Blend If sliders. RGB and CMYK don't need any crutches to eliminate this type of cast.

● But if we wait until we get to CMYK to fix the cast, it will be harder, because the color boost in LAB will have made the cast worse. Therefore, we should work on the cast in RGB.

That Old Savoir Faire— and How to Get It

Color-correction experts remind me of the characters played by Cary Grant and Maurice Chevalier—imperturbable, never a hair out of place, confidently ready for any situation. It is frustrating for the rest of us not to be able to match their sophistication.

Yet when we analyze how they behave, there's no magic at all. The only thing that separates them from us (other than good looks, which don't count) is that they deliver their ripostes immediately, whereas it might take us five minutes to think of them, causing us to feel stupid and frustrated.

And so it is with this chapter. Many concepts are surpassingly obvious, like that a bride wears white. Yet this is the most frustrating area of all for non-experts, and after more than a decade of teaching small classes, I think I have figured out why.

It doesn't take much study of curves and sharpening for an inexperienced user to be able to create work that's at least as good as an expert's, although usually an expert would make fewer errors and therefore be a bit more consistent. An inexperienced user, though, may take five minutes to analyze an image in the manner taught in this chapter, whereas an expert does it in seconds. Whereupon the inexperienced person feels stupid and frustrated.

I am not ordinarily one for pep talks, but listen up. The objective is to create images that look as good as if they were worked on by somebody who has done 50,000 more images than you have. You cannot seriously be upset if that person can figure out what he wants to do with the image considerably faster than you can. Now, if the person can make the picture look a whole lot better than your effort, *that's* something to be upset about. Take all the time you need before you start your Photoshop magic.

• With such a large, deeply colored sky, we need to be alert to the type of noise in the red channel described in the box on page 188, particularly considering that we have been told this capture is from an older digicam.

And so, we have a plan. Kill the cast in RGB; move to LAB to boost the colors and to sharpen, then on to CMYK for final output.

♠ *If it turns out that some kind of noise reduction and/or color change is needed for the sky, in which colorspace should we do it,* *and how do we avoid affecting the rest of the image?*

The sky, which is nearly a flat color, can be changed in any colorspace. Certain types of tricky blurring work better in LAB, but this wouldn't be one of them—nothing subtle is needed, because there's no real detail that can be obliterated.

Keeping the blur out of the rest of the image is another story. This is why we have to be able to visualize channels. In every RGB and CMYK channel, certain other objects will be the same darkness as this sky. Ditto the L of LAB. The sky is slightly more magenta than green in the A, but so are a lot of other things. But it's *far* more blue than yellow in the B, much more so than the only other blue object, the hotel at right. So LAB

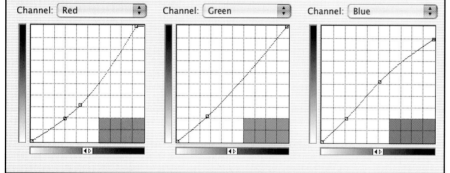

Figure 9.7 *On an adjustment layer, RGB curves are applied to reduce the cast in Figure 9.6, using several sampling points with readouts set to LAB for convenience. The version at bottom left appears to have lost some detail, so the adjustment layer is set to Color mode, producing the version at bottom right.*

A   B

is where we can most easily distinguish the sky from the rest of the image.

First, however, there is business to attend to in RGB. For reasons that will shortly become apparent, we should make a curves adjustment layer, at least temporarily, rather than applying the curves to the base file.

This cast vanishes as the image gets darker, so it's well to use the color sampler tool to choose

Figure 9.8 *The red channel (enlarged top left) is noisy. To compensate, the green channel is blended into the RGB in Luminosity mode (top right). The file now moves into LAB, where curves produce the version at bottom left. The sky remains quite noisy (bottom right).*

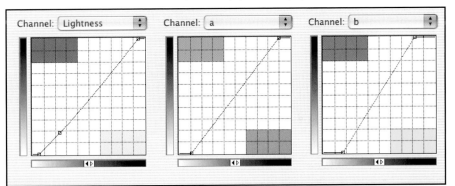

several reference points to evaluate the success of the curves. In Figure 9.7, #1 is the lightest part of the umbrellas, #4 is the gray windbreak, and #2 and #3 are both in the hotel itself. Although the file remains in RGB, I have set all of them to read LAB equivalents, where it's easy to see whether they are seriously away from 0^A0^B. The top left reading, a section of the beach, remains in RGB.

It's too much to ask for a perfect 0^A0^B in each of these sample points. Nevertheless, the numbers to the right of the slashes—the new values—are much closer to neutrality than the originals, which are to the left. The result is Figure 9.7A.

Controlling this many points with curves is somewhat difficult. I was so preoccupied with getting the color right that I ignored the contrast issue, allowing the curves to get steeper or flatter wherever the cards fell. I'd certainly accept any added contrast that these curves might happen to provide, but am also willing to revert to the original contrast if that proves to be better. That's the justification for the adjustment layer. The

color of Figure 9.7A is better, but I think it's a step backward in detail. Therefore, I changed the adjustment layer's mode to Color, the opposite of Luminosity, restoring the original contrast in Figure 9.7B.

♥ *Before moving out of RGB, what should our workflow check for?*

Since RGB offers unique opportunities for the sort of channel blending shown in Chapters 7 and 8, we should see if anything suggests itself before leaving that space. We ordinarily use the red channel to strengthen skies, but this sky has no interesting detail and is more than dark enough already. In any event, Figure 9.8A shows that we were right to worry about the possibility of a very noisy red. The blue would not be a good choice to replace it because its sky is missing and its trees are very dark. The green is a good choice: relatively free of noise, fairly light trees, a moderate sky, and sand with good detail. Figure 9.8B shows it, with contrast slightly enhanced, applied to the RGB file on a luminosity layer. After flattening that, we are ready to move into LAB.

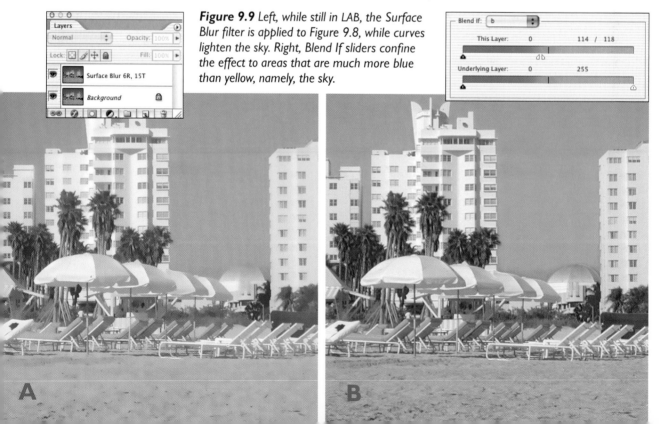

Figure 9.9 *Left, while still in LAB, the Surface Blur filter is applied to Figure 9.8, while curves lighten the sky. Right, Blend If sliders confine the effect to areas that are much more blue than yellow, namely, the sky.*

Figure 9.10 *Left, on a duplicate layer, the L channel of LAB is sharpened heavily. Right, the file is converted to CMYK and the lightening impact of the sharpening is reduced by placing it on its own layer and reducing opacity.*

The L curve sets the highlight in the umbrella and adds slight steepening in the beach's range. With another shot at correction coming up later in CMYK, there's no point in trying to achieve a perfect shadow in the relatively clumsy L.

The AB curves are simple: they both remain straight lines rotated around the midpoint, which the RGB curves had made sure is now correct. I thought it looked better to emphasize the yellow component of the warmer tones more than the magenta, so I used a steeper angle on the B curve. That's a matter of taste, as is the question of whether I made Figure 9.8C too colorful or not colorful enough.

◆ *The relatively smooth green channel replaced the noisy red in Figure 9.8B. So, after the LAB move, why is the sky still so noisy in Figure 9.8D?*

The poor-quality red channels contributed not just the darker areas of noise that are evident in Figure 9.8A, but also a nasty color variation. The dark blotches make for a bluer sky; the lighter ones are more purple. Blending the green into the red on a luminosity layer minimized the darkness variation but not the color shift.

As noted in Chapter 1, we humans aren't nearly as sensitive to variation in darker colors as when they're lighter. The sky is so dark in the original, Figure 9.6, that we barely notice the blue and purple mottling, but now that we've lightened things so much, it's a lot more evident, requiring us to use some sort of blurring filter.

If you have Photoshop CS2 or later, the most attractive option is Filter: Blur>Surface Blur, which has a Threshold setting in addition to the Radius found in most blurring filters; the higher the Threshold, the more blur is allowed, which is the opposite of the way Unsharp Mask works.

Here, though, we just want to blast away, so the Gaussian Blur, Median, or Dust & Scratches filters will work about as well. Figure 9.9A shows Surface Blur applied on a duplicate layer to all three LAB channels at a 6.0 Radius and a 15 Threshold. I also decided that I wanted a lighter sky, so I curved the L.

The filter is designed to hold edges, up to a point. But the sides of the hotels have lost nearly all detail, just as the sky has. To restore it in Figure 9.9B, we use the Blend If sliders, excluding everything that originally wasn't at least slightly blue, meaning everything but

Figure 9.11 *Curves to establish the desired shadow value create this final version.*

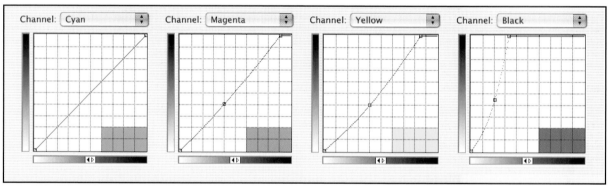

the sky. Notice that there is still detail in the mildly blue area of the right-hand hotel.

After flattening the image, we add a duplicate layer for sharpening. Again, the layer is for flexibility. We know that because of its many edges, this image wants as much USM as we can give it. Since it's hard to determine what that magic quantity is, and because it's so important to the image, the best course is to oversharpen and then cut back on it by reducing layer opacity or some other swindle.

Sharpening in LAB is always applied to the L only. Having selected that channel, I used settings of 500% Amount, .9 Radius, 10 Threshold to get to Figure 9.10A.

We saw in Chapter 6 that USM in images like this is often more effective when the lightening effect of the sharpening is reduced. Unfortunately, Darken and Lighten modes don't currently work in Photoshop's version of LAB.

Therefore, we move into our final destination, CMYK. Normally, when we change colorspaces, we want layers to flatten, because certain operations will otherwise be canceled. Adjustment layers, for example, are discarded altogether.

Here, though, in response to a prompt, we decline to flatten. On arrival into CMYK, we duplicate the top layer, leaving Figure 9.9B

Figure 9.12 *This image's yellow cast is concentrated in the light and middle ranges.*

on the bottom layer and copies of Figure 9.10A on the top two. Now, as shown earlier in Figure 6.10, we set the middle layer mode to Darken. The top layer may be left at Normal, or, if you need a reminder of what it's there for, to Lighten. I recommend setting the opacity of this top layer to 50% and assessing the situation. When I did so, I was fairly happy with the result. I left the top layer alone, reduced the middle layer's opacity to 90%, and got Figure 9.10B.

The best advanced techniques are useless without a foundation. A bridge player, no matter how brilliant, still has to follow suit and count to 13. We still have not verified that Figure 9.10B is correct by the numbers.

If this image had a distinct focus of interest, we'd try to put it into the steep parts of CMYK curves. As it doesn't, all we need do is verify that highlights are correct (yes; $4^C2^M2^Y$ in the nearest umbrella), that neutrals are portrayed correctly (yes; that's what the curves of Figure 9.7 were all about), and that shadows are full and balanced (no; they're too cyan and much too light, because we have been ignoring this issue until now).

Since there isn't much shadow detail in this image, and since the literally darkest areas are too small for the ink police to measure, I went for a shadow of $80^C70^M70^Y85^K$. The cyan needed no adjustment at all. The intermediate points in the curves prevent the light half of the image from getting darker and offer the sunny Figure 9.11 as the final alternative to the murky Figure 9.8.

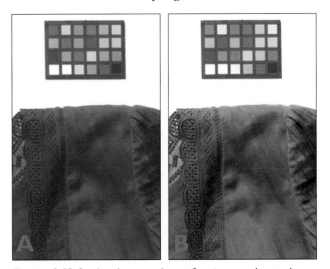

Figure 9.13 *Studio photographers often insert color cards to aid in later correction of the file. Which of these versions probably has more accurate color?*

Establishing a shadow is easiest in CMYK, just as luminosity blending is in RGB, and enhancing color is in LAB. So, this image made good use of all three colorspaces. As that can be mentally tiresome, we'll close this chapter with an image that requires only one.

A Card Laid Is a Card Played

Figure 9.12 arrives in sRGB. For the sake of argument, we'll say that that's what's eventually needed. Should we leave RGB at all?

At first glance, no. Without checking the numbers carefully, it seems that the obvious yellow cast doesn't affect the shadows, so it would be hard to fix in LAB. Also, we certainly don't need brighter colors as we did in the South Beach example. That's another strike against LAB. There's no obvious reason to make a CMYK copy to use the black channel for luminosity blending, and the faces are too small for the CMYK advantage in unsharp masking to make much of a difference. So, here's a toughie:

♣ *Granted that this image will never leave RGB, why might someone with a lot of CMYK experience do better with it?*

It's good practice, when possible, for photographers to shoot gray cards with their originals. These cards, which are commercially available from many sources, can give crucial guidance by providing a neutral reference that's missing in the scene itself. Some go further, and shoot a color reference card, such as the ones shown in Figure 9.13.

The theory is a good one. This chapter shows that it's not always easy to find reliable reference points in an image. The purpose of the card is to add some artificial ones.

Reliance on the card works well—if the colors being relied on are critical to the image. Otherwise, it can be worse than useless. These images, enlarged, are borrowed from Figures 2.17A and 2.19, raw and corrected versions of a studio shot of a purple blouse with a blank background.

♠ *Which of these versions has a more accurate color card? Which has a better blouse?*

Of course, the answers contradict one another. In bridge, players who cheat are ostracized. In Photoshop, cheaters make the money. The best corrections sacrifice fidelity in areas that are of little concern in favor of better detail and color in more significant parts.

A fleshtone color in the upper left of Figure 9.13A's card is gray in Figure 9.13B. A light green and an orange are portrayed as almost the same color. Why anybody would care is beyond me, since there are no fleshtones, greens, or oranges in the actual image, only dark purples. We live and die by what happens to that color. Any other is irrelevant.

Suppose this color card had been inserted in each of the images of this chapter so far. Some parts of it would have been useful, especially the neutral areas. You may recall the discussion in the first pages of Chapter 7 that demonstrated the futility of looking for a fixed formula to determine the appropriate darkness after a conversion. That chapter was about grayscale images, but the concept applies to color as well. Therefore, it's not important here whether any of the darknesses in the corrected card match the original.

In all of the originals so far, though, the gray areas of the card would have needed to reproduce as gray. Maybe a lighter gray, maybe a darker gray, but no other color. Otherwise, there would have been a cast in the final version. This blouse image is the only exception. As purple is the only color for which we give a hoot, it's irrelevant whether original grays remain that way. And, in fact, the medium gray in the lower right of Figure 9.13A reproduces as blue in Figure 9.13B.

Similarly, third from left in the third row of this color card is found a bright red. As no bright reds have yet appeared anywhere in this chapter, this swatch is a waste of energy—so far. In the image we're about to work on, however, bright red is important, since three of the little girls are wearing something approximating the color of that swatch. It would therefore have made our lives somewhat easier if such a card had been included in Figure 9.12, but it wasn't, so we'll have to muddle along without it. Fortunately, there's a suitable substitute, if you know where to look.

How Many Tricks Can We Count?

It's easy to say that Figure 9.12 is too yellow. The disciplined approach is instead to start by listing the colors we know and then proving what is wrong.

• The class is not being led by a schoolteacher, but by a U.S. congressman. His hair is certainly white. Furthermore, its lightest area is the lightest significant part of this image.

• The darkest significant point is either his jacket or the hair of the little girl at right. We should choose the hair as the shadow, because we know for reasons of ethnicity that it's black, whereas the man's jacket could conceivably be some other subdued color.

• All the other children have brown hair, except for one girl whose face is hidden, who may be a blond.

• Several children wear pants that are known as *blue jeans* for a reason.

• Fleshtones, as discussed in Chapter 3, must be red, and generally biased toward yellow. Young children like these may have, in CMYK terms, equal magenta and yellow. One would expect, but not bet the image, that the teacher, who is much older, has yellower skin.

When an image has as many interrelated parts as this one does, further inferences present themselves. Although this is an RGB file, we'll continue to read LAB values from the Info palette. For example, the man's hair at its lightest point is $99^L(6)^A23^B$ and at its darkest $75^L3^A35^B$. Translation: the hair starts out very yellow and slightly green. As it gets darker, it

gets even yellower, but becomes slightly warmer, acquiring a slight bias toward magenta rather than green. I consider it easier to make these judgments from the values of the A and B channels than to try to scope out what $254^R255^G207^B$ and $206^R181^G119^B$ mean.

Since we know that we want the hair to be gray or white, the desired values are 0^A0^B. So these readings confirm what we already know, that the image has a severe yellow cast.

The cast, however, is lessened as the image gets darker. The leftmost girl's jeans read $30^L(3)^A3^B$. The positive reading in the B means that they're slightly more yellow than blue, which is ridiculous. However, they're not 35^B too high, like the man's hair is—half that at best. And the rightmost girl's hair reads $5^L1^A5^B$, only slightly too yellow.

Stumbling Blocks: Positive and Negative Inferences

•**Knowing what a color must be, and knowing what it must not be.** Don't get into the habit of forcing things to be a specific color unless you're certain that you know what that color is. Often we know that the current value is wrong without knowing specifically what is right. In that case, we're on a guess. Example: the teacher's hair in Figure 9.12 is certainly white, so we should force it to be neutral when we correct. If he were a much younger man with dark hair, however, we could not be so sure. It might be neutral and it might not. However, it could not be even slightly green or blue, so if the Info palette indicated negative values in either the A or B channel, we'd have to correct the color to something else, even if we didn't know what that something else should be.

•**When no inference is available.** These techniques are similar to reading a mystery novel. In such novels, however, the detective invariably figures out whodunit. We do not always have such success. If you can't draw any inferences from a certain picture it's probably because there are none to be drawn, as there weren't in the tightly cropped house of Figure 9.4A. In that case, just set highlight and shadow and move on.

Figure 9.14 *The original green and blue channels confirm the yellow cast.*

We also pick up another known color. Her shirt is white. We don't know this by looking at Figure 9.12, but by measuring its darkest part, across her stomach, at $71^L1^A27^B$. That's similar enough to the congressman's hair that we must judge they're the same color.

And the numbers give us a surprise. The man's typical fleshtone is $75^L20^A36^B$, but the lighter-skinned girls come in at around $75^L10^A36^B$. The man must be quite pink-skinned indeed, if his A channel is more positive than that of a child.

♥ *How do we know that the man's pinker face is not a trick of the lighting conditions?*

If it were, the parts of his hair that are as dark as the skin would have a magenta cast, and they don't. Also, if the girls were in greener lighting than the man is, that would account for their skin not being as pink—but it would make their brown hair greener as well. It measures 0^A35^B, which is just about what we might expect, considering the known yellow cast. And we have already seen that the rightmost girl's white shirt matches the man's hair. If they were in different lightings, it wouldn't.

We could also confirm these numbers by looking at the individual channels. As with all face pictures, we expect a pretty good green. That's what we see in Figure 9.14, but the blue channel is clearly much too dark, which suggests a method we haven't considered before.

We've done most of our blending on luminosity layers, since we're usually trying to increase contrast without changing color. If we blend the green into the blue of Figure 9.14, however, it won't just be contrast that improves—it will reduce the cast as well, by forcing a bluer appearance.

This image's cast is considerably worse than the blue cast in the beach scene of Figure 9.6. It's hard to eliminate a cast so severe with curves. The preliminary blend isn't intended to solve the problem, but to lessen it so that the curves can do their thing.

So, with the blue channel exposed, Image: Apply Image, specifying the green as the source. It doesn't matter in this picture, but mode should be Lighten. If the leftmost girl's shirt were any purpler, it might be darker in the green than in the blue, and we wouldn't want the blend to affect it.

Opacity is a guess. The blue channel is supposed to be darker than the green in the faces, so it wouldn't do to use 100%. To create Figure 9.15A, I chose 50%. Then, I made a curves adjustment layer, reduced the cast further, and, after looking at the result, changed layer mode to Color as shown previously in the South Beach image, Figure 9.7.

Figure 9.15 *Top, the cast is reduced by blending the green channel into the blue at 50% opacity, Lighten mode. Bottom, curves are applied on an adjustment layer set to Color mode.*

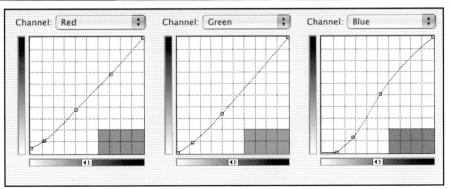

Blend If:	Green ⬍		
This Layer:	0		255
Underlying Layer:	93 / 114		255

Figure 9.16 *Top, the green channel is blended into the RGB composite on a luminosity layer. Bottom, the red areas are restored with Blend If sliders.*

This produced Figure 9.15B, which now is close enough for our standard maneuver with faces—blending the green channel into the composite, fully discussed in Chapter 8. So, after flattening the image, I applied the green channel to a duplicate layer in Normal mode at 100% opacity, changed layer mode to Luminosity, and reached Figure 9.16A.

Although it added depth to the faces, this maneuver destroyed much of the red areas, particularly the shirt of the second girl from the left. This occurred because the green

channel is very dark in such an intense red. Blending such a blob into every other channel instructs Photoshop to keep the color but make it as dark as the man's jacket, which Photoshop can no more do than a bridge player can beat the ace of trump.

Fortunately, it was easily restored in Figure 9.16B with Blend If sliders. True, the faces are red, too, but they're so much lighter than the red clothing that it's easy to differentiate them in the green channel. There's no difference between using This Layer and Underlying

Layer here, because every channel on the top layer is a copy of the green.

♦ *If it were against the rules to use Blend If sliders on the green channel, what other channel(s) could you use instead?*

Dark, pure colors like these are easy to isolate. If green were unavailable, five of the remaining nine channels could do it. In RGB, it would be tough to isolate it in the red. It could be done in the blue, although not as easily as in the green, because the face is darker and the leftmost girl's shirt lighter.

In CMYK, the green's close relative, the magenta, could do this easily, and so could the yellow, which corresponds to RGB's blue. Also, don't forget LAB. The L channel wouldn't help, but the A and B, being color only and not affected by darkness, can often isolate objects easily where RGB has problems. These red garments are much more magenta than green and much more yellow than blue compared to anything else in the picture.

Figure 9.17 *Top, a further blend of the green channel into the blue, Lighten mode, similar to that of Figure 9.15A. Bottom, sharpening is added.*

Measurements at this point indicated that the yellowness had been battered but not vanquished. I therefore flattened the image and once again blended the green into the blue, Lighten mode, this time at 40% opacity. Blending is not like curves or sharpening, where we try to avoid multiple applications of similar moves. Figure 9.17A is an expansion of Figure 9.15A, not a contradiction of it.

If an image is headed for either LAB or CMYK anyway, those spaces are where it should be sharpened. Figure 9.17A was first sharpened conventionally, then hiraloam, both with a high Threshold to avoid bringing out unwanted detail in the faces.

Cards on the Table

Card players occasionally get an unfair advantage when they accidentally or otherwise get a peek into an opponent's hand. I would have had such an advantage in correcting Figure 9.6, because I happen to know that the Delano Hotel is white, which would have saved me the trouble of deducing it.

Anyone with a lot of CMYK experience has a similar crutch to lean on here. Graphic artists who design books for children believe that any red that is not $0^C100^M100^Y$ is not a red. I am more sure that the back cover of the book is that formulation than I am that the bride was wearing white. I say that not just because the use of $0^C100^M100^Y$ is a cliché, but because it appears to match the stripe on the flag on the front cover, which prepress folk know is close to $0^C100^M100^Y$ too.

The second girl from left wears a shirt of the same color. So, we set up the right half of the Info palette to read CMYK, not LAB, equivalents, and measure her right shoulder. We learn that the ratio is a proper 100^M100^Y—accompanied by 13^C2^K of red-killing garbage. This allows the inference that, even though all other numbers seem to be correct, the red areas have a cold cast. That would include the faces.

I don't see how this could have been attended to previously, at least not in RGB. So now there are two choices. If we don't wish to leave RGB, we can use Image: Adjustments> Hue/Saturation or Image: Adjustments> Selective Color, each of which allows us to target any one of the RGBCMY colors for

Review and Exercises

✓Quickly interpreting the AB values of LAB in the Info palette can make drawing inferences much more efficient. For each of the following items, state roughly what the *desired* AB values are (example: A should be 0^A or slightly positive, B should be quite negative).

1. The light green gown of the second woman from left in Figure 9.1C.
2. The foreground beach in Figure 9.11.
3. The fabric of the blouse in Figure 9.13.
4. The red shirts of the three girls in Figure 9.18B. (Extra credit: how do they vary from one another?)

✓We haven't covered retouching yet, but what tools would you use to get rid of the yellow stain across the upper bodies in Figure 9.1C?

✓Collect a dozen of your own images at random. How often do you find (a) known colors such as the neutrals in Figure 9.1; (b) unknown colors where certain possibilities can nevertheless be excluded (for example, green hair); (c) no clue at all?

Figure 9.18 *Two attempts to make the shirts and faces redder. Top, the Hue/Saturation command in RGB. Bottom, converting to LAB and applying the curves shown.*

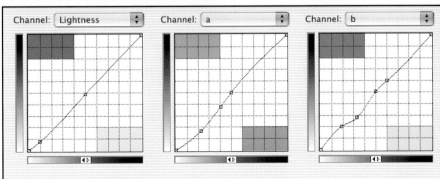

correction. Hue/Sat is the better option here, because we can target even more precisely by, after choosing Reds, Option–clicking the shirt to indicate that it is the focus of change. Figure 9.18A did this, with settings of 0 Hue, +13 Saturation, +9 Lightness.

The other option is to buy a round-trip ticket to LAB, which specializes in this type of color enhancement. I produced the curves shown by Command–clicking the faces, neutrals, and bright reds. This is the trickiest kind of LAB curving but also the most powerful. The bulge just below the center point bottom half of the B pushes the fleshtones toward yellow. The bottom point, however, limits the move toward yellow in things that were already extremely yellow, namely the red objects. Without LAB, it's hard to move the faces away from blue without pushing the reds toward orange.

Looking at the original, Figure 9.12, it's hard to argue against either version of Figure 9.18, but beta reader Clyde McConnell, a graphic arts professor, adds the following thought.

"The exercise that concludes with Figure 9.18 is excellent, and very clear, but if I were doing it with my students I might advocate a simple layer mask. I grant the wisdom of not going down that route much, if at all, in the book, but what is missing from this picture is a sense of the color—a layperson might say *warmth*—of that domestic tungsten lamp in the background, which says so much about the kind of environment the school is trying to provide for those kids. So I just duplicated the final version, set it to 50% opacity and then did a modest gradation in a layer mask for the top edge. Some people may use the book to overall good effect but drift toward a puritanism about some of the amazing moves they've learned. If, in a casual way, you were to lend a sense of 'permission' at a spot like this I doubt that anyone would take it as permissiveness, and it certainly wouldn't divert the reader from the central issue, really *looking* at images rather than processing them by some imagined set of rules."

Getting Ready for the Next Hand

By now, you know how I was able to wow the audience with my precision knowledge of exactly what color a tree should be. Said knowledge consisted almost exclusively of a surmise that it was probably green. On opening the file, the tree was yellow.

And so, with great smugness and an impressive aura of knowing precisely what I was doing, I took a wild guess at what green it might be. And, of course, it was much better than the original, because in that context, any green, regardless of how putrid, is better than any yellow.

Any time one eliminates colors that can't possibly be right and replaces them with ones that are at least conceivable, the improvement will be dramatic.

It's all, in a way, a confidence game. The first step is to screw up the courage to state that a bridal gown should be white, period. If you're able to take such a categorical position, it won't be long before you, too, can see through the backs of the cards.

The Bottom Line

Identifying areas that must be or that cannot be a certain color allows corrections to be more precise. The process of drawing inferences about color is not limited to experts—certain inferences are so obvious that we don't realize we're taking them, like inferring that a bridal gown is white.

The hardest decisions are those involving neutrality. Overeager assumptions that certain areas are neutral are responsible for a lot of color casts.

Take the time to analyze the whole picture. In context, in relation to other objects in the image, you may be able to pinpoint an object whose color would be unknown if taken in isolation.

10
Every File Has Ten Channels

Being able to work in three colorspaces offers an abundance of tools to improve quality. To avoid eyes-glazed-over syndrome, we have to learn not just to work in these colorspaces, but to think in them.

n the early days of desktop publishing, when electronic components were not as reliable as they are today, a video card failed on one of my Macintoshes around a week after I installed it. I called the vendor, was transferred after an interminable hold to a technical representative who appeared to be in his first week of employment, and run through an inquisition that would have made Torquemada proud.

Was I certain the Macintosh was plugged in? Yes. Is the monitor's cable connected? Yes. Are you sure it is turned on? And after a few other questions of this general level, I let drop the news that I had actually swapped the card with an identical card in an identical machine, and the problem had followed the card.

The representative mulled this disturbing information over for at least a minute, when the solution dawned on him. "Tell me," he purred, "did you have any problem seating the card in its socket?"

Having worked in prepress for as long as I did, I rarely address abusive language to outsiders, only subordinates. I am proficient, however, in adopting an icy tone of voice, and my response conveyed all the hundred kilograms of iciness that I was then capable of mustering.

"Yes," I told him. "Now that you mention it, I *did*. But then I realized that the hammer I was using wasn't big enough. Once I got a bigger one, the card went in just fine."

I got the new card.

Whether in Photoshop or home repair, when people use the wrong tool for a job, the explanation is usually one of two things: they don't know any better, or they can't find the right tool. Personally, I tend to have the first problem in Photoshop and the second in matters of hardware; and because so many other people can't find their tools, either, there's a big market for tool kits and organizers. The one shown in our first example, because of the revolting loss of detail in its critical shadow region, is an ideal way to start a discussion not just about choosing the proper tool but about how to get good results with it.

A Very Small Toolbox

If you've gotten through the first nine chapters, you should be ready for color correction on a professional level. The second ten chapters constitute almost a different book, fleshing out some of the concepts that the first half has developed.

To get these results, we have to date used few tools, outside of methods that have been used only once and anything pertaining to making or merging layers. Other than those, if I recall correctly, we have used only three commands—Curves, Apply Image, and Selective Color—and one filter, USM. We have not made any formal selections, alpha channels, or masks, although we have done something similar with the simpler procedure of Blend If.

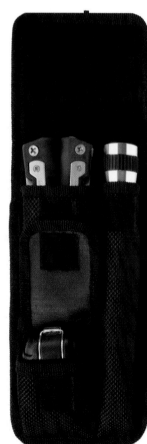

Each of this fab five is quite configurable, plus we have the choice of applying any of them in any of three colorspaces.

Figure 10.1 Many images have plugged shadows, but the impact usually isn't as disagreeable as it is here.

Sometimes there's only one correct option, and sometimes there are many. So it's no surprise that there can be confusion about which tool to pick up for what job.

Just choosing what colorspace to work in can cause one to reach for the blood pressure medication. Everybody nowadays starts with an RGB file. If a CMYK file is eventually needed, we can work in either space, or in LAB. If the final output file is to be RGB, we'd prefer to remain in RGB throughout, but we should be willing to buy a round-trip ticket to LAB, and every now and then to CMYK.

When making this choice-of-colorspaces decision, the possibilities are three.

●   It makes no difference. Example: setting highlight and shadow. All three colorspaces do this well.

●   One or more colorspaces has technical advantages that may or may not have any real impact. Examples: curves to increase contrast in localized areas, which often are better in CMYK; sharpening, which is occasionally superior in LAB.

●   Clear reasons exist to prefer one colorspace. Examples: the channel blending of Chapter 8, which should definitely be done in RGB rather than CMYK, and the black blob of the following exercise, where CMYK is clearly the tool of choice even if your final goal is an RGB file.

This chapter concludes the first half of the book. Chapter 1 was about concept, and Chapters 2–8 about specific tools. The final two chapters discuss when and how to use them. Chapter 9, which is color analysis, talks about what colors we *want* to achieve. This chapter talks about how to get there.

Figure 10.1 is an in-house studio capture, tagged sRGB, from a manufacturer of tools. The destination is a catalog, for which a CMYK file is required.

For form's sake, we have to go through the Chapter 9 analysis. What colors do we know here? And the answer is as obvious as it

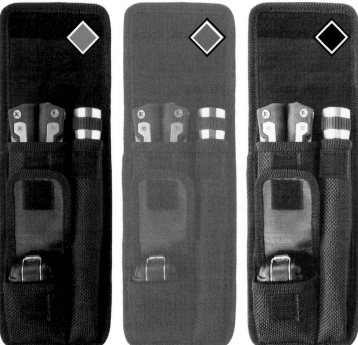

Figure 10.2 *RGB channels, like the green above, have detail throughout the shadow range. Their CMY cousins, like the green's relative, the magenta, have almost none, because it transfers into the black.*

ink on press, and the catalog printer would refuse to accept it.

There's no such effect in RGB, which has neither a black channel nor an ink limit. To verify this statement, compare the green channel to its close relative, the magenta, in Figure 10.2. In the darker areas, the magenta carries no detail at all. Everything shifts to the black.

It is highly convenient to so divide the image between useful information and garbage. We need only emphasize the black channel more while reducing the impact of the CMY. This can be done in several ways, of which the most straightforward is the following:

In CMYK, open Image: Adjustments>Selective Color. The default choice is Reds,

was in the wedding image of Figure 9.1. Everything in this image should be just as neutral as if it were a bridal gown or a black tie. Fortunately, for all its other shortcomings, the color in Figure 10.1 starts out correct.

Also, we ordinarily consider a luminosity blend while in RGB, but there's no point here. With everything being neutral, the three channels are nearly identical.

As discussed in Chapter 5, CMYK files are the best for bringing out shadow detail, because of a unique effect created by the limit on total ink. In dark neutral areas (for instance, in about three-quarters of the image we're working on) the CMY channels get ghosted out during the conversion from RGB. We live and die by what happens in the black. If this CMY ghosting were not done, the file would produce illegally high amounts of

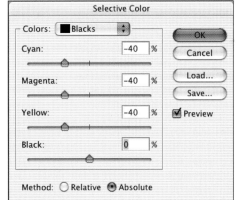

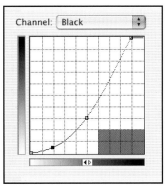

Figure 10.3 *A selective color move to reduce CMY in blacks, followed by a steep curve to the black channel, enhances shadow detail.*

which we change to Blacks, method Absolute. There, we subtract equal amounts (so as not to mess up the color balance) of CMY. I chose settings of –40 for each one, lightening the shadows in an intelligent fashion, by getting rid of worthless mud.

It's now time to attack the black with a curve. There is no need to worry about blowing light areas away altogether, since Photoshop didn't consider those areas to be black in the first place and therefore didn't lighten their CMY during the Selective Color move.

After these moves, I applied USM to the black channel only (why bother to sharpen a blur?) at settings of 350% Amount, .7 Radius, 12 Threshold; your taste may vary. Now we're at Figure 10.3, a dramatic improvement.

The black channel is the right tool to select in this image; the problem is, as always, to realize it before beginning to correct. Our life was made somewhat easier by the conditions of contest. I specified that the image was to be printed in a catalog. That announces up front that we need a CMYK file sooner or later. It doesn't take much thought to realize that sooner is better in this particular case.

But now, let's change the rules. Suppose this image is not going to press, but rather to some kind of device that requires an RGB file. So there is no black to adjust with our screwdriver, and no CMY to smash with our Selective Color hammer. What now?

Different Colorspace, Different Tools

If you accept for the sake of argument that the way just described will create the best possible CMYK file from the given RGB, then the way to produce the best possible RGB file is to follow exactly the same steps—and convert the CMYK file back to RGB when we're finished.

The idea of converting back and forth from CMYK is harder to swallow than doing the same with LAB. First, there are fewer reasons to do it. LAB is a completely different environment with several unique advantages. CMYK is basically RGB with a black channel attached, so it has most of the same strengths and weaknesses. Except in images like this one, where we really, really want a black channel, there's not much point in an unnecessary conversion.

Second, converting a photo from RGB to LAB and back isn't dangerous. Going to CMYK can be—under certain circumstances. LAB contains the entire gamut of RGB colors; CMYK doesn't. Any RGB color that CMYK can't hit will be toned down during the conversion, and may lose detail as well. Taking an eviscerated CMYK file back into RGB is likely to require some effort to get the colors back. CMYK notoriously does a terrible job with blues, but brilliant reds, greens, and any light, pure pastel colors won't survive the transition, either.

When in doubt about whether colors will be lost, be conservative. But the image we're working on is almost a black and white. There's less chance of the RGB file of Figure 10.3 holding a color that can't be matched in CMYK than there is of the pictured kit accommodating a jackhammer.

Also, some people rightly fear conversions to CMYK because it's hard to know whether our Photoshop definition of CMYK corresponds to the conditions of real-world printing. This point is irrelevant if we're going to reconvert to RGB. Photoshop will use the same definition in both directions, so it doesn't matter whether it's "accurate."

In fact, some people are so enamored of doing their curving and sharpening in CMYK that they avoid the gamut issue by converting their images into an artificial CMYK—one whose inks are defined as so impossibly pure that, in theory, no RGB color could ever be unprintable, so it would be safe to convert back and forth between RGB and CMYK. We'll discuss this further in Chapter 15. One such profile is on the CD; it comes from the developers of the Curvemeister plug-in (PC only), which allows writing curves that appear to be in CMYK or LAB without ever moving the document out of RGB.

A single-colorspace philosophy may have been acceptable ten or even five years ago. But today the world is different. As a singer popular a while back said, you don't need a weatherman to know which way the wind blows.

Pigeons Out on a Limb

The box on this page summarizes the strengths of each of our three colorspaces. We just saw an example of an image that clearly suggests using CMYK. In the rest of the chapter, we'll be looking for similar suggestions.

The west coast of British Columbia is breathtakingly beautiful. In real life, we see (or imagine that we see) far more variation in colors than any camera does. Figure 10.4 screams out to be handled in LAB, as most landscape shots do.

This does not mean that we either begin or end with LAB. It means that one of the key parts of the correction will involve it, because breaking similar colors apart is what LAB does best. We'll still look for other, additional options. But let's drop this image for a moment and move into one where we draw the opposite conclusion.

LAB is for creating differentiation between colors. In Figure 10.5A, we need that capability about as much as a jeweler needs a monkey wrench. There's plenty of difference between bird and cat already.

The cat's black fur suggests CMYK for the same reason that Figure 10.1 does. But what of the parrot? Couldn't we brighten it in RGB or LAB?

The photographer tells me that this is a Brazilian bird known as a sun conure. We know nothing about its color beyond that it is bright orange, but we certainly know that

the cat's fur should be black and white. In the original, the fur is typically a slightly blue-green $(2)^A(1)^B$ in both light and dark areas, but that's trivial to fix whenever we want. We next should look for a luminosity blend. You already know, I trust, what the parrot's RGB channels look like. The red is very light, and blue very dark. All detail is concentrated in the green.

Which Tool to Use?

The three colorspaces that Photoshop fully supports have different strengths. Keeping them in mind can guide you to the right one to use for each job.

CMYK:
- Best space for enhancing shadow detail, which is localized in the black channel.
- Good for sharpening images with one dominating color (sharpening of black plus the weak ink).
- Most precise control of curves of any colorspace.
- Can target small areas of complex images for contrast boosts.
- Directly addresses the colors that are in use on press.

LAB:
- Excellent for quick corrections where there's no time to fine-tune every number.
- Best sharpening space for images not dominated by one color.
- Allows cost-free blurring of colored noise.
- Convenient space for experimentation when unsure of what the final colors should be.
- Easily eliminates gross color casts.
- Steepening the A and B is the most natural-looking way of creating color variation or more intense colors.

RGB:
- The best channel-blending space, both in conjunction with reversions to luminosity and to correct casts.
- Better than CMYK for gross color changes when countercasts would prevent making them in LAB.
- Amenable to changes made in Color mode as a prelude to further correction in LAB.

Before deciding what to do with it, we need to agree that the bird should be as vivid as possible, particularly if we must end up in CMYK, where light, pure colors like this orange are a problem. Obviously we can't just put down the brightest possible orange; otherwise we'd just have a blob that wasn't a bird. But *some* parts need to be that color. It seems clear that the most vivid parts in the original are the top of the wing (yellow) and the top of the head (more orange). Those areas become known colors or, at least, two-thirds of known colors.

If the eventual file is to be CMYK, those vivid areas should measure $0^C?^M100^Y$. We have to guess at magenta because we don't know the exact shade of orange required. Whatever it is, though, killing cyan and adding yellow will give it more life.

If, on the other hand, we needed an RGB file, we'd shoot for $255^R?^G0^B$ in those areas. It's quite mad to attempt to achieve such specific values in anything other than the final space. Since I need to give CMYK to this book's printer, I did nothing in RGB or LAB at all. The first step was conversion. Then, the measurements. The highlight, near the cat's mouth, is a perfect $5^C2^M2^Y$. The shadow, above his right eye, is $83^C62^M72^Y72^K$, blue-green as the initial LAB readings led us to expect. The top of the

Figure 10.4 *Images that feature relatively dull colors generally are corrected most effectively in LAB.*

bird's head is $1^C31^M87^Y$ and the top of the wing $2^C17^M88^Y$. That suggests four steps.

- I applied the magenta channel to the cyan, Darken mode, 8% opacity, hoping to introduce slightly more detail in the less colorful areas of the bird's head and chest. This move does not make a huge difference.
- Curves: cyan, blowing out anything below 2^C and reducing the shadow to 80^C; magenta, increasing the shadow to 70^M (note that the bird is redder in Figure 10.5B); yellow, locking points at 50^Y, 60^Y, and 70^Y, but moving the top right endpoint inward to force 100^Y anywhere that was previously 82^Y or higher; black, the same curve shown in Figure 10.3, to add detail to the dark fur.
- Selective Color to the blacks as in Figure 10.3, this time using values of −10 in all three CMY channels.
- USM to the black.

Now, suppose the assignment had been to create an RGB file. You might suppose that this is the sort of image that shouldn't go to CMYK first. After all, we know that CMYK can't produce vivid oranges. Moving out of RGB and back will make the bird duller.

But why should you care? You are committed to applying RGB curves to strengthen the bird anyway, because the original file is not $255^R?^G0^B$ where it needs to be. A duller sun conure merely means that the curve screwdriver gets twisted an extra turn. So, I would produce Figure 10.5B just as before, then return to RGB and establish the brighter bird.

It should take longer to think of what the strategy of this technical exercise should be than to actually execute it. Photographers who are used to inkjet printers and brilliantly white paper may rightly feel that the bird in Figure 10.5B isn't particularly vivid. It is, however, absolutely as vivid as it can be

Figure 10.5 *The bird should be as brilliant as possible, but in the original, top, the darkest channel is not at maximum and the lightest is not at minimum. These colors are adjusted in the corrected version, bottom.*

under the printing conditions of this book—solid yellow, no cyan or black in its brightest spots. And so, while the original is not a bad picture, anybody is going to prefer the modest improvements of Figure 10.5B.

It's All Over Now, Baby Blue

The improvements will be rather more substantial as we return to the western Canadian coastline of Figure 10.4. This image is tagged ColorMatch RGB, and it exhibits the partial cast that is so typical of today's digital cameras. With the Info palette set to read LAB, the clouds show up as a slightly dark but nicely neutral $90^L(1)^A0^B$. As the picture gets darker, though, the news is quite grim. Canadians may not be able to spell *color,* but trees are nevertheless green in that country. Not the ones on these islands, however. In the center of the bottom island I find $25^L(10)^A(25)^B$. That's not even a bluish green—it's a cyanish blue. The A value isn't bad, but the B needs to be positive, not negative.

The cast is confirmed by what I take to be the shadow, at the bottom of said island: $15^L0^A(32)^B$. That's too light. Judging by the 0^A, this area is probably also neutral and should be 0^B as well, which would make the greener areas B–positive, as they should be.

This is the worst cast we've yet seen. Sometimes we try to reduce casts in RGB, but here we can dispense with the jeweler's screwdriver and proceed to the sledgehammer. Also, I would forgo looking for a luminosity blend until the cast is knocked out. At present, all the channels will be too flat because the dark half of the image is so tediously monochromatic.

Off to LAB, then, for the curves of Figure 10.6, on an adjustment layer perforce. The L curve ignores the lightness of the shadow. As noted earlier, it's safer and easier to darken a shadow in CMYK than elsewhere. There's no objection to lightening a highlight in LAB, though, so the bottom left of the curve moves over slightly to make the clouds lighter.

The A curve passes to the right of its original center point, moving the entire image slightly away from green and toward magenta. It's so steep, though, that the greenest areas (at the top of the curve) become greener in spite of the overall move.

The B curve is the cast-killer. It's shifted radically to the right, away from blue and toward yellow. The two internal points of the S are designed to separate the bluest areas of the water from the islands. The result of these LAB curves is Figure 10.7A.

As expected, the light half of the picture has gotten too yellow. The most flexible way to fix this is to create a layer mask to restore the original image where desired, but here there's no need for such complexity. Since the cast gets worse as the image gets darker, we can just use Blend If sliders to exclude the entire lightest part and establish a relatively long transition zone, creating Figure 10.7B.

With speculative curves like these, it's always better to overshoot than not go far enough. As I thought that Figure 10.7B was too much of a good thing, I reduced layer opacity to 75% and got Figure 10.7C.

Figure 10.6 These curves knock the blue cast out of the shadows but create a yellow cast in the highlights.

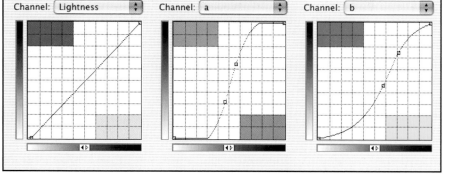

Take What You Have Gathered...

Now, we should consider a luminosity blend. Finding one here isn't nearly as obvious as in some other examples we've looked at. To help out, we'll check out channels from four different versions of this image: the original RGB of Figure 10.4, and three copies of Figure 10.7C, one remaining in LAB, one reconverted to ColorMatch RGB, and one converted to CMYK using Medium GCR.

It would have been bad to do the blending too early. The original red channel, Figure 10.8A, is plugged in

Figure 10.7 *Top left, after applying the curves of Figure 10.6 to Figure 10.4. Bottom left, the move toward yellow is excluded from lighter areas by these Blend If sliders.*
Bottom right: layer opacity is cut to 75%.

the shadows, due to the horrific blue cast. If we want to take advantage of its good detail in the water, we're surely better off using Figure 10.8D, which is the red of the file reconverted to RGB from the LAB file of Figure 10.7C.

We observe a couple of other clunkers in the set. There's nothing to be said for the new blue channel, Figure 10.8F. Also, I only bother to show the black channel, Figure 10.8C, because later in the chapter there are a couple of examples of where using such a black pays dividends, and I wanted to show a case where it doesn't. We certainly don't

Figure 10.8 *Blending possibilities. Top row, left to right: the original red channel of Figure 10.4; the L of Figure 10.7C; the black of a duplicate file converted to CMYK using Medium GCR. Bottom row: the red, green, and blue of a copy of Figure 10.7C reconverted to RGB.*

Figure 10.9 *The red channel of Figure 10.8D is blended, with contrast enhanced, into the L of Figure 10.7C at 40% opacity.*

Since the color (AB) channels are identical on both layers, Luminosity and Normal modes do the same thing here.

The result was much too dark, so I lightened the quartertone on the top layer, adding contrast to the water and the trees. I also reduced layer opacity to 40%, and applied light hiraloam sharpening to the L channel.

Figure 10.9 isn't the end of the line, but the next step is better understood if we temporarily switch images.

...From Coincidence

From the very first page, we've stressed the difference between what a person sees and what a camera does. There's also a third player: what the person *remembers* having seen when the time comes to open the file in Photoshop.

People's recollections are revisionist in two well-known areas. We usually recall skintones as being somewhat healthier than they actually appeared at the time. We also often recall most plant life as being greener than what we saw.

The first category is a relatively small distortion. The second can call for big moves—maybe too big for curves, even in LAB. Such curves can drive colors apart, but it's one thing to put distance between colors and another to introduce a color that isn't even close to what's found in the original photo.

We generally use Apply Image for channel blending as opposed to Channel Mixer, because we often need to blend from different layers or even from different files. To make Figure 10.9, for example, we needed to blend from an RGB file into an LAB one. Channel Mixer can't do that.

Nevertheless, Channel Mixer has an important advantage that specifically pertains

want to darken the green areas, so this black goes into the trash along with the blue.

The interesting comparison is between the L, Figure 10.8B, and the new red, Figure 10.8D. The L is slightly lighter. It therefore has less detail in lighter areas, which is bad, but holds the shadow better, which is good. In my opinion, the best luminosity for this image is some combination of these two channels.

We can therefore stick with the LAB version of Figure 10.7C, although the reconverted RGB file needs to be open. After flattening the adjustment layer, we create a duplicate layer and expose the L channel only, either in the Channels palette or with Command–1. Now, Image: Apply Image. Choose the RGB image, red channel, as the source, Normal mode, 100% opacity. Photoshop doesn't care if a blend is across colorspaces as long as the documents are the same size. A channel is a channel; every file has ten of them.

We now have Figure 10.7C on the bottom layer, and (in effect) a luminosity layer on top.

A

B

C

Channel Mixer

Output Channel: Green

Source Channels

Red: 0 %

Green: +140 %

Blue: -40 %

Figure 10.10 *Channel Mixer can be used to intensify greens. Left, the RGB original. Center, with Green=+140% Green. Right, with the settings changed to Green =+140% Green, –40% Blue.*

to greenery. It allows us to *subtract* one channel from another, often in combination with a multiplication of the first channel. This is easier shown than explained. Figure 10.10A is found a short distance from Figure 10.9. It's near the Museum of Anthropology of the University of British Columbia, likely the finest collection of Native American art in the world.

The totem is a nice off-brown, but so is the tree. Regardless of its color in the original scene, we'll remember it as greener. In this RGB original, the tree hangs around $90^R100^G60^B$, which is scarcely a green at all. To get something more credible, the green channel needs to be lightened, but only in the

trees; otherwise the whole image will become too green. (Remember, in RGB a higher number is a lighter channel, so we want the green value to go up, not down.)

Channel Mixer works on channels, not colors as Hue/Saturation and Selective Color do. In Figure 10.10B, I specified that the green channel should be 140% of itself. All green values throughout the picture are multiplied by 1.4. The tree becomes $90^R140^G60^B$, which is very nice, and the whole rest of the image becomes a green mess, which is not.

I compensate in Figure 10.10C by redefining the green as +140% of itself *but –40% of the blue*. Let's do the calculation ourselves, just as Channel Mixer does. The tree starts at 100^G, which the +140% command changes to 140^G. From that, we subtract 40% of the original 60^B, or 24 points. That leaves 116^G, considerably greener than the original.

Meanwhile, little else has changed. In neutral areas, green and blue are equal, so adding anything to one and subtracting the same amount from the other does nothing.

In the original totem, the green and blue are also nearly equal, so adding 40% of green and subtracting 40% of blue has little impact. It's only where the two channels originally had major differences that the command does anything.

This idea, as far as I know, works only with greenery. The problem with subtracting a channel is that very dark areas can lose contrast. This is again easier to show than to describe. Look at the shadow areas of Figure 10.8D. Plenty of detail, right? If we subtract that shadow from some other channel, the darker parts of it will get lighter faster than the rest, and the result will be flatter as well as lighter.

In natural greens, however, the blue channel is usually featureless, as it is in Figure 10.8F. Subtracting it from the green channel just lightens the area as a block.

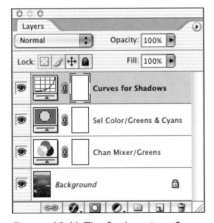

Figure 10.11 *The final version of Figure 10.4, after a Channel Mixer move to augment the greens, Selective Color to add yellows to greens and cyan to cyans, and a curve to establish a properly dark black shadow.*

Mixed Up Confusion

This business of making greens greener is highly applicable to the correction that's currently on hold. The bottom of Figure 10.9 is far greener than the original of Figure 10.4, but the tools we've used so far haven't quite been powerful enough. By the numbers it's still too desaturated, still too blue.

Unlike other types of channel blending, which generally work better in RGB, this green boost is equally applicable in CMYK. We just subtract yellow from magenta, rather than blue from green. So I took the document there for three final steps, which are shown as three adjustment layers in Figure 10.11. Because the first is a prelude to the others, it's probably easiest to explain the steps in reverse order.

• On the top layer (the final move), a curve to the black establishes a properly dark shadow. If your workflow requires a CMYK file, you shouldn't make a practice of setting shadows anywhere else. The black is always much lighter than either the L or any RGB channel. Forcing darkness into the image in either of the other colorspaces is apt to produce a muddier shadow than manipulating CMYK's black alone.

There's no waste of time in doing this. Even if, as in this picture, we do almost all of the work elsewhere, minor tweaks are invariably necessary once entering CMYK. Here, the magenta and yellow were fine, but the cyan was slightly too low in the clouds and too high in the shadows. So I had to go into the Curves dialog anyway.

• Selective Color (middle layer) puts needed yellow into greens and subtracts magenta. Also, I added cyan to cyans, trying to get even more of a break between the water and the greenery.

Selective Color and Hue/Saturation do much the same thing. H/S is more flexible in that we can target a particular color (such as yellowish greens and anything yellower, but

not anything bluer), but less flexible because we can't target blacks or neutral colors. When working in CMYK, Selective Color is more powerful in that we can adjust inks directly rather than hoping for the best when messing around with sliders that don't correspond to any of them.

It seems to me the correct workflow is to use Selective Color when certain of what we're trying to do, and H/S when feeling more experimental. Here, I was absolutely positive that I wanted to put more yellow in the greens, so I used Selective Color. I was less sure of what I wanted to do with the water. I would have used H/S to do it if that had been the only change. As it was, the two are so comparable in functionality that it didn't seem worth it to have an extra layer, so I just stuck with Selective Color since I was using it anyway for the greens.

• And the first move was one like that described in Figure 10.10, Channel Mixer with Magenta=+125% Magenta, −25% Yellow. It may seem that this is an extra command that could have been avoided by making a bigger Selective Color move on the next layer up. It's not.

Photoshop does not have an internal crystal ball. It also lacks a setting for "Forests" in either Selective Color or H/S. When we specify "Greens," it will only change things that it believes are green based on current pixel values. Without this preliminary Channel Mixer move, the islands may seem green to a human being. They don't seem that way to Selective Color, which treats them as cyans.

Figure 10.12 (opposite) An artificial black channel can often be used to add depth to an image because it is typically blank in brightly colored areas such as the flag in the original, top left. There is no need for the base file to be in CMYK. Top right, this black is from a copy of the image converted using Medium GCR. Bottom left, the original is converted to LAB, and the black is blended into the L in Multiply mode. Bottom right, the same blend is repeated twice more.

To get this large break between greens and blues, I think LAB is necessary. CMYK is not, although given that I needed to be in CMYK eventually anyway for this book, it made sense to do these last three moves there. There is another class of images in which CMYK is more important—whether we need a CMYK file or not.

Take Me As I Am

Our eyes tend to focus on brightly colored objects. In professional work, we often want viewers to focus on such objects even more than they would in real life. That presents a problem in the muted world of print.

The brightest part of the Chinese flag in Figure 10.12A has no cyan or black ink at all. In that respect, it's like the bird of Figure 10.5B. Neither object causes us to turn back somersaults by its brilliance. Definitely we would like them even more vivid, much as I would like to have a few extra million dollars and a smaller first digit in my age. Unfortunately, there's nothing to be done about any of the above. These two objects are as brilliant as they can possibly be, given the constraints of this book.

If you're printing on photo-quality paper instead of a sheet that permits Peachpit Press to sell this book for less than $100, you can get marginally brighter colors, but you are still likely to be dissatisfied. When you want to make the bright colors brighter but can't, the next best thing is to make the dull colors duller and darker. So, we go to Image: Adjustments>Tone Down Dull Colors, only to find that somebody forgot to include that command in Photoshop.

For the sake of argument, we'll assume that an RGB file is required. Nevertheless, we duplicate the image and convert it to CMYK. But not just Mode: CMYK. That would give a skeleton black, which would be close to being a blank in this case. Instead, we choose Custom CMYK, and Medium (or heavier) GCR (review Chapter 5, if necessary, for instructions on how to do this). I used Medium GCR. The black channel it produced is Figure 10.12B. It is almost nonexistent where the flag and boat are, somewhat darker in the river, and distinctly darker in the background hills.

There are several ways of marrying this black to the existing RGB. The following works as well as any.

- Convert the RGB file to LAB.
- Paste a copy of the black channel from the duplicate file to the clipboard, and paste it on top of the LAB file, creating a new layer.
- Change layer mode to Multiply.

This procedure produces Figure 10.12C. If the effect

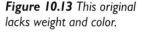

Figure 10.13 This original lacks weight and color.

Figure 10.14 *Top, a corrected version relying mostly on LAB curving. Bottom, using multiplication by an artificial black channel instead.*

is not sufficient, go to the Layers palette, grab the top layer's row, and drag it down to the page icon at the bottom of the palette to duplicate the multiplying layer. And again, and again, if you like. Figure 10.12D has three identical multiplying layers, instead of the one of Figure 10.12C. And, of course you could have an effect in between two and three multiplying layers by reducing the opacity of one of them.

Using a false separation to generate an artificial black has many variants. This flag image was a good example of how it works because it shows how brilliant objects are unaffected by such blends. It would not be difficult, however, to achieve the same result using different methods.

The black channel has unique strengths in blending, however. As images get more complex, it's harder to find a substitute. For our next example, we'll move away from Dylan and toward the Beatles. Figure 10.13 is a Norwegian wood.

When I Awoke, This Bird Had Flown

The sRGB original is dull, light, colorless. Before asking you to stay and telling you to sit anywhere, I'll offer two possible fixes. I prefer Figure 10.14B to 10.14A, because the trees, leaves, and mosses are better defined, even though the two versions are roughly of the same darkness.

Figure 10.15. Top left, the green channel of Figure 10.13 replaces the L in a copy that has been converted to LAB. Center left, curves steepen the A and B radically. Bottom left, opacity is reduced to 22%. Below right, three possible starts of a multiplication blend. Top, a Maximum GCR black from a separation of version B. Center, still with Maximum GCR, version C is used for separation instead. Bottom, a Heavy GCR black from another separation of version C.

Getting to either takes a few steps, and a few colorspaces. First, we recognize that when the colors start out dull, as they do here and did in the maritime scene of Figure 10.4, we probably need LAB. Before going there, we check for color issues and for the possibility of a luminosity blend.

I can find nothing wrong with the original color other than that it looks like it crawled off to sleep in the bath. As for the channels, the image is fairly neutral, so there isn't much difference between them. The green is better than the others, but it's scarcely worth the bother of making a new layer.

Rather than biding our time drinking wine, however, we can take advantage of a previously undisclosed LAB anomaly. In the next two chapters, we'll be discussing the concept of *gamma,* which roughly means how dark Photoshop construes a value of $128^R128^G128^B$ to be. It is not a fixed value; different definitions of RGB have different darknesses.

LAB is construed as darker than any of them, or at least the L channel is, since the A and B don't affect darkness. To compensate, the L channel usually has to be lighter than any RGB channel. This makes blending to and from the L a nuisance, as it can have a significant effect on perceived darkness.

Happy coincidence, is it not, that darkening the image is exactly what we're after. So,

● Make a copy of the image and convert it to LAB, keeping the RGB file open.

● Activate the L channel of the copy. Image: Apply Image, using the RGB file, green channel, as the source, Normal mode, opacity 100%. This adds depth and produces Figure 10.15A.

● While we know we would like more color, we don't know how much. In such cases, I advocate overkill. By steepening the AB curves drastically on an adjustment layer while holding their center

points constant, we can produce more vivid colors than anybody would ever want, and then we can adjust opacity to taste. There is normally no need to go as far as Figure 10.15B, but I had my reasons here.

● Choose a pleasing opacity for the adjustment layer. The dart that I threw at Figure 10.15C landed on 22%.

Now comes further experimentation. Making a bogus CMYK version of a copy of the file seems likely to pay dividends, but an infinite number of separation parameters can be changed. The last time we tried this, in the river scene of Figure 10.12A, we got by with Medium GCR. Figure 10.15A is much lighter. We may need a bigger hammer.

As we saw in Chapter 5, Maximum GCR is a poor choice for photographs, because it puts in absolutely as much black and as little CMY as possible. This forces an untenable shadow value of $0^C0^M0^Y100^K$ and renders the setting unusable for anything except linework—and false separations like this one,

---

Stumbling Blocks: The Fear Factor

●**"I just can't picture what to do."** If you don't see how to make moves like this on certain of your own pictures, it probably means that they wouldn't work, any more than a pair of pliers can be used as a screwdriver. When in doubt, go back to the basics.

●**Forgetting Custom CMYK.** For a black multiply layer like those of Figures 10.12C and 10.14B, don't convert with the Photoshop default of SWOP v2. It yields too light a black and too heavy a shadow. Use Custom CMYK to generate a Medium GCR (or heavier) black. Don't worry about whether it matches your printing condition: if you're only using the black for blending, whether the CMYK file would print properly is academic.

●**The dangerous CMYK/RGB conversion.** If a file must end up in RGB, don't be afraid to go to LAB and back again. If you see an advantage to moving to CMYK, be careful. Examine closely for any pastel or brilliant colors that might be lost. If in doubt, make a spare copy, convert it to CMYK and back, paste it onto the original RGB file, and see if you can tell the difference.

Figure 10.16 *Attempts to add weight to Figure 10.15C. Left, a curve to the L channel. Right, Figure 10.15E is multiplied into Figure 10.15C's L channel at 66% opacity. Both efforts plug the shadows, a defect corrected in Figure 10.17.*

where we have no intention of ever using the CMYK result as anything other than a source of blending channels.

Experimentation may be in order. Figure 10.15D is a Maximum GCR black generated from the psychedelic Figure 10.15B. As no black is found in brilliant colors like those reds and greens, this black is lighter than Figure 10.15E, which was generated using the same settings from the more sedate Figure 10.15C. And Figure 10.15F is more conservative still. It's also derived from Figure 10.15C, but uses Heavy, rather than Maximum, GCR.

In real life, any of the three would improve things and, unless it was a critically impor-

tant image, we'd be disinclined to try three alternatives. For this image, I chose the in-between look of Figure 10.15E.

To see what this gets us, let's look at a comparison. Figure 10.16A is the conventional way of treating a washed-out image. Using Figure 10.15C as the base, I raised the mid-tone of the L curve until satisfied with the overall weight; similar effects are possible in RGB or CMYK. Figure 10.16B is the black multiplication. We paste Figure 10.15E as a new multiply layer on top of Figure 10.15C, or else make a duplicate layer, choose the L channel, and use Apply Image, Multiply mode, to blend in the bogus black. I found

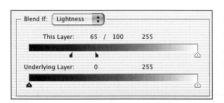

Figure 10.17 *Excluding by color is often more effective than by darkness. These two Blend If settings try to restore the shadows that were lost in Figure 10.16B.*

the result too dark, and reduced opacity to 66%.

The original had too much separation between the light and dark areas of the forest. In getting beefier overall, both competitors now have developed a case of plugged shadows. That's why the need for the separate layer, because the next step is Blend If, and another illustration of why being able to answer the picture-the-channels quiz of Figure 1.5 is a good idea.

Using Figure 10.16B as a base for the sake of argument, Figure 10.17A tries to rectify matters by excluding areas that are dark on the top layer. The operation is not entirely successful. We need a long transition zone because the two layers are so different from one another that harsh edges are possible where they meet. But with the setting shown, the two join as a blur, albeit a lighter blur than in Figure 10.16B.

A better solution is to use a color

Figure 10.18 *Left, a studio capture intended for magazine advertising. Below, the three channels.*

channel, which usually defines the original shadow more accurately. As an area gets darker, it gets less colorful. The sliders in Figure 10.17B leave anything that was originally neutral alone. So, the very darkest areas of Figure 10.16A, which don't have detail on either layer, are retained. But the falloff is rapid, because in all but these darkest areas, the lower layer is somewhat green.

The B channel, Underlying Layer, is the

correct slider choice. We want to exclude objects that were originally green or red, which are both B–positive. We don't mind if the background sky gets darker. These sliders will permit that, as blues are B–negative.

Therefore, I used these settings on Figures 10.16A and 10.16B, and also applied identical USM to get to the versions shown earlier as Figures 10.14A and 10.14B.

This original was flawed, as indeed all of the ones so far in this chapter are. But the lessons are also applicable to images of impeccable quality. Figure 10.18 is a high-end capture for high-end advertising, shot under controlled lighting conditions. The same moves that have improved our lesser images will also make a difference with it.

Figure 10.19 Left, drastic curves increase contrast in the wine at the expense of everything else. Right, the curves are assigned different values for color and luminosity, and a further blend adds more shape.

Tangled Up in Blue

Whether the original is good, bad, or indifferent, we start looking at the numbers, which are, as you might expect in studio conditions, all fine, and by examining the channels. This file is tagged Adobe RGB. The green is probably best of the three overall, but overall is not how professionals look at such images. We look at the product, which is the glass of bubbly. (The French co-owner of this California vineyard would throw a fit if this beverage were referred to as *champagne.* Personally

I wouldn't call it that either, particularly not in comparison to the better ones coming out of the Finger Lakes region of New York, which give the French a good run for their euro.)

Although the blue is too dark, it has more detail in the wine than the other two. On a luminosity layer, I moved the lower left point of its curve almost halfway over, drastically lightening the channel but increasing the contrast in the wine greatly. Because the blue plays such a small role in overall image contrast, the apparent change at this point was

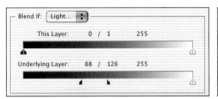
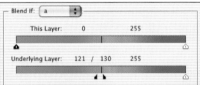

Figure 10.20 *Left, these Blend If options, and a reduction in opacity to 82%, modify Figure 10.19B. Right, extreme LAB curves are applied to create color variation.*

so trivial that I won't waste space showing it, but it was the key to the whole operation, as it forced enough bubbles into all three channels for further corrections to work.

I now made a copy of the image, and created a duplicate layer—not an adjustment layer—and went back to Chapter 2. Back then, we applied enormously steep curves to one image of a damaged car and another of a purple blouse, bringing out more contrast than we would ever need in either. In one case the background was irrelevant, and in the other it didn't exist at all. I pretended that such was the case here as well, making each channel's curve nearly vertical where the wine lives in each channel. The result is Figure 10.19A, which has, naturally enough, an outstanding glass of bubbly. Everything else appears to be a disaster area but is in fact just too much of a good thing.

Or rather, it's too much of two good things, color and contrast. I now duplicated the curves layer, wanting to investigate the possibility that the two good things were not equally excessive.

That gave me something similar to Figure 10.18 on the bottom layer and copies of Figure 10.19A on two layers above it. I set one of these to Color mode and the other to Luminosity. The curves had not just added contrast to the wine, but had driven the background colors away from it—so effectively, in my opinion, that Figure 10.19A is closer to being right for color than it is for detail.

Therefore, I set the color layer to 60% opacity and the Luminosity layer to 40%. I then pasted a merged copy of what was underneath onto a fourth layer. To it, I applied the augmented blue channel from the original RGB file, taking it from the top layer of that file, rather than from the default merged version, which is toned down considerably

Review and Exercises

✓Assume that you own a good-quality consumer-level printer that prefers RGB files as input. Explain, in terms of color theory, why you are likely to get a more vivid orange in the bird of Figure 10.5 than the one shown here. (Hint: how much are you spending on paper?)

✓In Figure 10.5, the magenta was blended into the cyan in Darken mode at a low opacity to try to increase detail in the bird. Why is it technically better to make this particular blend in CMYK, as opposed to the analogous move (green into red) in RGB?

✓Find a picture of a forest or other natural greenery, preferably with an overly light shadow value. (If none of your images have weak shadows, make one artificially by bringing down the top right endpoint of the master RGB curve.) Now, make three copies, one each in CMYK, RGB, and LAB. Attempt to restore the shadow with curves. The exercise should demonstrate that better color and better detail can be retained by manipulating the black channel only of CMYK.

✓In Figure 10.12, we made an artificial black channel and multiplied it three times into the L of an LAB file. If you want to avoid moving into LAB, how would you prevent a color shift when you multiply the artificial black into the RGB file?

✓Go through the exercise of building a deeper forest, ending with the plugged shadow of Figure 10.16B. Instead of using the B channel Blend If sliders to exclude the darker shadows as shown in Figure 10.17B, can you see how to do it with the A?

because the top layer is in Luminosity mode. Looking for an opacity that would be more than enough, I chose 25%. When this fourth layer was itself set to Luminosity mode, it produced Figure 10.19B.

Californians love their watercress, but not when it's as dark as it is here. Furthermore, the advertiser will be crabbier than the crab cakes are unless something is done to make its bottle more green and less black.

I now cut the file down to two layers by merging the top and bottom pairs. It would, I believe, require a layer mask in RGB at this point to try to restore the green areas, because as the bottle gets darker, so do a lot of other things. Better to convert to LAB, without flattening the layers. It's easy there to use the Blend If sliders to exclude anything that's A–negative, which is to say, more green than it is magenta.

I decided to use two sliders, one to exclude the very darkest parts of Figure 10.19B, the second to kill anything that's A–negative on the underlying layer. Note that both sliders have been split to produce a smoother transition. After doing this, I felt things were still too contrasty, so I reduced the top layer's opacity to 82%. That produced Figure 10.20A.

The original, Figure 10.18, didn't look bad at first glance, but it seems monochromatic now. As long as we're in LAB, we should try to drive the colors even further apart. That's what Figure 10.20B does, using AB curves that are very steep yet pass through the original center point, ensuring that anything that's neutral (such as the foamy top of the sparkling wine) stays that way.

Of course, these curves are on a new adjustment layer, since the idea is to make a final decision on what looks good by adjusting layer opacity. I cut it to 30% and added some USM to reach Figure 10.21. To get an idea of how far things have progressed, that figure also shows versions of the original and final glass at the original size for which reproduction was intended. I had to rez the image down for this exercise to keep within a manageable number of pages.

Figure 10.21 *Top, a final version, with opacity reduced to 30% and sharpening applied to Figure 10.20B. Bottom, the final and original versions are compared at the size for which the advertisement was originally prepared.*

The Times, They Are a-Changin'

On three occasions during the last correction, I deliberately overshot the mark, intending to limit the move later by reducing opacity. This is a modern strategy. I proposed it a few years back. Later, I recommended using extremely steep AB curves, like those that produced Figure 10.15B, as a way for people to introduce themselves to the power of LAB. Because the example picture was of a man whom the curves made blue, yellow, green, and purple, I called it the Man from Mars Method, which has caught on in some quarters.

I initially saw this as being for beginners. It became clear, particularly after the publication of my last book, that a lot of people who were not beginners thought that it was a valuable technique. Now that I've played with it more, I agree. I don't believe I could have gotten to Figure 10.21 four years ago.

The Bottom Line

RGB is good for channel blends. CMYK is the best place to add shadow detail. LAB drives similar colors apart in a pleasing way. Choosing which one to use is not always obvious. This chapter is about strategy. It treats each file as one that potentially has ten channels, and talks about how to decide which one(s) to employ.

The last three images have not involved work in CMYK. It goes without saying that at this point we would convert into RGB if they were going to the Web or to a printer that requires RGB, to CMYK for press or a RIP-equipped output device. And if we don't know where they're going—which is another feature of our changing times, it rarely used to happen—we leave them as they are.

Today we must be prepared to output in any colorspace. When we appreciate the strengths of each, we add many tools to our kit. Of the seven images shown in this chapter, I would say that it was important to work in LAB in three, including our last two. In the three other images, LAB would have been a bad idea.

Similarly, I feel RGB was important in four images and not recommended in two others, and that CMYK was helpful three times and should have been avoided (except for final touchup) twice. One of the seven, the maritime scene of Figure 10.4, needed help from all three colorspaces. Another, the totem of Figure 10.10, didn't offer any great reason to prefer or avoid any one of the three.

The key to knowing which one to use is being able to visualize the channel structure of each—ten channels in all. A plumber or a computer technician would never be caught with a half-empty tool kit. Neither should we.

11
Making Things Look Alike

The book's second half begins by discussing how to make the capture match the monitor and the monitor match the print, and how to make all three meet our expectations. The concept is a revolutionary one: if you want to know how something looks, open your eyes.

asters and servants are both tyrannical; but the masters are the more dependent of the two.

*   *   *

So goes one of the *Maxims for Revolutionists,* an audacious appendix to *Man and Superman,* the greatest work of the greatest writer the English language has produced since Shakespeare, Bernard Shaw.

In addition to being an authority on music and fine art, Shaw was into print quality in a big way. He micromanaged the production of his books of plays, demanding that they be set in Caslon and no other typeface, specifying precise amounts of letterspacing for words that were to be emphasized, forbidding the use of apostrophes, and imposing his own ideas of spelling. He had no color in his own works, but offered plenty of commentary on that of his contemporaries, William Morris and Dante Gabriel Rossetti. So there is no disconnect in invoking Shaw in a chapter about color. And if we're going to do it, it is certainly right to choose his most philosophical, most savagely irreverent work (including a couple of segments from the play-within-a-play, *Don Juan in Hell),* because we need to be both philosophical and irreverent, if relentlessly common-sensical, for the topic we're about to discuss.

Something very similar to Figure 11.1 appears in a text on color management published by the Graphic Arts Technical Foundation. Figure 11.2 was prepared by a professor at the Massachusetts Institute of Technology. In keeping with our ongoing themes, one of these examples is a question of color and the other of contrast.

The color scientist who prepared the GATF textbook invites us to

Figure 11.1 *Are the two green rows the same color? How would you prove it?*

compare the two rows of green stripes. The MIT professor directs our attention to the squares on the checkerboard labeled A and B. Both then advise us that these pairs, which are as obviously different from one another as Shaw's prose is from Dan Brown's, are in fact the same. It is as if they were arguing that Des Moines is the largest city in the United States, or that the current prime minister of the United Kingdom is Kaiser Wilhelm II.

The academics, who should be the masters, achieve this stupefying feat of illogic by becoming dependent upon their servants.

The phrase *circular reasoning* describes a proof that depends upon its own assumptions. Here, the assumption is that two colors are the same if an artificial color-measurement device declares them to be so. The proof that these two colors are the same is that an artificial color measurement device says so. The proof depends upon the assumption. Each is worth less than a copy of Photoshop 2.

The color scientist who presented Figure 11.1 states, "To most people the green segments at the top appear to be darker than the ones at the bottom, but both are the same." Both halves of the sentence are wrong.

It's not just *most* people who would perceive the top greens as darker. It's every member of the human race, including color-blind people. The reasons are explained in Chapter 1, in our discussion of the old survival instinct of simultaneous contrast.

The second half of the sentence confronts us with a pure conflict of technologies. The technology that the academics rely on is around a century old. Reliable specimens of it can currently be purchased for less than a thousand dollars, and will last for several years if well cared for. This technology uniformly reports that the two greens in Figure 11.1 and the two grays in Figure 11.2 are in fact identical.

The competing technology is very much older, and very much more expensive. It has a longer mean time between failures; it works under a much broader range of lighting conditions; it has the unique ability to evaluate colors in context; and best of all it has been continuously improved over the last million years or so by the forces of evolution. This second technology (including, as noted above, defective units thereof) uniformly reports the two pairs of colors as different.

So, which technology gives the correct answer? I would suggest that it depends upon the audience. If the audience consists of spectrophotometers, colorimeters, and densitometers, then the first technology's answer is probably correct; the colors are the same. If, however, the audience is one of human beings, then who cares what the machine thinks? It's the second technology that counts.

Does this uncertainty make you uncomfortable? If it does, refer back to Chapter 1. In a professional context, a Photoshop correction improves an image if, and only if, the client declares that the picture now looks better. Your opinion, my opinion, and the opinion of a machine are not relevant. What the client says goes.

In many of the pictures we've seen thus far, it's hard to predict what a client would say.

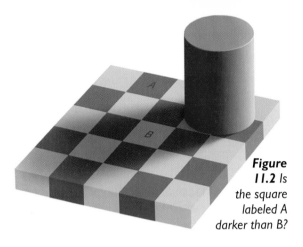

Figure 11.2 Is the square labeled A darker than B?

Here, there is no such problem. Clients are human beings, and all human beings see these two pairs of colors as different, wherefore they *are* different.

An Introduction to Calibration

The man who listens to Reason is lost: Reason enslaves all whose minds are not strong enough to master her.

We have now reached the halfway point of our travels. The first 10 chapters were heavy-duty color correction. We are about to take a break. When we resume in Chapters 15–19, the difficulty level increases substantially. This is not merely my opinion, but that of the beta readers, who, regardless of their Photoshop ability, rated those chapters as the hardest but also the most rewarding, particularly Chapters 16 and 19.

Meanwhile, five of the next six chapters will not necessarily be of interest to all readers. Chapter 16 is on handling of digital captures that are in a raw format. If you never confront such files, then you don't need to look at it. Chapter 14 covers image resolution; if the topic doesn't interest you it can safely be skipped.

This and the next two chapters deal with one of the most vexing—and overrated—issues in image manipulation, namely, how do we make sure that things look alike?

This question may be restated as "What is a match?" It has several subquestions. Does what your monitor shows adequately match what will eventually be output? Does the output match your expectations for it? If you had been given a proof of the final output before the actual job was run, does the proof match the reality? If we are outputting to two different conditions, say a newspaper and a magazine, how do we know that the colors will match? And, in the background, the unspoken question: did what the camera captured match the real-life scene?

Like Shaw, these chapters are highly political, especially Chapter 13, which discusses how to deal with commercial printers in the real world, not in some theoretical construct.

This chapter makes the shocking, if not revolutionary, suggestion that before you decide to calibrate, you ask yourself what you hope to accomplish by it and whether the tools you have chosen are likely to help you do it. It discusses theory, concepts, but few specifics. If you are looking for advice as to how to calibrate and configure your particular model of desktop printer, it's not here. In fact, we won't be discussing Photoshop at all. That will wait until Chapter 12, when we will go into the specifics of the Color Settings dialog.

These issues are much deeper than many authorities realize. That is one reason you may wish to staple these three chapters together and proceed directly to Chapter 14.

The second reason is that this subject has often been controversial, and whenever anybody else discusses it with any degree of heat, my name is ordinarily dragged in, preceded and followed by expletives printable and otherwise. Most readers, I suspect, find this as tiresome as I do, except that the conventional wisdom has changed dramatically since the last edition of this book, to the point that those who continue to call me names now occupy positions basically indistinguishable from the views I've been enunciating for around ten years.

Be that as it may, this is the one chapter that can most easily be skipped because the advice it offers is not immediately useful but rather requires reflection. I do, however, suggest reading it if you, like many readers, normally get predictable results when your work is printed, but occasionally receive nasty surprises when vivid colors are involved.

First, though, I'll throw a proposed diplomatic solution on the table. If I and the two aforementioned academics got together to craft some type of compromise language to describe the pairs of colors in Figures 11.1 and 11.2, we might emerge with the following: *the two don't look alike.*

Fine—except this chapter is about how to make things look alike, and we start off with a machine saying that things that very obviously don't look alike *are* alike. Who cares? Why should we value the machine's opinion, when it is that stupid?

Why Should We Care?

A revolutionist is one who desires to discard the existing social order and try another.... Every man is a revolutionist concerning the thing he understands. For example, every person who has mastered a profession is a sceptic concerning it, and consequently a revolutionist.

The idea that machines cannot be trusted to make aesthetic judgments about color, eminently correct as it is, represents starting from scratch in many ways. It seems reasonable that we should extend that philosophy to everything we discuss here. Before we begin, a disclaimer. Very few people take calibration as seriously as I do. When I've criticized other people's schemes, it has been because they are full of words and music but don't deliver quality. We will see a number of instances over the next three chapters where the proposed modern solution is worse than the traditional method.

Nevertheless, it's fair to ask, why do you want the monitor to match the output at all? How close would it have to be to satisfy you?

What are you trying to achieve by getting it that close, and how much good will it do you?

The obvious answer is that in Figure 11.1 I refer to two rows of *green*. This will make me look quite stupid if they are printed as orange or purple.

But that obvious answer doesn't hold up. Nothing that a reasonable person can do to a monitor, including putting in weird Color Settings, can possibly make those rows any color other than green. A different green than we expect, yes. A non-green, no. The fact is that a monitor right out of the box is calibrated well enough for most work—at least it is if we think about what we're trying to achieve.

Monitor calibration is overrated in terms of its actual impact on image quality. Mastering the main topic of *any* of the first ten chapters of this book will give somebody who doesn't calibrate far better results than somebody who does but doesn't understand how to color-correct. Nevertheless, conscientious users calibrate, because it can't be denied that bad results sometimes occur otherwise.

Suppose you are, as I am for this book, depending upon what you see on your screen to predict what will appear on output. When you get that output into your hand and compare it to what was expected, there are four possible outcomes, or phases.

- The actual output is so far off what you were expecting that you would do the job over, if it's possible to do so.
- The output doesn't surprise you so much that you would go to the trouble of redoing the job, but if you had known the truth in advance, you would have prepared the file differently.
- The output is not exactly what you expected, but if you had the chance to do the job again, you would not alter what you did.
- The output matches what you saw on your screen almost perfectly.

If you have achieved Phase Four, you doubtless feel all warm and fuzzy. Your name will be mentioned in trade publications, and vendors will hold you up as an example of the new order.

Personally, I feel that Phase Three is good enough. I do not care about Phase Four, particularly since it is apt to lead to useless arguments about whether it's a perfect match or not. If we would not have done the job any differently, then that's my definition of satisfactory calibration. This goes not just for monitors, but for any type of proofing of the final result.

Also, we have to admit that certain traps will still exist, no matter how well-behaved the monitor. It is, for example, very difficult to evaluate unsharp masking. The monitor produces a deceptively harsh look, particularly on an LCD screen. Exactly what we can get away with depends on the output conditions, on the resolution, and on the character of the image. If you don't believe this, check out the sharpening sections of most Photoshop texts. They usually show one or two examples of "oversharpened" images, and it is clear from the discussion that the authors regard them as *seriously* oversharpened. Often they look just fine in print, because the author was deluded by monitor appearance. You want seriously oversharpened images, you can find some in Chapter 6.

Then again, I've compared screen renditions of well over 100,000 images to their results in print. Eventually, confidence develops, but it isn't an easy road to navigate.

For that matter, you yourself have gone through such a learning experience with your own screen. When you get right down to it, a monitor and a printed product don't match at all. One generates its own light, one reflects it, and that's just the start.

I first began to use a monitor (a very expensive one) to eliminate unnecessary hard proofs back in 1981. By the late 1980s, monitor soft-proofing was well established in the prepress industry. Those experienced with

it had no problem getting good monitor-to-proof agreement as soon as Photoshop became capable of handling serious color correction in the early 1990s.

Adjusting the color on that 1981 monitor required removing the back panel, inserting a jeweler's screwdriver, and rotating one of several potentiometers. If you are interested in calibrating your own monitor today, you need to develop this skill about as much as a professional photographer needs to know how to develop a daguerreotype. Go forward ten years, though, and the skills that might seem ancient become anything but.

For this reason, I'd like to start talking about various kinds of calibrating. We will not, for the moment, allow the use of any third-party software, or any artificial color-measurement instrument. There's time enough to add these refinements—if you want them.

When Options Are Limited

The golden rule is that there are no golden rules.

When I have to give a speech in front of large audiences, I am naturally concerned that the projector, which will be connected to my computer, should give an adequate representation of the images. I usually get around five minutes, if that, to verify whether it does. If it doesn't, the options are limited. Most of the projectors I've had to deal with take a direct, unedited video signal from the host computer, so any attempt I might make to "calibrate" from my own computer would be irrelevant. As there is no time to purchase all the hardware and software that would be needed to do the job properly, I am reduced to doing my color management by means of adjusting the projector's internal settings.

I just used a phrase that hasn't been defined yet—one that has caused no end of trouble to uninitiated users. *Color management* is the science of making things look alike, particularly in scenarios where a variation would be undesirable. *Color correction,* the topic of this book, is the craft, the art of making things look better than they did previously. The relationship between the two is incestuous.

If a picture looks flat and washed out on the screen and it also appears flat and washed out in print, this is a failure of color correction, but it's a success for color management. If we hit an image with curves that make it look much better on our monitor, but in print it appears darker and muddier, this may be a successful color correction, but our color management leaves a lot to be desired.

In the real world, the two are sometimes difficult to separate. Camera Raw, which we will discuss in Chapter 16, has features that look similar to some of the color-correction tools we discussed Chapters 2 and 3. Chapter 15 describes how to use a color management technique for a purpose that is clearly color correction. And, in sensible workflows, many tools that nominally pertain to color management are used to make subsequent color correction easier.

But for present purposes—calibrating an unknown projector quickly—there's no need for that. I am not looking to improve a printed result, but to give the audience a reasonable facsimile of what I see on my own screen. An exact match is impossible. A monitor generates its own light; a projection system bounces it off a screen that isn't particularly reflective. The monitor gets a whiter white, and a blacker black as well. So, at best the audience will see a flatter image even than the one on my laptop, which is pretty bad.

My procedure is first to verify that my Color Settings in Photoshop are the ones that I use for lectures, which are not the same ones I use for live work. If the existing settings are different, then after loading the correct ones I always quit and relaunch Photoshop, so that if I happen to have a crash during the speech, Photoshop will remember the settings.

Second, I turn the lights way down in the hall, annoying the audience and causing people to trip over things as they attempt to find their seats.

Third, I open Figure 11.3, jump down from the stage, and take a look at it from the audience's perspective.

Finally, if dissatisfied, which is the natural state of a revolutionist, I drag a technician, normally kicking and screaming, over to the projector and we start adjusting settings that he previously didn't know existed.

These settings are similar to those found on any monitor. There's always one called *Brightness* (or occasionally *Gamma),* which controls the weight of the image midtone. It doesn't make the white point lighter or the black point darker; it can't. But it does make the overall image lighter or darker.

The critical setting is *Contrast.* The higher the setting, the more highlight and shadow detail is sacrificed in favor of more life in the midtones. For my purposes, this setting is often too high. People who are doing Power-Point presentations make very different demands of a projector than those who teach color correction.

Manipulating these two settings is enough to let me get by, more or less. It had better be, because sometimes they're the only adjustments available. Most of the time, fortunately, there are also settings for white balance, letting me make "whites" bluer or yellower, and also individual controls, similar to Brightness, for the red, green, and blue guns. With these, I can compensate for color imbalance, if any. And if these color-balancing tools are available, I've always been able to get close enough so that the audience can make intelligent judgments about the color, although it makes me crazy when they attack me for oversharpening based on what they see on this wretched ghastly primitive display.

A Vote for the Multidisciplinist

No man can be a pure specialist without being in the strict sense an idiot.

I describe the above situation at such length not because it is very good color management but because it exemplifies the types of challenges all of us sometimes face and how we have to be able to improvise solutions when more conventional methods are unavailable.

To solve a new color management problem requires a disciplined thought process. The same questions always present themselves. It is no waste of time to go through them even for this very simple exercise.

- **What do you hope to achieve, and why?** This is always the key question. Why bother to calibrate at all? What bad things will happen if you don't? What are you trying to match, and how close must the match be?

In the current case, I'm trying to match my own monitor—kind of. The audience won't know if the match isn't good, because they don't have access to my screen. I don't need a precise color match or even a darkness match because I'll be taking my bearings from the projection system just as the audience does.

I do, however, need known neutrals to display properly. If not, by-the-numbers color correction as described in Chapters 2 and 3 won't seem to work. And I can't afford to lose highlight or shadow detail, because a lot of the techniques I show emphasize those areas.

- **What special problems are present?** Not as many as you might think. Granted, a projector is not going to achieve the same vivid colors a monitor can, and contrast

will be an issue. But the audience realizes this, and cuts the speaker a break.

The real problem in color management comes when the thing we're trying to calibrate has certain specific weak points, like CMYK's inability to produce vivid blues even though it makes good reds. That isn't happening here. A projection system produces an overall lower-quality image than a good monitor does, but otherwise the two devices have the same strengths and weaknesses.

- **What conversions and distortions are taking place?** Since the projector takes a direct video signal that is unaffected by my own monitor calibration, the only players here are Photoshop and the projector itself. We have to be sure that Photoshop's Color Settings are what we want. Beyond that, it's whatever feeble tweaks the projector's software will permit.

- **What are the options?** Don't make the mistake of thinking that nothing more can be done without third-party software. True, I can't do anything from my computer to directly affect how the projector operates. If, however, I conclude that my test image is not displaying as I wish it to, I can color-correct it until it does. If I record everything I did, I can

Figure 11.3 *This image tests highlight detail, shadow detail, overall weight, and fleshtones. It's therefore a good start at checking whether a monitor is adequately calibrated.*

save it as a Photoshop Action and apply it to every image I intend to display. Or, along the same lines, I could create new Color Settings that would distort file appearance to compensate for the projector's vagaries.

With an infinitely sophisticated audience and an unlimited amount of time, I might consider one of these approaches. Given the few minutes that I actually have, they can't be considered. It's the twiddle the internal settings method, or nothing.

- **How will the result be tested?** More people go wrong with this step than any other. Either they test with things whose appearance isn't knowable, or they test irrelevant things, or they refuse to put confidence in their own eyes.

I know exactly what Figure 11.3 is supposed to look like, since I have been using it for years. Whether a machine agrees with my assessment is as irrelevant as the machine's delusion that the two greens of Figure 11.1 are the same.

And Figure 11.3 is not a collection of swatches. Rather, it contains the most critical elements for the intended use. Granted that the image may not display accurately under the best of circumstances, I don't particularly care about what happens to the woman's hat. But I need good fleshtones. I need the highlight detailing in the upper right and the shadow detailing in the lower left to be visible. And there are enough midrange areas to judge whether overall appearance is too dark.

- **How much drift can be expected over time, and how often will I have to repeat this procedure?** Easy, in this case. I just need the projector to be stable for the two to eight hours I'll be speaking. I have no reason to believe that it won't.

We have now taken three pages to analyze a problem that afflicts perhaps two dozen readers. It was a much, much simpler problem than the more general-interest ones we are about to study.

And yet, on at least two different occasions at trade shows, I've followed speakers who are recognized experts in the field of color management, who have concluded their talks by apologizing to the audience for how the screen previews were so deceptive, and, in effect, criticizing the show sponsors for not having bought a better projector.

"Even easy color management problems are hard," adds beta reader John Ruttenberg, who is also a Shaw fan, "if you don't have the right goals in mind from the start."

The Price of the Perfect World

Do not do unto others as you would that they should do unto you. Their tastes may not be the same.

Go to a doctor, whether quack or scholar, and you're likely to be advised to get more exercise, eat a balanced diet, and cut back on vices such as smoking, drinking, and dreaming of revolution. Go to a color expert, whether real or self-appointed, and you'll be told to calibrate your monitor.

That nobody questions the desirability of these recommendations strongly suggests that they are sensible. That a revised image is better than the original, however, doesn't prove it's a good correction. That eating spinach is good for the health doesn't guarantee you will be healthy if you eat more of it. That calibrating your monitor is a good idea doesn't guarantee you'll get adequate color if you do it.

Unfortunately, both in health and in color, easy answers are tempting. It would definitely be a better world if a calibrated monitor improved quality drastically, just as it would be a better world if ice cream had negative calories or if auditorium projectors had better calibration routines than the hokey one just described. We nevertheless must accept the world the way we find it.

In speaking of monitor calibration, therefore, we start from scratch. We accept that it is a nuisance. To justify spending time on it, we need to do the same analysis as I did with my projector. In following these steps, we are not discussing your monitor or mine. No specific brand, no specific display technology, just general principles.

- **What do you hope to achieve, and why?** I can think of four scenarios, listed in order of easiest to toughest. First, you might just want to review your own digital photographs on a monitor, without ever wanting to print them. Second, you might be planning to post something on the Web, and wish to know how it will look to other people. Third, and most common, you could be planning to output your images, and don't wish any surprises when you do. Fourth, you could be working as part of a team, in which case someone else may occasionally be using your screen, or which calls for you to evaluate images that have been prepared on different monitors.

If you're in the first group, consider another of Shaw's maxims: Never resist temptation: prove all things: hold fast that which is good. You have the unique advantage that the monitor doesn't have to match anything in particular, as long as you're happy with what you see.

The second group poses the annoying problem of trying to outguess a situation over which we have little control. Most Web surfers have no idea of how to calibrate monitors. Nobody knows what they may be seeing. This is similar to the problem of sending a file to an unfamiliar photo lab or printer. It requires a different philosophy. Instead of creating something that looks good to us, we strive for something that won't look bad if viewed in an unexpected way.

The following discussion is therefore limited to the third and fourth cases. The third is somewhat like the first, in that nobody else needs to be satisfied with your calibration as long as you are. Conceivably, you could calibrate in some messed-up way that resulted

in a good preview of your own work but would not be satisfactory for some unknown type of work in the future. If so, no harm, no foul. If somebody else depends on your settings, you have to be more careful.

- **What special problems are present?** Most of us are so accustomed to using the monitor as a proxy for what will eventually be printed that we forget how much imagination is involved. When you get right down to it, a monitor display looks no more like a print than Shaw looked like Shakespeare.

One of the most cherished early tenets of the mindless, counterrevolutionary philosophy that I call *calibrationism* was that hard proofs and by-the-numbers color would fall by the wayside as it became possible to rely totally on monitor appearance.

While a calibrated monitor is much to be recommended, relying on it *totally,* without reference to any numbers, doesn't work, because of the human visual system's inconvenient insistence on recalibrating itself to whatever light source may be hitting it. We react to brilliant highlights by desensitizing ourselves to them, allowing us to overlook objectionable detail. And the more we look at an image with a cast, thanks to the human phenomenon of chromatic adaptation, the more the cast vanishes.

Furthermore, judging delicate contrast issues accurately on screen is possible but, in my view, extremely difficult. Just as we adjust to a color cast, we adjust to the brilliance of the light shining into our eyes where the screen is attempting to portray highlights. We desensitize ourselves and don't notice detail (possibly offensive detail) that will appear in print.

In shadows, it's the opposite. Regardless of how well calibrated the monitor, when we stare into a darkly lit area, we become *more* sensitive. And so we pick up detail, and wonder where it all went once the job is output.

A well-maintained screen can be accurate

for relations between colors and, especially, to give a sense of overall darkness. By all means, calibrate it—just don't rely on it for highlights, shadows, or neutral colors. That is why we have an Info palette.

●   **What conversions and distortions are taking place?** A whole gang, and a villainous gang at that, of factors affects monitor performance. Start with the viewing environment. Is your screen's desktop set to a solid gray background? If not, it's altering your perceptions. Think simultaneous contrast. If the background is blue, all images will seem too yellow on screen; your unconscious compensation during correction will result in printed images that are too cool.

Similarly, are your walls painted gray? Are your carpets neutral? And is the lighting around the monitor consistent at all hours? If not, you have some calibration issues.

Then, the hardware. If you have an LCD monitor, probably only a few internal settings can blow your calibration. Expensive CRTs can have more than a dozen.

The operating system, particularly on Macintoshes, offers several opportunities to foul up. For example, one Macintosh keyboard shortcut changes the setting in the Universal Access module, which is designed to make screens more intelligible to the visually impaired. The shortcut drastically increases screen contrast, over and above the monitor's own settings and whatever calibration may be in effect. The particular land mine can be disabled, but by default it's there, waiting for a viewer with normal vision to step on it.

●   **What are the options?** Similar, but more extensive, to those for a projection system. We can use the factory defaults. We can go into the monitor's internal settings and make some alterations. We can buy a monitor calibrator, which will generate its own profile that the system can then use, or, with a Macintosh, we can do it ourselves by eyeball.

Or, we can use the Adobe Gamma utility on either platform.

●   **How will the result be tested?** Ultimately, the test is whether you are satisfied—whether you think your setup gives you the ability to predict the next step in the process. It's not whether I think, or a machine thinks, that you're in a calibrated state. If you never feel inclined to redo work because the monitor misled you, you're as calibrated as you can meaningfully be.

It follows, much to the chagrin of those who would like us to spend a lot of money on this endeavor, that a monitor calibrated for one person may not be for another, or at least not without an adjustment period. I, for example, am doing much of the color evaluation for this book on a nine-year-old monitor. Its physical capabilities, like mine, have changed for the worse in those nine years. Chances are that a mechanical calibrator would throw in the towel, as the colors would be so far out of specification that it would not know what to do.

As we have grown older together, however, the monitor and I have become accustomed to one another. It tolerates my swearing at it when it displays an ugly image. I tolerate its tepid colors, and do so without difficulty, although I can no longer make it match any of my other, newer screens.

Could *you* come in and do professional-quality work on such a screen? Probably not right away, unless you've had a lot of experience shifting from computer to computer.

You would, however, be able to adjust within a day or so. The revolutionary thing about evaluating image quality on the monitor is that you can do it at all. A light-emitting screen is so radically different from a light-reflecting print that it is a tribute to the human imagination that we can see *any* resemblance, let alone one strong enough to make intelligent color decisions from. If you have that kind of imagination—and you ought to, after all, you're human—then you should have no trouble adjusting to mildly deficient monitors.

● **How much drift can be expected over time, and how often will I have to repeat this procedure?** The chances of a physical change in the monitor are less than those of a change in lighting or, worse, an unintended change in either the internal monitor settings or those of Photoshop. If it weren't for these possibilities, I'd be content to check the monitor once a week. As it stands, however, I check against a known standard, such as Figure 11.3, every time I sit down to work.

The Black and White of Color

Happiness and Beauty are by-products. Folly is the direct pursuit of Happiness and Beauty.

We now move into the hard area of making a monitor and a print match one another. Let's start by reconsidering Chapter 7, which covers one of the most troublesome color management issues of all: RGB to grayscale.

It may seem crazy to think of black and white as being color, but it's no more so than supposing that the two greens of Figure 11.1 are the same. All the requirements for a color management showdown are in place. The two spaces don't match up. One can say that color is missing in black and white, or be a revolutionist and say that an RGB file is excessively colorful. Either way, the idea is to create a figurative match, as obviously a literal match is impossible.

So, what's the best way to convert into grayscale? Without knowing more about the individual picture, my answer would be to use the formula Photoshop does, three parts red, six parts green, one part blue.

Now suppose that some other joker comes along and says that instead of 3–6–1, a better formula would be 4–5–1. In support of this proposition, he supplies two conversions of the parrot of Figure 7.1, and sure enough, his way is better—more accurate. A third person

shows up claiming that 3–3–4 is best of all, backing up her position with the Canadian flag of Figure 7.4. And an old-time scanner operator, showing us the man of Figure 7.17, advocates 0–10–0.

How would you resolve this issue? The only logical test would be to get 100 or so typical images together, convert each of them all four ways, and get a jury to decide in each of the 100 cases which of the four was the most accurate. I have never tried this, but imagine that 3–3–4 and 0–10–0 would be the clear losers and that 3–6–1 would probably win.

It would, however, depend on the images. If they are supplied by a portrait photographer, 0–10–0 might be in first place.

One thing's for sure: the winner wouldn't even come close to a clean sweep. If one method was judged superior in 70 of the 100 images, it would be a stunning upset.

But who cares if 3–6–1 is the correct conversion formula for a file we've never seen and aren't allowed to work with first? Probably not you, if you've bought this book. You'll be blending channels first. But in that case, how often will you literally be using the 3–6–1 formula? Once in a lifetime? 3–6–1 is irrelevant, no more than a convenience, a known result when you execute Image: Mode>Grayscale. If the formula were something else (provided we knew what it was), the impact on workflow would be precisely zero.

Black and white has no color and is therefore more absolute than CMYK, which merely has no blue. But the same considerations apply—in a more complicated form.

The Colors That Are Missing

The difference between the shallowest routineer and the deepest thinker appears, to the latter, trifling; to the former, infinite.

It's hard to come up with logical solutions when the technology does not behave logically. At least black and white is egalitarian: we get no colors at all. In any kind of color printing, from newspapers to inkjets using the most expensive paper, we achieve some colors but not others.

Furthermore, the missing colors are sometimes accepted as normal behavior, sometimes not. Have you noticed what terrible blues this book's images have, in comparison to their reds and yellows? Probably not, because you have never seen good blues in other books or magazines either, so you aren't expecting anything else here. If Peachpit Press were willing to spring for a good blue ink in addition to CMYK, you'd notice in a big hurry the first time it hit a sky.

But what if viewers are not so willing to forgive the missing colors? Blue areas are so common in images that you must be aware, at least subconsciously, of the problem in print. But what about pinks?

Figure 11.4 In the RGB original of this image, which can be found on the CD, the pink flowers are far more intense than they appear on this page.

Two factors delude us. First, CMYK has a magenta ink. Put down a solid layer of it—100^M—and you achieve a color that's out of the gamut of most RGBs, including your monitor. Shouldn't a lesser amount of magenta ink also produce a vivid color? And second, faces are pink. There doesn't seem to be any problem printing faces, does there?

Faces are deceptive because they're not pure enough to cause a problem. Even natural blonds, who have the pinkest skin of any humans, have a red-killing cyan component, plus a substantial amount of yellow. The color we might describe as bubble-gum pink, which is the color of many flowers, is what causes the problem.

To get a full idea of what's happening, you need to open the CD and look at the RGB original that converted into Figure 11.4. If you can't be bothered to do that, the file is much, much more colorful than it is on this page, because the color being called for is well out of the CMYK gamut. Yet this is a magenta flower, and magenta ought to be a CMYK strength. Let's discuss why this surprising result occurs.

Nobody can make a white whiter than the paper being printed on. Whiter whites equal more contrast just as blacker blacks do. Very expensive paper normally has both. Printing on paper like that of this book is destined to look flat by comparison. But the real difference is in pastel colors. Open that CD file, go Image: Mode>CMYK, and watch it turn gray. Chances are you could get something more vivid by feeding an RGB file to your desktop inkjet, with its brilliant substrate.

Magenta ink is quite potent. A swatch of solid magenta on this page is a color too intense for a monitor to display. Then again, that color never occurs in nature. There are lots of magenta flowers, but they're light magenta, like in Figure 11.4.

Or, at least, they *were* magenta, when they were in RGB. Now, they're quite gray, and

Figure 11.5 *This image was created in RGB, using the equivalent of 100ᴹ as the base color for the gradient. Compared to the RGB original on the CD, this printed version does well in the darker areas, but poorly as the color gets lighter.*

any photographer who had told a client that CMYK prints nice magentas would have a lot of explaining to do at this point.

Viewers perceive magenta when their eyes are flooded with red and blue light. The most intense magenta would be as much red and blue light, and as little green, as possible. On a monitor, this is accomplished by firing the red and blue guns at full intensity and turning green off altogether. In CMYK, laying down a solid coating of magenta ink blocks reflection of green light while permitting red and blue.

In RGB, a lighter magenta is made by adding green light, since red and blue are already maxed out. In CMYK, the lightening is achieved by reducing ink coverage and exposing more paper. That only works as well as the RGB method when the paper is absolutely, totally, blindingly white. Anything less achieves its non-whiteness by blocking reflection of not just green light, but some of the critical red and blue as well. The darker the paper, the more pitiful the light magenta. The dollar-a-sheet stuff is quite white. Paper that costs a 20th as much absorbs 20 times as much red and blue.

Consequently, if you convert the gradient at the top left of Figure 11.5 to CMYK, the dark square, which was originally defined as the RGB equivalent of solid magenta ink, doesn't appear to change on your screen. But the lighter areas of the gradient are distinctly grayer after the conversion than they appear in the original file on the CD. That effect is what's eviscerating Figure 11.4's flowers, which are so vividly pink in RGB.

What's a poor photographer to do? There are several possibilities, but all involve understanding why CMYK is incapable of doing what is wanted. To get a purer-looking color, we need to leave less paper exposed. That means we have to use more ink. We can add magenta to make the flower darker, or yellow while eliminating cyan to make it redder, or cyan while eliminating yellow to make it bluer. It depends on what lie we wish to tell. But any of these three lies, in my view, would be better than leaving Figure 11.4 the way it is.

Having done these experiments, I can tell you that not only do audiences prefer the darker versions aesthetically, but they also—unanimously—regard them as more accurate renditions of the RGB color.

Color, Contrast, and Revolutionism

A learned man is an idler who kills time with study. Beware of his false knowledge: it is more dangerous than ignorance.

We clearly have no chance of matching the original file in print. Yet, in terms of the two main topics of our book, Figure 11.4 is a reasonably close match in terms of contrast. However, it misses badly in color.

Those who have evaluated this image feel that we should take liberties with the contrast, by making the flowers darker, so as to come closer to the original color. It takes us back to the hog in Figure 1.2, where similar concerns led some to prefer one version and others a second. These two examples vary in one important particular. The majority, although not everybody, was willing to forgo a color match in the hog if the contrast improved. Here, the vote is nearly unanimous that we can junk some of the contrast in the interest of getting more attractive color.

That vote makes this an unusual picture. Generally, people assign more weight to contrast accuracy than to color match—contrary to what you might think, and to what you might read.

The most revolutionary thought in the color field has traditionally come from people without a strong color background but who understood several disciplines. We can go further. Almost everyone who has made a contribution of any significance has demonstrated a clear appreciation for not just the sciences but the arts.

The theory of neutralization of shadows was sketched out by the artist Leonardo da Vinci, who also began the study of simultaneous contrast that was fully enunciated in the 1830s by the chemist Michel Eugène Chevreul. Understanding of visual perception owes much to the work of the playwright and novelist Johann Wolfgang von Goethe and the biologist Charles Darwin. Goethe and Leonardo were hardly the only nonacademics to put in their oar. Shaw himself took a strong interest in color; so did Beethoven, among many others.

Some of our fundamental understanding comes from the profoundly multidisciplinary Isaac Newton, but probably the deepest book on color ever written was by Ogden Rood, a 19th-century American physicist, and like Chevreul, an art fancier. In *Modern Chromatics,* this revolutionist wrote,

> We forgive, then, a partial denial of the truths of colour more easily than those of light and shade, which probably is a result of the nature of the optical education of the race. For the human race, thus far, light and shade has been the all-important element in the recognition of external objects;

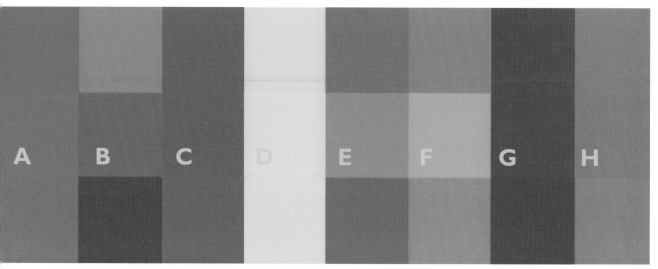

Figure 11.6 *Machines and humans often come up with different answers about how closely colors match. For each swatch in the center row, state whether you think that its top or bottom neighbor (or neither) is a closer match.*

colour has played only a subordinate part, and has been rather a source of pleasure than of positive utility.

We must recognize that our preference for a darker, more vivid color to represent these light purples has to do with the unique nature of the subject. If this purple were anything but a flower, and a big, important flower at that, we'd probably think that the color of Figure 11.4 is a better choice than something darker.

The idea that there is no one correct way to convert this purple for output sounds revolutionist, but we've seen it before, back in the chapter on the other form of color management, color to black and white. The parrot's chest of Figure 7.1E was the same red as found in the Canadian flag of Figure 7.4. The most accurate translation of this color was the light gray of Figure 7.1B, but also the much darker gray of Figure 7.1C.

When it's possible to match the RGB file's color in CMYK, usually we want to do so. When it isn't, *accurate* is not a fixed target, and this is the demise of calibrationism, which believes that said target must be fixed.

If a human audience unanimously believes that one method gives a more accurate result than another, then that method is, by definition, more accurate. From the votes in the two images described above, it is a short leap to the realization that the first method is more accurate than the second, but the second is more accurate than the first.

A machine is incapable of coping with such a simple concept. So are some humans. The beta readers accepted the above paragraph. This book's copy editor, Elissa Rabellino, flagged the last sentence, saying, "These seem to be contradicting each other."

Peace. We are doing images here, not mathematics. It is hard to accept that two plus two is most accurately described as four but simultaneously as seven or the square root of 19—if we look at it from the wrong point of view. But it happens all the time in colorspace conversions.

Then again, being a revolutionist, I believe that the greens of Figure 11.1 are two different colors, spectrophotometers, densitometers, colorimeters, and cameras to the contrary notwithstanding. Are you getting to that point yourself?

Win Some, Lose Some

Men are wise in proportion, not to their experience, but to their capacity for experience.

Color-measurement devices are excellent for retaining calibration once it has been established. They do not have an aesthetic sense, however; they can't compensate for differences in context or characteristics of an individual image. They also don't have a very good sense of when colors match—and of which colors are more important than others.

Today, most methods of conversion originate with machine measurements of a series

---

Worksheet for Figure 11.6

On the facing page are eight columns of three swatches apiece. The center is the reference row, and the question is whether the top or bottom sample is a better match to each center swatch. You may also rank it a tie. My own answers, and those of the leading mathematical formula, are in the box on page 265. Obviously, the point is to show that you and I often disagree with machines, but in some cases here we likely agree. Also, the top and bottom rows are random; neither I nor the machine voted for all top or all bottom versions.

Col.	Closest	Col.	Closest
A		E	
B		F	
C		G	
D		H	

of swatches (more complicated than, but along the same lines as, Figure 11.6), which measurements are then compared to desired values in some reference colorspace, such as LAB. Then, software decides the least evil way to render the colors when the desired value is impossible to match.

Me, I would try to match swatches A, F, and G. It would be overstating things to say I don't give a hoot about the others, but A, F, and G are vastly more important to a successful calibration. They represent fleshtones and plant life. In professional work, we live and die by the quality of work in those areas. If small lies need to be told about the other five, so be it. The human profiler will do it, and get better results on the whole than a machine would—unless, of course, the test is how well the pro-

CRT and LCD Monitors

The question of whether professional-quality color work can be done on an LCD as opposed to the traditional CRT screen strikes me as very similar to the question of whether digital cameras are capable of achieving the same quality as film, or whether CD sound is better than that of a vinyl LP. The actual answer to each question is irrelevant, because the market has already decided the issue.

LCD monitors are cheaper and lighter, and require less desktop space. Their main problem at present is that colors vary based on the viewer's angle. Also, the appearance is higher contrast than that of the CRT monitors that have been the professional standard for two decades. There are usually fewer controls, so it is often difficult to avoid perceiving plugged shadows and/or blown highlights.

Someone accustomed to working on a CRT monitor usually has a tough first day adjusting to the LCD look. Then again, the first predigital craftsmen who had to adjust to looking at a monitor rather than a hard-copy proof had a tough time adjusting as well. It can be done. If I were buying a screen for high-quality work today, it'd be an LCD—I'd prefer to get my exercise with free weights rather than slinging some enormous CRT around the room, and in any event the writing is on the wall.

file prints swatches. As we don't sell swatches, only images, this consideration is not a particularly weighty one.

Again: no method is perfect all the time. Our job is to get the one that is right most frequently for the type of work we do. For me, that means my fleshtones and greenery are going to be where I plan to beat the machine. I understand that I will lose on certain other categories of images, and don't care.

Similarly, in calibrating a monitor, take a tip from Ogden Rood: luminosity is much more important than color. Hearing clients claim that they were misled by a badly calibrated monitor, and then having to investigate whether it is true, is an area in which I am considerably experienced. I can tell you that usually the monitor is fine; the problem is that the viewer adjusted to a cast and was too lazy to look at the Info palette, or else misinterpreted highlight and/or shadow detail.

When a miscalibrated monitor truly is to blame, it is almost invariably a contrast, not a color, issue. Overwhelmingly, the problem is that the monitor predicted something lighter than the client got.

Consequently, when calibrating a monitor, a sensible human always gets the darkness right, even if the color gets shortchanged slightly. A machine may be more doctrinaire.

The Red Flag of the Revolution

All who achieve real distinction in life begin as revolutionists. The most distinguished persons become more revolutionary as they grow older, though they are commonly supposed to become more conservative owing to their loss of faith in conventional methods of reform.

The machine's lack of aesthetic judgment becomes painful when we move from a larger to a smaller colorspace—as we do whenever we convert from RGB to CMYK.

In principle, we want to come as close as reasonable to the original colors. Sometimes it's obvious. More than half of all nations use a strong red in their flag. It's often somewhat beyond the gamut of the output device, unless it's been flown in the sun too long. On converting this red to CMYK, we almost certainly want values near $0^C100^M100^Y$. And that goes for *any* kind of CMYK—a newspaper, a magazine, an inkjet printer, an annual report—as well as for a book like this one.

Then again, the reds found in flags aren't all that far out of gamut. The blue of many flags is another story. It's so far beyond the capabilities of most printers that many solutions are possible. And something as unreasonable as the original flowers, as we have seen, could be many things, too.

We find it so easy ourselves to determine what is a close match that we forget how difficult it is for non-humans. Figure 11.6 illustrates. The center row is the reference. Each center swatch is the desired color. The question is whether its top or bottom neighbor (or both, if you consider it a tie) is a closer match. This is similar to the process of considering alternatives that a machine goes through in generating a profile—and strongly suggests why that process is so dubious.

After all, how does a mere machine make the decision about which of two colors matches a third better? Do you suppose it was born with aesthetic instincts like ours?

If you think the decision is easy, try explaining it in terms that a machine could understand. For example, you could say that misses in the green channel of RGB look worse than if they were in the red—but if the underlying color is red, they may look better.

Machines like it better if you express things in LAB, which is designed to be *perceptually uniform,* which means that a variation of, say, 5^A from the desired value theoretically looks just as bad whether plus or minus, and regardless of what is happening in the other two channels.

In practice, whether all this is true depends on the colors being discussed. If it's a rich

How Far Off Can We Be?

Color-correction techniques don't require precision knowledge of output conditions. Mild variations between photo labs or commercial printers won't turn a good correction into a bad one. The same is true of monitors. I'm in a position to know.

In my classes, seven or eight students work on the same images on computers and monitors supplied by the course sponsor. When completed, they transfer their work to my own monitor, where we gather round and compare them side by side.

The monitors on which the students work may or may not be the same model. Some may be much older than others. Some may be CRT and others LCD. Before the class begins, I have about 30 minutes to get all eight or nine to a condition of rough—and that means *rough*—equality, without the use of any supplementary hardware. They are all Macintoshes, which means that I can—if there's time—calibrate through System Preferences. In Mac OS X v10.3 and up, this is a powerful tool that, in the right hands, delivers calibration superior to that of a machine—provided you have the time to play around, which in this case I don't.

Nevertheless, the best image looks best no matter which monitor it's viewed on—even when the calibration is as rudimentary as what I just described. It gets worse, though.

In certain classrooms, three or more slave monitors are hooked up to mine, so that students can watch what I'm doing without everybody having to crowd around my screen. I've always resisted using the slave monitors because, since they take unedited video direct from my monitor, the only way to affect their appearance is with whatever internal controls for brightness, contrast, and whatnot they may offer. I sometimes find one of the slaves so poor that I steal another from somewhere else. But if the internal juggling gets the picture anywhere close to mine, people will make the same decision about which picture is best that they would if viewing my screen.

The only exceptions have been with LCD screens (see box, facing page). Such monitors can have such a drastic effect on highlight and shadow appearance that it is possible a certain image might look unacceptable on one monitor and fine on another. But with CRT screens, I've never seen the problem.

blue, subtracting 5^A will yield a closer match than adding it, but in most reds, the opposite is true, and in cyanish blues, adding and subtracting 5^A are about equally evil. Changes in the A channel are customarily more noticeable than equal ones in the B, except for the cases in which the opposite is true; or unless the result is being evaluated by persons who are partially or totally color-blind, who see far more variation in the B than the A.

Note that we haven't even hit the two most obvious problems. First is context: conversions headed for the Web, for example, where the background is often vivid, need to be more vivid themselves than if they were to be placed on a white background.

Second, the calibration appropriate for one person may not be for another, and not just because of differences of perception. If you shoot lots of flowers, the conversions will be more accurate on the whole if magentas come out relatively dark. If you don't, lighter magentas are more correct.

I once worked on a coffee-table book by the brilliant photographer Robert Bergman. He specializes in portraits of street people, poor and often homeless. His work received support from many of the leading vendors in the field. No expense was spared to create the greatest possible color management package, one that would have the most sophisticated conversions of out-of-gamut colors into ones that the high-quality printing conditions would support.

It was one of the great wastes of time ever seen in the graphic arts. These photographs are, as you might expect, depressing. Their colors are dull. Other than neon lights, which have to be handled separately anyway, Mr. Bergman's images spotlight unprintably bright colors about as often as MTV presents a production of *Major Barbara*. None of the problems we've been spending so much time on exist; no finesse solutions are necessary. Essentially every RGB color in his photos

can be matched in CMYK, so very simple methods of calibration would have worked fine. Instead, many of Mr. Bergman's CMYK moves were counter-corrections for the fancy footwork his color management system had indulged in to dance around hypothetical colors that didn't happen to exist in any of the artwork.

In Favor of the Machine

To a mathematician the eleventh means only a single unit: to the bushman who cannot count further than his ten fingers it is an incalculable myriad.

Using a color-measuring machine to verify that your hardware is performing in the way that you wish it to is so obviously sensible that it might be called revolutionary. To use such a machine to *decide* how the hardware should be performing is as sensible as to let it decide what movies you like or what type of food tastes good to you. It is to rely on hardware that does not see color as accurately as humans do, and cannot evaluate the context, using a really lame set of rules programmed in by humans who may not know that much about color themselves—rules designed to allow the machine to ape how humans match colors. When this process finishes, the quality will be evaluated by actual humans who *are* aware of context and who *do* see colors as humans do. Is the inadequate result somehow shocking?

When the things we are trying to match have much the same color gamut—a digital proofer and an analog film proofer, for example—it's easy to create a satisfactory match. But the more different the devices, the harder it is to pull off the scam, and the more a human needs to intervene. Getting a good match between two monitors is easy, between a monitor and a projector fairly easy, between a monitor and a high-quality print moderately hard, and between a monitor and newspaper color quite difficult indeed.

Difficult, that is, to those who believe that the two greens in Figure 11.1 are the same color. Where we have two dissimilar conditions and want optimal results in both, there's no way to avoid human intervention at least some of the time. To expect one master file to magically metamorphose into versions suitable for both a newspaper and an annual report, let alone for a newspaper and the Web or for a magazine and a film recorder, is ridiculous. The sharpening issue alone would torpedo the idea, even if the insurmountable color issues didn't exist.

The conclusion that machine measurements make for poor conversions, obvious though it is, has not always been accepted to the extent that it is today. Those who have not accepted it, historically, have been so violent in their criticism of me that in the last edition of this book the chapter that corresponds to this one was wrapped around references to hell, whose executive officer I was continually being likened to. If you'd like a chuckle, it's included on the CD. Meanwhile, however, I must add two disclaimers.

First, calibrating different devices without the aid of machine measurements seems very easy to me, because I've done it with literally hundreds of different devices in the last two decades, and all methods seem alike after a while. If you haven't done it that often, you may not be as comfortable doing it as I am. In that case, a machine-generated profile is a reasonable way to start—just don't be intimidated, be ready to fix its problems.

Second, the proponents of machine calibration were putting out for belief that I was rejecting their profiles not because they were considerably inferior to the ones I was currently using (and more expensive to boot), but because I hate machines. In point of fact, few people are as exigent about the use of machines to retain calibration as I was running prepress companies.

The reason has been stated in earlier discussion. When you analyze any calibration decision, ask what the consequences are if you do a poor job, and also how rapidly the devices drift once they are calibrated.

For a graphic arts service provider, poor calibration costs money. Jobs are wasted, clients offended, business lost. Also, many devices (notably presses) are subject to constant fluctuations. The way to keep them in sync is with regular, frequent machine measurements. Figure 11.6 might serve as one of the targets. We, the humans, decide when it is printed correctly—and then we take a measurement, and record it. Tomorrow, when we print it again, the machine will have a better memory of what it looked like today than we will, and will be able to give us a better answer as to whether it is extremely close to today's version.

If Not Victory, Is Yet Revenge

Activity is the only road to knowledge.

While writing this chapter in August 2006, I took time off to give a two-day seminar in Costa Rica, a country with the revolutionary idea of having no army, much to the benefit

Quiz Answers

In Figure 11.6, the challenge was to state whether the top or bottom version in each column was closer to the middle, or whether it was a tie. The following are my votes, and those of the most commonly used computer formula.

Group	Man	Machine
A (green)	Top	Top
B (rose)	Tie	Bottom
C (purple)	Top	Bottom
D (yellow)	Top	Bottom
E (blue)	Top	Tie
F (flesh)	Tie	Bottom
G (olive)	Bottom	Top
H (dark flesh)	Top	Tie

of its populace. I usually prefer to teach groups of six to eight, where everyone can have a computer and compare results with others; I haven't done a full-day speech for a large group in the U.S. in a long time. The rest of the world, yes. Inasmuch as I only get to Central America once every few years, we did everything possible to make the thing accessible to local professionals, and got an audience of around 200. I suggested that the best way to handle questions was to reserve the entire second half of the second day to answer them, and have people give them to me in writing at the lunch break so that we could eliminate duplication. I was not expecting as many as 50 questions, but twice that number materialized.

What was astonishing was, with so many challenging topics to choose from, around a quarter asked why files from LAB never hold their colors when entering CMYK, or how can we tell when there is going to be a conversion problem from LAB, or words to that effect.

To that, I can only respond with the theory of the eminent color scientist, Yogi Berra, who remarked, "You can observe a lot just by watching."

Files move from LAB (or RGB) into CMYK just fine, thank you, provided that they don't call for colors like those of the original RGB of Figure 11.4, colors that are beyond CMYK's capability to reproduce. If they do call for such colors, we may get an unpleasant surprise, because no method of conversion does the right thing all the time.

To figure out whether an image might have such a problem does not require a spectro-photometer, a lumihumitron, or even the Info palette. It requires opening your eyes. You are looking for areas of pure, light colors; of reasonably intense blue; and of extremely intense anything else. Sometimes you can be certain there will be a problem (like, the minute you open the RGB original of Figure 11.4). Sometimes it's unclear; for example,

in the wedding image of Figure 9.1 all the women except the bride wear light pastel colors that may or may not present conversion problems; we'd have to examine the RGB file carefully to know whether there was any loss.

The ugliness of what can follow a mismatch—a loss of detail, a nasty color shift, or both—hides a revolutionary secret. Such mismatches don't happen that often.

To prove it, let's go back to Chapter 10, and consider the images shown there. This being a color-correction textbook, it might be expected that the images would present more problems than normal. Let's see.

• Figure 10.1, a tool kit, is almost dead neutral. There is not the slightest chance of a conversion problem.

• Figure 10.4, a sea scene from British Columbia, is primarily blue, although not particularly intense. We should pay attention to the conversion, but not expect damage. Maybe it will turn out slightly less blue than the RGB, but if so, there won't be anything to be done about it. Detail won't suffer.

• In Figure 10.5, everything is subdued except an exceedingly orange bird. As yellow is a CMYK strength, we don't expect any particular problem, although we keep our eyes open.

• In Figure 10.10, an image of a wooden totem with trees, nothing can possibly present a conversion problem.

• Ditto Figure 10.12, a Chinese river scene. The background is dull. There's a red flag, but it's not brilliant enough to be an issue.

• Figure 10.14, a Norwegian wood, is all subtle colors, nothing problematic.

• By the time we're done with Figure 10.21, a food shot featuring a bottle of sparkling wine, the colors are rather snappy—but there's nothing even close to being an unprintable color.

If you are a sports photographer (many teams have intensely colored uniforms), or if you specialize in pictures of flowers, or undersea images, then the problem of making the print look like what you are expecting is a major one. For most of the rest of the world, it's not all that frequent, yet the problem is so terrifying when it hits that it seems more important than it is.

In the introduction and in Chapter 1, I mentioned that of the reader requests for this edition, there was a clear vote for more coverage of channel blending, of sharpening—and of getting difficult colors to print correctly. The first two, I can understand. They are technically difficult topics whose techniques are not exactly intuitive.

To have a problem with conversions, though, is another story. Everybody has enough technical knowledge to avoid it, if they just refrain from being intimidated.

It's just like the conversions to black and white in Chapter 7. If you don't take proper precautions prior to converting, you may be stuck with a grayscale image that's difficult to fix. It's the same way here. I don't particularly want to fix the flowers of Figure 11.4, now that the conversion to CMYK has wrecked them.

So, here's a piece of advice. If you don't like how your method of conversions handles brilliant colors, don't let it handle any of them. Tone them down in RGB or LAB first. If it's not possible to reproduce the color you'd prefer, then at least get the next best choice—not the ninth-best choice, like Figure 11.4.

Maxims for Color Revolutionists

- If you can color correct, you can color manage, but you can't color manage if you can't color correct.
- The objective is predictability, not perfection.
- There is always a conversion somewhere, and probably more conversions than you think.
- There are more devices that we would conceivably like to calibrate than time that we could conceivably spend in calibrating.

- Distrust anyone whose arguments are analogies rather than images. If an image were available to prove the point, you'd be seeing it, not the analogy.
- Profiling a printing press is like profiling the wind.
- The successful color manager does not believe that two plus two is four, but rather that it simultaneously equals five, seven, and the square root of 19.
- If you don't understand how to calibrate, you tempt fate, which will take vengeance sooner or later by arranging for your career to depend on understanding how to calibrate.
- All men are created equal, but some colors are more equal than others.
- The proper reproduction of test swatches is very low on the list of priorities.
- If you don't like the way algorithms solve problems, don't give them problems to solve.
- He who can, does. He who cannot, blames color management.
- Nobody ever got rich selling histograms.
- Not every image is alike, not every conversion presents the same problems, and not every problem has a solution.
- Perception depends upon opening one's eyes.
- Of all the areas of color reproduction, this is the one most amenable to common sense, yet is the one in which the conventional wisdom has been the most consistently wrong.

Look for the Pattern

The DEVIL (angrily). You throw my friendly farewell back in my teeth, then, Don Juan? DON JUAN. By no means. but though there is much to be learnt from a cynical devil, I really cannot stand a sentimental one. Señor Commander: you know the way to the frontier of hell and heaven. Be good enough to direct me. The STATUE. Oh, the frontier is only the difference between two ways of looking at things. Any road will take you across it if you really want to get there.

For calibration to be at fault, there has to be some kind of pattern. It may be gross, as in almost all images are too green, or something very subtle.

Either way, there's a simple test. Ask yourself, is there a pattern? And if so, would you be able to correct for it in Photoshop?

Suppose that you are trying to make your monitor agree with the results you're getting back from a certain print shop. If that is not currently happening, it's probably a bad CMYK setting on your part, but it could be a lot of other things—it doesn't really matter.

It also doesn't matter whether you think the printed product looks good or bad. The question is, can you call up the file and apply some kind of curves or whatnot to make it look on screen the way it looks in print, or at least to be a closer match? If you can't, it's probably not a calibration issue, but one of gamut, of capabilities. If you can, then the question is whether that same series of commands would also make most other images match the print more closely.

If it wouldn't, the issue is probably one of process control. If half of the images show up too light and the other half too dark, and half are too colorful and the other half too gray, you can try to calibrate until hell freezes over and only succeed in making matters worse.

But if you've gotten this far in the book, you should be able to detect whether there's a pattern; you should be able to calibrate your monitor with any one of several options; and, assuming that your final output is CMYK, you should be able to generate a plausible Custom CMYK for every printer you deal with, especially after you read the next two chapters. And that Custom CMYK is an ICC profile, which can be exchanged with other applications or reused in a variety of ways.

Remember: without a pattern, there's no point in doing anything. If somebody shows you a single image and says that you're calibrated, you're not.

The Superior Measuring Device

DON JUAN. Just as Life, after ages of struggle, evolved that wonderful bodily organ the eye, so that the living organism could see where it was going and what was coming to help or threaten it, and thus avoid a thousand dangers that formerly slew it, so it is evolving today a mind's eye that shall see, not the physical world, but the purpose of Life.

Our perception of color has proven too complicated to be reduced to rules understandable even by humanity's best minds— let alone a machine. We've already shown several examples of *simultaneous contrast*— the idea that the background affects the foreground colors. *Chromatic adaptation* explains why we can't trust what we see on screen for neutrality without the aid of the Info palette. And we haven't even considered the Stevens Effect, the Hunt Effect, the Bezold-Brücke hue shift, the Helson-Judd Effect, the Abney Effect, and, lest we forget, the Helmholtz-Kohlrausch Effect.

If somebody asks you what all these effects mean, give the same answer that I would. They mean that machines don't see things the way we do.

Calibration is the art—and to a much lesser extent, the science—of making images look alike. The idea that something other than the human eye can make this determination is highly dubious. Use the eye, not the machine, and your profiles will be not just cheaper and faster to produce, but *better.*

Some scientists argue for artificiality, but the scientists with artistic sensibility have long known better. Charles Darwin voted for anticalibrationism as follows.

> It is scarcely possible to avoid comparing the eye to a telescope. We know that this instrument has been perfected by the long-continued efforts of the highest human intellects; and we naturally infer that the eye has been formed by a somewhat analogous

process. But may not this inference be presumptuous? Have we any right to assume that the Creator works by intellectual powers like those of man? If we must compare the eye to an optical instrument, we ought in imagination to take a thick layer of transparent tissue, with a nerve sensitive to light beneath, and then suppose every part of this layer to be continually changing slowly in density so as to separate into layers of different densities and thickness, placed at different distances from each other, and with the surfaces of each layer slowly changing in form. Further we must suppose that there is a power always intently watching each slight accidental alteration in the transparent layers; and carefully selecting each alteration which, under varied circumstances, may in any way, or in any degree, tend to produce a distincter image. We must suppose each new state of the instrument to be multiplied by the million; and each to be preserved till a better be produced, and then the old ones to be destroyed. In living bodies, variation will cause the slight alterations, generation will multiply them almost infinitely, and natural selection will pick out with unerring skill each improvement. Let this process go on for millions on millions of years; and during each year on millions of individuals of many kinds; and may we not believe that a living optical instrument might thus be formed as superior to one of glass, as the works of the Creator are to those of man?

*   *   *

Understanding evolution is much like understanding color. We know Darwin was on the right track, but he demonstrated that we are still in the dark ages. Every year we learn more about his field and refine his teachings, just as we now understand where Newton, Chevreul, Goethe, and even Leonardo fell short in their appreciation of how color works.

With due respect to our incomparable optical system, the most impressive attribute of our species is our ability to sift through concepts, reject some, accept others. Darwin forced us to confront that, to think about where we came from. But to do so, we have to make our life far more uncomfortable by giving up certain things that we used to accept on blind faith.

A lot of the time, if not most of the time, you'll be calibrating to new printing conditions using the by-guess-and-by-gosh method. That is, you get no swatches, no profile; what you get is a bunch of images that look too green and too dark, so you tweak a few settings and hope they work better on the next job.

You therefore will learn to calibrate by eye, or you'll never be able to adjust to certain print realities, and you'll never be able to convince your print vendor that your proofs are reliable enough.

Beyond that, if you wish to calibrate by machine, go ahead; like almost all other color management methods, they're compatible with the general approach of this book. But even if you refuse to rely on what your eyes tell you, rely on your common sense, a commodity that is often lost in these arguments.

If Our Substance Be Indeed Divine

The reasonable man adapts himself to the world: the unreasonable one persists in trying to adapt the world to himself. Therefore all progress depends on the unreasonable man.

As I hope this chapter has indicated, I *do* believe fairly strongly in calibration. But I do not make a religion of it; I insist that science and mathematics be my servants and not my master; when I see an image that looks lousy I say so, even if a machine says it looks good. And so, I am not a calibrationist, but I am a color manager.

If someone offers you what seems like a plausible scientific argument, such as, say, offering to trot out an artificial instrument to measure whether the two greens of Figure 11.1 are the same, think it over before buying into it. If you allow yourself to be buffaloed by technology into believing things that your own eyes and intelligence can tell you are false—well, then, beware. Tomorrow's calibrationist could be *you.*

You can do better. To start on the path to righteousness, stand up straight, take a deep breath, and let the world hear it: those two greens are different colors.

This chapter has indulged in a lot of name-dropping. It's to remind you that you have become involved in a topic that has fascinated humanity's finest minds for centuries. We've learned a lot in that time, but there is a lot we still don't get.

Not everything about this field is fiendishly complex. If you go over everything I've said

here, it seems quite innocent enough—provided you don't get intimidated by jargon or by machines. If that starts to happen, please remember that there is no area in the entire graphic arts in which most of the experts have been so consistently proven wrong.

For this reason, a certain cynicism is in order, and this and the next chapter feature quotations from two of the leading cynics of the 20th century. Here's what the featured artist of the next chapter, H. L. Mencken, had to say about the star of this one:

> Practically all of the sagacity of George Bernard Shaw consists of bellowing vociferously what every one knows. …Why is he regarded as an arch-heretic, almost comparable to Galileo, Nietzsche, or Simon Magnus? For the simplest of reasons. Because he practices with great zest and skill the fine art of exhibiting the obvious in unexpected and terrifying lights—because he is a master of the logical trick of so matching two apparently safe premises that they yield an incongruous and inconvenient conclusion. …Therein lies the secret of the continued vogue of Shaw. He has a large and extremely uncommon capacity for provocative utterance; he knows how to get a touch of bellicosity into the most banal of doctrines; he is forever on tiptoe, forever challenging, forever sforzando.

With that, it's only appropriate to let Shaw himself have the last word:

> I believe in Michelangelo, Velázquez, and Rembrandt; in the might of design, the mystery of color, the redemption of all things by Beauty everlasting, and the message of Art that has made these hands blessed.

The Bottom Line

This chapter is the first of three discussing calibration and conversion issues. Rather than discussing specific products, it is philosophical, asking what the purpose of the calibration is, what methods are available to achieve it, and what are the consequences if it is omitted.

Conversions only become problematic when colors are called for that are out of the gamut of the destination space and therefore cannot be output accurately. Most people are aware that intense blues are difficult in almost all printing scenarios, but this chapter discusses several other weaknesses that must be dealt with.

Machines are valuable in ensuring that calibrated systems remain that way, but it is inappropriate to use them to make subjective decisions, an unfortunate trend in color management software.

Managing Color Settings

The Color Settings dialog has some good choices, some bad ones, some that are matters of opinion, and some that used to be, but are no longer, controversial. Selecting the proper settings requires not only a grasp of theory but an understanding of the choices others make. Ironically, this subject, which has caused more than its share of foul language, is best explained in terms of how people swear.

Photoshop uses different terms in different languages. The Italian version translates *black generation* into *function of gray.* The program sold in Spain uses *Superimpose* mode rather than *Overlay,* but if you try to use that term in Latin America, nobody will understand you, because they all work with English-language Photoshop. In the German version, *Overlay* becomes the incomprehensible *Ineinanderkopieren,* and the History palette is the *Protokol* palette. And on and on. It causes endless trouble in online discussion groups, which know no national borders.

It also plays the devil with translations of books and other technical documentation. Most professional translators are not Photoshop experts. If, in a book for an area where non-English versions of Photoshop are in use, I say "Custom CMYK," the translator may recognize it as a specific term but also may have a hard time finding where it's located in the program. If, in a book being translated for a place where people work in English-language Photoshop, I say "sponge out the color," the translator is unlikely to know whether *sponge* should be left in English.

That my own writing style has driven so many professional translators to drink qualifies me to write this chapter, which is about the Color Settings dialog, which is in turn about translations between colorspaces, and sometimes between colorspace dialects. This discipline has so many similarities to the field of linguistics that advocates of one type of color translation often explain its use by references to language translation.

Before getting started, we need to agree on some language of our own, because although almost all of these phrases were recently coined, not everybody concurs with the following definitions.

How the Phrases Are Defined

• *Color management* is a phrase coined, I believe, in the early 1990s, although I am not sure of the source. I understand it to mean trying to ensure predictable results when translating between color definitions, or between different devices, such as a monitor and a press, or between my monitor and yours. It is not the same as *color correction,* the subject of this book, which tries to make pictures look better, or as *process control,* which tries to ensure that today's result can be repeated tomorrow or next year.

In the late 1990s, *color management* was used by some to describe a paradise-like situation, often called *the universal language of color,* where each and every file bears an embedded tag specifying its color unambiguously. That idea has gone the way of Windows 95, leaving the original definition intact.

• *Calibrationism* is a word coined by me in 1994 to describe the religion of those so worshipful of color-measurement devices and their capabilities that they turn off their mental processes when confronted by anything that has a number or a histogram in it. It is a pejorative term.

Early calibrationism believed that the objective of all reproduction was to create as close to a literal match to the original photograph as possible, an idiotic idea that hasn't been heard of in more than a decade.

Calibrationism was noted for its belief that perfect translations are possible. It was at odds with common sense, which realizes that for any translation (as was demonstrated emphatically in the examples shown in Chapter 7 and 11) there may be some good general guidelines but there will also be a lot of ifs, buts, exceptions, and whereases.

• The *Conventional Color Management Wisdom,* or CCMW, is a phrase coined by me in 1998 to describe a composite of the opinions of the published views of color consultants and Photoshop authors who comment on these matters. It is not intended to be a pejorative phrase, because generally this is a responsible group, free from all but the occasional calibrationist impulses. I needed the term in 1998 because I wanted to point out that many of my positions were not (yet) widely accepted. At that time the CCMW was homogeneous, and disagreed with me on certain key points.

As time has gone on, the CCMW has become more fragmented, with a distinct radical wing but with the remainder edging ever closer to my positions. As in the last two editions, we'll discuss the things that both the CCMW and I have changed our minds about.

• The *booboisie* is also a coined term, around 90 years old. Its father was one of the great authorities on language, the cynical American journalist H. L. Mencken. It refers to the most influential group in current digital imaging development. It sounds pejorative, but it isn't: it simply refers to people who are disinterested in knowing anything about current affairs. I use it because I know of no easy substitute. *Fools* is too strong, and *less sophisticated users* is not accurate.

Fortunately, you yourself cannot be a member, because just by cracking this book you have indicated a desire to learn something. You and I are, however, greatly affected by them, because there are so many more of them than of us that vendors tailor their products to them. They are a critical factor in digital camera design, and also in the structure of Camera Raw and similar acquisition modules. In the next five chapters, we will see how features that are aimed at allowing the booboisie to get good pictures don't always work for us, followed by a discussion of how to shut those features down.

• *Profile* is a term coined in the late 1980s and now used in too many different ways. A profile is an assumption about how certain devices behave; it also is used to describe how an existing file should be interpreted.

That last sentence screams out for a hypothetical example, so here goes. You have just printed out 20 pictures, doesn't matter where or how, and you are dissatisfied with the quality and think they should be redone, to which end you hire me to fix the problem. I examine your output and conclude that all 20 pictures look too green.

Now, I open the files on your monitor. If they also look too green there, I give you a copy of this book and tell you to read Chapters 1–10. And I go home. Your files are bad, but your color management is good. It accurately predicted the appalling result that you deserved and received.

If, on the other hand, the files look good on screen, then it's bad color management. I solve this problem by writing a Photoshop Action that applies the same curves to each of your files, darkening the green channel and/or lightening the red and blue if in RGB, darkening the magenta and/or lightening the cyan and yellow if in CMYK. And I go home.

This is color management. It eliminates the unexpected result. It isn't a particularly desirable form of color management, because it doesn't address the possibility that your monitor is to blame, in which case you will have the same problem with different output conditions in the future. But the difficulty for which you summoned me is history.

This form of color management involved a profile—the supposition that the output condition was greener than we thought. It isn't a particularly desirable form of profile, because it's in my head and nobody else can make use of it. But it's probably fairly sophisticated. To make my Action workable, I have to know whether the image is too green at every darkness level or only, say, in the midtones to the shadows. I also must decide whether the results are overall too dark, too light, or just right. These findings will dictate whether my profile calls for darkening the green channel, lightening the other two, or a combination.

Unfortunately for those desiring to understand this murky subject, partisans of one approach often assert that any form of color management other than the one they endorse is not a form of color management, and that any profile other than a profile that is compatible with what they endorse is not a profile. To that, there is a simple reply. Any document that says such a thing is not a document. Anybody who says so did not say so.

How the Color Is Defined

Until now, we have thrown about the terms *RGB* and *CMYK* indiscriminately. Sometimes we have noted that a certain original is *tagged* without explaining what that means. I seriously doubt that as many as half the readers of this book know.

When you were in first grade, your teacher doubtless gave you a crayon and told you it was *red.* It is unlikely that you were informed what the LAB values were for that crayon, with which you could have enlightened us as to what color she really meant.

In any RGB, $255^R0^G0^B$ produces red, no doubt about it. But whose red? Yours? Mine? That of the color scientists who screwed up so badly in Figures 11.1 and 11.2? One person might have a more brilliant red, another a more orange one. Yet Photoshop has to take some position; otherwise, when the time comes to translate into CMYK, it won't know what do with anything that happens to be $255^R0^G0^B$ or any other shade of red.

For that matter, it needs to know what *cyan* means. The cyan ink used by North American commercial printers is lighter and bluer than that found in Europe. Magenta varies even more around the world.

Above all, Photoshop needs to know not just what color certain values will produce, but how dark it will be. No doubt for the sake of confusion, the darkness factor is called *gamma* in RGB and *dot gain* in CMYK.

The good news is that there are many ways to set up these preferences acceptably. The bad news is that many of these seemingly acceptable ways rapidly become unacceptable when the booboisie get involved.

Our definitions of RGB and CMYK are profiles; everyone in the industry calls them that. We can change each one individually, or we can change them both, along with all our grayscale and color management preferences, in one fell swoop by replacing the entire Color Settings File, or .csf. The only thing that never changes is the definition of LAB. Other LAB variants exist, but Photoshop will have no part of them.

Figure 12.1 is what the Color Settings dialog looks like when first accessed in Photoshop CS2, where it is found in the Edit menu. The dialog is virtually unchanged since Photoshop 6 (2000) but it is found in different places in different versions.

Assigned, Assumed, and Embedded

Mencken was contemptuous of Americans' skills in many intellectual areas, notably cursing. In his textbook *The American Language,* he wrote, "Of all the nonprofane pejoratives in common American use, *son of a bitch* is the hardest-worked, and by far....But *son of a bitch* seems as pale and ineffectual to a Slav or Latin as *fudge* does to us. The dumbest policeman in Palermo thinks up a dozen better ones between breakfast and the noon whistle. Worse, it is frequently transmogrified into the childish *son of a gun.* The latter is so lacking in punch that the Italians among us have borrowed it as a satirical name for an American: *la sanemagogna* is what they call him, and by it they indicate their contempt for his backwardness in the art that is one of their great glories. In Standard Italian there are no less than forty congeners of *son of a bitch,* and each and every one of them is more opprobrious, more brilliant, more effective."

To that, there are three responses. First,

Mencken would not have dismissed the American skill level in this art had he known my wife, who, when provoked, uses locutions that would shock a gunnery sergeant, or possibly even a pressman. Second, he lived in Baltimore, not New Jersey. That would have changed his opinion, too. And third, if you think you've just wasted time reading two long paragraphs so that I can lead up to some lame punch line about how profiling issues have caused more cursing than anything else about Photoshop, think again. After years of frustration at being unable to get my students to understand how assigned, assumed, and embedded profiles relate to and interact with one another, I finally found success by telling a story about swearing.

I was once teaching a class that consisted of five persons from the province of Ontario, who speak a relatively subdued dialect known to grammarians as Standard Canadian English, and two New Yorkers. For any international readers who may not know this, New Yorkers, and particularly residents of nearby suburban New Jersey, are noted for their creative and aggressive use of foul language, Mencken's views notwithstanding.

Every student submits a corrected version of a given original. The seven are then compared, and the group votes on which is the best. Usually the vote is unanimous, but sometimes the winner is not obvious and a debate ensues. This time, the New Yorkers clearly had the best two versions. Each argued his own case passionately, to the point that when one restated his argument for the umpteenth time, the other directed a comment at him that doesn't even come close to meeting Peachpit Press's standards for decency. The words were so vile that the Canadians actually gasped, and thought that the next step would be a challenge to a duel, or whatever the custom is in Canada these days. I had to step in and explain that no offense was meant, that New Yorkers talk to each other that way routinely, and that the true meaning of the phrase was, "Are you pulling my leg, sir, eh?"

If we had to translate the unprintable New York/New Jersey language into Italian, we'd face a problem that has a color cognate. The translator would absolutely have to know that the English words need to be interpreted as if spoken by one New Jerseyan to another. Otherwise, the translation would be some horrible obscenity, similar to the printed result when a properly embedded color profile is ignored by someone down the line, or an improperly embedded one is honored.

Our Color Settings show that our input (read: RGB) is the New Jersey dialect, and our output (read: CMYK) is Italian, or perhaps the Neapolitan dialect thereof. As long as we stay on our own system and never change these settings, little can go wrong.

Similarly, there is no problem if we are passing out our Italian result files to others. Once the words are in Italian, nobody knows or cares what they used to be in English, any more than clients who buy printing care what the original RGB file looked like.

The problem is if we pass out the original English words, and somehow the information that they must be interpreted as if spoken among New Jerseyans is lost.

In theory, this is prevented by embedding a profile, or *tag,* into the file. This tag can override the next user's own settings and preserve the critical information as to how the file is to be interpreted. In real life, this system often breaks down, as we will discuss later in the chapter under *Color Management Policies.*

The really tricky part comes not when converting from one language to another, but from one dialect to another—as with going from New Jersey

to Canadian English, or from sRGB to Adobe RGB. Two commands that many people mix up control this process.

Edit: Assign Profile (CS2; Image: Mode> Assign Profile in previous versions) does not change the file, or, if you like, the words. It overrides our standard settings and instructs Photoshop to *interpret* the file in a different way. That interpretation does not become permanent, however, until somebody translates the file into some other language or dialect. Until then, the original information stays intact, ready to cause trouble.

Assigning a new profile therefore potentially changes the future meaning of the phrase without actually changing anything. It is dangerous, because if the original profile is correct, assigning a new one renders any future translation incorrect. It is, however, powerful if used properly, as we'll see in Chapter 15.

The complementary command, Convert to Profile, is more of an everyday tool. We already have used it extensively in Chapter 5. Unlike Assign Profile, it changes the *current*—but not the future—meaning. In our example, it would be like telling Photoshop to change the words identified as those a New Jersey speaker would use into those that a speaker

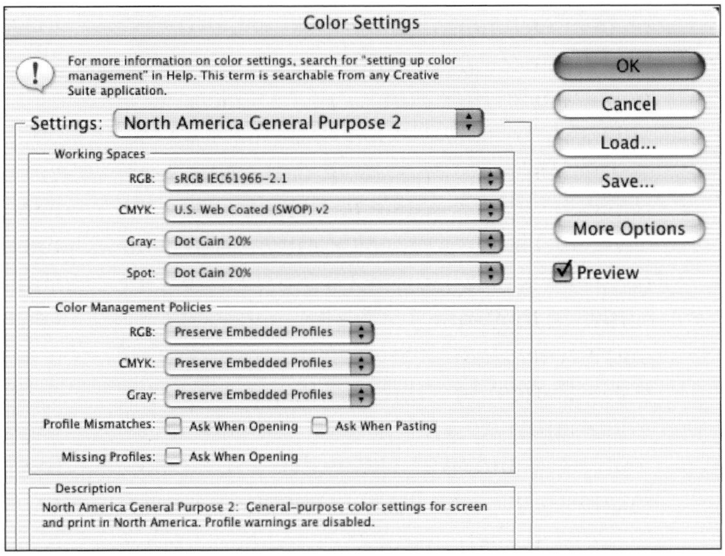

Figure 12.1 *The Color Settings dialog.*

of Standard Canadian would. If those properly tagged Canadian words later needed to be translated into Italian, the result should be the same as if the properly tagged New Jersey phrase were. If all goes well, that is. If all does *not* go well, then we are much safer after this application of Convert to Profile. Not much bad can happen if the relatively inoffensive Canadian words are misinterpreted as being spoken by somebody else. The danger case is the original, where the New Jersey words could be misunderstood as having a most unpleasant meaning.

There's a color cognate to this issue, as well. Certain RGBs are inherently safer than others because the consequences of misinterpretation are not as severe.

The RGB Working Space

Click RGB Working Space, and four officially preferred choices pop up: Adobe RGB, Apple RGB, ColorMatch RGB, and sRGB. If More Options (CS2 and later; Advanced Mode in previous versions) is checked, umpty-nine more become available.

The setting defines the purity of red, green, and blue, which in turn governs how vivid or dull images appear. Also, it controls gamma. It isn't necessary to have a technical understanding of gamma other than to know that a higher one implies darker-looking files. Apple RGB and ColorMatch RGB carry the traditional Macintosh gamma of 1.8. Adobe RGB and sRGB use the 2.2 that is normal for PCs.

The same file opened in one of the latter two will therefore seem darker than in one of the first two. As for color, Adobe RGB is the most intense of the four by far. sRGB is quite subdued. Apple RGB is slightly more colorful and ColorMatch RGB slightly more colorful still. None of the three is in the league of Adobe RGB.

In addition to some RGBs that are intended to address flaws in the above four, we'll mention two exotic alternatives in this chapter.

Both are ultra-wide gamut—more colorful than Adobe RGB and in some cases even more than LAB. These two are Wide Gamut RGB, which has a gamma of 2.2, and ProPhoto RGB, whose gamma is 1.8.

First, though, a quiz. Figure 12.2 presents six variants of the same original, each interpreting the file as being in one of the six RGB definitions just discussed. Your first mission is to determine which is which.

The second question: one of these variants, it doesn't matter which one, was in my own current RGB working space, so all I had to do to prepare it for printing was change mode to CMYK. For the five others, did I have to use Assign Profile, or Convert to Profile?

The quiz is not as difficult as some of the others in this book. The answers are in a box on page 283. Meanwhile, let's discuss what your RGB should be. In all of these settings, we need to pay attention to what our colleagues do, even if they are doing it for the wrong reason.

- **What everyone else does.** In 2002, I described RGB working spaces as "the most unsettled area of all the settings." No more. The war has ended with two victors. I've surveyed about a thousand trade show attendees recently, and around 90 percent use either sRGB or Adobe RGB. This is a change from five years ago, when I doubt that any RGB space enjoyed more than 30 percent support. Now, people appear to be evenly split between the two biggies.

Of the people who even know why they've chosen one or the other, those favoring sRGB often are Web oriented. Or, they may have to share RGB files with strangers, for whom sRGB is a safer choice than Adobe RGB. Professional photographers heavily favor Adobe RGB, as do most people who have to produce physical as opposed to electronic copies of their work.

- **History and development.** The historical Photoshop standard was, loosely speaking, Apple RGB. In 1998, Adobe unwisely changed this to sRGB in Photoshop 5. At that time, both the CCMW and I called the sRGB default unusable. I have since recanted this view, but the CCMW has become even more violently opposed. Commentary by its members often refers to this option by such witticisms as stupidRGB, sickRGB, sadRGB, sillyRGB, and one other designation that would provide even more fodder for Peachpit Press's censor, who has been given quite a workout in this chapter already.

The European Color Initiative, a group comprising persons prominent in the color management field who advocate better standards for commercial printing, is just as obdurate. It states flatly, "If quality is important, sRGB is not an option."

As a result of this mindless rejection of a perfectly sensible alternative, sRGB is one of the few remaining areas with a real consensus in the CCMW, which actually believes it to be evil. Also, it is one of the few areas in which the CCMW has not yet adopted my position, which in this case is that sRGB is a better choice than Adobe RGB for most readers of this book.

Before discussing why that is, let's remark on some areas of agreement. sRGB is a narrow-gamut, or not particularly colorful, workspace. Adobe RGB is a wide-gamut one. The CCMW and I agree that neither one is a particularly good representative of its class— sRGB because it is unreasonably narrow, Adobe RGB because its definition of green is too wide for practical purposes.

We also agree, however, that even if we dislike both, there is a case to be made for choosing a workspace that a large percentage of our colleagues use. Later, we'll discuss other, potentially better, RGBs. For the moment, however, it's easier to pretend that sRGB and Adobe RGB are the only available definitions and we must choose one or the other whether we like it or not.

sRGB is the best choice for those whose work is headed for the Web. Windows browsers read images in sRGB. At present, the Macintosh OS doesn't permit this; it uses a user-specific color model, meaning that what users may see is even more open to question than on the Windows platform, if possible.

For those who print their images, photographically, laser, offset, or otherwise, Adobe RGB is a good choice—for the booboisie, that is. People who are not skillful at color correction will get more colorful results if they work in Adobe RGB, for much the same reason that they would get duller results in CMYK if they worked with files with the heavier GCR options described in Chapter 5. The price for this added color would be a loss of detail in saturated areas, but that's a fair price for a novice. For this reason, I'd recommend that beginners use Adobe RGB even if they have to output in CMYK. If the choice is between bright, happy, detail-free colors, and contrasty dullness, I vote for the colors.

We have to be somewhat more careful in applying curves and similar corrections in Adobe RGB, because it's easier to provoke bright colors. When trying to make neutrals, sRGB is more tolerant of slight inaccuracies. In preparation for this chapter, I corrected several images in both spaces and concluded that the problem isn't significant, although it becomes a serious headache in something like ProPhoto RGB or Wide Gamut RGB.

The real issue is suggested by the red handbag and shirt in the three most colorful variants of Figure 12.2.

- **A gamut warning.** Some readers produce files that are viewed only on the Web or on a monitor, but most are more interested in some type of hard copy. Every such copy has been translated into CMYK, either by the user or by the output device itself.

A lot rides on the success of the translation. RGB and CMYK are different languages. Like all languages, each has particular strengths.

As Mencken noted, it is hard to translate Italian vulgarities into English, which does not offer nearly as many ways of disparaging one's ancestry. He forgot to mention the converse: most English vulgarities refer to bodily functions, and they do not pass gracefully into Italian.

It works that way in colorspaces, too. The particular strength of our two languages is in their fully saturated primaries. No real-world CMYK can produce the vivid reds, greens, and blues of any of the RGBs. Many RGBs do not have equivalents for the colors CMYK produces by laying down solid cyan, magenta, or yellow.

In a perfect world, these problems would

Figure 12.2 *When in RGB, each of these images had the same numerical values, which were interpreted through one of the six different profiles mentioned in the text. Can you match the profile with its image?*

not exist. A fully saturated red would be either $255^R0^G0^B$ or $0^C100^M100^Y$. A fully saturated magenta would be either $255^R0^G255^B$ or $0^C100^M0^Y$. In our vale of mortal sorrows, there are enough impurities in colorants to derail this system.

This mismatch between color languages is every bit as difficult to cope with as the New Jersey–Canadian mismatch in terms of abuse. If it didn't exist, calibrationism would have won. Without this mismatch, the perfect conversion the calibrationist theology depended on could in fact have been made every time.

The mismatch is worst in blue, where CMYK is a notorious disaster area. For all colors, it gets bigger as the colors get lighter. As we discussed in Chapter 11, CMYK processes depend on reflections off blank paper to add lightness, whereas RGB actually adds light. Because the white of paper is not as pure as white light, the CMYK gamut dissipates where pastel colors are concerned. We saw this earlier in the light magenta flowers of Figure 11.4, where even sRGB seriously exceeds the gamut of the most ambitious CMYK.

The CCMW, which has made so much progress in other areas, remains true to its calibrationist heritage in this one. It pooh-poohs the idea that translations are difficult—just press the button, and presto! the system takes care of the rest.

What it *does* feel is an insurmountable problem is an RGB that's smaller than any part of CMYK. It considers sRGB to be unacceptable because it can't equal the deepest CMYK cyans, magentas, and yellows.

We will examine that issue shortly, but first we should consider the problem that the CCMW won't acknowledge. If you insist that RGB has to exceed the CMYK gamut even in the colors in which CMYK is at its best, then you are insisting on an *enormously* larger gamut in the colors in which CMYK is at its worst.

- **718,900 and counting.** For simplicity's sake, until further notice we will put the other options on the back burner and assume that sRGB and Adobe RGB are the only two options in the world. For the next example, we simplify further, by limiting the discussion to those whose only interest is commercial offset printing.

Figure 12.3A displays the most intense yellow-green possible in CMYK—$60^C0^M100^Y$. A higher cyan value would make the color too blue.

Bright as that color may seem in isolation, when it comes to greens, Adobe RGB hasn't even had its morning coffee yet. According to Photoshop's calculations, it renders the same bright green as $140^R190^G79^B$. The most intense green in any RGB is $0^R255^G0^B$. So, any Adobe RGB formulation in which green is higher than 190^G and the others are lower than 140^R and 79^B makes a color that is unprintably bright, if Photoshop's numbers

Worksheet for Figure 12.2

Each version on the facing page is produced by assuming that the same file is tagged with one of the six RGB definitions discussed on page 276. Identify which is which. (Answers, page 283.)

Bonus question: these variants were created by initially applying what command to the base RGB file?

☐ Assign Profile ☐ Convert to Profile

Profile	Version
Adobe RGB	
Apple RGB	
ColorMatch RGB	
ProPhoto RGB	
sRGB	
Wide Gamut RGB	

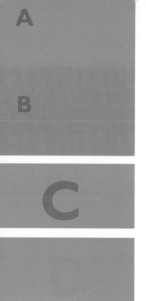

Figure 12.3 The Adobe RGB gamut is much larger than the CMYK used in this book. Sample A is $60^C0^M100^Y$, the most vivid yellow-green that we can print. Adobe RGB can describe more than 700,000 greener colors. To leave room to distinguish all of them in print, the sample would have to be toned down to the much duller green in B, $45^C25^M69^Y$. The bottom two versions were created by converting the top one to Adobe RGB (C) and to sRGB (D). In each, the letter was inserted at $0^R255^G0^B$, and the file was reconverted to CMYK. The results do not resemble the RGB files.

are correct. That's an awful lot of colors, 718,900 of them to be precise.

How, then, do we translate these 718,900 colors if they all occur in the Adobe RGB file? If we translate them all to the greenest green we can make, we'll have 718,900 copies of Figure 12.3A, and all detail will vanish. If something the color of Figure 12.3A actually exists in the file, there will be no way to differentiate it from something much greener.

A common proposal to lessen (but certainly not eliminate) this problem is to have the separation algorithm tone down all greens, so that the hypothetical brilliant greens that may or may not be found in the Adobe RGB file will stand out.

This approach is much like spitting into the ocean in an effort to make the tide come in. True, if an object is supposed to be the color of Figure 12.3A, we can probably dull it down a little without anyone noticing. That would gain us a few extra colors, but hardly enough to accommodate the missing 718,900.

To allow separate values for each of the 718,900, we'd have to force anything that ought to be the color of Figure 12.3A to be the color of Figure 12.3B instead—$45^C25^M69^Y$. That formulation allows 718,900 more intense CMYK greens.

As nobody in their right mind would ever consider going that far, the only question is

whether to leave things the color of Figure 12.3A alone, in which case anything greener will suffer a catastrophic loss of detail, or to tone them down slightly, in which case the damage will only be horrendous.

Personally, I think the above explanation is satisfactory and that we should move on. Unfortunately, the beta readers (who, you may wish to know, thought my discussion of swearing and profiling was right on target) bit my head off, demanding a further hypothetical example of the grief out-of-gamut colors can cause.

In response to these complaints, I have created two additional versions. Figure 12.3A was created in CMYK, but I converted it to Adobe RGB for Figure 12.3C, and to sRGB for 12.3D. In each of the two new files, I inserted the appropriate letter, specifying its value as $0^R255^G0^B$, maximum green. Then I reconverted to CMYK for printing.

Both letters stand out prominently—while the files are in RGB, that is. In Figure 12.3D, we get a ghost, not a letter. In 12.3C, you can see the letter, but there's one small difficulty. In the original, the letter is much lighter than the background.

Repeat, for the benefit of the Peachpit editor who would otherwise query it and for anybody else who suspects that it's a typographical error: *the letter C is supposed to be much lighter than the background.* If you don't believe it, the source files are on the CD. While you're there, look at Figure 12.4A, too. If you don't, you'll have no way of knowing what it's supposed to look like.

In real life, this green lantern practically glows in the dark. We have as much chance of reproducing that as Mencken did of being elected president of the Women's Christian Temperance Union. There's plenty of detail in the Adobe RGB file, but almost all of it lives in the 718,900 greens that CMYK can't reach.

Consequently, Photoshop maps everything to just about the same color, and Figure 12.4A is hopeless. We saw the same effect, albeit to a lesser extent, in Figures 12.2B, 12.2C, and 12.2E, where assigning a colorful RGB profile ran many reds out of the CMYK gamut, killing detail in the red shirt and handbag.

• **A counterintuitive countermeasure.** I returned to the original Adobe RGB file and chose Image: Adjustments>Hue/Saturation. There, I reduced master saturation by applying a value of –35.

This, along with Figures 12.3C and 12.3D, is the kind of joke you have to get used to if you persist in preparing RGB files with colors well out of the CMYK gamut. This Hue/Saturation move is supposed to drastically dull all colors. And it does, in RGB. But Figures 12.4A and 12.4B are almost the same color. The move is not supposed to add detail, but Figure 12.4B appears to have gained a lot of it, because it was translated from RGB greens that CMYK understands as opposed to some of the 718,900 that it doesn't.

All other ways to get this kind of result require intelligent intervention. Occasionally we hear that during the conversion of such images, the Perceptual rendering intent should be used. We'll discuss this more fully later in the chapter, but Perceptual is an attempt at the finesse approach alluded to earlier: deliberately toning down colors that ought to be $60^C0^M100^Y$ so that they can be differentiated from greener greens.

Unfortunately, no such approach would ever dream about toning them down as far as the color of Figure 12.3B, which is how far we'd need it to go to get more detail. So, all Photoshop gives us is Figure 12.5A. If you look hard, you will see that it shows slightly more detail than Figure 12.4A. But it fires a cap gun where a howitzer is needed.

Figure 12.4 *Top, the lantern has plenty of detail in Adobe RGB, but it's almost all out of the CMYK gamut and goes away during the inevitable move to CMYK. Bottom, the same Adobe RGB file has its saturation sharply reduced before the conversion.*

Figure 12.5B is another vain effort. Before the conversion, I assigned sRGB as the profile even though the shot is known to be in Adobe RGB. In addition to shifting the color slightly, this method failed because even sRGB greatly exceeds the CMYK gamut in this range of colors. It was therefore far out of gamut, as

opposed to the Adobe RGB file, which was far, far out of gamut. And with that, we close the discussion of why excessive RGB gamut can be a bad thing, and move on to why inadequate gamut is supposed to be a bad thing.

• **The missing example.** I am generally against using non-photographs to illustrate

how photographs work. The swatches of Figure 12.3 are an exception; they're useful in setting the stage for what comes next, which is a real-world image that is affected by the problem being described. Indeed, this lantern printed in a catalog just about as badly as it did in Figure 12.4A.

Someone trying to explain why the sRGB gamut is a problem would probably start out the same way. The equivalent of Figures 12.3A and 12.3B would be three swatches, one each of $100^C0^M0^Y$, $0^C100^M0^Y$, and $0^C0^M100^Y$. He would explain that all three are out of the sRGB gamut. It would therefore be impossible to find these colors in the CMYK immediately after conversion; and even if they were corrected to the proper numbers after conversion, the stint in sRGB would probably have lopped off much of the detail.

Then, the equivalent of Figure 12.4A—the real-world image that illustrates the problem that the theory suggests must occur.

But that image would never come.

*   *   *

To demonstrate that the problem exists, he'd need a good CMYK file—one containing the colors that sRGB is supposed to have trouble with. Convert that file from CMYK to sRGB and back again, and it should show a quality loss.

The first try might be Figure 12.6A, which was prepared without any visits to sRGB. Its brightest yellow is outside of the sRGB gamut.

Yellow is such a light ink that we don't see contrast problems in it easily. Figure 12.6B is the conversion and reconversion. The result is no worse than if we had taken any other CMYK file and converted it back and forth. The impact of the mismatch is that areas that were previously $0^C5^M100^Y$ have become $2^C5^M99^Y$.

Figure 12.5 *Top, converting the original Adobe RGB file into CMYK using the Perceptual rendering intent does not improve Figure 12.4A markedly. Bottom, an sRGB profile is assigned before the conversion.*

Whenever we construct a really brilliant color in CMYK, we check the final file to see that the brightest part is blank in the weakest channel and solid in the strongest. After converting Figure 12.4B to CMYK, for example, we are supposed to verify that no magenta or black ink appears in the greenest areas, and that yellow is at 100^Y. I omitted the step to avoid an unfair advantage over Figure 12.4A.

That mandatory step would make Figure 12.6B functionally identical to 12.6A, if it is not so already. Even if the file had been converted to LAB, which has no gamut issue, this restoration step would still be needed.

In short, the limited sRGB gamut is irrelevant in yellow objects. But the mismatch is greater in magenta and much greater in cyan, and detail in those colors is far more visible than in yellow objects.

With the aid of Channel Mixer, I've produced a cyan and a magenta pepper for Figures 12.7A and 12.7C, just as dark and saturated as the yellow one of Figure 12.6A was. This time, when we convert to sRGB and then back, the damage is clear. If Figures 12.7A and 12.7C are what we want, we will have a tough time getting there from Figures 12.7B and 12.7D.

There's only one problem. Peppers come in green, red, yellow, even orange. Never, though, as far as I know, in magenta or cyan. These are not real images.

Because CMYK does so badly with light colors, the only places that the sRGB gamut can be a limiting factor are where all CMYK channels are either blank or solid, with perhaps 10 points of variation allowed.

Such colors do exist in nature. The yellow pepper of Figure 12.6A is one example. If you'd like another, return to the congressman and schoolchildren image of Figure 9.18B.

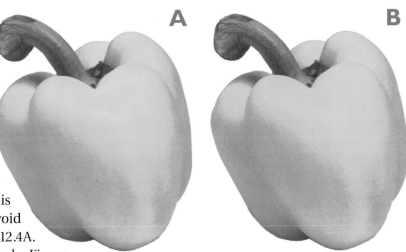

A **B**

Figure 12.6 *The pepper at left is a CMYK file that contains yellows that are out of the sRGB gamut. When it is converted to sRGB and reconverted to CMYK (right), the differences are minor, indicating that the mismatch is not severe.*

Three girls are wearing clothing that falls between 10^{C}90^{M}90^Y and 0^{C}100^{M}100^Y. The same red appears in the Chinese flag of Figure 10.12, as it would if there were a fire engine in the image, or Santa Claus. The color is common, and if it fell outside of the sRGB gamut, there would be serious repercussions.

Red, however, is a primary RGB color, so sRGB exceeds even the best CMYK. To provoke a problem, we need a magenta or cyan as intense as these reds.

Good luck finding such an image. I have

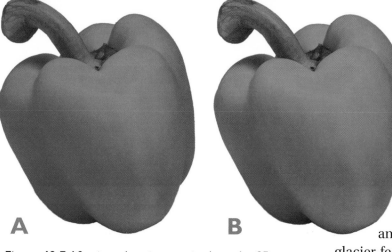

A   B

Figure 12.7 *After interchanging certain channels of Figure 12.6A, the pepper becomes cyan or magenta (above left and below left). After the same CMYK to sRGB back to CMYK maneuver that produced Figure 12.6B, the two right-hand versions are much worse in comparison to the originals than when the pepper was yellow.*

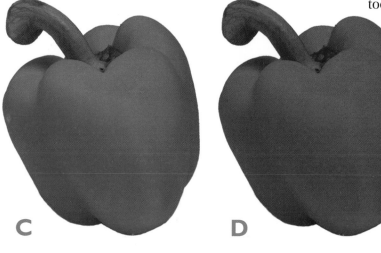

C   D

These four images may indicate that such pure magentas appear every now and then, but they all fall short of the darkness shown in Figure 12.7C's pepper, where the sRGB gamut would become problematic. And cyans are so rare in nature that nobody could give me anything better than Figure 12.8B, a glacier-fed Swiss lake that owes its unusual color to minerals in melted snow.

Lakes of similar color are found in the Canadian Rockies, where glaciers also exist for the time being, but you can't find anything much more cyan in nature, and this cyan is too light and too green to fall within the enormous range of cyans that sRGB can't portray.

So, as for the claim that sRGB has an unduly limiting gamut: "In brief," as Mencken once wrote in a slightly different context, "the whole story is apocryphal, bogus, hollow and null, imbecile, devoid of substance."

And with that, let's come up with some recommendations. Remember, please, that we have been assuming that sRGB and Adobe RGB are the only two choices in the world.

• **The input of output.** If you receive a tagged file from somebody else, nothing stops you from continuing to work on that specific image in its own RGB definition. You do, however, need a general choice of workspace for your own work. The most important factor by far is how much control you have over who will handle your RGB files. Many of us can guarantee that nobody will receive one of our tagged RGB files without our knowing that they are getting the type of RGB they want.

If you aren't in that situation, don't even think about anything other than sRGB. Photo

been looking for one ever since the last edition of this book in 2002. Tens of thousands of images have crossed my screen since then, but not a single one featuring a magenta or cyan that was outside the sRGB gamut yet achievable in CMYK.

I also requested the help of my colortheory list in the search. Two people submitted non-sRGB files featuring very magenta objects. Figure 12.8A is one; the other appears later as Figure 15.14. I also have several pictures of cactus flowers whose color is similar to that of Figure 12.8A. One of the DVDs sent by a photographer who contributed images to this book contained a similarly colored dress.

labs, commercial printers, and the booboisie all regularly assume that any RGB file is sRGB even when tagged Adobe RGB. In that case, if you expect Figure 12.2C, you'll get Figure 12.2F instead. Having this happen on even one important job will far outweigh any conceivable benefit you might have from working in any other RGB for the rest of your life.

Next, a skilled person gets better results from working in a narrow-gamut space like sRGB, where all moves are subtler than in something as wide as Adobe RGB. But if you don't have those skills, it's easier to get pleasing results with the wider-gamut Adobe RGB.

If you *are* skilled, but so pressed for time that you will be taking lots of shortcuts, my recommendation is not to use RGB at all, but to convert the files to LAB, where you can get a bigger and quicker bang for the buck. You may want to review the workflow chapter of *Photoshop LAB Color,* which has pointers for the retoucher in a hurry.

If you have decided to adopt a workflow that often features quick and dirty forays into LAB, then your RGB working space should be Adobe RGB for self-protection. Working hastily in LAB is apt to inadvertently produce colors that are out of the sRGB gamut.

If nothing described above makes the decision for you, your output conditions may.

Figure 12.8 *Cyans and magentas as deep as seen in the "peppers" of Figures 12.7A and 12.7C are unheard of in nature. Below, the flowers are quite magenta, but too light to provoke the problem seen in Figure 12.7D. Cyans like that of the lake at right are lighter and greener than Figure 12.7B.*

If you are only concerned with generating CMYK files for commercial printing, then sRGB has no disadvantages. Adobe RGB does.

If you may have to deal with better conditions than this, the choice becomes more problematic. With much whiter paper, like the kind that many people use to feed their inkjet printers, a color more intense than the magenta flower of Figure 12.8A may be achievable, and the sRGB gamut may start to become limiting.

All output, including photographic prints, is based on CMY colorants, but many devices won't accept CMYK files as input. They insist on an RGB file, which is converted into CMYK internally by a process we can't control.

That costs us a safety valve. Say that we actually encounter something like that cyan pepper, where we want Figure 12.7A but sRGB limits us to 12.7B. If we are still able to intervene after the conversion to CMYK, we may be able to recover by applying a curve to darken the cyan channel to match that of Figure 12.7A. But if the system doesn't permit it, there isn't much else we can do.

If the output device is truly CMYK, it's not that much of an issue because it's so uncommon to find anything that sRGB can't hit. But if the output device uses extra inks (often a pink and a light cyan), many more pastel colors become available. For example, the light magentas shown in the gradients of Figure 5.10 and 11.5 and the flowers of Figure 11.4 are as vivid as our current CMYK condition allows, yet aren't even close to achieving the color that an sRGB file might call for. Add

Choosing an RGB Workspace: A Flowchart

Here is the recommended procedure for choosing an RGB workspace, on the assumption that Adobe RGB and sRGB are the only two available choices.

1. Are you reasonably certain that your RGB files will not fall into the hands of a stranger who may have no clue what an embedded profile is? If not, then **STOP HERE**. You should use sRGB.

2. Are you proficient at color correction? Or did you jump forward to this chapter without getting a good grasp of Chapters 2–6? If you are *not* proficient, but you have answered Yes to question 1, **STOP HERE** and use Adobe RGB.

3. Are you concerned enough about the quality of your images that you would be willing to spend at least a few minutes apiece in correcting them if needed? If you aren't, **STOP HERE**. Convert your files to LAB, work on them there, and then, if necessary, reconvert them to Adobe RGB, not sRGB.

4. Are you much more interested in commercial CMYK printing than any other type of output? If you are, **STOP HERE** and use sRGB.

5. Do your images almost all come from one source, such as a single camera, that always tags its images or that appears to work better in one RGB than another? If so, **STOP HERE** and use that space.

6. Does your work often feature brilliant and exceptionally vivid colors that are important to the image? If YES, use Adobe RGB, but be sure you know the techniques shown later in the discussion of Figures 15.11–15.15 in case you need to bring such colors into a smaller gamut. If NO, use sRGB.

a pink ink, however, and all bets are off. We could get a substantially more intense color—perhaps one that sRGB couldn't match.

• **Reasonable alternatives.** sRGB was designed as a description of how cheap monitors behave. Adobe RGB was created by typographical error, when someone intended to copy an existing RGB specification into Photoshop but didn't proofread the numbers. It is hardly a surprise that neither is an optimal color-correction choice.

Apple RGB and, especially, ColorMatch RGB compensate for many of sRGB's deficiencies. If you want something along the lines of Adobe RGB but more logically organized, at least three other definitions are widely available, but you have to find them on the Web, download them, and put them into your profiles folder. The aforementioned European Color Initiative has one; my friend Bruce Fraser formulated one called BruceRGB; and a German group has issued a high-gamma one called L-Star RGB, trying to stress a similarity with the L channel of LAB.

All three are technically better than Adobe RGB if we're starting from scratch, but we aren't, and I don't see a big enough benefit to warrant adopting them. Also, I think all four are excessively wide gamut. Until shortly before publication, I'd never seen a photo for which the moderate-gamut ColorMatch RGB was insufficient for *any* output condition. See page 499 for a description of this exceptional image, which is also found on the CD.

If *I* were starting from scratch, I might choose ColorMatch RGB, or possibly invent some RGB with a slightly wider gamut. Instead, I use Apple RGB. Before 1998, it was a pain to use anything else. When 1998 came, I certainly wasn't going to switch to sRGB or Adobe RGB before they had established themselves. I thought about ColorMatch RGB, but compare Figures 12.2A and 12.2D. I find it hard to tell them apart. I surmise that in the decade or whatever since that decision was made, one or two pictures might have worked out better with the slight extra gamut that ColorMatch RGB provides. But I hardly think it is worth losing compatibility with several years of existing files.

Had I not fessed up to this horrible secret, you would be unlikely to know, because I would never be so foolish as to allow an Apple RGB file to enter the hands of a stranger. I prefer to hand out LAB, which is unambiguous, but if RGB is necessary, I convert to sRGB before distributing the file.

• **Exotic alternatives.** When theory is taken to mindless extremes, we see stuff like the two final alternatives. First, the practice of using an ultra-wide RGB, one that greatly exceeds the gamut (not gamma) even of Adobe RGB. The second is the use of an ultra-low gamma (not gamut) of 1.0.

Original digital captures sometimes contain (or at least the camera can be persuaded into thinking that they contain) very intense colors, possibly outside of the gamut of even Adobe RGB. It is a good idea to store this information somewhere. The customary way is to record the values in LAB, XYZ, or some other academically inspired colorspace, but it's reasonable to substitute an ultra-wide RGB. That is, in fact, what Photoshop's Camera Raw module does. Its reference space is ProPhoto RGB.

Using one for color correction is a different story. Such spaces are so volatile as to make precise moves difficult to impossible. If you'd like to see why, go back to some of the exercises in Chapters 2 and 3. Convert the files to Wide Gamut RGB or ProPhoto RGB before working on them. You will discover that it's harder to avoid casts. Neutrals are supposed to have equal RGB values. In sRGB or Adobe RGB, we are likely to get away with being off by four or five points. In an ultra-wide RGB we may have only half that tolerance.

These spaces are as big as LAB, but harder to control. For example, keeping colors close

to neutral is easier in LAB, where we can, if necessary, flatten the A and B curves near the center point. An ultra-wide CMYK, if it existed, would also be easier to handle because of the presence of the black channel. Either LAB or an ultra-wide CMYK would handle certain files better, and others worse, than sRGB or Adobe RGB. There are no such advantages to working in an ultra-wide RGB.

The common excuse for these spaces is that it is possible to find colors that only they are capable of reproducing, and that may be possible to reproduce in print in a few years. If somebody says that to you, I would ask to see an example of the sort of image that he is referring to. If one exists, which I doubt, then I would ask whether it looks like a rare enough commodity that it could just be handled in its own private RGB when the time came, rather than adopting a ham-handed ultra-wide definition as my permanent RGB working space.

The other exotic definition, using an ultra-low gamma, is only for the brave. Many techniques operate in unfamiliar ways at low gamma. Blurring usually works better. We'll see why in Chapter 15. Sharpening is generally worse. Highlight detail is more easily handled, but shadows break apart easily. For this reason, I wouldn't even consider this option unless the files are headed for CMYK, whose black channel may be able to compensate for problems in the shadows.

The CMYK Working Space

We have just burnt 15 pages discussing workspace and profiling options in RGB. The bad news is that there are many more options in CMYK and the structure is more complex. The good news is that there's less controversy, plus the next chapter will cover some of these options.

Photoshop proper offers two basic choices, both flawed. Custom CMYK dates from the early 1990s and was last improved in 1998.

You can make quite passable profiles with it. The defaults, however, are poor, and they aren't compatible with any form of instrument measurement, such as that recommended by the CCMW.

The alternative is to use a ready-made profile, of which several are packaged in Photoshop, or one provided by a third party. But these profiles can't be edited at all. If you need a different black generation for any of the several reasons stated in Chapter 5; if you need a lower or higher total ink limit because that is what your printer demands; if you want to create a customized black channel for blending, as shown at the end of Chapter 9; if you find that the profile creates files that are marginally too light or too dark for your own conditions—if you ever expect to face any one of these scenarios, you are out of luck.

• **What everyone else does.** Experienced CMYK users hold their noses and use Custom CMYK. Those who are not familiar with the power of CMYK generally use the built-in Photoshop profile called U.S. Web Coated (SWOP) v2. Some also use this profile for previewing but not separations, and others, like me, use it some of the time for both.

The CCMW and I agree that adding the capability of editing modern profiles is something that should have been done in 1998. As Adobe refuses to listen to reason on this point, all alternatives are bad. The CCMW tepidly endorses buying third-party software to generate alternate profiles when needed. Suggesting paying for something that takes a long time to reproduce what Custom CMYK already does in seconds for free, that's a pretty hard sell.

• **The shortcomings of the two approaches.** Choosing which of these poisons to ingest largely depends on your tolerance for their shortcomings. Custom CMYK has a long learning curve. Unless you read Chapters 5 and 13 carefully, you are unlikely to get good results.

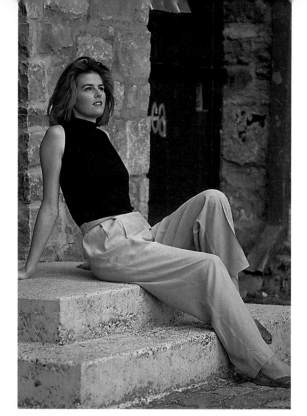

Figure 12.9 *This type of image previews badly with the SWOP v2 setting.*

Custom CMYK has, if you look hard enough, values that purport to reflect LAB values of various inking combinations. If you are thinking of measuring swatches with a spectrophotometer and entering them into these tables, forget it. This engine was cobbled together a long time ago, and it has many kludges, among which is that these numbers don't really correspond to anything. To correct them, you have to adopt the philosophy I do when I find that the air conditioning has made the room too cold. I go to the control panel and increase the temperature by two degrees. I do not assume that the temperature readout has any connection with reality; I assume that I want to make the room warmer.

Also, screen previews are deceptive, because in drawing the preview, Custom CMYK assumes that black ink is *absolutely* black. 100^K and $100^C100^M100^Y100^K$ preview as the same color. So, darkness is overstated in any area with heavy black coverage. (One possible cure: separate using Custom CMYK, then

Figure 12.10 *Because bright blues are often out of the CMYK gamut,* competing profiles often yield different results. These four blues were separated with five profiles that all claim to target SWOP printing conditions. The large black numbers show by how many percentage points cyan exceeds magenta ink, a key to keeping the color blue and not purple. The lower the number, the purpler the result. Photoshop's SWOP v2 (B, above) consistently produces the purplest blues.

use Assign Profile to preview the printing using one of the supplied profiles.)

* * *

The shortcoming of the built-in profiles has already been alluded to: you can't change them, not even in a minor way. Some people think they can, by loading the built-in profile first and then going to Custom CMYK, but that's an illusion. Doing so builds an entirely new profile from scratch, starting with the default settings of Photoshop 5. With these profiles, it's take it or leave it.

To me, that's a deal-breaker, although I do use the SWOP v2 profile on some occasions, including for most of the non-CMYK corrections of this book.

As for the others, Photoshop includes profiles that purport to be suitable for European and Japanese printing conditions. I have never tested them. The four U.S.-oriented profiles aim at sheetfed and web (rollfed) printing, on coated and uncoated stock.

The Convert to Profile command was introduced in 2000, in Photoshop 6. It was a benefit to CMYK users because it enabled alternate black generation on an image-by-image basis, as opposed to changing Color Settings. Since then, there hasn't been any effort to add CMYK features—for CMYK purists, Photoshop 6 is arguably a better program than Photoshop CS2.

These four profiles as a group are surprisingly weak. It is no exaggeration to say that anyone who knows the first thing about printing knows that dot gain is much heavier in web than in sheetfed printing. We'll discuss this more in the next chapter; for now it's enough to say that a separation prepared for sheetfed printing needs to be much darker than for web printing, for the same reason that an RGB file prepared for Apple or Color-Match RGB has to have a darker channel structure than it would for the higher-gamma sRGB or Adobe RGB.

Instead, Photoshop's sheetfed coated profile delivers a *lighter* separation than the web coated (SWOP v2) does. As it allows ink coverage of up to 350%, which web printers won't accept, it serves no useful purpose.

On the uncoated side, there's a different twist. The sheetfed and web profiles are identical. The results in separating the same file with each of them don't vary from one another by as much as a pixel.

Both sheetfed profiles, in short, are worthless. The web profiles are better. In comparing them, the uncoated one should (and does) deliver a lighter separation, with cleaner colors, than SWOP v2 does, to compensate for the muddier, higher dot gain conditions when a poorer-quality paper is used.

The following comments are limited to SWOP v2, but I believe they would also apply if you were printing on uncoated paper and using the uncoated web profile.

• **Singing the blues.** The translation between RGB and CMYK is difficult, almost as bad as the grayscale conversions discussed in Chapter 7. Too many holes in the dike, not enough fingers. The only question is where the inevitable unplugged holes lurk. Custom CMYK profiles are often inaccurate for bright colors. SWOP v2 does a good job with reds and most greens, but not with blues.

Figure 12.9 has appeared as a curving exercise in the last three editions of this book. This time, there are no curves, just the CMYK file enclosed on the CD. When you open it, Assign Profile>SWOP v2 if that's not already your CMYK workspace. My prediction is that your monitor will show you something much bluer than the printed image.

SWOP v2's belief that things are more blue than they actually are leads to a more significant issue.

In CMYK, we are always trying to find equivalents for colors that we can't really match. The biggest offenders, by far, are blues, where the CMYK gamut is tiny indeed. On a clear day, the sky is bluer than CMYK can accommodate. In that case, we improvise. There's no right answer, any more than there would be a single correct translation for an obscenity that doesn't exist in English.

Trust SWOP v2 to give good blues, though, and the obscenities may indeed fly. Figure 12.10 compares the work of five different CMYK profiles that each claim to be targeted at SWOP printing conditions, which are supposed to be in effect for this book.

The swatches were derived from four blue images I used in a recent lecture about LAB. The top swatch is the color of a lake; the bottom three are skies taken by three different photographers in three different seasons. Top to bottom, they are: an autumn shot; a cloudless summer day at high altitude; a winter day where the sky has a distinct cyan flavor. If you want to see what was actually desired, the original LAB file from which these conversions was made is on the CD.

You can see by the near-total absence of yellow and black ink that these are absolutely the bluest blues that CMYK can produce. Differences in translation shouldn't be surprising, but would you really expect to see as much variation as there is on the second line?

The profile for Figure 12.10A is more than a decade old. It's from Linotype-Hell, the successor to one of the most distinguished manufacturers of drum scanners in the pre-desktop publishing days. Figure 12.10E is nearly as old—it's the default setting of Photoshop 5 from 1998. Figure 12.10C is a Custom CMYK profile I made in 2000 for *Professional Photoshop 6,* and 12.10D is a modern profile supplied by ColorBurst, a RIP manufacturer.

Figure 12.10B is SWOP v2, and it's the odd man out. In each swatch, the large number indicates the excess of cyan ink over magenta. As we know, equal magenta and cyan would make a nice blue if inks were as pure as we would like, but in our world they make purple. Figure 12.10B is slightly more purple than 12.10C, and much more purple than the other three.

This performance is typical of machine-generated profiles. During the discussion of Figure 11.6, we noted that machines are not good judges of how close one color is to another, often disagreeing with what humans would perceive. The machine here was thinking in LAB. It knew that it would never be able to match in print the strongly B–negative value that the LAB file asked for, but it saw no reason to tone down the A channel to match. A human—and humans tweaked all four of the other profiles—would know instinctively that if the blue-versus-yellow B channel was being toned down, then the magenta-versus-green A needs to be toned down as well.

Whatever the reason, anyone using SWOP v2 needs Selective Color, Hue/Saturation, or some other way to remove magenta from blues after conversion. Clients can be finicky about overly purple blues, much more so than if the blues are too cyan.

In the last edition, an exercise featured one of the most dazzling sights in the United States. I did not feel equipped to describe it, since the brilliant travel writer Alexander Theroux had already done so as follows: "The deep blue of Oregon's enchanting Crater Lake, the deepest lake in North America, almost intolerable in its beauty, can swamp with emotion the flickering power of analysis. The lake is 1,932 feet at its greatest depth. Fed only by snow and rain—and drained by sun and wind alone—the lake suffers no silt from running water, the sunlight striking it reflecting the blue rays, while the rays of the other colors are absorbed, all serving to make it the bluest blue lake in the world."

In short, this lake is really, really blue, possibly the bluest object in all of nature. Figure 12.11A is the uncorrected original, separated using the same profile that produced Figure 12.10C. I suggested forcing yellow into the sky and background shore to try to talk the viewer into seeing a bluer lake.

We'll forgo that here in favor of comparing three very different separations. Figure 12.11B is by SWOP v2 and 12.11C is produced by the same Linotype profile that made Figure 12.10A. The results say a great deal about conversion philosophy.

- **Insurance policies and recommendations.** I think that Figure 12.11B will print too purple. Nobody will know for sure until ink hits paper. When it does, it will be too late to change the prediction.

Figure 12.11A came out the way I hoped last time. The uncorrected photo, which is on the CD, is a reasonable rendition of the lake's actual colors. The printed result was somewhat duller perforce, but still satisfactory.

Figure 12.11 This uncorrected image is separated with, top to bottom, the profiles illustrated in Figures 12.10C, 12.10B, and 12.10A.

Will I be lucky again? I'll find out when the job is printed. While I don't know that Figure 12.11B will be *too* purple, it can be confidently predicted that it will be more purple than either competitor. Unless, of course, the printer has figured out a way to make magenta ink print as some other color.

The other thing that can be said for sure: if something unexpected happens on press, Figure 12.11B is the most vulnerable.

In the next chapter, we'll be discussing how variable commercial printing is. We will also be reiterating one of the sad refrains of professional life: if the printer screws up the job, the client is apt to blame us.

The logical response, and the one that the most successful CMYK practitioners adhere to, is that the best file for printing is not the most accurate one, but rather the one that is least likely to print badly.

Suppose you like Figure 12.11B. Ask yourself, what will happen if magenta ink comes down too heavily? What if cyan ink does? What if the same things were to happen to Figure 12.11A?

The answer, I think, is that only one of these occurrences would be really, really objectionable, and that is if Figure 12.10B took more magenta than we expected. In that case, this lake, which we are committed to portraying as blue, will be definitely purple and the client will likely reject the job. If you agree, then Figure 12.10A is the better choice—the insurance policy.

Figure 12.11C is an expression of that philosophy. Remember, this profile comes from a company with a great deal of printing and prepress experience, and from times when presses were even less reliable than they are today, if possible. Figure 12.10C is an out-and-out defensive separation, one that leaves plenty of room for whatever blunder the printer may dream up. Ink coverage that's too heavy is more probable than too light; and Figure 12.11C can absorb it gracefully, in addition to being able to take whatever blow the pressman may deal with the magenta ink.

I think this approach is too extreme for today's world, but ten years ago it made eminent sense. There would have been a good argument that Figure 12.10C was the best choice of the three. Let's summarize.

If you want to use the powerful techniques of Chapter 5, among others, you currently have no choice within Photoshop but Custom CMYK. Similarly, if you print sheetfed, on newsprint, or some other less common CMYK condition, or if you print duotones or CMYK grayscale images, Photoshop proper has no answer other than Custom CMYK.

For those remaining, SWOP v2 is a reasonable choice. Remember, though, that all profiles have strengths and weaknesses, and the weakness of SWOP v2 is blue. We just saw an example of where it delivered a poor separation, but if Figure 12.11 had been red rather than blue, SWOP v2 would probably have given a better result than the majority of the other profiles, including mine.

Gray and Spot Working Spaces

The default for conversion to grayscale (Gray, under Color Settings: Working Spaces) is 20% dot gain. If you primarily prepare grayscale images for RGB output or for the Web, you should change this setting to 2.2 gamma, to agree with the majority.

If you have an RGB background and are preparing grayscale documents for print, think of dot gain as being a form of gamma. If it's set higher, your grayscale conversions will produce lighter files—by the numbers, that is. They'll preview darker, to make up for it. And, if you were correct that the dot gain setting should have been raised, the printing will be darker, too, matching the preview.

Black ink usually has more dot gain than the others, so 20%, which is reasonable for CMY, is a little low for black. (Note: this setting doesn't affect how black gets generated when we separate to CMYK, only to grayscale.)

If you have nothing better to go on, change the Gray working space to Custom Dot Gain, which brings up a curve within a dialog. The definition of dot gain is not particularly logical: 20% means that a 50^K dot appears to have darkened to 70^K. Increase it to 73^K, thus giving you a dot gain of 23%.

When preparing for a printer with whose color work you are familiar, you can be more accurate, provided you have both the CMYK file and the printed result handy. Open the file and go to Color Settings: CMYK>Custom CMYK. Change the dot gain setting (the next chapter shows how) until you think you have the best match to the image's *darkness,* not color. For example, forgetting the color issues, Figure 12.11B is darker than 12.11C. If you have trouble blinding yourself to the color, open Hue/Saturation and desaturate the whole picture while you work.

Once you have estimated dot gain in CMYK overall, a good guess is that the black dot gain is around four points higher. So enter that value in your Gray working space.

The Spot working space pertains to those who have to prepare CMYK files that have additional printing channels. It does not apply to alpha channels (masks) or to devices like the many desktop printers that have extra inks beyond CMYK but which insist on an RGB file as input. In that case we have no control over how the extra inks are generated. The Spot setting governs extra inks that we *can* control. For example, suppose the client insists on printing a logo in green ink rather than as a mix of cyan and yellow. If we're enterprising, we can deliver a CGMYK file that might print better than just CMYK.

There used to be a full chapter on this topic, together with duotones. As this skill is needed by a smaller percentage of the reading audience, we took it out to save room. However, the original chapter (from *Professional Photoshop 5,* 1998) is still valid. It's in PDF on the CD, in the Chapter 5 folder. It explains the circumstances under which the Spot setting should be changed.

As far as I know, there is no CCMW on either the Gray or Spot setting.

Conversion Options: Rendering Intent

We bypass Color Management Policies in favor of a more logical next item, Conversion Options. There was once controversy over the Intent item, but no longer. The CCMW now agrees with me as follows:

- **Engine** is inconsequential. Leave it at the default, Adobe (ACE).
- **Intent** should be Relative Colorimetric.
- Check **Use Black Point Compensation**.
- **Use Dither** (very fine noise added during the conversion process as an antibanding measure) is unimportant unless the file contains a computer-generated gradient, in which case it should be checked. I suggest it be kept on unless you plan to convert a specific file multiple times between LAB and RGB. In that case, use Convert to Profile with Dither unchecked.

Intent applies, at present, only to conversions into CMYK. The CCMW used to think that it should be set to Perceptual. That choice is an attempt to finesse gamut issues by toning down almost all colors to differentiate them from such wild animals as the greens in the lantern of Figure 12.4A.

When this mode appeared in 1998, the CCMW, and Adobe itself, stated that it was *the* correct way to handle conversions. However, as Mencken remarked, one horse laugh is worth ten thousand syllogisms. In *Professional Photoshop 5,* I called it the PCCM (Politically Correct Calibrationist Method) and described it as "a recipe for mediocrity."

I advocated, instead, the EIAM (Every Image an Adventure Method), which is to match every RGB color that can be matched and worry about the colors that can't be matched when they rear their oversaturated heads, and not until. This EIAM rejoices in a more academic name; it is called Relative Colorimetric, which is such a pain to pronounce that almost everybody calls it *relcol*.

Relcol is the better way to go if the RGB file doesn't have any out-of-gamut colors, since Perceptual would then be toning everything down for no gain. Relcol is also better if the out-of-gamut colors aren't important.

Perceptual is innocuous. It has to be, or nobody would ever have recommended it as a general method for separating all files. The theoretical argument is that it might help something like the aforementioned Figure 12.4A, which contains important detail that's outside of the CMYK gamut. But in such cases, Perceptual is of no practical use. Such images need *major* surgery. Figure 12.5A was converted using Perceptual (you can do this through the Convert to Profile command without changing your base Color Settings file) and you can hardly tell the difference

between it and the unsatisfactory Figure 12.4A. If someone demands that we say which one is better, why, we must respond Figure 12.5A, but the truth is that it would be no harder to correct one than the other.

In 2004 and 2005, several members of the CCMW gracefully conceded that they had been mistaken all along, and that relcol is a better choice.

The other two intent possibilities have no attraction for us. Saturation intent supposedly holds the brilliance but not the accuracy of the colors. The theory is that it's useful for PowerPoint presentations.

The final option, Absolute Colorimetric (abscol), is best explained in terms of a different setting. So far, we've been speaking of how to translate colors. There's also the question of how to translate darknesses. LAB and RGB support much darker blacks than CMYK does—out-of gamut-blacks, if you will.

Unlike out-of-gamut greens, there's no case for destroying shadow detail by smashing all such blacks into only a few levels. The sensible thing is to translate the darkest incoming black to the darkest CMYK black and tone down everything lighter. This technique is activated by checking Black Point Compensation. Uncheck it, and your shadows will plug during conversion.

There's no white point compensation, because the odds against your wanting to translate $255^R255^G255^B$ or $100^L0^A0^B$ to anything other than $0^C0^M0^Y$ are large. There is however, a catch. RGB and LAB, being expressed as light rather than ink, have a defined white point, which is usually not white. In the unlikely event that you want an RGB or LAB white to convert to something like $1^C0^M0^Y$, choose abscol.

Choosing this option by mistake (which is easy to do, because it's right under relcol in the Convert to Profile

---

Stumbling Blocks: Whom to Ask?

•**"Editing" an uneditable profile.** This topic is such an, er, black art, that those who don't understand it wimp out and suggest that we ask the printer what Photoshop settings to use. Personally, I would prefer to ask an electrician or a plumber, or possibly even a lawyer, because while these worthies probably know as little as the typical printer about the subject, they would be less inclined to bluster their way through an answer. Every modern printer deals successfully with many variants of GCR. The number of commercial printers who know their own dot gain is small, and the number who have any clue what GCR does is less.

•**Assign Profile and Convert to Profile.** These two are likely the most often mixed-up commands in Photoshop. Assign Profile changes the appearance, but not the reality, of the file—until it's translated into another colorspace, when it becomes real. Convert to Profile keeps the appearance constant, if possible, but alters values to do so.

•**Relative and Absolute Colorimetric.** If you don't know what the Absolute Colorimetric command is, it holds nothing but dangers for you. Use Relative instead.

dialog) is a good way to destroy silhouetted images, such as the pepper of Figure 12.6. The CCMW and I agree that abscol should be hidden someplace where the booboisie can't find it and where experts in too much of a hurry won't invoke it accidentally.

Color Management Policies

As with every other section of this chapter except RGB workspace, the CCMW has migrated to my position, and there is no longer any serious dispute as to the proper settings:

* For **RGB,** choose Preserve Embedded Profiles. For **CMYK** and **Gray,** choose Off.

Unlike the controversy about rendering intent, which resolved itself in a civilized fashion, reaching this consensus has been bloody. I've put the chapter that corresponds to this one in each of the last two editions on the CD, to illustrate how much has changed in people's thinking over that time.

The idea of tagging every file with information that identifies what colors the preparer actually intended is quite old. It was implemented, more or less, in Photoshop 5.0, released in 1998. At this time, users were encouraged to let a thousand different RGB workspaces bloom; previously it was very difficult to use anything other than Apple RGB.

Photoshop 5.0 dealt two fatal blows to the entire concept. First, it changed the default to sRGB, replacing a definition that some didn't like but most could tolerate with something that was condemned almost universally. So, people scattered in all different directions with their RGB definitions with disastrous results; some universally understood "RGB" is a practical necessity.

Worse, Photoshop 5.0 wildly overestimated the capabilities of the booboisie. Its default was, without warning, not to assign, but to convert any file the user opened into the current working space.

It would take at least 100 pages to explain how much trouble this misguided default caused 1998 users. Suffice it to say that a corrective update came out within a couple of months, but it was too late to get anyone ever to trust anything that smacks of profiling or "color management" again. Both the CCMW and I believe that converting automatically on opening is so unlikely to be right that the option shouldn't even be where it is. As with abscol rendering intent, it should be available, but not in waters in which the booboisie are likely to run aground.

If you work only with your own files, it won't make any difference what your setting for opening files is. The question is what to do when you open somebody else's file that contains a tag that doesn't agree with your own settings. The whole linchpin of the system was that users would notice, and either convert to their own settings or (this became possible in Photoshop 6) continue to work using the other person's definition.

Service providers rejected this workflow, preferring to ignore all incoming profiles. Explaining why this happened is a waste of space; the point is that even today, eight years after the extremist wing of the CCMW promised us that service providers who refused to adapt would die within a year, the chances of a printer or a photo lab honoring an embedded RGB profile are slim to none. A tagged Adobe RGB file will be opened as if it were sRGB, and will look dull, washed out. To get them to pay attention, you have to call them up and tell them, or better yet, give them a file that can't be misinterpreted, such as untagged CMYK or LAB.

The preferences in Color Management policies refer both to opening and saving files. If you choose Preserve Embedded Profiles, the incoming file will open in whatever RGB or CMYK workspace is embedded. When you save a file, your standard profile (or any profile that has been assigned directly to the file) gets embedded unless you tell Photoshop not to in the Save dialog.

For RGB files, embedding a tag costs around 4K. There are no known reports of bugs or other technical difficulties in converting or handling RGB files that contain tags. If the tag is not honored—if, typically, Adobe RGB is misinterpreted as sRGB—the result may be very bad. While there is no guarantee a stranger will pay attention to it, a tag can do no harm.

There is also no guarantee that a tag on a stranger's RGB file means anything. It could have been put there by mistake; it could mean nothing because he was trusting a miscalibrated monitor; or it could actually be intended. One way or the other, it costs us nothing to open it and take a look. If we doubt that the profile is accurate, we Assign Profile>Don't Color Manage to insert our own.

The CCMW's biggest mistake has always been in assuming that CMYK follows the same rules as RGB. All the arguments in favor of using RGB tags are arguments *against* using them in CMYK. A CMYK tag can add as much as a megabyte to a file. One assumes that CMYK files will be output as is, not translated. Translations out of any CMYK, because of the vagaries of black generation and gamut reduction, are inherently less reliable than from RGB. Embedding CMYK tags, especially ones that didn't originate in Photoshop, has caused glitches in certain RIPs and certain applications. It's not like it would happen every day or even every week, but it occurs enough so that a high-volume user would conclude that there's a reliability problem.

The forms of CMYK are so close to one another that if one is mistaken for another (as, for example, a file prepared for printing in Europe as opposed to North America), in all probability no one will notice. CMYK files are normally printed exactly as given; we do *not* want a conversion. In any event, no competent service provider would convert based on a CMYK tag without consulting with us. So, unlike an RGB tag, which can do only good, a CMYK tag in a file going to a stranger can do only harm.

Similarly, any CMYK tag in a document provided to you is almost certainly a mistake. It may be some profile used for proofing, or just an outright error. Remember, also, that the best CMYK practitioners don't provide the file as they want it to print under best conditions—they make files that are unlikely to print badly. The most obvious examples are the Crater Lake variants of Figures 12.11A and 12.11C, which are purposely too cyan and too light in comparison to what is really wanted. Embedding a tag would be quite wrong, since it would imply that the look when printed normally is what the user wants.

Opinions have changed on this point over the years. Few have ever doubted that tags should be embedded in RGB files. In the 2000 edition of this book, I advocated CMYK tags only in files prepared for newspapers or similar conditions that are unusual enough to cause a disaster if someone assumed they were for normal printing; the CCMW still believed that they should always be embedded. By 2002, I had withdrawn the recommendation in view of repeated reports of accidental conversions. I reported then that "The CCMW is of two minds on CMYK tags. It likes the idea in principle, but understands that the CMYK world doesn't, and that attempting to ram it down people's throats may be counterproductive. The CCMW is not as doctrinaire on this point as I have become."

By 2006, however, even the most extreme members of the CCMW refrain from embedding CMYK tags, albeit with nasty comments about how the printer is to blame.

You can always override your base setting when you save a file. The save dialog will suggest that you embed if that is your preference, but you can uncheck that option. And, if you ever use Assign Profile, Photoshop will assume you want to embed unless you tell it otherwise during the save.

The Sahara of the Bozart

As new techniques develop and new challenges arise, books like this one have to get bigger. This one, for example, is well over twice as long as the original 1994 edition.

This and the preceding chapter, however, have been getting shorter in recent years—until now. In this area, progress has lagged. The industry has grown more sophisticated even as its most prominent voices have preached an outdated, stagnant philosophy.

Now, finally, the conventional wisdom about these matters is essentially correct, even if the rhetoric is still a little steamy. Consider the following items that used to be controversial but now are agreed upon by everyone. (Most of these items were in dispute even at the time of the last edition in 2002, although some were resolved before then.) Some of these changes in attitude have already been explored in this chapter.

• Strangers, such as unknown printers and photo labs, cannot be relied upon to honor embedded profiles. It is best to give them files in whatever their final output space is.

• An untagged file must have some presumed meaning. In the absence of other information, untagged RGB files should be considered to be sRGB. Untagged CMYK should be considered to have been prepared for SWOP conditions. This varies from the CCMW of five years ago, which dismissed such files as "meaningless mystery meat."

• As a corollary, photographers, designers, and all others who now need to prepare files for commercial printing have to acquire CMYK knowledge. This replaces the previous dogma that a properly tagged RGB file should be provided to the printer, who might, the CCMW mistakenly thought, have some kind of clue about what to do with it.

• A further corollary: the person preparing the file needs to know not just how to separate, but how to make at least rudimentary edits in CMYK, because of examples like Figures 12.4 and 12.11B. Previously, it was felt that the perfect profile would yield the perfect separation, little or no subsequent editing required.

• And still another: the separation method is not aimed at color accuracy so much as it is at producing something workable. Typically this means going for a slightly desaturated separation, to allow more room to add color, which is easy, as opposed to trying to put detail into brilliant areas that lack it.

• CMYK files should not be tagged.

• Under Color Management Policies, use Relative Colorimetric intent, not Perceptual.

• The full impact of the 1998 release of Photoshop 5 in preventing the adoption of a profiled workflow has finally been appreciated. At the time, I wrote that its color defaults were so damaging that the entire release had to be considered "a major disservice to the industry." This resulted in a

Review and Exercises

✓ What is the difference between gamma and gamut?

✓ What is the difference between gamma and dot gain?

✓ If your file is intended to be Adobe RGB, but someone else opens it as if it is sRGB, what will it look like? What setting would you recommend changing on this someone else's system?

✓ Which two of the following four objects are the most likely to fall outside of the CMYK gamut?
   (A) a banana   (B) a pink flower   (C) a green leaf   (D) the sky on a cloudless day

high volume of public personal abuse. Since then, the CCMW has not just reversed its position on this but gone significantly beyond my own.

I was the odd man out at a recent color management panel with two members of the CCMW. The question of the impact of Photoshop 5 came up. One of the color management advocates called it "the most incompetently designed interface in the history of the graphic arts." The other said, "It could not possibly have been worse. Wait—if Photoshop 5 had formatted your hard drive when you booted it up, that would have been worse. Otherwise, it was as bad as it could possibly be." I said nothing.

- A machine-generated profile is not sacrosanct, but needs to be reviewed and possibly edited by a human being.
- Many of the best printing systems use their own proprietary calibration methods as opposed to some kind of open standard. The CCMW now approves, a big reversal.

The Bottom Line

Translations between colorspaces are governed by choices in Photoshop's Color Settings. No perfect method of conversion between RGB and CMYK is possible; the two spaces have different strengths and weaknesses. The correct choice of RGB definition depends on individual circumstances. Most users have settled on either sRGB or Adobe RGB.

Virtually all printers and photo labs ignore embedded profiles. All RGB files are likely to be interpreted as sRGB. When dealing with an unknown service provider, you should supply an sRGB, LAB, or CMYK file—never a different RGB.

In CMYK, the choice is between the difficult Custom CMYK, which has not been updated since 1998, and canned profiles supplied by Adobe or third parties. These profiles cannot be edited within Photoshop for such things as black generation, dot gain, and total ink, which sharply limits their utility.

- In designing a system to guarantee good results in offset printing, we should not attempt to calibrate or profile the printing press, as the CCMW strongly believed only a few years back, but rather the proofing system that feeds it. We'll discuss this further in the next chapter.
- Except for those shooting in a studio or other very repeatable conditions, there is little point in attempting to profile a camera. It's better to use an ad hoc profiling method during the acquisition of the images. Photoshop's Camera Raw module, for example, which we'll discuss in Chapter 16, is in many respects a profiling tool.
- Most important of all, calibration is much less important than process control. If process control is absent, no form of color management works; if it's there, almost any form works.

For these reasons, if you find these topics challenging, don't let your eyes glaze over. Remember that the conventional wisdom has a long history of being wrong in this area.

Mencken wrote of our profession, "Nine times out of ten, in the arts as in life, there is actually no truth to be discovered; there is only error to be exposed. In whole departments of human inquiry it seems to me quite unlikely that the truth ever *will* be discovered. Nevertheless, the rubber-stamp thinking of the world always makes the assumption that the exposure of an error is identical with the discovery of the truth—that error and truth are simply opposites. They are nothing of the sort. What the world turns to, when it has been cured of one error, is simply another error, and maybe one worse than the first one. This is the whole history of the intellect in brief."

Keep an open mind, use common sense, ask yourself what you are trying to achieve with your color settings, and you can prove him wrong.

Politics, Printing, and the Science of the Skosh

Preparing files for commercial printing is a minefield for the unwary. Good advice is hard to come by. There's lots of name-calling, lots of magic bullets being peddled. Nevertheless, prepress experts get good results—but not by treating printers as if they were photo labs.

ommercial printing, like the declarations of politicians, is inherently unreliable. Unexpected complications continually manifest themselves. When they do, both printers and politicians inevitably look for somebody to blame them on.

Let us assume that the job has just printed—unsatisfactorily, in your view and/or your client's. Let us also exclude problems not related to imaging, such as font substitution, or printing your client's job with her competitor's logo. No, just say that one or more critical images are unacceptable.

The causes are, in rough order of likelihood:

- You trusted your monitor instead of the Info palette, and handed in a file with a color cast, not realizing that your own eyes adjust to the image, whether your monitor is calibrated or not.
- You did not give full range to each image as described in Chapters 2 and 3, so that it looked flat in print as opposed to the peppy appearance that your calibrated monitor deluded your eyes into expecting.
- The printer actually messed up the job. His inking was too heavy or too light, the inks had become contaminated and changed color, and/or he lost control of his dot gain, among several thousand other possibilities.
- You were asking for something impossible, either by calling for a critical color that was out of the press's gamut, or by laying out the job in such a way that it became impossible to print correctly.
- The printer printed the job correctly to his own standards, but you did not have a good handle on what those standards were.

Of these five possibilities, three are your fault and one has enough blame to go around. But, in charity, let's assume that it's the one listed third, the one that's truly the printer's fault, the one that is, technically speaking, inadequate printing.

Now, the hard question: how do you know? And who do you expect will believe you if you tell them?

We will add to the fun by assuming, first, that the client demands a personal explanation from the printer, and also that you are a professional photographer, because there is no group that commercial printers take greater joy in sticking with the blame.

In all probability, the printer's explanation will sound to the client very much like the following: "This photographer that you're working with has no idea how to prepare a digital file. You can see it for yourself right here in this fleshtone, where he used the Slithy Toves filter instead of complying with the SWOP three-quartertone viscosity standard. How stupid is that, I ask you? Same way over here. There's a bisynchronous bitflop because he didn't gray balance his black limit when he turned left on the Whitestone bridge, plus his snicker to doodle ratio is all [messed] up."

In real life, this explanation sounds better than it does in writing, because commercial printers are so practiced at blaming photographers for their own shortcomings that they can do so *very* convincingly.

Confronted with such balderdash, the client can react in three ways, two of which are bad. He can fall for it, or he can decide that you and the printer are a bad match and that one of you needs to go. Which one do you suppose that will be?

- **Rule One**: If the printer does a poor job, *you* are likely to take the fall for it.

Nonprinters rarely appreciate the economics that make printing firms different from other graphic arts folk. The most striking example: if you hire an independent photographer, or designer, or layout artist, or photo lab, or advertising consultant, and you can't get along with that individual or

that firm, the relationship is likely to be short-lived. With a printer, this is not the case. The decision of who prints is often out of our hands altogether. Even if we want to move and have the authority to do so, we frequently can't. There may be no other printer between here and Shanghai who has the proper equipment and the ability to do the job when you want it at the price you want to pay.

Printers are often said to be heartless and cruel, not customer-oriented. It's not true. I know some very incompetent printers, as well as incompetent photographers, designers, color management consultants, even Photoshop book authors. I have never met anybody in any of these fields who wasn't made happy when their customer liked their work, or didn't feel bad when their work was criticized.

There is, however a big difference between a commercial printer and all these other fields. If you work elsewhere, it is virtually certain that at some, probably many, points in your career, you have given away work or heavily discounted it for reasons that were mostly the client's fault.

Printers rarely do that. If you or I have to eat a job, it probably doesn't cost us all that much for supplies. We lose the free time that we would otherwise spend in some other unsavory enterprise. But a printer may have laid out several thousand dollars for the paper that your mistake is now forcing him to sell to a recycler. And presses are very expensive. Printing companies make money by running them 24 hours a day, seven days a week, scheduling work far enough in advance that the press never goes idle. If they have to redo your job, they have to turn away other work.

Pressmen are known, as alluded to in the last chapter, for their creative use of foul language. They know of no more vile pair of words than "nonchargeable remake." Yes, if it's absolutely clear that a mistake has taken place that is *entirely* the fault of the printer, there will probably be little argument that you are entitled to a rerun. But if they have the slightest wiggle room—like, you signed off on a proof that contained a heinous error that no reputable printer would have ever allowed to sneak in—why, you're out of luck. You sign off, it's your fault.

- **Rule Two**: You're not getting the job rerun unless it's absolutely incontestable that the printer has made a serious error that you could not have known about in advance.

The Origin of Political Parties

Speaking of nasty language, this chapter has its share. What great fun for the author, to write a chapter about politics, particularly when there are so many windbags around to make fun of! No stumbling blocks, no exercises, no need for diplomacy.

This is a technical book, and technically speaking, this chapter doesn't belong here. Yet a section on how to prepare for the *realities* of commercial printing is one of the most demanded topics.

One reason is that too many easy answers are being peddled. Here's one: read the rest of the book, give the printer a good CMYK file. What's the problem?

Here's another: give the printer a good RGB file, let him take care of the rest.

This chapter will cover some of the real-world reasons why printing does not come out as expected, what practical people can do to compensate, the differences between color management and process control, how to be polite to printers, what dot gain is all about, why most of what you've read anywhere else on these topics is uninformative, why photographers and printers hate each other, why photo labs are worse than commercial printers, and why understanding the concept of the skosh is a critical element in quality reproduction. In our spare time, we will discuss the Custom CMYK dialog.

Many of the realities of printer-client politics are hard to understand without knowing some history, which, for our purposes, starts in the mid 1980s.

Offset printing—this chapter is not going to tackle gravure or flexo, which play by slightly different rules—was developed in the first half of the 20th century but did not become commercially common until the 1960s. There have been incremental improvements in press technology since then, but the basic design is the same. Presses last a long time—20 or more years is not uncommon.

Drum scanners took hold in the 1970s, but they output film. Color correction was a manual operation, mostly executed by dedicated prepress companies. Digital color correction became feasible in the early 1980s at a horrendous cost, somewhat cheaper later in the decade. This work was done at prepress companies, not printers.

Photoshop, the Macintosh, and cheap scanners killed this model.

Why do we go through the stress of dealing with these obstreperous printers at all? It would be much easier if we could just put the press in our offices and do the work ourselves, without paying them their ripoff prices and dealing with their surly attitudes and lousy work.

Unfortunately, to avoid the experience, we would have to lay out several million dollars on plant and equipment, so let's be real. The printer holds us hostage.

It used to be the same way with the prepress house. Unless you had a million dollars and a semi-industrial workspace, you could not do the kind of work that we take for granted in Photoshop today. And so, you (I say you, not we; I was working for the enemy back then, thanks) were also held hostage. If the prepress company did good color correction and (since it also took care of relations with the printer) got good results on the printed page, you looked good. If not, the best original art in the world would look amateurish.

Early pioneers occasionally got passable results with Photoshop 2 and a desktop scanner. As time went on, software and hardware got much faster and much better, to the point that companies that were farming out a lot of prepress work began to wonder why they were doing so. And, as they got still better and still faster, individuals joined the exodus.

Few could justify giving a prepress company $100 or more to process a single image that could be handled in-house for a small fraction of that, even assuming that quality would be better, which wasn't always true. So the market gradually collapsed, and though many companies have in-house graphics departments that rival the size of some prepress houses, the large independent prepress suppliers were pretty much finished by the turn of the century.

Politics Abhors a Vacuum

The absence of the middleman led to near civil-war conditions. It's a long way between a photograph and a press, and most of the knowledge of that route lived with an industry that had become extinct.

Some large companies outside of the graphic arts knew what they were doing; some printers had enough prepress skills to give sensible advice as to what sorts of files worked for them.

Both, however, were the exception. Instead, we had clients (including you, perhaps) who were used to having their hands held, being forced to work directly with printers who are not good hand-holders.

Worse, there was every incentive for each side to dislike the other. Clients would ask questions that seemed perfectly reasonable about things like ink limits and dot gain, and printers would have no idea what they were talking about. Meanwhile, instead of getting work from companies whose business was to prepare work to a printer's satisfaction, printers were confronted with new clients who wouldn't know a fountain from a flying paster and who were used to getting jobs redone for free when they themselves had messed up.

This was a tinderbox, and plenty of matches got thrown into it.

Now. Who *should* have stepped up to the podium and offered themselves up to be the next prepress experts? A lot of photographers nominated the printers, who promptly pulled a Sherman.

Granted, some printers, typically of the smaller variety or those who had existing departments, answered their party's call. More did not. For those who cannot understand why, it was partially laziness but there were also two valid reasons.

First, remember Rule Two. The printer absolutely does not want to give you your money back unless the error is incontestably his fault. If he gives advice on prepress, or works on a file, and later it proves that the file had some defect, there may be an argument over who should pay for the rerun. There is no percentage in this for the printer: whatever profit he makes on 100 prepress jobs more than vanishes if he has to remake one press job.

Also, there is a cultural difficulty. Large printers need large buildings not just for their presses. They also need to find a place to store several hundred tons of paper, which does not conveniently fit in one's closet. So a good deal of land is needed, preferably in close proximity to railroad tracks. You rarely find large printers anywhere near urban centers—they'd have to charge an arm and a leg to make up for their rent.

The labor force in East Bandersnatch County, or wherever these printers reside, may not feature too many skilled retouchers. Furthermore, it's going to be difficult to find any other prepress work to justify having any kind of sizable operation.

All of which means that a very sad rule is about to be announced.

- **Rule Three**: Unless you have learned otherwise, you must assume that the printer knows less about how to prepare a file than you do.

The Power of the Media

Of course, there do exist printers who can be of great assistance in these matters. It behooves us to find out—if we can. We may be confined to talking to a customer service representative who thinks that a mouse is some kind of foot pedal.

If the printer *does* employ somebody who actually knows something about file preparation, that person is likely to be very busy, and hard to get hold of. If we can't do it, and can't find out any other way, we're probably stuck with assuming the likeliest scenario, which is that the printer knows nothing about prepress.

Most Photoshop books, in the three paragraphs they allot to preparing files for press, recommend asking the printer what to do. I would not wish to insult other Photoshop authors. I don't see how they could know even less about preparing CMYK files than most printers do, which is ordinarily zero; but I do not want to insult the printers by suggesting they might know more.

The advice about asking the printer what to do, though, deserves the following serious warning. If you ask an electrician or plumber about how to prepare your Photoshop files, at least you will get a frank admission that they don't know what you're talking about. Ask a printer, who probably is no more versed in the subject than the aforementioned electrician or plumber, and embarrassment may become a factor. He may have read that this is a subject you are supposed to ask him about, so he may spout gibberish in the hope that you'll buy it.

The first Photoshop book of any significance appeared, if memory serves, in 1992. It was written by David Biedny, a retoucher, and Bert Monroy, a digital artist who specializes in the relation between Photoshop and Illustrator. Like me, these two have worked in Photoshop for a living. This is rare for authors of software books, who tend to be professional writers skilled at explaining how things work, but not necessarily qualified to do the work themselves.

That is the sort of author responsible for most Photoshop books of the late 20th century—adequate writers, Photoshop tyros. It may have been a good time for people just learning the program, but these books hardly were a service to experts.

Today, this is no longer the case. Pick a Photoshop book off the shelf at random, and it's more likely to be written by a knowledgeable person than at any point in the past. Readers benefit from the hard times afflicting the technical book industry. Digital photography is so hot that publishers, badly hurt in their other areas by the downturn, look to put out more Photoshop books.

Not quite so desperate, however, as to hire professional authors to write them. Over 1,000 Photoshop titles are now on the market. Publishers have to be quite bold to take on new ones without verifying that the author is technically competent. Meanwhile, those eyeing a career as Photoshop educators find they need to have published a book to gain professional credibility, and they take care to make it a good one.

But where do all the experts come from? The National Association of Photoshop Professionals runs a biannual show called Photoshop World. Their instruction staff contains, by anybody's reckoning, most of the leading Photoshop authorities. I have the roster for the September 2006 show, which has 35 instructors besides myself.

Of these 35, 16 are or were professional photographers. 13 others are what I would classify as professional experts: they have always trained people or written about the topic, without having significant actual production experience. They tend to be the most polished and most popular speakers. Two others, of whom Bert Monroy is one, have done heavy-duty production work in Photoshop. I am not sure about the other four.

I learn new things from these talented 35 at every show. They truly represent the leading figures in the field. But how balanced is that field?

Of the 35, to my knowledge two have what I would term serious experience at preparing CMYK files. Not one, as far as I know, has ever been a full-time retoucher, or worked for a commercial printer, or worked full-time in Photoshop for a service provider.

On the one hand, polls of the attendees indicate that somewhat more than a third are more comfortable working with CMYK than RGB files. On the other, all 36 instructors, present company excepted, are more comfortable with RGB. What does this tell you about the quality of information you're likely to find about commercial printing? It also explains why there are so many glib answers on the topic that don't quite hold up under examination, the bloodcurdling one of asking the printer about Photoshop settings being one. Another is in what

Figure 13.1 *The printing industry has its standards, but the variability inherent in the printing process works against them.*

colorspace to supply the file. To me, this is a no-brainer. Whoever knows the most should be doing the conversion to CMYK. If you've come this far in the book, and you're about to deal with an unknown printer, the odds against the most knowledgeable person being the printer are very high. As we've seen in the last two chapters, conversion to CMYK is not always easy. We do not need to allow anybody else to do it for us if there is any doubt as to their ability to do so correctly. Give the printer CMYK files.

Pollsters, Printing, and Predictability

Commercial printing is much less reliable than any other method of output we commonly use. The *specifics* of why this is so are not well documented.

Figure 13.1 appeared in a column I once wrote about industry standards. It was called "Breakfast of Champions," because the three most widely used standards are—ready?—SNAP, GRACOL, and SWOP.

We are about to go on a quick tour of an operation that, for the sake of argument, prints on a web (roll-fed) press, such as the one used to print this book. Chances are, the printer claims to adhere to SWOP, which stands for *Specifications for Web Offset Publications.* (GRACOL applies to sheetfed printing, SNAP to newspapers).

This *claim* of SWOP compliance is, in my experience, worth nothing. It does, however, suggest that if we separate RGB files using any of the settings described in the last chapter, the printed result will have a passing similarity to what we were expecting.

SWOP encompasses several requirements, but the three most important should seem familiar to RGB users. One specifies the colors of the inks, the second their densities when printed solid, the third how dark they appear when printed at 50%. These three, taken together, are exactly analogous to the way we define an RGB working space. For ink colors and densities, read *primaries;* for the 50% dot, the term is *gamma* in RGB and *dot gain* in CMYK. We'll be discussing the key dot gain setting at length later. But first, let's talk about what can go wrong.

These days, printing plates are imaged directly from computer files, a more controllable approach than the old way of pulling film and exposing the plates through it. The plates are made largely of aluminum, dark in the printing area, light elsewhere. The dark areas attract ink and repel water, the light ones the opposite. The plates gradually wear down during the pressrun, adding variation to what already sounds like an unreliable process.

Each plate is large—eight full pages of this book. It gets locked onto a heavy metal cylinder, which spins around (and bounces) at high speed during the run. It is opposed by a similar cylinder wrapped in a piece of rubber called a *blanket.* Meanwhile, one ink is entering the scene, being forced through a bunch of holes whose width varies during the pressrun, through a series of most unreliable rollers whose performance is affected by the layout of the document being printed—large areas of solid ink force the rollers apart by the microscopic amount needed to permit more ink to pass through in other areas than we would like.

The ink hits the spinning plate, which transfers (or *offsets,* get it?) its image to the spinning blanket, which thus receives a wrong-reading (mirror) image. The spinning blanket deposits a right-reading image on the paper, which is simultaneously being caressed by a different blanket-plate combination on its other side. After this experience, the paper sashays onto the next printing unit to receive the next color ink, then a third unit, then a fourth. This all happens at tens of thousands of impressions per hour, which is to say that the cylinders usually run through around ten full rotations per second.

What's wrong with this picture? Let me count the ways. Inks vary by batch, but they also vary in color during the pressrun if press maintenance is not what it should be. If the press has just been cleaned, the color will not be the same as if the inks have been left to contaminate one another. The blanket is sensitive to heat, humidity, and age. Its performance depends on the packing between it and its cylinder, and how tight the bolts are that hold it. If these last two procedures aren't done carefully, dot gain will be considerably more in the center of the sheet than on the edges. The entire process changes depending on not only the speed at which the press is being run, but also whether other presses are simultaneously being run nearby, and if so, what types of particulates they are throwing off. Even an excessive pollen count can change color.

As if this isn't enough, the paper is also affected by the climate conditions, and by the conditions in the area in which it was stored before being brought into the pressroom, by how tightly the mill wrapped it, and by which side of the sheet is being printed.

Pressmen, aided by computers, are continuously monitoring and adjusting ink flows during the run. The speed of adjustments is hampered by the pressmen having to scream at one another to make their wishes known, because the press is so loud that they are required to wear hearing protection.

A Party and Its Platform

GRACOL has it right. Its slogan is, "Variation is the sum of all the variables." The whole secret of quality printing is to keep this convention of variables as somnolent as possible. But even under the best conditions, variability will be far greater than we would like, or than we would accept from, say, a photo lab. A good commercial printer's results will be somewhat variable, a bad one's horrendously so.

Figure 13.2 *These images appeared in six different publications, all using the same source CMYK file.*

Before we decide how to react, let's take a look at the variation in the real world. I've seen a lot of it, because many of my own jobs, including my magazine columns, have seen the same files printed by multiple printers in several countries. And, for sport, I did a bit of field research for this book. I prepared a tough little set of 25 sRGB images and, masquerading as a member of the booboisie, presented them to a dozen different photo labs, in three different states, plus some self-service kiosks and online services, to see how much variation there would be in comparison to what printers deliver. The results were instructive.

The woman of Figure 13.2 appeared several years ago in six different publications at very close to the sizes you see here. Each used the same digital file. For publication here, all were scanned with the same settings. Although I have corrected them to eliminate problems associated with re-screening, the same moves applied to all six, so there was no change in relative colors. In the background area around each image, you can see the color of the paper.

Figure 13.3 is from my test of photo labs, again scanned and handled identically. Eliminating results from companies that used exactly the same brand and model output device, these come from the first six labs I tested.

We'd *like* to see six identical images on each side of this spread. So much for pious

Figure 13.3 These prints were produced by six different photo labs from the same sRGB file.

hopes. However, there's more difference between the two sets than meets the eye.

Starting with the print side, speaking as your friendly former press quality control officer, the bane of sloppy presswork, the champion of the intimidated, and the enemy of variation in all its evil incarnations, I accept Figures 13.2D and 13.2F as a match. Figure 13.2A does not match; its dot gain is slightly heavier, but is acceptable on the assumption that one of the other two is the desired result.

Figure 13.2B is a special case. I knew about the printing conditions in advance and was aware that it would print lighter than the others. So, this is the expected result, also acceptable.

That leaves two. Figure 13.2E is garbage, too light and too blue. Figure 13.2C is too saturated. Many printers would defend it. It probably falls within the liberal tolerances of SWOP. (A PDF of the full SWOP guidelines is in the folder for this chapter on the CD, together with a recent errata file.)

I was not expecting the results from photo labs to be much better than from a random selection of printers, but I certainly wasn't prepared for them to be this bad. No two of these six match one another as closely as Figures 13.2A, 13.2D, and 13.2F do.

Figure 13.3A is close enough to what I was expecting. I could, holding my nose, say that Figures 13.3C and 13.3F are somewhat close. As for the others. Figure 13.3B is great if you like green hair and Village of the Damned eyes, the woman of Figure 13.3D looks like she's just been visited by Count Dracula, and the lab that produced Figure 13.3E believes that if boosting the contrast setting is good, then taking it off the scale is better, by God.

Not only that, when I came back with the same files to test these labs a month later, the results were just as bad. And that is the enormous difference between photo labs and printing firms.

The Opposition Is Heard From

Poor-looking images, like election losses, can be accounted for by one of two factors: unforeseen circumstances and stupid decisions. Poor printing usually is a result of the first factor, poor results from a photo lab or other imaging service the latter.

The distinction is a major one. If you take a file to an unknown offset printer and also to an unknown photo lab, the odds are greater that you will get something like what you wanted from the printer. I'm convinced of this from my own testing.

That is, you will get a better result from a printer *the first time*. On subsequent passes, it's a very different story.

Consider Figure 13.4, which shows the same six photo labs having a go at a different picture for a second time, a month after the first test. The labs are in the same order as before, but even if they were randomized, it would be easy to pick out which was which. Figure 13.4D blows out the clouds just as Figure 13.3D blows out its own highlights. Figure 13.4B has the same yellow-green cast as 13.3B. Figure 13.4A is closest to my expectations just as 13.3A was; in comparison, Figure 13.4F is warmer and higher contrast, just as 13.3F was.

Some of the poor results are the fault of machines. These output devices are self-calibrating. A human being would be very unlikely to approve the calibrations of the

companies that produced either the B or C versions of these images. Sometimes it's a shrewd business decision. The warmer, high-contrast look of the F versions doesn't do much for these two images, but would likely enhance the average picture brought in by the booboisie.

In short, we know what each of these labs will do with our files, and we can take countermeasures. If I've got a hundred new images where I want the look of the A versions but prefer to go to one of the other labs, getting the hundred images prepared will take less than an hour. I'll write a Photoshop Action that corrects for, say, the yellow-green cast of the B versions, run that Action on the hundred images, burn the CD, hand it off to the B vendor, and be fairly sure that it's going to look acceptably close to what the A vendor would have produced.

Offset presses, however, are vastly harder to maintain than photographic imagers. If I reran the image of Figure 13.2 with the same six printers on the same presses with the same paper, it would still be almost the same crapshoot it was in the beginning. *Repeatability*—that's the key factor we are accustomed to seeing elsewhere that is lacking in commercial printing. There's too much room for human error.

You'd need a loupe and a copy of the original magazine to verify it, but Figure 13.2C is too red because the press has trouble holding highlight dots, like the red-killing cyan found in a person's face. Therefore, while the result is undesirable, we'd be likely to get something similar if the same job went to the same press.

Figure 13.3E, on the other hand, is sloppy presswork. I've checked. The density of the yellow ink is far lower than it should be. If the same printer had at it again, there's no telling what would come out the second time. This type of unpredictable yet inevitable human error is what drives the politics of printing.

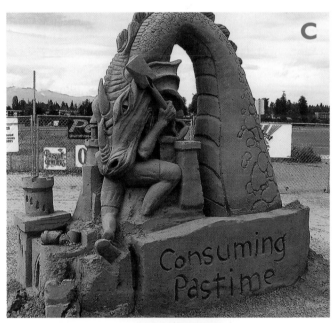

Figure 13.4 *The same six labs as in Figure 13.3, in the same order, produced these from a single source file.*

Figure 13.5 *This thumbnail image was printed in eight consecutive issues of the same magazine, using the same press and paper each time.*

I am no great admirer of the company that used to print my magazine column. Figure 13.5 should give a hint as to why. It's the same thumbnail image (don't ask me why it is recropped and resized each time) printed on the same press and the same paper, over eight consecutive issues.

This is a book about pressroom realities, so a bit of pressroom language is appropriate. These people are bleeping incompetents. Whoever is in charge of quality control at this company should be replaced by a hog, because even a hog would be repulsed at how infrequently they perform press washups. I hope that hornets nest in that press during downtime, and when the crew starts it up again I hope their sorry butts get stung big-time as they run into the arms of the police who are waiting to bleeping arrest them on charges of impersonating pressmen.

Rhetoric and Substance

This last set has three important reminders about the realities—and the politics—of printing, and why it is different from most other forms of output.

- **No choice.** We usually have control over who outputs our digital files. The photo lab that produced Figures 13.3D and 13.4D can expect to see the next job from me right around the time of the next presidential election in which Utah goes Democratic. But the printer of that magazine? Nobody asked my opinion, and they wouldn't have paid any attention if I gave it. Professionals frequently don't even know who's going to print the job, let alone have the ability to change the choice.

- **Guess where the blame goes.** Look at it this way. In the course of this book, you have seen some pretty poor original photographs taken by others. I presume that it never crossed your mind to blame *me* for them, although I could certainly have had an impact. But you've now seen almost 50 of my color corrections, and, presumably, you like some of them more than others. If you didn't like one, did it ever occur to you that it might be because it was poorly printed? Short of something as dramatic as printing with green ink where the black is supposed to be, I seriously doubt it. I think you blamed me.

- **Cursing helps.** It definitely calms one, as does fantasizing physical violence against the pressmen. (That last has to remain a fantasy, because pressmen push around half-ton rolls of paper all day, and have biceps like bricks. You don't want to mess with them.)

Unfortunately, swearing doesn't make it any more likely that you'll get a predictable result next time, or that anybody will blame you the less if it happens. Instead, you should ask yourself how so many prepress professionals manage to get quality results. The answer is pretty easy.

- **Rule Four**: Hope for the best, but expect the worst.

If you can identify the ways sloppy presswork can hurt you, you can take precautions. Think defensively—particularly if you're not familiar with the company that's going to do the printing. If we are preparing for a photo lab with a track record of consistency, then we can shoot for what we want. For an unknown press, we attempt to avoid what we don't want. There's a difference.

Here are questions about some hypothetical images—so hypothetical that you will get only the vaguest description of them—but you don't need any more than that, in my opinion, to know the correct answer.

• Your picture is one of a fashion model. Would you prefer her face to be too beet red, or too pale?

• In a picture taken in the open spaces of a national park, would you prefer the sky to be too cool (cyan) or too purple?

• A landscape shot features lots of greenery. Would you prefer it too light and clean, or too dark and muddy?

• A shot of a cityscape at night shows the dark edges of the skyscrapers barely outlined against the sky, although the lights and stars are clearly visible. Is it better that this image print too dark, or too green?

• Substitute a shot of silver jewelry. Should this one be too dark, or too green?

A Skosh of Prevention

Printed results are assuredly going to be erratic. The only question is, *how* erratic? Variation as bad as in Figure 13.5 is, sadly, common. But the buyer can't be forced to accept it. If ads in the publication come out as bad as these thumbnails suggest, agencies will demand a rerun or a credit. So conceivably you are able to get some redress.

Variations not as large as this, but nevertheless quite significant, are considered acceptable. For example, go back to the Assign Profile test and compare Figure 12.2A (Apple RGB) to 12.2F (sRGB). If you were promised one and got the other, you'd be within your rights to complain. If the difference were only half as much, though, you'd be out of luck. If necessary, the printer would wave the SWOP tolerances in your face.

The Stoic philosopher Epictetus said, "Do not ask for things to be as you wish; wish for them to be as they are." A true stoic hands the printer the file as he hopes it will be printed and pretends afterward to like whatever the result is. A sensible person tells Epictetus to take a hike, and takes action to undermine the printer's capability of messing up.

The *skosh* is a crucial unit of measurement for anyone serious about doing so. In technical terms, a skosh is .313 of a tad, or 3.24 weenzies. It is the experienced person's insurance policy against an undesired result on press.

How did you answer that last little quiz? Did you, like me, vote against purple skies and beet-red fleshtones? If you think that the alternative is more palatable, the solution is obvious: a skosh less magenta than you would send to an output device you were more confident of. That's what the magazine should have done with my thumbnail picture in Figure 13.5. Granted, my skin is quite dark; a couple of images there are actually pretty close. But in view of this enormous variation, the set of eight would have looked better as a group if all eight were lighter.

If you'd rather have park colors that are too clean than too muddy, or if you'd rather a cast than added darkness in a nightscape, take insurance by making the file a skosh lighter than you think it will print. And, if you'd rather chance a file being too dark than too colorful, you use another trick that confounds the RGB-centric. We discussed it in Chapter 5, but it bears repeating.

In RGB, there's only one way to define colors. In CMYK, everything except brilliant colors can be constructed in many different ways, by adjusting the amount of black up and the CMY down, or vice versa. If the subject is something neutral, like jewelry, give the printer more black ink, which can't print as any color but gray, instead of inks that impart an ugly cast with ease, if he is as careless as the printer of Figure 13.5.

- **Rule Five**: On press, the object is not to get what you want, but rather to eliminate the possibility of getting what you *don't* want.

The skosh is a variable unit of measure. The printer of this book is the same one that did *Photoshop LAB Color*. Their process control is good, so my skoshes are relatively small. When I was working with the printer of Figure 13.5, they were pretty big skoshes.

Along the same lines: many jobs are printed without the benefit of contract proofs. In those, I would recommend a full tad of prevention, rather than a mere skosh. If a proof is going to be available and the printer will be held accountable if he doesn't match it, revert to only a skosh.

The science of the skosh, large or small, governs the art of preparation for print. Calibration, as such, takes second place to common sense. That brings us back to politics, where common sense finds no home, and to more discussion of the aforementioned proof.

The Contract and the Proof

For printers, reducing variability on press requires major, usually costly effort, and often serious detective work to figure out which of the dozen or so likeliest mechanical culprits is responsible for the fluctuation. Some printers care enough to try; for others quality is but a minor consideration. It seems obvious that those who wish to make suggestions on how the printing industry could improve itself would concentrate on changing those attitudes.

Instead, the focus has been on three bogus issues. We have already discussed one: the notion that somehow these printers—many of whom, as we have just seen, have a difficult time just printing—should become responsible for learning how to teach their clients to prepare files in Photoshop. The others are the role of the proof, and the need (or lack thereof) for more calibration.

Misunderstandings about the objectives of the thing called a *contract proof* usually derive from an inability to fathom what the two simple-sounding words mean.

That so many factors alter press performance mandates a system where pressmen are constantly making minor, sometimes major, adjustments in ink flow. The motivations for so doing fall into three categories.

- Color bars and other quality-control swatches appear outside of the job's trim area, on the theory that if they print properly, then the job itself will, too. The pressman may observe or measure weirdness in these areas, and attempt to compensate.
- The pressman may make a unilateral artistic decision. Confronted with Figure 13.3B, for example, he may reflect on the fact that in 30 years as a pressman he has yet to encounter a client who liked green hair and fleshtone. So he may up the flow of magenta ink and decrease the flow of cyan to that zone of the form.
- There is a more tangible reason to think that the client wants some change. The source of this feeling could be a contract proof that doesn't look like what's being printed, or it could be something much simpler: a desktop inkjet print, a page ripped out of a magazine, or a written instruction like "make sure this doesn't go too red."

None of these scenarios requires a very high-quality proof—but another party needs one—us. Otherwise, we can't hold the printer accountable. If we are spending thousands of dollars, it's really hard to accept the idea that we have no recourse at all if the job turns out badly.

Note that I have never stated what qualifies as a contract proof. The term is associated with certain brand names, like Matchprint, Signature, or Cromalin, but it doesn't have to be. A contract proof is what it says it is: a contract between client and printer. The printer agrees to match it, within reason. The client agrees to pay for the job if he does. If the two agree that something off a color copier is a contract proof, that's what it is.

- **Rule Six**: The contract proof protects you, not the printer.

To understand that rule fully, we have to go back to Rule Two. The economics of printing dictate that jobs cannot be run for free except where the error is clearcut and provable. The contract proof is a Sword of Damocles, hanging over the printer's head. Once he has agreed to match it, he has to go through whatever gyrations it takes to do so, or the blade will descend.

Two obvious consequences: the printer is going to be very careful in establishing his own proofing system, because his business won't survive if he can't match his own proof; and the printer will be reluctant beyond all names of reluctance to accept as a proof anything that he does not know for a fact is matchable—like, for example, output from your inkjet printer. They'll almost always accept one of the big brand name contract proofs regardless of who prepared it. Also, SWOP offers certification of certain proofing systems, and if the proof is so certified, most printers will take it.

Meanwhile, the lithographic landscape is littered with companies with excellent, reliable proofing systems and nonexistent quality control in the pressroom—bringing up the steamiest source of rhetoric.

The Platform Is Developed

Even in the days when printers made their proofs from film, the process was quite reliable. The nonimpact proofers available today make life easier. They're exceptionally stable, if treated well.

To summarize, the proofing system is reliable and repeatable; the press is not. If the proof is good, the printed job will be good, or the printer will be in big trouble.

The conclusion is obvious from our point of view: we shoot for a good proof, and let the printer worry about what happens next. We don't try to outguess his press conditions. If he has to change a blanket or call in a mechanic so that his cylinders don't bounce so much, that's his problem, not ours.

It's also obvious from the printer's point of view. Get the proofing system to a point where the pressmen feel comfortable that it can be matched, then keep it there. Do not alter the proofing system to chase changes in press conditions; alter the press conditions to comport with the proofing requirements.

That an accurate proof is the objective was not obvious, however, to the self-appointed theoreticians of the 1990s. This resulted in the political schism that still creates great hostility today.

The theory—which Adobe supported, although they did not originate it—was that individual presses behave differently, which is true enough. From this observation came the mind-boggling leap that every press should be profiled, and every CMYK file should bear a tag identifying the characteristics of the press it was intended for. Then, if printed in a different setting, the file would undergo a CMYK to CMYK conversion, resulting in a perfect match to the intended appearance.

These theorists mistook the real problem—that careless printers don't get the same result from day to day—for generalized chaos. Remember, much if not most professional CMYK work is prepared without knowledge of who the printer will be. Remember, printers were accustomed to accepting Matchprints and Cromalins from third parties as contract proofs. Neither of these general practices could have developed if there had been huge differences from firm to firm.

The chaos shown by the photo labs in Figures 13.3 and 13.4—that's what the theorists thought they were facing in commercial printing. But they weren't. The printers, as Figure 13.2 suggests, had (and have) *the basics* down well. If they print properly according to their own specifications, one firm's work matches that of another's closely enough that nobody would want to worry about conversions. If they don't print properly, if they pull one of these Figure 13.5 kinds of deal, then all the accurate conversions in the world wouldn't help.

The theorists, who then as today could not grasp that CMYK was not just RGB with another letter, overlooked a killer. Converting CMYK to CMYK regenerates the black. If somebody has made a special black for purposes described above or in Chapter 5, it gets wiped out, and whatever kind of black the profile specifies is substituted. Being able to make unusual blacks is necessary for quality reproduction. This lack of control made the whole concept a nonstarter.

Also, they forgot to provide a working mechanism. The theory might have sufficed for photo labs, because photo labs want RGB input, and RGB to RGB conversions have proven completely reliable. The mathematics of CMYK to CMYK conversions are far more complex. Errors are not infrequent. Adobe once made the argument that at least 95 percent of such conversions are successful, which is probably correct. Time to look again at Rule Two, about refunds for printing, and you can understand why printers were not impressed with such a success rate.

Finally, the theory grossly overestimated how interested the printers (not to mention the booboisie) would be in cooperating. To see how wrong they were, we need only turn away from printers and back to the photo labs.

These labs *do* have the problem that the theorists mistakenly thought the printers had. Send files to an unknown lab today, and you have almost no idea what's going to come back. The solution being offered—

embedded profiles, RGB to RGB conversions—is proven, and lacks the technical issue of black generation. The equipment the labs run, unlike printing presses, stays fairly predictable from day to day.

Therefore, the theorists offer an effective, reliable solution to a real problem, as far as photo labs are concerned. This is as opposed to the printing field, where they offered an ineffective, unreliable solution to a problem that did not exist.

And when the votes were counted: In 2006, eight years afterward, not only do printers not honor embedded tags, neither do photo labs. Some of my RGB test images had such tags, others didn't. Every single lab ignored them. Not one even asked whether I wanted them honored.

The Cost of Negative Campaigning

Expecting CMYK users to adopt a workflow that failed even in the much simpler RGB world was naive even by the standards of politicians. After all, it delivered worse quality, was more expensive, required an extensive learning curve, and was error-prone, all in one package. The market reacted as it usually does to products with these attributes. However, the basic idea, although misapplied, made sense.

The idea of attempting to profile the press, rather than the proof, on the other hand, was the last sigh of calibrationism, the plaintive belief that as long as there is an instrument measurement, no matter how obviously unreliable, no matter how incontestably irrelevant, fortune will smile.

Unfortunately, the press won't stand still. Even under the best-controlled conditions, measurements taken now are invalid in 15 minutes.

Meanwhile, the proofing system is stable. The printer agrees that the press can match it. The knowledgeable prepress types don't use a divining rod to predict what the press may or may not do. How difficult is it to realize that the thing that needs to be measured is the proof, not the press?

We'll move to politics now, back to 1998, shortly after the release of the troubled Photoshop 5.0. Adobe, which as far as I know does not employ anyone with commercial printing experience, publicly berated the printing industry as Luddites. They suggested that users should avoid printers who did not profile their presses and supply the profiles to clients. An online user wanted to know why, if all this was so, the experienced CMYK types seemed to be aiming their efforts at the proof, not the press.

Chris Cox, a programmer who has been Adobe's most visible spokesman on color, replied, "They're trying to achieve reliable, quality color while dealing with brain-dead print shops who refuse to even consider using color management…if I give them data that prints a good proof, then they can match it on press without having to worry about all that new-fangled calibrationist colorsync crap we don't need because we know the numbers and my daddy didn't need it or his daddy before him blah blah blah. Having reliable presses and a profile of the press would be better—but this is one way to do things until the print shops wake up."

The user then quoted me (I had recently noted that trying to profile an offset press is like trying to profile the wind) and asked, possibly rhetorically, "DM is dense? (not)"

Mr. Cox replied, "Yes. Quite. And stuck in the stone age of printing…Dan's views on color management are going to sink him and his followers just about the way computer typesetting sunk all the die-hard hot lead typesetting houses. I just don't want to see too many innocent users sunk with him."

And when the votes were counted: Around four weeks later, the corrective update 5.0.2 was released, changing the color management behavior of 5.0 that I had complained

about. The entire 5.0 settings interface was junked in Photoshop 6, in favor of the one we have today. Today's mainstream view of the merits of Photoshop 5.0 is discussed on page 298. Mr. Cox reversed his view, coming out in favor of profiling proofs rather than presses, right about the time of our next whistlestop on the campaign trail, the release of Photoshop 7.0 in 2002.

Stereotyping Is a Form of Printing

When opening a file that has an embedded tag, we can accept it, or ignore it and use our own. As discussed in the last chapter, the sensible approach is (with some exceptions) to accept RGB but ignore CMYK tags. Allowing users different defaults for opening RGB and CMYK files should have been in the Color Settings dialog for a long time.

In Photoshop 7.0, Adobe incomprehensibly decided that if we opened a file merely to look at it and ignored the embedded tag in doing so, it should count as a change to the file. We could not close it without being prompted to save nonexistent changes.

Most Photoshop users, who don't have to open CMYK files coming in from strangers, weren't affected. It did, however, make the program unusable for commercial printers. When they open a client's CMYK file for inspection, or placement into a page-layout program, they *have* to ignore the tag, as otherwise it will not preview as it is to be printed. Relatively unskilled people have to open hundreds of files a day in this fashion. Ignoring the waste of time in responding to hundreds of bogus prompts, if an invitation to save these changes were inadvertently accepted (and the default answer was yes, save the changes), there would be a record that the client's file had been changed before it hit press, which could be catastrophic in the event of a dispute over print quality.

Also, Photoshop 7.0, unlike previous versions, recognized a type of RGB "tag" found in the EXIF data of certain cameras. Nobody from Adobe investigated whether these tags actually meant anything, which they didn't. The tags identified almost all cameras as supplying sRGB, when they were doing nothing of the sort. Anyone owning one of these cameras could not batch-open files for inspection into the proper workspace without running into the same problem as the printers.

After I pointed out these difficulties publicly, one user posted to an online group, "The new 'Photoshop always complains if you don't have the composite turned on when saving in PSD format' and 'Photoshop always marks a file changed if you open a file and discard the embedded profile' bits are EAB (excessively annoying behavior). Fix that, and I may upgrade, but for right now I'm afraid that I'll take a pass."

Mr. Cox replied, "It sounds like you listened to Dan Margulis's piss and vinegar before getting any real facts…Dan's little rant should not be treated as a review—just a list of things that Dan doesn't like, and things that don't fit with Dan's narrow world view."

Jeff Schewe, a photographer who is closely associated with the Photoshop team, added, "While he's right that 7.0's behavior is different from 6, he's wrong that this is wrong (from his narrow point of view). The vast majority (in fact I can't remember anybody on beta who agreed with him) expects that if you open a file and do *anything* to it, such as ignore a profile, it should be considered [changed]. This was actually considered by many to be a wrong behavior in 6.0 and now fixed in 7.0.

"Dan's up to his old tricks of trying to spread fear and uncertainty. One can only assume that Dan's worried that his relevance in the industry is slipping so he has to make some loud noise to remain noticed. Take what he says with a *very* large dose of salt."

And when the votes were counted: The corrective upgrade 7.0.1, reversing the opening-is-changing behavior, arrived three weeks later. The other new item the user referred to, a superfluous warning each time a new layered image was saved without a file-bloating composite, was reversed in Photoshop CS.

The Adobe hostility to the printers continues even now. In 2006, Mr. Schewe disputed a user who was saying that preparing files for CMYK was somewhat complex. He wrote,

"If today's printing industry had half a clue, the problem would already be solved…For political reasons, I do not save CMYK files with a profile because I don't want to telegraph to the printer that I know what I'm doing—printers won't generally do *anything* you don't pay them to do so the odds are *real good* that if you give them a CMYK file, they'll just print it.

"Talk about using Photoshop's old and crusty Custom CMYK settings—which are way last millennium in terms of CMYK separation capabilities—is really unfortunate. Generally, I view old features in Photoshop such as Custom CMYK and Gamut Warnings as features Adobe was too chicken to remove, even though they should have. CMYK profiles and Photoshop's soft proofing have superseded those old features."

*   *   *

I spend two pages quoting these icons of diplomacy so you can see what type of attitudes you are up against, if you are attempting to get quality printing in the real world.

The suggestion of abolishing Custom CMYK, which Mr. Cox also endorses, is unabashedly punitive. That'll teach those printers for not liking Photoshop 5!

The ability to edit separation method is fundamental. Without it, there is no defense against registration errors such as the disaster of Figure 5.11. Without it, there is no defense against shifting of neutrals on press, as is needed in Figures 3.6 and Figures 5.7B. Without it, if we're not confident of the printer's ability, we can't change something like the

SWOP v2 profile, which assumes best-case conditions, to something safer, like the profiles shown in Figures 12.11. Without it, if we are satisfied with current results but are shifting to a new paper that certainly has higher dot gain, we have no way to compensate.

I quite agree that Custom CMYK leaves a lot to be desired, as might be expected of a product that was last improved in 1998. If Adobe would devote the two days of programming—that's all it would take, it's technically easy—to making a substitute that could edit anybody's profile in the ways described above, I'd be happy to embrace the new method. Right now, however, users are like the driver who has the choice between a 1992 Chevy that runs and a new Mercedes without an engine.

We will therefore spend most of the rest of the chapter discussing Custom CMYK, but we'll take a brief pause to discuss how to have better relations with printing firms than Adobe does. And before leaving this section, we may let Dashiell Hammett state one important rule about life, not just printing.

- **Rule Seven**: The cheaper the crook, the gaudier the patter.

Welcome to the Team

My late mother was fond of informing me that one attracts more flies with honey than with vinegar. With printers, you need a bit of both—and some discretion.

We assume that a printer has been chosen for your job. Somebody else did the choosing, since you yourself would unquestionably have chosen a good printer. The quality of this one is unknown, but one thing is for sure.

- **Rule Eight**: Like it or not, the printer is your teammate. You win together, you lose together.

Everyone who has ever played any competitive sport has been saddled with inadequate teammates from time to time. The winners are the ones who get the best performances out of the poorer performers. The winners find out what their teammates are capable of, and what is too difficult for them. If no information is available, winners don't risk the game by assuming that anybody else is as good as they are.

Your teammate is going to have to put the ink on the paper, that's for sure. You need to assess what the probabilities are of his doing it accurately. If you think the chances are not very good, then go into full defensive mode. Give files that are as bulletproof as they can be, even if that means they won't look as good if printed well.

Also, go into the game with the assumption that your teammate cannot help you with file preparation. Most printers can't—they know how to match their own proofs, but not how to convert files so that the proof looks like the RGB original.

But if they do happen to know, what a boon to the team, particularly if they are willing to share the information! Many printers are—the only trick is to figure out whether the information is worth anything.

If you are one of the ones who demanded this chapter, it's probably because you are to some extent intimidated by having to adjust to a process that you don't fully understand. Just when you think you're getting a handle on things, the printer's customer service rep starts whipping out terms like *slur* or *wet trap* as if you are expected to understand them.

When this happens, do you say you don't understand? Or do you, like most people, nod your head in embarrassment and hope that nobody realizes how ignorant you are?

Printers are, surprisingly enough, human beings also. They are subject to the same emotional pressures you are. If you ask them something that they don't know—like what kind of dot gain to insert in your Custom CMYK—some will do the right thing and say they don't have any notion. Others will, 100^M100^Y-faced, make up something. Still others may actually know the answer and give you information you can use. It's up to you to sort it out.

Unless you go on a press check, the chances of your being permitted to talk to any of the purported craftsmen is small. Pressmen are notorious for saying things to clients that had best be left unsaid, so you'll probably be stuck with a salesperson or a CSR, if in fact you're allowed to talk to anybody at all.

The Investigation Proceeds

Even if you're not allowed to speak to the printer, and are not able to locate anyone who can give you references, you should still be able to find something on the Web. The type of work a printer does offers a hint as to quality level. A magazine printer probably adheres to higher standards than one specializing in books, because book publishers rarely reject product for color, but magazine advertisers do. A commercial printer who does corporate work is likely to be better than either. A book printer who claims to do a lot of coffee-table products may be better than the average book printer. This is a start.

Printers who publish the specific models of presses they run are more likely to be using modern equipment than those who don't. While the basic technology is the same, modern presses often have more sophisticated on-the-fly controls that help reduce variation.

If the printer publishes any kind of file preparation guide, you can probably get it even if you yourself are not permitted to speak to the printer. Chances are, this documentation will not be very good. If it advocates that you use Photoshop default separations, or if it tells you what RGB definition to use while insisting that you submit CMYK files, you can safely ignore it.

At the opposite extreme, I once received a package from a commercial printer that I would have liked to put on this CD, but they won't give me permission. It is dated 2004, and contains PDFs describing color management settings in Acrobat, Illustrator, InDesign, Photoshop, and QuarkXPress. It adds instructions on how to make press PDFs in one version of InDesign, two of Acrobat Distiller, and three of Quark. Then come 42 different CMYK profiles (for gloss coated, matte coated, and uncoated stock, each for 70-pound and higher and 60-pound and lower paper, each with several GCR variants, plus grayscale conversions for each condition). There is a large spreadsheet summarizing the aim points (for example, the desired shadow value) for each of these profiles.

The existence of such a document is a strong indication of the possibility of intelligent life on this printer's planet. Certainly, it could have been assembled by some renegade who is no longer with the company. And this printer would not be the first to have a good prepress department and incompetent pressmen. But preparing for print is a series of gambles. If this is all I have to go on, instead of moving my files a skosh in the safe direction, my gamble would be to cut it down to a weenzie.

The Personal Touch

CSRs are trained to be polite, respectful, and helpful. They are taught how to make small talk to put the client at ease. This training is given them not because the printing company wishes to give them a break from the tedium of their everyday job, but because it has been found that clients are more cooperative when treated that way.

Take a tip from this. CSRs are human, too. You want them to cooperate. You also want them to respond to your complaints. The surest way to prevent this is to complain about things over which they have no control.

Do not ask for a copy of their instructions to clients on how to prepare files. Instead, say, "Those boys in the back wouldn't by any chance have anything that would help me with my Photoshop work?" If they don't, under no circumstances express ire or even click your tongue. There is no percentage in it. If nobody at the company knows anything about Photoshop, they're not going to learn it by the time your job runs.

- **Rule Nine**: You are allowed only a limited number of complaints. Make sure they are in areas—like print quality—in which the printer can actually respond.

The CSR is ordinarily happy to provide samples of the company's work. Make sure to ask for products that are printed on the same press you're going to use and on the same paper, or something close. Otherwise, you'll receive a copy of the most expensive job they've ever done, because quality stock makes an enormous difference. Having that sample may give you a strong clue as to the quality level. If the product generally looks good but one or two images appear badly casted or too washed out, bad printing is more likely than a file prep error.

The Holy Grail would be to get some of the files that were in use to print that sample. Look at it this way. Suppose that a lot of the printing looks like Figures 13.3B and 13.4B. The yellow-green cast could be the fault of bad input files, or of bad printing. The odds favor adding a skosh of magenta to every file in case it's the printing. But if you can get hold of even a couple of files, you will know for sure, and then you can jigger your files to take account of the probable cast.

I have been more successful extorting such files out of the boys in the back than from the CSR, who may know that they're confidential. I get to talk to the boys in the back because I call the printing company after hours, when the CSR is not available. I explain that I have an emergency because I have to show the work to my client in the morning.

It's helpful to know who the technical people are. The way to find out that, and considerably more, is to make it a practice to, politely and in a nonthreatening manner, ask a question that is too hard for the CSR. This will get you the valuable information as to whether she is inclined to bluff her way through, or to simply own up, say she doesn't know, and ask whether you want her to find out the answer.

I would start out simply by asking about the proofer. If she doesn't know the brand name, that's a bad sign. Then I'd ask whether it uses the same inks as the press does. If I am told that it doesn't, then I'll ask whether it lays down the colorants in the same order as the press, and what order is that, anyway?

The chances are that the CSR can't answer that, but if she can, and the answer is anything other than the standard YCMK, find somebody who can explain why they are using a nonstandard ink rotation.

Some of these CSRs are difficult to stump, because they've had production backgrounds themselves. If so, the following always works. Ask about the brand name of the platesetter, or whatever department you are interested in. She tells you. Now say, "Oh. Wait a minute. Isn't that the one where they just discovered the bug in the cyan three-quartertone when it encounters InDesign transparency?" Guaranteed that such a question will get you the name of the responsible party, although if you are sporting, you will call back half an hour later to explain that you had confused their platesetter model with a Linotron 202, so never mind.

Politicians Sometimes Tell the Truth

The world of commercial printing is a cruel one. Methods that play fast and loose with the truth or involve skoshing and/or other brigandry are reasonable responses. It used to be worse: in the age of film, I would, every once in a while, throw away one of the pieces of film from which the Matchprint had been pulled and substitute a new, lighter, magenta, this to cause the pressman to panic at the green cast and up the flow of magenta ink. By coincidence, these jobs always contained brilliant reds that benefited from having more magenta ink than press standards were supposed to permit.

If you consider yourself an ethical person who would never stoop to such tactics, ask yourself if you're honest enough, because there are two common areas in which clients forget to be honest with printers, and never realize how high a price they pay.

Every job contains certain elements that are much more important than others. Often it's one or two images; sometimes it's whole areas. For example, I don't care how badly the screen grabs in this book come out. Also, if any chapter is printed badly, I hope it would be this one, rather than one of those showing difficult color correction.

It is very much to your advantage to communicate such information to the printer. If you single out a couple of images, they're sure to get special attention. If your job has multiple forms, your honesty can compensate for an area in which printing companies are often untruthful.

Every printer I've ever worked with (along with every other service provider) advertises that it is staffed exclusively by quality-conscious, hard-working and conscientious craftspeople, who maintain the old world traditions of their discipline, etc., etc. Fair enough. But those printers who operate 24 hours a day (and most of them do) often tell us that it doesn't matter which shift prints the job, because they're all good.

Not to put too fine a point on it, this is a crock. Presswork is a skilled operation. There are no, repeat, *no* printers whose shifts produce equal quality. The best is typically but not always the first (day) shift, because the most senior employees get to work it. Sometimes the advantage is small, sometimes huge, but it's always there.

If you rate your forms in order of difficulty/importance, the printer may not tell you it's happening, but the hard ones will be scheduled for the best shift.

This book, for example, consists of 33 forms, 16 pages apiece. The 33rd form is black type only. I want it printed by the worst press crew, rather than letting them muck around with one that has pictures on it. The sixth and seventh forms, by contrast, contain the end of Chapter 3 and most of the LAB moves of Chapter 4. It's very important that these be printed correctly.

So, shortly before the run, I'll divide all the forms into four categories of importance, and give the list to the printer.

At quality-oriented firms, all jobs have some kind of color bars or other color reference outside of the trim area. The densities of solid swatches of each of the four inks are regularly measured to ensure compliance with the company's standards. Nowadays, an on-press scanner connected to a computer is likely to adjust inking on the fly. If that's there, even bad press crews can comply with the numbers, just as even bad Photoshoppers now can get good highlights and shadows.

Good press crews earn that name in ways that people don't notice, just as good retouchers do. Optimal measurements do not guarantee optimal printing. Alert pressmen see and compensate for changing conditions, and they also make changes not just when directed, but when they feel certain that the client will like the change.

We've seen such moves time and again in this book. How many times have I had to put in a disclaimer, saying this last move that I just showed is subjective? But how many other times have we looked at something that was indisputably the right thing to do?

Press crews don't get to make moves of quite the same magnitude that we do, but still they are entitled to more information than most clients give them.

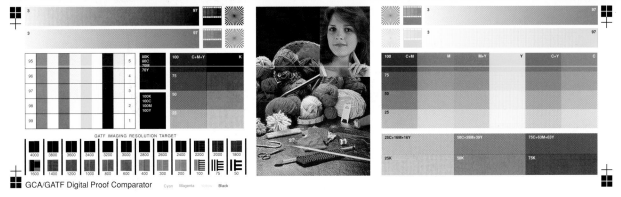

Figure 13.6 *A quality-control reference like this assists in accurate printing.*

Suppose, for example, that we give the CMYK file that made Figure 13.3A, and a copy of this book in lieu of a proof, to some other printer. The natural behavior of their press may not match the one that printed this book. If the crew tries too hard to match the woman, the background may change color.

It would be fine with me if that happened. I'd accept the background from any one of the other five variants of Figure 13.3 provided that the woman looks good.

The problem is that the pressmen lack a crystal ball. They understand that the background is less important than the woman but they can't take it upon themselves to declare that it's meaningless. Only we can do that, which is why we should clearly mark on the proof, "OK if background color changes."

The Gamma–Dot Gain Alliance

In short, we want good press crews to be able to help us with minor inking adjustments. *Major* adjustments, on the other hand, indicate that someone has done something wrong. It could be the file itself; maybe we submitted an image with such an obvious cold cast that it needs to be "corrected" by using less cyan ink. More likely, it's technical. If process control is poor, the press's performance may be different in one area of the form than the other, and the press crew may have to alter inking to compensate. Or, it can be the topic of the rest of the chapter: we submitted a file that wasn't properly prepared for this particular press because it assumed the wrong dot gain, and now the pressmen

have to go through all sorts of gyrations to try to save it.

Readers who are more comfortable with RGB should start by assuming that dot gain is CMYK's version of the gamma setting discussed in Chapter 12. The higher the dot gain, the darker the image is expected to print. If you Convert to Profile to a CMYK with higher dot gain, its channels must be lighter, since the *interpretation* of the file is darker. If you Assign Profile to designate a CMYK with a higher dot gain, it looks darker, but its underlying numbers don't change.

If you've been using one of the Photoshop built-in CMYK profiles, such as the SWOP v2 that we put through its paces in Figures 12.10 and 12.11, the dot gain setting is invisible, fixed, unchangeable. If you need to change the setting, you have to use Custom CMYK to generate an entirely new profile.

Let's now discuss the ways in which dot gain is *not* like gamma, along with some ways in which Convert to Profile and Assign Profile have different ramifications in CMYK.

- Gamma is a computer-generated adjustment that follows a predictable form. Dot gain is a physical phenomenon, difficult to measure, and idiosyncratic.
- For our purposes, gamma is always the same in all three RGB channels. Dot gain is never the same in all four CMYK channels.
- Converting from one RGB to another is painless. Converting from one CMYK to another may not be accurate, and will certainly generate a new black channel, which may not be desirable for the particular image.

- For RGB files that eventually will go into CMYK, assigning a new gamma changes appearance but in effect changes the output as well—the new profile will be taken into account when the file is translated into CMYK. Assigning a new dot gain to a CMYK file changes appearance on screen, but that's all. CMYK files undergo no further translation, so the output will look exactly the same as if the new dot gain had never been assigned.

- Although gammas can be of any value between .75 and 3.0, in the real world it's unusual to see anything other than 1.8 or 2.2. Dot gains range from roughly 10% to 40%, and can be anything in between.

- Few people use more than one RGB setting for files they generate themselves, although they may honor embedded tags in documents they receive from others. People who do business with many printers, however, often have many CMYK settings.

- And most important: we rarely *convert* anything into our own RGB—the definition simply gets assigned to incoming files. But we always have to convert into our own CMYK settings. You can't assign a CMYK profile to an RGB document.

Voting for a Change

Image: Mode>CMYK is such a simple command that it can hide the inadequacies of our CMYK setting. If you are consistently being disappointed with the way your CMYK files turn out in print (and this includes situations where the output device is not a press), consider the possibility that the culprit is your CMYK working space.

If it is, you will be able to detect a pattern. If some images come out too light and others too dark, some too green and some too orange, then you're dealing with a tribe of baboons like the ones who printed Figure 13.5. But if almost every printed image strikes you as, say, too dark, then the onus is on you. Your dot gain setting is too low.

- **Rule Ten**: A series of images that are unsatisfactory in a predictable way is ordinarily the fault of the client, while if the defect is unpredictable it is the fault of the printer.

Asking the printer for advice is quite useless. Not only do most printers not know what their typical dot gain is—why should they?—those that do know frequently understate it. Higher dot gains are commonly associated with poorer printing, so certain printers are embarrassed to speak the truth.

From our perspective, dot gain is what it is. If somebody is going to mislead us about it, it's much better that we think it's too high than too low. If we submit a file that's too light (because we expect more dot gain than is actually the case), the pressmen will add ink to compensate. This will close up shadow detail—which may or may not be critical, depending on the image. It is still possible we'll be satisfied. If the image we send is too dark, on the other hand, they'll have to cut inking back. When they do, our shadows will look cheesy and the overall appearance will definitely be too flat.

If you find you need a new CMYK workspace, your three choices are to buy profile-editing software from a third party, hire a consultant to make you a new setting, or use Custom CMYK.

The providers of the first two options would have you believe that this is a highly scientific process that requires, at the very least, a spectrophotometer. And, as you have seen, Adobe suggests that if you use Custom CMYK, you are a dinosaur.

This is all politics. Do you need a spectrophotometer to tell you whether your images look consistently too dark? Do you think it's a reasonable request that Photoshop should be able to lighten its separations if that's what you need? Do you think it's technically too difficult for Adobe to code a separation module better than the one it developed in 1992?

Anyhow, Custom CMYK consists of two halves. The bottom pertains to black generation and total ink limit. We covered that in Chapter 5. The top half is about dot gain and, if you are ambitious, ink formulations.

There's no urgent reason for you to know the technical definition of dot gain any more than there is to know the technical definition of gamma. In both, the higher the setting, the darker the appearance, and the lighter the conversion has to be to compensate.

If you care, however, whenever liquid hits paper, some of it is absorbed. The more absorbent the paper, the more the liquid spreads; this is how Procter & Gamble, the manufacturer of Bounty paper towels, makes a great deal of money.

The above rule of physics is not suspended just because the liquid happens to be ink. If our Photoshop file calls for a 50% dot, that's what will appear on the plate, in theory—neat little squares, neatly covering exactly half the area, leaving half blank.

A lot more than half of the surface area of the paper will be covered when the ink actually hits it and spreads. Compare the printed piece to the plate, and it will appear darker. And the more absorbent (read: the cheaper) the paper, the darker the effect will be.

The technical definition of dot gain is mathematically repulsive: the amount (not the percentage) by which a 50% dot appears to increase, as measured by a complicated formula known as the Murray-Davies equation. 20% dot gain means that a 50% dot appears to cover 70% of the paper.

Commercial printing on coated paper has dot gains between 15% and 25%. Uncoated paper, which absorbs more ink, tends to be about 5% higher than coated. Newsprint dot gains range from 30% to 40%.

To get an idea of what these numbers mean—and also what is considered acceptable variation in commercial printing—I

previously suggested comparing Figure 12.2A (assigned profile of Apple RGB) to 12.2F (same file with sRGB assigned). The difference between the two as printed is the equivalent of around 6% dot gain. That is, if you were after the look of Figure 12.2A and separated it on the assumption that dot gain was 20% when it actually was 26%, your screen preview would look fine, but in print you'd get something similar to Figure 12.2F.

SWOP's standard dot gain is 22%, but it has a tolerance of 3% in either direction. So, if you were looking for Figure 12.2A but got 12.2F instead, you'd be entitled to gripe, because it's outside the stated tolerance. But if what you were looking for was halfway between the two, then either Figure 12.2A or 12.2F is acceptable, as both fall inside the permissible area.

Appalling, isn't it, that on two different days you could get these two results from the same printer, and still have both be considered correct according to industry practice? This is why listening to all the palaver about precision measurements and embedded tags and brain-dead printers is ultimately a waste of time. A CMYK setting that's close is good enough, because exact is a contradiction in terms if this amount of variation is acceptable, which it is.

Setting Up in Custom CMYK

You possess, then, several CMYK files that have, over a period of time, consistently printed darker than you expect. (If you calibrate to a single image or even a single press-run, that's certain to be the one that ran while the head pressman was out for a beer or on the day some lamebrain spilled black ink in the magenta fountain.) We also have to assume that you believe your monitor is properly calibrated so that your RGB files are being accurately represented.

● Open a few of the CMYK files. Have the darker printed results handy for comparison.

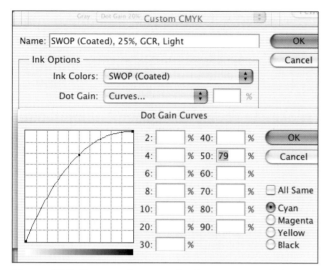

Figure 13.7 *Choosing Curves in the Custom CMYK dialog brings up a familiar interface. Dot gain is defined as the percentage of the sheet that a 50% ink coverage is perceived to cover, minus 50%. The cyan curve above calls for 29% dot gain, even though this Custom CMYK is set for only 25%.*

• Custom CMYK can be accessed through Convert to Profile, but that's a one-shot deal, more appropriate to changing the GCR setting for a single image. For dot gain maneuvering, go to Color Settings: Working Spaces>CMYK>Custom CMYK. If you've never made a Custom CMYK setting before, you're looking at the default settings of Photoshop 5: dot gain at 20%, Medium GCR, 100% maximum black, 300% total ink limit, 0% UCA. Chapter 5 explains why Light GCR with 85% black ink limit are better choices.

• Ink Options: Ink Colors defaults to SWOP (Coated), which is probably what you want. There are 11 other options, the most useful of which are settings for newsprint and for uncoated stock. Choose the setting most appropriate for your work.

• Optional information for experts only. By choosing Custom in Ink Colors, you can edit LAB or xyY values of the inks, starting with the values of whatever was in Ink Colors before, SWOP (Coated) by default. Do *not* attempt to enter these numbers based on machine measurements. The engine is old; the numbers are kludged. If you want a yellower magenta ink, then increase its B value by a skosh. I used to reduce the saturation of most inks in this menu, lying to Photoshop to force it to produce more colorful separations. Now, I'm more inclined to just correct in LAB. Again, stay away from these settings unless you're brave.

• When satisfied with all settings except Dot Gain, click OK to both Custom CMYK and Color Settings. Naturally, you have a backup copy of your original settings in case you need to restore them later.

• Now that the other changes to the dialog are locked in, reopen Custom CMYK and increase the dot gain setting until the image previews start to match the printed pieces. Ignore color issues; you're looking only for overall darkness. Concentrate on the midtones; that's where dot gain is most pronounced. When you think you're close, click OK and exit Color Settings. Carefully examine the open images, toggling back and forth to the previous setting with Command–Z, to see whether you want to go back and add or subtract a point or two from your new dot gain

The Bottom Line

Preparing files for commercial printing is difficult because of the likelihood of unexpected variation on press. As bad printing is frequently blamed on bad file preparation or bad photography, the field is highly politicized, with lots of name-calling.

Printers are frequently lambasted for poor color management, but an output comparison indicates that commercial printers are closer than photo labs are to a uniform standard. The problem, instead, is one of process control, day-to-day variation.

This sad reality means that we must prepare files defensively, guarding against certain errors that we think would ruin the image.

Altering expected dot gain in separation settings is an important element in file preparation. Unfortunately, the only way to do so within Photoshop is to use the elderly Custom CMYK dialog.

setting. When satisfied, reopen the Custom CMYK dialog.

- Let's say you have decided that 25% is the proper setting. Now, under Ink Options: Dot Gain, change Standard to Curves, bringing up the dialog of Figure 13.7. The cyan curve has a single point bringing 50% up to 79%. By the definition given above, that's a 29% dot gain, whereas you have specified 25%. This is a bug in Custom CMYK, which always tries to set cyan dot gain four points higher than the others. There are no printing conditions on this planet for which such a treatment is correct.

- In real life, dot gain is slightly heavier in darker inks. A good general policy is to make the magenta dot gain one point heavier than the cyan, the yellow one point lighter, and the black four points heavier. In our example, we should change the 50% point to 75% on the cyan curve, 76% on the magenta, 74% on the yellow, and 79% on the black.

- Click OK and reevaluate. Occasionally you will want to make further adjustments for color, not darkness. It is fairly common to see magenta printed consistently too heavily. If your printed pieces still look warmer than your screen, you may wish to increase magenta dot gain even further, or adjust its curve in places other than the 50% point.

- Type in a descriptive name, perhaps the name of the printer for which you have created the setting. When finished, click OK to Custom CMYK but leave the Color Settings dialog open. Your CMYK workspace should now reflect the newly assigned name. Change it to Save CMYK (note: this is not the same as hitting Save in the Color Settings dialog). You will be prompted to save into the folder that contains other profiles.

Congratulations! You have now created an ICC profile, one that can be used as often as you like. Even if you change your CMYK definition to something else, the profile you just made remains accessible.

Making Use of the Settings

Having these Custom CMYK profiles around means that you can target your separations to different printing conditions easily. For example, many high-volume digital copiers like CMYK files. These machines compete with presses, but they don't behave exactly like them. You can have one Custom CMYK setting for the copier, another for the press.

Even if you have an existing profile that you like, I'd recommend making the 25% dot gain one that we just discussed, and also a 20% dot gain one, for reasons very much in line with the title of this chapter.

If you are preparing for web offset, make the separation into CMYK as you usually would. Then assign SWOP v2, if that's not the

Merging Custom CMYK And "Uneditable" Profiles

CMYK profiles from third-party software are of limited utility in a professional context because they can't be edited. Not having added such editing a long time ago puts Adobe, in my opinion, squarely in the company of the printer responsible for Figure 13.5, but as in that lamentable case, we have to make do. A cumbersome method (but one that can be scripted for batch processing) of merging the flexibility of Custom CMYK with the potentially superior color of the canned profile is as follows:

Luminosity layers in CMYK compute the CMY channels and the black separately. If you would like to use, say, the SWOP v2 or some third-party profile for color accuracy, but you need a heavier GCR or a different total ink limit, make a Custom CMYK separation that does those things and paste it as a luminosity layer on top of the normal separation. The darker black on the top layer totally replaces the lighter one on the bottom. The CMY on the bottom layer is recomputed to retain color but match the darkness of the top layer. The result is a lighter CMY, since the top layer's CMY is light to accommodate the heavier black. The resulting total ink will be similar, though not identical to, the total ink of the top layer.

method you used. Then assign the 20% dot gain profile and then the 25%.

All of this assigning has no impact on the printed result, because nobody is going to do any further translations. It does, however, change the screen preview, which gives you a good idea of what might happen when ink hits paper. These three profiles pretty much bracket the possibilities. A good printer might produce something that looks like any one of the three, just because of normal variation.

You should ask yourself not which one of the three you like best, because you're going to get what you're going to get. You should ask yourself whether any of the three are particularly offensive. If so, you should assume the

Figure 13.8 *These randomly ordered images derive from a single RGB file. One was separated with SWOP v2, the other five with the Custom CMYK settings in the box on the facing page. Can you match the separation setting with its image?*

worst, and correct away from the potential problem. For example, we saw in the last chapter that SWOP v2 makes purpler blues than other profiles do. If your file features important blues, assigning either Custom CMYK profile will hint at whether you are in trouble. If the blues still look acceptable, you have no problem; otherwise you take insurance by reducing magenta.

Assign Profile, again, does nothing after the file is in CMYK. Convert to Profile, however, changes everything. Here's a quiz.

Figure 13.8 uses the same original file as Figure 12.2 did. It's in the Chapter 12 folder on the CD if you wish to follow along. First, as the RGB file has no tag, I assigned Color-Match RGB. I then separated it in six different ways, five Custom CMYKs plus SWOP v2. The Custom CMYKs all use unedited SWOP (Coated) ink colors and the black settings recommended in Chapter 5. They vary only in dot gain setting. The five sets of values are given in the worksheet box. Can you tell which setting made which separation?

Clues That Dot Gain May Increase

Before revealing the answers, let's talk briefly about factors that might cause you to increase your dot gain setting preemptively.

First, dot gain increases slightly as screen ruling gets finer. If you are used to printing with a 150-line screen but suddenly decide to change to 175- or even 200-line, you should add a point or two to your dot gain setting.

If your paper is changing, check it out carefully. The smoother the surface, the lower the dot gain will be, and vice versa.

If the press is young, dot gain tends to be lower, for several mechanical reasons. And, if you've heard that the printer has a bad reputation for quality, that suggests higher dot gains, too. You may have to guess—but that's really the story of this chapter, no?

The quiz illustrates a little-appreciated fact about dot gain—its inordinate effect upon faces. The leftmost woman's white shirt doesn't vary much in these six versions. Nor does the center woman's dark hair. But compare the faces in Figures 13.8A and 13.8D!

- **Rule Eleven**: The biggest impact of misestimating dot gain is in fleshtones.

Dot gain saves its full fury for the midtones. The dots in light areas are so small that any increase is hard to see. In dark areas the dots already cover almost the entire surface area of the paper. But the range between 30% and 60% is strongly impacted. This is why the center woman's blouse and the large handbag are not as affected as the faces, even though all these objects are red. The blouse and handbag are darker. Magenta and yellow are too heavy for dot gain to have much impact, and cyan and black are too light.

When you see an unduly red face in print, then, it probably doesn't mean that the subject is embarrassed but that the person who separated the file underestimated dot gain.

In solving the quiz, remember that a

Worksheet for Figure 13.8

Each CMYK file was separated from the same RGB source. One used the SWOP v2 profile. The other five used Custom CMYK, assuming SWOP inks and the dot gain percentages for cyan, magenta, yellow, and black given below. Can you match each setting with its separation? Answers, next page.

Setting	Version
15, 16, 14, 19	
15, 25, 25, 29	
20, 30, 20, 24	
22, 23, 21, 26	
30, 31, 29, 33	
SWOP v2	

darker image implies a *smaller* assumed dot gain. If we've said that dot gain is heavy, Photoshop has to prepare a lighter separation to compensate for the anticipated heavying on press.

One of these versions assumed a drastically lower gain in cyan than the other three. That results in an unreasonably heavy cyan plate. Another assumed a drastically larger gain in magenta than the others. That makes for an unreasonably light magenta plate. Can you tell the resulting green cast from the cyan one caused by the other weird setting?

The two that look the most alike are the 22% dot gain Custom CMYK and the SWOP v2. You can tell them apart by the latter's characteristic purpling of the denim shirt. One of these two will be the most accurate rendition of the RGB original. We'll have to wait until press time to find out, but my guess is that it'll be SWOP v2, which tends to do a better job with reds than Custom CMYK does.

Realpolitik and the Skosh

Preparing a file for press is always a guess, always a gamble. Understanding the dot gain setting, and being willing to change it, is a fine way to improve the odds.

Yes, the concept is difficult. Yes, plenty of people create good color without under-

standing it. Yes, the methods of Chapters 2–10 will make your images look better whether you have a correct dot gain setting or not.

But, once you get it, changing the settings is so easy! What on earth is the point of having every picture print darker than the monitor shows? Why lose detail in the darker areas of every image because the original separation stank? Why have every face print too red? Why, when you can make the adjustment in seconds?

The crapshoot nature of the printing game dictates that we will be disappointed some of the time. But if you are getting disappointed *all* of the time, there's something wrong.

This chapter has run through some of the practical ways that you can reduce the chances of disappointment, not in the imaginary world where everything works like clockwork, but in the real world, with all of its technical problems—and politics, which we can now refrain from for the rest of the book.

Success in print depends to some extent on luck, but a lot is common sense. Remember that the printer is your teammate—you succeed or fail together. If you find out that he is skilled enough to be captain of the team, that's great, but if he is not, the role falls to you. Do not be intimidated, or you will let the team down.

If you know that your teammate is competent, by all means let him carry the ball. If it's an unknown printer, and you suspect that he might be better at image preparation than you are, you should ask yourself whether you like that situation and what you are prepared to do about it. And if you could carry the ball yourself but insist on forcing the printer to do it because you think he's unprofessional if he can't, take a look in a mirror, and ask yourself whether you are fighting for what you think is right or casting blame for your own deficiencies, and—whatever your answer is— whether doing so is truly in the best interests of the team.

Quiz Answers

Each version of Figure 13.8 was produced by different separation methods applied to a single RGB file. All images look the same on the monitor, because they are seen through the profile that separated them, but they print very differently. The higher the presumed dot gain, the lighter the separation needs to be to compensate. The SWOP v2 version can be differentiated from the others by its purpler denim shirt.

A	15, 16, 14, 19	D	30, 31, 29, 33
B	15, 25, 25, 29	E	SWOP v2
C	22, 23, 21, 26	F	20, 30, 20, 24

Resolution for the Multimegapixel Era

Today's professionals frequently receive images that have too little resolution for their intended use—or too much. We don't need as much data as we used to in the days of film. What is the impact of the amount of information on file size, and on image quality?

Shortly after dawn, the honeymooning couple awakens, but not for the usual reasons. Their oceanfront suite in Phuket seems to have become a bit more oceanfront than they had in mind: seawater is entering through the walls, almost to the level of their bed.

The thought that this is charming, rustic, and romantic ends when the husband looks out the window and observes their car floating out to sea, along with a good percentage of the rest of the village.

Honeymooners of this century, of course, carry digicams. Soon enough, they are able to find a dial-up connection, and are able to send their worried friends Figure 14.1A. The file size is 216 kilobytes.

Newspapers and magazines are like hungry wolves with pictures of the aftermath of a catastrophe. So attempts to print them at sizes for which they were never intended are common. They can be improved, but the quality of Figure 14.1B is only impressive if you have seen the source.

The original (among other, more serious problems) lacks adequate resolution for what I'm trying to do with it. Resolution is one of the trickiest topics in all the graphic arts. It casts its tentacles into such areas as the "resolution" of an inkjet printer or a platesetter, or the halftone screen of a printing press. The terminology is also confusing. For that reason, in past editions there's been a full chapter sorting out all the types of resolution, and suggesting more precise terms. That chapter is still valid and still recommended, but in this edition, we've put it in PDF and relegated it to the CD, so that there is more room to cover the single topic of the resolution of the Photoshop file.

This topic is more important today than in the past, because we are

A

being attacked from two directions: we get lots of files with not enough resolution, and others with too much.

On the one hand, clients today often want print projects prepared based on images that they've downloaded from the Web. The thought that these images are of much lower resolution than they ought to be

Figure 14.2 *The conventional wisdom suggests that this is the maximum size at which Figure 14.1 should have been printed. Do you see any of the defects that are so obvious when the image is larger?*

rarely occurs, and so we are forced to make the best of it, as we did with Figure 14.1A.

On the other, the claimed resolution of digital cameras keeps going up. Claimed capture resolutions of 10 megapixels are now common, and presumably 100 megapixels is just around the corner.

The word *claimed* is used advisedly. A file's *resolution* is sometimes expressed as its total number of pixels, but more frequently as the number of pixels per inch. The problem is that we don't always know the source of these pixels or how accurate they are.

For example, Figure 14.1B has a resolution of 300 pixels per inch (PPI)—which is greater than that of most of this book's images. A fat lot of good it does. The extra resolution was generated artificially, which does little to address the file's inherent defects.

The Many Types of PPI

Upsampling, scaling, and screen ruling can be confounding to the resolution novice, so I'd like to go slowly through what happened to this file.

As received, Figure 14.1A was 500 pixels wide by 375 tall, therefore 187,500 total pixels. To see how little that is, at the moment many consumer digicams are delivering around

Figure 14.1 *(opposite) Top, an original digital capture whose resolution is not adequate for printing at the size shown here. Bottom, a corrected version attempts to compensate for some of the deficiencies.*

2560×1920, or 4,951,200 pixels total, slightly less than 5 megapixels, a megapixel loosely being defined as a million pixels. As mentioned early, 10-megapixel models are now becoming standard, so the 188 (or 183, depending on your definition) kilopixels we have to work with here seem pretty scrawny.

The conventional wisdom for commercial offset printing is that the file's *effective resolution*—which is a different animal from its actual resolution—should be between 1.5 and 2 times the screen ruling. Magazines and books typically screen at either 133 or 150 halftone dots per inch; this book uses 150. Therefore, the conventional wisdom calls for a minimum of 225 PPI (1.5 times the screen ruling) and a maximum of 300. Our actual 500×375-pixel file allows printing at 1.67"×1.25" at the conservative end of the conventional wisdom or 2.22"×1.67" (the size of Figure 14.2) at the radical end. Unfortunately, the required print size is 7"×5".

We check the file's original resolution by opening Image: Image Size. Figure 14.3A announces a starting point of 6.94"×5.2"—at a resolution of 72 PPI.

Even at such a horrifyingly low resolution, the file is slightly too narrow. Also, the printer requires a *bleed*—the image has to continue for around four points, or about an 18th of an inch, over the left margin so that no thin white line can appear to the left of the image should the page be trimmed badly.

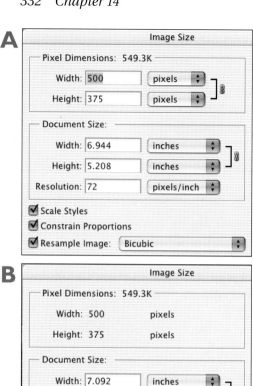

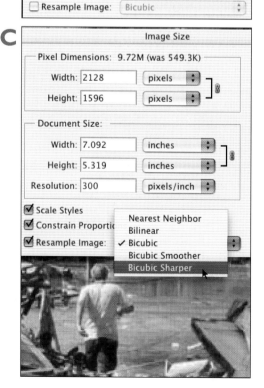

In real life, we would probably specify 102% magnification when placing the image in our page-layout program. To see how this changes the effective resolution, however, let's assume that we wish to change its size in Photoshop instead, and place it at 100%.

This process does not contemplate any physical change to the pixels—at least not in Photoshop. We therefore uncheck Resample Image. We specify either new image dimensions or a new resolution, and Photoshop fills in the other. In Figure 14.3B, resolution is changed to 70.5 PPI; changing width to a bit over 7" would have done the same thing. Anyhow, now that we've specified that the pixels are larger (slightly fewer of them fit per inch), Photoshop tells us that the theoretical size has grown to 7.09"×5.32", which we'll crop to 7"×5" in the page-layout program.

The next steps involve black magic and are largely hidden to us. A raster image processor constructs halftone dots out of this incoming data and sends a map of them to the platesetter. The RIP needs to fill the 35 square inches of this graphic with 150 halftone dots per linear inch. That's $7×5×150×150=787,500$ dots per channel—or around four times the number of pixels currently found in the image. Most RIPs insist on the reverse, files in which there are between three and four pixels for every halftone dot.

RIP manufacturers are secretive about how their products work, but often the file is resampled internally. This can be because the file is, as here, too small, in which case the existing pixels are made smaller and new ones are added by interpolation; or, less commonly, it can happen because the RIP believes that the incoming image is too large, in which case it is downsampled, resulting in fewer, but larger, pixels.

It is unduly risky, in my view, to allow a RIP to do major resampling. Nobody knows how sophisticated a method it uses. Meanwhile, Photoshop, as Figure 14.3C shows, offers five different ways.

Bicubic, which analyzes 16-pixel areas before generating each new pixel, is the default. The cruder Bilinear (four pixels) and the primitive Nearest Neighbor (one) are relics of a time of slow computing, when resampling via Bicubic could take a very long time. The last two, Bicubic Smoother and Bicubic Sharper, were introduced in Photoshop CS. They use an edge-sensing algorithm to slightly de-emphasize

Figure 14.3 *Top, the original resolution. Middle, changing either size or resolution while Resample Image is unchecked does not alter total pixel count. Bottom, resampling generates new pixels and a new file size.*

and emphasize edges, respectively. Granted that there will be later corrections, I don't think there's any problem using Bicubic all the time, but inasmuch as Figure 14.1A has lots of edges, I chose Bicubic Sharper anyway.

Where Did the Pixels Come From?

Before taking a camera vendor's resolution claim at face value, consider what you have just seen. By hidden resampling, you could construct a camera that spits out gigapixel, even terapixel files. The vendors jealously guard their decoding secrets. We don't know whether they're resampling, or how much blurring they're doing to try to compensate for the noise of inferior optics.

As the resampled Figure 14.1B indicates, the sheer number of pixels doesn't matter—the question is how good the pixels are. Thanks to the photographers who contributed files to this book, I've had a chance to look at several different models that all claim to deliver about the same resolution. Without naming names (because whatever I say will be obsolete in six months, as new models are introduced), some cameras look to me like they're delivering the kinds of real resolution they promise, and others seem to be delivering pixels of doubtful provenance.

To me, this whole area is one of the more discouraging in imaging, because so few people are interested in investigating the topic. Particularly, the conventional wisdom about how much resolution is necessary was developed in the age of scanned film. At that time it was basically correct, but digital captures are a lot cleaner. They clearly don't need as much. Nobody knows *how* much less, because, as far as I know, nobody has run tests.

The autumn scene of our next example is one of these 10 megapixel-

plus (3528×4704) files. I've cropped it in four different ways, yielding effective resolutions of 75, 150, 225, and 300 PPI.

The conventional wisdom suggests that Figure 14.4C, being 1.5× screen ruling, is as low as we dare go, particularly in images as full of fine detail as this one. I observe the following about these four variants.

- Figure 14.4A (.5× screen ruling) is seriously ill, but it is better-looking than Figure 14.1A, which is approximately the same effective resolution. Mostly it's because at this unreasonable magnification we can see some artifacts the JPEG compression inflicted on the tsunami image. But it also has to do with the quality of the camera and the photographer. One is shot by a professional with a professional instrument; the other is not.

Coping with Poor Resolution

Dealing with absurdly low resolutions takes time. A full discussion is beyond the scope of this book, but the basics can be summed up in a single sentence: add as many visual distractions as possible, and make the edges credible.

Creating loud colors is always desirable, because it diverts attention from the inevitable poor detail. This is a strong argument for working in LAB, because the A and B channels can be heavily blurred before attempting to increase saturation. Also, don't ignore the sponge tool. In Figure 14.1B, I used it to saturate the reflection of the man's pink shirt in the water.

The file should always be upsampled, because some retouching techniques—and a lot of the necessary blurring—will be obstructed by overly large pixels.

Everyone seems to have their own favorite method of resampling. I have tried several, and find little difference in quality regardless of colorspace used, or whether the resampling is done all at once or in increments, or in a third-party plug-in.

The Surface Blur filter (CS2 and later), which tries to recognize edges, can be very helpful, particularly in the L channel of LAB.

Be prepared to create edges by hand. During resampling, colors tend to bleed outside of the objects that hold them. In Figure 14.1B, I erased some of the color around the man, the flag, and the red letters to the left of it. And, as there was no luminosity edge between the man's upper body and the background, I drew one in manually, emulating what unsharp masking does.

Remember, Figure 14.4A is a tiny piece of a much larger image, whereas Figure 14.1A is full frame. That *should* give it an advantage, but it doesn't seem to. One way or another, resolution, though significant, is not as important as the other features of the images.

• It's unfair to compare Figure 14.4B (1.0× screen ruling) to Figure 14.4C, because the sizes are so different; of course the smaller one looks better. The real question is, how large can this picture appear before major surgery is needed? I am no fan of Figure 14.4B, but we've all seen a lot worse in print, and it hasn't even been corrected yet. I would be quite comfortable with a version between Figures 14.4B and 14.4C—that is, at a resolution of something like 1.3× screen ruling.

• If you don't believe it, go back to the

Figure 14.4 *(opposite) Sections of a single file, shown at effective resolutions of 75, 150, 225, and 300 pixels per inch. Above, the full scene, downsampled.*

woman pictured in Figure 8.7. I thought it was a particularly good example of how Blend If works, but in choosing it for this book, I didn't realize that the file was so small. As printed, it's at the same effective resolution as Figure 14.4B—1.0× screen ruling. Did you notice any problem?

• It is unfortunate that nobody has run full tests like this on a variety of different images. Softer originals like that woman give us some leeway; those shot under difficult lighting conditions may need higher resolutions. Plus, we don't know whether the camera that shot this image is more aggressive in noise reduction than other models. Tests *were* run in the days of film, and resolutions below that of Figure 14.4C got bad results.

• Preparing files for photo labs and for most inkjet printers appears to require the same resolution as for commercial printing. Some labs ask for 400 PPI, but this is overkill, possibly a relic from the days of film. As noted in Chapter 13, I tested a lot of photo labs with a suite of images for color variation—and also for resolution issues. The paper being used makes a difference—matte finishes generally showed a slightly sharper look that might require more resolution than a gloss finish would. But I had no difficulty with any digital image at an effective resolution of greater than 200 PPI, which is about the same as I'd expect for this book. A couple of images at 150 PPI showed barely the hint of a problem.

This last statement, incidentally, threw several beta readers, including George Harding, who reports that he cannot see differences on his own inkjet between printing at effective resolutions of 180 and 240 PPI. He wrote, however, "I was a bit surprised by the remark that matte finishes show a sharper look, requiring more resolution. Based on entirely unscientific observation I would expect that a glossy print would be able to show more detail and benefit from a higher resolution file."

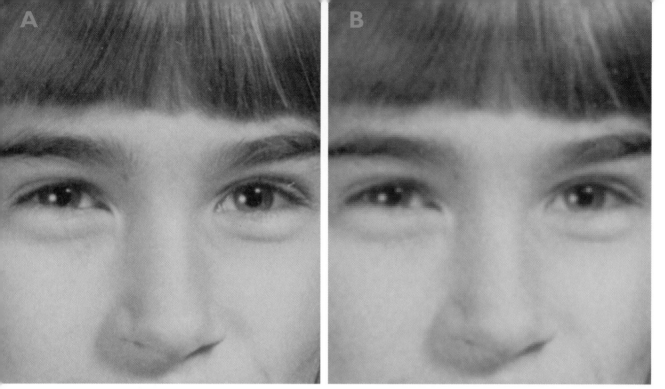

Figure 14.5 *These two images were printed from film at two different sizes, then scanned at identical settings. Left, an effective resolution of 100 pixels per inch. Right, the effective resolution is 40 PPI.*

Supporting extra detail is one animal and looking oversharpened is another. Inadequate resolution can be misinterpreted as oversharpening. The smoother overall look that glossy papers offer can tolerate a lack of resolution reasonably well—better than matte stocks can.

More Information Means Less Variation

The impact of resolution can be confused with that of unsharp masking. The artifacts that show up when we work without enough resolution are reminiscent of those introduced by sloppy USM.

To see why this happens, we need a direct, unadulterated comparison of the effect of two different resolutions. We don't have that in Figure 14.4 because the sizes are different. I have a couple of good examples, but we have to retreat to the age of film.

Figure 14.5 is a schoolchild's portrait, exposed onto film at several different sizes and then printed on a single sheet. I have scanned the sheet in a single pass and cropped one large and one small version out. Figure 14.5A is 2.5 times larger than 14.5B. At the enlarged sizes shown here, its effective resolution has been reduced to 100 PPI.

This means that Figure 14.5B weighs in at a paltry 40 PPI—far worse even than the tsunami scene of Figure 14.1.

A child's skin is soft, smooth. For the opposite effect, we turn to the busy scene of Figure 14.6. This was originally a 35 MM chrome, drum-scanned to two different resolutions. Again, the lower-resolution version is on the right. Figure 14.6B is correctly sized at 300 PPI; 14.6A is a 900-PPI gorilla. The roles are reversed when the file size triples. Now Figure 14.6D is an underweight 100 PPI and 14.6C is printing as the scanner operator intended.

These direct comparisons emphasize a concept that applies to much more than just image resolution: *The more information in the file, the more uniform the result.*

Smoothness is a virtue in a child's face and many other images. We have more chance of achieving that with a higher resolution, because of the law of averages. Pixels are not perfect. They can represent dust, a voltage fluctuation, noise, or intervention by space aliens, in addition to the occasional accurate one. The smaller the pixels are in relation to the print, the less likely that aberrant ones will be noticeable.

In Figure 14.6B, the resolution is almost exactly twice the screen ruling—two pixels for every halftone dot in both the vertical and horizontal directions, therefore four pixels per dot total.

Figure 14.6A has three times the resolution, but because of that same squaring effect, the file size is nine times as large as 14.6B. Furthermore, instead of four pixels per halftone dot, there are 36—six in each direction.

Even in an age of cheap storage (me, I once spent $17,000 for a 25-megabyte, yes, megabyte, drive, how's that for dating oneself!), excessive resolution eats space in a hurry. If you are using 300 PPI

Figure 14.6 *This film original was drum-scanned twice, once at three times the resolution (nine times the file size) of the other. Above and below, each scan appears at two different magnifications; the left-hand version of each pair is the high-resolution file. Above, the effective resolutions are around 900 and 300 PPI. Below, 300 and 100 PPI.*

where 200 PPI is enough, your file size is more than twice as large as it need be. At 400 PPI, it's four times as large.

The Law of Averages

Toss a coin four times, and the odds of 75 percent heads—that is, three—are pretty good. Toss it 36 times, and the odds of getting 27 heads are bad, and if you toss it 100 times and get 75 heads, look for a new coin.

Lower resolution is a move in the direction of action and variability. Resolutions that are much too low have so much variability that they turn the image into garbage like Figures 14.1A and 14.4A.

That variability is visible in both of our current example images. The strands of the girl's hair are well defined in Figure 14.5A. Figure 14.5B can't resolve them. The eyes, however, are big enough for its pixels to de-

fine—and that definition is harsher, heavier, than in Figure 14.5A.

Meanwhile, do you see the extra mottling in Figure 14.5B's skin? That's the impact of these rogue pixels not being averaged out.

On the other hand, we're looking at high magnifications, in which the pixel size is actually less than that of the halftone dot. I could show Figure 14.5B at a normal size, and downsample Figure 14.5A to match it, but it would be a waste of space. The variability is so limited that you'd be hard-pressed to tell the two apart.

Figure 14.6B tells a different story. It is printed at the size intended by the scanner operator, and comes out noticeably better than the much higher-resolution Figure 14.6A. The blue objects, particularly the feathers, seem better defined.

These feathers, unlike the girl's hair, are too tiny for either version to portray accurately. The enlargements, particularly Figure 14.6D, show that what we take for extra detail is nothing but harshness.

How Much Is Too Much?

In the pre-digicam era, the concept that too much resolution might be as bad as too little was well known. In the last edition, I showed a similar image, featuring a large grassy area. The individual blades of grass were too tiny to resolve, and again the more active low-resolution version talked viewers into thinking they were seeing more detail.

Given these results, not to mention the space savings, I've theorized for some time that it might make sense for digital photographers to deliberately shoot at lower resolutions by backing off their targets and then cropping. A digital camera, after all, is no more than a scanner with a variable focal length.

This being a subject of great interest to photographers, several professionals

---

Stumbling Blocks: How Many Pixels?

•**Stated vs. effective resolution.** Effective resolution is stated resolution divided by magnification. For example, a 300 PPI file placed at 110% magnification has an effective resolution of 270 PPI.

•**Resampling vs. resizing.** Changing resolution in the Image Size dialog only changes pixels if Resample Image is checked. If it isn't, the file's stated resolution will change, but the pixels remain intact.

•**Type and vector graphics** need much more resolution than photographs do, but it's a different kind of resolution. Type or graphics that are rendered into a photographic file can look jagged. This is why Photoshop permits us to keep separate vector objects within a raster file. For a full discussion of this topic, see the resolution chapter from the last edition, which is included in PDF on the CD.

•**Inkjet printers, presses, and viewing distance.** The rules about how much resolution to use antedate desktop printers and are usually expressed in terms of a halftone screen ruling, which inkjet printers don't have. For prints that will be viewed close up, it's reasonable to use the same resolutions as for high-quality offset printing. If the product is to be viewed at a considerable distance, however, the resolution can be drastically decreased.

volunteered to try to prove or disprove it. Darren Bernaerdt, Stuart Block, Ric Cohn, and David Moore each shot several series of images to try to come up with the answer, and deserve our thanks.

This extravagant expenditure of human resources resulted in a decisive conclusion.

You should shoot at the size that produces the best photograph.

The effect exists. Other things being equal, you should avoid shooting at a resolution that is wildly excessive for the intended use. Alas, other things are never equal. Even the slightest variations in lighting, angle, or any of several other factors outweigh the impact of resolution.

Figure 14.4E, for example, was one of several shots of the same autumn graveyard setting at different distances. Despite the photographer's care, the individual shots weren't directly comparable in the sense that the two halves of Figures 14.5 and 14.6 are. And so it was with all the other sets.

Our next example may illustrate the point somewhat better. Figures 14.7B and 14.7C are two separate photographs, each containing two pieces of jewelry. The client's intent is to reproduce the image at the size shown here.

The photographer shot Figure 14.7B as he normally would, zeroing in on the products

and shooting at the full resolution of the camera. This produced a file of 127 MB. He downsampled it by entering a size of 21 percent in the Image Size dialog.

The alternative was also an enormous file, which is shown downsized as Figure 14.7A. Figure 14.7C is cropped out of it without resizing.

As you can see from the original, I've had to rotate and correct Figure 14.7C to approximately match the color and tonal range of 14.7B. This doesn't affect the overall conclusion, which is that Figure 14.7B is better. The lower resolution of 14.7C works in its favor—

Figure 14.7 This jewelry was intended to be printed at the sizes shown below. One pair was shot close-up at the full resolution of the digital camera, resulting in a file size of 127 megabytes. The other is cropped, without resizing, from the capture shown at drastically reduced size above. Which pair is better?

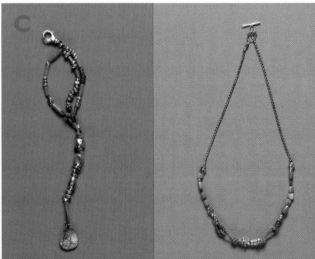

but it's outweighed several times by the slight lack of focus. Figure 14.7B is better because it is a superior photograph, not because of its extra resolution.

We have not even considered another argument. The client says that the photograph is to be reproduced at this size. The chances of her later deciding to repurpose it for some kind of output that requires a much larger file are not high, but they are not zero, either.

For these reasons, a sensible photographer should ignore the resolution issue when shooting, provided that what is shot is sufficient for the probable use. It's more important to capture the best possible image.

Double the Bits, Double the File Size

And, how big was the downsampled RGB file before being converted into CMYK for Figure 14.7B? (It's placed at 100% magnification, and the resolution is 300 PPI.) The answer: 2.6 MB. The original file had about 4.8 times as much resolution (100÷21). As file size increases with the square of resolution, it should have been about 23 times as large, or around 60 MB. In fact, however, it was 128 MB, approximately double what is expected. (Photoshop-format files use a form of compression, so we can't predict a precise file size.)

This doubling occurred because Photoshop permits files to be encoded (and worked on) in 16-bit per pixel mode as well as the normal 8-bit. For computerphobes, a brief technical explanation is in order before getting to the uses or lack thereof of this option.

Computers think in terms of binary objects, or *bits,* often described as 0 or 1, or as on or off: two, and only two, possible states. All storage, and all programming, is based on manipulation of these bits.

Take a grayscale image and choose Image: Mode>Bitmap. You're now working in 1-bit mode. The image is dithered into tiny black dots. It may look continuous-tone when viewed from afar. But it is a *real* black and

white: every pixel is either black, or it's white, unlike the grayscale images we normally think of as B/W. As the name suggests, they have many levels of gray.

If we reserved two bits for each pixel instead of one, file size would double. We would also be able to make a more accurate image, because instead of two possibilities per pixel we would have four: black, white, light gray, and dark gray.

And so on. Each time we reserve one more bit per pixel, the number of possible tones each pixel can portray doubles, and the file size increases. Three bits provide eight possibilities, four bits 16. The term *levels* is often used to describe these possibilities; in previous editions I have suggested *varieties of tone.*

When drum scanning was introduced some 30 years ago, images were captured as analog voltages, not as bits. Consequently, VOT was infinite—at least until the file got output. To do that (and scanners had their own output unit, which produced halftone film), the analog file was converted into bits, eight bits (256 VOT) for each pixel in each CMYK channel, 32 bits per pixel altogether.

As noted earlier, in those days computing power was prohibitively expensive. Using more than eight bits would probably have driven the cost of a drum scanner over a million dollars, but there really wasn't a need for more. 8 bits for output is still the standard, because it has proven sufficient. Even today, with rare exceptions, all output files must be in 8-bit form.

Most people believe, however, that 8 bits is not accurate enough for capture. Many cameras use 10 bits internally—1,024 VOT per channel. When drum scanners went digital, some of them used 12 bits—4,096 VOT.

So far, this is similar to the question of file resolution—extra data, extra size. The topics vary, however, in the following particulars.

• Photoshop lets us adjust resolution in almost infinitely fine increments, but gives us only two choices for bit depth. If we want more than eight, we have to use 16. If we open a 10-bit camera file, Photoshop tacks on an additional six bits.

• The impact of major differences in resolution is easy to see, but the impact of extra bit depth is almost invisible.

• Only now are we starting to question whether the large resolutions that cameras claim to record are actually capturing meaningful data—it seems that some do, and others may not. It's been clear for a long time, though, that cameras and scanners don't capture slight tonal variations as accurately as all these bits allow. In skies and deep shadows, for example, it's doubtful that any cameras are accurate beyond six bits, let alone eight.

What the Tests Have Shown

Whether the additional bits are helpful during the vendor's acquisition process is unimportant, inasmuch as we have no choices to make. If you work in Camera Raw, as we will in Chapter 16, you will be working on a 16-bit file. The same goes for the raw acquisition modules of most other vendors. The choice comes when the file enters Photoshop. If the camera or scanner supports it, we can open the file in 16-bit, and we can work on it there; we can also convert to 8-bit immediately. If we have an 8-bit file, we can convert it to 16-bit at any point. Presumably at some point all files must enter 8-bit, because they can't be printed otherwise.

Every method discussed so far in this book works equally well in either mode, provided you're working with a photograph and not a computer-generated graphic. Use whichever you like—there will be no difference of any significance. In previous editions, and also in *Photoshop LAB Color,* I've shown page after page of enormous corrections done both ways, including individual channels at high magnifications. And I've invited readers to pick out which was which. Nobody can.

Extended discussion of this issue has been consigned to the CD, where there is a summary of a controversy which went on for nearly a decade but now is dead in all but a few minds. Very briefly: in the early days of desktop publishing, banding in computer-generated gradients was a major headache. The problem was ameliorated by the expedient of adding noise—a few random pixels—to gradients, noise being extremely effective at disguising banding.

It would also have been possible to defeat the problem with brute force, by using more bits to define the gradient, increasing the available VOT and reducing the possibility of a gap showing up on output. That would surely have improved things, and some of us (yes, me, too) also thought that adding extra bits might make color correction more accurate.

Tests showed that there was no advantage at all—but not before Adobe had invested a substantial amount of programming time retooling Photoshop to handle 16 bits. Many commands (but not layering and most filters) made it into Photoshop 6; almost everything else was added in Photoshop 7.

Supporters of working in 16-bit made extravagant claims about massive increases in image quality, asserting a "night and day difference" that anyone could see. Such hype, we know, is par for the course in the graphic arts—it's no worse than what today's camera manufacturers say about why there is an urgent need for ever-increasing resolutions.

As it turns out, the quality difference is nonexistent. I have tested the concept quite extensively in the intervening years. Around 20 people, to my knowledge, have run tests similar to mine. The results have always been the same: no significant difference with any real-world types of correction, no matter how extreme, no matter how far-fetched the scenario. Those who advocated the workflow have admitted that they ran no tests and have offered no serious counterexamples.

Individuals frequently emerge online with a claim of personal knowledge of examples that *do* show a 16-bit superiority. I have privately contacted about 50 such people. Not one had actually tested the concept.

In summary, there is not, to my knowledge, anyone anywhere who claims to have an image that (a) is a color photograph free from massive retouching; (b) was manipulated in a standard colorspace, however incompetently, excluding only moves that are obviously intended to damage the image; (c) clearly looks better because it was worked in 16-bit as opposed to 8-bit.

If you have the space available, there's no reason *not* to correct in 16-bit mode if you feel more comfortable—but at this point the evidence is overwhelming that there isn't any benefit, either.

As to why there is such a decisive 16-bit advantage with gradients and none with photographs, I could go into a long technical discussion, and have done so elsewhere. But what is the point? If the theory were correct, it would be possible to come up with a credible example to back it up. Since it is apparently not possible, and a lot of people have tried, it is sufficient to know that there is something deficient in the theory.

Meanwhile, you shouldn't shy away from putting 16-bit to constructive use. Here are three important ones—two of which don't even require that you start with a 16-bit file.

Shifting In and Out of 16-Bit

- **Gradients** should be created in 16-bit. If you are inserting them into a file that is currently in 8-bit, there's no need to worry: moving them in and out of 16-bit causes no issues.

Important note, though. 16-bit does not solve all problems of colorspace conversion. Whenever possible, the gradient should be built in the destination colorspace. If the file is headed for commercial printing, you should be inserting the gradient *after* the file

hits CMYK—if possible. It isn't always. If you are preparing files for an inkjet printer that insists on an RGB file, then you're out of luck. When I was preparing Figure 11.5, I faced the same problem. I would have liked to produce the magenta gradient in CMYK, but the whole point of the exercise was to illustrate the problems of translating into CMYK. Since I didn't wish to have banding problems in addition to the ones I was attempting to illustrate, I prepared the file in 16-bit, and only converted to 8-bit after getting to CMYK.

- Some **proprietary raw capture modules** don't do a good job of converting 16-bit to 8-bit. They simply ignore the last eight bits when they export the file into some type of 8-bit format that Photoshop can read. This is like ignoring all numbers to the right of a decimal point when rounding to a whole number. We want $19.99 to round to $20, not $19. Camera Raw, among others, does this properly, but some modules don't. If you are affected by this problem, you should export from the raw module in 16-bit and convert in Photoshop when you are ready. Detecting whether you are affected is easy. A description of how to do it is given in the Notes & Credits section on page 500.

- **The march of progress** can create needs that previously did not exist. This book's contribution to that march is a series of maneuvers involving heavy blurring that will be fleshed out in Chapters 18 and 19.

We already have seen one move that requires use of a massively blurred copy to affect an image. It was the hiraloam (high Radius, low Amount) sharpening technique described in Chapter 6. We never see the blurred copy, but it's used in the background to create subtle haloing. We will extend that technique in Chapters 18 and 19, using enormous blurs to help us not just with hiraloam sharpening, but with layer masks, overlays, and the Shadow/Highlight command.

Figure 14.8A is the green channel of one of

these files. From it, the technique described in Chapter 19 required that I make Figure 14.8B, which is 14.8A inverted, and Gaussian Blurred at a healthy Radius of 50.0 pixels.

The result no longer has the characteristics of a photograph. Its transitions from light to dark have become perfectly smooth—like a computer-generated gradient. For the record, Figure 14.8B is not shown in Chapter 19, but it is the overlay referred to in the description of Figure 19.17 on page 466.

Gradients and other computer-generated graphics are first-generation. Their data is perfect, without flaw. Natural photographs—even photographs of computer-generated gradients—are full of raggedness that disguises any type of banding; this is one of the main reasons why all the tests are so decisive that there is no advantage in using 16-bit for the techniques shown so far.

Correcting *gradients* in 16-bit can create a better-looking result in the real world and can never create a worse one. (Correcting a photograph in 16-bit *can* theoretically be worse than doing it in 8-bit, although in the real world it never happens.) Hence, the recommendation to use 16-bit when constructing gradients, particularly if doing so outside of the destination colorspace.

The serious questions, then: is Figure 14.8B a photograph, or is it a computer-generated graphic? And is there any consequence if we choose the wrong answer?

It gets worse. As noted, I applied Figure 14.8B to my destination file just as you see it, and it worked fine. But now, suppose that for some reason a higher-contrast version were needed, like Figure 14.8C, which applies a big curve to 14.8B. In the upper right corner, you may notice banding—or maybe not. Presses add many imperfections.

I recommend that you grab the CD and follow along. You'll find the actual TIFFs used here to print Figures 14.8A and 14.8C. The banding will be evident on your screen, and if you print it on your inkjet, too. In this book, I'm not so sure. So that you can see the source of my doubts, I'm also enclosing a similar B/W print file from the last edition—it's identified on the CD as PP4E Figure 15.13C. It displays similar banding, which was evident on the proof. And on the plate, too. I know this, because I stopped the press and got underneath the black unit with a wrench in my hand to look. The overall darkness of the print matched the proof, but the banding was completely gone, even when examined under magnification, even after we changed the blanket, which is techspeak for something pressmen do when they can't figure out what the bleep is going on.

Getting back to Figure 14.8C, the problem can be avoided in at least three ways:

● Apply the blur after, not before, the curve. This would produce the much smoother Figure 14.8D.

Review and Exercises

✓What's the difference between a file's stated resolution and its effective resolution?

✓What is the traditional rule on how much effective resolution is required for a file prepared for offset printing? Why is the validity of this rule in doubt today?

✓What is the function of the Resample Image box in the Image Size dialog?

✓If a file's resolution is much larger than necessary, why is it preferable to downsample it in Photoshop before placing it in a page-layout program?

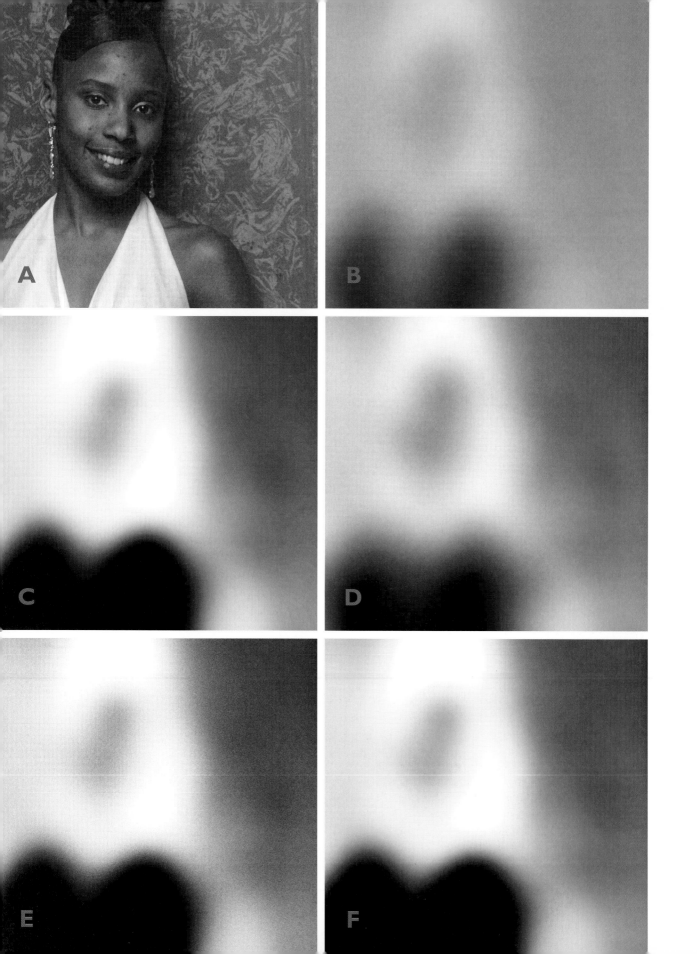

- Apply noise first, then the curve (Figure 14.9E).
- Save the channel to a separate file, convert it to 16-bit, then blur, then curve, then reconvert to 8-bit (Figure 14.9F). Or, you could just convert the entire RGB file to 16-bit and do everything there.

Final Food for Thought

Now, granted, I am not printing Figure 14.8C, I need it to modify a color picture that you haven't even seen yet. Also, I don't need something as extreme as Figure 14.8C; and even if I did, the texture of the natural image's upper right corner would defeat any banding.

Occasionally, however, photos have large expanses of very smooth areas—usually bare skin—that at least theoretically might be affected by such things. And two of the three antibanding tactics listed above aren't available against what hiraloam or Shadow/Highlight do with their big blurs. Should we use the third?

Chapter 19 happens to have just such a seminude image (the original appears on page 458, if you'd like to look ahead). Unrelated to that exercise, I've done two different sets of bogus corrections here, just as food for thought. Also, I did both corrections two ways. I had no 16-bit file to start with, but I converted the 8-bit original to 16-bit, and repeated what I had done in 8-bit.

There is no need to show the results side by side, because, as always, there was no visible difference between the 8-bit and 16-bit versions, even at high magnifications. But the pixels were not identical, and Photoshop lets

us augment detail in ways for which *drastic* is an insufficient adjective. The two versions of Figure 14.9 compare the 16- and 8-bit corrections—with the differences magnified literally thousands of times.

The "correction" that led to Figure 14.9A was a very steep curve, followed by a heavy conventional sharpen. The infinitesimal differences being shown here represent grain and other real detail in the image. There is no conceivable set of circumstances in which they could make a quality difference.

The differences in Figure 14.9B were produced by hiraloam USM (35.0 Radius). The effect is reminiscent of the banding of Figure 14.8C, or of various kinds of moiré.

As it happens, the actual Chapter 19 exercise involves not one but four massive blurs. In addition to hiraloam sharpening, there's an overlay, a layer mask, and an application of Shadow/Highlight. Could the four, in combination, provoke a defect in the skin if the file is not converted to 16-bit before applying them? Can this possibly be the one image, after so many years, that shows that something one might actually do to a color photograph undeniably works better in 16-bit?

I know the answer, since I've done the exercise three times, once in 8-bit, once in 16, and once in 8-bit with added noise. But my

Figure 14.8 (opposite) A heavily blurred alpha channel is similar to a computer-generated graphic and may benefit from extra bits. Top left and right, the original channel was blurred and inverted. If higher contrast were needed, the wrong way would be to apply a steep curve to the result (middle left). Better results are possible by applying the curve before the blur (middle right); by adding noise before the curve (bottom left); or by repeating the process in 16-bit (bottom right).

The Bottom Line

Traditional wisdom about how much image resolution is needed is not necessarily correct today, when digicams deliver smoother files than in the age of film. Files without sufficient resolution appear more active, sometimes offensively so. Drum-scanning film at very high resolutions has been proven to create excessively soft files. This chapter attempted to show whether a similar effect might exist in digital photography. The results indicate that the photographer should concentrate on getting the best possible image rather than trying to shoot at an optimal resolution.

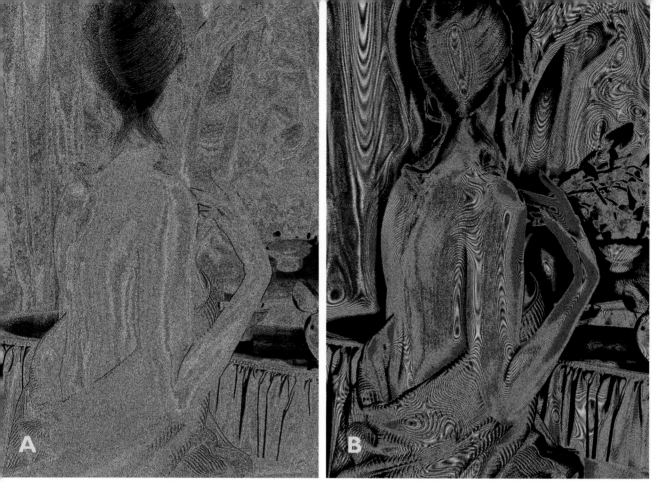

Figure 14.9 *Exaggerated several thousand times, these graphics show the differences in files corrected by identical moves in 8- and 16-bit. Left, curves plus conventional unsharp masking were applied to the two files, which were then compared. Right, starting from scratch, the two files were hit with hiraloam sharpening, Radius 35.0 pixels.*

lips are sealed, and I won't broach the subject in Chapter 19 itself. You can try it all three ways, if the topic interests you. But do keep it in perspective.

These blurring techniques have never been seen anywhere else before. They offer a dramatic improvement over previous methods. Questions of resolution (of which bit depth is a subset) are, as we have seen throughout the chapter, of almost no importance in comparison to what can be achieved through proper technique.

It should also be remarked that writing a book on color correction and doing real-world production are two different things. In the first case, I am not averse to creating three (or more) different versions if that's what it takes to understand what goes on. In the second, forget it.

If this exercise had crossed my desk as a live job, I would have said to myself, Look. I've done experiments with every category of photo and have never found one where there was the slightest benefit to working in 16-bit. This image, given how I plan to approach it, is absolutely screaming out that it might be the first. What do I care if it is or isn't? It costs me 10 MB or so to play it safe in this once-in-a-lifetime instance, not the extra couple of petabytes I would currently be sitting on if I had taken the advice of the 16-bit crowd way back when. So, I just convert to 16-bit, correct it, reconvert to 8-bit, and move on.

Speaking of which, as we leave this chapter on data and return to pure image manipulation, its lesson must be: in the race for better image quality, the importance of the horse pales in comparison to that of the jockey.

15

The Art of the False Profile

If an image appears too dark, it could be because your expectations are too light. Change the definition of RGB, and a Wonderland of possibilities opens up. Ditto for images with colors so brilliant that they lack detail—just find an RGB where they get it back.

fter a four-chapter hiatus, we revert to hard-core color correction with a dicussion of specific problems that have developed recently. As Chapter 7—converting color files into grayscale—served as a foundation for the following three chapters, which had nothing to do with grayscale, this chapter is the introduction to the two that follow.

We start with two questions. First, take a look at Figure 15.1, which, it goes without saying, is uncorrected. It shows the opening moment of a surprise party that so surprised the camera that the flash did not go off. How can you tell this is a digital capture, and not shot on film?

The second question is a quiz about a quiz. Refer back to Figure 12.2, where you were asked to identify various profiles that had been assigned to the same RGB image. At first glance, this quiz looks a lot like several others in this book, but there's one significant difference. Can you name it?

*   *   *

Politics pervades the industry, as we discussed in Chapters 12 and 13. We get blamed for bad printing; the printer gets blamed for getting ugly results from ugly files; the photo lab gets blamed when muddy shots print muddily. And the camera gets blamed when an amateur photographer produces something that looks like it was shot by an amateur.

It is therefore vital to camera manufacturers that the booboisie be able to get good-looking pictures with a minimum of effort. This implies simple, easy-to-understand setup, which is nice. Unfortunately, it also implies behind-the-scenes processing that improves the average amateur shot. Sometimes, it improves ours as well. Sometimes it scrambles it.

Figure 15.1 is a benign example. In a picture this dark, it's preposterous that the white stripes in the man's jacket should be blown out. They wouldn't be, if this photo had been exposed onto film. But the digicam's logic told it that every picture needs a white point, and one was accordingly wedged in.

Since most pictures depend on midtone detail, digital cameras, unlike their film predecessors, intentionally shortchange the highlights and shadows in the interest of more action in the midrange. Therefore, the detail in these stripes is suppressed. Inasmuch as there wasn't anything there in the first place, it's no big loss.

Alas, shadow detail gets sacrificed as well, which is unfortunate because the kissing man and woman are so dark that the camera considers them to be shadows.

Correcting this image would be technically difficult, but not complicated to plan. We don't care what happens to the light areas, so we just find a way of opening the shadows as much as possible, and then somehow address the flat, brownish color.

Our actual assignment, Figure 15.2, is just as dark as Figure 15.1, but not as boring. The shadow is critical, and on a wintry evening in Prague, we can't ignore the highlights. In the age of film, the blowing snow in the

foreground would have been far darker, and a single set of curves might have gotten us to within striking distance of where we want to be. But the digicam's logic has in effect broken this unfortunate image into two pieces, a very light one and a very dark one.

Before putting Humpty Dumpty together again, let's answer the second question.

A Word Means What I Want It To

In almost all previous quizzes, the original was identified and the other versions were variations. In Figure 12.2, six different profiles were assigned to the same original—but there was no indication of which was, in fact, that original.

The reason is that the original is whichever one you like. When we open a tagged RGB file, Photoshop treats it as if its tag had been assigned. If there is no tag, it assigns whatever our current RGB setting is. But no law requires us to accept either decision. We can override it by assigning something new, remembering that the file itself won't really change until we change colorspaces or convert to another RGB.

This chapter refers extensively to the Tweedledee and Tweedledum of color management commands, Assign Profile and Convert to Profile. Please recall that they are found in different places in different versions: under Edit in CS2 and later; under Image: Mode in earlier versions.

Figure 15.2 arrives tagged. As explained in Chapter 12, I personally open such images into Apple RGB. Like most overly dark photos, it lacks color.

We might consider, then, Assign Profile> Adobe RGB, which would define all colors as being more vivid than Apple RGB does. We can forget that option, though, because Adobe RGB is also interpreted as *darker*

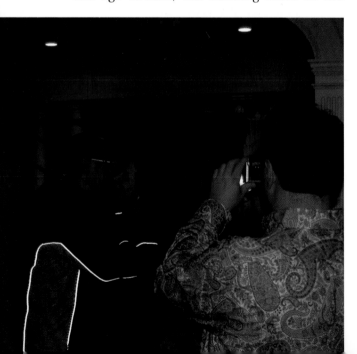

Figure 15.1 *Digital cameras often insert artificial-looking white points, like the light fixtures and the white areas of the man at left's jacket.*

Figure 15.2 *The image is too dark overall, yet important highlights are almost blown out. This defect in digital captures (it didn't happen in the film era) is best addressed by splitting the image into two halves and correcting them separately.*

than Apple RGB—2.2 gamma rather than 1.8. Figure 15.2 needs to get darker about as much as I need to go on a high-carbohydrate diet.

Speaking of which, my doctor, whose opinion of my lifestyle is similar to, but stronger than, my own views on calibrationism, once presented me with a spreadsheet representing the American Medical Association's ideas on the proper weight for a person of a given height, and asked me what I thought of it.

After querying whether the recommended weights were in pounds or kilograms, and getting the wrong answer, I replied that evidently I was too short. If I were a foot taller, I told her, there would be no problem with her spreadsheet.

Since her response was not printable, let me return to the analogous case of these two pictures. You think they are too dark. I reply, your expectations are too light.

* * *

Back in Figure 10.12, a Chinese river scene, and in Figure 10.13, a Norwegian forest, we created false separations—CMYK files with bogus black generations that we never intended to use in the usual way but only as a means to an end—to wit, channel blending.

Those exercises required creative use of Photoshop's Custom CMYK. There's also a Custom RGB, although most people aren't aware of it, which can be used to set up similarly valuable false profiles.

We are looking for more color, so we want to use Adobe RGB, which, as Humpty Dumpty once remarked, is "a stupid name enough. What does it mean?"

"Must a name mean something?" Alice asked doubtfully.

"Of course it must," Humpty Dumpty said with a short laugh. *"My* name means the shape I am—and a good handsome shape it is, too."

We will now proceed to make an Adobe RGB of a different shape. Or, rather, of *two* different shapes, because we need two versions, one that will produce something lighter than Figure 15.2 so we can recover shadow detail, and a second to produce something darker, to augment all that detail in the snow.

The Meaning of the Numbers

As always with difficult images, we start by planning where to do the work. We certainly want brighter colors, which suggests LAB. And critical detail is found in black areas, which suggests that we should be in CMYK, exploiting the black channel. Also, images as underexposed as this one are usually very noisy in the shadow, which we will need to fix somewhere along the way.

Before getting anywhere, however, we need a better starting point than Figure 15.2. The plan is to produce two halves, one for the highlights and one for the shadows, and then merge them together. There are several ways

to do this, some less complicated than (but not as flexible as) the one I'm about to show. This procedure assumes you've neither made such a false profile before on your system nor loaded the ones that are enclosed on our CD, as otherwise certain steps would be unnecessary.

- Open three copies of Figure 15.2. For convenience, they will be called Base, For Shadows, and For Highlights.
- Enter the Color Settings dialog, which is located in places that depend on the version of Photoshop (the keyboard shortcut, Shift-Command–K, is constant). Note the description at the top. If it's a Photoshop default, like the North American General Defaults shown in the screen grab of Figure 12.1, you can always reinstall it after you're done. If not, you should save yourself a copy of your full color settings (a .csf file) by clicking Save on the right side of the dialog.
- Change the RGB workspace to Adobe RGB, if that's not what it is already.
- The following option is only available when More Options (CS2 and later; Advanced Mode in previous versions) is checked.
- Change the RGB workspace from Adobe RGB to Custom RGB. The dialog in Figure 15.3 appears. It shows the basic settings of whatever the previous RGB workspace was, in our case Adobe RGB.
- Enter a new value under Gamma. For present purposes, choose 1.0. As soon as you do, the Name field changes from Adobe RGB to Custom RGB. Replace this with a new, more informative name, like Adobe RGB 1-0 Gamma. (Certain operating systems don't care for a decimal point in the middle of a filename.) The three images visible behind the dialog are now much lighter. All three look like Figure 15.4A.

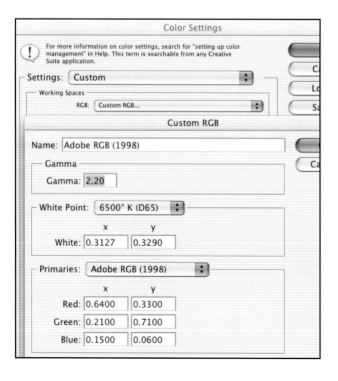

Figure 15.3 *When Custom RGB is selected in Color Settings, it brings up a dialog showing the current values, which can then be edited to create a previously unknown definition of RGB.*

Click OK to return to the Color Settings dialog. The working RGB is now shown as Adobe RGB 1-0 Gamma. Change it to Save RGB (not the Save button on the right of the dialog). You will be prompted to save your new profile into the place where all others are kept, which varies with platform, operating system, and version of Photoshop.

Since you have never OK'd the Color Settings box itself, click Cancel, restoring your original settings. All three images now revert to Figure 15.2.

Repeat all the preceding steps, except that when the time comes to enter a gamma value, enter 3.0 rather than 1.0. When this happens, all three images darken, this time looking like Figure 15.4B. Save this RGB as well, and cancel Color Settings again.

An Invitation to Play Croquet

We have just spent a page apparently accomplishing nothing. The three copies look exactly the way they did when we started, although we have demonstrated that appearance in RGB is transitory, ephemeral. The files first seemed to get lighter, then darker, then returned to their original appearance, all without any change in the underlying numbers.

Figure 15.4 Top, a false profile based on Adobe RGB, but with a gamma of 1.0, is applied to Figure 15.2. Bottom, gamma is changed to 3.0. The normal gamma of Adobe RGB is 2.2.

Plus, if we really wanted to make Figures 15.4A and 15.4B out of 15.2, quicker ways suggest themselves—or at least they did before we went through that exercise. We now possess some new tools.

Click into the For Shadows file. Open the Assign Profile command, and scroll down into a list of miscellaneous RGB definitions. The two we recently saved should now be among them. So, assign Adobe RGB 1-0 gamma and click OK.

Previously, the three files had no specific profile, so they were governed by whatever the RGB working space is. Change the working space, change the appearance.

Now, however, a profile has been assigned to For Shadows, overriding the workspace settings. This file now looks lighter than the other two—but *looks lighter* is a deceptive phrase. It's still the same file, because there's never been a translation—an important advantage in the next step.

At Figure 15.4A's size, it's hard to see the shadowy noise, but enlarged in Figure 15.5A the problem is evident. Getting rid of it seems to have nothing to do with the topic of this chapter. Let's do it first, and then discuss why it's on topic.

Blurring and Gamma

Killing this noise requires some type of blurring filter. Before Photoshop CS2 (2005), the options were limited. Several methods permit limiting the blur to relatively dark areas, but still may kill detail that we're not anxious to lose. Filter: Blur>Gaussian Blur or Filter: Noise>Dust & Scratches can wipe out the shadow noise, but at any setting high enough to do so, they wipe out most of the statue as well.

The better solution in CS2 is Filter: Blur>Surface Blur, which can be understood as Gaussian Blur with an edge detector added. The blur is disallowed in places that the filter thinks are edges, such as the windows, or where the light and dark areas of the statue meet.

The dialog is reminiscent of the Unsharp Mask filter described in Chapter 6. It has Radius and Threshold settings (and, one

hopes, someday an Amount as well). Unlike USM, however, increasing Threshold in Surface Blur makes the filter more active. The higher the Threshold, the less apt the filter is to classify something as an edge, and the more objects get blurred.

● With the For Shadows file active, create a duplicate layer. To it, apply Surface Blur at Radius 14, Threshold 9. These values are subjective, so you don't have to like mine; you can experiment with the full-resolution JPEG on the CD. My settings produce Figure 15.5B.

Where did these numbers come from? The strategy to find the right values is roughly the same as with USM: start with ridiculously high settings and fix them one at a time. So, start with a Threshold of 150, so high that you might as well be using Gaussian Blur, as Surface Blur won't recognize any edges at all.

Now, find out what kind of Radius it will take to blur away the noise. Then, start reducing the Threshold. The objective is to get it low enough that it sees edges in the buildings, but not low enough that it thinks the noisy pixels are edges.

● Leaving For Shadows blurry, switch to

Figure 15.5 *Left, magnified, Figure 15.4A exhibits noise in dark areas. Right, the Surface Blur filter eliminates it, along with much detail in other areas.*

Figure 15.6 Left, if the same Surface Blur settings as in Figure 15.5A had been applied to Figure 15.4A after it had been converted to 3.0 gamma. Right, after the conversion to 3.0 gamma, Blend If options confine the effect of Figure 15.5B to shadow areas.

For Highlights. Assign the 3.0-gamma profile, restoring the file's original look.

- Apply curves to increase detail in the highlight areas. This plugs the shadows even further, which means nothing since that area is coming from the other image.

But how? Remember, all these assigned profiles are merely tentative definitions. These three files all look different now, but if we were to discard the profiles (by Assign Profile>Don't Color Manage, which returns the file to whatever is called for by the RGB workspace definition in Color Settings), they'd all be of the same darkness. It wouldn't do, therefore, to paste For Shadows on top of For Highlights—the instant we did, For Shadows would be For Gotten, as it would become just as dark as For Highlights.

The look of the assigned profile becomes permanent only when we translate.

- Back to For Shadows. Now, not Assign Profile, but Convert to Profile>Adobe RGB 3-0 Gamma, being sure that Flatten Image is unchecked so that the layers will be retained.

For the first time, one of the three files has been altered, not just given a new appearance. For Shadows has been lightened drastically, translated so that *when looked at in 3.0 gamma,* the file resembles Figure 15.2. It can now be united with the much darker For Highlights, but there's housekeeping to take care of first. We still haven't restricted the effect of the blur shown in Figure 15.5B.

- Double-click to the right of the top layer's icon in the Layers palette to bring up the Blend If sliders. Use Underlying Layer, the unblurred version, rather than This Layer, because in the blurred top layer, the noise is indistinguishable from its surroundings. It is, however, darker on the unblurred layer. Move the right-hand slider to the left to exclude areas that are light. When satisfied, split the slider by Option–clicking it, and spread the two halves to create a transition zone to avoid an obvious break.

We have now reached Figure 15.6B, and For Shadows is ready to emerge from its rabbit hole. Time to unite the two versions.

Blending with a Layer Mask

• Return to For Highlights. Paste it on top of For Shadows, which can be flattened first if you like.

• Layer: Layer Mask>Reveal All, or choose the layer mask icon at the bottom of the Layers palette.

The task is to marry the light areas of the top layer to the dark ones of the bottom. Blend If is a possibility, but when, as here, a soft transition is imperative, it's better to use an existing channel as a selection. Here, that takes the form of a layer mask, allowing most of the For Shadows layer to peek through, while retaining the light areas of the For Highlights top layer.

Layer masks are Photoshop's most potent retouching tool. Where white, they keep the top layer intact; where black, they show what's underneath. Where the layer mask is

gray, we see a combined version; the lighter the gray, the more it favors the top layer. We have started with a white mask, meaning that we see the top layer only.

• As long as you haven't done anything since establishing it, the layer mask is the current active channel. So, Image: Apply Image, and apply something. You have a lot of choices—there are three documents open, and each has three channels and some have extra layers. Applying anything, including the composite RGB, to the layer mask will give approximately what we want. All these channels are much lighter in the foreground than in the background, meaning that the For Highlights layer will be favored in the foreground buildings and not in the sky.

Since Photoshop continually updates the preview, we may as well toggle through the various options while the Apply Image dialog is open. I had expected that the choice would be the red channel of the file called Base, which was why I had kept a copy open. I did not think I wanted to use For Highlights after I had applied the contrast-enhancing curve to it. As it turned out, I was wrong. So, I chose the RGB composite of For Highlights as the source. Apply Image doesn't let us choose the target; the target is whatever the active channel(s) may be. In this case the layer mask is what's active.

The merged version is Figure 15.7. Do you see a line of transition where the two halves meet? When masks are formed by existing channels, we usually don't.

The home stretch starts with the translation that finalizes the gamma changes we have been at such pains to produce.

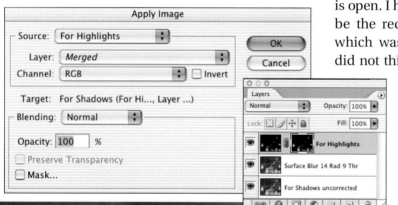

Figure 15.7 *After the For Highlights version is pasted on top of For Shadows, a layer mask merges the two.*

Figure 15.8 *After converting Figure 15.7 to LAB and applying the curves shown.*

• Convert Figure 15.7 to LAB, accepting the invitation to flatten the image first. At this point we no longer have to worry about profiles—assigned, converted, or embedded. There is only one LAB, and we're there now.

• Apply curves to increase color variation, as described in Chapter 4. The L curve of Figure 15.8 is aimed at increasing variation in the sky. As is normally best practice with LAB files that are headed for CMYK, I left the shadow rather light, intending to darken it later with a curve to the black channel.

The A curve emphasizes variation in magentas and greens, while moving the entire image slightly toward warmth. In the B, I felt that

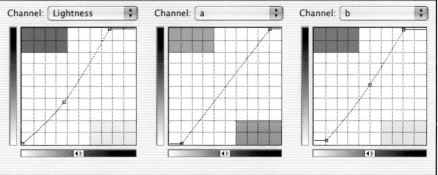

the whole image could move toward blue, away from yellow. The original sky was dead neutral. I think that night skies are very dark blue, B–negative, not quite 0ᴬ0ᴮ. These curves produced Figure 15.8.

• Apply hiraloam sharpening (conventional USM won't work on a picture this noisy) to the L channel. Hiraloam (high Radius, low Amount) is discussed in Chapter 6.

• Convert to CMYK. Apply final curves to neutralize the highlight (which was made too red by the LAB curves) and to add depth to the black. The final image is Figure 15.9.

I'll Be Judge, I'll Be Jury

The steps leading up to Figure 15.7 seem unduly convoluted. The case for taking them, rather than just generating two half-images with curves and uniting them with a layer mask, is as follows.

• This isn't the last ridiculously dark image that we'll ever have to work on. The next one will go much faster, because the false profiles we just made stay in our system forever. We just make two copies, assign 3.0 gamma to one, assign 1.0 to the other and convert it to 3.0, and merge. Crack the book's CD, and you can have many more options: profiles with the primary values for Apple, Adobe, and Wide Gamut RGBs at gammas of 1.0, 1.4, 1.8, and 2.6. A gamma of 2.2 is unnecessary because "real" Adobe RGB and Wide Gamut RGB live there, and because Apple RGB with a 2.2 gamma is close enough to sRGB for the purposes of this technique.

• If the image just needs to be lightened drastically, this method beats curves, which tend to blow out all light areas. Furthermore, there isn't any need to save backup copies: if we ever think we need to go back to the original, we just reassign the original gamma.

• Having these false profiles available is a useful diagnostic tool. Figures 15.10A and 15.10C, shot deep inside lush forests, appear just as bad as the Prague original, Figure 15.2. Can they be salvaged? The easy way to find out is to waste the two seconds necessary to assign the same 1.0-gamma profile used earlier. I'm not saying that this is the profile to use in an actual correction, but rather that Figure 15.10B indicates that there's plenty of available detail if we care to exert ourselves. Figure 15.10D shows that it would be a waste of time to try to fix 15.10C, as the trees are totally plugged.

• Most important from the quality point of view, working in two radically different gammas can sometimes be beneficial. The explanation is complex.

At low gammas like 1.0, the image is interpreted as being very light. If we *convert* a file to 1.0 gamma—not merely *assign* that profile to it—the underlying pixels must become darker, to compensate for the lighter interpretation. For example, a medium gray that's $128^R128^G128^B$ in sRGB or Adobe RGB (both of which are 2.2-gamma) converts to the hugely darker, if that's the word, $55^R55^G55^B$ in a 1.0-gamma space. It would be $153^R153^G153^B$ in our 3.0-gamma false profile.

This has big ramifications for the Surface Blur filter, which looks for edges. The objective was to kill as much of the shadow noise as possible while limiting the effect on the lighter parts of the image. As the above number indicates, shadow values in 3.0 gamma occupy almost three times as much space as in 1.0 gamma. In the lower-gamma setting, therefore, the shadow noise is only a third as far from the value of its surroundings as it would be at 3.0 gamma. So, we can set

Figure 15.9 The final version incorporates hiraloam sharpening and curves to the magenta and black channels of CMYK.

Surface Blur's Threshold quite low, allowing it to consider the shadow noise as noise but foreground noise as edges that must be maintained.

Compare Figure 15.5B, which was surface blurred not at 1.0 but at 1.8 gamma, to Figure 15.6A, in which the same settings were applied instead after the conversion to 3.0, and the quality gain is clear. And yes, I lied. In the interest of preserving your sanity, I said that I blurred the file after *assigning* the 1.0-gamma false profile, which would be the same as applying the filter to the original medium-gamma file. In real life, though, I assigned 1.0-gamma Adobe RGB *and then converted* to 1.0 gamma Apple RGB (we can't convert to the same profile we're already in) before blurring. That was the version I used to make the final merge in Figure 15.7.

Beta reader George Harding termed the above paragraph "border-line sadistic." He added, "This was the hardest going of any of the chapters so far. The discussion and explanation flows logically, and the explanations are clear, but that doesn't mean it will sink in on the first reading. It's a very powerful technique, though, and I can see using it with a lot of the files I have to deal with. The only change I'd suggest is including the step of converting the 1.0-gamma file before blurring it in the step by step explanation. Your concern for the reader's sanity is greatly appreciated, but the fact that we're traipsing through the world of false profiles shows that we're not worried about it. After grinding through the example, when I saw the 'I lied' paragraph my head damn near exploded. Since the blurring of the dark noise works better in 1.0 gamma it isn't really an optional step."

I'm leaving it this way, thanks. The key statement is that this is the hardest chapter so far. It's about to get worse, much worse, not just in my opinion, but also that of the beta readers who have finished Chapters 17–19.

Horsing around with gamma for blurring purposes is a move that nobody has ever heard of before, one that is minor in the context of the overall correction. If any heads are going to explode, they can

Figure 15.10 *Dark pictures aren't always unusable. Temporarily assigning a false profile can show whether there's enough detail to warrant going on (B)—or not (D).*

do so *after* we've gotten a good result with a difficult original, not in the middle of the correction so that we have to call somebody with a mop to clean up the mess, and then still have to finish the work ourselves.

We've added contrast with false profiling, so let's move on to color, with two examples that have not gamma, but gamut problems.

Curiouser and Curiouser

Back in Figure 12.2, the challenge was to identify which of six different profiles had been assigned to a single RGB file before conversion to CMYK for printing. This time, we use the same six RGB definitions, but the files have gone through Convert to Profile, not Assign Profile.

There is no point in showing the six color originals, which would all look alike after conversion to CMYK. Remember, Convert to Profile maintains overall appearance, while modifying the channel structure.

So, in Figure 15.11, can you identify which red channel belongs to which profile? Hint: this is a Chinese New Year celebration. The fabric dominating the right side of the picture is a brilliant magenta that's more or less the same color shown in the flower way back in Figure 12.8A. It will be very hard to hold detail in this area when it enters CMYK, which may provoke a sneaking suspicion as to why this exercise is included.

We'll be back to this little walk in the park later, but first let's turn to another original that was produced without the limitations of CMYK in mind but is suddenly confronted with the exigencies of that color-starved space. Figure 15.12A arrives in Adobe RGB. It's not as bad as the green lantern we saw back in Figure 12.4A, but the problem is the same. The orange in the original RGB file (which you can see for yourself on the CD) is too intense to reproduce in print, so detail gets lost.

Figure 15.11 (opposite) Red channels of a single RGB file that has been converted to six different profiles.

By now, we should know the final step. When we have a large, brilliant object that we can't make as colorful as we would like, we have to be sure that some part of it is as colorful as we can possibly make it. Such an orange requires values of $0^C?^M100^Y$. The magenta is a question mark because we don't know how much to move this color toward yellow or toward red. But whatever color we decide upon, cyan will kill it and yellow intensify it.

No conversion can hit exactly $0^C?^M100^Y$ in exactly the places we want. That commits us to doing at least some work in CMYK, so we don't have to worry about a modest color shift when we convert, provided that we have the needed detail.

The quick way of getting the needed detail is to assign the narrower-gamut sRGB before converting to CMYK. Figure 15.12B looks too dull because the fabric now contains a lot of cyan. This is an advantage. Figure 15.12A is so

Worksheet for Figure 15.11

Six RGB images were generated from a common parent, using Convert to Profile to bring each into one of the spaces listed below. The six composite color images look identical, but their channel structure varies. The swirling fabric is a magenta so intense as to be out of the CMYK gamut. The six variants on the facing page are the red channels of each file. Identify which is which. (Answers, page 363.)

Converted to	Version
Adobe RGB	
Apple RGB	
ColorMatch RGB	
ProPhoto RGB	
sRGB	
Wide Gamut RGB	

Figure 15.12 *Above left, the Adobe RGB original contains colors outside the CMYK gamut. Above right, prior to conversion to CMYK, sRGB is assigned as the profile. Below left, instead, the file is converted from Adobe RGB to LAB and the curves of Figure 15.13 are applied. Below right, after the LAB curves, the image is converted to CMYK for a final set of curves that force the brightest areas to the extreme values of 0^C and 100^Y.*

featureless because it's 0ᶜ almost throughout, which is what happens when we bring out-of-gamut reds and oranges into CMYK. The easiest procedure is to produce more cyan detail, and then lighten it with CMYK curves.

Something similar to Figure 15.12B could be gotten with Hue/Saturation in slightly more time. If you have a few minutes more than that, the best results without channel blending involve a trip to LAB.

After converting the Adobe RGB original to LAB, we should insert four fixed measuring points with the color sampler tool and take stock. Since we're concerned about what happens when we enter CMYK, we click the eyedropper in each of the six value boxes in the Info palette (except for the top left, which should usually be set to Actual Color) and configure them to show prospective CMYK, not LAB, values. The points should represent areas near the brightest parts of the image.

The L curve should attempt to add contrast. The AB curves are the opposite of the ones shown in Chapter 4. There, we were

trying to intensify the colors by steepening the curves. Here, we want to tone the colors down, so we flatten, being sure to hold the center point constant. (Beta reader André Dumas suggests locking the center by placing a point and typing in equal numbers in the Curves dialog—50=50 in this book's orientation, 0=0 with darkness to the left. He notes, "In LAB, even a fraction of a millimeter makes a big difference.")

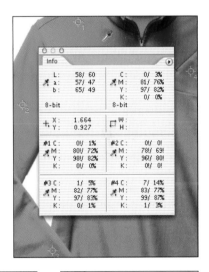

Figure 15.13 Below, the LAB curves that produced Figure 15.12C, and the subsequent CMYK curves that produced Figure 15.12D. Right, the Info palette during the application of the curves, showing how more cyan is entering the image to create more detail in the orange.

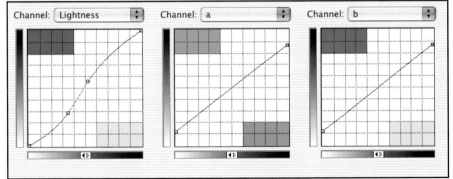

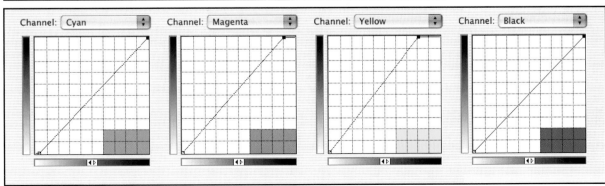

Figure 15.14 *The composite color image that produced the variant red channels of Figure 15.11. The magenta fabric is far out of the CMYK gamut. Detail is lost and color has shifted in this rendition.*

The top right of Figure 15.13 shows the four sample points plus the position of the eyedropper. This Info palette was grabbed with the curves open, so before and after values, separated by a slash, are shown for each sample point. The exclamation points in the left-hand sides of the #1 and #2 boxes indicate that the CMYK value is merely an approximation, because the color that the LAB file is calling for is out of gamut. Compare these two original values with the top value (see eyedropper for position), and it becomes obvious why Figure 15.12A is so lacking in detail. Two distinctly different out-of-gamut colors, plus another that Photoshop says is in gamut, convert to the practically indistinguishable: $0^C81^M97^Y$, $0^C80^M98^Y$, and $0^C78^M96^Y$. (Notice that even if we were willing to put up with this lack of contrast, we'd still have to go in after conversion and correct this, because nothing is quite at 100^Y.)

The LAB curves produce Figure 15.12C:

more detail than 15.12A, but lighter and duller. That is corrected after we enter CMYK with simple straight-line curves that establish the desired color. Since this is a studio capture, there is no reason to doubt that the original orange is correct, so we look at what the values would have been in CMYK if we had converted with no correction at all. The three values cited are close to 80^M100^Y. In the lower (CMYK) Info palette of Figure 15.13, we see several initial values that are lower, particularly in the yellow.

The difference between the final version, Figure 15.12D, and the original, Figure 15.12A, shows the power of the weak CMYK channel (in this case, the cyan) in creating shape. The magenta and yellow values are almost unchanged between the two versions. But the cyan in Figure 15.12A (in our five testing points including the present position of the eyedropper, reading from top to bottom in the left columns of the top Info palette) is 0,0,0,1,7. In Figure 15.12D (right columns of bottom Info palette), these values have morphed into 5,0,0,2,14. The extra orange-killing cyan makes the darker areas of the shirt more believable.

Return of the Red Queen

For another way to restore detail to out-of-gamut colors, let's solve the quiz of Figure 15.11, in which we were to identify the red channels of what is now presented as Figure 15.14, when converted to six different RGB definitions.

Differentiating *gamma* from *gamut* is the key. If you have done so, this is the easiest quiz in the book. If not, it's likely the hardest.

Three of these RGBs use 1.8 gamma, three use 2.2. The 2.2 gamma spaces are *interpreted* as being darker; therefore the underlying image must be lighter if it is to match the look of the lower-gamma versions.

The confusion comes in the portrayal of the fabric. Some of these spaces have narrow gamuts, in which this magenta is a wild color. It would have to be extremely light in the red channel for the same reason that a good rendition of Figure 15.12 has to be extremely light in cyan.

Resist, therefore, the temptation to look at the fabric first. Instead, concentrate on the dancer's hair. We know by her ethnicity that it must be black, or close to it. Black, being neutral, has equal values in all three RGB channels, no matter what definition is in use. The only variable is the gamma. sRGB and Wide Gamut RGB are as different as the March Hare and the Mad Hatter, but they should be nearly identical in the hair. So should Adobe RGB, and all three should have it lighter than any of the three 1.8-gamma versions.

That cinches it. Figures 15.11 B, 15.11 D, and 15.11 E are the 2.2-gamma spaces, and *now* we can compare the colored fabric in each of the three. The darker it is, the wider-gamut the space must be, as it can apparently accommodate even more extreme colors. So the lightest of the three, Figure 15.11 E, must be the narrowest gamut, sRGB. Figure 15.11 D, considerably darker, is Adobe RGB, and Wide Gamut RGB, Figure 15.11 B, is darker still.

Of the other three, Figure 15.11 C is obviously the darkest, hence ProPhoto RGB. That leaves the toughest two to distinguish, but Figure 15.11 F, ColorMatch RGB, is slightly darker than 15.11 A, Apple RGB.

Now that we've seen the composite, we know that the quiz is not just academic. Open the RGB original on the CD, and you'll appreciate what a train wreck Figure 15.14 is. This is exactly the type of image that frustrates photographers and all other quality-oriented people who haven't had much CMYK experience—the type of image that has provoked the most requests for information on technique among those who study this book, the type of image that poses technical difficulties but surely merits saving. We have sort of been leading up to it with the flowers of Figure 11.4, the lantern of Figure 12.4, and the orange shirt we just did in Figure 15.12. This image is harder because the out-of-gamut areas aren't the only important part. Any move to tone down the fabric is likely to turn the woman's skin gray.

Through the Looking Glass

The following is one of many possible approaches. It makes use not just of false profiles but of several techniques we learned in the first ten chapters. Plus, it emphasizes much of the color management philosophy of Chapters 11–13. For the purposes of this exercise, we are assuming that this file needs to be converted to CMYK for appearance in this book, but afterward we will talk about how it would be prepared if the output circumstances were different.

In real life, we would probably not start with six different versions of the image, but

Quiz Answers

Each version of Figure 15.11 was produced by applying Convert to Profile to a single RGB file. Although the six results were interpreted as looking alike for the purposes of future translations, they had different numbers and channel structure, which is why these red channels vary. If Assign Profile had been used instead, all six red channels would look alike, but after conversion to CMYK the six images would be radically different. The profiles to which the image was converted are as follows:

A	Apple RGB	D	Adobe RGB
B	Wide Gamut RGB	E	sRGB
C	ProPhoto RGB	F	ColorMatch RGB

Figure 15.15 *Left column, top to bottom: Apple RGB is assigned to an sRGB version of Figure 15.14; a contrast-enhancing curve is applied to the green channel; the curve is reverted to Luminosity mode. Top right, Apple RGB is assigned to a ProPhoto RGB version of 15.14. Bottom right, curves are applied to its red and green channels.*

who looks gift hares in the mouth? In Figure 15.11, it seems that the ProPhoto version sports the best detail in the fabric—better than, for example, Adobe RGB. That observation should provoke a reconsideration of the last image. Figure 15.12B showed detail being recovered when an Adobe RGB file was assigned a false profile of sRGB. Are you devious enough to have considered converting the Adobe

RGB file to Wide Gamut RGB first, and *then* assigning the false profile?

Inasmuch as we have Figure 15.11 to look at, it appears that the ProPhoto RGB has the most to offer for the fabric. To make use of it, we must assign a narrower-gamut profile. It should not be sRGB, though, because the gamma is different. sRGB is what we'd use for the 2.2-gamma Wide Gamut RGB; for the 1.8-gamma ProPhoto RGB, we should assign Apple RGB.

Doing that will destroy the face. You might suppose we could steal a new one from the "authentic" Apple RGB version of the document, but that would ignore the fact that there's a gamma, as well as a gamut, issue in Figure 15.14. We are so dazzled by the magentaness of the fabric that we can overlook that the face is much too dark. This image calls for not just one false profile, but two.

- If you don't happen to have six versions of the image handy, convert (not assign) one copy of the image to sRGB (not Apple RGB) and another to ProPhoto RGB.
- To the sRGB version, Assign Profile>Apple RGB. This lightens the appearance, producing Figure 15.15A; note the improvement over Figure 15.14.
- As we saw in Chapter 8, faces usually benefit from blending the green channel into the entire document on a luminosity layer. That won't work here because the face is still too dark and the blend would darken it more. Instead, on a new layer or adjustment layer, apply a simple contrast-enhancing curve to the green channel by lightening its quartertone. We are now at Figure 15.15B.
- As the skin has now become too green, restore the original color by changing layer mode to Luminosity, producing Figure 15.15C.
- Paste or drag the ProPhoto RGB copy onto the document we're working on. No need to assign a new profile; it automat-

ically happens when it enters a document with a different profile. All colors are drastically desaturated, and we get Figure 15.15D.

- Now, the move that couldn't be done without the false profile. In the Apple RGB document that created Figure 15.15C, the red channel is nearly blank in the fabric and the green is solid, as you would expect in a color this extreme. It can't be improved much with curves. But in the warped world of ProPhoto RGB, this magenta is *not* an extreme color. The red and green channels are not at the end of their ranges, and we *can* apply contrast-enhancing curves to them, which I did on an adjustment layer for Figure 15.15E. I considered changing it to Luminosity mode, but decided it looked better as is.
- Figure 15.16 advertises color variation, the LAB specialty, as well as more luminosity contrast. The key is the A curve. Its center point is shifted left, away from magenta and

Stumbling Blocks: Command Syntax

•**Save RGB and save .csf.** The Save button to the right of the Color Settings dialog saves *all* the settings described in Chapter 12, not just the RGB, as one giant file. This .csf (color settings file) can be loaded if you want to replace everything at once, but not to assign an RGB profile that otherwise is nowhere in the system. To do that, change your RGB workspace from 1.0 gamma Adobe RGB (or whatever you may have named it) to Save RGB. That will prompt you to save the false profile for future use.

•**Why not an LAB false profile?** Unlike RGB and CMYK, which can mean whatever you and Humpty Dumpty decide, only one LAB is permitted in Photoshop.

•**Why not a CMYK false profile?** If dissatisfied with the look of your CMYK file, you can try assigning a new profile. But pass it on to a printer, and you'll get the same sorry result as if you hadn't assigned. Remember, the new look is made permanent only by a translation. If you assign an RGB profile and then convert to LAB or CMYK, you'll get what you expect. But if you assign it and simply pass the RGB file on to a photo lab that ignores profiles (as most of them do), the assigned profile will have no impact. Same way in CMYK—almost all printers discard CMYK profiles.

toward green. The purpose is to make the relatively dull areas even less magenta. The brightest areas, meanwhile, become even more vivid, because they fall lower on the curve and are affected by the bottom point.

- Last, another LAB specialty. Figures 15.15C—still on the bottom layer—and 15.16 need to be wed. Since the fabric is far more magenta than anything else, it can be isolated with Blend If options in the A channel, as shown below the final version, Figure 15.17.

This image enters CMYK with excellent numbers for highlight and shadow, a rarity after applying the relatively crude curves of LAB. The fabric is also acceptable, with the necessary 0^Y0^K in the brightest areas. Any change would be subjective. You might want to add more magenta for the sake of making it more colorful, or perhaps drive it toward purple by adding cyan. Me, I just left it alone.

The Final False Profile

Someone looking at the original RGB file can easily be disappointed by Figure 15.17. But that's the reality of commercial printing. The brightest areas cannot be made any brighter than they are at present. The only question is whether you prefer something with shape, like Figure 15.17, or a colorful blob, like Figure 15.14. (Tip: in images like this, it's helpful to have both alternatives. Do one conversion to CMYK without any correction at all, and one the hard way. You may wish to blend them. Would it make sense to apply Figure 15.14 to 15.17 at 10% opacity?)

If you were preparing this file for some more favorable output condition—a photo-quality desktop printer, for example—there's good news and bad news. The good news is that paying 50 times as much for your paper as Peachpit Press does has its benefits. Because your paper is so much whiter, it doesn't absorb as much of the red and blue light that is so critical to this image, and you should be able to achieve a more vivid fabric without difficulty.

The bad news is that you may not get the detail you want. I know that there will be detail when Figure 15.17 gets printed, because I have the CMYK file and I can look at the cyan and black channels, which are the ones that give shape to this fabric. But if your desktop printer or photo lab requires RGB input, as most do, it will be generating its own CMYK file, using uncontrollable, unchangeable, un-knowable, and probably irresponsible rules.

In Chapter 13, I described testing several photo labs with a battery of challenging images. One was a flower of approximately

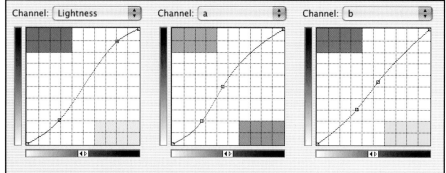

Figure 15.16 *These LAB curves, applied to Figure 15.15E, aim at getting more contrast in the fabric.*

this same magenta, nicely detailed just as Figure 15.17 is. About half the labs did reasonably well with it. The other half had set up their systems to slightly saturate everything. The booboisie, who make up most of their client base, don't know better than to submit muddy-looking files. Adding saturation helps a lot more of their pictures than it harms. However, these labs made *my* flower look as formless as Figure 15.14. Does your desktop printer, or your photo lab, cater to the booboisie in the same fashion? Test it, and find out.

Once you have accepted the warped logic of the false profile, something like Figure 15.18 becomes inevitable. It's a CMYK file produced directly from the same LAB file that made Figure 15.17, but, obviously, the CMYK profile was different. I've seen profiles made by machine measurements that weren't all that much better, but this one takes the cake. Why does it exist? Who thought it would be useful?

The answer is the same as for the ProPhoto RGB version of this last image, or for the Medium GCR version we produced for blending purposes in the river scene back in Figure 10.12. It is an entirely bogus file that is a means to an end and is never intended to influence the final color of the output.

Correcting in CMYK has advantages in certain images, chiefly where delicate curves and/or sharpening are needed, or where it's convenient to have a big black. So much so,

Figure 15.17 *These Blend If sliders unite the fabric from the top layer, Figure 15.16, with the face and background from the bottom layer, Figure 15.15C.*

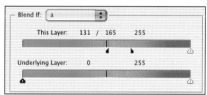

that some people prefer to work there even when the final file needs to be RGB.

CMYK obliterates bright colors. If, for example, we took the file we've been working on from any RGB to CMYK and back, it would

Figure 15.18 *This CMYK file was separated from the same LAB document that produced Figure 15.17, but using a false profile that assumes all CMYK inks are incredibly vivid.*

sedate the fabric. We'd have to figure out a way to restore those tepid colors. Unless, of course, we use a little imagination. This chapter has liberated us from the concept that gamma has to be 1.8 or higher, even though that's how the rest of the world operates. Similarly, we just have to imagine a world in which cyan ink isn't so pathetic and magenta so impure. That bright blues are impossible in real-world CMYK doesn't stop us from inventing a CMYK in which they're mock turtle soup.

Wide Gamut CMYK, a profile that's on the CD, expands on this. The magenta fabric is so dull in Figure 15.18 because it is in fact a relatively dull color in Wide Gamut CMYK's Wonderland of eyeball-searingly brilliant inks. So, if you're in Adobe RGB, for example, but would like to buy a round-trip ticket to CMYK, this profile is a large bottle labeled *Drink Me.*

Wide Gamut CMYK was produced by Mike Russell, the developer of Curvemeister, a useful Photoshop plug-in available for Windows only. Curvemeister's interface permits curves in RGB to have the look and feel of either CMYK or LAB, and vice versa, thus avoiding having to make formal conversions. A demo copy is on the CD.

The Golden Key

For our final example, we return to the pre-digital era, for the photographer's nightmare, an image so spectacular in positive film that no CMYK rendition can do it justice. Yet once again, to CMYK it must go. Today, it teaches an entirely different lesson, one that we'll continue in Chapter 16.

The shot is taken from the ocean into Waikiki Beach and its skyscrapers. The water is blue, and boats with brilliantly colored sails litter the foreground. The tropical sun is directly overhead, giving a golden feel to the skyscrapers on shore. The sky is a rich blue at the top of the image, but large, well-defined cloud formations on the horizon are butting green hills behind the buildings.

Unfortunately, the amazing tonal range of film is gone. In print, we can probably portray some of these attractive features, but not all. The likely tradeoff is that the buildings, inadequately lit, will be too dark, because

Review and Exercises

✓Considering that the two files would look identical if viewed in composite color mode, explain why the fabric in the red channel of Figure 15.11B, the Wide Gamut RGB version, is so much darker than in Figure 15.11E, the sRGB version.

✓What is the difference between the Save command in the Color Settings dialog and the Save RGB setting in the RGB workspace field?

✓Find one of your own originals that is clearly too dark, and another that is too light. Try correcting them once with curves, and once with a false profile assigned before curving. (If you'd like examples from this book, try Figure 2.8, the bathtub products on a white towel, and Figure 3.9, the grieving man.)

✓You have a picture that features brilliant colors and must be converted into CMYK. Even assuming that you prefer to correct in RGB and/or LAB, what final checks (and possible adjustments) do you have to make after the file enters CMYK?

any attempt to lighten them will damage the clouds.

In the good old days, scanner operators did what we do today in Photoshop—they were creative, trying to correct the image before it ever entered the digital world. Their biggest tool was curves, but they also used the equivalent of Selective Color, and it could be argued that they used false profiles as well. Let's see how two such operators dealt with this image.

To me, it's a choice between poison and having the Red Queen order my head chopped off. Figure 15.19A has a cyan cast. A sail that should be yellow isn't. The buildings are much too dark. But we do get a good sense of color intensity.

Figure 15.19B, in fixing these problems, jumps out of the sinking ship into the whirlpool. Now the colors are tepid, there's a purplish cast, and worst of all, the beautiful sky has been suppressed.

I prefer a third alternative. Figure 15.19C is something that the booboisie are never meant to see. It's the uncorrected capture file lurking internally in the scanner that produced Figure 15.19B.

Choosing this monstrosity over the other two seems crazy. Indeed, it would be, if we didn't know its origin. We couldn't be sure that there's any detail in the buildings to bring out, or that lightening them wouldn't cause a symphony of noise.

The weak spot of today's digicams is shadow detail. When a capture is truly underexposed—as the first four original images shown in this chapter are—the shadow areas are almost random pixels. No matter how expensive the digicam, trying to lighten an underexposed photograph always exposes serious

Figure 15.19 *Top and middle, two different scans of a brightly colored film original. Bottom, the raw file that the scanner used internally to produce the middle version.*

noise. If you don't believe it, return to Figure 15.5A.

Figure 15.19C, however, is not an under-exposed photograph. It has merely been stuffed into a relatively dark package for the convenience of a machine. The shadow will be forgivingly full of detail.

Figure 15.19C is attractive precisely because it's so virginal. Nobody has tried to impose any kind of correction on it yet. What the scanner operators did to Figures 15.19A and 15.19B might get in the way.

The plan of attack must surely start with a false profile. We will then need to lighten the buildings. As this will inevitably damage the sky, we need to think back to Chapters 7 and 8. Just as the generalized solution to washed-out fleshtones is a luminosity blend with the green channel, the way to cure overly light skies is to blend with the red.

So much for contrast. We turn to color. The omnipresence of blue suggests that LAB may be called for, but we don't know. There doesn't seem to be anything that

Figure 15.20 *Top, a false profile of Wide Gamut RGB, .8 gamma, is assigned to Figure 15.19C. Left, after converting back to Apple RGB, curves establish a better highlight. Below, the red, green, and blue channels after those curves.*

suggests CMYK, but noting that anything that needs to be emphasized is relatively dark, we have to think about sharpening in a way that emphasizes dark halos.

Figure 15.19C is so dark that even a gamma of 1.0 would leave it muddy. And Adobe RGB may not be sufficiently bright when there are so many happy colors. For Figure 15.20A, I assigned a false profile of Wide Gamut RGB, .8 gamma. As my experience in working in such an extreme definition is limited, I immediately converted back to an RGB I'm more comfortable with, in this case Apple RGB.

The lightest part of the clouds now measured $218^R216^G195^B$—too dark, too yellow. But the darker parts of the clouds were rather blue. Countercasts like that are a warning that a color correction in LAB won't work, so I did some preliminary curving in RGB.

Setting a normal highlight can be dangerous when further corrections are known to be forthcoming. I did lighten the lightest clouds in all three channels, but only to about $230^R230^G230^B$. I bulged the blue curve upward to force more yellow into the image, but I didn't lower the center of the other two for fear of losing cloud detail before the protective blend. Figure 15.20B is now better, but there's still a slight blue cast.

As expected, the sky is much stronger in the red than the other two channels—but look at how light the sails are! I made a duplicate layer and used Apply Image to apply the red, specifying Darken mode, which orders Photoshop to replace the green and/or the blue only in areas where the red is darker. The blend may replace one, both, or neither.

In items that are magenta, red, or yellow, the red channel is the lightest of

the three. In blue or purple items, it's lighter than the green but darker than the blue. This accounts for the failure to replace the sails in Figure 15.21A, in the process of turning the rest of the image black and white.

I then changed the layer to Luminosity mode (Figure 15.21B) and converted to LAB. There, curves lightened the buildings and created more color variation—note the yellow reflections that have appeared in the water.

I applied USM to the L channel of a duplicate layer at 500% Amount, 1.2 Radius, 15

Figure 15.21 *Top, the red channel is blended into Figure 15.20B in Darken mode. Bottom, the blend is reverted to Luminosity mode.*

Figure 15.22 *The final version, after curves in LAB and mild sharpening.*

Threshold, the high Threshold being needed to avoid noise in the sky, and copied the sharpened layer to a third layer.

Lighten and Darken modes don't work in LAB, so I first converted to CMYK, then changed the second layer to Darken and the third to Lighten, using opacities of 80% and 45%, respectively.

A final set of curves lowered the quarter-tone in magenta and cyan while holding the shadow, reducing the bluish tinge in the darkest clouds. They also corrected the black, which was a few points too low in the shadows. The result is Figure 15.22, and with that we come to the end of our discussion of how to make *RGB* mean whatever we want it to.

* * *

"When *I* use a word," Humpty Dumpty said, in rather a scornful tone, "it means just what I choose it to mean—neither more nor less."

"The question is," said Alice, "whether you *can* make words mean so many different things."

"The question is," said Humpty Dumpty, "which is to be master—that's all."

The Bottom Line

The definition of RGB is transitory. If an image appears too light, we can correct it—or we can change the definition of RGB so that, upon conversion to the next colorspace, it will appear darker. If it's too dull, we can assign a more colorful profile.

Assigning false profiles is attractive because it's fast. *Converting* copies of files into false profiles is a powerful correction method, because the channel structure of the resulting file may be eccentric enough to be of use in blending back into the original, even though the composite file is useless.

16
What Comes Around, Goes Around

Camera Raw and similar acquisition modules let us return to the original scene as the camera saw it, before automatic corrections were applied. It's analogous to the role of a scanner in the age of film: if you don't like the scan, go get the negative and scan it again.

In photography as every other artistic discipline, people talk about the good old days. Arguments start, and nobody can agree whether those days were really all that good. Everybody concedes, though, that they were old.

Such is the fate of the argument over whether film or digital photography delivers better quality. It is as valuable as the argument over whether digital sound is better than the LP, or whether Mondale is a better presidential candidate than Reagan. Right or wrong, what's happened has happened.

It is, however, not a waste of time to discuss specific technical differences. In most respects, digital captures are smoother than film, but, as we saw in the opening of the last chapter, they don't do as well in deep shadows, and back on page 188 we saw proof that they don't do as well with skies.

These deficiencies don't affect the philosophy of color correction. If the shadows are noisy, we fix them. We're more likely to encounter the problem with a digital capture, but the solution is the same either way.

On the other hand, certain types of correction were seldom seen in the age of film. To understand why, it's best to return to our last example, the Honolulu scene of Figure 15.19, which represented a traditional way of doing things. The film was given to a scanner operator who was presumed to be a part of the creative process. Most scanners can color-correct to some extent; expensive drum scanners rival many of Photoshop's own capabilities. So, the scanner operator would at least set highlight and shadow, and probably also do things analogous to the contrast- and color-enhancing curves of Chapters 2 and 3.

Before photographers horned in by getting computerized and learning Photoshop, this system was a great equalizer. Scanner operators could rescue bad originals with good curves, just as we can today. This was a great boon to the incompetent photographer, for whom these were, in fact, the good old days.

On the other hand, bad scanning decisions can turn a good original into a bad digital file. This was a source of great frustration among those whose images were so victimized, and who had no recourse at all.

The More Things Change

In the aforementioned old days, when the scan was unsatisfactory, it was redone. In effect, that's what we did with the Honolulu image at the end of the last chapter. Whether it would have been possible to make something good out of the bad scan of Figure 15.19B is irrelevant. It certainly would have been harder, and taken more time, than starting over without having to compensate for the scanner operator's poor decisions. And here is where the discussion turns very modern indeed.

Film records information dispassionately. If the lighting is yellow, the capture is yellow. If the film is underexposed, the result is too dark.

Then, somebody *interprets* it. If the interpretation is done well, everybody is happy; but if it's done badly there can be a real mess, like a picture that's half too yellow and half too blue, or one that's half too dark and half too light. In that case, it may be easier, or give higher quality, or both, to start from scratch rather than try to counter-correct.

In today's world, we face the same problem, but the enemy is not a scanner operator, but an algorithm. Digital captures are *interpreted* by the time we open them. Most of the time, we don't even notice, any more than we would notice when a scanner operator did a good job capturing what was on film.

The digicam algorithms are there because they make most images better.

When they don't, we are back in the counter-correcting business. We saw it most recently in the Prague night scene of Figure 15.2, where it was our job to join together what no man had rent asunder, or, to be less opaque, to reverse the camera's decision to make half the picture too light and the other half too dark.

Algorithms don't take the characteristics of the image into account, so they commit these aesthetic howlers more frequently than scanner operators used to. Consequently, this book features a lot of corrections the like of which would never have been seen in previous editions.

Almost as soon as it became clear that the future of photography was digital, software companies realized that there was value in the 21st-century equivalent of Figure 15.19C, which was the internal scanner capture file that we used to bypass the bad scanning decisions made in Figure 15.19B. That is, we would like access to what the camera saw before the algorithm started setting white and black points and messing about in other ways of which we might not approve.

This uninterpreted information is commonly called a *raw* file. The most widely known way to manipulate it is with Camera Raw, which became an integral part of Photoshop in CS (2003). However, raw manipulation is currently the hottest area of imaging software development. Most camera vendors have similar modules. Apple released Aperture; Adobe countered with Lightroom; Microsoft has something up its sleeve for its Vista operating system.

I thought about covering all these products, but realized that it would take a book, not a chapter. Also, it would require an update every few months. Photoshop, QuarkXPress, Illustrator, Flash, InDesign: these are all mature products. Most of the obvious improvements have already been made. Consequently, I have no difficulty writing *Professional Photoshop* at four- or five-year intervals. We've covered some new techniques that I wasn't aware of in 2002, and talked about certain digital file characteristics that have made themselves apparent since then, but as for Photoshop itself, everything up until this chapter could have been done in Photoshop 6.

These raw packages are different. They are improving rapidly both in performance and capabilities. Making fun of their deficiencies would be like criticizing Photoshop 2.0 for not having layers. Plus, the workflow is new enough that the software vendors don't yet have a good handle on what kinds of workflows will survive.

Accordingly, this chapter will cover Camera Raw only. The feature set will be that of CS2, with the warning up front that major improvements are to be expected.

Warnings and Exclusions

Whether a photographer should shoot raw at all is a question beyond the scope of this book, which assumes that the photograph has already been taken by the time our services are required. If the file is in a format that only a raw module can read, then we have to talk about how to proceed. If it's not, then the rest of the chapter is irrelevant and you can safely skip it. We will, however, discuss the interesting case where the camera delivers *both* a raw and a non-raw file.

Generalized approaches to a series of images are also beyond our scope. This chapter comes right after the one on false profiling for a reason: what Camera Raw does is very like assigning a new profile, one with many more options than just gamma and primary colors. Plus, like a false profile, that Camera Raw setting can be saved. It can then be applied to similar images, typically ones that were shot under the same lighting conditions. We can

configure Camera Raw to open all these images automatically to the desired setting. While this is an important feature, we have to keep on topic. Our focus will be on single images, not groups of them. We will therefore not be exploring batch processing.

The case in favor of raw manipulation has already been stated: it gives us a chance to preempt undesirable changes inserted by artificial intelligence, a chance to (using archaic but accurate terminology) rescan the image, a chance to return to the original film, as it were. Adobe promotes a raw format known as DNG, for *digital negative,* a very appropriate name.

The case against is that it kills time. A raw file requires many times as much space as the JPEG that the camera would presumably deliver instead. It takes the camera longer to save the file and prepare itself to shoot the next one. All the packages are extremely slow. Camera Raw, which operates glacially, is like a starving coyote on speed in comparison to some of the others. Also, its color-correction capabilities leave much to be desired.

All these deficiencies will presumably go away in time. Meanwhile, the poor user must suffer through massive hype, as Adobe and other vendors strive to convince us that this workflow makes for massive improvements in quality, is the wave of the future, etc., etc. Shortly before writing this chapter, I learned why from the technology section of a leading newspaper: "Resolution in itself is no longer a powerful selling feature. ...Nearly all cameras now provide five megapixels—enough for high-quality prints of at least 8.5 × 11 inches. So vendors are expanding other abilities. The [name of camera], for instance, can capture photos either in the JPEG format used by all cameras or as raw files, which can be processed into higher-quality prints."

He was doing all right up until that last sentence, which is a crock. I don't think anybody who knows anything about correction technique has ever tried to figure out how much benefit there is to raw manipulation, if any. Since I would like to know the answer, this chapter has been a lot of work.

How one camera's raw files behave doesn't prove much about how another's will. I solicited contributions from my colortheory list, and got a dozen DVDs of raw files from ten different models of five different manufacturers. I looked for challenging images, and when I found them, tried several different ways of handling them, looking not just for the best result but also for the quickest acceptable one.

My ideas of what raw modules are good for changed during these experiments. Over the past few chapters, it has seemed like correcting images gets more and more complicated. With a raw module, it can be made easier—provided we remember the simplest concept of all: if we don't like how an algorithm is correcting our files, we shouldn't let that algorithm correct them.

When There's a Choice

Seeing when and how to use a raw module is easiest when we consider the case of the people who have the option of using one or not. That is, your camera produces *both* a raw file and a JPEG. Which one should you use? How would you demonstrate that your conclusion is correct?

The first answer is easy: we'd like to use the JPEG. Going into Camera Raw is a big time-waster, unless we think we need it for some nefarious purpose.

The second answer is not so easy. Camera Raw files don't hatch themselves. Somebody has to decide how the images will be opened before we can save them into a format that Photoshop proper can read. If we disallow every automated correction and create what could truly be called a *raw* file to work on in Photoshop, it almost certainly won't look as good as the JPEG because it

won't have had its endpoints set or its color balanced. It may be easier to *correct* than the JPEG, though.

On the other hand, if we hand-tweak the file while it's in Camera Raw and *then* open and compare it to the JPEG, it will probably look better. Most corrected versions do.

Alternatively, we can match artificial intelligence with artificial intelligence and allow Camera Raw to analyze the image and open it as it sees fit. I have done so with many images, and it seems that in half or more cases there is little difference—both find the same light and dark points and leave it at that. Of the ones with significant variance, the cameras' versions were better than Camera Raw's around three-quarters of the time. Figure 16.1 shows one victory for each side; the Camera Raw auto-adjusted versions are on the left and the camera JPEGs on the right.

The Camera Raw algorithm is aggressive in attempting to create contrast. In Figure 16.1A, that approach doesn't work. The fur on the back of the darker bear is almost gone.

Also, Figure 16.1A demonstrates the perils of applying the same move to all three RGB channels simultaneously, which is the lame way that Camera Raw does things. Where one channel is significantly lighter than the other two (as in, for example, the darker bear's back and the lighter one's belly), a lightening move like the one Camera Raw is applying has a disproportionate effect on the lighter channel. Here, the redness is emphasized too much. It may not look bad yet, but the animals' coats are no longer consistent. This introduced defect will be problematic in later correction. Other raw modules don't have this defect.

And of course we assume that there *will* be a subsequent correction. If these were two final versions, the case could be made for Figure 16.1A. As matters stand, both are poor—and Figure 16.1B is easier to work with.

Figure 16.1 *Camera Raw's automated correction routine is more aggressive than that of most cameras. These two scenes compare files opened with Camera Raw's auto adjustments (top and bottom left) to out-of-the-box JPEGs.*

The flip side is the pathetically light Figure 16.1D, a JPEG from a different camera. Anybody would prefer to start with the Camera Raw auto adjustments version, Figure 16.1C.

So, if you are lucky enough to have both a camera JPEG and a raw file available, open the JPEG, but be alert. Raw may have advantages if there is critical detail in the highlights and/or shadows (these can get wiped out by the camera's booboisie-friendly algorithm) if there is an obvious color cast (introduction of an artificial white point into such an image makes it much harder to correct); or if, as we'll see in the next example, brilliant colors are in play. The shot of the two bears has none of these characteristics, unlike the flower.

I'll go off limits for a moment and point out that if you dislike shooting raw generally because of the inconvenience, but have the option to do so, the above rules can be a useful guide. You should be able to recognize that a raw file would be unlikely to be useful in the case of the bears but might very well be so for the flower. For that matter, for most flowers.

The Multi-Channel Approach

We'll examine three images in the rest of the chapter. All three are on the CD in raw form. If you choose to follow along, I am always exporting from Camera Raw into sRGB, but if you choose some other colorspace, there should be no impact on quality. In all three cases, no camera JPEG was provided, so we have no option but to open in some raw acquisition module and resave them into a format that Photoshop proper can read.

Camera Raw's tools don't always sport familiar names, but they're analogous to

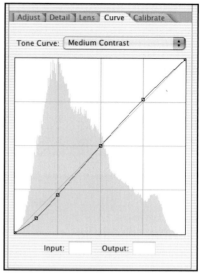

Figure 16.2 *The basic Camera Raw color-correction interface.*

some old friends. Most of the interesting stuff is under the Adjust tab shown in Figure 16.2.

- **Exposure** sets the lightness, but not the color, of the highlight.
- **Shadows** does the same for the file's dark point.
- **Brightness** adjusts the midpoint of what remains. It appears to lighten or darken the image without actually changing its light and dark points.
- **Contrast** trades detail in the highlights and shadows for more action in the midtones.

The first three sliders can be seen as the equivalent of the master (same correction applied to all channels) Levels command, or of a master Curves dialog where we can only access the two endpoints and one point halfway between them.

All four of these sliders are impacted under the Curve tab. It's another master adjustment, this time in the more flexible form of a curve. Unlike the ones shown in this book, lightness is to the top right, so lowering the curve darkens the image. By default, its setting is the booboisie-friendly, expert-hostile one shown

in Figure 16.2, adding further midtone contrast beyond what is specified in the Contrast slider described above.

A useful set of two White Balance sliders, used to correct casts in lighter areas, lives on the Adjust tab. A rough counterpart, Shadow Tint, is on the Calibrate tab. Several saturation sliders on other tabs roughly equate to Photoshop's Hue/Saturation and Color Balance commands.

Our choices for all these sliders can be saved as a single setting, which can then be applied to other files, or can, through Bridge, be applied to batch-open Camera Raw files.

If you're able to apply identical Camera Raw corrections to a dozen files or so, then it's probably worthwhile to do so. If you instead are working on individual images, then these are the three possibilities:

- Open the file with Camera Raw's auto adjustments, allowing the module to analyze the image and pick its own settings for the four major sliders. As we have seen, this process is similar to what digicams do to make JPEGS, if a bit more aggressive. Most of the time the picture looks better; sometimes, as with camera JPEGs, it gets damaged.

• Uncheck every automated correction, set the curve to linear, and open the file in as near to a "natural" format as possible. It will definitely look flat now, because nobody has set a white or dark point. It may, however, be easier to correct than any other option.

• Adopt a combination approach of opening the dialog, seeing what Camera Raw proposes to do if noboby intervenes, and adjusting the sliders to compensate for any deficiencies.

The third option seems like the obvious choice. That was the one I expected to favor when I started working on these images. I don't think that way anymore.

Back to the Future

The third option is problematic, considering the competition. Camera Raw's correction tools compete with those of a mature and powerful application, namely Photoshop itself. This is like pitting a high school baseball team against the New York Yankees. Photoshop is state of the art in the second half of the first decade of the 21st century. Camera Raw offers less than what its predecessors, drum scanners, had in the mid-1980s.

Scanners of 20 years ago were able to address channels individually. Camera Raw currently cannot. In Chapters 2 and 3, we saw that this is an inferior approach.

Treating all channels in the same manner works when the image is black and white. It is also acceptable when the important parts of a color image are nearly neutral, as they were in the pelican of Figure 2.13. But the more vivid the colors, the more differently each channel behaves, and the more incapable a master-adjustment system is of coping. And, of course, the type of image that would cause the most problem is the type of image we've been focusing on ever since the middle of Chapter 12: where the focus of attention

is some brilliant object that's near or over the edge of what the output conditions can reproduce.

Even before we look at the digital file, we can tell that the poppy depicted in the Figure 16.2 screen grab is going to present a problem that Camera Raw won't be able to cope with. The flowers must reside in the lightest part of the red channel and the darkest of the other two. The background greenery cannot be found in these areas because it is not a brilliant color. It must live in the center, with the green channel slightly lighter than the red and the blue slightly darker.

Under these circumstances, the ability to adjust each channel individually is indispensable. An all-channels-treated-alike policy can't improve anything without hurting something else.

Opening this image with Camera Raw's auto adjustments produces the shapeless Figure 16.3A. Naturally, we would like to get more detail, but how? Moving the Exposure and Shadow sliders would serve no purpose. If we move the Brightness slider to the right, it damages the critical detail in the red channel, but if we move it to the left, it hurts the other two. Decreasing saturation would hurt the brightest parts of the poppies more than it would help the more detailed areas.

Nor can the master curve help. Getting more flower detail in the red would require steepening the highlight area, but this would kill the other two, which need to have the shadows steepened. And if we try to do both, by making a master curve in the shape of an inverted S, the background is annihilated.

In short, this correction is simplicity itself in RGB, but a problem without a solution in Camera Raw. So, we want to get out of there as quickly, and with as little damage, as possible.

If the idea is to avoid having Camera Raw damage the file, the best way is to prevent it from making any decisions. We therefore

click off all four of the automated adjustments and set the curve to Linear. The result is Figure 16.3B.

Without all the automated adjustments that make typical images look better, this atypical one is too flat, possibly even worse than Figure 16.3A, assuming those are our only two choices. But they aren't. The client won't care *what* this picture looked like when it emerged from Camera Raw. The question is what it looks like when we print it. It's

certainly easier to set proper endpoints for Figure 16.3B than it is to extract detail from Figure 16.3A.

There's one last move, though. Figure 16.3B uses Camera Raw's defaults for uncorrected images, except for setting the curve to Linear. But even those defaults have the Contrast slider set to +25, fair enough for most images but not for this one. We do *not* want to suppress highlights and shadows, because those are the areas where the flower lives.

Figure 16.3 *Opposite top, Camera Raw's automatic adjustments lose detail in the flowers. Opposite bottom, the image is opened without automated correction. Above, without automated correction and with Contrast set to 0. Below, this top version is corrected with the curves shown at right.*

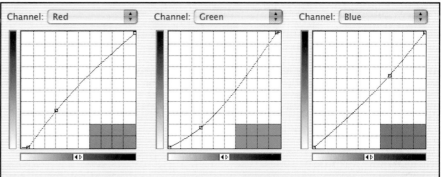

We should set the Contrast slider to 0, giving us Figure 16.3C. Compare it to 16.3A, and note the smoother detail in the flowers and the softer transition into shadow.

From there, the curves are straight out of Chapter 2. In the red channel the flowers are light and the greenery is in the mid- to three-quartertone; both ranges are in the steep part of the curve. In the green the leaves are quarter- to midtone and the flowers are dark; again the curve steepens both ranges.

The Mind of the Machine

If you think this last example is some kind of defeat for raw processing, think again. We don't have a camera-produced JPEG, but it would probably be similar to Figure 16.3A. If such a thing were given to us as a starting point, the last few chapters have shown several ways of attempting to cope. If curves and standard blends don't work, we can assign a narrower-gamut RGB. Or we can convert a copy of the image to an ultra-wide RGB, which would create a better-detailed red channel that we might be able to use for blending. Or we can convert to LAB, use a specialized curve to exaggerate color variation in the flowers, and derive some blending channel(s) from that.

I've tried it with this image, and while I can make a huge improvement over the original, I'm not readily able to match the detailing of Figure 16.3D. Even if it were possible, who cares? Going through Camera Raw is much quicker—provided you know what to turn off.

The same rule applies to images with strong color casts.

The sliders we have looked at so far ignore color issues. To attack the cast in Camera Raw, we'd turn to the two White Balance sliders. We can configure them ourselves, but presets are provided as well. I applied the Tungsten setting to make Figure 16.4B, without altering anything else.

This preset supposes that the image has a warm cast, which it corrects by pushing the image toward cyan. As the actual cast is better described as yellow than warm, the setting isn't quite right. It's worth showing, though, because of a surprise: Figure 16.4B is unexpectedly much lighter than 16.4A.

This sort of thing can happen when we allow automated adjustments. Remember, Camera Raw tries to make a pleasing picture by smoothing the overall range. Figure 16.4A has the complicating factor of large catch-lights over the man's left shoulder and in his glasses and forehead. These catchlights hornswoggle the algorithm into thinking that the overall darkness of the picture is satisfactory and that there is a danger of blowing highlights out. Such mistakes are common among machines (and among humans who rely on histograms, too).

The new setting forces cyan into these catchlights, darkening them. There is now less luminosity distance between the catchlights and the highlight that a human being would choose, which is the lightest part of the woman's hair. Camera Raw now concludes it can safely lighten the image.

If carefully chosen, new White Balance settings can take casts out relatively safely. If you wish to mix your own, it's probably best to start by setting White Balance to Auto, which lets Camera Raw estimate the desired values. Then, adjust the Temperature and Tint sliders to your taste.

The names are misleading. The two sliders roughly correspond to the B and A of LAB, respectively. Moving the Temperature slider to the left forces the image toward blue; to the right, toward yellow. The Tint slider is green at the left, magenta at the right.

Let's introduce a third competitor. Figure 16.4C is the equivalent of the earlier Figure 16.3B. It's a "natural" open, with no automated adjustments. As there is no attempt to set proper endpoints, the picture is too dark.

(I did not bother to set the Contrast slider to 0 as I did in Figure 16.3C, because there is no critical highlight or shadow detail.)

Assume that we have chosen a better white balance for Figure 16.4B than the Tungsten preset, so that no overall cast remains. In that case, which of the three contestants would you choose to correct?

The Duckling Becomes a Swan

Theoretically, someone might not have the time or the inclination to do a subsequent correction and would be willing to settle for whatever Camera Raw could give. In that case, the best alternative is the hypothetical improved version of Figure 16.4B.

I wonder, though, how often that workflow occurs in the real world. Camera Raw has no ability to fine-tune endpoints, or blend channels, or enhance contrast in selected areas. Anyone who forgoes the opportunity to make these improvements has decided that saving time is more important than optimizing quality.

We are all sinners in that regard. I've never heard of a graphic artist who didn't have to cut corners from time to time to meet deadlines. But the question suggests itself: if saving time is so important that we will permit quality to suffer, why in the world would a person be killing so much of it by shooting in raw format in the first place?

Assuming that we are willing to proceed further in Photoshop, the easiest comparison is between Figures 16.4A and 16.4C. Most people presumably think that Figure 16.4A looks better and would therefore be easier to correct. The first statement is true, but the second does not follow from it.

Whether we correct in RGB, CMYK, or LAB, the darkness variation between these two images is irrelevant. Our curves will correct either one in exactly the same amount of time; the curves will merely be more drastic in Figure 16.4C.

LAB is the most inviting choice for this particular image. The faces lurk in a temptingly short range of the L channel, easy to target for added depth. The colors are tepid, and should respond well to steepened AB curves. And those same curves should be able to knock the cast out—unless some preemptive machine correction has made it impossible.

If we convert Figure 16.4C to LAB, it's easy to jump to Figure 16.4D. The curves shown are the basic ones discussed in Chapter 4. The lower left point of the L curve moves to the right to establish a highlight in the woman's hair. The internal point goes below the faces, ensuring steepness in the critical range. The A and B curves are straight lines, steepened to increase color variation. The A curve passes slightly to the left of the original center point, moving the image slightly away from magenta and toward green. The B curve is farther to the left, moving the image strongly away from yellow and toward blue.

Now, suppose we had started with Figure 16.4A. It would seem that we could get the same result by moving the bottom of the L curve to the left to compensate for the original being lighter. There would, however, be a color difficulty, caused by the automated adjustment.

To explain requires some detective work along the lines of that described in Chapter 9. What color is the woman's shirt? Most likely white, but based on Figures 16.4A and 16.4C it could conceivably be ivory.

We can prove or disprove this by comparing its values to the man's and woman's hair. If all three are approximately the same color, either all three are white, or we are looking at the strangest coincidence since Enron executives unloaded their own stock at the same time they were telling the world what bright prospects they foresaw for the company.

As it happens, the shirt is white in the original. Or, rather, it's yellow, just as the hair is.

Camera Raw, as we know, has lightened Figure 16.4A by means of the same correction applied to all three channels. As we also know, such an approach intensifies any colors with one or two particularly light channels, because these channel(s) are lightened proportionally more than the darker one(s). The lighter the hair and the shirt become, the more Camera Raw exaggerates their yellowness.

I have measurements from the lightest part of the woman's hair, and in a medium area of the center of the shirt. In LAB, as reported in the Info palette, the hair is $87^L2^A13^B$ in Figure 16.4A and $82^L2^A17^B$ in 16.4C. The shirt, which is darker, is $71^L2^A16^B$ in 16.4A and $62^L2^A15^B$ in 16.4C.

The L numbers are as expected; we know that Figure 16.4A is the darker (lower L value). The A figures are identical. Figure 16.4C seems to be the yellower (higher B value) of

Figure 16.4 *Opposite top, a version opened with Camera Raw's auto adjustments. Opposite bottom, the Tungsten setting for White Balance is added, unexpectedly lightening the image. Above, the image is opened without automated correction. Below, the top image is corrected with the LAB curves shown at right.*

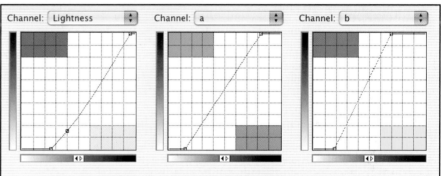

the two, but there's a surprise. Figure 16.4A has the shirt significantly yellower than the hair. Figure 16.4C has the hair yellower than the shirt. We could produce the following variations from this pair of images:

* Hair slightly blue-purple; shirt white.
* Hair white; shirt slightly yellow-brown.
* Hair white; shirt slightly blue-purple.
* Hair slightly yellow-brown; shirt white.

The first two choices require starting with Figure 16.4A; the second two require 16.4C. I believe that the fourth choice is obviously the correct one. The automated adjustment has degraded Figure 16.4A enough that using it for further correction would produce a result inferior to Figure 16.4D.

I would also prefer to avoid correcting the hypothetically more accurate version of Figure 16.4B. Since it is lightened more than Figure 16.4A is, we'd expect even more color variation issues. More to the point, though, it would be a waste of time. If we are committed to correcting in LAB (as we should be, to get the livelier colors and stronger faces seen in Figure 16.4D), then we will surely measure the hair and shirt to see whether we should move the A and B curves to the left or right in addition to steepening them. Even if spending time adjusting the White Balance sliders makes these LAB adjustments smaller, those subsequent curves take just as long to write either way.

Before leaving this image, it should be pointed out that the advantage of the "natural" capture, Figure 16.4C, would have been even more pronounced had it not been for the catchlights. Without them, a white point would have been forced into the image. The woman would have had yellow hair with white highlights, and it probably couldn't have been corrected without a mask or selection.

Figure 16.4D is not a final image, but rather a necessary stop on the way. Getting there would have been possible starting with either Figure 16.4A or 16.4C, but it would have taken longer. If there had been a camera JPEG available, it might have been a toss-up whether to work on it or to take the trouble of opening up the raw file.

The Monster from the Deep

Under most professional circumstances, the photographer decides when the picture gets taken. When the photographer is being approached by a large wild animal, the animal gets to make the decision.

This explains our next original, which is shot by a very good photographer. This is not one of his better-quality efforts, perhaps understandably in the circumstances. All we can see from Figure 16.5, which was opened with Camera Raw's auto adjustments, is that something big is emerging from the water, but whether bear, Loch Ness monster, or mirage cannot yet be determined.

As people gain experience in color correction, images start to fall in patterns. This one is reminiscent of Figure 15.2, the Prague night scene: a very dark half and a very light half with almost nothing in between. In that exercise no raw file was available, so we had to make the best of a bad situation by creating two half-images and merging them.

Now that we have a raw file, we could try to move the two halves closer together and thereafter treat the file as a single unit. I don't think that would work here, because what the camera saw is too different from what we would have.

How a camera evaluates this scene is not typographically interesting. Human beings in the same position as the camera would see water, rocks, plant life, and ***an animal that might be able to inflict grievous bodily harm on human beings***.

Our visual system is the child of evolution. Being able to bring potential threats into immediate sharp focus is one of its endearing inheritances. To emulate that, we will have to

Figure 16.5 *This original image was opened with Camera Raw's auto adjustments.*

put so much contrast in the dark half of the image that the light half will vanish.

Accordingly, we need a version with strong highlight detail that can be used for a later merge. Fortunately, this is a strong point of raw acquisition modules.

Capture algorithms that are designed to let amateurs get the best-looking pictures don't just stop with setting a full range. They actually allow some highlights to blow out and shadows to plug. The theory is that discarding this detail will rarely be noticeable enough to make up for the contrast it adds to the rest of the picture.

In a raw capture, no detail has yet been discarded. It could be that Figure 16.5 will be good enough to restore the highlight once we're done lightening the image. If we think it might not be, we need only ram the Exposure (highlight) setting well to the left, put the light areas in a steeper part of Camera Raw's curve, and save a copy of whatever results. We don't care that it completely plugs what little there is of shadow detail, because we're not going to use that part. And we don't care that the highlight detail is excessive because we can always blend it into the final picture at a low opacity.

We therefore save Figure 16.5 in a format that Photoshop can read, and reopen the raw file to produce the file we'll need for the darker half of the merge. For the sake of argument, I'll do this two ways: once using Camera Raw's manipulation capabilities, once without.

The first option is to open the file without automated correction. That file is not shown, because it's similar to Figure 16.5. To get Figure 16.6A, I adopted the same strategy used in the Hawaii image of Figure 15.19C: a false profile of Wide Gamut RGB, .8 gamma. As with the earlier example, because I am uncomfortable with this strange setting, I immediately used Convert to Profile to return the newly lightened file to sRGB.

The competition, Figure 16.6B, uses the sliders and curves of Camera Raw to produce a lighter original. This move requires caution, as the sliders and the curve interact. We don't want the nearest rocks or the animal's haunches to disappear. I would have liked to lighten the shadow even more, but the Shadows slider is already as far left as it can go.

The mystery of the animal's species is now resolved, giving us valuable information

A

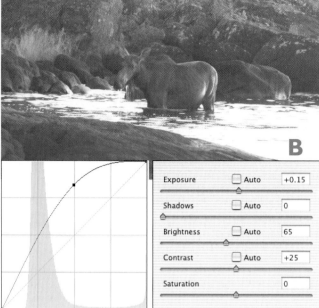

B

Figure 16.6 *Two ways to prepare the dark half of the file for further action. Left, a file is exported to sRGB from Camera Raw without automated correction, and a false profile of Wide Gamut RGB, .8 gamma, is assigned. Right, the image is acquired in Camera Raw using the settings shown.*

Exposure	Auto	+0.15
Shadows	Auto	0
Brightness	Auto	65
Contrast	Auto	+25
Saturation		0

about color. If this animal were a bear, it could be light cinnamon, black, or anything in between. But we now know that it's a female moose, which must be a dull brown. That color, a very desaturated red, occurs so often in nature that it bears repeating the numbers that produce it. In RGB, approximately equal green and blue, red slightly lighter. In CMYK, approximately equal magenta and yellow, cyan slightly lighter. In LAB, A and B approximately equal and slightly positive. In any colorspace, if the paired channels aren't equal, they almost invariably favor a yellower rather than a purpler brown.

Both these versions are too purple. Although the files are in RGB, there is so much variation in the animal's darkness that it's easier to read colors in LAB, which darkness doesn't affect. The moose averages $7^A(6)^B$ in Figure 16.6A and $6^A(9)^B$ in 16.6B.

This is a mild surprise. Remember, I assigned Wide Gamut RGB to Figure 16.6A when the file actually was in sRGB. That should really have lit off some bright colors. But Figure 16.6B's moose is the bluer of the two.

The news is worse in the shore areas.

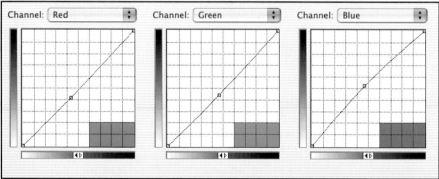

Figure 16.7 *Moose are a dull brown, but the one in Figures 16.6A and 16.6B is distinctly purple. Curves to create the lower left version are shown; the ones for the right-hand version are more drastic.*

A

B

Figure 16.8 In red objects such as this moose, the green channel frequently has more contrast than the other two. Left, a copy of Figure 16.7A is converted to LAB. The green channel from the original image is then applied to the L of the copy, creating a darker, snappier original. Right, Figure 16.7B starts out dark enough, so the blend is accomplished in the more usual way of applying the green channel to a duplicate layer of the composite RGB, and changing mode to Luminosity.

The foreground is typically $3^A(8)^B$ in Figure 16.6A and $3^A(12)^B$ in 16.6B; the background is $4^A(10)^B$ versus $5^A(12)^B$. The differences, which are caused by Camera Raw's all-channels-are-equal approach, aren't a big deal—yet. We still have a long way to go with the image.

The blue-purple cast that these numbers indicate is probably better taken out in RGB or CMYK than LAB, since it doesn't appear to affect the water. I prefer RGB, because both versions are still so bland that I would like to have a chance to hit them with steep LAB curves to bring out more color. I would much rather eliminate the cast in RGB and then go to LAB than go unnecessarily in and out of CMYK.

The curves that transform Figure 16.6A into 16.7A are mild. The green channel lightens, the red lightens less. The blue gets darker, to add yellowness. The curves to correct 16.6B, not shown, are similar, but more drastic. Unfortunately, they can't fully neutralize the foreground and background without making the moose too red.

Reds, Saturated and Otherwise

Now that the casts are eliminated, more or less, we should be thinking of luminosity blends, which we first discussed in Chapter 8. There, we saw that the green channel is usually the best in faces. I recommended blending the green into a luminosity layer.

A moose's fur isn't nearly as saturated a red as a human face is, but it's still a red, and the same rules apply. The green channel should have marginally better contrast than the other two. The difference between Figures 16.7B and 16.8B may not be much, but it's there, and it only takes a minute, so we may as well do it.

Figure 16.7A, being so much lighter than 16.7B, can be handled in a better way: duplicate the image, convert to LAB, and then apply the green from the first file directly to the L, rather than to a luminosity layer in its own document. Notice how much fuller the resulting image (Figure 16.8A) is than 16.7A.

This method works because the L channel is interpreted as being very dark, almost as if a false profile of 2.6 or 2.7 gamma had been applied to it. (Gamma is a poor description of the L's behavior; it is somewhat eccentric in the highlights and shadows, which need not concern us here.) Since the interpretation is dark, the channel itself must be light—lighter than any RGB channel. So replacing the L with the green must darken the image.

Figure 16.8A, then, is already in LAB, and we now put 16.8B, which was created in RGB in the more conventional way of putting the green on a luminosity layer, there as well. The most important part of the correction is coming up. It makes sense to review why we are in LAB in the first place.

LAB is good at breaking colors apart and making dull pictures look livelier. Of the three pictures we have worked on in this chapter, two of them—this moose image and the previous one of the elderly couple—have that problem. Figure 16.3, on the other hand, was dominated by brilliant poppies, a strong clue that we want to do the work elsewhere.

Simple casts are also easy pickings for LAB. Figure 16.4C had one. All we had to do was push the entire image away from yellow, and the man and woman came to life. It was easier to do this in LAB than in RGB or CMYK. In Figures 16.7A and 16.7B, the cast was more complicated: too blue-purple in the midrange, but correct in the highlight. That's why we curved it in RGB before entering LAB.

LAB, or rather the L channel thereof, also does well when the main interest object falls in a narrow range, as this moose does. Figure 16.9A owes its great shape in the animal to the impossibly steep L curve. We can't go quite that far in Figure 16.9B, because the base file (Figure 16.8B) is darker. Also, we can only go half as far in steepening the A curve. The background is already too purple, and a steeper A would aggravate it. As a consequence, note that the reddish area of rock above and to the left of the moose's head is redder in Figure 16.9A, more orange in 16.9B.

Both of these are creditable pictures, particularly when we consider the disaster we started with in Figure 16.4. I prefer Figure 16.9A because of the extra snap in the animal and because she stands out better against neutral rocks than the purpler ones of Figure 16.9B. I do not quibble about Figure 16.9B, but if I had wanted to achieve it with the false-profile workflow I could have done so. It is much harder to get from Figure 16.9B to 16.9A if the lightening is done in Camera Raw.

If you decide you want as much snap as Figure 16.9A has, you're probably committed to a false profile. But if you are going to use a false profile to lighten, the question must be, why go to the bother of making the Camera Raw adjustments of Figure 16.6B when just opening an uncorrected version of the image would probably give a better result?

This is the question I continually found myself asking as I plowed through my test files. Before answering it, let's finish this last correction.

Merging with a Layer Mask

Assuming you agree that we should forget about working with Figure 16.9B and proceed with 16.9A, the next step is to retrieve Figure 16.5, convert it to LAB (or convert Figure 16.9A to RGB), and paste it on top, giving us nice water but covering up the animal and background that we have been at such pains to produce.

At first glance it seems we might merge the two layers with Blend If options that exclude all areas that are dark on the top layer. It wouldn't work, though, because some of the ripples in the water are darker than the lightest areas of the water, not to mention the animal's haunches. Instead, we need a layer mask: white where the water is, dark for the moose and the background, gray where the two layers merge.

By that definition, we need look no further for the start of a mask than the top layer itself. Here are the steps to finalize it:

• With the top layer (Figure 16.5) active, Layer: Layer Mask>Reveal All.

• The layer mask is now the selected channel, so Image: Apply Image. Source is the merged image itself, 100% opacity, Normal or Multiply mode.

• Option–click the layer mask's icon in the top layer line in the Layers palette. The screen now displays the layer mask rather than the composite image.

Figure 16.9 *These curves transform Figure 16.8A into the top version. Similar curves, although not as steep in the L channel, transform Figure 16.8B into the bottom version.*

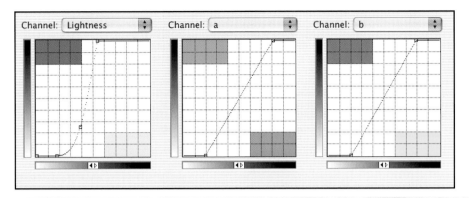

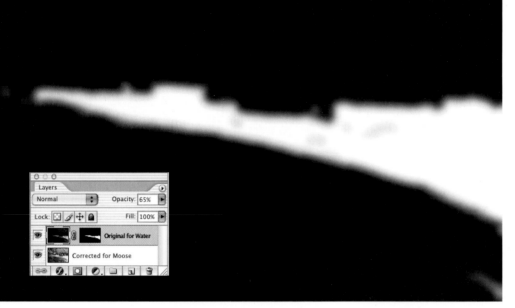

Figure 16.10 Merging the water of Figure 16.5 with the moose and background of Figure 16.9A calls for a layer mask. The one at left is based on Figure 16.5 itself, with contrast enhanced and imperfections removed. With the layer structure as shown in the inset, white areas allow the top layer to show, black ones the bottom.

- Apply a curve to drive the lightest areas to pure white and the darkest to pure black.
- The lightest parts of the background and the animal won't yet be fully black. Paint over them, or lasso and delete them to black. Do the reverse for any nonwhite areas in the water.
- Filter: Blur>Gaussian Blur with a Radius of around 10 pixels. The idea is to soften the edge where the water hits the bank, allowing the two layers to merge smoothly there.
- Option–click back to the composite image, and decide on an opacity for the top layer. I chose 65%, feeling that anything higher made the water look unrealistically dark in comparison to the animal.

Figure 16.10 shows the completed layer mask. After the merge, some mild hiraloam sharpening of the L channel and a slight adjustment to the shadow once in CMYK produced the final version, Figure 16.11.

Summing Up: The KISS Approach

It's difficult to prove which of two different approaches to an image is better when there is as much operator control of the process as in the last example. If you like one version of Figure 16.9 better than the other, it could be because a superior method was in use, or it could be some error or eccentricity on my part. Nevertheless, based on these and several dozen correction attempts that are not shown in this chapter, some generalizations are possible. I had some questions in mind before I began, and answered them to my own satisfaction as follows.

Review and Exercises

✓Create a new version of the poppies image (Figure 16.3) by manipulating the file in Camera Raw as you see fit, but doing all subsequent work in LAB rather than RGB. (Hint: the process is similar to the one that produced Figures 15.12C and 15.12D in the last chapter.)

✓In the raw capture of the couple (Figure 16.4), manipulate the Temperature and Tint sliders (under White Balance) to achieve a more accurate color than that of Figure 16.4B.

✓What two settings in Camera Raw favor midtone contrast at the expense of highlights and shadows?

Figure 16.11 *The final version of Figure 16.4, after merging the water back in through the layer mask of Figure 16.10.*

• *Do most images benefit from entering Camera Raw or a similar module?* No. The standard automated adjustments that a raw module can bypass are standard because they usually work.

• *Do ANY images benefit?* Yes. The clues that a raw approach may be better are: the presence of important, brilliant colors, like the poppies of Figure 16.2; pronounced color casts, as in the man and woman of Figure 16.3; seriously troubled originals, such as the moose that was nearly invisible in Figure 16.5.

So far, these findings are about what I expected. The next one is not.

• *Does it pay to do preliminary correction in Camera Raw before opening the file?* With the current feature set, I don't think so. I am unable to identify any images where better quality results from doing anything other than opening an uncorrected version or just accepting Camera Raw's auto adjustments.

The major benefit is being able to open uncorrected images, not manipulating them before entering Photoshop. For example, I don't think that the final flower image, Figure 16.3D, would have been achievable starting with a camera JPEG.

• *Would it nevertheless be easier for some users to employ these tools?* Some users would find it easier to reduce casts by using Camera Raw's white balance eyedropper tool than by exporting the image into Photoshop proper and correcting there. For those too snooty to use an eyedropper, I would say that the White Balance sliders are attractive for some minor casts. But the relation of these two sliders is not intuitive—anybody who understands it probably doesn't think curves are very hard, either.

The contrast-related adjustments, on the other hand, are comparable to using the Levels command in all-channel mode. Some may find such an interface easier, but it can't be recommended for serious users, for the reasons developed in Chapters 2 and 3.

• *What is the biggest surprise?* I had forgotten how easy color correction is. We have seen some complicated curves in this book—

but not in this chapter. There have been four sets of curves, 12 channels total, *and not a single curve has had more than one internal point.* The content of this chapter, particularly in conjunction with the introduction of false profiles, seems a little heavy, but all three exercises use beginner-level curves comparable to the easiest examples in Chapters 2–4. Granted, the moose image needs a false profile, a luminosity blend, and a merge via layer mask, too, but that's what happens when we get a very bad original that's too interesting or has too much sentimental value to throw away uncorrected.

The first two exercises, though, are easy. Have another look at Figure 16.4C, the uncorrected, overly dark capture of the elderly couple. It can be fixed in seconds with the

The Bottom Line

Capture modules such as Photoshop's Camera Raw bypass automated correction and allow us to work with files in which endpoints have not yet been set. These capabilities are particularly useful in images that are seriously under- or overexposed, contain brilliant colors, or have casts.

At present, raw modules are slow, and their correction capabilities are rudimentary. Therefore, it's generally better either to accept their automated corrections or to turn everything off and start with the file in a natural state.

Raw modules are currently the hottest area of imaging-software development. It should be anticipated that capabilities and speed will improve rapidly over the coming years.

simplest form of LAB curves. To see what a big deal this is, you may wish to glance ahead to Figure 19.6. It's a superficially similar image—older woman, yellow cast. But no raw file is available. We have to work with the camera's JPEG. It can be fixed, but not quickly, and it's in one of the late chapters because it's not easy, either.

In color correction as in so many other human endeavors, one of the best approaches is known as KISS—Keep It Simple, Stupid. It's never truer than with raw acquisition modules. The main benefit of using them is that it avoids having an algorithm precorrect our images rather than allowing easy fixes in Photoshop. The best way to enjoy the benefit is to prevent any algorithmic or non-Photoshop corrections by opening the file out of the raw module in close to a natural state.

When confronted with a new tool, it's wise to ask ourselves how we would proceed if the tool weren't available. That was the whole purpose of going back to the age of film with the Hawaii image of Figure 15.19 just before commencing this chapter. The concept of being able to revert to an uncorrected capture of the image was useful then; it's even more useful today.

The old days were not as good as sentimentalists remember. The age of digital photography has given us power that was undreamed of two decades ago. To take full advantage of it, we need to understand the few ways in which the old days were better. Raw capture modules are a form of retro chic—one we would do well to appreciate.

Blurs, Masks, and Safety in Sharpening

Effective use of unsharp masking depends on understanding that sharpening and blurring are close relatives—and on exploiting the channel structure that allows us to merge two different types of sharpening into one harmonious whole.

n life as in Photoshop, the most tempting things are the riskiest. The best steaks are loaded with cholesterol, the best wines make you tipsy, the best outdoor adventures are dangerous, and the most heartfelt expressions are likely to backfire, particularly in matters of love, about which I have nothing further to say in this book.

Photoshop's great temptation is unsharp masking. Everybody wants to do it, but all but the most dissolute of desperados, of whom I count myself one, fear doing too much of it. Handled properly, sharpening makes a contribution to believability that rivals that of curves and channel blending. Handled badly, it can wreck an image. Fortunately, ways of avoiding this exist, but in presenting them another problem emerges.

Chapter 6 described how the Unsharp Mask filter creates the distinct halos that characterize the traditional, conventional kind of sharpening. I also suggested a form called *hiraloam*—very high Radius, very low Amount—that creates very diffuse halos. Some say that the effect is so different that it blurs the distinction between what constitutes sharpening and some other form of image improvement.

That verb *blur* is a most apt one. We have learned that the haloing depends on blurring, a hidden blurring process that most users aren't aware of. But things are about to get blurrier still, because hidden blurs have more uses than mere unsharp masking. It is now hard to say where sharpening begins and ends. The next three chapters will explore the frontiers and suggest a unified approach.

Risky behavior is addictive. People who learn to sharpen well want to learn better, braver ways. Chapter 6 is really sufficient for the average user,

but not for the desperado, many of whom have asked for the sort of extended coverage that previous editions have not offered.

Consider Figure 17.1B. It looks like USM has been applied to Figure 17.1A, and curves as well. Neither was. It's Shadow/Highlight, a powerful but underutilized tool introduced in Photoshop CS. To use it properly—and to realize when better alternatives exist—requires understanding both why it is so like hiraloam USM and how it in effect is making a selection of certain areas. (The setting for this image is on the CD, if you care, but read Chapter 18 first before playing with it.)

Above all, these chapters are about channel structure—if you ever had any doubt about why you need to be able to solve the channel-identification quiz of Figure 1.5, you won't after getting through Chapter 19.

Why are people so interested in this arcane topic? The archperfectionist Ansel Adams explained as follows:

> Some photographic issues seem to defy precise explanation. Visual impressions are difficult to assess in verbal form, and we grope for words that encompass the qualities of the medium. One such elusive concept is *sharpness.* It is worthwhile…to consider sharpness and related concepts in physical terms, but in discussing mechanical or optical issues we must not lose sight of the much greater importance of image *content*—emotional, aesthetic, or literal. I believe there is nothing more disturbing than a sharp image of a fuzzy concept!

Limiting the Damage

These next three chapters are unified by the hidden blur, and can't easily be separated. In principle, this one is about sharpening,

Figure 17.1 *The advent of new tools makes it hard to say what constitutes sharpening. The bottom version was created with the Shadow/Highlight command, but it shows many characteristics of unsharp masking.*

Chapter 18 is about the Image: Adjustments>Shadow/Highlight command, and Chapter 19 is about the use of selections and masks to marry pieces of images that have been treated in two separate ways. In practice, the three are so closely linked that each topic spills over into the others.

The desperado does not look at the areas in which sharpening does well. Instead, the focus is on areas in which it often creates problems. Then comes the search for ways to accentuate the positive while removing the cholesterol of the rest.

For reasons brought out in the last two chapters, digicams create more problems in the highlight and shadow regions than their film predecessors did. Proper sharpening of these areas is a bigger technical challenge. Also, *highlights* and *shadows* do not mean just whites and blacks. Strongly colored objects are highlights in the lightest channel(s) and often are shadows in the darkest one(s).

Before getting started, two warnings. Some lily-livered cowards employ the USM equivalent of training wheels by using one sharpened and one unsharpened layer, and then using a layer mask or the history brush to paint in the sharpened areas, leaving the rest of the image looking weirdly neglected. If you want to sharpen the foreground more than the background, fine. But there are ways to *limit* what happens to the background without leaving the impression that the foreground has been cut out of the image and pasted back in.

Second, recall that taste in sharpening is highly personal, and also that for purposes of this chapter you need to be able to *see* the sharpening. So, the settings for these examples are chosen with a heavy hand. Everything is on a layer, though. If you think the image is oversharpened, just imagine a version with lower opacity.

In point of fact, *desperado* and *500% Amount* go together like mushrooms and

A

D

E

garlic, like Chateaubriand and Château Pétrus, like channel blending and Luminosity mode, like color management and hype. Some people are so intimidated by such gargantuan USM Amounts that reading this chapter could be more hazardous to their health than skydiving without a parachute. So, when sharpening conventionally during the rest of the chapter, let's keep the Amount a secret. I'll just say YKW, for You Know What. That way, no heart attacks.

Now, a quiz. Figure 17.2 previews the six images we'll be working on in the rest of the chapter. Each exercise relies on channel structure to limit sharpening to areas where it can do the most good.

By now, you should not need to make copies of the image and examine each channel. Looking at these thumbnail versions should tell you which channels are likely to be the most helpful.

For each, the worksheet poses a question about differentiating objects. Your job is to say which RGB and which LAB channel has the best separation between two stated areas.

Waterfalls and Sharpening Highlights

Adams wrote,

> A waterfall is but an episode in the life of a whole singing stream, pouring from the high stone fountains of the summit peaks to the blending with the greater river below. We can trace its exuberant life from glittering fields of ice and snow, through clean alpine meadows, the clear pools, cascades, and the flower groves of the high country, and the longer passage through the timbered valley to the rim of Yosemite. Then suddenly the prodigious leap—and the frothy gathering in the tranquil reaches on the valley floor.

Figure 17.2 The key to successful sharpening can be finding a channel that strongly differentiates the important objects.

Professional retouchers, who are more laconic, would use simpler terms, like, when you find the bottom of a waterfall, sharpen it to death.

Figure 17.3A, the bottom of a waterfall in Adams' favorite national park, could benefit from a massive conventional sharpen, something that Adams would have approved of had it been available in his time.

Monstrous USM settings of YKW Amount, 4.0 Radius, 0 Threshold are therefore wheeled out for Figure 17.3B. The big Radius setting is standard practice with violent water scenes: it can make rainstorms or blizzards more intense, or, as we'll see in Chapter 20, put more carbonation in a glass of beer. Big Radii are the enemy of detail, but in the above-described images, and this one as well, we aren't after real detail, we're after an appearance—in this case, churning, foaming water.

That most people would find Figure 17.3B oversharpened is not an issue. When we

Worksheet for Figure 17.2

The six images on the facing page may look oversharpened if USM is applied without a limiting mask. Each has two main areas where sharpening needs to be emphasized or limited. For each, name the one RGB channel and the one LAB channel in which you expect to find the most separation between the two objects described below. Answers, page 406.

Image	Channels
A The water and the foreground rock.	
B The snow and the foreground greenery.	
C The water and the leaves.	
D The yucca plant and the background.	
E The faces and the background greenery.	
F The letters and the background.	

Figure 17.3 Top, the original image of the bottom of a waterfall. Bottom, in an effort to create turbulence in the water, heavy unsharp masking is applied.

What's Not to Like?

Once having decided that a certain part of an image needs less sharpening than the rest, our knowledge of channel structure comes into play. I'll show you the way I prefer to put it to use, but there are other alternatives.

The choice in sharpening is often between conventional and hiraloam. Conventional is usually more convincing but full of the potential for trouble. Hiraloam, if done with even the slightest care, is rarely offensive.

Figure 17.4A is such a hiraloam effort, with the soft values of 60%, 25.0, 0. New York retouchers describe this as a WNTL document. It stands for *What's Not to Like?*

The answer is, nothing in particular is not to like. We can certainly imagine better detail in the water, but there's nothing objectionable in what we have. If we are required to say whether the original (Figure 17.3A) or this Figure 17.4A is better, it's not a real head-scratcher. Yet a choice between Figure 17.3A and 17.3B might produce a split vote.

In such situations, I advocate a three-layered document. The bottom is the unsharpened original. In principle, it isn't needed. In practice, it's an insurance policy. Sometimes our opinion of sharpening changes when we see alternatives.

sharpen this heavy-handedly, we do so on a separate layer, so that we can later reduce its opacity to whatever looks good. The problem is that the foreground rock looks so stupid in comparison to the water that if we must reduce opacity enough to take care of it, we won't be able to get as much action in the water as we want.

The middle layer is the WNTL version—the one with no obvious defect, the one that we would prefer on all counts to the original.

The top layer is the speculative one, the one with strengths and weaknesses, the one that we expect to have the most trouble merging into the document.

Here, Figure 17.3B is on top of 17.4A, with 17.3A on the bottom just in case. Now is when we need a good answer to the quiz's query of how to differentiate the oversharpened foreground rock from the more acceptable water.

The temptation is just to say that the rock is darker than the water and that any channel will do. In fact, it's darker *and yellower.* The most differentiation is found in the blue of RGB and the yellow of CMYK. Either is better than using something based on pure darkness.

I happened to work this file in RGB, so the next move is Blend If options that favor the middle layer over the top one in areas where said middle layer is dark in the blue. The exclusion of the top layer is not complete, because the sliders have been split to create a transition zone. The rocks now have a small amount of the flavor of the top layer, but the water is top layer only. At this point, with the rock no longer a worry, we decide how much we like

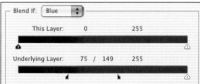 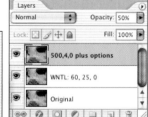

Figure 17.4 *Top, hiraloam USM of Figure 17.3A. Bottom, the two sharpened versions are united with Blend If options and a reduction of opacity.*

Figure 17.5 *In the original, top left, the bottom objects have distinct edges. This favors conventional sharpening, top right. There are no such edges in the water, suggesting hiraloam, bottom left. The two sharpened images are merged to create a final version, bottom right.*

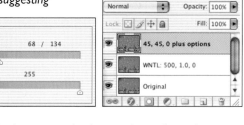

the extremely crisp water of Figure 17.3B. To produce the final version, Figure 17.4B, I cut the top layer's opacity to 50%.

Still Waters Run Deep

The recipe just given is a good general one. The specifics vary with the image. Figure 17.5A again features water, but this time we want to sharpen it in a different way, the WNTL layer is not the one we would usually expect, and the Blend If exclusion comes in a different colorspace.

In Chapter 6, we found that conventional USM works best when it finds well-defined edges. The bottom half is full of such edges—the leaves hitting the background, the tiles and the mortar butting the concrete. Figure 17.5B improves these areas.

Hiraloam works best when the edges are amorphous or nonexistent, as they are in the water. Figure 17.5C has better shape, more pronounced rippling.

RGB and CMYK do not offer easy ways to merge the two. The water is dark in the red and cyan channels. So are the leaves. The blue and yellow channels don't distinguish the two halves well, either.

LAB's color channels often solve selection problems. Here, we can forget the A: the water is more green than magenta, and so are the leaves. But the water is much more blue than yellow, and everything in the bottom half is more yellow than blue. They can therefore be separated by Blend If options in the B channel.

Also, the choice of middle (WNTL) layer is different. The water in the conventionally sharpened Figure 17.5B is not as attractive as in the hiraloam 17.5C, but it's better than the original. What's not to like? In Figure 17.5C, I dislike the darkening of the leaves, although the water is nice. So, this time the layering is: original on bottom, conventional sharpen in the middle, hiraloam on top.

To produce the corrected version, Figure 17.5D, I used the Blend If sliders to exclude everything that isn't strongly blue on the top layer, and a layer opacity of 75%. This means that the bottom half of the image comes from the middle layer, but the top half, the water, is a combination of the top and middle layers.

The final question is whether the middle layer, Figure 17.5B, is *too* sharp. Personally, I don't think so, so I left it alone. However, if you disagree, that's why there's a bottom layer, Figure 17.5A. Just change the middle layer's opacity to 80% or whatever looks good, moving it back in the direction of the unsharpened original.

Sharpening, Shadows, and Workflow

Sharpening the L channel sometimes gives better results, even better than when an RGB sharpen is done on a luminosity layer. *Photoshop LAB Color* has a long discussion of this effect. The bottom line is that we should prefer to sharpen the L when convenient, but with rare exceptions I wouldn't bother to convert for no other purpose than sharpening. Blurring, yes; LAB is *much* better than RGB, but sharpening, no.

Sometimes, however, the workflow puts us there already. In this last example, the obvious way to unify the two types of sharpening was with a Blend If based on the B channel, a move with no easy counterpart in RGB. This put us in LAB anyway, so it made sense to do the sharpening there as well.

To see how sharpening fits into the overall scheme of things, let's do a full correction this time, one that involves not just sharpening but curves.

In highlight areas, we're sensitive to color variation and not so much to contrast; in shadows the reverse is true. Sharpening highlights is reserved for situations like Figure 17.3A, where we want a harsh, disagreeable appearance in the water. When sharpening dark areas, which we have to do much more frequently, we often want more precision than Blend If offers.

Figure 17.6A arrives in an untagged RGB, and with a problem we just saw in Chapter 16. Most of the image has a cyan cast, as measured in the darker areas of the snow. But the very lightest areas have fallen victim to the camera's algorithm and are white.

Relatively dull colors, not to mention a lot of greenery, suggest an LAB correction, but that won't work here because of this, er, half-cast camera. If we make the darker snow neutral, the lighter snow will go red. In Figure 16.4, a portrait that exhibited the same kind of problem, we used Camera Raw to short-circuit the whitening, whereupon it was very easy to correct in LAB as planned. But here, no raw file is available—the image was shot as a JPEG.

Sighing, I foresee the following:
- Preliminary curves in RGB to neutralize the snow. Because this will entail lightening the cyan, which would blow out detail if done in Normal mode, these curves will probably have to be on a layer set to Color mode, to preserve luminosity.
- When the cast is gone, move to LAB for the usual steepening curves to boost color variation.
- Since we are bound for LAB anyway, that's where we should sharpen. But this image has a split personality just as the others in this chapter have had: the background should not take as much sharpening as the foreground.

We certainly don't want the snow to look like the churning water of Figure 17.3B.

The progression, then: Figure 17.6A is the original image, Apple RGB assumed as usual. In Figure 17.6B, a curves adjustment layer set to Color mode obliterates the cast in the snow without harming detail.

We now flatten and convert to LAB, so that we can steepen the AB curves in the usual manner to produce Figure 17.6C.

Now, the two types of sharpening. Figure 17.6D is the conventional (low Radius, high Amount), at settings of YKW, 1.0, 8. It shows promise for the foreground, but creates havoc in the background snow. Figure 17.6E is hiraloam, at settings of 60%, 25.0, 8. What's not to like?

We again work with a three-layered document, Figure 17.6C on bottom, 17.6E in the middle, 17.6D on top. So far, we've been merging the top two layers by Blend If with satisfactory results. For more accuracy,

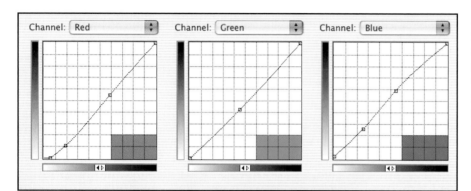

Figure 17.6 *Left, the original. Right, RGB curves are applied in Color mode. Opposite, top left, LAB curves add color variation. Top right, conventional USM is added. Bottom left, the alternate hiraloam USM. Bottom right, the final merged version.*

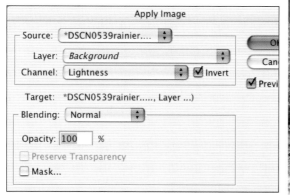

Figure 17.7 *To unify Figures 17.6D and 17.6E, a layer mask is added to the top layer, and an inverted copy of the base L channel is applied. In the light areas of the mask (right), the top layer takes precedence; in the darker areas, the middle layer is favored.*

however, we can consider the alternative of a layer mask, which can easily be modified by a curve if needed.

When part of the correction is done in RGB and part in LAB, I recommend holding a copy of the RGB, just in case one of the channels is needed for blending or masking. Here, there's marginally more variation, but also more noise, in the blue than in the other two. I'd say it's not worth the bother of getting rid of the noise. We are trying to limit the

conventional USM to the darker half of an image that doesn't feature brilliant colors. Any channel at all should give us a decent start—including the L.

• With the top layer active, add a layer mask, either from the bottom of the Layers palette or by Layer: Layer Mask>Reveal All.

• Image: Apply Image. Unless we've clicked into some other area in the Layers palette, the layer mask is active, and therefore the target. For Source, choose the L channel from the *bottom* layer, which has not yet been sharpened. The Invert box must be checked, because lighter areas of a layer mask favor the top layer, darker ones the one(s) below. Without inverting, we'd see more conventional USM in the lighter areas and more hiraloam in the foreground, the opposite of what we want. The mask needs to be a negative, like Figure 17.7.

• The layer mask can be edited. For example, it can exclude conventional sharpening of the snow altogether, instead of leaving the slight impact shown in Figure 17.6F. We would apply a curve that renders the darkest parts of Figure 17.7 completely black. Or, we could lighten the mask's midtone, allowing sharper snow and background cliffs.

While a layer mask offers the most flexibility, it also takes the most time. Let me suggest a simpler route for images that don't warrant such premium treatment.

High Risk, High Reward

As pointed out in the box on page 139, some photographers regard oversharpening as a mark of ill breeding at least as appalling as ordering one's steak tartare medium well. This attitude accounts for the popularity not just of hiraloam, but of sharpening the black only, if you happen to be working in CMYK. Both approaches are relatively forgiving. It's obvious when we've gone too far—the whole image looks strange.

Conventional sharpening is more dangerous, because its damage is easier to overlook. It's annoying to make something look nice on gross inspection only to discover eight steps later that the filter has chopped some small area to smithereens.

Based on what we've seen in this chapter and in Chapter 6, we can apply a bit of USM to improve the focus of the above paragraph. The dangers of conventional sharpening usually show up either in naturally light areas or in areas that have taken excessive lightening halos. One countermeasure was shown in Figure 6.10B, a cactus: putting the lightening and darkening halos onto separate layers and adjusting their opacities separately.

A similar maneuver is available for those who don't like to take chances, but want a faster workflow that combines conventional and hiraloam sharpening. It involves sharpening conventionally

through an inverted luminosity selection, and then sharpening the entire image hiraloam.

I'll show this quick and dirty procedure in RGB, but it works in any colorspace. Let's say that Figure 17.8, which is untagged, is OK for color and contrast. All that's needed is USM.

● Choose the appropriate channel to load as an inverted selection. Say to yourself, the dark parts of my channel are the ones that will show the most sharpening; the light parts the least. We would like to sharpen everybody's hair, which is dark in any channel we

---

Stumbling Blocks: Safe Sharpening

•Finding the right hiraloam Radius. Do it, and the filter will create shape; pick the wrong Radius and it will simply lighten and darken randomly. To choose the right one, set Amount to something extreme, even YKW, and judge how different Radii affect shape. When satisfied, reduce Amount to 50% or thereabouts.

•The two Blend If lines. All the Blend If sliders in this chapter except Figure 17.5 are shown on the Underlying Layer line, meaning that Photoshop examines the bottom layer to see whether the criteria are met. That's where it's usually easiest, but it's occasionally more efficient to use the This Layer sliders. Those often are best in LAB, when curves on an adjustment layer drive colors farther apart. In such cases, the ranges in the top layer are longer, so it's easier to be accurate with the top sliders.

•Layer mask workflow confusion. Those without much experience in editing layer masks inevitably have to redo work because they thought they were editing the mask when they were editing the image itself, or vice versa. If you're editing a layer mask, keep checking the Layers palette to verify (the mask or the image will be highlighted when active) that your edit is being applied to the right place.

•Forgetting the invert step. Finding the right channel is the hard part. Sometimes people forget the easy part, which is to know when to invert it. Where selections or masks are light, they permit corrections (or allow the top layer to show); where dark, they restrict corrections or exclude the top layer. Inverting a mask or selection takes only a single keystroke—it's just a matter of realizing, as in Figure 17.7, that the dark parts of the channel need to be made light and vice versa.

Figure 17.8 *Many images can be sharpened more heavily in dark areas than in light ones. The hair could use conventional USM, but it might damage the faces.*

way is to Command–click the red channel icon in the Channels palette, followed by Select: Inverse.

• Sharpen conventionally. I chose settings of YKW, 1.3, 0. Figure 17.9A shows these values applied to 17.8 without modification; 17.9B with an inverted copy of the red used as a selection.

• Select: Deselect to return to global sharpening.

might pick. We'd like to avoid sharpening the faces themselves, which are dark in the green and blue but light in the red.

• The keyboard shortcuts to load the inverted red are Command-Option–1 (load the first channel as a selection); Shift-Command–I (invert the selection). The long

Apply hiraloam USM to the image that has already been sharpened once through a selection. I used 55%, 30.0, 9 to make Figure 17.9C.

Two final points about this method. First, until now we've applied conventional and hiraloam to separate files, which were then merged. Here, the two filters were

Review and Exercises

✓What is the general rule for knowing when hiraloam, rather than conventional unsharp masking, is appropriate?

✓In a two-layered document, what rules are followed when we load a channel as a layer mask?

✓In applying conventional USM to a portrait, what channel might an RGB user prefer to load as a selection or layer mask? Should it be inverted, or not?

✓In Figure 17.12C (among other variants) the layer mask is black in the lightest areas of the flowers, so the sharpening is all hiraloam, no conventional. How would you edit this version if you were told that at least *some* conventional sharpening was needed in every area? (For this exercise, assume that the minimum acceptable blend is 20% conventional, 80% hiraloam.)

✓Find a normally lit photo of a forest or other greenery, or go back and pick up Figure 6.1. On a duplicate layer, apply massive conventional sharpening. Experiment with the different impacts of loading the red, green, blue, black, and L channels as a layer mask—and of taking the file into LAB and using Blend If to exclude anything that isn't A–positive.

applied consecutively. If you do this, conventional should come before hiraloam, as even subtle presharpening can make later conventional USM problematic.

Second, virtue sometimes has to be its own reward. I was going to offer another variation of Figure 17.9, showing what would have happened had we made the selection with the green rather than the red channel. When I tried it, there was almost no difference. I could have magnified a section and showed that using the green allowed more noise in the faces without any compensating benefit, but what would have been the point? Our knowledge of channels tells us that the red must be technically the better choice. We need not investigate whether using the green would be much worse, slightly worse, or nearly indistinguishable.

To show how experimenting with the inverted luminosity selection *can* make a difference, an example is coming right up. So is a quiz.

Figure 17.9 Top, a conventional sharpen of Figure 17.8. Middle, an alternate version, in which the same settings are used after an inverted copy of the red channel is loaded as a selection. Bottom, after deselecting, hiraloam USM is added to the middle version.

Figure 17.10 *The original image.*

The Search for the Layer Mask

Figure 17.10 shows one of the prettiest sights in the desert, the ivory-and-red blooms of the yucca plant. As it summarizes many of this chapter's issues, let's discuss our options before proceeding.

In my opinion, the flowers are the focus, which is unfortunate because they feature very dark reds as well as the predominant whites. As we have seen, conventional (low Radius, high Amount) USM often has trouble with highlights. Figure 17.11A is on the table as an example. It savages the delicate white flowers at the same time that it does well with the red areas. Also, the green stems are, in real life, rather waxy, not as sharp as this.

The countermeasure is a second version of the original, this time sharpened hiraloam (Figure 17.11B). Neither the values nor the colorspace that produced these two sharpened versions is particularly relevant yet. But for the record, the USM was applied to the L channel of an LAB file; the conventional sharpen used values of YKW, 1.3, 0, and the hiraloam 40%, 22, 0.

If you produced your own versions, you'd use numbers more to your liking, but our reactions to the two versions would probably be the same. In the conventional Figure 17.11A, I like the dark parts and dislike the white ones. The hiraloam Figure 17.11B is less dramatic, but it is superior to the original in every way, even if I don't like the red parts as well as in 17.11A. The trick is how to merge the stronger parts of 17.11A, or your equivalent thereof, and the inoffensive 17.11B.

I can think of at least five different ways to do it, all starting with a three-layered document. As with the other examples in this chapter, the original goes on the bottom, the less offensive sharpened version (the WNTL layer) in the middle, and the dangerous version on top. What mask, or Blend If selection, might merge the two appropriately?

• We could load an inverted copy of the L channel as the mask for the top layer. Being inverted, it would be darker in what used to be the light areas, preventing the top layer from showing through. Therefore, the lighter the original object, the more the hiraloam sharpen would be favored.

• Instead, we could use an inverted copy of the original green channel of RGB. This is technically a better approach, because the white parts of the flowers would be light and the red parts dark, with the green leaves as midtones. In the L channel, the reds and greens are about the same darkness. So, using the inverted green channel rather than the inverted L would emphasize sharpening the red areas more.

• We could convert a copy of the file to CMYK, Medium GCR, and use an inverted copy of the resulting black as our layer mask. It's a more conservative approach than the last two, restricting the conventional sharpening's impact exclusively to dark areas like the reds of the flowers.

• The replacement could be based on color, not luminosity. This method would use a LAB file and Blend If sliders, not a layer mask. In the green-versus-magenta A, the leaves are dark, the white areas 0^A (50% gray), and the reds of the flowers light. In the B, everything is more yellow than blue, but the leaves and the reds are much yellower than the lighter parts of the flowers. So, we could start with a B slider that toned down the sharpening of the whites without affecting the reds and the greens, and then turn to the A if we decided that the leaves were still too sharp. We could even add an L channel slider to exclude the very lightest areas of the image.

Figure 17.11 *Three styles of sharpening Figure 17.10 without a selection or mask. Top, conventional. Bottom left, hiraloam. Bottom right, a version to be used for masking only, sharpened with settings of Amount YKW, Radius 250.0, and Threshold 0.*

• And now for something completely different: way back in Figure 6.7J, the lengthy series of sharpens involving a gull, we saw how applying USM with a sufficiently insane Amount and Radius could, in effect, select certain objects. Figure 17.11C, sharpened in RGB, uses the Photoshop maxima: YKW, 250.0, 0. It is the USM equivalent of a false profile: something never intended to be seen, but only used for blending or masking purposes. As the leaves have become totally yellow and the flowers driven to black and white, the blue channel of this work of art seems like a possible masking choice. When inverted, it will emphasize the conventional USM of the reds, the hiraloam of the whites, and something in between in the greens.

Now, the quiz. Figure 17.12 shows, in a random order, the last four ideas presented above for merging the two sharpened versions. (Forget the first option, an inverted L channel as the mask; if you like that, you must like the second option, an inverted green, better.)

Three of these moves involve layer masks. One is an inverted green from an untouched RGB version; one is an inverted Medium GCR black from a CMYK conversion; the last is the inverted blue from the ultra-sharp Figure 17.11C. The fourth version uses Blend If in the A and B of LAB rather than a layer mask, trying to emphasize the top (conventional USM) layer in areas that are strongly positive in both A and B, emphasize it less for things that are both A–negative and B–positive, and deemphasize it for more neutral objects.

Can you pick out which is which? Which do you prefer?

This is a hard quiz, in my opinion. If you want a hint (or, to quote the beta readers, who also thought it was hard, a giveaway), turn to Figure 17.13. There, in the same order,

Figure 17.12 *Four styles of merging the conventional USM of Figure 17.11A with the hiraloam of 17.11B. For magnified versions and answers, turn the page.*

are magnified versions of the document plus the appropriate layer mask or Blend Ifs. Remember, the darker the mask, the more it favors the WNTL version on the middle layer. Note that all masks are dark or semidark in the white areas of the flowers.

So, which is best? Here's Adams's vote.

There are situations when it is desirable to emphasize a certain subject by isolating it from its surroundings; minimum depth of field is one way to accomplish this. By selecting a large f-stop, the depth of field will become small, and foreground and background objects will definitely be out of focus and may be less distracting. This effect, called differential focus or selective focus, can be enhanced by any means that reduces depth of field: changing to a long focal length lens, decreasing the subject distance, or using a larger aperture.

Me, I favor the mask based on black. You can tell which one that is because black is

Worksheet for Figure 17.12

Each version on the facing page is based on a document with the conventional USM of Figure 17.11A layered on top of the hiraloam of Figure 17.11B. In one case, Blend If options restrict the use of the top layer whenever it is either A– or B–negative. The other three use layer masks—inverted copies of the original green, a Medium GCR black separated from the original, and the blue of the weirdly sharpened Figure 17.11C. Match each version with its layer mask or Blend If setting. Answers, page 413.

Layer Mask	Version
Black, Medium GCR, inverted	
Blue from Figure 17.11C, inverted	
Green from original image, inverted	
LAB Blend If to exclude cool colors	

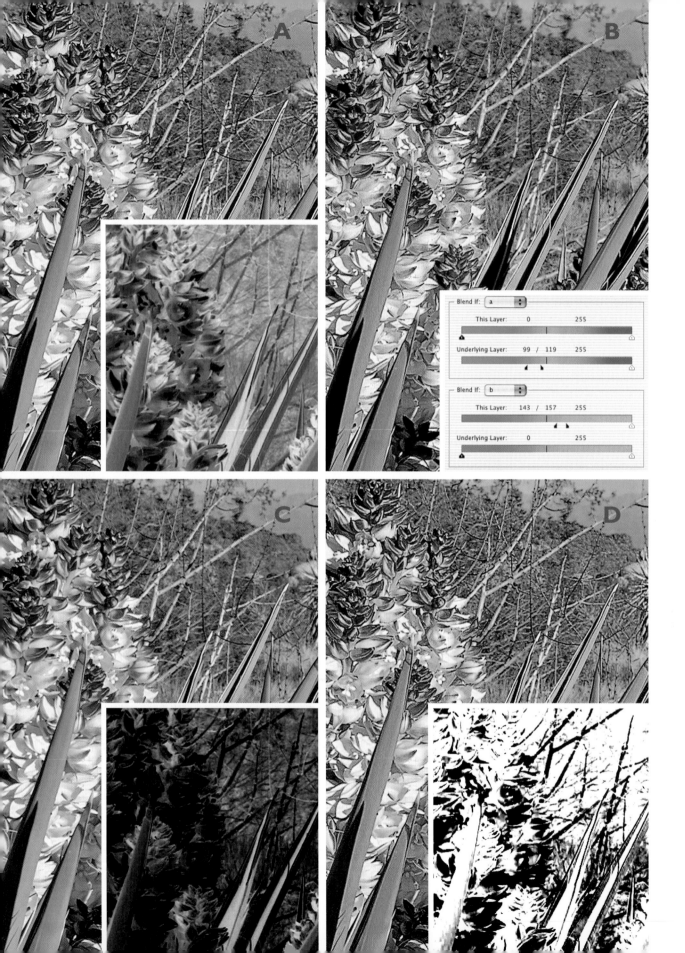

A

B

Blend If: a

This Layer: 0   255

Underlying Layer: 99 / 119   255

Blend If: b

This Layer: 143 / 157   255

Underlying Layer: 0   255

C

D

always the lightest channel, meaning that it would make the darkest mask when inverted and therefore yield the most conservative version. I also like the Blend If exclusion based on color, which is the only one that really keeps the entire background soft while allowing some nifty sharpening of the flowers.

You, of course, can choose whichever of the four you like, change the opacities, do weird things with the layer masks, and so on. We could show ten more pages of examples of variations on this one image, too.

The percentage of space devoted to images in this chapter is much higher than in the previous 16. It needs to be that way: tastes vary greatly on this topic, and one can't evaluate sharpening at thumbnail sizes.

There's also the question of how much time you're willing to spend. To warrant throwing as much time examining options as we just did at this last exercise, you'd better be quite good at the basics of color correction. One slightly inadequate curve or blend will outweigh whatever slight gain you might get from picking the best version of Figure 17.12.

Betting on the Sure Thing

Remember, also, that these images were chosen for a chapter on advanced sharpening techniques. Most images don't need to be sharpened twice.

Nevertheless, how tempting, how irresistible, is the thought of doing something, anything, that makes the image undeniably look better. Let's end with a difficult implementation of a simple concept.

The historical marker of Figure 17.14A is full of the pronounced edges that indicate conventional USM will be better than hiraloam. There is, however, no reason to refrain from using both.

Figure 17.13 (opposite) Enlarged sections of the four variants shown in Figure 17.12, together with corresponding sections of their layer masks.

This untagged image prints here at a resolution of 240 pixels per inch. Figure 17.14B applies robust USM settings of YKW Amount, 2.0 Radius, 0 Threshold. And we again see the same problem that has been afflicting us throughout most of the chapter: the highlights can't stand all this love. The letters have lost their color. Gold on blue is compelling; blah on blue, boring.

Since this is the last example, we could use a summary, and a confession. Cascades of sharpening are for desperados, buccaneers, perfectionists. We have to be able to improvise, which is why I started the chapter with a scam, two images that are not typical of the problems we face. Aiming conventional sharpening at the highlights, as we did in the waterfall of Figure 17.3, is rare; we're far more likely to want to use hiraloam or leave them alone altogether. Hiraloam sharpening is the safe, if not always the preferable, way

Figure 17.12 Quiz Answers

Opposite, magnified, are the four versions of Figure 17.12, in the same order, with their masks. One might reasonably solve the quiz by starting with C, which favors the hiraloam version more than any other. It must have the darkest layer mask, and since black is always the lightest channel, an inverted black makes the darkest. Similarly, D favors conventional sharpening, and must have the lightest mask, which would be the inverted blue of Figure 17.11C.

B, the LAB version, can be distinguished from A, the inverted green, by observing the softer background. The Blend If sliders exclude everything that isn't more yellow than blue, which kills the mountain and sky, and tones down things that are more green than magenta, which subdues the leaves, particularly in the background.

The answers, therefore, are:

A inverted green

B LAB Blend If

C inverted black

D inverted blue from oversharpened version.

A

HISTORIC NEW YORK

THE CHIPPEWA BAY AREA

This area was settled early in the 1800's by immigrants from Scotland. They were encouraged to come here by agents of George Parish, a large landholder in the North Country. These conscientious farmers and tradesmen came up the St. Lawrence River from Montreal with true pioneer determination. The hardships of the frontier were especially severe since much of the land had to be redeemed with the axe.

As the trials of the first years passed, fields of grain replaced the forest and gave way to prosperous farms. Gradually, the original log cabins were replaced by stone houses, many of which survive to this day. Superb workmanship, firmness of principle and industriousness were part of this Scottish tradition that is now part of our heritage.

EDUCATION DEPARTMENT   STATE OF NEW YORK   1969   DEPARTMENT OF TRANSPORTATION

B

HISTORIC NEW YORK

THE CHIPPEWA BAY AREA

This area was settled early in the 1800's by immigrants from Scotland. They were encouraged to come here by agents of George Parish, a large landholder in the North Country. These conscientious farmers and tradesmen came up the St. Lawrence River from Montreal with true pioneer determination. The hardships of the frontier were especially severe since much of the land had to be redeemed with the axe.

As the trials of the first years passed, fields of grain replaced the forest and gave way to prosperous farms. Gradually, the original log cabins were replaced by stone houses, many of which survive to this day. Superb workmanship, firmness of principle and industriousness were part of this Scottish tradition that is now part of our heritage.

EDUCATION DEPARTMENT   STATE OF NEW YORK   1969   DEPARTMENT OF TRANSPORTATION

C

HISTORIC NEW YORK

THE CHIPPEWA BAY AREA

This area was settled early in the 1800's by immigrants from Scotland. They were encouraged to come here by agents of George Parish, a large landholder in the North Country. These conscientious farmers and tradesmen came up the St. Lawrence River from Montreal with true pioneer determination. The hardships of the frontier were especially severe since much of the land had to be redeemed with the axe.

As the trials of the first years passed, fields of grain replaced the forest and gave way to prosperous farms. Gradually, the original log cabins were replaced by stone houses, many of which survive to this day. Superb workmanship, firmness of principle and industriousness were part of this Scottish tradition that is now part of our heritage.

EDUCATION DEPARTMENT   STATE OF NEW YORK   1969   DEPARTMENT OF TRANSPORTATION

of doing things. Images where conventional USM has less chance of causing offense, as it did in the pool of Figure 17.5, are unusual.

Shots like this marker, accordingly, are the ones that confront us all the time. We decide where the conventional USM is causing a problem (usually in lightening things, or in highlight areas) and devise a strategy to finesse it—usually by thinking of a logical way to explain to Photoshop what we're trying to accomplish, in terms that a computer might be able to understand.

That explanation is easy in this image. We want to sharpen blue things and avoid sharpening yellow ones. The solution is also easy. We can work in any colorspace we like, because every one has a channel that strongly differentiates yellows from blues: the yellow of CMYK; the B of LAB; the blue of RGB. I'll sharpen this image in RGB, but either of the others would do.

If in a hurry, you can Command-Option–3, Shift-Command–I (load the blue channel as a selection; invert the selection), and proceed. That deprives us of a move worth knowing about, so we'll eschew the shortcuts in favor of the scenic route. Figure 17.14B goes on a duplicate layer; in Figure 17.14C an inverted copy of the blue channel is loaded as a layer mask. There are several ways to get it there. I just created a blank layer mask, and used Apply Image to apply the blue from the Background—not the default Merged— layer, mode Normal, checking Invert.

Figure 17.14 *Top, the original RGB image. Middle, conventional USM is applied on a separate layer. Bottom, a layer mask is added to the middle version: an inverted copy of the original blue channel, preventing much of the sharpening to the golden letters.*

The result is a step in the right direction. The lettering is preserved and emphasized. But no reason to stop here. If we're careful, we can apply hiraloam *after* conventional, rather than doing the two separately and then merging. With the layer mask still in place, I clicked into the top layer's icon (otherwise I'd be editing the layer mask, not the image) and resharpened Figure 17.14C with settings of 50%, 25.0, 2, producing Figure 17.15A.

Hiraloam sharpening works its magic with wide halos that are so subtle as to be almost invisible. It doesn't work well in busy images where the halos on one important object can intrude on some other.

If the background butting the interest objects is large and relatively flat—a sky, say, or the spaces between the letters in the current exercise—another option emerges: sharpening with an *ultra-high* Radius. Figure 17.15B is 17.15A resharpened with settings of 40%, 100.0, 2.

Three types of sharpening ought to be enough. All that remains is to decide whether the effect is excessive. If so, we can reduce the sharpening layer's opacity, but here there's a subtler way. If you think Figure 17.15B is too sharp, it's probably because it's become too obvious that the yellow letters were excluded from the process. To correct this, click into the layer mask and blur it slightly. I used Filter: Blur>Gaussian Blur at 1.5 Radius to make the final version, Figure 17.15C.

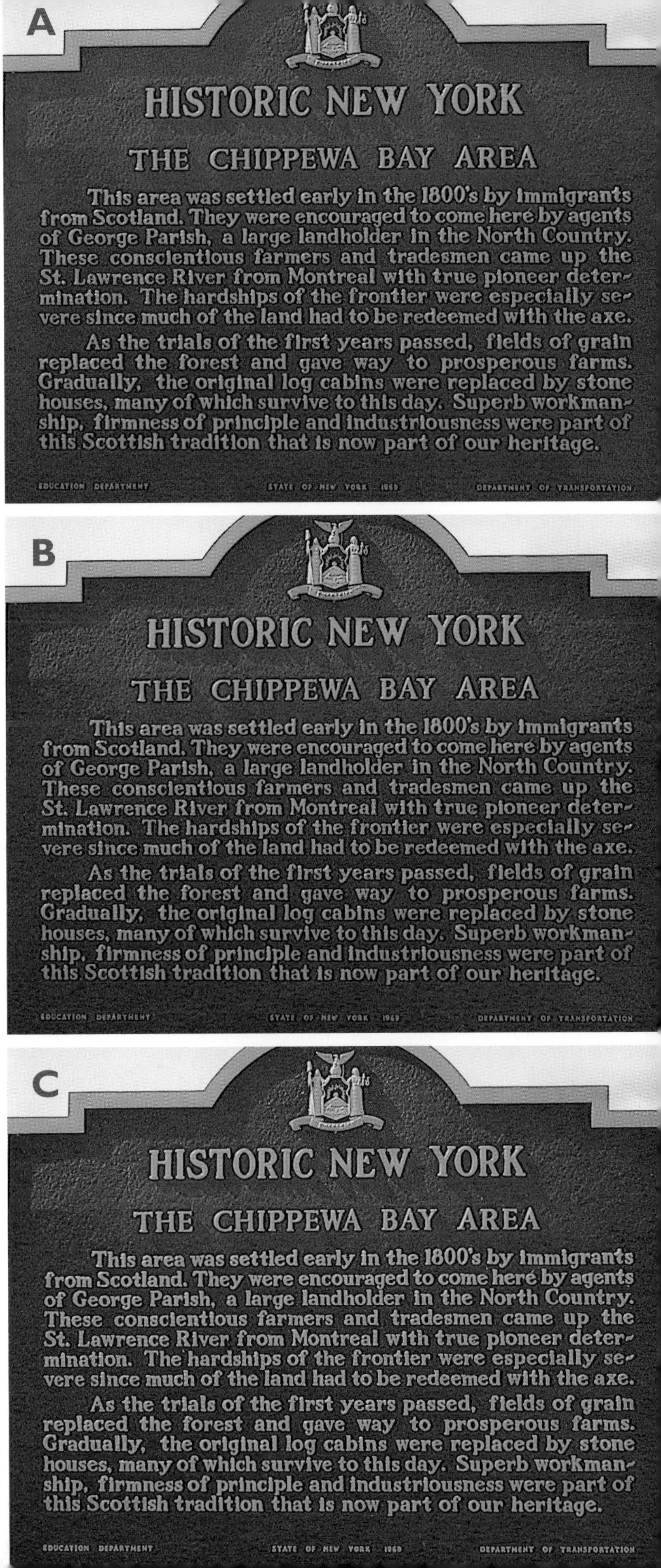

Figure 17.15 *Top, with the layer mask still in effect, hiraloam USM (Radius 25) is added to Figure 17.14C. Middle, USM with an ultra-high Radius of 100 is added to the top version. Bottom, the layer mask is blurred with a 1.5 Radius, softening the sharpening halos.*

Sharpening, Past and Future

Unsharp masking has an unsavory reputation under the best of circumstances—let alone when we start introducing these wild techniques. Most of these were unthinkable a decade ago, because we could have gone out for a beer during the time that Photoshop would have needed to perform the calculations for some of these operations. And, without the ability to experiment with new ideas, nobody was able to come up with much more than the conventional sharpens described in Chapter 6, which closely mimic the way drum scanners used to behave.

But if anyone starts to grouse about this being some kind of space-age chicanery, unsuitable for those of sophisticated taste, tell them to get a life. Unsharp masking in

the conventional sense—narrow, perceptible light and dark halos—was originated, as far as I know, by Michelangelo, and taken to extremes by El Greco. The 20th-century ideas of sharpening by channel or in Luminosity mode are mine, as are the mixing methods shown in this chapter. Hiraloam sharpening, alas, is not. I pirated it from Velázquez.

The idea of mixing two varieties of sharpen to minimize the problems of each is new, but there's nothing wrong with innovation in a good cause. Before we return to our search for a calorie- and cholesterol-free dessert to complement our hangover-free libation, let's give the last word to Adams.

The Bottom Line

Conventional sharpening with high Amount and narrow Radius became conventional for a reason. Unfortunately, in certain types of images—or rather certain *areas*—it can become obtrusive. High Radius, low Amount (hiraloam) sharpening isn't as dramatic, but it's less likely to be offensive.

Some images benefit from a combined approach, beginning with one conventional and one hiraloam version. The two styles of sharpening are merged from separate layers, either by Blend If or a layer mask, putting each into areas in which it delivers a more effective sharpen.

This is the first of three chapters discussing the related topics of sharpening, blurring, and Shadow/Highlight; and selections, masks, and merges.

I give full credit to the excellent scientists and technicians involved in the photographic industry. The research, development, and design aspects, as well as production, are extraordinary. However, very few photographic manufacturing technicians comprehend photography as an art form, or understand the kinds of equipment the creative person requires. The standards are improving in some areas, however: in my opinion modern lenses approach the highest possible levels of perfection, and today's negative and printing materials are superior to anything I have known and used in the past. I am sure the next step will be the electronic image, and I hope I shall live to see it. I trust that the creative eye will continue to function, whatever technological innovations may develop.

Overlays, Hiraloam, and Shadow/Highlight

In the mind of a digital camera, midtones reign. The endpoints—shadows and highlights—need resuscitation more frequently than they did in the age of film. Fortunately, Photoshop has just the tool for it, provided you know your sharpening and blurring basics.

The left-hand side of the span shown in Figure 18.1 meets the back of Venice's Palazzo Ducale, the most opulent building in the world in its time. On the right, it hits a dungeon of the darkest and most depressing category.

After standing trial in the palace, prisoners would be led across the water. On the way, they would be tortured by one last, limited glimpse of the Grand Canal before being thrown in a cell to rot. Consequently, it is known as the Bridge of Sighs.

This area of Italy is the fatherland of all commercial publishing, printing, and typography. All originated elsewhere, but the Venetians were the first to make a business of them, in the late 15th century, and tough businessmen they were, too. In fact, those who challenged the government-approved printing monopolies occasionally found themselves heading the wrong way across the Bridge of Sighs.

The left half is in sunlight and the right side in shadow. The camera, therefore, saw the picture as half too light and half too dark. You and I wouldn't have, because the human visual system is more tolerant of weird lighting conditions than cameras are. Plus, we aren't prisoner to the dubious logic of digicam technology: fixing a white point and adding contrast to the midtone, something this image needs about as much as Venice needed to be invaded by Turks.

We have been dealing off and on with this kind of image for several chapters. The methods we've come up with so far all fall a bit short this time. We can't apply contrast-enhancing curves to the highlight without making the rest of the picture too dark; we can't disallow the camera's contrast enhancement by opening a raw file because we don't have one

A

B

C

D

Figure 18.1 *(opposite) Top left, the original. Top right, curves applied through a luminosity mask strengthen the highlight. Bottom left, an alternate correction using Overlay blending. Bottom right, a Darken merge between the two left-hand versions.*

to open, and no channel blend suggests itself because, the marble being neutral, all channels are approximately equal.

We can improve things with the techniques we tried with the overexposed images of Chapter 15. That is, we admit that we have to treat the document as a light half and a dark half. We load a channel (any channel, they're all about the same) as a selection or layer mask, and *now* run our curve to enhance contrast in the highlights.

Such a luminosity mask might work if the highlight consisted of a snowbank. But a lot of what we take for a "highlight" in the Bridge of Sighs is nothing of the kind. The bridge itself may be white, but the fine lines in the ornamentation are midtones. They won't be fully selected by the mask, they won't darken as much as the rest of the marble, the difference between background and ornament will be reduced, and we'll get Figure 18.1B.

What's needed is something like Figure 18.1C, or, if you prefer, Figure 18.1D, which is 18.1C applied to 18.1A in Darken mode.

We haven't seen this move before, but there's something very familiar about it. Figure 18.2B shows an inverted, heavily blurred, mask, just like the ones we were using in Chapter 17. And look at the sky underneath the bridge in Figure 18.2C, which is an enlarged version of 18.1C. That wide, subtle light halo suggests that hiraloam sharpening has been applied, no?

Figure 18.2 *Top, an enlarged version of Figure 18.1A. Middle, a blurred, inverted copy of the red channel, used as an overlay. Bottom, an enlarged version of Figure 18.1C shows characteristics of hiraloam sharpening in the sky.*

The Most Serene Command

Techniques that use computer intelligence to assist in image processing—like Auto Color, or the algorithms that cameras employ to produce white points—are of limited use to professionals, and often actually counterproductive, as we've seen in the last two chapters. The present topic, the Image: Adjustments>Shadow/Highlight command,

is the exception. Introduced in Photoshop CS (2002), it's Photoshop's most significant color-correction tool since adjustment layers (1996).

Regrettably but understandably, it's underused. Most people are afraid to venture far from its default setting, which is no surprise since the key field is both counterintuitive and undocumented.

The reputation of Shadow/Highlight is that of a desperation measure to resurrect grossly under-exposed garbage such as that shown throughout Chapter 15. This is actually one of its poorer uses.

Instead, S/H should be a regular part of your life. It doesn't appear earlier in this book because to use it properly you have to understand Chapter 17, complete with inverted layer masks and merges of hiraloam with conventional sharpening.

Don't believe it? Return to the start of the last chapter, and look at the opening teaser, a desert scene. Figure 17.1B is S/H. Do you see the telltale hiraloam halos where the mountains meet the sky, and where the greenery meets the mountains?

More to the point, Figure 17.1B is a pretty effective correction, considering that it took around a minute. To equal or exceed that effect of increasing the range of the clouds while lightening the greenery would require substantial time from a sophisticated person.

Figure 18.3 Top, the original sRGB image. Middle, a false profile of Apple RGB, 1.4 gamma, is applied. Bottom left, an alternate version prepared with Shadow/Highlight defaults. Bottom right, sharpening with a 30-pixel Radius is applied to the false profile (middle) version.

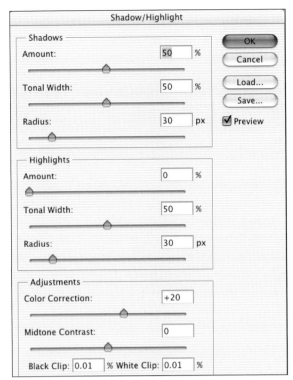

Figure 18.4 The Shadow/Highlight defaults.

The method that produced Figures 18.1C and 18.1D is S/H in slow motion: a more flexible approach for those who want to milk the most from the image. That approach is usually indicated when the image has strong colors. We'll show why that is, and how this slow-motion method works, after we illustrate S/H's operation. Our example will come from a courtroom in the United States, half a millennium after Venetian judges sentenced prisoners to a one-way march across the Bridge of Sighs.

The Overall S/H Look

I don't know the judge in Figure 18.3A, but he looks like the kind of jurist who might not have a great sense of humor about flashbulbs that disturb his sentencing hearings. So we can pardon the overly dark original.

As we know, digicams shortchange highlight and shadow detail because they feel that it usually is not all that important. This image is a good example of why the philosophy is correct. The shirts, the cup, and the judge's hair and moustache are not big-ticket items. Similarly, although it would be nice to have detail in the judge's robe, true shadows are not as important as the faces. The problem is that the picture starts out so dark that the faces count as shadows.

To fix this mess, we would, if we had never heard of S/H, turn to the false profiling described in Chapter 15. Figure 18.3A arrives in sRGB; I produced Figure 18.3B by assigning Apple RGB, 1.4 gamma, one of the profiles found on the CD. Apple RGB and sRGB are close enough that we don't notice a color difference. I chose 1.4 gamma not because I think it's best but because it happens to produce something roughly as dark as Figure 18.3C, which applies the S/H defaults directly to Figure 18.3A.

Although the darknesses are similar, the two have three major differences. First, Figure 18.3C is noisier in the shadows than 18.3B; second, it is more colorful; third, the face seems to have better shape. Let's find out why.

The Meaning of the S/H Defaults

The simplified version of the Shadow/Highlight dialog that greets us when we open the command for the first time should be forgotten about immediately. Click Show More Options, and Figure 18.4 appears.

Highlight and shadow adjustments are treated independently. If Amount for either is set to 0, regardless of the other settings, nothing happens to that side. By default, as you can see, there is no highlight adjustment, which is fine for this image.

The command tries to get more detail in the shadow (and in the highlight, too, if we ask for it) by lightening what it construes to be the affected region, while holding the darkness of its darkest point. It will in fact darken the dark point if given a flat enough image, but this effect is usually invisible.

What happens next is part blend, part curve. A copy of the image is inverted and used to lighten the existing image. In effect, although we don't see it, S/H is doing what we did the hard way in our first image. Let's return to that hard-way move now.

Figure 18.2B is a blurred, inverted version of the red channel of the Bridge of Sighs image. It goes on its own layer, which is then set to Overlay mode. This mode lightens the underlying image wherever the overlay is lighter than the equivalent of 50% gray, darkens where the overlay is darker than 50% gray, and does nothing at all where exactly 50% gray.

This overlay move therefore both darkens the highlights and lightens the shadows, as opposed to Shadow/Highlight, which manages the two independently. To match the control that S/H offers, we need to add a third layer, a copy of the original file. We set this third layer to Darken mode to restrict the correction to the highlights, or Lighten to restrict it to the shadows. (If you wish to forgo the possibility of re-blurring Figure 18.2B, you can do the same thing in only two layers: on the top layer, use Apply Image to apply it in Overlay, not Normal, mode, allowing us to choose Lighten or Darken mode for the layer itself.)

The key to this method—and to the proper use of S/H, too—is the blur. Without it, we'd get the relatively flat look of Figure 18.1B. The white marble would get darker, but the lines that define the bridge might actually lighten.

The solution is to hit the overlay with a big enough blur to obliterate those dark lines. Then, when the overlay is applied, it darkens the entire area, not just the white parts.

This method implies rather a big blur. Most applications of the Gaussian Blur filter use Radii in the low single digits. But even though the lines in the highlight area of the Bridge of Sighs are unusually skinny, it took a Radius of 11.5 pixels to make Figure 18.2B.

For more typical images, like that of the judge, an even higher number is needed. The blur has to be big enough to obliterate the eyes, which otherwise wouldn't be lightened. We'll see in a minute what happens if they aren't.

The S/H default blur is a sensible 30 pixels. The result is hauntingly reminiscent of hira-loam USM—why wouldn't it be, since they both use the same blurring computation?

To demonstrate, the 1.4-gamma version, Figure 18.3B, is sharpened with the same wide-Radius blur setting (USM filter values: 80%, 30, 2). The result, Figure 18.3D, is now more like the S/H version, Figure 18.3C. The main difference is in the color of the face. Note that the defaults of Figure 18.4 show +20% in the Color Correction field. This is a booboisie-friendly, expert-hostile setting. It acknowledges that most pictures that are too dark or too light are usually too gray as well. So it adds saturation to all colors.

In isolation, Figure 18.3C is preferable to the monochromatic 18.3D. It has, however, developed a big warm cast that will be a pain to get rid of. So if you have any intention of correcting the image further, be careful with this setting. It can help sometimes (we're about to see an example), but unless you're in a hurry, the assumption must be to axe it by setting it to 0.

The slider beneath it, Midtone Contrast, is an all-channel operation, which, as we know, is usually deadly. If you have enough time to mess with it, you have enough time to apply a sensible set of curves.

The three settings above these, though, Amount, Tonal Width, and Blur, are subtle and useful.

A Blur and a Blend

To illustrate how these fields interact, and also how to choose the proper settings for each image, Figure 18.5 has eight variants. We've already discussed the Blur field, and its close relation to hiraloam USM. Indeed, all unsharp masking is based on blurring: the opening graphic of Chapter 6, you may recall, looks like it was conventionally sharpened, but the only filter used was Gaussian Blur. (The convoluted steps to do this are listed in the Chapter 6 folder on the CD.)

The Amount and Tonal Width fields of S/H are readily confused. Amount governs, as it does with USM, the strength of the effect. Tonal Width limits the darknesses to which the effect applies. The lower the Tonal Width, the more the command confines itself to pure shadows and/or highlights.

Figure 18.5A shoots Amount up to the maximum 100%, while leaving the other two fields at the default 50%, 30. The picture looks silly. The dark parts have been lightened too far in relation to the rest of the image. And the noise is really objectionable.

Driving Tonal Width up to 100%, while leaving Amount at its 50% default and Blur at 30, is more acceptable (Figure 18.5B). The only thing is, it amounts to an overall lightening of the image, not an attempt to open the shadow. If you want to do that, there are better ways to accomplish it.

To choose the proper settings, I suggest a workflow similar to that recommended for hiraloam sharpening way back in Figure 6.12. That is, we set two fields to extreme values, pick the third, and then adjust the other two. In S/H, I establish Tonal Width first, by setting Amount to the 100% and Blur to 3. In Figure 18.5C, I married these two preposterous settings to the conservative 30% Tonal Width. Easy to see now why the blur has to be big enough to erase the judge's eyes!

When deciding the Tonal Width setting, it's actually an advantage to have the face so formless. Tonal Width's function is to set the darkness of the head in relation to the background. The sharpening effect of a decent Blur setting might confuse us.

I felt that 30 was too low a setting, but

A Smarter Sharpen Filter?

The Unsharp Mask filter dates from the early 1990s. It was an impressive feat back then, but much more is known today about the mechanics of sharpening. Also, back when computers were limited to 8 megabytes of RAM and operated at a tiny fraction of today's speeds, a complicated filter was out of the question—Unsharp Mask itself took forever on large files.

Granted that USM is, if not the most important filter Photoshop has, at least in the top three, a much stronger filter is overdue. Attempting to answer this need, Smart Sharpen was introduced in Photoshop CS2. It falls short of the mark in several ways. The basic function is the same as USM, but inexplicably, the critical Threshold field is omitted—it's just Amount and Radius.

The innovation is separate fields for shadow and highlight, with fields that resemble those for the Shadow/Highlight command discussed in this chapter: Fade (read: Amount), Tonal Width, and Blur. Unlike S/H, where the Blur setting is critical, Smart Sharpen's Blur has almost no impact. However, with proper adjustments of Fade and Tonal Width, we can cut back the sharpening in light and dark areas.

This capability is sometimes useful, particularly if we have a number of images that all need to be sharpened in the same way. In that way, it's like Camera Raw, whose correction capabilities are more useful to batch-process similar originals than individual images. As a one-shot tool, unfortunately, Smart Sharpen is a disappointment. The lack of Threshold is crippling. The highlight and shadow fades are handled better by Blend Ifs, which can apply to any channel. For more critical work, the channel-based layer masking methods discussed in Chapter 19 offer nearly infinite flexibility.

The current USM filter could best be improved by having it provide independent control of light and dark haloing. Chapter 6 shows some of the contortions we have to go through to get this effect.

Drum scanners of the 1980s did USM on the fly. Some had the equivalent of a Radius control; others Amount only. But all were able to treat the lightening and darkening halos as separate entities. If it was an important enough feature to have been standard 20 years ago, it's important enough to include now.

when I went to the more ambitious 60 Tonal Width in Figure 18.5D, it seemed to me that the head had gotten unrealistically light. So I settled for 40, in Figure 18.5E.

Just as in hiraloam sharpening, too low of a Blur setting damages the image, and too high simply lightens and darkens huge blocks without adding shape. We've already seen a 30 Blur in Figure 18.3C, so I went to 20 in Figure 18.5F and 50 in 18.5G, which is the one I vote for.

Finally, we lower Amount to taste. I favor the 60% shown in Figure 18.5H, and prefer this result to any of the four variants of Figure 18.3.

This image is a good one for demonstrating how S/H works, but a poor one for actually using it, with one large exception. Many times in professional work we have to get results much faster than we would like. This picture may be an example, for it was taken for a daily newspaper, where having enough time is as rare as an autostrada in Venice. Figure 18.3C takes ten seconds; 18.5H less than a minute. If that's all the time you've got, I heartily endorse S/H.

If time permits, however, starting with S/H is a bad idea. Instead, we'd proceed along the lines of a similar picture seen much earlier in Figure 3.9, an image of a grieving man who also had white hair. In both images, the camera was suckered into putting a white point where it didn't belong. There, it was a catchlight in the background. Here, the reflection off the top of the judge's chair has sold itself to the camera as a white point. As we know, the white point must be set in the lightest *significant* area. In both images, that happens to be the men's hair. Curves, possibly in conjunction with a false profile, handle this easily without S/H's assistance.

Trying to use it in this case would be counterproductive. In Figure 18.5H, the lightest hair is at $200^R170^G125^B$, far too dark. Setting it to a proper $245^R245^G245^B$ will drastically open up the entire image. In doing so, it will emphasize the noise that S/H thoughtfully provided in the shadows. That's why I don't show such a version—it would be impressive only in comparison to Figure 18.3A, not to a correction that started with a false profile.

Also, we know we should try to postpone a sharpening decision until near the end of the correction process, for fear that later

Figure 18.5 *Below, the roles of the Amount and Tonal Width settings are compared. Opposite, a suggested workflow for choosing the proper settings, deciding upon the Tonal Width first by viewing with an extremely high Amount and low Blur, then picking an appropriate Blur, and finally establishing the Amount.*

A (100,50,30)   B (50,100,30)

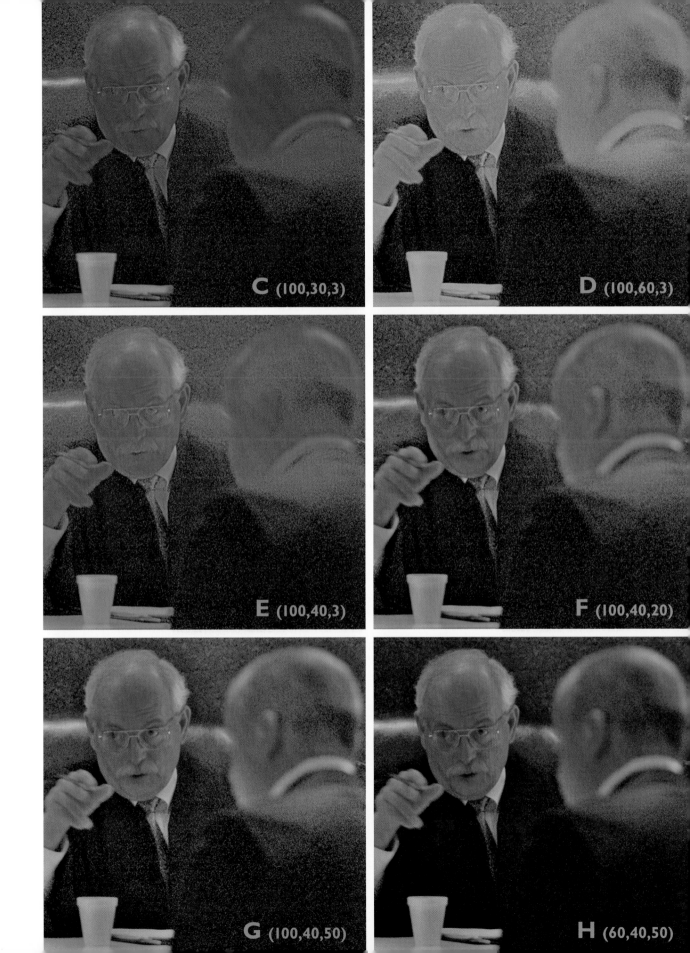

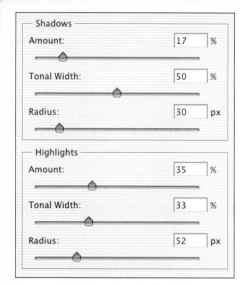

Figure 18.6 These Shadow/Highlight settings transform the original, top, into the version at bottom.

moves may transform an acceptable sharpen into a horsy-looking one. S/H requires us to make that sharpening decision up front when we declare a Blur setting.

To summarize, this image is not a good advertisement for S/H because, first, we are looking for a very big move. S/H may make a good appetizer, but Photoshop has a luau of tools for making big moves.

Second, we are using S/H for overall lightening, not for what it's best at, namely, opening highlights and shadows. We now will look at an image that *does* need those corrections.

Half Shadow, Half Highlight

The opening Bridge of Sighs shot needed work because of one of those nagging disparities between how cameras and humans evaluate scenes. The left side of the picture was in sunshine, the right half in shadow. Something like Figure 18.1C, which darkens the highlights while lightening the shadows, is on the right track. In my opinion, it goes too far in the shadows, which is why

I offered Figure 18.1D, which doesn't touch them. I'd prefer a version midway between the two. Shadow/Highlight would have been able to provide that.

Similar moves make sense in other sunlight/shade contexts. The most important case involves faces. Figure 18.6A, typical of the class, is not awful, but the left side is somewhat too light compared to the right.

Later in the chapter, we'll wrestle with a similar portrait where the problem is more severe than it is here. There, it would be dangerous to try to make S/H do more than it's capable of. But Figure 18.6A is the type of modest adjustment that S/H excels at but causes trouble for conventional methods.

With faces, we are accustomed to blending the green channel on a luminosity layer, as discussed in Chapter 8. That technique works wonderfully on most faces, but not here. It would darken the left half, as desired, but the right half would darken as well.

The highlight settings shown bring the two halves of the face closer to equality, closer to what we would have seen if we had been in the position of the camera. I chose them with the method shown in Figure 18.5: Tonal Width first, then Radius, then Amount.

The Shadows half is an afterthought this time. No drastic move to bring out contrast in the shirt or clothing is needed. But since the opportunity to make a pleasing tweak in almost no time flat has knocked, we might as well open the door. With Amount at only 17%, there's little point in trying to fine-tune the other settings—the result would have been nearly the same.

This time, the Color Correction setting of +20, which saturates colors as it darkens or lightens them, is helpful—somewhat. It demonstrates that the hair is not black, but brown. It makes the left side of the face redder. We could particularly debate whether the dimple to the left of the woman's nose is too red.

We can hope that in future versions the Color Correction field can be applied to either half of the S/H command, rather than to both as at present. In the interim, nothing stops us from applying S/H twice, once for highlights, once for shadows. Or, if you find the dimple in Figure 18.6B really objectionable, you could paint over it with the sponge tool, set to Desaturate mode and a low Flow. That would tone down the redness without doing any lightening.

So far, all the images in this chapter have showcased relatively dull colors. When they get more vivid, S/H still works—but you have to know your channels, and you have to know your options.

S/H and Colorspaces

The examples in this chapter are all RGB, but Shadow/Highlight works in LAB, too. Since Photoshop CS2, it has also been available in CMYK.

Although some exceptional cases are out there, CMYK is generally a bad place to run S/H. The highlights have already been damaged by the dot gain adjustment applied during separation; the shadows have no detail in the CMY, for reasons discussed in Chapter 5. If you want to enhance shadows in CMYK, apply curves and/or sharpening to the black channel.

LAB gets slightly better results with the Shadows half of S/H than RGB does: the higher the gamma, the better it handles shadows and the worse highlights. I show examples in *Photoshop LAB Color* of the LAB advantage in enhancing shadows. The RGB advantage in highlights, although present, is hard to see.

Images that require S/H usually need colors boosted, which is why the Color Correction field is +20 by default. However, it's more accurate to do this boosting in LAB, if convenient. Therefore, I apply S/H in LAB most of the time. It's not a big deal.

If you're not planning to intensify the colors and have no other reason to go to LAB, I'd stay in RGB unless it was a critical part of correcting a critical original, in which case I'd do the highlight work in RGB and the shadows in LAB.

The Channel with the Difference

The black handbag in Figure 18.7A is the kind of thing that used to give ulcers to the RGB-centric. It's never been hard in CMYK: such dark, neutral objects, as we learned in Chapter 5, migrate into the black channel, where they are easily dealt with. Until the advent of S/H, there was no easy RGB solution.

Today, though, if you need to fix the handbag and aren't headed for CMYK, you can always go to a separate Shadow/Highlight move limited to shadows only. The difficult part of this image is the woman's pink outfit, which is nearly blown out at its edges.

Nothing stops us from using S/H in the normal way on this image. I used settings of Shadows: 20%, 50%, 90 and Highlights: 30%, 45%, 15. Note the narrow Blur radius in the Highlights setting: the detail in the fabric is so fine that it doesn't take much blurring to obliterate it.

Overall, Figure 18.7B is a step in the right direction, but there are two quibbles. First, even with the Color Correction adjustment, the pink is rather dull. Second, the outfit has darkened, which is what we wanted, but the woman's hand has darkened also, which is undesirable.

The channel structure gives us the solution. Pink is a species of red; thus the green and blue channels must be darker than the red. If you would describe the red as being an angrier or more orange color, then the blue would be darker than the green, but if, as here, it's a rosier or purpler color, the green is darker.

Figure 18.7 Below, the original and its red, green, and blue channels. Opposite: top left, an application of S/H to the composite RGB. Top right, S/H is applied instead to the green channel only. Bottom left, the layer on which the top right version appears is changed to Luminosity mode. Bottom right, a final option: S/H applied to the green and blue channels.

In either the green or the blue channel, however, the hand is darker in comparison to the fabric than it is in the red channel. That suggests we may be better off applying S/H to individual channel(s). If we apply it to the composite color image, the weak red channel is averaged in and the hand is light enough to be counted as a highlight.

Figure 18.7C shows what happens when we apply S/H to the green alone. Since the other two channels are untouched, I went to the stronger Amounts of Shadows 30% and Highlights 40%, leaving the other settings alone. The hand is more reasonable.

Unfortunately, the handbag is now green. Because such color shifts often happen when we sharpen or apply S/H to a single channel, we always make such moves on duplicate layers, so that, if necessary, we can change to Luminosity mode to restore the original colors. That's what I did in Figure 18.7D. The hand is darkened, but not as much as in Figure 18.7B. The detail in the blown-out areas is better, too.

We now cast a wistful look at the color we just threw away. Figure 18.7A is too bland; surely the suit must be pinker than that. Figure 18.7B, because of the Color Correction setting, intensified the pink, whereas Figure 18.7D reverted to the original color.

We could try a two-layered document with Figure 18.7B on bottom and 18.7C, set to Luminosity mode, on top. In my opinion, there's a better way. The color of Figure 18.7C is exciting, but it's too purple, especially in the hand and buttons. To make it more of the light red that it should be, we apply S/H not just to the green but to the blue as well, and forget about the luminosity layer. That's what's happening in Figure 18.7E, which we can, of course, tone down slightly if we think it's too colorful.

I did have to omit the Shadows half of the S/H command (the Highlights Amount is 35%). Otherwise, with the red channel

excluded from the mix, the handbag would have become cyan. But, as mentioned earlier, there is no shortage of ways to improve the handbag, the easiest of which being an all-channel application of shadow-only S/H.

This is yet another example of how the digital camera, with its incessant search for midtone contrast, can be our enemy. That's why the original pinks were so blown out, and the handbag so dark, and that's why Shadow/Highlight is such a valuable command today.

USM, Pseudo-USM, and Shape

The Unsharp Mask filter is appropriate for most images, but every so often, particularly when highlights are critical, even hiraloam sharpening won't work. In that case, we can exploit the pseudo-sharpening abilities of S/H—or even look for a more sophisticated alternative.

Figure 18.8, a product shot for print advertising, has enough weight in the highlight, but the client would no doubt be pleased if shape were added to these flat-looking containers. S/H can do it, but if you, like me, consider this the critical part of the image, we should look for even better options.

Let's start by pretending that Shadow/Highlight does not exist and that we need to find a similar solution elsewhere. As usual, a knowledge of how the channels behave is the key.

The following fleshes out the procedure already used in the Bridge of Sighs image of Figure 18.1. The idea is to use a blurred, inverted copy of one of the channels (or possibly of the composite color image) to overlay the original, creating shape.

I do not think that darkening anything blue is on the agenda. Therefore, we should work with the red channel, which has the most distance between the white and blue areas. The background wall is as light as the darkest white areas in either of the other two

Figure 18.8 *The original image and its three channels. The red channel is the key to the forthcoming blends because it has the best separation between the white and blue areas.*

channels. Even the blue labels themselves might be construed as partial highlights and darkened.

We work with a three-layered document, in which the top and bottom layers are copies of the original, and the middle an inverted, unblurred copy of the red channel. Photoshop allows this to be done in many ways, such as: start with three identical layers, make the top layer invisible, activate the middle layer in the Layers palette, then Apply Image, using the red channel from any layer as the source, Normal mode, with Invert checked.

The fun begins when the top layer is made invisible and the middle layer's mode goes to Overlay, producing Figure 18.9A and presumably the sinking sensation in your stomach that this is some kind of bad joke rather than a correction. The overlay is drastically lightening all the blue areas. Even

the lighter parts, which are what we're trying to improve, are worse. They're just darker, not shapelier.

Figure 18.9B is the unblurred original inverted red. The next three versions Gaussian Blur it at Radii of, respectively, 20, 40, and 60.

The impact of these different Radii is pronounced, but extremely difficult to comprehend without a lot of practice, so I will go slowly, and resort to an unusual graphic before showing the final results.

Overlay mode lightens wherever the overlaying layer is lighter than 50% gray. One look at the labels of Figure 18.9B, and we understand why the blues in Figure 18.9A have been destroyed: the overlay lightens them as much as it possibly can.

We don't want any of this lightening at all. That's why there's a top layer, which, as the Layers palette shows, is invisible in Figure 18.8A—a copy of the bottom layer, but set to

A

Figure 18.9 *Above, a blurred, inverted copy of the red channel is applied to Figure 18.8 in Overlay mode. Right, top to bottom, the overlay channel is seen unblurred, then blurred at Radii of 20, 40, and 60.*

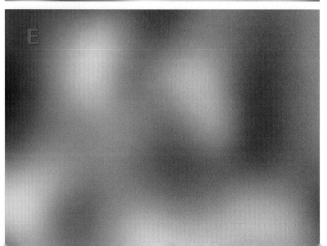

Darken mode. We now make it visible, which prevents any lightening but allows the middle (overlay) layer to darken as much as it likes.

Even with that layer reinstated, though, Figure 18.9A would be calamitously flat. Among other things, the white word *milk* in the middle of each label would darken unacceptably—look how dark that type is in Figure 18.9B.

This is why we need to blur the middle layer at least as much as the 20

A

of Figure 18.9C, which barely eliminates that type; it just becomes part of the blue label and hence off limits for alteration.

Figure 18.10 helps visualize the impact of each of the blurs of 18.9. I've enhanced and colorized the overlays to show where, and how strongly, they do their work. The original image appears in areas where the overlay has been disallowed because it would have lightened the area. (The white background, which is completely blown out in the original, remains that way, as overlays don't affect blank areas.)

Notice that a bigger Radius doesn't mean that a bigger area is affected. All three versions appear to be darkening roughly the same amount of real estate, but they aren't always doing it in the same

Figure 18.10 These three versions show the effect of overlaying, respectively, Figures 18.9B, 18.9C, and 18.9D onto the original image, with an additional copy of the original on top to restore the darkness of any areas that have been lightened. The reddish areas indicate where the image will be darkened. The other areas will remain unchanged.

B

C

places, and each emphasizes certain areas more than the others do.

It's easiest to compare the two extremes—and to look at what happens in real life (Figure 18.11), too.

The 20-pixel blur, Figure 18.10A, shows a darkening in the center of the skin cream that is not present in the 60-pixel Figure 18.10C. That darkening is clearly visible when we go real-world and compare Figures 18.11A and 18.11C. The jar is similarly affected. Look at the where the blue and white parts of the label merge, right above the word *milk*. Figure 18.10A shows that the darkening from the overlay reaches that area. But in Figure 18.10C, the reddish blur clears that line of transition by a wide margin.

Figure 18.11 *The results of the blurred inverted overlays shown in Figure 18.10.*

Result: the jar is darker in Figure 18.11A than it is in 18.11C.

The smaller blur reserves its biggest impact for the lightest areas, which is not a good idea in this image. Figure 18.10A indicates intense darkening on the left sides of the two rightmost bottles. The left sides therefore get darker in Figure 18.11A faster than the right sides do. In Figure 18.10C, the darkening is more uniform across the product. There is more life in Figure 18.11C's bottles.

All in the Family

For these reasons, if it's between the 20- and 60-pixel blurred versions, it's an easy choice for me and presumably for you as well. Choosing between Figures 18.11B and 18.11C is more difficult. You can pick whatever you want, as this image is on the CD at full resolution. Me, I split the difference and chose

Figure 18.12 *Top, a version prepared with a 50-pixel blur, plus slight sharpening and curves. Other options are less palatable. Bottom left, Shadow/Highlight does not offer the same shape. Bottom right, hiraloam USM blows some areas out.*

A

B

C

a 50-pixel blur. After some modest touchup (sharpening and curves to lighten the highlight), my final version is Figure 18.12A.

Compare this result to two competitors. If you see a family resemblance, it's because they both use the same blurring strategy, and I chose a setting of 50 both times, to match Figure 18.12A. With Shadow/Highlight, the closest I could come was Figure 18.12B, with Shadows turned off and Highlights settings of 25%, 45%, 50.

It's nice, but the white containers don't have the depth of Figure 18.12A. Also, since S/H has to work on overall image darkness (as opposed to using the red channel, which separates the whites and the blues well),

there was no way to prevent darkening of the blue areas. We would be able to mask out the darker blues easily, but the lighter background blues would create a problem.

Figure 18.12C reminds us of why we need a surrogate method of hiraloam sharpening (which is what the process we have just been through amounts to): the real thing won't work with detailing this light. USM settings of 60%, 50, 50 blow out parts of the products and darken the blues excessively. Still, the strong points are apparent. The overlay blur method allows us to retain them, without the drawbacks of direct sharpening.

Forcing this faceoff is misleading. Sharpening, Shadow/Highlight, and selections are teammates, not competitors. If one of them can do everything we need, then we don't waste time by bringing the others into the act. Often, though, they can reinforce one another. Let's have a look at how they can interact to dispose of a considerably nastier specimen of the blown-out fleshtone problem we confronted earlier in Figure 18.6.

Balancing Blur and Blend

Pasty-looking fleshtones are usually fixed right up with a technique demonstrated in Chapter 8: apply the green channel to a new layer set to Luminosity mode. This works well, up to a point. That point comes when the skin is as washed-out as it is in Figure 18.13A.

We are not, however, without options. We'll turn to a Shadow/Highlight solution in a moment; first let's try to cobble together a blending method. The green appears to be too light to do much good. The blue is usually too dark in faces for blending, but given how pale the original is, it might work—if modified.

Stumbling Blocks: The Five-Run Homer

•**Looking for a miracle.** Shadow/Highlight works best in small doses, as an enabler of further corrections rather than a blunderbuss attempt to solve all problems at once. Notice that in the most effective S/H corrections shown here, the Amount is less than the default 50%. It is true that the command can make an impressive change for the better in a seriously under- or overexposed image. Impressive, that is, until you look closely and discover that there are easy ways to get better quality.

•**Speed versus Quality.** When do we use S/H rather than the three-layer overlay blending shown in Figures 18.3 and 18.9? The answer is easy. Never! That is, of course, on the assumption that you have an unlimited amount of time for each job. The overlay blend method is stronger and more flexible. You would never get a worse result, because you could always use a straight luminosity mask just the way S/H does. Sometimes the results would be equivalent, and sometimes there would be a benefit, and occasionally a *big* benefit, in using overlays. It also takes 20 times as long as S/H. That's why we study both methods in this chapter, not because there's ever a case where S/H is superior.

•**The overlay must be one channel.** This chapter suggests enhancing shadow and highlight by putting a single inverted, blurred channel on a layer that's set to Overlay mode. Don't try substituting a blurred and inverted copy of the entire file. If you do, certain colors will be neutralized because their light components will darken and their dark components lighten. If you use a single channel as the overlay rather than all three, that can't happen. Either all channels will darken or all will lighten. The big question, of course, is which channel to use for the overlay.

Figure 18.13
Top right, the RGB original, with its channels at left. Right center, the blue is applied to a luminosity layer to deepen the fleshtone. As this creates overly dark hair, a layer mask— a copy of the red channel—is added to make the bottom right version.

WARNING: Don't use the blue channel for such blending if the file has ever been JPEGged. That method of compression damages the blue channel much more than the other two. Before applying the blue in this image, I looked at it carefully, at 300% magnification on screen, to make sure there weren't nasty artifacts that could blow up in my face if applied to the other two channels. I then proceeded to make Figure 18.13B.

The fleshtone is definitely improved, but the hair has become black in spots. We saw one way of dealing with a similar problem (a red dress that the luminosity blend had made too dark) back in Figure 8.7—the Blend If options. We could experiment with those here to exclude the top layer in areas where, say, its blue channel is dark.

A more flexible option was discussed peripherally in the last chapter and will be the main topic of the next one. We can restrict the top layer not with Blend If but with a layer mask. Or, if we're in more of a hurry, we can blend directly through a selection. To make Figure 18.13C, I loaded the original red channel from the bottom layer as a layer mask for the top one.

To review why this works: we start with two layers. The original, Figure 18.13A, is on the bottom. A copy of the blue channel is on top, but for our purposes we can assume that what's on top is Figure 18.13B. Although the top layer is grayscale (since every channel is a copy of the blue), it has been set to Luminosity mode to revert to the original color.

A blank layer mask is there automatically if we make an adjustment layer; with a standard layer like this one, we have to add it ourselves with Layer: Layer Mask>Reveal All or by clicking the layer mask icon at the bottom of the Layers palette.

Where the layer mask is white, we see the top layer, where black the bottom layer, where gray a combination. At the outset, the layer mask is blank—pure white—so there's no change. We still are seeing Figure 18.13B.

Here, first making sure that the layer mask was highlighted so that it was the active channel, I used Apply Image to insert a copy of the red channel, Background layer, the same channel shown on the top left of Figure 18.13. Since the face is almost blank, it leaves Figure 18.13B in control. The hair is darker. If, for the sake of argument, it is at 50% gray, then the resulting hair will be an

Review and Exercises

✓Why are you more likely to need the Shadow/Highlight command with a digital photograph than one that was scanned from film?

✓By default, S/H applies a strong correction to shadows and none to highlights. If you wish to work on highlights only, how do you prevent the command from affecting the shadows?

✓What does Shadow/Highlight's Color Correction field do? Why and when is it a good idea?

✓Return to Chapter 17's opening image, a desert shot. Can you reproduce the effect of Figure 17.1B with Shadow/Highlight, without referring to the actual settings, which are on the CD? Would you prefer to work this image with S/H, or with overlay blends as in Figure 18.11?

✓For blurring out noise, the Surface Blur filter (Photoshop CS2 and later) is often preferred because it avoids blurring edges. In this chapter, we use Gaussian Blur instead. Why?

✓From our pink suit exercise, you have produced for your client's approval Figures 18.7D and 18.7E. She examines them and says to use the handbag from Figure 18.7D, but to make the rest of the image a blend: two-thirds 18.7E, one-third 18.7D. How would you carry out her instructions?

even split between the two layers. That's about what we see in Figure 18.13C—hair midway between the darknesses of the two previous versions.

It's true that there's a quicker way: before blending the blue into the top layer, load the red channel as a selection (Command-Option–1, or Command–click the red icon in the Channels palette) rather than as a permanent mask. It works, but it takes away a certain amount of flexibility. For example, suppose we feel that the hair in Figure 18.13C, although better than 18.13B, is still too dark. Rather than editing the image itself, we can alter the layer mask. We apply curves to darken its shadow. As the hair gets darker in the layer mask, it moves the final result closer to the bottom layer (Figure 18.13A) and its lighter hair.

One final note. In keeping with the theme of this chapter, the layer mask should be blurred. Otherwise, detail gets lost in the hair. It's not a big deal, but the effect is there. The reason is the same as found in much stronger form in Figure 18.9, where an unblurred inverted overlay caused unacceptable closing up of similar detail.

Don't Try Too Hard

Now, let's begin again, this time using Shadow/Highlight.

This original is very like the judge of Figure 18.3A. In each, S/H can make an impressive change. But trying to get a perfect result with it is criminal. S/H is best used to open shadows and highlights—*real* shadows and highlights, not artificial ones that have been created by poor photography. The judge image was too dark, so things that shouldn't have been shadows were. This

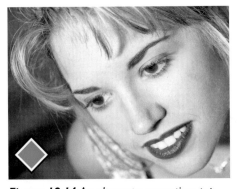

Figure 18.14 *An alternate correction: top right, S/H is applied to Figure 18.13A. The resulting green channel (above) can now be used on a luminosity layer to produce the bottom right version.*

original is too light, so the fleshtone falls in the highlight range.

Try to use S/H to equal the facial detail of Figure 18.13C, then, and you'll have a mess. Downsize your expectations, and you can do better.

To make Figure 18.14A, I used Highlights settings of 15%, 40%, 50. I left the Color Correction field at +20% to allow a pinker skintone. And, foreseeing that the hair might get darker later, I took preemptive action by adding a Shadows correction of 10%, 50%, 30.

Some may find the result more aesthetically pleasing than Figure 18.13C. It's just another battle in the never-ending war that commenced with our examination of the hog of Figure 1.2. The color is better in Figure 18.14A, but clearly there is more detail in Figure 18.13C. Who can say which is the better picture?

We might think of putting one on top of the other in Luminosity or Color mode as the case might be. There is, however, a more effective way.

Remember, the normal procedure is to use the green on a luminosity layer. It wasn't

The Bottom Line

The Shadow/Highlight command, introduced in Photoshop CS, is a powerful tool to open detail near image endpoints. It addresses a major problem of digital captures, which emphasize midtones at the expense of highlights and shadows.

Some perceive S/H as a means of resurrecting hopelessly underexposed images, but in fact it is better at more modest moves. This chapter proposes a more powerful, but more time-consuming, alternative: single-channel overlay blending, a method that gives shaping control characteristic of hiraloam sharpening. The clues that this method may be better than S/H are large areas that need to be improved and/or the presence of brilliant colors.

possible with the original image, but Figure 18.14A has added enough spice that the *new* green is good enough. So, we put it on a luminosity layer as usual (I chose an opacity of 70%, believing that the picture was now dark enough), and get Figure 18.14B. I rate that as a better version than Figure 18.13C—temporarily. That isn't a final effort, either. It has solved the major problem of the blown-out skintone; the rest is routine.

An Embarrassment of Riches

In summary, we have just seen two separate ways to get an effect that most professional retouchers would not have been able to achieve even five years ago. And that's leaving aside the different ways to mask that we could have used. Plus, we never considered the overlay blend method shown in the skin-products image of Figure 18.9, which would certainly have worked, nor the false-profiling approach of Chapter 15, which probably would have worked too.

Many, if not most, examples of this annoying category of images can be handled with the Shadow/Highlight command in a fraction of the time needed to do the overlays shown here—provided you can figure out what to do with with the critical Blur setting. To summarize the lessons of this chapter: *The blur has to be big enough to kill fine detail, yet small enough to retain shape.*

If, at the start of this chapter, you'd have been willing to settle for slight improvements in highlight and shadow detail, pretend you're eating in Italy. Be a bit more greedy, because now there are a lot of other tasty options on the table. Most of the images in this chapter could be interpreted in several different ways. Master the blur and the blend, and you can have whichever interpretation you like.

Blur, blend, and stride briskly back across the Bridge of Sighs, into the palace.

Color, Contrast, and Safety in Masking

When the objective is to completely change the art—or to make a subtle reinterpretation of it—it is sometimes necessary to correct through a selection or mask. The best masks are based on existing channels. Here's how to find them.

The battleship USS *Missouri*, which some thought was obsolete 60 years ago, has not yet outlived its usefulness. Today it is a floating museum, anchored at the place most associated with the reason for its existence, Pearl Harbor. Built incredibly rapidly, the *Missouri* entered World War II long after there was any doubt which side would win, but it did see action off Japan, where it justified its reputation as the most formidable naval weapon yet developed.

Its three batteries of 16-inch guns, one of which is shown in Figure 19.1, could fire half-ton projectiles 20 miles or so with remarkable accuracy. The *Missouri* was so intimidating that it was chosen as the site to receive the Japanese surrender that ended the war.

The age of the battleship was then thought to have come to a close, because in an age of air power they were nothing more than big targets, at least if the enemy was another superpower. The Soviet Union did not bother to build battleships for this reason, and nobody else added to their fleets, either. Nevertheless, it was discovered subsequently that not all wars are fought against other superpowers, and that battleships have their uses against enemies who cannot sink them. Consequently, the *Missouri* was brought out of retirement no less than three times, using its huge guns to pulverize significant portions of Korea, Vietnam, and Kuwait before being finally decommissioned—we think—in 1992.

This vessel teaches so much about where we have been that any image of it deserves to be treated with respect. For one thing, we should be sure the ship is the right color. Fortunately, we're pretty sure of what that color is. The naval term for it is *battleship gray*. I'm not certain of the exact formulation of that paint but am willing to bet Canadian dollars to navy beans that it isn't as blue as in Figure 19.1.

Finding the Excuse to Use the Mask

For all the fancy sailing of the last two chapters, with their inverted, blurred masks and other legerdemain, this exercise is back to basics. It could have come right out of Chapter 2. The ship doesn't need sharpening as much as it needs the contrast boost that only curves can give. Since we have to make some adjustments anyway to get the color right, it should be simple to put the *Missouri* in the steepest part of each curve.

Contrary to the strong recommendations of Chapters 2 and 3, however, these curves, like every other correction in the rest of this chapter, will be applied through a mask that emphasizes changes in certain areas and restricts them in others. Masks are the Photoshop equivalent of 16-inch guns—absurdly powerful, but counterproductive when used in the wrong context. Corrections through masks are usually bad tactics, so before getting involved in one, we have to come up with some kind of justification.

The most obvious such justification is what retouchers call a *move away from the art*—putting in a new color that has nothing to do with the original photograph. Later in this chapter, we'll change a dress from green to orange. That's a move away from the art. We don't have to feel guilty about using a mask to accomplish it.

Using a mask without a satisfactory reason unbalances the image. Many pages ago, I made the case against selections, pointing

Figure 19.1 This battleship is known to be gray, but the original capture has it blue.

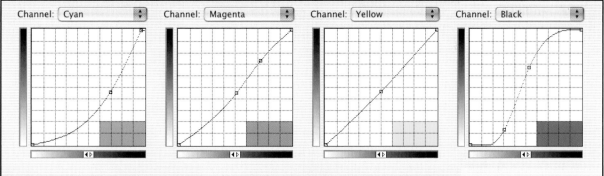

out that the pink horses of Figure 3.12 indicated that the whole light part of the image was too pink, and that isolating the horses to correct them would result in white horses on a pink background.

The same is true in the case at hand. If the battleship is too blue, then everything else of approximately that darkness is also too blue. We must assume, therefore, that the sky is too blue in Figure 19.1.

That reasoning may float in the calibrationist navy, but it sinks in mine. I like the sky

Figure 19.2 *These curves, modified by an inverted copy of the blue channel of the original RGB as a layer mask, bring the ship to a proper gray and add contrast, without affecting the sky.*

the way it is, a fitting backdrop to an important piece of history. As long as the clouds are white (and they are, in the original), I am ready to make a move away from the art toward a bluer sky.

This file arrives in untagged RGB; it must be prepared for CMYK. Where should we apply the curves, and what channel(s) should we use for the mask?

We know from previous channel-blending voyages that skies are always strongest in the red (RGB) or cyan (CMYK) channels. These two are therefore to be avoided for masking purposes, since their skies might be just about as dark as the battleship. Instead, we would choose the blue or the yellow, as these are more direct opponents of a sky than the green or the magenta. A third option is the black of CMYK, possibly of a separate copy converted with Heavy GCR as described in Chapter 5. All three of these possibilities would have to be inverted for use as a layer mask, the sky of which needs to be black to permit the lower layer to show through.

There's no case for correcting this file in LAB, as we have no need for color variation. And there's not much for doing it in RGB, either. We saw in the discussion of the blouse of Figure 2.17 that when all we care about is detail, we can get more of it with four channels than three. Moreover, when the prime object is supposed to be neutral, the black channel can serve as an anchor to keep it that way.

Accordingly, the procedure:

- Convert the file to CMYK.
- Add a curves adjustment layer.
- Apply curves like those in Figure 19.2, steepening the ship's range in every channel and creating a gray rather than a blue.
- Click the layer mask that the adjustment layer automatically created, activating it.
- Image: Apply Image, using whatever source you've decided on. In my case, I saved (and kept open) an RGB copy of the file and applied its blue channel, inverted. This is a slightly better choice than the yellow of CMYK, which is not as dark in the ship for the ink limit reasons discussed in Chapter 5.
- Re-evaluate the ship to see if the layer mask has driven it off neutrality. If it has,

apply a curve to the layer mask, forcing its lightest areas closer to white, thus ensuring that the curves of Figure 19.2 take full effect. This is why using an inverted copy of the yellow or black would work, even if the blue would be technically more pristine.

Red Sky in the Morning

Before embarking on the rest of the chapter, midshipmen are politely but firmly requested to listen to the following safety briefing:

- Clients do not care whether the picture was taken with a Hasselblad or a cell phone. They do not care whether the image was corrected with Brightness/Contrast, a set of curves, or an ICC profile. They are not impressed by fancy Photoshop techniques because they have no idea what they are. If you use a mask, you may consider yourself a more sophisticated person. That, plus 20 quarters, buys you a five-dollar bill, as far as the client is concerned. You get no prize for having used a mask, unless it's a booby prize for having wasted time with it in the course of producing worse quality than if you had done the correction globally.
- The surest indication of incompetence in image handling is the discovery in the middle of correction that a selection or mask is necessary. If you need one, you should know (or at least strongly suspect) it the minute you open the image.
- The use of masks, even when appropriate, does not excuse you from following the rules laid out in Chapters 1–10, particularly the by-the-numbers requirements of Chapters 3 and 9. If your competitor doesn't know how to make a mask but does go by the numbers, all the masks in the world won't save you from losing business to her—unless you get good numbers yourself.

Bearing these stern advisories in mind, there are two excuses for using masks. The first is to re-correct something that somebody else, or some machine, has corrected badly. The most common example is the algorithmic insertion of a white point into a document the rest of which isn't properly color balanced.

The second is to put something into the file that the camera never saw. As the last two chapters have made clear, the term *unsharp masking* actually does imply the presence of a mask. The mask is present in the Shadow/Highlight command as well. Both commands aim at manufacturing detail not present in the original image, and thus qualify as moves away from the art. In Chapter 17, we went even further, using another mask—a layer mask—to merge two different varieties of the masking we call unsharp.

In the more conventional kinds of color correction—curves and channel blending—masks tend to be appropriate in the three areas in which human memory often doesn't agree with what the camera saw. And, given that Missouri is the Show Me state, examples of each will be forthcoming. The three categories are:

- **Skies**. We like them blue, deep blue.
- Greenery, **plant life**. We usually remember it as being a more saturated color than the camera does.
- Above all, **faces**. Whether obsessed with our own mortality or for another reason as yet undetermined, we remember faces as being healthy-looking. In light-complexioned individuals, this implies a suntanned, yellower look; in darker-skinned individuals, a redder appearance often seems more accurate.

If these or comparable factors are present, the mask hunt may commence. If we're in a hurry, we may dispense with the mask and work with a direct selection based on a single channel. Or, we may work on a separate layer, modified by Blend If sliders.

It is probably more understandable to explain masking in terms of the two types of correction we've grappled with for the last 450 pages. Some masks are for contrast,

others for color. The contrast masks are usually found in RGB, occasionally CMYK. The color masks always come from the AB of LAB.

The Scanner Operator Takes the Helm

A selection based on contrast is often referred to as a *luminosity mask,* or, when used as in Figure 19.2, an *inverted luminosity mask.* We've already seen such masks several times in the last two chapters. For example, we often use inverted luminosity masks to limit conventional USM to darker areas. We just saw an uninverted luminosity mask in Figure 18.13, where I tried to deepen an objectionably pale fleshtone (see the list of common masking exceptions above) with a blend, without darkening the hair.

The word *luminosity* suggests loading the composite color channel (or, in LAB, the L) as the selection or mask. That's a good practice sometimes, but if it's worth loading a mask at all, it's worth looking for the right channel to use for it. Most of the time it's obvious. Just look at the *Missouri* image and we know the three channels that are best for masking it; just look at the face of Figure 18.13 and we know that it should be the red.

Sometimes, though, it's not so apparent. Fortunately, experimentation is easy.

Figure 19.3A is professional architectural photography. It originated in film, was drum scanned, and arrives in CMYK. Therefore, somebody has already corrected the image, just as today's digicams do, although this time it's a human being, who is presumably more discreet than an algorithm.

Without seeing the original film, I'm betting that the scanner operator deliberately tried to intensify the rich colors. If so, I endorse the decision in view of the context in which the image is to be used.

There is, however, a technical error. The scanner operator either chose the wrong highlight or else didn't understand how to handle a nonwhite light point. If he paid

attention to the light from the lamp, or to the face of the statue, he shouldn't have. They're both speculars, and even if the statue isn't, it's white areas are too small for us to care about detail. That leaves the bolster—the long, narrow cushion at the foot of the bed—as the lightest significant object.

If its light areas were believed to be white, they should have been set to $5^C2^M2^Y$ or thereabouts, as recommended in Chapter 3. Apparently, however, the operator thought they should be warmer, more orange-yellow. So he chose $5^C5^M15^Y$.

I agree with the thinking but not the execution. If the bolster's cover contains whites, the pillowcases and the sheets must also, and if we force whiteness into them, the picture will get very cold if in fact they shouldn't be white. However, if it turns out that the highlight really should be slightly yellow, it still shouldn't be *darker* than $5^C2^M2^Y$. Instead, we choose something like $1^C1^M8^Y$.

On a curves adjustment layer, I pushed the bottom left CMY endpoints to meet these desired values in Figure 19.3B. Maybe you feel this should be the final version. Personally, I'm happier with the darker wood and wall found in Figure 19.3A. So, I click into the layer mask that the adjustment layer automatically creates. By default, it's blank and has no effect.

Choosing the Right Channel

Assuming we don't bother to convert a copy of this image to RGB, there are five—not four—CMYK channels from which to choose a layer mask. (The CMYK composite itself can be used as the source, provided the file itself is in CMYK; otherwise only the obvious four are available.) Can you put them in the correct order, lightest to darkest, just by looking at Figure 19.3A? Any of the five will retain the lightness of the pillow. But which gives the best overall image?

Figure 19.3 *In the original, top, the lightest significant area (the bolster) is too dark. Bottom, straight-line curves make it lighter, but also lighten the rest of the image.*

As we saw all the way back in our original channels quiz of Figure 1.5, the black channel is always the lightest one. If we load that as the layer mask, the result will be the most like Figure 19.3B. Choose any of the other four, and the result will start to resemble Figure 19.3A. Lightest to darkest, the other four are: cyan, composite CMYK, magenta, and yellow.

Fortunately, it only takes a couple of seconds to try all five. Just open the Apply Image dialog and toggle through the source channels, first making sure that the layer mask is the target. The image preview changes each time, and we take our pick. Two examples are shown here. Figure 19.4A uses the black as the layer mask, 19.4B the magenta.

In professional contexts, it's often best to be conservative. The client makes the final call, and the client may have different tastes than we do. As pointed out in Chapter 1, certain corrections (normally those involving color changes) are matters of taste, but others (usually range extensions) would be universally accepted.

The differences shown here are mild. Stating a preference among the three corrected versions is your role, or your client's. I can imagine clients criticizing Figures 19.3B and/or 19.4A (which is my own favorite). If the choice, however, is between the other two, it is hard to imagine that anyone would prefer the original, Figure 19.3A, over the conservative Figure 19.4B.

How Green Is My Valley

If people who do a lot of work in LAB agree on one thing, it's that the presence of large natural green areas is an indication that we should not just be entering LAB but also steepening the AB curves considerably.

This move away from the art recognizes that we don't see greens the way a camera does. For simultaneous contrast reasons, we want to see more flavors of green; for sentimental,

Figure 19.4 *Top, Figure 19.3B is modified by using the black channel as a layer mask. Bottom, the magenta channel is used instead.*

Figure 19.5 Opposite, the original (top) could use brighter greens, but standard AB curves knock the flowers out of gamut, costing detail (bottom). Above, Blend If options restrict the change to areas that were originally green.

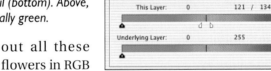

romantic reasons we often remember the greens as also being more saturated than the camera recorded.

Although this justifies a mask if one is needed, they usually aren't in LAB. We either jigger the curves so that they affect greens only, or we don't mind that other colors get brighter along with the greens.

This image, however, is uncooperative. LAB is usually ineffective where brilliant colors are present, and Figure 19.5A has a lot of them. Chapter 4 showed us the basic LAB curve structure: steepened straight lines in the A and B, moved slightly to the right of the original center point here because the road, which presumably should be 0^A0^B or something close, instead checks in as rather cool.

Just steepening the curves, however, produces Figure 19.5B. All the flowers have gone out of CMYK gamut, especially the red ones, which are now nothing but blobs.

It would be annoyingly difficult to mask out all these flowers in RGB or CMYK, but it just takes a second in LAB, provided you know your channel structure. In addition to the greenery, I see six other important objects: the road, the white arch, and four types of flowers. From top to bottom, they are pink, red, yellow, and bluish purple.

Consider the magenta versus green A channel. The road and arch are both neutral, therefore near 0^A. That's where the yellow flowers are, too. Although strongly colored, they're neither magenta nor green. The pink, red, and purple flowers are clearly more magenta than green, meaning they're A–positive.

Only the area that we want to correct is A–negative, greener than it is magenta. So to produce Figure 19.5C, we just need to do the curves on an adjustment layer and follow with a simple Blend If. That's why the selection is so easy, and that's why it's so important to get the LAB channels quiz of Figure 4.7 right. If you didn't do well then, you should go back and try again now.

The sliders shown exclude everything that's more than slightly A–positive. Anything more than slightly A–negative comes from Figure 19.5B. Things in the middle, like the walk and the arch, fall in a transition zone, partially Figure 19.5A and partially 19.5B. We use the This Layer rather than the Underlying Layer sliders because the steepened curves have made the ranges longer on the top layer. Anything slightly green is farther away from 0^A on the top layer than on the bottom. This gives us extra precision in deciding where to place the slider, as there is more differentiation between weak greens and neutrals.

The Double Whammy

Most of the time, we can get by without any mask at all, if you don't count sharpening or S/H. When needed, one is usually sufficient, either color or contrast. Occasionally, the age of digital photography forces us to use both.

To say that Figure 19.6 has offensive color is to say that the *Missouri* has offensive weaponry. But it's all part of the life of today's professional. When we're lucky, we get to work with good originals like the last two we've worked with. If we get them right, since no good deed goes unpunished, our reward is that our next job is garbage like this.

We've seen a similar picture recently: Figure 16.4, an elderly couple with a yellow cast nearly as bad as this one. That was in a chapter on Camera Raw, however. The solution was to acquire the image without any automated correction at all, whereupon we knocked out the cast in LAB without any more difficulty than a battleship would have in combat with a junk.

But, speaking of junk, we have no raw file to work with here. What you see is what you get, and it has already been "corrected" by the camera's algorithm. So instead of having a relatively flat file in which the yellowness appears stem to stern, we get one with full range and in which the yellow cast is about

Figure 19.6 *The obvious yellow cast in this original isn't uniform, thanks to automated "correction" within the digital camera. The lightest and darkest areas are close to being neutrally correct; the problem is in the midrange.*

as uniform as the position of an oceangoing vessel during a typhoon.

The original file is tagged ColorMatch RGB, but it's easier to verify the cast in terms of LAB values, so I have changed the right side of the Info palette to report them.

The following numbers run from lightest to darkest. All represent areas that should be fairly close to neutral. The light above the woman's head is completely blown out, $100^L0^A0^B$. The lightest spot in the hair, above her right eye, is $99^L(3)^A13^B$. The medium-white hair, high up on her left side, is $88^L5^A53^B$. The face in the background artwork, which I take to be a black and white print, is $80^L7^A52^B$. The darkest part of the woman's hair, near the left ear, is $73^L14^A56^B$. The dark background high up in the artwork is $59^L4^A39^B$, and the black ink on the cover of the woman's book is $13^L9^A14^B$.

The camera, in sum, has established a balanced white point that morphs into a serious yellow cast that reaches its zenith at roughly 75^L and then tails off. There is not a single B–negative value anywhere in the file; the only thing that is A–negative is, ridiculously, the lightest part of the hair, which is therefore greenish yellow rather than the orange yellow found in all darker areas.

Here's the drill.

- Make a copy of the RGB file—we may or may not need the original later—and convert to LAB.
- Add a curves adjustment layer.
- Apply the curves shown. They are very similar to the ones shown in a previous yellow cast exercise, Figure 16.4, which had been captured in Camera Raw. Unlike those of that docile example, these curves don't fix everything in one fell swoop. The dark half of Figure 19.7A is distinctly, disturbingly cool.
- Click the layer mask that the adjustment layer automatically created, activating it.
- Now, the experimentation. Remember, we've saved, and kept open, an RGB version

of the file in addition to the LAB one that we're currently working on. Since the two files are the same size, the Apply Image command recognizes both as potential sources for blends, or for the new layer mask. So, with the layer mask as the target, we use the Apply Image dialog to preview all three of the RGB channels and the L of the current file. Any of these choices will allow most of the correction in the lighter parts of the image and disallow most of it in the darkest parts; the only question is how rapidly the effect fades off. I felt that the best result came from loading the L as the layer mask, producing Figure 19.7B.

- The damage is now under control, except for the lightest areas of the woman's hair, which have become cyan, and the bluish light behind her head. For these, we turn to Blend If. Notice how this adjustment layer is modified twice: once by a contrast-based layer mask, once by Blend Ifs that are based on color. The two sets of sliders disallow the very lightest areas of the top layer, restoring the original blown-out lighting, and call for a smooth reduction, not an elimination, of anything that is more blue than yellow in Figure 19.7B.

The result of all this maneuvering is Figure 19.8. It's far from perfect, but it gives us something to start with.

Before moving into fleshtones, the final area in which masking is often necessary to compensate for the annoyance of cameras that don't see things the way humans do, let's look at a more complex way of creating a mask, one that applies to another area of human-camera disagreement.

Multiplication and Masking

Cameras don't have the human responses of simultaneous contrast and chromatic adaptation. Prudent application of curves, without masking, can make it look like they did. Skies, greenery, and fleshtones sometimes do need a mask, because we actually recall seeing

A

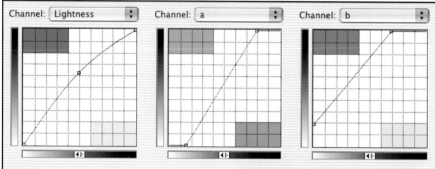

Figure 19.7 *Above, these curves are applied to Figure 19.6 on an adjustment layer without a mask. Because the dark half of the picture is now too blue, a copy of the L channel is loaded as a layer mask to produce the version below.*

B

different colors, not just more contrast or better color balance, than the camera did.

Cameras and humans also do not see eye to eye with respect to reflections. For obvious evolutionary reasons, we prefer not to be blinded, so our species has developed a mechanism to tone down bright sources of light, a mechanism that cameras lack.

The classic example of this is in faces, such as the one illustrated in Figure 1.4, with evil reflections off eyeglasses, as well as forehead, nose, or anyplace else that the skin secretes sufficient oil to reflect light.

As a rule, such reflections get retouched out in LAB (there's a section on how to do it in Chapter 9 of *Photoshop LAB Color*) but sometimes the reflections are too large to be painted away. That's what's happening in Figure 19.9, a shot to be used to advertise an expensive cabinet. The big reflection off the top center panel is not what the client had in mind.

All three channels are too light to load as layer

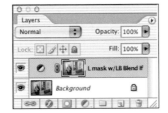

masks. They each have the reflection, but we can't correct through them without darkening other areas of the cabinet.

We could, say, load the blue as the mask, then apply a darkening curve. However, since all three channels treat the reflection in slightly different ways, a subtler result is possible by multiplying all three together into a single mask.

This masking channel can be created in several ways. It could be done directly into the layer mask, although it's more usual to make a separate channel. One possibility is Image: Calculations, using the red and green as sources, Multiply mode, 100% opacity, destination a new channel. When the new

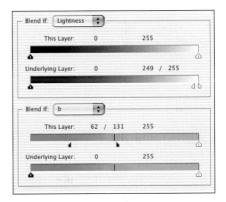

Figure 19.8
These Blend If options, added to the adjustment layer with layer mask of Figure 19.7B, prevent the lightest parts of the hair from turning blue.

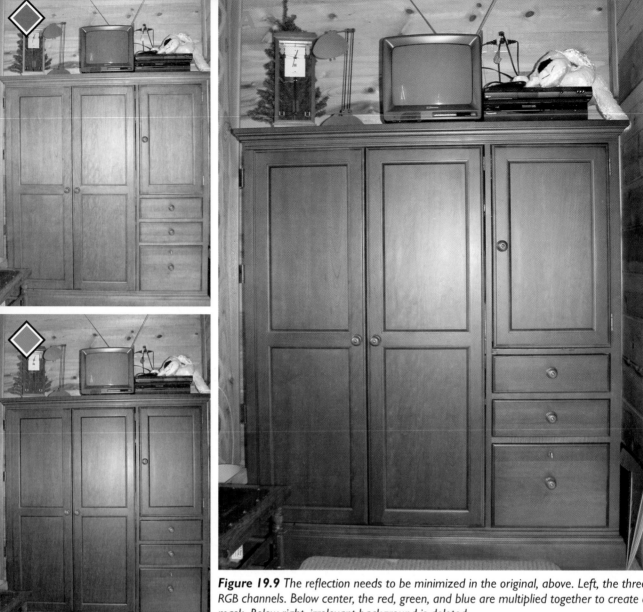

Figure 19.9 *The reflection needs to be minimized in the original, above. Left, the three RGB channels. Below center, the red, green, and blue are multiplied together to create a mask. Below right, irrelevant background is deleted.*

channel is created, open it, and Image: Apply Image, specifying the blue as the source and Multiply mode again. That extra channel is shown in Figure 19.9B, dark enough to exclude everything but the reflection.

The next step is to exclude the irrelevant objects on top. I used the rectangular marquee tool, set with a feather radius of 15 pixels, to make a selection of the cabinet, which I then inverted and deleted to black

(Figure 19.9C). This is a nauseating shortcut under normal circumstances, but with the sides of the cabinet as dark as they are in Figure 19.9B, nobody will notice an edge.

It's tempting now to make a curves adjustment layer and flood the image with red by

Figure 19.10 *Top left, Shadow/Highlight through a layer mask does not produce a red. Middle left, S/H is applied only to the green and blue channels. Bottom left, the layer mask is blurred. Below, after a Hue/Saturation move in the affected reds (right), the final file.*

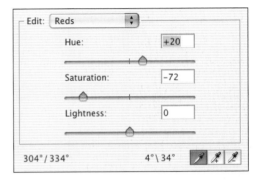

Figure 19.11 No white point has been set in this advertising shot, but establishing one will make the fleshtone too light.

make Figure 19.10A. The reflection has become dark enough, but too gray. The original was so light that it lacked any color for S/H to intensify, even with its Color Correction field jacked up.

For Figure 19.10B, therefore, I canceled the overall S/H and reapplied it to the green, then to the blue channel. Since the red channel is untouched while the other two get darker, overall the reflection is both darker and redder—too red, in fact, to match the rest of the cabinet.

Before dealing with that, we need to revert to a topic from the last chapter. We are trying to augment a highlight area without doing much to the rest of the image. For best results, we need to blur Figure 19.9C. If you look hard enough, it shows wood grain in the reflection. If we keep that grain darker than its surroundings when we load Figure 19.9C as a layer mask, the S/H move can't touch it. The light parts get darker faster than the grain does, and we get flatness, just as we did when a different mask was left unblurred in the last chapter in the Bridge of Sighs image, Figure 18.1B.

Note the extra focus in Figure 19.10C when the grain is blurred out of the layer mask.

The final step is to reduce the intensity of the newly created red. That can again be done in several ways. The most efficient is Image: Adjustments>Hue/Saturation. We choose Reds as the target, but are allowed to refine what types of reds we need by clicking the target area. The reds we are after are somewhat orange. We can also adjust how far we want the move to extend into yellower and/or redder oranges by adjusting the

darkening the light points of the green and blue channels. We could then apply Figure 19.9C as a layer mask to restrict the effect to the reflection. This strategy would work if the knobs were not present. Their neutrality has to be preserved, but these curves would make them red. We'd have to go back to the layer mask and paint each one out by hand to restore the appearance of the bottom layer.

Instead, we could make a duplicate layer (not an adjustment layer; Shadow/Highlight doesn't yet work on them) and give the highlight half of S/H a workout. I did so, at the swashbuckling values of 75%, 50%, 50, to sliders at the bottom of the dialog. It wasn't necessary here. Working on the top layer (which was still masked by a blurred version of Figure 19.9C), I desaturated the reds as shown and moved the hue toward yellow, producing the final version, Figure 19.10D.

The Tale of the Towel

A sky, a reflection, oceans of greenery, complicated casts: we've seen all of them in this chapter. In each case, we have to consider moving away from the original photograph, and thus using a selection or mask. The final category is fleshtones. We'll end with three shots that are posed somewhat similarly but exhibit different quality levels, different purposes, and different challenges. All, however, require separating fleshtone from the rest of the image.

We're nearing the end of our travels now. We have lots of choices, lots of ways to go wrong, lots of approaches that might please me and not you, or might please both of us and not your client. Figure 19.11 is a mood shot, so how it is handled depends on the mood you want to create, and I am no mind reader. However, certain absolutes are involved. Before we open fire with all the fancy stuff of the last three chapters, let's pause and analyze what we have and where we wish to go with it.

The original has a clear defect—no white point (or better stated, no *light* point). The lightest significant area is the tabletop to the right of the arm. It measures (this file is tagged Adobe RGB) $236^R221^G215^B$, too dark, and likely too red as well.

The propriety of the redness could be debated. The photographer is after some kind of warm look. Making the tabletop white is not, however, inconsistent with his approach. So, I'd put it at $245^R245^G245^B$ if feeling doctrinaire, or more likely, since it doesn't seem to have any detail to protect, at $250^R250^G250^B$. The towel is darker. Our curves can leave it slightly reddish if we want, or make it neutral. I vote for the latter.

If you don't agree that the cloth should be white, fine. But you can't leave it the way it is. If you feel it should be red, set it to $255^R250^G245^B$ or something along those lines. Not lightening it is poor technique, period, as we saw in the discussion of the bedclothes of Figure 19.3.

So, the linens will get lighter. When they do, the skin will, too. That is likely to present

Figure 19.12 *Left, on a luminosity layer, the blue channel is applied to the entire image. Middle, a blurred version of the red channel is added as a layer mask, resulting in the image at right.*

 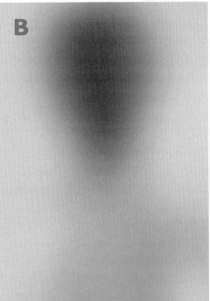 

a problem. The woman has reddish hair, which usually denotes a light complexion. We tend to prefer darker skin in print. So we could be looking at a selection or mask, because if we darken the skin without one, the hair may lose its redness.

It's tempting to say that one fleshtone is like another, but backs shouldn't be treated as if they were faces. Blending the green into the composite on a luminosity layer is something we often do to try to put shape into noses, cheeks, and chins. We use conventional USM to outline eyes. But this picture has no nose, chin, or eyes. We don't need to emphasize the difference between the darker, closer half of the back and the lighter one that's more to the rear.

I see nothing here that would favor correcting in LAB or CMYK, so we'll just do everything in RGB.

• Make a duplicate layer. To it, apply the blue channel, which is the darkest of the three in a fleshtone, and change layer mode to Luminosity, producing Figure 19.12A. The green is a more conventional choice, but since I intend to apply a layer mask later, I'm worried that it might not darken the skin enough. With this blue, if I think I've gone too far, I can always drop the layer opacity.

Repeating a warning from the last chapter: be very wary of making luminosity blends with the blue channel, which usually has much more noise than the other two, particularly if the

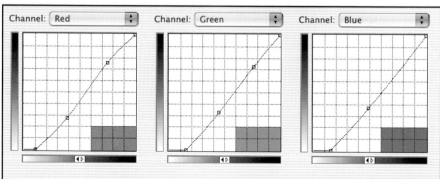

Figure 19.13 *Curves to lighten and whiten the linens are applied to Figure 19.12C.*

Figure 19.14 *Left, a blurred, inverted copy of the green channel is applied to Figure 19.13 to bring out more detail in the towel. Right, Shadow/ Highlight brings out the redness of the hair. Below, after hiraloam sharpening and mild CMYK curves, the final image.*

image has ever been JPEGged. Before concluding that I could use it for this blend, I checked out the blue carefully at high magnification, looking for artifacts that weren't visible when viewing the composite color but might cause problems if they get exported to the green and red channels.

• Add a layer mask. To it, apply the red channel. Blur it considerably (Figure 19.12B), to make sure that the hair is treated as a unit rather than a collection of individual strands. When applied, this layer mask produces Figure 19.12C.

• Add a curves adjustment layer, and make Figure 19.13, without using the layer mask. Moving the lower left endpoints lightens the table covering, and are in my view mandatory. The internal points are my idea of how much of the warm feeling of the image to retain; you may disagree.

• The skin is now satisfactory to my way of thinking, so I would flatten all the layers, although good practice suggests saving a backup copy somewhere. We next turn our attention to the towel and other fabrics. Enhancement with Shadow/Highlight, as we saw in Chapter 18, doesn't work well

when the areas involved are large and when distinct colors are present. Both of these factors appear here. Therefore, instead of S/H, we follow the steps shown in Figure 18.9, the advertising shot of skin products: start with three identical layers; to the middle one apply a blurred, inverted copy of a suitable channel (I chose the green); change its layer mode to Overlay and that of the top layer to Darken. The result is Figure 19.14A.

● On to the shadow. The enhancement there is similar to, but easier than, what it was in the highlights. It affects only the hair, which occupies a small area, and no conflicting color poses a threat. So, while making extra layers and blurring and inverting a channel would work, it would be a waste of time. S/H is all we need for something this simple. After flattening the image, I chose Shadows settings of 25%, 50%, 30, and left the Highlights and the Color Correction settings of the command disabled. The corrected hair is shown in Figure 19.14B.

● We have full range, and there seems to be no case for conventional USM. So, I chose hiraloam values of 25%, 60, 5, converted to CMYK, and applied final curves to neutralize the background. The result is Figure 19.14C.

There Are No Bad Originals

A perfect world would need no warships, and all originals would be perfect, too.

In today's professional world, we have to be ready to start with nearly anything. This chapter contains seven originals that might be part of a typical day's work. Three are quite good, one has poor color but adequate detailing, one has a defect that calls for a localized solution, and two are—well, I don't want to use the word, because, among other things, it isn't relevant. The only differences between an original of the type I will not name and a good one is that the final product will be less impressive in comparison to the starting point and that there may be an extra step or two along the way. The same problems manifest themselves; the only difference is how drastic the corrections are.

Our next challenge, Figure 19.15A, is very like the original we just finished working on, Figure 19.11. Fleshtone dominates; the starting white point is poor; highlight detail is critical; more definition is needed in the hair, which is the darkest significant part of the image. One picture probably has more value, at least in terms of emotion, than the others. Professional models get lots of assignments; high school girls only get one prom, unless they're recidivists.

Yes, if you compare Figures 19.15A and 19.15B, the difference is bigger than between Figures 9.11 and 9.14C. So what? Anyone who can fix one ought to be able to fix the other. In fact, working with something like Figure 19.15A, which obviously needs major work, is a good way to convince yourself that a much better original, like Figure 19.11, can still be improved considerably.

It's a Matter of Routine

The original is again tagged Adobe RGB. The channels are as expected, red lightest, blue darkest, best detailing found in the green.

The glittering stones in the dress have fooled the digicam, which stupidly supposes that they should be the white point. Consequently, the real lightest significant part of the image, the folds of fabric around the bustline, are an unacceptably dark $177^R160^G129^R$. So far, it's Figure 19.11 reincarnated: the fabric is not only too dark, but it's also a warm yellow, which may or may not be right.

Unlike Figure 19.11, this image has a face, which means we must consider conventional unsharp masking to emphasize the eyes. This is often done in the black channel of CMYK, which usually doesn't have the facial detail that might contain things we don't wish to emphasize. This skin is dark enough, however, that the black channel *will* show

Figure 19.15 Top, original and corrected versions of a photo taken on prom night. The procedure is much the same as that shown in the preceding example, just more extreme. Bottom, the green channel at three different stages of the process—from Figures 19.15A, 19.17A, and 19.18, respectively.

detail. So we might as well do it elsewhere, probably with a selection to limit the effect to darker areas.

In terms of color, we also may have to make more of a move, because of the human predilection for healthier-looking skintones. I've researched this topic as much as anybody else, and I'm pretty clear on what people prefer in general terms. In photographs, we do not approve of light complexions such as those found in blond individuals. Usually we find their skintone too pink as well, so we prefer a darker, yellower, more suntanned appearance, something more typical of the skintone of a medium-complexioned brown-haired Caucasian.

There is no objection to darker skintone as such; however, we often disapprove of the way the camera handles persons of African, Asian, or Hispanic ancestry, finding the originals too jaundiced-looking. I would add redness to this face, probably in LAB, because the kind of facial blemishes that teenagers are prone to are most easily retouched out there. Let's get started.

- There is no sense in avoiding a lighter profile. I chose ColorMatch RGB, which changed the appearance to that of Figure 19.16A. While this is still much too dark, I did not wish to go overboard by choosing a profile with an even lower gamma. There are two areas of interest in this picture—the skin and the gown. I want to get both of them into steep areas of subsequent curves, and am afraid that an extreme false profile might restrict that.
- As usual, the green channel has the best facial contrast. So, on a layer set to Luminosity mode, I applied the green channel.

Even before this last move, this picture is so dark that we may not visualize the dangerous shoals ahead. The face has to get much lighter sooner or later. When it does, the reflections that we can barely see now are likely to sink us. I'd like to do something to protect those areas from undue lightening, while permitting it on the sides of the face. The problem is finding a channel that might have that structure.

- Figure 19.16D is the original blue. If we invert that, it can be used to protect those light areas to some extent. So, I established a layer mask on the luminosity layer, and loaded an inverted copy of the blue into it.
- The impact of this last move is just about zero. The original blue is almost solid black, so the inverted copy is almost blank, doing almost nothing to restrict the top layer. However, I then forced the reflections to become black with a steep curve. Then, a 45-pixel blur, producing Figure 19.16E. At this point, the overall image looks like Figure 19.16B.

Sinking the Reflection

Having this layer mask brings us to the key moment in the whole correction. We now have a very soft selection of the sides of the face and the surrounding background. Lightening through that will establish hiraloam-like halos around the head. And, the skintone will appear to get lighter, but in fact the reflections won't, and the gown won't, either.

- Curves, applied through the same layer mask, create Figure 19.16C. The reflections are less prominent than they were in Figure 19.16A. The head stands out more prominently against the background.

With all that added shape, it looks like we've finally reached calm waters. The next step is a new set of curves, without the layer mask, to establish overall range. If you'd like to refer back to the preceding image, the cognate curves showed up at Figure 19.13. Both that set of curves and the ones we need now have the same objectives: place a white point somewhere in the fabric as opposed to some irrelevancy elsewhere; and adjust the picture's warmish cast to taste. The curves for this image also have to hold neutrality in the hair. In the previous one, we knew the hair

Figure 19.16 *Top left, a profile of ColorMatch RGB is assigned instead of the original's Adobe RGB tag. Top center, the green channel (Figure 19.15C) is applied to a luminosity layer, through a layer mask. Top right, these curves, applied through the same layer mask, give shape to the face. Bottom left, the original blue channel used as the source of the mask. Bottom right, the mask itself, inverted, with extreme contrast added, and blurred.*

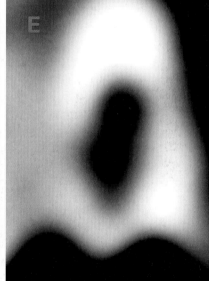

should be some kind of red or brown. Here, we know for sure it should be black.

In the previous example, we had the advantage of being nearly certain that the table covering we were using as a highlight was in fact white. We don't know that about this gown, which could be a pastel color of some sort. However, remember the detective work of Chapter 9? There's an important clue hidden in this image.

Highlights and Shadows Sail Again

Human teeth are white only in the distorted view of the Pepsodent people. Everybody else knows that they're slightly yellow. To find out what color the gown is, we need only compare values. If it's roughly the same B as the teeth, then it's an ivory dress. If clearly less yellow, then it's white. If it's *far* less yellow, it might be powder blue. My measurements find the second choice: the gown is yellow in the original, but not nearly as yellow as the teeth. It must therefore be set to white.

Figure 19.17 Left, straight-line RGB curves are applied to Figure 19.16C to create a white point. Right, an inverted, blurred copy of the new green is used as an overlay to create more detail in the gown.

• The lightest significant area is now known white, and the darkest, the hair, is known black. I applied the simplest possible curves: three straight lines that produced the endpoints recommended in Chapter 3. I was willing to stick intermediate points in if the dress didn't stay neutral, but it was better behaved than most prom attendees. The straight lines produced Figure 19.17A.

We continue along the same lines as with the woman by the mirror. There, we looked for more texture in the towel; here we need it in the gown.

Again, we reject the easier option of Shadow/Highlight: the area of concern is large, and contrasting colors surround it. All three channels are alike in the gown, but not in the skin. The red is so light that, if we used it as an inverted overlay, the face would take on almost as much extra detail as the gown, which would not be a good idea. The blue is so dark that the skin wouldn't change at all—the effect, when we invert the channel, would actually be to lighten it. So, again,

• Starting with a flat copy of Figure 19.17A, make two extra duplicate layers. The top layer should be set to Darken, to prevent any area from getting lighter during the next move.

• Activate the middle layer. Apply an inverted copy of the green channel. (For reference, the unblurred green is Figure 19.15D. To make it, I converted a copy of the

Figure 19.18 *Figure 19.17C is converted to LAB, where these curves force more redness into the skin.*

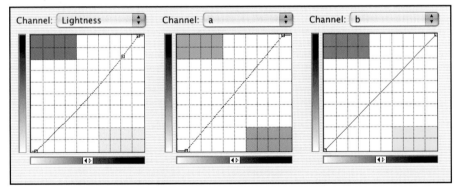

less yellow and more red. Since I've decided to go there anyway, it makes sense to do certain other things there as well.

- Convert to LAB, flattening the image on the way. Apply the curves shown in Figure 19.18.
- Load an inverted copy of the L channel as a selection (or as a layer mask, if you need to experiment) and apply conventional USM, to (as always) the L channel only. The selection limits the haloing to dark areas such as the eyelids and hair.
- After canceling the selection, I blurred the A and B channels to eliminate noise in the fleshtone. I considered Shadow / Highlight to improve the hair but found it did not help. I added light hiraloam sharpening, retouched out some blemishes, and headed for drydock, with one last port of call.

Whenever we see faces, we think of blending with the green on a luminosity layer. It didn't quite work this time; the original green, Figure 19.15C, wasn't all that great, and we had to restrict it further with a layer mask. But what about now? Convert Figure 19.18 back to Adobe RGB, and the green now looks like Figure 19.15E. *That's* a good blending channel. And so the final version, Figure 19.15B, puts it on a luminosity layer above Figure 19.18. It's analogous to the procedure used with the very light-skinned woman shown at the end of the last chapter, Figure 18.13. If you can't do the green blend at the start of the process, try it at the end.

image to Adobe RGB so that the comparison to Figure 19.15C would be fair.)

- Blur this channel at least enough to obliterate all facial features. Change the mode of its layer to Overlay to get to Figure 19.17B.

The reason for going to LAB is that it's the most natural-looking (and probably the easiest, as well) way to make the skintone

The final version is not just a lot lighter than the original. It's much shapelier, and most of that shape derives from identifying the channel that produced the layer mask of Figure 19.16E.

Yes, I would have preferred to start with a

Figure 19.19 The assignment: change the dress from the current green to Pantone 145C, a dull orange.

better original. Who wouldn't? But if the original *had* been better, is it realistic to think that we could have gotten something significantly superior to Figure 19.15B?

The third woman of our series also requires a selection, this time for a very different reason.

Changing Product Color with LAB

In each of this chapter's exercises, the justification for selecting was that we wanted to move away from the art—not just to extend the range, balance the lighting, add contrast to important areas, avoid impossible colors, and sharpen, but to change the context of how a certain object appears in the photograph. Sometimes this reasoning is subtle, as when we decide to alter the color of greenery or of a fleshtone. Sometimes it's clearer, as when we decide to leave a sky alone even though we know the rest of the image is too blue. And sometimes it's about as subtle as a 16-inch gun, as in Figure 19.19. The dress is green. The client says to make it orange.

This seemingly difficult assignment is a snap if you know your LAB channel structure.

Review and Exercises

✓ If you choose to avoid a layer mask in Figure 19.2, the *Missouri* correction, what Blend If settings might you use instead, assuming you work in RGB? And what if you decide to work it in LAB?

✓ Using the image from the CD, redo the woman of Figure 19.11 as indicated in the text, applying the blue on a luminosity layer, then limiting its effect by loading the original red, inverted, as a layer mask. Now, experiment with different blur settings for the layer mask, and watch what happens to the shaping of the back muscles. (Note: the image on the CD is lower in resolution than the one used for printing this book, so your blur will need a smaller Radius than the text suggests.)

✓ This chapter emphasizes the importance of being able to identify channels quickly. If you have any doubt of your ability to do that, you owe it to yourself to make CMYK, LAB, and RGB versions of some of your own pictures, pull grayscale prints of the channels without labeling them, and go through the same identification quiz that was presented back in Figure 1.5.

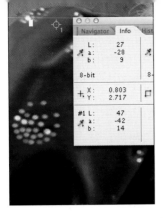

Figure 19.20 The color sampler tool places a permanent measurement point in the Info palette. The crosshair is placed in the most representative green of the dress.

Clients usually specify colors using the Pantone Matching System when ordering up such changes. We'll assume that the request is for the brownish orange Pantone 145C (traditionalists call it PMS 145). I pick this color because it makes the change harder than would have been the case if it were, say, purple. We'll see the problem that orange causes in a minute.

We can't just select the dress and fill it with a flat color. Instead, we have to locate a *typical* area of the current green, change that value to the orange, and let the rest of the dress fend for itself. Since most of this garment is in shadow, its eventual overall appearance will necessarily be darker than a swatch of PMS 145; the question is whether we can get a close match in the top of the dress nearest to us, where the lighting is more normal.

To make this (or any similar change) happen, the procedure is:

- Convert the file to LAB, if it isn't there

already. With the Info palette open, activate the color sampler tool, and place a measurement point on a typical green: nothing too dark, nothing too light. I chose a point in the near shoulder. As shown in Figure 19.20, the reported values are $47^L(42)^A14^B$.

- Open the Color Picker, and click Color Libraries (CS2 and later; Custom in earlier versions). Change the Book setting to Pantone Solid Coated, if that's not what it is already.

- Type in the desired PMS number. As seen in Figure 19.21, Photoshop reports back the LAB equivalents, in this case $59^L31^A71^B$.

- Make a duplicate layer. Then add a curves adjustment layer. We'll see why the intermediate layer was necessary shortly.

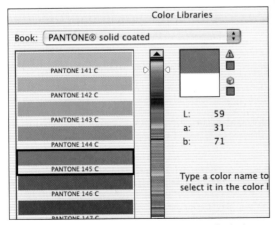

Figure 19.21 When a PMS color is specified, the Color Picker reports LAB values.

Stumbling Blocks: Blurs and Blends

- **Blurring the layer mask.** Small blurs to layer masks are needed when there is grain or other fine detail. A larger blur is sometimes useful for special purposes, and usually requires experimentation. Some pictures, like the ship of Figure 19.1, don't need it, but a small blur is rarely harmful.

- **When a selection, when a mask.** A mask is nothing more than a portable selection that can be loaded whenever we like—and edited, if we wish, using any of Photoshop's tools. The only reason to prefer selections to masks is one of time and convenience. We can load channels as selections with a single keystroke, for example. Masks are for those who will trade time for flexibility.

- **Blend If vs. layer mask.** These two commands go hand in hand. Blend If can be edited to a considerable degree, but it doesn't allow retouching. If a layer mask doesn't work the way you want to on a certain area, you can always fill it with white or black. And you can't do the blurring magic we saw in this chapter with Blend If. Knowledge of Blend If is nevertheless essential for those working in LAB, because making a layer mask out of the A or B channels isn't easy. In RGB or CMYK, it's also hard to base a mask on characteristics of more than one channel, but Blend If does so easily. Even when only based on a single channel, if the isolation is easy to achieve in Blend If, it takes much longer to construct a mask. Most of the time an effect can be achieved either way, but both techniques should be part of your workflow.

A

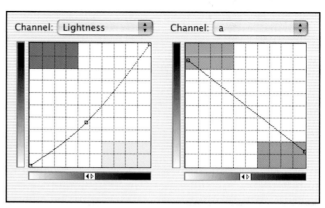

Channel: Lightness   Channel: a

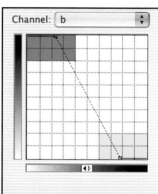

Channel: b

Figure 19.22 *The progression of the color change. Top, the L and A curves establish the desired values for the dress. Bottom left, because the original B is too flat to accept the needed curve, it is replaced by a copy of the original A. Bottom right, the B curve is added to the bottom left version.*

B

C

• This adjustment layer converts the measured point to the known LAB values for PMS 145. The L curve is easy enough: we lighten the quartertone until the fixed point in the Info palette reports that 47^L has lightened to 59^L. The original A value is negative, whereas the desired value is positive. To fix this, we invert the A curve: move the bottom left point to the top left, the top right point to the bottom right, converting $(42)^A$ into 42^A. It does not affect neutrals, as 0^A inverted remains 0^A.

• Since the desired A value is less (closer to 0^A) than the current one, the curve needs to be flattened, the opposite of what we're accustomed to doing. When the L and A are properly adjusted, the result is Figure 19.22A. The B is as yet unchanged.

To change the current value of 14^B to 71^B would require a nearly vertical curve, one that would be prone to posterize the colors. Fortunately, since all detail lives in the L, we can mess around as much as we like with the A and B. You may remember the quiz back in Figure 4.7, where we replaced A and B channels with each other or inverted copies of one another. The colors looked very odd, but the effect was realistic, perfectly suitable for live jobs if the situation warrants.

It does here. The B is too flat. So we will replace it with the original A. (Now you can see why purple would have been easy.)

• Activate the middle layer, but expose only

the B channel. Apply Image, specifying the source as the A channel, Background (not the default Merged) layer, Normal mode, 100% opacity. Figure 19.22B shows the result, including the corrected L and A channels.

• Going from the new $(42)^B$ to the desired 71^B requires only the slightly steeper curve shown, and finalizes the dress's color in Figure 19.22C.

There remains only the slight matter of restoring the background to put the dress in its proper context. This looks complicated, but of course it's just the same as the procedure in the flower image of Figure 19.5. The original dress is A–negative. The entire background is 0^A or A–positive, so the two can be distinguished with Blend If sliders. But can you say which channel and which layer?

The top two layers of this document, counting the adjustment layer, feature no less than four channels descended from the original A. Two of these (the A and B of the

Figure 19.23 *These Blend If sliders remove the background of Figure 19.22C and produce the final version at right. The background below is a swatch of the desired color of the dress, PMS 145.*

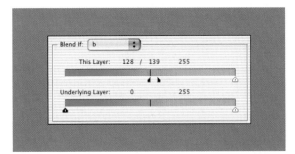

middle layer, remembering that we replaced the B with a copy of the A) are in fact the un-modified original A. The two on the adjustment layer have been modified.

We should choose the one with the longest range, and the curves of Figure 19.22 tell us which it is. The A curve has been flattened, the B steepened. So the longest range is on the B of the top layer, and we should choose that slider for the most accuracy. The setting is shown in Figure 19.23, together with the final image and a swatch of PMS 145 to verify that we got the right color.

A Swift and Swelling Ship

Sharpening, Shadow/Highlight, selecting. These, our topics of the last three chapters, interrelate, strengthen and support each

The Bottom Line

Masks and selections become appropriate when we wish to move away from the meaning of the photograph, not merely to correct its lighting, sharpen it, or reallocate contrast. Assigning a new color to a product is an obvious example. The nonobvious ones come in the areas in which humans and camera disagree—chiefly skies, natural greenery, and fleshtones. In each of the three cases, the human observer invariably recalls more attractive colors than the camera does.

The most flexible method employs a layer mask based on one or more channels. Being able to visualize channel structure is therefore a huge time-saver in planning such a mask.

Selecting is a discipline closely related to the sharpening and Shadow/Highlight topics discussed in the last two chapters.

other, suggest new directions in which to sail off. You'll have to be your own navigator on those seas; you've seen most of the perils and also the potential, but you have to take it from here, because your job is now to satisfy yourself or your client, not me. Everything from Chapter 11 on should help you do that, with the reminder that if you don't follow the basic rules of Chapters 1–10 your work won't satisfy anybody.

There are not as many fixed rules in the disciplines of these last three chapters as there were in the first ten. I've laid out some of the considerations that might make us choose one approach over another, but a lot inevitably depends on what you see in the image. Selecting and masking are both overused, but when they work, they work really well, and there isn't a ready replacement.

Consequently, this is one of the two longest chapters in the book, yet on looking back, I am nagged by the thought that it didn't say enough. It ends a process that began 15 years ago when I wrote that a monkey could be taught to correct color. At that time, it was perfectly possible to use Photoshop to make the same green-to-orange change we just worked through. Neither I nor anybody else would have dreamed that it could be done, but it was there all the time.

Just when we think we're getting the hang of color, it's time to move on. Life itself is like that, too.

Among the many valuable lessons that the history of the mighty battleship *Missouri* teaches, though, is that you never know when your final chapter has been written.

20
There Are
No Bad Originals

We wrap up with a proposed thought process for how to approach an image, one new and one old correction, and some speculation about the future of our field.

The stormy west coast of Vancouver Island features some of the world's most extreme tidal conditions. At low tide, the ocean recedes hundreds of feet. It leaves, in indentations in the beach, pools containing just enough water to support life.

These tidal pools are explosions of color, inhabited by aquatic life forms that have evolved to survive a nearly waterless environment for several hours at a time. Green anemones, bluish black mussels, pink sea stars: each species huddles together with its own kind, reducing the community's total surface area to preserve what little water remains, as they wait for the sea to return.

A little girl circles the pool. She holds a small digital camera. She stops, focuses, frowns, refocuses, changes position. She presses a button that seems to call up some kind of menu that changes exposure settings, and enters a few responses. She takes several shots, calls in her mother for consultation, moves to a new angle, and the process begins again.

As it becomes increasingly evident that the child knows what she's doing, it becomes very doubtful that she cares so little about these pictures as to permit them to be output uncorrected. Perhaps she has a copy of Photoshop Elements at home; possibly even Photoshop itself.

Back at the wedding of Figure 9.1, we made an unspoken assumption. It was obvious to us that the bridal gown needed to be white, and we acted on it without being aware we had begun to analyze the image. Did you notice the similar unspoken assumption of the last paragraph?

I assume that the girl is computer-literate. How could she not be, in the 21st century? But the idea that a new generation, sophisticated in digital imaging, is upon us—that's a little unsettling. I am not good at guessing

children's ages, but it's safe to say that when the first edition of *Professional Photoshop* appeared, this girl had not yet been born.

This realization does not make me feel old—taking advantage of a life in computing, I express my age in hexadecimal notation, where I am still in my 30s. It does, however, call for a moment of taking stock, of remembering where we have been and how far we have come.

The camera that little girl is using is almost certainly technically capable of producing images of quality sufficient to print in advertising. And, there's the infinite-number-of-monkeys factor. If she only shoots enough, at least a few of her exposures are bound to be good enough for professional purposes.

Over the life of this series, we have had to adjust to some big changes—but none as big as the one represented by this little girl.

I regret to report that it is questionable whether our planet is a better place today than when this girl entered it. In the insignificant part of it that pertains to color photographs, however, we are very much better off, with only one or two exceptions. Inasmuch as I remember those days well, it is irritating to hear people say that quality has slipped since then.

Sure it has—if you count all the children, and all the other nonprofessionals who would never have done such work previously but have suddenly been empowered to produce images superior to anything accessible to them in the past.

The Two-Edged Sword

The original title of this series referred to its audience, which was assumed to be professional retouchers. At that time, it cost hundreds of dollars to create even one file that was ready for press (and why else would you be working on a digital file back then? Neither inkjet printers nor the Web were any kind of factor). Today, the little girl doesn't need to buy film, or spend money to have it drum scanned, or pull expensive proofs. And she doesn't need a press, either.

If you want to compare eras, be fair. Compare the people who worked in Photoshop for a living back then to the ones who do so today. Don't compare them to children or other earnest amateurs.

At the professional level, believe me, we are incomparably better off today. Back then, the first edition of *Professional Photoshop* shook the industry—because it advocated setting appropriate highlights and shadows, looking for neutrals and other known colors, and putting interest areas in steep parts of the curve. Believe it or not, those concepts were virtually unknown at the time, and of course when they were adopted, they made a huge difference to image quality.

While those are still the irreplaceable fundamentals, today's arsenal contains many more weapons—generally weapons and tactics that have been discovered by experience, as opposed to capabilities that have been added to Photoshop.

In 1994, the battle lines were drawn in a chapter called "Calibrationists and Buccaneers." You may guess which side I came down on. The favored weapon of the buccaneer is a sword, but the amazingly improved models we swashbuckle away with today have two edges. One side gives us better images than ever before; the other offers us more possibility for confusion.

Will this photographer grow up to be a desperado, a buccaneer? She's shooting a difficult scene now. It is, however, a memorable one. Will she know what to do with her files when she gets them back to her computer?

We'll talk about how to handle Figure 20.1, but rather than learning how to fix one specific image, it's more valuable—particularly for a young person—to develop an attitude, a means of evaluating what needs to be done and how to do it. Now that we've reached

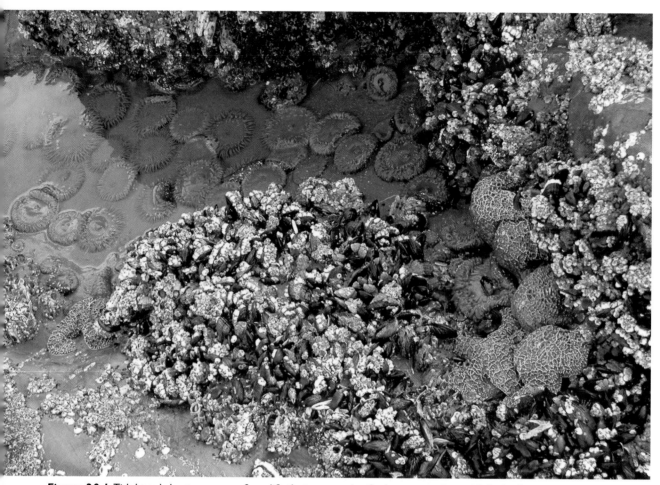

Figure 20.1 *Tidal pools host an array of sea life that can survive for hours at a time with limited seawater.*

the final chapter of the final book, it's time to summarize that approach.

The best way to do things right is not to do them wrong. Back in Chapter 6, we were asked to prepare a strategy, sight unseen, for a hypothetical picture in the 21st chapter of this 20-chapter work. Since we knew nothing about the picture, we couldn't decide whether channel blending would be involved, or hira-loam sharpening, or fancy GCR moves, or LAB curves to increase color differentiation.

Nevertheless, we knew a lot. We knew that we would look for the lightest and darkest significant objects, and set them to certain predetermined values. We knew that we would inspect the picture for any known colors (usually neutrals) and adjust if they were incorrect.

We knew also that we would identify the most important parts of the image and try to arrange steepness in the parts of all curves that affect them. We knew that we would consider several sharpening options, largely based on whether and where we see edges. We knew that certain channels are more important than others, so we might allow problems in the blue channel that we'd never permit in the black.

Effective use of our other tools requires opening our eyes and seeing what kind of image confronts us. I've tried to summarize the thought process on pages 478–479.

Running through all these options mentally doesn't take as long as you might think. For example, one of our tools is the use of a heavier GCR than normal. Approximately

.38 nanoseconds after opening Figure 20.1, we should dismiss the possibility of using it. GCR helps guard against the appearance of bright colors, but we've been told that we need this sea life to be strongly colored. And so forth with our other options, eliminating some immediately, considering others.

This is a complex image, with a lot of elements competing for attention. It arrives in untagged RGB; a CMYK file is required eventually. What do you see in this picture? What are your objectives, and what tools will you use to reach them?

On Opening a File for the First Time

When I outlined the chapter, I set this image aside. I'd never worked on it before, so I didn't know the exact steps I'd use. I just corrected it now, but instead of proceeding by instinct, I wrote down what was going through my head as I got started. These observations are in the order in which they occurred to me, so it may seem disorganized. You might disagree with some of them, or see other points of interest that I don't. Or, you might use a different thought process. And you may certainly find other ways of addressing the problems you find. But for what they're worth, here are my notes.

• Like the Bridge of Sighs image of Figure 18.1, this tidal picture is loaded with what some might call highlight detail but in fact is no such thing. It's a bunch of white areas interspersed with much darker detailing.

Applying steeper curves to these barnacles won't be effective, because the range between their lighter and darker portions is too great.

Also, as in the Bridge of Sighs, some of the image is in shade and some is not. Humans, as we know, don't see the sharp demarcation that a camera does. I will want to decrease the difference between the two halves.

The factors in the above two paragraphs strongly suggest the use of Shadow/Highlight

or overlay blending like that discussed in Chapter 18.

• Shadow detail is critical. The mussels are an important aspect of the scene. Also, the large dark area in the center of the background threatens to plug. Both of these inconveniences suggest careful adjustments to the black channel once I reach CMYK. I will not, accordingly, attempt to darken the shadow before getting there—it will, in fact, be easier to enhance detail if the black is too light when I enter CMYK.

• The scene is so busy that every part of the tonal range is in use. Attempting to bring out detail in the L of LAB will therefore not work, because something important would have to be sacrificed. If there's any way to target the anemones and the sea stars with curves, CMYK, with its fourth channel and its shorter ranges, is certain to be better at it than RGB, for the reasons discussed in Chapter 5.

• The human imagination affects this image, as does simultaneous contrast. The appearance of vivid animal life in a tiny, dark pool is so unusual that we remember it as being much more brilliant than a camera does. The opening paragraphs described these tidal pools as being "explosions of color." This one is a dud. The anemones are green, but not particularly bright; the sea stars are supposed to be pink, and they aren't; the mussels are described as blue, and we can barely detect it. This lack of color looks like a prescription for curves in LAB's A and B channels.

• Sharp edges are everywhere, so this is a candidate for conventional, not hiraloam, USM. As no color dominates, it's better to sharpen overall than in specific CMYK channels, so since I'm scheduled for a stop in LAB anyway, that's where I'll do it.

At this point I start measuring. Although the file is still in RGB, I prefer to look at LAB numbers. The light areas are in some cases blown out, so I don't need to check highlight

The Final Curves

THE STRATEGIES FOR APPROACHING AN IMAGE

THE EVERY-IMAGE TOOLS

If you haven't done these things every time, you won't have first-quality images.

Full Range
No Impossible Colors
Proper Shaping of Curves
Good Black Plate
Good Detail in the Weakest Channel of Strongly Colored Objects
Good Sharpening

THE OPTIONS

Here are some of the unusual techniques that show up from time to time. They aren't appropriate for every image. Look for the right opportunity to bring them into play.

Using variant GCR settings for ease in correction or to guard against press variation
Channel blending to change color
Steepening or flattening the AB curves
Altering the picture to put in a cast and then putting in a false highlight
Selecting and desaturating the background
Sharpening in some unorthodox way, such as emphasizing the darkening, or hiraloam (high Radius, low Amount)
False RGB profiles, or a false separation
Putting in a false highlight or other detail via a layer mask
Using an unusual black plate to emphasize shadow detail
Selecting an area and correcting it locally
Correcting once for color and once for contrast
Channel blending in Luminosity mode
Splitting the image into light and dark halves, correcting each, and merging them
Using overlay blends or Shadow/Highlight to enhance detail in the lightest and/or darkest areas

THE CHECKLIST

Ask yourself these questions before you do ANYTHING.

•   **What is the object of the correction?** This is such an obvious question most of the time that when the exceptional case comes up, there's often a problem. So, before starting, try to look at the image from a different perspective. What, from the client's point of view, is likely to be the objective? What parts of the image need to be spruced up, and which can be sacrificed?

•   **Are there obvious problems that need to be fixed?** This will govern your overall strategy. If there's one crying problem with the image, go with the method that fixes it even if other strategies might otherwise be appropriate.

•   **Is there any critical highlight detail that an aggressive correction may damage?** If there is, be careful about correcting outside of CMYK.

- **Are the shadows in this picture important?** Look also at the three-quartertones. Is there any delicate gradation there that you'd be afraid of losing? If not, jack up the shadow value by adding more black.

- **Does the image have problems with color, contrast, neither, or both?** If only color or only contrast is a problem, think about a correction in LAB. If both color and contrast are wrong, ordinarily think RGB or CMYK. Before using LAB to correct color, make sure that the cast you are correcting is uniform—that is, that it affects highlight, midtone, and shadow in the same way.

- **Is the image obviously too light/too dark/too colorful/not colorful enough?** You can often make life a lot easier by assigning a new profile in RGB before beginning the correction.

- **Are bright colors bad?** If so, think about heavier GCR. Most pictures look better with bright colors; if you have the exceptional one that won't, compensate with a heavier black plate.

- **Is the most important object lighter than a midtone?** If so, normal sharpening may not work well. Consider a multistep sharpening process that emphasizes dark haloing.

- **Is the most important object light and neutral?** If it is, think heavier GCR, to prevent any color cast from developing and to make bringing out the detail with curves a bit easier.

- **Is the most important object a brilliant color?** If it is, double-check the weakest channel in RGB or CMYK to make sure it has detail, as otherwise the color will be shapeless. And if going to CMYK, check the brightest area of the object. It should be set to 100% coverage of the strongest ink and 0% of the weakest.

- **Are you reasonably certain you know what the colors should be?** If not, LAB (and perhaps the Hue/Saturation command) are easy to experiment with.

- **Is some type of local correction going to be necessary?** If you discover halfway through the correction that you need a selection, you didn't plan well. Life is much easier if you know in advance that a selection will eventually be necessary: you can then, in effect, work on two separate images.

- **Is one color by far the most important in the image?** If so, this suggests avoiding sharpening the darkest channels. Think about sharpening black plus the weak color. When colors are of more equal importance, an overall sharpening reverted to Luminosity mode, or in the L channel of LAB, is usually better.

- **Is the original halfway decent, or are major moves going to be needed?** The worse the original, the more you should avoid starting in CMYK. Try to bring the image closer in LAB or RGB before converting it.

- **Is there an atrocious color cast?** If so, it suggests LAB, but before doing so, see whether you can minimize the cast with an RGB channel blend. For example, if the image has a gross yellow cast, it can often be softened by blending some red into the blue.

- **Is there critical detail in the darkest shadows?** This suggests special handling of the black plate. Remember that detail in the CMY channels will be suppressed because of the total ink limit. Consider starting with a weak black plate and then applying a drastic curve. Also consider, at the end, using Image: Adjust>Selective Color to reduce the CMY component of blacks. Even though this will lighten the shadow, it will probably add detail.

- **Is there a lot of greenery?** Think steepening the A, and possibly the B, channels of LAB.

- **Are there important fleshtones?** This is the only major class of image where bringing out detail is usually undesirable. Never sharpen the blue, green, magenta, or yellow channel. Expect to have to do a channel blend into the cyan. Think about a preliminary luminosity blend of the green into the entire image. Avoid taking fleshtone readings in any area where makeup may be present. Be prepared at the end to minimize hot spots that the camera may have picked up in the face.

- **Does the image feature pronounced edges?** If so, conventional sharpening works best. If the edges are vague, however, think hiraloam.

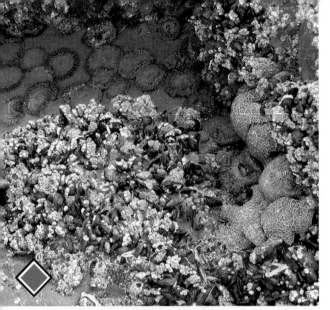

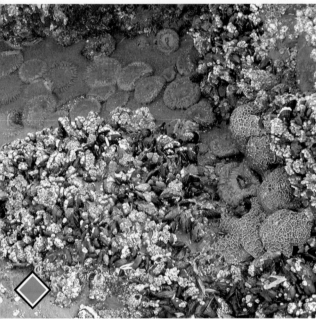

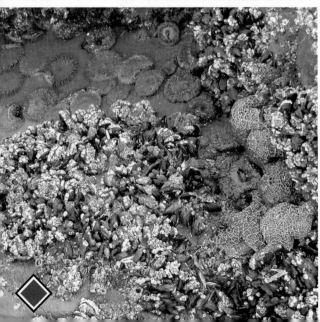

values. The deepest shadows at top center show a lot of color variation, but the average is around the 0^A0^B that one would expect. I don't care how dark it is, because I intend to set shadow in CMYK.

As for the aquatic life, the anemones are essentially pure green, $(25)^A2^B$, rather than the yellowish green of most plant life. The sea stars are always A–positive and near 0^B, but some are slightly more blue than yellow and others the opposite. The barnacles are slightly warm at 2^A2^B. The lighter mussels average $(5)^A(17)^B$, greenish blue as advertised.

All these values make sense to me, so I conclude that there's nothing wrong with the original color other than that it isn't vivid enough. This means there is no need for RGB curves to adjust color before entering LAB.

Sounds like a plan. As always, I'll look for a luminosity blend while in RGB. Then, I'll use an overlay blend as in the Bridge of Sighs image to bring out detail in the lightest areas. I will convert to LAB to drive the colors apart and to sharpen the L, and finally apply curves in CMYK, first being careful in the separation to get the sort of black I want.

Looking for Friend and Foe

In several of the late-chapter exercises, I've announced that I wouldn't take the space to show the individual channels because by now it should be obvious to you what they look like. It is not possible to behave so snootily here. I have an idea of how dark each channel is, but not how they distinguish some of the subtleties that we might want to emphasize with a blend. So I, for one, need a look at Figure 20.2.

For blending purposes, the red channel is the worst of the three. Its shadows are plugged, its highlights weaker than the other two. The green looks like the best choice because it has good shadows and offers some curving chances to increase contrast in both the anemones and the stars. There is, however, one problem.

Creating a luminosity blend requires us to think as if we were creating a black and white. Chapter 7 taught us that we need to look for the contrast that

Figure 20.2 The channels of Figure 20.1.

will be lost when color vanishes, and replace it with luminosity contrast. Here, there's no problem with the barnacles, mussels, and stars, all of which are significantly lighter or darker than their surroundings.

The anemones, though, are perhaps the most important part of the image, and a lot of their impact comes because they are so much greener than the water they're resting in. That added greenness, of course, is worth zilch in black and white.

To compensate, we have to decide which should be darker, the anemones or the water. From Figure 20.1, it's clear that it should be the anemones.

Chapter 7 says that the next step is a friend-or-foe analysis of the channels, to see which ones can be counted on to help us with our plan of lighter water and darker creatures. Unfortunately, the green appears to be the foe. The red is an ally in the anemones, but it carries a lot of baggage.

Remembering that the green is responsible for 60 percent of overall luminosity, anything that weakens its malign impact is welcome. The blue isn't great, but it's better than the green. So, we're good to go.

● Add a duplicate layer. Using either Channel Mixer or Apply Image, replace the green channel with the blue, creating Figure 20.3A.

● Change the layer's mode to Luminosity. Also, in view of the slight loss in shadow detail, add Blend If options that exclude the deepest shadows from the blend. The sliders in any channel should be suitable. We now have Figure 20.3B.

Compare Figures 20.1 and 20.3B. They don't look that much different—unless you concentrate on the anemones and the foreground barnacles. Shape has been added to both, perhaps enough to make a real difference later.

● After flattening the image, we move on to the overlay blend. We look for the channel with the most pronounced break between the light and dark areas. This time, no problem in making the choice: Figure 20.2 shows that the red wins easily.

● Add a copy of the red as a fourth channel, either by dragging the red to the page icon at the bottom of the Channels palette, or by Command-Option–1; Select: Save Selection.

● Activate this new channel by clicking it in the Channels palette or by Command-

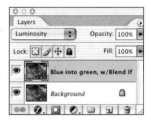

Figure 20.3 *Left, on a duplicate layer, the green channel is replaced by a copy of the blue. Right, layer options exclude extremely dark areas from the blend, and the layer mode is changed to Luminosity.*

Option–4. As in the earlier Bridge of Sighs image, this fourth channel needs to be blurred so heavily that all highlight detail vanishes. Here, it took a Gaussian Blur at Radius 25.0.

● The blurred channel needs to be inverted. We can do so on the fly when we apply it, but I find it easier to visualize what is about to happen by inverting it beforehand. This is Figure 20.4A.

● Return to the composite color image. Make a duplicate layer. To it, Image: Apply Image, using the fourth channel as a source, Overlay mode, 100% opacity. This produces Figure 20.4B.

The object of this last move was to build detail in the lightest areas. Getting more shadow detail was secondary. That was why I suggested applying the channel in Overlay mode as opposed to applying in Normal mode and changing the layer mode to Overlay. By invoking Overlay mode while applying, we can later set the layer itself to Darken.

Figure 20.4 *Top right, a blurred, inverted copy of the red channel. Bottom left, this channel is applied to Figure 20.3B in Overlay mode. Bottom right, a new copy of Figure 20.3B is placed on top, Darken mode, with opacity set to 40%.*

● Until now, the moves have been uncontroversial. We are now faced with a subjective decision about how well we like the enhanced highlights and shadows of Figure 20.4B. My own answer is that I'm happy with the former and of two minds about the latter. It does not bother me that the shadows are now too light, because the plan calls for darkening them as much as needed in CMYK. And it seems that the mussels now have more impact. As a compromise, I decided to put a copy of the background as a third layer on top

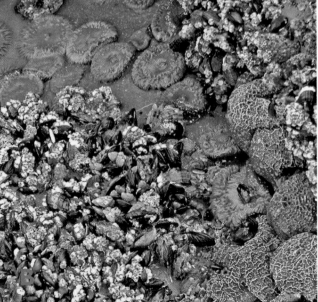

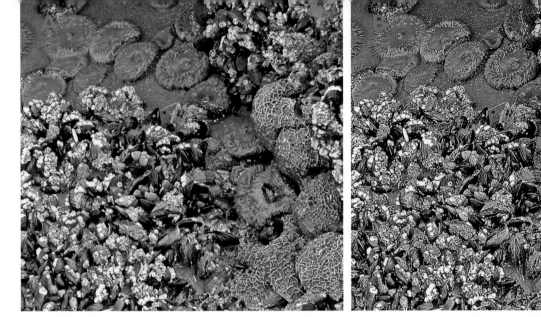

Figure 20.5 Above left, after entering LAB, the curves at right are applied to increase color variation. Above right, heavy conventional unsharp masking is applied to the L channel on a duplicate layer.

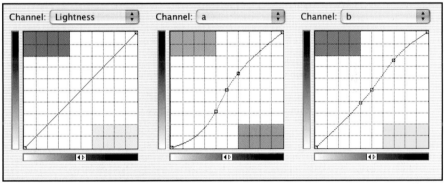

of the overlay. By setting its mode to Darken, I preserved everything that the middle layer had strengthened in the highlights. I chose 40% opacity, making Figure 20.4C use every part of Figure 20,4B that is darker than Figure 20.3B, but only 60% of the lighter areas. On to LAB.

Finding the Color Variation

• Flatten the image, and convert to LAB. The plan is not to touch the L, but rather to establish color variation in the A and B. Also, I intend to sharpen the L, possibly restricting it to darker areas. If I were planning to curve the L, it would be better to do the sharpening afterward.

• Inasmuch as the curves won't touch the L, create one duplicate layer for the USM and put a curves adjustment layer on top of the whole thing, making three layers in all.

• Without touching the bottom two layers,

create Figure 20.5A with the illustrated curves to the A and B of the adjustment layer. Both have three points: one to hold the center and the others to give independent control of two objects.

I moved the center point of the A curve microscopically to the left, toward green, feeling that the picture was overall slightly too magenta. The bottom point affects the sea stars, which are more magenta than green; the top point governs the anemones, which are more green than magenta. Everything else in the picture is practically 0^A, thus unaffected by whatever these two points do. I felt that both could use more color, but that the stars could use even more, hence the added steepness below the center point.

Not many things are more yellow than blue in this image. Increasing the slope of the B curve below the center point might be counterproductive if it makes the foreground

Figure 20.6 *Figure 20.5B is oversharpened, but the effect is most objectionable in the highlights. Blend If sliders eliminate the sharpening in the lightest parts and then gradually introduce it as the image gets darker. Overall opacity is set to 40%.*

barnacles more yellow. The mussels, however, are more blue than yellow. The top half of the B curve is aimed at bringing out more of that blueness.

• With the curves out of the way, return to the middle layer for sharpening, activating the L channel only. Since the layer's opacity can always be reduced, and the lightening can be further restricted with Blend If options, there's no need to be shy. I chose settings of 500% Amount, 1.2 Radius, 6 Threshold, producing Figure 20.5B.

• Assuming you find the effect excessive, as I do, double-click the layer's icon to bring up Blend If, splitting the Underlying Layer> Lightness slider by Option–clicking it. Everything to the right of (lighter than) the right half is excluded; everything between the two

halves is a combination of both layers, and everything to the left of the left half uses the sharpened version at full intensity. Placement of these sliders is purely personal preference.

• Ditto for the adjustment of the sharpening layer's opacity. To make Figure 20.6, 40% looked good to me, whereupon I flattened the image in preparation for the move into CMYK.

The Final False Separation

• Now that we've played to the strengths of RGB (channel blending) and of LAB (color variation and sharpening), we move on to the things CMYK does best, which are

Figure 20.7 *Left, these separation settings for the LAB file of Figure 20.6 intentionally suppress shadow detail to enable steeper contrast-enhancing curves. Center, the resulting composite image lacks depth. Right, the black channel.*

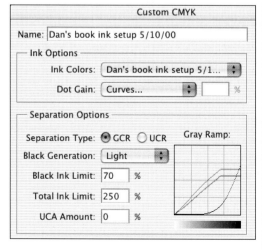

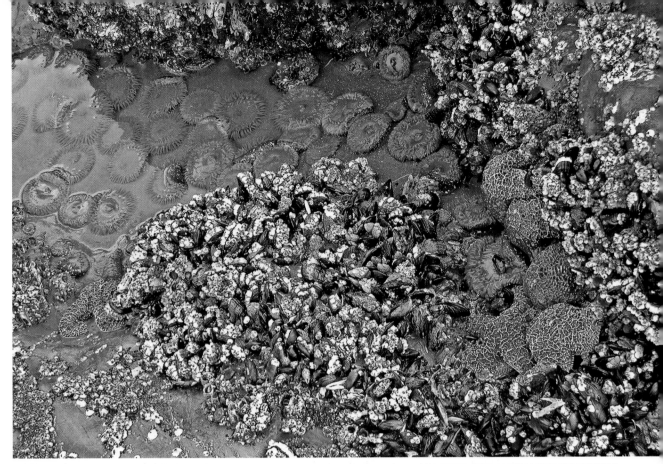

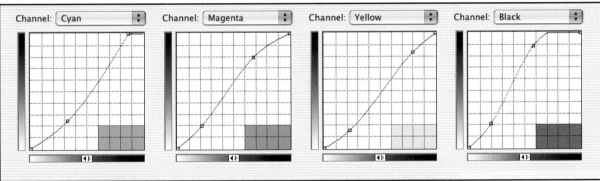

Figure 20.8 *The vivid colors of the tidal pool return in this final version, for which the curves are shown. Left, the final black channel.*

bringing out detail in specific areas, and setting a shadow. But getting there calls for a little planning. I chose not a standard mode change, but Convert to Profile, using the abnormal settings of Figure 20.7.

The ultra-low maximum black ink setting is to permit an extremely steep curve later. It guarantees that nothing can be as dark as 70^K immediately after we separate the file. Thereafter, we can raise the black endpoint to 90^K or even 95^K if we like, to bring out the critical shadow detail.

The unnecessarily low total ink limit of 250% (this book's printer accepts 300%) is to prevent the CMY from getting too

Changes Since Last Time

The 1994 *Professional Photoshop* showed a mountain forest image that had been scanned on both a drum scanner and a primitive desktop unit. I pointed out that while the cheap scan could be improved, it could never reach the quality of the drum scan. By the 1998 edition I had learned enough about LAB to correct the poor image to be *better* than the drum scan. So I showed both versions, with a few snorts at my own ignorance.

Every installment in this series has seen exposure of such errors and/or significant changes in recommended workflow. This time is no exception. Here are some of the ways I've changed my approach since the last edition in 2002.

• Looking for a luminosity blend, although I knew about it before, is now my normal first step in RGB.

• Similarly: instead of trying to achieve perfection with aggressive moves, I find it more convenient to exaggerate them on a separate layer and then reduce opacity.

• Many corrections are much easier when separated into color and contrast halves, and then merged.

• The overlay blend to enhance highlight and shadow detail described in Chapter 18 was developed in response to digicam deficiencies.

• Hiraloam sharpening, which did not appear in the last edition, is fully developed, and a sensible strategy offered for merging it with conventional USM.

• The last edition recommended false RGB profiles to pep up tepid colors by, for example, assigning Adobe RGB to files that were actually sRGB. It is now clear that going to LAB is better.

• I now realize the power of a false conversion into an ultra-wide gamut RGB to create a source of channel blends for brightly colored areas.

• Shadow noise reduction is shown to be significantly improved by applying the Surface Blur filter at a low gamma setting.

• In the last edition, there were no new Photoshop commands of any significance to color correction. This time, we've had to develop strategies for three: Shadow/Highlight, Surface Blur, and Camera Raw.

• I now know how to generate a specialized black channel from an "uneditable" CMYK setting, by making a Custom CMYK layer in Luminosity mode.

dark in the shadows in an effort to make up for the inadequate black. I intend to improve detail in the anemones and the sea stars by raising the dark ends of at least the cyan and magenta curves, and I don't want the CMY to get too heavy in the real shadows, where it might interfere with the black.

(Note: this uses my own conversion setting. If you use a different Custom CMYK, you can alter the black generation as shown. If you use an uneditable profile, make one normal separation, and another using this Custom CMYK with 22% inserted in Dot Gain. Paste the Custom CMYK version as a layer on top of the other, and change mode to Luminosity.)

• Apply the curves of Figure 20.8, save, and close. The black is being held in its lightest areas and then steepened drastically to bring out detail in the mussels. The magenta and cyan curves vary in shape because the anemones and stars are both in the midrange of the magenta, but the anemones are in the shadow range of the cyan.

Back to Square One

These last curves were straight out of Chapter 2—find the interest objects, steepen the regions that contain them. It is only fair, then, that we go back even further—to the very first page of this book, in fact.

In real life, these tidal pools do seem very colorful. Compare Figure 20.8 to the original, Figure 20.1. Which do you prefer? Don't tell me how you could do better; your must choose one or the other. If you, like the rest of the world, agree that Figure 20.8 is better, it proves that the original has been *corrected,* which is what we said about Figure 1.1B, and what the book is all about.

This correction took more steps than usual, because it is a complex image, but at the end of the day it's just a correction like any other. Developing the instinct that tells which techniques to use, and in what order, takes practice. But it isn't magic. As I said in 1994, a monkey can do it. As I say today, somewhat more diplomatically, even a small child can do it.

Provided, of course, that the child has the right attitude. Professionalism, like youth, is a state of mind.

My own state of mind is fine in both respects, thank you. I have spent my life in the steep part of the curve, which is all I could have asked for when I was the girl's age. However, it must regretfully be conceded that the future belongs to her generation, not mine.

If she chooses to, she can produce beautiful images, whether she calls herself professional or hobbyist. She can build on what the digital pioneers left as a foundation.

This girl will never meet me in person. If, however, she stays committed to creating beautiful photography, I console myself with the thought that she is likely to make my acquaintance nevertheless, and thus endorse, on behalf of her generation, the principle that every image is a new adventure.

* * *

Progress in color correction is a never-ending process of trying out new approaches, discarding those that don't work, replacing others with better solutions when they become available. The book's philosophy has not changed over five editions, but its recommended techniques certainly have.

This time is no exception. The box on the facing page details my changes in approach since the last edition four years ago, things that I now believe I know how to do better. The evolution of technique will continue for as long as you and I process images.

The solutions being offered this time are also different than in the past, owing to the rapid ascendancy of digital cameras. Digicams in many cases deliver better quality than film cameras ever did, but they also create certain problems that were rarely present in film, like images with partial casts, or plugged shadows or blown highlights.

Yesterday's techniques don't always give the best results with today's problems. Yet it does not follow that something new is necessarily better. The hardest part for all of us is to distinguish the real improvements.

As production of the book winds down, Peachpit Press's marketing department wants to know how different it is from *Professional Photoshop Fourth Edition.* I answer, about 90 percent. They refuse to believe it. I tell them where to stick their doubts, because I happen to have it spreadsheeted. Forgetting corrected versions, intermediate steps, and screen grabs, there are 142 original images in this book, this chapter having the fewest with only two. Of the 142 files, 125 did *not* appear in the last edition. And much of the text that goes with the other 17 has been rewritten.

This reprehensible level of image replacement comes about neither because I have obsessive-compulsive disorder nor because I feel a need to practice typing. It is because I know more now than I did then, and I believe that the new images are more instructive than the older ones.

As against that, it would have been easy enough to go the extra mile and throw *everything* from past editions away. Thanks to the photographers who so generously donated images to this project, I have more than enough images to replace the 17 holdovers. The only problem is, I don't believe they're as good. I'm thinking of the three grayscale cats of Chapter 3, the wedding image of Chapter 9, the parrot and flag that opened Chapter 7, and the hog of Chapter 1. I can replace them—but not with anything better. And so they stay—on merit.

I would be happy to end this series with

something new, but if the old way is better, I say, stick with the old way. So for our final example, we will go back not to the fourth edition, but to the second. These next three pages, other than the updated figure numbers and one reference to a new image, are what I had to say then.

*   *   *

This book has emphasized the use of traditional methods, updated for the needs of today's images. As we have come to the end, I suggest that we honor another long-standing graphic arts tradition by celebrating with a cold beer.

Unfortunately, the beverage of Figure 20.9A resembles apple juice more than it does the kind of thing I'd like to down after a long day of Photoshop work. The color is approximately correct, but what happened to the fizz?

Is it a bad original? It can't be, if it can be brought to the state of the pint on the right. Particularly, if it can be brought there in a minute or less, scarcely enough time for the head to settle.

The image is provided in LAB. Recalling similar examples with yellowish objects in the past, we save a copy, and convert the original to RGB. An examination of the channels (Figure 20.10) indicates that the bubbles in this beer exist only in the green. The head in the green is adequate but not as good as in the blue. The red channel, like certain of my relatives, occupies space without serving any useful purpose.

Figure 20.9 *The original beer at left looks flat in more ways than one. The correction, right, adds fizz.*

A   B

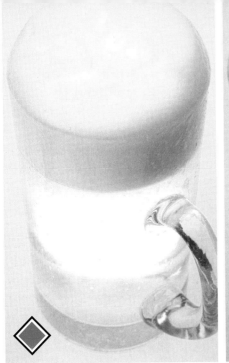
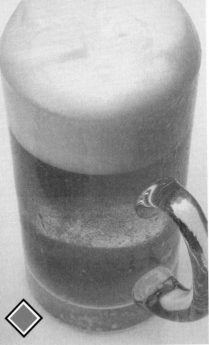
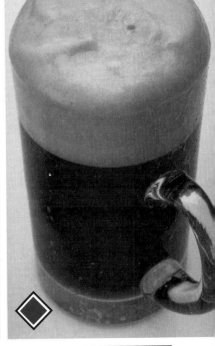

Figure 20.10 *Above, the red, green, and blue channels of Figure 20.9. Right, the curves applied to the green and blue channels (the red having been discarded).*

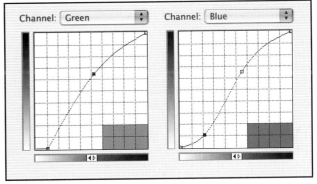

We now know that we will work this image at least partially in RGB, because two problems are conveniently isolated. The red channel needs to be liquidated, and the green channel must get special sharpening attention because in it, we have isolated the bubbles we are so interested in improving.

First, we need to make the two useful channels even better. The steeper the curve, the more the contrast, so we apply the curves of Figure 20.10, steepening the green where the body of the beer falls and the blue where the head is. As for curving the red, forget that. That channel is history.

The blue and the green are two separate sharpening problems. In the green, we are trying for the bubbles in the beer. They aren't subtle, so we need a wide Radius of 3.5, with a 400% Amount, Threshold of 5. The foam that is the blue's strength, on the other hand, has fine gradations that a wide Radius would kill. So, we lower the setting to 1.5.

Now it's just a question of getting the blends right. I chose to replace the red with a 65–35 blend of green and blue, feeling that the beer

was more important than the head. For the same reason, I then blended 25% of the green into the blue.

The situation at this point is Figure 20.11. Happy St. Patrick's Day! But we are long since past the point where such trivialities as green beer cause us grief. We simply convert to LAB, where a copy of the original awaits us. The old and the new L channels are compared in Figure 20.12. Replace one with the other, convert to CMYK, and we're done.

A Toast to Professional Color

And with that, we come to the end of a long journey. This image is an appropriate one to finish with, not so much because it is an effective correction but because it is an easy one—for those in the know.

The battered and bleached-out tidal pool of Figure 20.1 will take anybody a while to repair. This beer image should take about a minute. And yet (I can tell you this for a fact because I've seen many people work these two images) the typical professional gets much better results from the tidal pool image than this one.

Although our field is in many ways a highly technical one, it's very different from most technical fields. It takes someone with a background in numbers to know whether a mathematician's work is credible. It takes a background in music to understand why Vladimir Horowitz played piano better than Liberace. But with us, it isn't that way. What expertise does it take to tell that Figure 20.9B looks a lot better than 20.9A?

Not too much—that's why we call it a *correction.* You know it's better, I know it's better, even if we can't put our finger on why. And, as we are talking *professional* Photoshop, this presupposes that we have clients. They will think the corrected beer is better, too; how could they not?

This image had no highlight, no shadow, no neutrals, no fleshtone, and no unwanted color. It's therefore a most atypical problem, and this may account for why professionals do so badly with it.

Throughout this book, I've tried to suggest a general way of approaching correction by the numbers. That is indeed the best way, the time-proven way, to give your images the snap they deserve. Now and then images requiring special treatment pop up, like the one we just worked on. Certainly, experience with this kind of image helps.

But even without that, an intelligent artist can often work out the proper strategy. Making the following mental checklist, I find, is useful:

- What is the object of the correction? (To make the beer look appetizing.)
- Are there obvious problems that need to be fixed? (You can't see the bubbles.)
- Is there any critical detail that an aggressive correction may damage? (The lightest area of the foam.)
- Does the image have problems with color, contrast, neither, or both? (Just contrast; the original color is acceptable.)
- Is some type of local correction going to be necessary? (Not here.)
- Is the original decent, or are major moves going to be needed? (The original is terrible.)

All these answers suggest both that we need to study the channels carefully and that sharpening will be a critical issue.

Figure 20.11 *After the curves and channel blending, the beer is appropriate to serve on St. Patrick's Day. But the skilled Photoshop user has no problem restoring the original color.*

But no matter what strategy you use, no matter what colorspace you work in, no matter what version of Photoshop you use, certain goals are constant. Ignore them, and you condemn yourself to mediocrity. Achieve them, and you'll have professional color. They are:

- A full tonal range
- Interest areas falling in steep parts of the correction curves, where possible
- Strong detail in the unwanted color, if there is one
- Accurate unsharp masking
- The right kind of black plate

Do these things, and you will be able to shrug off changes in Photoshop and laugh at what some call bad originals.

If you don't foresee spending a career working on images, may those you do correct be vivid, lifelike, full of detail. And if this is going to be your lifetime interest area, may it always fall in the steepest portion of fortune's curve. Let's raise our glasses to that.

A Buccaneer's Farewell

We return—briefly, I promise—to our own century for an update. Not of the correction technique; it was good in 1998, and as far as I know it is still the correct approach today.

What needs to be changed is the assertion that few professionals would know how to get a result as good as Figure 20.9B. It was surely true in 1998, but today channel blending is

Figure 20.12 *The L channels of the files shown in Figure 20.9.*

A

B

mainstream, and this is an easy example compared to many of the others we've seen.

Learning curve is an apt phrase for us, because that curve is just like every other curve we've looked at. Once it's made steep, problems start to vanish. Anyone who can't get a good result on this beer image would certainly not get one on a considerably more difficult bubble-bearing beverage, the sparkling wine image of Figure 10.21.

That image would have been too difficult for me in 1998. Then again, I expect to be able to correct certain images a few years from now that are too difficult for me today.

*   *   *

All we want to do is make the picture look better. The phrase sounds so simple, and yet it seems like we've hardly begun to explore it.

The next steps of that exploration are up to you, and to the little girl, and to everyone else who wants to make the image look more natural, more lifelike, more convincing. That story is a book that has no final page.

The tides of knowledge and of change sweep in and withdraw. We can gasp, grope, huddle together, or choose to sail with them, hoisting the brave black flag of beauty as they carry us away on waves of color and contrast.

Notes & Credits

The images in this book represent most of the categories that professionals work with today. Some are mine; more come from the photographers who supported this project by offering libraries of images for me to choose from. These people are recognized by name in the Introduction.

Unless otherwise noted in the text, all images are uncorrected digital captures, acknowledging the reality that digital has replaced film in most professional contexts.

About the CD

The CD enclosed in this volume is for your private use in practicing and perfecting the techniques discussed here. You are permitted to manipulate the images however you like for your own edification, including printing them to test how well you did. However, these images are copyrighted. You may not publish them, post them, share them with others, or allow any reproduction other than what you yourself need for learning purposes.

The photographers who supplied images for this book have graciously consented to have their images included on the CD. In most cases, however, the images have been downsampled to prevent commercial reuse. Therefore, you may not be able to duplicate the exact numbers referred to in the text.

Unless otherwise indicated in the text, the format of RGB files is as received from the photographer. Where the original file contained an embedded profile, it is included. The absence of a profile means that there was none in the image as supplied. (For exercises requiring the use of LAB or CMYK, the conversion has already been done.)

Images that are for display purposes only and do not illustrate color correction, such as many of the images in Chapter 1, are not included. In the one case where the original image for a correction exercise is omitted, a note appears in the following chapter credits.

Chapter 1

The pictures of the woman and the Venice scene that both have purple reflections are mine, as are the flowers used in the exercise of Figure 1.4 and the man whose face is ruined by reflections in Figure 1.5. The guitarist comes from the *Knoxville News Sentinel*. The hog and the single rose are royalty-free stock photos from more than ten years ago, no longer available as far as I know.

Review and Exercises

- *Simultaneous contrast* describes the human visual system's propensity to perceive colors as being more different from their immediate neighbors than a camera would.
- *Chromatic adaptation* refers to the human visual system's instantaneous adjustment to the color of the ambient light, which is always perceived as being neutral.
- The most powerful RGB channel in terms of the contrast it adds to the picture is the green; however, this does not mean that the green is necessarily the best-looking channel.
- The red channel of RGB is closely related to the cyan of CMYK. The green and magenta are also cousins, as are the blue and yellow.
- Figure 1.8B has information only in the red channel; the green and blue are blank. Therefore, we see as much green and blue light as possible, but varying amounts of red.
- Chromatic adaptation makes it impossible to rely on a monitor, however well calibrated, to judge whether neutrals are really neutral. Our visual system adjusts so rapidly that near-grays quickly become pure grays.

- In RGB, objects are neutral if they have equal values in all three channels.

Chapter 2

The appallingly flat image of Figure 2.1 is mine, as are the car that was involved in an accident, the black and white pelican, and the yellow and green fields near Guilin, China. The cats are royalty-free stock photography from the defunct Corel Professional Photos library, which is now owned by Hemera Technologies Inc. The advertising photographs are by Ric Cohn (the toiletries) and David Moore (the purple blouse). The Niagara Falls image was taken by Gerry Shamray on his honeymoon.

- *CD Note:* The thread from my colortheory list concerning how to refer to keyboard shortcuts (Mac vs. PC) is enclosed.

Review and Exercises

- The purpose of the unusual twist in the shadow half of the red curve in Figure 2.12 is to create more contrast in the blue slickers, which are dark in that channel.
- Any sequence of commands can be applied to standard layers, but once the file is saved, they can't be undone. Adjustment layers allow only a single command, normally curves. The command is editable forever, but the adjustment layer itself can't be painted or otherwise retouched.
- If endpoints are set to extreme values, contrast is enhanced, but detail is lost in shadows and highlights. In certain images this is no big deal because the detail is unimportant or missing totally from the original file.

Chapter 3

The macaque was photographed in the wild by David Cardinal. The neutral statue is from the Corel library. I sabotaged one of my own images to make the purple cat. The woman standing outside is by Marty Stock. The grieving minister is courtesy of the *Knoxville News*

Sentinel. The ancient royalty-free picture of the horses will not be identified in fairness to the vendor, whose quality improved dramatically in the years following that release. The Irish castle was shot by David Xenakis.

- *CD Note:* My 1994 permission to use the horses image did not include the right to reproduce it electronically, so it is not provided. An Excel spreadsheet, prepared by David Riecks, compares fleshtone values in CMYK and various RGBs.

Review and Exercises

- Moving the lower left point of a curve to the right increases contrast uniformly in all areas of the image that it doesn't blow out. Lowering a higher point to lighten the highlight emphasizes midtone contrast at the expense of lighter areas.
- All 8-bit Photoshop channels have 256 levels. CMYK and grayscale values are reported on a 0–100 scale only for reasons of tradition. There is no lessened accuracy.
- Setting the shadow to $0^R0^G0^B$ plugs whatever information may be found there. It is appropriate in images where the shadow and three-quartertone range contains no important detail at all.

Chapter 4

The opening and ending canyon images, as well as the flower image for the exercise of Figure 4.7, are mine. The Yellowstone sunset is by John Ruttenberg. The prairie scene is by Darren Bernaerdt. The image of antique autos was provided by the *Knoxville News Sentinel.* The shots of soap floating in a bathtub and of jewelry on a fanciful background are both by Ric Cohn.

Beta reader Les De Moss prepared the useful schematic that appears as Figure 4.4 to help him as he learned how LAB works.

The beta reading team found the quiz of Figure 4.7 to be extremely difficult. In response to their urgent suggestion, here is how I would go about solving the quiz, remembering that we are given that Figure 4.7A is the original, meaning (to use the terms of the worksheet) 1,3.

We key on the original yellow (which, since their color changes, I'll call the *primary)* flowers. To construct a yellow, the A channel must be near 0^A but the B must be quite positive. Armed with that information, we can break the 16 variants into three groups, as follows.

Four versions have copies of the A in both channels. Therefore, they are close to 0^A0^B in the primary flowers, which must be much less colorful than in any of the other 12 versions. This group is clearly 4.7B, G, J, and N.

Eight images have copies of the A in one channel and the B in the other. Since the A had little color to begin with in these primary flowers, whether it is inverted doesn't change them. We expect to see four colorful pairs, which are 4.7A and H, F and P, K and O, and L and M.

The final four versions have copies of the B applying its strong influence to both channels. Each of the four is uniquely colored; none of the four match anything else on the page. These four singletons are 4.7C, D, E, and Q. You can use Figure 4.4 to identify them if you have trouble. Figure 4.7C is violet, meaning A–positive, B–negative, so its answer is 3,4. Figure 4.7D is cyan, negative in both, so 4,4. Figure 4.7E is red, positive in both, 3,3. And Figure 4.7Q is yellow-green, A–negative, B–positive, hence 4,3.

For the eight half-breeds, we need to look at what I'll call the *secondary* flowers, the ones at lower right that are magenta in Figure 4.7A and therefore A–positive but near 0^B. We are given at the start that Figure 4.7A is 1,3; inverting the A channel produces yellow primary and green secondary flowers, so Figure 4.7H is 2,3.

When the B channel is inverted, the primary flowers become blue but the secondary flowers remain almost unchanged. Figure 4.7K, with its magenta secondary flowers, is 1,4, and 4.7O, where the secondary flowers are green, is 2,4.

When the A is based on the B and vice versa, the primary flowers are green if the B is inverted and magenta otherwise. The secondary flowers are blue if the A is inverted and yellow otherwise. So, Figure 4.7F is 4,1; 4.7P is 4,2; 4.7L is 3,2; and 4.7M is 3,1.

Where both channels are based on the original A, the secondary flowers will have the same four variants that the primaries did when both channels were based on the B. The secondary flowers are yellow-green in Figure 4.7B, which is therefore 2,1; red in 4.7G, which is 1,1; cyan in 4.7J, which is 2,2; and violet in 4.7N, which is 1,2.

- *CD Note:* Les says that he keeps a copy of his graphic by his monitor to help him when he works in LAB. If you'd like to do the same, the file is included.

Review and Exercises

- Curving the L channel of LAB to increase contrast is advisable when the important object is strongly colored. Such objects fall in the middle of the L but at the ends of the RGB channels. Objects with subtler, less brilliant colors are likely to be improved by curves in the AB, but increasing their detail is better handled in RGB or CMYK than LAB.
- The quiz answers: 1-C; 2-D; 3-B; 4-A; 5-F; 6-E.

Chapter 5

The flowery outdoor scene printed in CMY only is by David Moore. The woman wearing western clothing was photographed by Mike Vlietstra for Hobby Horse Clothing Co. The woman used for GCR comparison was photographed by Mike Demyan, and the Gorham forks that accompany her by Ric Cohn. As to the name of the magazine in which the out-of-register screen grab appeared, my lips are sealed, except for the comment that anyone who uses the master Levels setting deserves whatever he gets.

- *CD Note:* A PDF of a complete chapter on the preparation of duotones and spot color channels, taken from previous editions of *Professional Photoshop,* is included.

Review and Exercises

- The total ink limit in CMYK dictates that the cyan, magenta, and yellow stop short of their natural values in dark neutral areas. This wipes out almost all detail; all shadow contrast information transfers into the black. The effect does not occur in RGB, which has no ink limit, or in colored areas of CMYK. A navy blue, for example, is almost as dark as a black, but contains so little yellow ink that there is no danger of going over the total ink limit, so there is no reason to suppress the cyan and magenta shadows.

- Drop shadows that are specified while in RGB separate to CMYK in the same manner as any other gray—typically with little or no black ink. As we would like these shadows to contain some black ink to prevent color shift, it is better to create them and specify their values after the file has entered CMYK.

- GCR is a defensive mechanism against press error. If a job is printed incorrectly, we normally prefer a color shift to a muddy result. However, when the main objects are neutral (like jewelry, metals, or white fabrics) we may prefer to chance extra darkness rather than risk a color shift. In such cases we use more GCR. In color correction, we usually like to produce vivid, pleasing colors; black ink is a hindrance. In the less common images where vivid colors are not on the agenda, correcting with a heavier black channel can avoid problems.

- Separation settings created using Custom CMYK are editable for dot gain, ink color, and black generation. Premade profiles such as SWOP v2 cannot be changed, at least not without third-party software—it's a take it or leave it situation.

- Maximum GCR is not useful in photographs, but it is helpful when trying to separate fine black lines, such as type or cartoons, because on conversion to CMYK they will become pure black, $0^C0^M0^Y100^K$, instead of a combination of four inks, which could cause registration difficulties.

- The reader who asked why the Bodoni type in the box on page 118 wasn't separated with Maximum GCR did not understand that the text of a book has nothing to do with Photoshop or color separations. The text is generated in a page-layout program, which by default spits out text at $0^C0^M0^Y100^K$.

Chapter 6

Areca vestiara is from student David Leaser's book, *Palm Trees: A Story in Photographs.* The woman whose skin I devastatingly over-sharpened is by Calgary-based glamour photographer Mark Laurie, as are the two eyes featured in Figure 6.11. The man is from the *Knoxville News Sentinel*, and the seagull is by David Xenakis. The shots of Capitol Reef National Park, the flowering cactus, the boats, the sea scene, and the flags are mine.

- *CD Note:* To aid in testing, the images are enclosed at the same resolution used for printing this book. The two portraits have been cropped to prevent unauthorized reproduction. There is also a text file containing the 23-step recipe used to sharpen Figure 6.1B using blending modes and the Gaussian Blur filter only. Reminder: this method is a joke, merely to prove that it can be done. You can do as well in a tenth the time with the USM filter.

Review and Exercises

- Figure 6.3B, the version sharpened in the L channel, appears to have lighter leaves than the original (Figure 6.3A) because the USM process lightens the inside edges of each leaf while darkening the background edge. It also seems lighter than Figure 6.3C, which was sharpened only in the magenta and black. Black is largely absent in leaves, so the impact was only in the magenta, rather than in the combination of all channels that generates the L. Note the color change in Figure 6.3C: magenta kills green, and magenta is getting lighter in these leaves. Therefore, the leaves seem greener than in either of the other two versions.

● Most objects that we might wish to sharpen are either close to neutral, or else red or green. If the image contains several such colors and all are of similar importance, we sharpen overall. When we believe that red is the most important color to sharpen, however, we apply USM in the two weak CMYK channels, in this case cyan and black. If green is the most important, we use magenta and black. Doing this prevents color shift, because the dominating inks (magenta and yellow in red, yellow and cyan in green) don't change.

● What I have called *conventional* sharpening uses Radius settings that are usually lower than 2.5, and rarely exceed 4.0. They are coupled with Amounts of 200%–500%. The combination produces distinct halos, which are effective in emphasizing transitions but can be offensive if overdone, particularly halos that lighten rather than darken. *Hiraloam* (high Radius, low Amount) sharpening operates with Radii about ten times higher than and Amounts a tenth as high as conventional. The halos are much softer and more difficult to detect. While poor hiraloam is generally less offensive than poor conventional, if the Amount is set too high, lighter areas, such as the whites of a person's eyes, may blow out.

Chapter 7

The parrot and the Canadian flag are from the Corel library. The man with the canoe is from the *Knoxville News Sentinel*. All other images in the chapter are mine.

Review and Exercises

● RGB is generally a better blending space than CMYK because its channels are fuller, as no detail migrates into the black channel.

Also, the total ink limit suppresses shadow detail in the CMY channels.

● To convert a color image to grayscale, Photoshop creates an idealized RGB file and averages the channels, roughly at a ratio of 3–6–1: three parts red, six parts green, one part blue.

● Figure 7.10B has the type layer in Lighten mode. Since the word *BLEND* is blue, it is light in the blue channel, dark in the green, and medium in the red. Therefore, since no darkening is permitted, the green on the top layer does not replace the bottom layer's green. The top layer's blue wipes out the bottom layer's, and the top layer's red replaces the bottom layer's in some places but not others. What remains is blue type (because the blue channel is that of the top layer) with a texture contributed mostly by the green channel, and to some extent by the red.

● To convert the flag of the United States from color into grayscale, we first acknowledge that the blue is currently darker than the red. We must increase the variation between the two, presumably by lightening the red. Acceptable ways of doing this would be to use the Hue/Saturation or Selective Color commands to lighten all reds; or to delete the blue (RGB) or yellow (CMYK) channel, both of which contribute much more darkness to the reds than to the blues.

Chapter 8

The striking image of the two bighorn rams is by David Cardinal. The portrait of the African-American woman is by Pamela Terry; the Caucasian woman is by Jim Bean. The woman with the red jacket is from the *Knoxville News Sentinel*. The man at sunset is by John Ruttenberg. The images of the boys on the slide, the flags, and the castle come from previous chapters.

Review and Exercises

● We could use Blend If sliders to prevent the red-channel Darken move in Figure 8.6C from affecting anything other than the sky. We could use the B channel sliders to eliminate the greenery, which is B–positive (more yellow than blue) while the sky is B–negative. We could use the L slider to limit the effect to things that were originally light, like the sky, excluding the much darker blue flags.

• On the top layer of Figure 8.11, all channels are identical—they're copies of the green. Since we wish to apply exactly the same correction to each, there is no reason to avoid the master curve.

• The blend in Darken mode to correct face color in Figure 8.13B is safer when applying magenta into cyan than green into red, for a subtle technical reason. The hair appears to be slightly brownish. If so, it needs to be heavier in the green than in the red, and the blend might fail. But in CMYK, where extra cyan is needed to achieve equality, equal CMY values create this type of dull brown. The blend would therefore not darken the hair in the cyan channel, the way it would in the red.

Chapter 9

The wedding scene is a real-world restoration job furnished by Jim Bean. The Pledge of Allegiance scene is from the *Knoxville News Sentinel*. All other images in the chapter are mine, except the color card image picked up from Chapter 2.

Review and Exercises

• You were asked to give approximate AB values for several of the items appearing in this chapter. Correct answers are: The beach in Figure 9.11, 3^A17^B. The blouse in Figure 9.13A, 50^A5^B. The three red shirts in Figure 9.18B, from our left to right, 50^A40^B, 64^A51^B, and 64^A50^B. The left-hand shirt is therefore less colorful than the others, but the other two vary only in darkness, not color. The "light green" gown in Figure 9.1C is a trick question. The top half *appears* green because of the presence of the yellow stain that also

affects the top half of the bridal couple. The dress is actually blue, as can be seen from the waist down. At the bustline the measurement is $(2)^A2^B$, but at knee level it's $(2)^A(8)^B$.

• The easiest way to retouch out the yellow stain across the white areas of Figure 9.1C is with the sponge tool set to desaturate. Alternatively, you could make a rough selection of the affected area and, with the Hue/Saturation command, choose Yellows and desaturate and lighten.

Chapter 10

The overly dark toolkit is courtesy of Alltrade Tools LLC. The British Columbia coastline was photographed by Darren Bernaerdt. The totem and the scene of China's River Li are mine, and the foggy background in the latter is air pollution, not lousy photography.

The cat and bird were shot by Marty Stock. The Norwegian wood scene is by Kim Müller. The champagne and crabcakes layout was photographed by Ric Cohn.

Review and Exercises

• You would be likely to get a brighter orange on your desktop printer than I could in Figure 10.5, not because your printer is better, but because you use more expensive paper. Your paper is presumably a brilliant white, much more reflective than this book's paper. A paper that is less white does not reflect as much red, green, and blue light. The poor reflectivity with respect to red light will force either a yellower or a darker bird in comparison to what is possible on a whiter paper.

• The Darken blend in Figure 10.5 works better when applying magenta to cyan than green to red because the objective was to put detail in something very light and not to affect darker areas. The cyan channel is darker than the magenta in neutral and near-neutral areas, so these areas are not affected by Darken blends. The red channel and the green channel are equal in such areas, meaning that changes might be possible.

• To use a bogus black channel for blending in RGB mode without changing color, convert a copy of the RGB document to CMYK at the desired GCR setting. Returning to the RGB file, create a duplicate layer. Apply the black to it in Multiply mode. Then, change the top layer's mode to Luminosity.

• In Figure 10.17B, the darkest part of the top layer, the shadows of a forest, was excluded by Blend If sliders in the B, which specified that the top layer should not take precedence where it is much more yellow than blue. To do this in the A instead, we would exclude things that are significantly more green than magenta. (The B move is technically superior because it encompasses some red leaves, which are more yellow than blue. In the A, they are more magenta than green, hence unaffected by the sliders.)

Chapter 11

The impractical comments about the graphic of Figure 11.1 appear in Adams and Weisberg, *The GATF Guide to Practical Color Management* (GATFPress, 1998).

The excellent checkerboard graphic of Figure 11.2 was prepared by William H. Adelson, professor of visual science at MIT, who graciously gives others permission to use it. The other graphics in the chapter are mine.

The Darwin quotation is from *The Origin of Species.* Mencken's essay on Shaw, *The Ulster Polonius,* appears in his *Prejudices: First Series.* In my own maxims, I could not resist pirating one from Shaw, although I modified it slightly. The original: "He who can, does. He who cannot, teaches."

• *CD Note:* An interesting colortheory thread, in which a graphic arts instructor asks for agreement about certain aspects of monitor calibration and gets anything but, is enclosed. Also, for comic relief, a PDF of the corresponding chapter in *Professional Photoshop Fourth Edition,* written at a time when I was regularly being referred to as the devil, who accordingly plays a prominent role in the chapter.

Chapter 12

Further discussion of the blue issue with SWOP v2 is found in Chapter 13 of *Photoshop LAB Color.* Alexander Theroux's description of Crater Lake is found in his book of color essays *The Primary Colors.*

The lantern with the gamut problem is from Alltrade Tools LLC. The yellow pepper and the woman with the blue cast are from the Corel library. André Dumas provided the image of the magenta flower. The three women and both lake images are mine.

• *CD Note:* The corresponding chapters from the last two editions are included in PDF, to show the development of the conventional color management wisdom. Also, there's an interesting raw image by Vladimir Yelisseev. I received it too late to include in the text. Its yellow flower is the only image I have yet encountered that contains colors that may be printable yet require a working space at least as wide as Adobe RGB.

Certain vendors claim copyright on their profiles, for which reason they are not included on the CD.

Review and Exercises

• *Gamut* refers to all the colors that a given space can portray; colors too brilliant to portray are referred to as *out of gamut.* Gamma is a mathematical formula that alters how the darkness of an RGB file is interpreted for display and subsequent conversions.

• Dot gain is roughly the CMYK equivalent of RGB's gamma. As commonly used, it's a midtone adjustment, just as gamma is. However, dot gain is a mechanical phenomenon—the ink spreading into the paper and creating a darker appearance than anticipated—and as such it is not always amenable to being represented by a mathematical formula.

• A file prepared in Adobe RGB but opened as if it were sRGB seems about as dark as expected, but all colors are washed out. The person who opened it incorrectly needs to change the RGB setting of Color Management Policies to Preserve Embedded Profiles.

● A banana is yellow enough to be close to 100^Y. If anything, it's out of the RGB gamut, not that of CMYK. A pink flower, on the other hand, is so light that CMYK needs to leave a lot of the paper blank, which means it probably can't match certain colors that RGB can. A leaf is not a problem, because its color is not very saturated. Skies on cloudless days are often out of the gamut of CMYK, which does poorly with all saturated blues.

Chapter 13

The process control bars of Figure 13.6 are available from the Graphic Arts Technical Foundation (www.gain.org).

Information about the Specifications for Web Offset Publications (SWOP) is available at www.swop.org.

The Hammett quotation, made more famous by Humphrey Bogart as Sam Spade, is from *The Maltese Falcon.*

The printed image of the bare-shouldered woman was originally from the Corel library. The woman in the photo lab exercise was originally photographed by Hunter Clarkson. The sand sculpture is mine.

● *CD Note:* The quizzes of Figure 13.8 and Figure 12.2 use the same original. It's found in the Chapter 12 folder. The file is untagged; to follow the exercise in this chapter, assign ColorMatch RGB. The Chapter 13 folder contains no images. However, a PDF of the tenth revision of the full SWOP standard (June 2005) is included, plus an errata sheet.

Chapter 14

The aftermath of the tsunami was photographed by Nikolay Malukhin. The autumn leaves are by Stuart Block. The jewelry shots were taken by David Moore. I would like to thank Geoff Shearer and Vladimir Yeliseev

for files that don't appear in the book but were very useful in analyzing differences between processing 8-bit and 16-bit files.

The procedure to determine whether your raw capture module is converting 16-bit to 8-bit files correctly is as follows:

● Export the file from your module in both 8-bit and 16-bit. Convert the 16-bit to 8-bit in Photoshop.

● In this newly converted file, make a duplicate layer. Then make a duplicate copy of the two-layered file.

● Using the Apply Image command, apply the raw module's 8-bit version to the top layer of one file, at 100% opacity, Lighten mode. Do the same to the other file, but use Darken mode instead of Lighten.

● Change the mode of the top layer of each file to Difference. Both files will now appear solid black.

● Flatten both files, and apply Image: Adjustments>Auto Levels. This will bring out what appears to be noise, representing the difference between what used to be the two layers before they were flattened.

● Compare the two results. If each shows approximately the same amount of noise, you have no problem. If, however, one file has far more noise than the other, it probably means that your module is discarding the final eight bits when it converts from 16-bit to 8-bit, an inferior method. In that case, you should always export from the module in 16-bit, and convert to 8-bit in Photoshop when ready.

● *CD Note:* The much longer resolution chapter from *Professional Photoshop Fourth Edition,* dealing with many facets of resolution not covered in the present text, is included in PDF. Also, the original grayscale TIFF that produced Figure 15.13C of that chapter is included. It shows considerable banding—but in print it was invisible even under magnification, although it was clearly evident on the plate. For the same reason, the actual print files for Figures 14.8A and 14.8C of this edition are also included. Is the banding visible in print this time?

Additionally, there is a history of the 16- versus 8-bit controversy that I wrote in late 2005 when one of the more prominent 16-bit advocates announced that bit depth was "possibly a non-issue" for those working in Adobe RGB or sRGB. Many additional threads on this topic are available at the colortheory list archive: www.ledet.com/margulis/ACT_postings/ACT.htm.

Review and Exercises

• A file's effective resolution is its stated resolution divided by the magnification on output. Outputting a file at double size (200% magnification) halves its effective resolution. In evaluating whether you have enough, use effective resolution, not the value found in Image: Image Size.

• The traditional rule is that the effective resolution should be between 1.5 and 2.0 times the halftone screen ruling of the printing process. The rule is in doubt today because digital cameras deliver a significantly smoother file than is obtainable by scanning film. Also, printing at higher screen rulings is more common now than in the past, and it is known that the needed ratio goes down somewhat as the screen gets finer.

• The Resample Image box governs whether Photoshop merely restates the size of an image at a different resolution or actually calculates new pixels. Example: you have a file at 4"×6" at a resolution of 300 pixels per inch (PPI), and type in a new size of 6"×9". If Resample Image is not checked, Photoshop will restate the resolution as 200 PPI. If checked, it will calculate new pixels to maintain an actual resolution of 300 PPI. The file size will more than double.

• When a RIP encounters a file that it considers to have grossly too little or too much resolution, it ordinarily resamples it. We don't know what method it uses to do so, so it is prudent to do the resampling in Photo-shop, which probably is using a less primitive algorithm.

Chapter 15

The night scene of Prague's Old Town Square is by Jason Hadlock. The bright orange shirt is by David Moore. The Chinese dancer was provided by the *Knoxville News Sentinel.* The Waikiki Beach scene was photographed by Errol de Silva.

Information about the Curvemeister plug-in is available at www.curvemeister.com.

• *CD Note:* In addition to the four images, the folder contains a demo version of Curve-meister (PC only) and all the profiles used in the chapter.

Review and Exercises

• Where the red channel is as light as possible, the RGB manufactures its reddest possible color. sRGB reaches that point long before wider-gamut RGBs do, so an extremely light red channel would become darker (without changing the overall color) when an image converts from sRGB to a wider-gamut space.

• The Save RGB command saves a new RGB profile that can be converted to or assigned in future images. The Save choice in the Color Settings dialog saves *all* settings for all colorspaces. It is not a profile itself (although it contains four profiles). It is used to restore predetermined workspace choices when needed.

• Since CMYK does poorly with brilliant colors, you should check after conversion to see that in their brightest points the lightest channel is zeroed out and the darkest channel is solid.

Chapter 16

The quotation about raw as a selling point came from the May 5, 2006, edition of the *New York Times.*

The Camera Raw versus camera JPEG comparisons in Figure 16.1 were provided by David Cardinal (the two bears) and Kim Müller (the white flower).

The original raw files for the three main example images of this chapter are included. The photographers are David Xenakis (the poppies), Marty Stock (the elderly couple), and Fred Drury (the moose).

Review and Exercises

• Camera Raw confusingly has two controls that each favor midtone contrast at the expense of highlights and shadows. The Contrast slider (Adjust tab) and the Tone Curve (Curve tab) both are set up to emphasize this contrast by default. If highlight and/or shadow detail is critical, they should be changed.

Chapter 17

All images in this chapter are mine. The Adams quotations are from his books *The Camera, My Camera in Yosemite Valley,* and *Examples.*

Review and Exercises

• Hiraloam sharpening is indicated where the subject displays few emphatic edges, as, for example, in rippling water or in a person's flesh.

• Where the layer mask is white, it permits the top layer to take precedence. Where black, the top layer is suppressed and the bottom layer is seen. Where gray, the two layers are merged. The lighter the gray, the more it favors the top layer.

• If applying conventional USM to an RGB portrait, it might make sense to load the red channel as a selection or mask, because it has the biggest variation between flesh, in which conventional sharpening is undesirable, and eyes, eyebrows, and hair, where it is beneficial. Because a selection permits changes in its light areas and prohibits them in dark ones, the red would need to be inverted before loading.

• To edit a layer-masked file to guarantee that all areas contain a minimum of 20

percent of the information of the top layer, find the darkest point in the layer mask and reduce it to 80%. In the case of Figure 17.12C, certain areas of the layer mask are solid black, so you would apply a curve in which the top right point was moved down by two grid lines.

Chapter 18

The images of the judge and of the woman in pink are from the *Knoxville News Sentinel.* The dark-haired woman was photographed by Marty Stock, and the light-haired one by Mark Laurie. The product shot of the skin-care products is by Ric Cohn. The Bridge of Sighs is mine.

Review and Exercises

• The Shadow/Highlight command is more important today than it would have been in the film era because digicams often suppress highlight and shadow detail in the interest of snappier midtones.

• To prevent S/H from affecting dark areas of the image, set a 0% Amount for Shadows.

• Shadow/Highlight correctly assumes that seriously over- or underexposed images are usually too gray as well. Its Color Correction field automatically intensifies colors where the command takes effect. When quality and flexibility are at a premium, you should turn it off and go to LAB. However, doing so takes considerable time, so Color Correction makes sense when the adjustment is slight and when we are in a hurry to finish.

• The blending shown in this chapter applies the Gaussian Blur filter to the overlaying channel. The blur is needed to obliterate any detail found in the highlight and shadow areas so that the blend will enhance the entire area and not just its lightest and darkest parts. Since the Surface Blur filter tries to avoid damaging real detail, it would not yield as smooth a result and would be inappropriate for this type of blend.

• In a two-layered document with Figures

18.7E on top and 18.7D on the bottom, the assignment is to use 18.7D's handbag but elsewhere establish a blend in which two-thirds is 18.7E. The easiest way to do this is to set the top layer's opacity to 67%, and add Blend If sliders, This Layer, to exclude objects that are dark in the red channel. This Layer is chosen because the handbag is darker, and hence easier to isolate, on the top layer. The red channel is chosen because the suit is lightest there, hence easier to distinguish from the handbag.

Chapter 19

The ladies of Chapter 19 were supplied by the following sources: the prom night and the big yellow cast are both from the *Knoxville News Sentinel,* the scene at the vanity is by Ric Cohn, and the woman whose dress color was changed is by John Ruttenberg.

The bedroom scene was photographed by David Moore. The *Missouri,* the flowers, and the cabinet are mine.

Review and Exercises

* If correcting the *Missouri* image of Figure 19.2 in RGB with Blend If rather than a layer mask, the slider should exclude anything light in the blue channel. The blue channel is chosen because it is probably blank throughout the sky, whereas the sky in the others might be mistaken for the battleship. Either the This Layer or Underlying Layer slider should work. If the correction is done instead in LAB, the sliders should exclude anything that is *either* very light in the L channel (the clouds) *or* strongly negative in the B (the sky).

Chapter 20

All images in the chapter are mine, except for the beer, which is from the Corel library.

Applied Color Theory, the Course

In 1994, a chain of department stores bought some very expensive hardware (not personal computers, which weren't nearly powerful enough in those days) to bring advertising work in-house rather than sending it to pre-press houses at a cost of millions of dollars per year.

This was done based on a vendor's assurance that all the chain had to do was retrain its secretaries and receptionists to run the new equipment, and all would be well.

In real life, it turned out to be a little more difficult than that, as the vendor learned when the buyer asked to return all the equipment. In desperation, the vendor offered to arrange training in color correction for the buyer's staff. This also turned out to be more difficult than the vendor thought, as most Photoshop trainers then tended to specialize in demonstrations of fancy filters rather than how to fix pictures, and it was not feasible to Google up somebody with more practical knowledge, as Google did not exist.

The vendor learned by word of mouth that I had a reputation for being able to teach people how to get good color (I was running a plant in New York City at the time) and, in desperation, brought me to Atlanta. For three days, I sat with six members of the store's staff, learning in what I was already convinced is the best way: everybody works on the same images, then we compare results and decide whose work is the best. Then, the inquest: what did the people who were successful do right, and what did the losers do wrong?

The improvement in quality was so immediate and so dramatic that a second session was scheduled, but a couple of seats were sold to other companies to defray expenses. Suspecting that there might be a broader market for this type of color-correction knowledge, the vendor scheduled a third session, open to the general public, and then a fourth, and on and on.

I have now taught this class nearly 200 times, never the same way twice. The first class used Photoshop 2.5, and everything was scanned from film. As technology has changed (and, more important, as I've learned more tricks), so has the curriculum. It's still three brutally long days, still heavy on comparisons of different versions, still limited to seven or eight students. It usually sells out months in advance, catering to professional photographers, in-house retouchers, serious hobbyists, and anyone else who simply wants to make their pictures look better.

For a fuller description of the course, along with current scheduling, pricing, and locations, visit www.ledet.com/margulis. The site also features dozens of my magazine articles and edited, advertising-free threads from the Applied Color Theory newsgroup.

Sterling Ledet & Associates

In the United States, my color-correction courses have always been marketed by Sterling Ledet & Associates, originally a tiny Atlanta operation that has grown into one of the largest providers of graphic arts training services in North America, with classrooms in many major cities. Its extraordinarily deep course list is found at www.ledet.com.

Other Countries, Other Languages

As the pictures in the book indicate, I enjoy traveling the world. I have taught classes in many countries, in, so far, Spanish, German, and Italian as well as English. If you would like to arrange an engagement outside of the United States, contact me directly.

The Applied Color Theory List

In 1999, Sterling Ledet & Associates launched a newsgroup to support those who had attended or were thinking of attending my color-correction course, or who are interested in my writings. It currently has 3,000 members and averages 250 messages per month. The emphasis is on discussions of practical applications of color knowledge using Photoshop. Signup for the list is available at http://tech.groups.yahoo.com/group/colortheory or at www.ledet.com/margulis.

The list has had a history of distinguished commentary. Around 200 of its most important threads are at www.ledet.com/margulis/ACT_postings/ACT.htm.

Reaching the Author

My address is dmargulis@aol.com. While I try to reply to all correspondence, a three- to six-week delay has regrettably become the norm. If you need a quicker answer to a technical question, I recommend joining and posting it to the Applied Color Theory group (details above). Please note that due to the volume of e-mail I receive, I cannot accept images or any other form of attachment.

A Note on the Type

The text type of this book is one I prepared for the first (1994) edition of *Professional Photoshop*. Each subsequent edition, however, featured a new text face, this tactic being a good way to force me to read every single line again instead of blithely assuming that all was well.

The letterforms are those of Utopia, designed by Robert Slimbach of Adobe in 1990. I stripped out all width and kerning information and substituted my own, as I prefer both a two-column format and large text type, a deadly typographic combination if the letterspacing isn't well controlled.

Index